Signs of Life in the U.S.A.

Eighth Edition

Signs of Life in the U.S.A.

Readings on Popular Culture for Writers

Sonia Maasik
University of California, Los Angeles

Jack Solomon
California State University, Northridge

BEDFORD/ST. MARTIN'S   Boston ◆ New York

For Bedford/St. Martin's

Vice President, Editorial, Macmillan Higher Education Humanities: Edwin Hill
Editorial Director for English and Music: Karen S. Henry
Publisher for Composition, Business and Technical Writing and Developmental Writing:
   Leasa Burton
Executive Editor: John Sullivan
Senior Developmental Editor: Adam Whitehurst
Editorial Assistant: Kathleen Wisneski
Senior Production Editor: Jessica Gould
Senior Production Supervisor: Lisa McDowell
Executive Marketing Manager: Jane Helms
Copy Editor: Jennifer Greenstein
Director of Rights and Permissions: Hilary Newman
Senior Art Director: Anna Palchik
Cover Design: Marine Miller
Cover Art/Cover Photo: Simon Evans, *Everything I Have,* 2008. Pen, paper, Scotch tape,
   correction fluid, and ink-jet prints of personal inventory, 60¼ × 40⅛ in., 153.04 ×
   101.92 cm © Simon Evans / Courtesy James Cohan Gallery, New York/Shanghai
Composition: Cenveo Publisher Services
Printing and Binding: RR Donnelley and Sons

8   7   6
f   e   d

For information, write: Bedford/St. Martin's, 75 Arlington Street, Boston, MA 02116
(617-399-4000)

ISBN: 978-1-4576-7025-1

Acknowledgments

Preface for Instructors

The more things change, the more they . . . intensify. For in the years since the publication of the seventh edition of *Signs of Life in the U.S.A.*, two profound interventions in American history — the Great Recession and the Digital Revolution — have only increased their influence on American culture and consciousness. Years of diminishing opportunities, of un- and under-employment, stagnant wages, and economic disruption persistently erode the national spirit, even as the explosive growth of digital technology continues its transformation of our culture into a vast social network: an always-on virtual society that has recast Marshall McLuhan's global village into a global hive. And there is little reason to believe that either of these forces will be abating in the foreseeable future.

In the midst of such interventions, the role of popular culture in our lives has equally intensified. No longer a mere cultural embellishment or ornament, popular culture now permeates almost everything we do even as it reflects back to us what we are becoming as a society and who we are. With digital technology blurring beyond recognition the line between everyday life and entertainment, transforming the traditional work spaces of school and office into virtual play stations and shopping malls, if we wish to understand America today we must learn to think critically about the vast panoply of entertainments and commodities that were once condescendingly dismissed as elements of "mass culture." And that is what *Signs of Life in the U.S.A.* has always been designed to teach your students to do.

Then and Now

The importance of thinking critically about popular culture has not always been apparent to the academic world. When the first edition of *Signs of Life* appeared, the study of popular culture was still embroiled in the "culture wars" of the late 1980s and early 1990s, a struggle for academic legitimacy in which the adherents of popular cultural studies ultimately prevailed. Since then, more and more scholars and teachers have come to recognize the importance of understanding what Michel de Certeau has called "the practice of everyday life" and the value of using popular culture as a thematic ground for educating students in critical thinking and writing. Once excluded from academic study on the basis of a naturalized distinction between "high" and "low" culture, which contemporary cultural analysis has shown to be historically contingent, popular culture has come to be an accepted part of the curriculum, widely studied in freshman composition classrooms as well as in upper-division undergraduate courses and graduate seminars.

But recognition of the importance that popular culture has assumed in our society has not been restricted to the academy. Increasingly, Americans are realizing that American culture and popular culture are virtually one and the same, and that whether we are looking at our political system, our economy, or simply our national consciousness, the power of popular culture to shape our lives is strikingly apparent. That is why, unlike most other popular cultural texts, *Signs of Life* adopts an interpretive approach — semiotics — that is explicitly designed to analyze that intersection of ideology and entertainment that we call *popular culture*. We continue to make semiotics the guiding methodology behind *Signs of Life* because semiotics helps us, and our students, avoid the common pitfalls of uncritical celebration or simple trivia swapping.

The Critical Method: Semiotics

The reception of the first seven editions of this text has demonstrated that the semiotic approach to popular culture has indeed found a place in America's composition classrooms. Composition instructors have seen that students feel a certain sense of ownership toward the products of popular culture and that using popular culture as a focus can help students overcome the sometimes alienating effects of traditional academic subject matter. At the same time, the semiotic method has helped instructors teach their students how to analyze the popular cultural phenomena that they enjoy writing about, and through these methods students have learned the critical thinking and writing skills that their composition classes are designed to impart.

Reflecting the broad academic interest in cultural studies, we've assumed an inclusive definition of *popular culture*. The seven chapters in *Signs of Life in the U.S.A.* embrace everything from the marketing and consumption of the products of mass production to the television programs and movies that entertain us. We have chosen semiotics as our approach because it has struck us that while students enjoy assignments that ask them to look at popular cultural phenomena, they often have trouble distinguishing between an argued interpretive analysis and the simple expression of an opinion. Some textbooks, for example, suggest assignments that involve analyzing a TV show or film, but they don't always tell a student how to do that. The semiotic method provides that guidance.

As a conceptual framework, semiotics teaches students to formulate cogent, well-supported interpretations. It emphasizes the examination of assumptions and of the way language shapes our apprehension of the world. And, because semiotics focuses on how beliefs are formulated within a social and political context (rather than just judging or evaluating those beliefs), it's ideal for discussing sensitive or politically charged issues. As an approach used in literature, media studies, anthropology, art and design coursework, sociology, law, and market research (to name only some of its more prominent field applications), semiotics has a cross-disciplinary appeal that makes it ideal for a writing class of students from a variety of majors and disciplines. We recognize that semiotics has a reputation for being highly technical or theoretical; rest assured that *Signs of Life* does not require students or instructors to have a technical knowledge of semiotics. We've provided clear and accessible introductions that explain what students need to know.

We also recognize that adopting a theoretical approach may be new to some instructors, so we've designed the book to allow instructors to use semiotics with their students as much or as little as they wish. The book does not obligate instructors or students to spend a lot of time with semiotics — although we do hope you'll find the approach intriguing and provocative.

The Editorial Apparatus

With its emphasis on popular culture, *Signs of Life* should generate lively class discussion and inspire many kinds of writing and thinking activities. The general introduction provides an overall framework for the book, acquainting students with the semiotic method they can use to interpret the topics raised in each chapter. It is followed by the section "Writing about Popular Culture" that not only provides a brief introduction to this topic but also features three sample student essays that demonstrate different approaches to writing critical essays on popular cultural topics. The introduction concludes with "Conducting Research and Citing Sources," a section to help your students properly document the research they've done for their writing assignments, including three articles that guide students in the appropriate use of the Internet as a research tool.

Each chapter starts with a frontispiece, a provocative visual image related to the chapter's topic, and an introduction that suggests ways to "read" the

topic, provides model interpretations, and links the issues raised by the reading selections. Every chapter introduction contains three types of boxed questions designed to stimulate student thinking on the topic. The Exploring the
Signs questions invite students to reflect on an issue in a journal entry or
other prewriting activity, while the Discussing the Signs questions trigger
class activities such as debates, discussions, or small-group work. Reading
Online questions invite students to explore the chapter's topic on the Internet, both for research purposes and for texts to analyze.

Two sorts of assignments accompany each reading. The Reading the Text
questions help students comprehend the selections, asking them to identify important concepts and arguments, explain key terms, and relate main
ideas to one another and to the evidence presented. The Reading the Signs
questions are writing and activity prompts designed to produce clear analytic
thinking and strong persuasive writing; they often make connections among
reading selections from different chapters. Most assignments call for analytic
essays, while some invite journal responses, in-class debates, group work,
or other creative activities. Complementing the readings in each chapter are
images that serve as visual texts to be discussed. We also include a glossary
of semiotic terms, which can serve as a ready reference to key words and
concepts used in the chapter introductions. Finally, the Instructor's Manual
(*Editors' Notes for Signs of Life in the U.S.A.*) provides suggestions for organizing your syllabus, encouraging student responses to the readings, and using
popular culture and semiotics in the writing class.

What's New in the Eighth Edition

Popular culture evolves at a rapid pace, and the substantial revision required
for the eighth edition of *Signs of Life in the U.S.A.* reflects this essential muta-
bility. First, we have updated our readings, including more than twenty-five
new selections focusing on issues and trends that have emerged since the last
edition of this book. We have also updated the exemplary topics in our introductions, which are used to model the critical assignments that follow, and
have adjusted the focus of some chapters to reflect the changing conditions
of students' lives and the ways they consume popular culture. Two new chapters, "Heroes and Villains: Encoding Our Conflicts" and "My Selfie, My Self:
Ma(s)king Identity in the New Millennium," explore the ways in which the
conflicts and contradictions in American society are reflected in video entertainments awash in heroes, antiheroes, and villains, even as our sense of our
selves is being reshaped in an era of online profiling and self-advertising.

From the beginning, *Signs of Life in the U.S.A.* has been based on the
premise that in a postindustrial, McLuhanesque world, the image has come
to supplant the printed word in American, and global, culture. That is yet
another of the reasons we chose semiotics, which provides a rational basis for
the critical analysis of images as the guiding methodology for every edition

of our book. Each edition of *Signs of Life* has accordingly included images for critical analysis; the eighth edition continues this tradition. The images included in the text supplement the readings, offering a visual perspective designed to enhance the critical understanding modeled by the texts. Yet the images are not meant to replace the texts—we strongly believe that while the semiotic interpretation of images can help students hone their writing skills, it should not be a substitute for learning critical thinking through the analysis of written texts.

At the same time, the way that students consume images has been revolutionized by digital and mobile technologies, and *Signs of Life in the U.S.A.* reflects this new reality both through the offering of an e-book version of the main text and through LaunchPad Solo for *Signs of Life in the U.S.A.*, a collection of digital resources referenced throughout the print book that includes reading and writing tutorials, quizzing on rhetorical and grammatical topics, and e-readings—from vintage TV ads and films to documentary clips that elaborate on the topics covered by the reading selections. LaunchPad Solo for *Signs of Life in the U.S.A.* is available as a free package.

Even as we revise this text to reflect current trends, popular culture continues to evolve. The inevitable gap between the pace of editing and publishing, on the one hand, and the flow of popular culture, on the other, need not affect the use of popular culture in the classroom, however. The readings in the text, and the semiotic method we propose, are designed to show students how to analyze and write critical essays about any topic they choose. They can choose a topic that appeared before they were born, or they can turn to the latest box-office or prime-time hit to appear after the publication of this edition of *Signs of Life in the U.S.A.* Facebook and Twitter may well have been replaced by such more recent sites as Snapchat, Pinterest, and Instagram within the life span of this edition (indeed, Facebook obliterated MySpace shortly after the publication of the sixth edition of this book), but such changes are opportunities for further analysis, not obstacles. To put it another way, the practice of everyday life may itself be filled with evanescent fads and trends, but daily life is not itself a fad. As the vital texture of our lived experience, popular culture provides a stable background against which students of every generation can test their critical skills.

Acknowledgments

The vastness of the terrain of popular culture has enabled many users of the seventh edition of this text to make valuable suggestions for the eighth edition. We have incorporated many such suggestions and thank all for their comments on our text. We are also grateful to those reviewers who examined the book in depth: Anna Alessi, Saddleback Community College; Suzanne Arakawa, California State University—San Bernardino; Nick Brittin, Lake Michigan College; Mary Ann Bushman, Illinois Wesleyan University; Jane Christensen,

University of Nebraska at Kearney; Amy Corey, Gonzaga University; Patricia Cullinan, Truckee Meadows Community College; Nicole Denner, Stetson University; Sarah Duerden, Arizona State University; Catherine Gillis, Napa Valley College; Lynda Glennon, Rollins College; Christi Hein, Colorado Mesa University; Shawne Johnson, Community College of Philadelphia; Terry Krueger, Central Oregon Community College; David McCracken, Coker College; Laurie Vickroy, Bradley University; Chris Warnick, College of Charleston; Edward Wesp, Western New England University; Paula White, Community College of Philadelphia; Eve Wiederhold, George Mason University; Joshua Woodfork, American University; and John Ziebell, Florida State College Jacksonville.

If we have not included something you'd like to work on, you may still direct your students to it, using this text as a guide, not as a set of absolute prescriptions. The practice of everyday life includes the conduct of a classroom, and we want all users of the eighth edition of *Signs of Life in the U.S.A.* to feel free to pursue that practice in whatever way best suits their interests and aims.

Once again, we wish to thank heartily the people at Bedford/St. Martin's who have enabled us to make this new edition a reality. We especially want to thank our editor, Adam Whitehurst, a real partner in our work who brings to the eighth edition of *Signs of Life* both a fresh perspective and a storehouse of creative energy that, in the tradition of our collaboration with Bedford's editors, has left its own imprint on the book. Jessica Gould ably guided our manuscript through the rigors of production, while Kathleen Wisneski handled the numerous questions and details that arose during textbook development. Susan Doheny expertly researched and obtained permissions for art, and Margaret Gorenstein cleared text permissions. Our thanks go as well to Jennifer Greenstein for her fine copyediting of this book.

Get the most out of your course with *Signs of Life in the U.S.A.*

Bedford/St. Martin's offers resources and format choices that help you and your students get even more out of your book and course. To learn more about or to order any of the following products, contact your Bedford/St. Martin's sales representative, e-mail sales support (**sales_support@bfwpub .com**), or visit the Web site at **macmillanhighered.com/signsoflife/catalog**.

LAUNCHPAD SOLO FOR SIGNS OF LIFE IN THE U.S.A.: *WHERE STUDENTS LEARN*

LaunchPad Solo provides engaging content and new ways to get the most out of your course. Get **unique, book-specific materials** in a fully customizable course space; then assign and mix our resources with yours. Visit **macmillanhighered.com/signsoflife8e**.

- **Curated content** — including readings, videos, tutorials, and more — is **easy to adapt and assign** by adding your own materials and mixing them with our high-quality multimedia content and ready-made assessment options, such as **LearningCurve** adaptive quizzing. LaunchPad Solo for *Signs of Life in the U.S.A.* lets students make connections between their reading and real pop culture artifacts, including TV commercials and film clips.

- LaunchPad Solo also provides access to a **gradebook** that provides a clear window on the performance of your whole class, individual students, and even individual assignments.

- A **streamlined interface** helps students focus on what's due, and social commenting tools let them **engage**, make connections, and learn from one another.

To get the most out of your course, order LaunchPad Solo for *Signs of Life in the U.S.A.* packaged with the print book **at no additional charge**. (LaunchPad Solo for *Signs of Life in the U.S.A.* can also be purchased on its own.) An activation code is required. To order LaunchPad Solo for *Signs of Life in the U.S.A.* with the print book, use ISBN 978-1-319-01383-7.

CHOOSE FROM ALTERNATIVE FORMATS OF SIGNS OF LIFE IN THE U.S.A.

Bedford/St. Martin's offers a range of affordable formats, allowing students to choose the one that works best for them. For details, visit **macmillanhighered .com/signsoflife/catalog**.

- **Paperback.** To order the paperback edition, use ISBN 978-1-4576-7025-1.
- *Bedford e-Book to Go.* A portable, downloadable e-book is available at about half the price of the print book. To order the *Bedford e-Book to Go*, use ISBN 978-1-4576-7084-8.
- **Other popular e-book formats.** For details, visit **macmillanhighered.com /ebooks**.

PACKAGE WITH ANOTHER BEDFORD/ST. MARTIN'S TITLE AND SAVE

Get the most value for your students by packaging *Signs of Life in the U.S.A.* with a Bedford/St. Martin's handbook or any other Bedford/St. Martin's title for a significant discount. To order, please request a package ISBN from your sales representative or e-mail sales support (**salessupport@bfwpub.com**).

SELECT VALUE PACKAGES

Add value to your text by packaging one of the following resources with *Signs of Life in the U.S.A.* To learn more about package options for any of the following products, contact your Bedford/St. Martin's sales representative or visit **macmillanhighered.com/signsoflife/catalog**.

LearningCurve for Readers and Writers, Bedford/St. Martin's adaptive quizzing program, quickly learns what students already know and helps them practice what they don't yet understand. Gamelike quizzing motivates students to engage with their course, and reporting tools help teachers discern their students' needs. *LearningCurve for Readers and Writers* can be packaged with *Signs of Life in the U.S.A.* at a significant discount. An activation code is required. To order *LearningCurve* packaged with the print book, contact your sales representative for a package ISBN. For details, visit **learningcurveworks.com.**

i-series. This popular series presents multimedia tutorials in a flexible format — because there are things you can't do in a book.

- *ix visualizing composition 2.0* helps students put into practice key rhetorical and visual concepts. To order *ix visualizing composition* packaged with the print book, contact your sales representative for a package ISBN.
- *i-claim: visualizing argument* offers a new way to see argument — with six multimedia tutorials, an illustrated glossary, and a wide array of multimedia arguments. To order *i-claim: visualizing argument* packaged with the print book, contact your sales representative for a package ISBN.

Portfolio Keeping, **Third Edition, by Nedra Reynolds and Elizabeth Davis**, provides all the information students need to use the portfolio method successfully in a writing course. *Portfolio Teaching*, a companion guide for instructors, provides the practical information instructors and writing program administrators need to use the portfolio method successfully in a writing course. To order *Portfolio Keeping* packaged with the print book, contact your sales representative for a package ISBN.

MAKE LEARNING FUN WITH RE:WRITING 3
bedfordstmartins.com/rewriting

New open online resources with videos and interactive elements engage students in new ways of writing. You'll find tutorials about using common digital writing tools, an interactive peer review game, Extreme Paragraph Makeover, and more — all for free and for fun. Visit **bedfordstmartins.com/rewriting**.

INSTRUCTOR RESOURCES
macmillanhighered.com/signsoflife/catalog

You have a lot to do in your course. Bedford/St. Martin's wants to make it easy for you to find the support you need — and to get it quickly.

Editors' Notes for Signs of Life in the U.S.A. is available as a PDF that can be downloaded from the Bedford/St. Martin's online catalog at the URL above. In addition to chapter overviews and teaching tips, the instructor's manual includes a sample syllabus, assignment and course organization ideas, and additional advice using semiotics in your writing course.

Teaching Central offers the entire list of Bedford/St. Martin's print and online professional resources in one place. You'll find landmark reference works, sourcebooks on pedagogical issues, award-winning collections, and practical advice for the classroom — all free for instructors. Visit **macmillanhighered .com/teachingcentral**.

Bits collects creative ideas for teaching a range of composition topics in an easily searchable blog format and includes "Teaching Popular Culture Semiotics," the blog by *Signs of Life in the U.S.A.* author Jack Solomon. A community of teachers — leading scholars, authors, and editors — discuss revision, research, grammar and style, technology, peer review, and much more. Take, use, adapt, and pass the ideas around. Then, come back to the site to comment or share your own suggestion. Visit **bedfordbits.com**.

Contents

🄴 LaunchPad Solo for *Signs of Life in the U.S.A.* takes advantage of what the Web can do, at **macmillanhighered.com/signsoflife8e**.

"Frontier; opportunity; more. This has been the American trinity from the very start."

"Everyone, from the architecture critic at the *New York Times* to kids in the hall of a Montana high school, knows what *Ralph Lauren* means."

"Retailers don't just want to know how shoppers behave in their stores. They *have* to know."

A popular play figure for girls makes a purchase.

macmillanhighered.com/signsoflife8e

🄴 macmillanhighered.com/signsoflife8e

Signs of Life in the U.S.A.

POPULAR SIGNS

*Or, Everything You Always
Knew about American Culture
(but Nobody Asked)*

Dawn of the Living Droid

"HARDER. BETTER. FASTER. STRANGER."

With these words, Marvel Comics introduced its new series, *Avengers A.I.*, in 2013, the same year that *Iron Man 3* busted the box office, Daft Punk's *Random Access Memories* topped the charts, and Google Glass became available in a $1,500 version for selected consumers.

And so, even as *World War Z* and *The Walking Dead* continued to demonstrate that the reign of the undead was far from over, American popular culture began to show signs of the advent of a new empire of the unliving, of intelligent machines whose long-anticipated arrival would push the world ever closer to the apocalyptic event that futurists have called "the Singularity": that posthuman moment when human intelligence will be surpassed by artificial intelligence and humanity itself will be replaced by robotic androids.

Now, whether the Singularity ever comes to pass (frankly, we are skeptical), it appears that after years of fascination with the living dead—first with vampires and then with zombies, who completed their migration from the margins of fantasy fiction to pop culture's center stage in the first decade of the new millennium—American popular culture is now preparing a similar movement for the figures of the cyborg and the android. This emergence of the man-machine—as with the zombies and vampires before him—is not an overnight occurrence (Iron Man, for example, was created half a century ago, and the Six Million Dollar Man was a creation of the 1970s), but it is picking up steam as we write these words. While you might easily assume that this development is natural and inevitable and has no particular significance, there is actually quite a lot of cultural meaning behind it. One of the purposes of this book is to help you find such meanings.

Indeed, the foundational principle of *Signs of Life in the U.S.A.* is that human behavior has meaning and that popular culture is particularly meaningful and should never simply be taken for granted. Treating popular cultural behavior as a system of **signs**, this book will teach you how to read—or interpret— these signs, while at the same time teaching you the critical thinking skills necessary to write strong university-level arguments. Accordingly, each chapter in this book focuses upon a particular segment of American popular culture and, through readings, images, and assignments, guides you through the process that will help you analyze the significance of the full range of our everyday lives, behaviors, and entertainments. We will return shortly in this Introduction to the prevalence of such inhuman, or even posthuman, figures as androids, zombies, and vampires as a prominent example of a popular cultural sign, but first we will look at just what we mean by the term "popular culture" and why it is important to think critically about it.

From Folk to Fab

Traditionally, popular or "low" culture constituted the culture of the masses. It was set apart from "high" culture, which included classical music and literature, the fine arts and philosophy, and the elite learning that was the province of the ruling classes who had the money and leisure necessary to attain it—and who were often the direct patrons of high art and its creators. Low culture, for its part, had two main sides. One side, most notoriously illustrated by the violent entertainments of the Roman Empire (such as gladiatorial contests, public executions, and feeding Christians to lions) continues to be a sure crowd-pleaser to this day, as demonstrated by the widespread popularity of violent, erotic, and/or vulgar entertainment (can you spell *Jackass*?). The other side, which we can call "popular" in the etymological sense of being of the people, overlaps with what we now call "folk culture." Quietly existing alongside high culture, folk culture expressed the experience and creativity of the masses in the form of ballads, agricultural festivals, fairy tales, feasts, folk art, folk music, and so on. Self-produced by amateur performers, folk culture is exemplified by neighbors gathering on a modest Appalachian front porch to play their guitars, banjos, dulcimers, zithers, mandolins, and fiddles to perform, for their own entertainment, ballads and songs passed down from generation to generation.

Folk culture, of course, still exists. But for the past two hundred years it has been dwindling, with increasing rapidity, as it becomes overwhelmed by a different kind of popular culture, a commercialized culture that, while still including elements of both the folk and the vulgar traditions, represents the outcome of a certain historical evolution. This culture, the popular culture that is most familiar today and that is the topic of this book, is a commercial, for-profit culture aimed at providing entertainment to a mass audience. Corporate

Traditional high culture: Deborah Voigt in performance at the
Metropolitan Opera in New York.

rather than communal, it has transformed entertainment into a commodity to
be marketed alongside all the other products in a consumer society.

The forces that transformed the low culture of the past into contemporary popular culture arose in the industrial revolution of the late eigh-
teenth century and its accompanying urbanization of European and American
society. Along with the rise of corporate capitalism and the advent of electronic technologies, these four, essentially interrelated, historical forces—
industrialization, urbanization, capitalism, and electronic technology—shaped the
emergence of the mass cultural marketplace of entertainments that we know
today. To see how this happened, let's begin with the industrial revolution.

Prior to the industrial revolution, most Europeans and Americans lived
in scattered agricultural settlements. While traveling entertainers in theatrical

troupes and circuses might have visited the larger of these settlements, most people, especially those with little money, had little access to professional entertainment and so had to produce their own entertainment. But with the industrial revolution, masses of people who had made their living through agriculture were compelled to leave their rural communities and move to the industrial towns and cities where employment could increasingly be found. Populations began to concentrate in urban centers as the rural countryside emptied, leading to the development of mass societies.

With the emergence of mass society came the development of **mass culture**. For just as mass societies are governed by centralized systems of governance (as the huge expanse of the United States is governed by a federal government concentrated in Washington, DC), so, too, are mass cultures entertained by culture industries concentrated in a few locations (as the film and TV industries are concentrated in Hollywood and its immediate environs). Thanks to the invention of such technologies as the cinema, the phonograph, and the radio at the end of the nineteenth century, and of television and digital technology in the mid to late twentieth century, the means to disseminate centrally produced mass entertainments to a mass society became possible. Thus, whether you live in Boston or Boise, New York or Nebraska, the entertainment you enjoy is produced in the same few locations and is the same entertainment (TV programs, movies, DVDs, or Netflix series) no matter where you consume it. This growth of mass culture has been fundamentally shaped by the growth of a capitalist economic system in America, which has ensured that mass culture would develop as a for-profit industry.

To get a better idea of how the whole process unfolded, let's go back to that Appalachian front porch. Before electricity and urbanization, folks living in the backwoods of rural America needed to make their music themselves if they wanted music. They had no radios, phonographs, CD players, iPods, iPads, smartphones, or even electricity, and theaters with live performers were hard to get to and expensive. Under such conditions, the Appalachian region developed a vibrant folk musical culture. But as people started to move to places like Pittsburgh and Detroit, where the steel and auto industries began to offer employment in the late nineteenth and early twentieth centuries, the conditions under which neighbors could produce their own music decayed, for the communal conditions under which folk culture thrived were broken down by the mass migration to the cities. At the same time, the need to produce one's own music declined as folks who had once plucked their own guitars and banjos could simply turn on their radios or purchase records to listen to professional musicians perform for them. Those musicians were contracted by recording companies that were in business to turn a profit, and their music, in turn, could be heard on the radio because corporate sponsors provided the advertising that made (and still makes) commercial radio broadcasting possible.

Thus, the folk music of the American countryside became *country music*. An amalgamation of the traditional songs that a predominantly Scots-Irish immigrant population brought over from the British Isles with such American

Traditional folk culture in transition: Bill Monroe is known as the father of bluegrass music.

traditions as "white" gospel music, cowboy songs, and rock 'n' roll, contemporary "country" preserves the rural working-class perspective of folk music even as it is performed by wealthy professionals. (Country music's working-class roots explain why it is so often filled with the broken romances and broken-down cars of the poor.)

So the performance of folk music, which had once been an amateur, do-it-yourself activity, became a professional, for-profit industry with passive consumers paying for their entertainment either by directly purchasing a commodity (for example, a CD) or by listening to the advertising that encouraged them to purchase the products that sponsored their favorite radio programs. It is still possible, of course, to make one's own music, but most people find it easier and perhaps more aesthetically pleasing to listen to a professional recording. Today we are, in effect, constantly being trained to be the sort of passive consumers who keep the whole consumer-capitalist system going. Without that consumption, the economy might totally collapse.

This is hardly an exaggeration, for postindustrial capitalism is making popular culture all the more dominant in our society with every passing year. With the American economy turning further away from industrial production and increasingly toward the production and consumption of entertainment (including sports), entertainment has been moving from the margins of our cultural consciousness — as a mere form of play or recreation — to its center as a major buttress of our economy. A constant bombardment of advertising (which, after all, is the driving force behind the financing of digital media, just as it was for radio and television a generation or two ago) continually prods us to consume the entertainments that our economy produces. That bombardment has been so successful that our whole cultural consciousness is changing: We are becoming more concerned with play than with work, even while *at* work. (Tell the truth now: Do you ever tweet, or post something to Tumblr or Instagram, during class?)

The result of the centuries-long process we have sketched above is the kind of culture we have today: an *entertainment culture* in which all aspects of society, including politics and the traditional elite arts, are linked by a common imperative to entertain. Indeed, as traditional high culture shrinks in social importance and becomes part of what might be called a museum culture (which is quietly marginalized and mostly ignored), popular culture itself has assumed its own "high" and "low" strata, with television programs like *Mad Men* and *Game of Thrones* enjoying a kind of high cultural status, while *Here Comes Honey Boo Boo* profitably entertains at the low end.

Congressman Paul Ryan poses with *Duck Dynasty* stars Willie and Korie Robertson at the 2014 State of the Union address.

Jewel Samad

Pop Culture Goes to College

Far from being a mere recreational frivolity, a leisure activity that our society could easily dispense with, popular cultural entertainment today constitutes the essential texture of our everyday lives. From the way we entertain ourselves to the goods and services that we produce and consume, we are enveloped in a popular cultural environment that we can neither do without nor escape, even if we wanted to. To see this, just try to imagine a world without cloud computing, TV, movies, sports, music, shopping malls, or advertising. The study of popular culture has accordingly taken a prominent place in American higher education — not least in American composition classrooms, which have taken the lead in incorporating popular culture into academic study, both because of the subject's inherent interest value and because of its profound familiarity to most students. Your own expertise in popular culture means not only that you may know more about a given topic than your instructor but that you can use that knowledge as a basis for learning the critical thinking and writing skills that your composition class is intended to teach you.

Signs of Life in the U.S.A., then, is designed to let you exploit your knowledge of popular culture so that you may grow into a better writer, whatever the subject. You can interpret the popularity of a TV program like *The Walking Dead*, for example, in the same manner as you would interpret, say, a short story, because *The Walking Dead*, too, constitutes a kind of sign. A sign is something, anything, that carries a meaning. The familiar red sign at an intersection, for instance, means exactly what it says: "Stop." But it also carries the implied message ". . . or risk getting a ticket or into an accident." Words, too, are signs: you read them to figure out what they mean. You were trained to read such signs, but that training began so long ago that you may well take your ability to read for granted. Nevertheless, all your life you have been encountering and interpreting other sorts of signs. Although you were never formally taught to read them, you know what they mean anyway. Take the way you wear your hair. When you get your hair cut, you are not simply removing hair; you are making a statement, sending a message about yourself. It's the same for both men and women. Why was your hair short last year and long this year? Aren't you saying something with the scissors? In this way, you make your hairstyle into a sign that sends a message about your identity. You are surrounded by such signs. Just look at your classmates.

The world of signs could be called a kind of text, the text of America's popular culture. We want you to think of *Signs of Life in the U.S.A.* as a window onto that text. What you read in this book's essays and Chapter Introductions should lead you to study and analyze the world around you for yourself. Let the selections guide you to your own interpretations, your own readings, of the text of America.

In this edition of *Signs of Life in the U.S.A.*, we have chosen seven "windows" that look out onto separate, but often interrelated, segments of the American scene. In each chapter, we have included essays that help you think about a specific popular cultural topic and guide you to locate and analyze related examples of your own. Each chapter also includes an Introduction written to alert you to the kinds of signs you will find there, along with model analyses and advice on how to go about interpreting the topic that the chapter raises.

We have designed *Signs of Life in the U.S.A.* to reflect the many ways in which culture shapes our sense of reality and of ourselves, from the products we buy to the way culture, through such media as television and the movies, constructs our personal identities. This text thus introduces you to both the entertainment side and the ideological side of popular culture — and shows how the two sides are mutually dependent. Indeed, one of the major lessons you can learn from this book is how to find the ideological underpinnings of some of the most apparently innocent entertainments and consumer goods.

Signs of Life in the U.S.A., accordingly, begins with a chapter called "Consuming Passions." Because America is a consumer culture, the environment in which the galaxy of popular signs functions is, more often than not, a consumerist one. This is true not only for obvious consumer products like clothes and cars but for traditionally nonconsumer items such as political candidates, who are often marketed like any other product. It is difficult to find anything in contemporary America that is not affected somehow by our consumerist ethos or by consumerism's leading promoter, the advertiser. Thus, the second chapter, "Brought to You B(u)y," explores the world of advertising, for advertising provides the grease, so to speak, that lubricates the engine of America's consumer culture. Because television and film are the sources of many of our most significant cultural products, we include a chapter on each. Chapters on the digital cloud, American heroes and villains, and personal identity round out our survey of everyday life.

Throughout, the book invites you to go out and select your own "texts" for analysis (an advertisement, a film, a fashion fad, a TV show, and so on). Here's where your own experience is particularly valuable, because it has made you familiar with many different kinds of popular signs and their backgrounds, as well as with the particular popular cultural system or environment to which they belong.

The seven "windows" you will find in *Signs of Life in the U.S.A.* are all intended to reveal the common intersections of entertainment and ideology that can be found in contemporary American life. Often what seems to be simply entertainment, like an action-adventure movie, can actually be quite political (consider the Native American response to *The Lone Ranger*), while what *is* political can be cast as entertainment as well — as in *House of Cards*. The point is that little in American life is merely entertainment; indeed, just about everything we do has a meaning, often a profound one.

The Semiotic Method

To find this meaning, to interpret and write effectively about the signs of popular culture, you need a method, and part of the purpose of this book is to introduce such a method to you. Without a methodology for interpreting signs, writing about them could become little more than producing descriptive reviews or opinion pieces. Although nothing is wrong with writing descriptions and opinions, one of your goals in your writing class is to learn how to write academic essays — that is, analytical essays that present theses or arguments that are well supported by evidence. The method we use in this book — a method known as **semiotics** — is especially well suited for analyzing popular culture. Whether or not you're familiar with this word, you already practice sophisticated semiotic analyses every day of your life. Reading this page is an act of semiotic decoding (words and letters are signs that must be interpreted), but so is figuring out just what a friend means by wearing a particular shirt or dress. For a semiotician (one who practices semiotic analysis), a shirt, a haircut, a TV image, anything at all, can be taken as a sign, as a message to be decoded and analyzed to discover its meaning. Every cultural activity leaves a trace of meaning for semioticians, a kind of blip on the semiotic Richter scale that remains for them to read, just as geologists "read" the earth for signs of earthquakes, volcanic activity, and other geological phenomena.

Many who hear the word *semiotics* for the first time assume that it is the name of a new and forbidding subject. But in truth, the study of signs is neither new nor forbidding. Its modern form took shape in the late nineteenth and early twentieth centuries through the writings and lectures of two men. Charles Sanders Peirce (1839–1914) was an American philosopher who first coined the word *semiotics*, while Ferdinand de Saussure (1857–1913) was a Swiss linguist whose lectures became the foundation for what he called *semiology* (which was later developed under the rubric of linguistic *structuralism*). Without knowing of each other's work, Peirce and Saussure established the fundamental principles that modern semioticians or semiologists — the terms are essentially interchangeable — have developed into the contemporary study of semiotics.

Reduced to its simplest principles, the semiotic method carries on Saussure's argument that the meaning of a sign lies, in part, in the fact that it can be *differentiated* from any other sign within the **system**, or **code**, to which it belongs. For example, in the traffic code, being able to distinguish the difference between green, red, and amber lights is essential to understanding the meaning of a traffic signal. But that's not all there is to it, because it is only within the code that green, red, and amber signify "go," "stop," and "caution." So in order to interpret a traffic signal correctly, you need to be able to *associate* any particular red light you see with all other red traffic lights under the concept "stop" that the code assigns to it, and any green light with all other green lights under the concept "go," and so on.

But outside of the traffic code, the same colors can have very different meanings, always depending upon the system in which they appear. For example, in the codes of American politics, green signifies not only a political party but an entire worldview in support of environmentalist policies, while red, rather paradoxically, can signify either communist sympathies or the conservative politics of the so-called "red states," depending upon the context. Amber, for its part, has no significance within the codes of American politics.

The fact that the color red has gained a new significance in the codes of American politics demonstrates the fact that systems, and the meanings encoded within them, can change—an important principle when you are interpreting popular cultural signs, because their meanings are constantly changing, unlike the more or less fixed signs of the traffic code. Here is where Peirce's contribution comes in, because while Saussure's structural semiology is static in its interpretational orientation, Peircean semiotics is dynamic, situating signs within *history* and thus enabling us to trace the ways in which meaning shifts and changes with time.

But neither Saussure nor Peirce applied their methodologies to popular cultural signs, so to complete our description of the semiotic method, we must turn to the work of French semiologist Roland Barthes (1915–1980), who, in his book *Mythologies* (1957), pioneered the semiotic analysis of everything from professional wrestling to striptease, toys, and plastics. It was Barthes, too, who established the political dimensions of semiotic analysis, revealing how phenomena that may look like mere entertainments can hold profound political or ideological significance. Since "politics" is something of a dirty word in our society, Barthes's politicization of pop culture may make you feel a little uneasy at first. You may even think that to find political meaning in popular culture is tantamount to reading something into it that isn't really there. But consider the way people responded to *Batman: The Dark Knight Rises* in 2012. Many conservative commentators were upset that the villain of the movie was named Bane—they insisted that this was an allusion to Bain Capital, the former employer of then–presidential candidate Mitt Romney. For them, the movie was a piece of liberal propaganda. Conversely, liberal commentators saw Bane's revolution as an insidious allusion to the Occupy Wall Street movement and complained that it demonized a legitimate desire for greater economic equality.

In other words, the political interpretation of popular culture, even when it is not conducted under the name of semiotics, is already a part of our culture. The semiotic method simply makes it explicit, pointing out that all social behavior is political because it always reflects some subjective or group interest. Such interests are encoded in the ideologies that express the values and opinions of those who hold them. Politics, then, is just another name for the clash of ideologies that takes place in any complex society where the interests of those who belong to it constantly compete with one another.

While not all popular cultural signs are politically controversial, careful analysis can uncover some set of political values within them, although those values may be subtly concealed behind an apparently apolitical facade. Indeed, the political values that guide our social behavior are often concealed behind images that don't look political at all. But that is because we have to look beyond what a popular cultural sign **denotes**, or directly shows, to what it **connotes**, or indirectly suggests. The **denotation** of a sign is its first level of meaning, and you have to be able to understand that meaning before you can move to the next level. The **connotation** of a sign takes you to its political or cultural significance.

Take, for instance, the depiction of the "typical" American family in the classic TV sitcoms of the 1950s and 1960s, which denoted images of happy, docile housewives in suburban middle-class families. At the time, most viewers did not look beyond their denotation, so to them those images looked "normal" or natural—the way families and women were supposed to be. The shows didn't seem a bit ideological. But to a feminist semiotician, the old sitcoms were in fact highly political, because from a feminist viewpoint the happy housewives they presented were really images designed to convince women that their place was in the home, not in the workplace competing with men. Such images—or signs—did not reflect reality; they reflected, rather, the interests of a patriarchal, male-centered society. That, in effect, was their connotation. If you disagree, then ask yourself why programs were called *Father Knows Best*, *Bachelor Father*, and *My Three Sons*, but not *My Three Daughters*. And why did few of the women characters have jobs or ever seem to leave the house? Of course, there was *I Love Lucy*, but wasn't Lucy a screwball whose husband, Ricky, had to rescue her from one crisis after another?

Such an interpretation reflects what the English cultural theorist Stuart Hall (1932–2014) called an *oppositional* reading. Such a reading of a cultural text like a sitcom challenges the "preferred reading," which would simply take the program at face value, accepting its representation of family life as normative and natural. The oppositional reading, on the other hand, proposes an interpretation that resists the normative view, seeking to uncover a political subtext that often contradicts any particular intended "message." The fact that so many cultural signifiers *appear* normative and natural, as transparent images of an apolitical social reality, can make oppositional reading look

The popular television show *Leave It to Beaver* (1957–1963) exemplified traditional family values of the 1950s.

The Kobal Collection at Art Resource, NY

"unnatural," or like "reading into" your topic a meaning that isn't there. After all, isn't a sitcom simply a trivial entertainment that distracts viewers from the concerns of everyday life? But given the commercial foundation of our popular culture, the fact that something is entertaining is itself significant, because only those scripts that are calculated to be popular with a mass audience make it to the screen (whether digital, "silver," or TV). In other words, popular culture appeals to audience desire, and so the fact that something is entertaining raises a fundamental semiotic question: *Why* is it entertaining, and what does that say about those who are entertained by it?

Abduction and Overdetermination

You may think that a semiotic analysis resembles sociological interpretation, and indeed cultural semiotics and sociology do not significantly differ. The differences are largely methodological. Sociology tends to be highly statistical in its methodology, often working with case studies, surveys, and other quantifiable evidence. Cultural semiotics primarily works by looking at broad patterns of behavior and seeking what Charles Sanders Peirce called *abductive* explanations for them. **Abduction** is the process of arriving at an interpretation by seeking the most plausible explanation for something. No one can absolutely prove a semiotic interpretation, but the more material you can bring into your systems of related and differentiated signifiers, the more convincing your movement from denotation to connotation will be.

As you build up your interpretation of a cultural signifier, you can often find more than one explanation for it. Is that a problem? Are you just having trouble deciding on a single argument? No, because cultural signs are usually **overdetermined**: That is, they can have more than one cause or explanation (another word for this is *polysemous*). This is especially true for what we consider "rich" cultural signs, ones that have had a long-standing effect on our tastes and habits. As we will see in the analysis that follows, the popularity of the "unliving" is especially overdetermined, with many interpretive explanations converging. Indeed, the more causes behind a cultural phenomenon, the more popular it is likely to be.

Interpreting Popular Signs: Androids and Zombies and Vampires, Oh My!

The essential approach to interpreting popular cultural signs is to *situate signs within systems of related phenomena with which they can be associated and differentiated*. Being attuned to the history that provides the background for a sign is also essential. To see how this works in practice, let's return now to those unliving protagonists of so many currently popular entertainments.

Now, the fact that vampires peaked in the first decade of the twenty-first century and were overtaken by zombies (who are very likely to have peaked and similarly declined by the time this book is published) not only is *not* a reason to dismiss them as yesterday's fad but, quite conversely, raises a number of interesting questions in itself: Why *did* vampires become so popular in the 1990s and 2000s? Why did zombies take over? And why does it appear that androids are next in line?

To answer such questions, let's first ask another very basic one: What do vampires, zombies, and androids all denote? There is a very simple answer to this question: *unliving humanoids* (there are, of course, some differences between them that we will return to shortly, but this is their basic common ground). The task of a semiotic interpretation is to move from such a denotational significance to a connotational one, and in order to do that, we must determine whether the popularity of all three of these beings reveals any pattern or system.

The fact that vampires, zombies, and androids all denote unliving humanoids provides us with the basis for such a system because it enables us to *associate* them together in a single category. So in what kind of stories do we find unliving humanoids as characters? This one is easy: in *fantasy* stories — stories that, like fairy tales, are about things that are not found in ordinary reality. Ordinary reality is the subject of a very different variety of story called *literary realism*, and this *difference* is highly significant. To see this significance, however, we have to turn to some history.

A little research will reveal that until the latter part of the 1960s, fantasy stories in America (including fairy tales, science fiction, cartoon superheroes, and horror tales) were regarded as kid's stuff: something for B movies, comic books, Sunday matinees, and children's literature. Literary realism, on the other hand, was for grown-ups. This distinction effectively marginalized fantasy as nonserious and trivial; thus, the relation between fantasy and literary realism was not unlike the traditional relation between low culture and high culture.

But with the appearance of Gene Roddenberry's *Star Trek* in 1966, along with the popular revival of J. R. R. Tolkien's *Lord of the Rings* trilogy and *The Hobbit* at the same time, the hierarchical relationship between realism and fantasy began to change. Add to this the appearance of George Romero's *Night of the Living Dead* (1968) and the makings of a cultural revolution were at hand, a revolution that was sealed in the 1970s with the enormous successes of George Lucas's *Star Wars* (1977) and Anne Rice's *Interview with the Vampire* (1976). Suddenly fantasy wasn't mere kid's stuff anymore.

This shift of fantasy from marginal to central cultural status has only intensified in the decades since it began, with realism being increasingly marginalized in a popular culture dominated by the many descendants of Tolkien, Roddenberry, Romero, Lucas, and Rice. Thus, we now have a striking historical difference to consider.

So let's ask: Is there any possible significance in this shift from realism to fantasy? To answer this question, we can go back to the years in which it all began, the decade when America's baby-boom generation first began to come of age. The first generation in history to be raised on television, the boomers were provided with a source of constant daily entertainment heavy on children's fantasy. As a result, they were responsible for the creation of the *youth culture* that has been inherited, and enhanced, by every succeeding generation in America, from Gen X to the millennials. And it is within the context of an emerging youth culture that we can situate the rise of fantasy.

The values of a youth culture include not only a preference for prolonging childhood and clinging to the physical appearance of being young, but also a desire to maintain the tastes of childhood, which include a strong attraction to the sort of fantasies with which the young have been traditionally raised. These fantasies provide an alternative to the realities of adult life: the dull grind of making a living, of raising families rather than having adventures, of not being free to do whatever one likes. In other words, we can abductively argue that the triumph of fantasy connotatively signifies a culture-wide rejection of the realities of everyday life in America, a disillusionment (or simple boredom) with what ordinary experience has to offer and a desire to escape into the imaginative fairylands of infancy.

But while this can explain why such fantasy figures as vampires, zombies, and androids are so popular today in mainstream entertainment, it doesn't explain why zombies surpassed vampires in popularity in the second decade of the new millennium, or why androids are a likely contender to supplant zombies in the near future (with such films as *Her* and a remade *Robocop* leading the way, along with TV's *Almost Human*). And here is where overdetermination comes in, because the popularity of vampires, zombies, and androids is not *solely* explained by the rise of fantasy in American youth culture; there are other determinants as well, specific to each. The way in which an overdetermined set of phenomena can branch out into further systems with their own meanings is one of the key elements of a semiotic analysis.

It would be beyond the scope of this Introduction to provide a separate interpretation of all three of these figures (a full analysis of vampires, for its part, would focus on their transition from hideous monsters to romantic and sympathetic lovers and high schoolers, and you can find an interpretation of zombies in Chapter 3). But to show how the differences within a system lead to further semiotic meanings, let's return to androids for a moment. The key difference between androids and the other fantasy figures we have looked at is that androids are machines while the others are, in some way or another, biological. That is, if vampires and zombies denote the "living dead," androids aren't alive at all—they are only "powered on or off." But there is a more important difference to consider here: Unlike zombies and vampires, who don't exist and won't ever exist, androids are actually close to existing. What is science fiction or mere fantasy today could be reality in some not so very distant future.

The development of androids was a lot farther off in the days of R2-D2, C-3PO, HAL 9000, and Roy Batty, as was the prospect of real biomechanical men like Iron Man and the Six Million Dollar Man. But now, with Google Glass portending the arrival of real-life vision-enhanced Riddicks (the protagonist in a series of Vin Diesel films), and AI researchers coming ever closer to the creation of independently functioning intelligent machines by downloading human

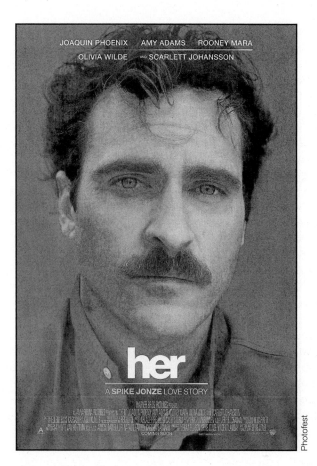

JOAQUIN PHOENIX   AMY ADAMS   ROONEY MARA

OLIVIA WILDE   AND SCARLETT JOHANSSON

her

A **SPIKE JONZE** LOVE STORY

COMING SOON

Photofest

The poster for the film *Her* (2013).

minds into computers, the android/cyborg is transitioning from fantasy to real possibility, a prospect at once glamorously exciting and naggingly worrisome.

In short, when we situate the android in the larger context of the growing dominance of technology in our lives, an abductively plausible interpretation emerges. That is, as "socializing" becomes "social networking," university classes become massive open online courses (MOOCs), cars become self-propelled robots, and the Singularity comes ever closer to arrival, the line between human and machine is becoming blurred. With our lives increasingly being conducted via cloud computing, just who we are as human beings is becoming less and less clear. In such an environment, we should not be surprised to see a host of androids storming the center stage of popular culture both as superheroes and as perplexed not-quite-humans who resent their

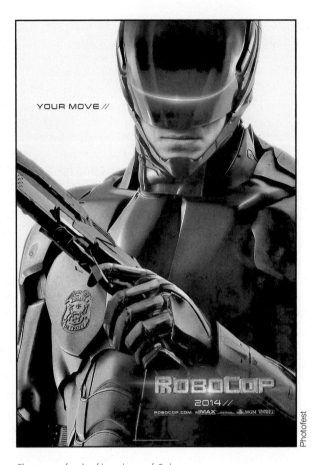

YOUR MOVE //

RoboCop
2014 //
ROBOCOP.COM IMAX MGM

Photofest

The poster for the film reboot of *Robocop*.

subservience to their creators, signifying at once a fascination with a looming brave new world of posthuman existence and a nervousness over what it all may lead to.

The Classroom Connection

This analysis of androids in popular culture could be extended further, but we will leave that for you to consider for yourself. The key point is that while the popularity of any particular fantasy characters, like androids or zombies, is evanescent, what such characters *signify* is not. The vampire fad is still significant, even if vampires today are old hat. The zombie fad is significant and will remain so after it has passed. All the fads of an ever-shifting popular cultural terrain remain significant, just as all the historical events in an ever-changing world are significant. In fact, performing a popular cultural analysis is essentially equivalent to writing interpretive history, but it is an interpretive history of the present.

Thus, semiotic analyses of popular culture are not different from the more conventional interpretive analyses you will be asked to perform in your college writing career. It is in the nature of all critical thinking to make connections and mark differences in order to go beyond the surface of a text or issue toward a meaning. The skills you already have as an interpreter of the popular signs around you — of images, objects, and forms of behavior — are the same skills that you develop as a writer of critical essays that present an argued point of view and the evidence to defend it.

Because most of us tend to identify closely with our favorite popular cultural phenomena and have strong opinions about them, it can be difficult to adopt the same sort of analytic perspective toward popular culture that we do toward, say, texts assigned in a literature class. Still, that is what you should do in a semiotic interpretation: You need to set your aesthetic or fan-related opinions aside in order to pursue an interpretive argument with evidence to support it. Note how in our interpretation of the android story we didn't say whether or not we like it: Our concern was with what it might mean within a larger cultural context. It is not difficult to express an aesthetic opinion or a statement of personal preference, but that isn't the goal of analytic writing and critical thinking. Analytic writing requires that you marshal supporting evidence, just as a lawyer needs evidence to argue a case. So by learning to write analyses of our culture, by searching for supporting evidence to underpin your interpretive take on modern life, you are also learning to write critical arguments.

"But how," you (and perhaps your instructor) may ask, "can I know that a semiotic interpretation is right?" Good question — it is commonly asked by those who fear that a semiotic analysis might read too much into a subject. But then, it can also be asked of the writer of any interpretive essay, and the answer in each case is the same. No one can absolutely *prove* the truth of an argument in the human sciences; what you can do is *persuade* your audience by including pertinent evidence in an abductive reasoning process. In analyzing popular culture, that evidence comes from your knowledge of the system to which the object you are interpreting belongs. The more you know about the system, the more convincing your interpretations will be. And that is true whether you are writing about popular culture or about more traditional academic subjects.

Of Myths and Men

As we have seen, in a semiotic analysis we do not search for the meanings of things in the things themselves. Rather, we find meaning in the way we can relate things together through association and differentiation, moving from objective denotation to culturally subjective connotation. Such a movement commonly takes us from the realm of mere facts to the world of cultural values. But while values often *feel* like facts, from a semiotic perspective, they derive from cultural systems that semioticians call *cultural mythologies*.

A cultural **mythology** is not some fanciful story from the past; indeed, if the word *mythology* seems confusing because of its traditional association with such stories, you may prefer to use the term "value system" or "ideology." Consider the value system that governs our traditional thinking about gender roles. Have you ever noticed how our society presumes that it is primarily the role of women—adult daughters—to take care of aging and infirm parents? If you want to look at the matter from a physiological perspective, it might seem that men would be better suited to the task: In a state of nature, men are physically stronger and so would seem to be the natural protectors of the aged. And yet, though our cultural mythology holds that men should protect the nuclear family, it tends to assign to women the care of extended families. It is culture that decides here, not nature.

But while cultural mythologies guide our behavior, they are subject to change. You may have already experienced a transitional phase in the myths surrounding courtship behavior. In the past, the gender myths that formed the rules of the American dating game held that it is the role of the male to initiate proceedings (he calls) and for the female to react (she waits for the call). Similarly, the rules once held that it is invariably the responsibility of the male to plan the evening and pay the tab. These rules are changing, aren't they? Can you describe the rules that now govern courtship behavior?

A cultural mythology or value system, then, is a kind of lens that governs the way we view our world. Think of it this way: Say you were born with rose-tinted eyeglasses permanently attached over your eyes, but you didn't know they were there. Because the world would *look* rose colored to you, you would presume that it *is* rose colored. You wouldn't wonder whether the world might look otherwise through different lenses. But in the world there are other kinds of eyeglasses with different lenses, and reality does look different to those who wear them. Those lenses are cultural mythologies, and no culture can claim to have the one set of glasses that reveals things as they really are.

The principle that meaning is not culture-blind, that it is conditioned by systems of ideology and belief that are codified differently by different cultures, is a foundational semiotic judgment. Human beings, in other words, construct their own social realities, so who gets to do the constructing becomes very important. Every contest over a cultural code is, accordingly, a contest for power, but the contest is usually masked because the winner generally defines its mythology as the truth, as what is most natural or reasonable. Losers in the contest become objects of scorn and are quickly marginalized and declared unnatural, deviant, or even insane. The stakes are high as myth battles myth, with truth itself as the highest prize.

This does not mean that you must abandon your own beliefs when conducting a semiotic analysis, only that you cannot take them for granted and must be prepared to argue for them. We want to assure you that semiotics will not tell you what to think and believe. It *does* assume that what you believe reflects some cultural system or other and that no cultural system can claim absolute validity or superiority. The readings and Chapter Introductions in this book contain their own values and ideologies, and if you wish to challenge those values, you can begin by exposing the myths that they may take for granted.

Thus, everything in this book reflects a political point of view. If you hold a different view, it is not enough to presuppose the innate superiority of your own perspective — to claim that one writer is being political while you are simply telling the truth. This may sound heretical precisely because human beings operate within cultural mythologies whose political invisibility is guaranteed by the system. No mythology, that is to say, begins with "This is just a political construct or interpretation." Every mythology begins, "This is the truth." It is very difficult to imagine, from within the mythology, any alternatives. Indeed, as you read this book, you may find it upsetting to see that some traditional beliefs — such as "proper" roles of men and women — are socially constructed and not absolute. But the outlines of the mythology, the bounding (and binding) frame, can be discerned only by first seeing that it *is* a mythology, a constructive scaffolding upon which our consciousness and desires are constituted.

Getting Started

Mythology, like culture, is not static, and so the semiotician must always keep his or her eye on the clock, so to speak. History and the passing of time are constant factors in a constantly changing world. Since the earlier editions of this book, American popular culture has moved on. In this edition, we have tried to reflect those changes, but inevitably, further changes will occur in the time it takes for this book to appear on your class syllabus. That such changes occur is part of the excitement of the semiotic enterprise: There is always something new to consider and interpret. What does not change is the nature of semiotic interpretation: Whatever you choose to analyze in the realm of American popular culture, the semiotic approach will help you understand it.

It's your turn now. Start asking questions, pushing, probing. That's what critical thinking and writing are all about, but this time you're part of the question. Arriving at answers is the fun part here, but answers aren't the basis of analytic thinking: Questions are. You always begin with a question, a query, a hypothesis, something to explore. If you already knew the answer, there would be no point in conducting the analysis. We encourage you to explore the almost-infinite variety of questions that the readings in this book raise. Many come equipped with their own "answers," but you may (indeed you will and should) find that such answers raise further questions. To help you ask those questions, keep in mind the elemental principles of semiotics that we have just explored:

1. Cultural semiotics treats human behavior itself — not what people say about their behavior but what they actually do — as **signs**.
2. The meaning of signs can be found not in themselves but in their relationships (both differences and associations) with other signs within a

system. To interpret an individual sign, then, you must determine the general system to which it belongs.

3. Things have both **denotative** meanings (what they *are*) and **connotative** meanings (what they *suggest as signs*); semiotics moves beyond the denotative surface to the connotative significance.

4. Arriving at the connotative significance of a sign involves both **abduction** (a search for the most likely explanation or interpretation) and **over-determination** (the multiple causes behind a cultural phenomenon).

5. What we call social "reality" is a human construct, the product of cultural **mythologies** or value systems that intervene between our minds and the world we experience. Such cultural myths reflect the values and ideological interests of their builders, not the laws of nature or logic.

Perhaps our first principle could be more succinctly phrased, "Behavior is meaningful," and our second, "Everything is connected," while our third advises, "Don't take things at face value." More simply, always ask yourself, whenever you are interpreting something, "What's going on here?" In short, question *everything*. And one more reminder: Signs are like weather vanes, they point in response to invisible historical winds. We invite you now to start looking at the weather.

WRITING ABOUT POPULAR CULTURE

Throughout this book, you will find readings on popular culture that you can use as models for your own writing or as subjects to which you may respond, assignments for writing critical essays on popular culture, and advice to help you analyze a wide variety of cultural phenomena. As you approach these readings and assignments, you may find it helpful to review the following suggestions for writing critical essays — whether on popular culture or on any subject — as well as some examples of student essays written in response to assignments based on *Signs of Life in the U.S.A.* Mastering the skills summarized and exemplified here should enable you to write the kinds of papers you will be assigned throughout your college career.

As you prepare to write a critical essay on popular culture, remember that you are already an expert in your subject. After all, simply by actively participating in everyday life, you have accumulated a vast store of knowledge about what makes our culture tick. Just think of all you know about movies, or the thousands upon thousands of ads you've seen, or the many unwritten "rules" governing courtship behavior among your circle of friends. Your very expertise in popular culture, ironically, may create a challenge simply because you may take your knowledge for granted. It might not seem that your knowledge can "count" as material for a college-level assignment, and it might not even occur to you to use it in an essay. You should certainly draw on your own knowledge, but to write a strong essay, you need to do more than just go along with the "flow" of your subject as you live it; instead, you need to consider it from a critical distance.

Using Active Reading Strategies

The first step in developing a strong essay about any topic happens well before you sit down to write: You need to make sure you understand accurately the reading selections that your instructor has assigned. You want to engage in *active* reading—that is, you want to get more than just the "drift" of a passage. Skimming a selection may give you a rough idea of the author's point, but your understanding of it is also likely to be partial, superficial, or even downright wrong. And that's not a solid start to writing a good paper!

Active reading techniques can help you understand the nuances of how an author constructs his or her argument accurately and precisely. You should question, summarize, agree with, and/or refute the author's claims. In other words, try to have a kind of *conversation* with the author. Studies have shown that such interactive learning simply works better than passive learning; if you read actively, you'll gain knowledge at a higher rate and retain it longer. With any reading selection, it can be helpful to read at least twice: first, to gain a general sense of the author's ideas and, second, to study more specifically how those ideas work together to form an argument. To do this, you can use some formal discovery techniques, or what are called *heuristics*. One of the most famous heuristics is the journalist's "five *W*s and an *H*": who, what, where, when, why, and how. By asking these questions, a reporter can quickly unearth the essential details of a breaking story and draft a clear account of it. For your purposes, you can apply the following questions to reading selections you will discuss in your own essays.

Active Reading Questions

- What is the *author's primary argument*? Can you identify a *thesis* statement, or is the thesis implied?
- What *key terms* are fundamental to that argument? If you are not familiar with the fundamental vocabulary of the selection, be sure to check a dictionary or encyclopedia for the word's meaning.
- What *evidence* does the author provide to support the argument? Is it relevant and specific? Does the author cite reliable, authoritative sources?
- What *underlying assumptions* shape the author's position? Does the author consider alternative points of view (counterarguments)?

---

macmillanhighered.com/signsoflife
LearningCurve > Critical Reading
Tutorials > Critical Reading: Active Reading Strategies

- What *style* and *tone* does the author adopt?
- What is the *genre* of the piece? You need to identify what kind of writing you are responding to, because different kinds have different purposes and goals. A personal narrative, for instance, expresses the writer's experiences and beliefs, but you shouldn't expect it to present a complete argument supported by documentation.
- Who is the *intended readership* of this selection, and does it affect the author's reasoning or evidence?

As you read, write *annotations*, or notes, in your book. Doing so will help you both remember and analyze what you read. A pencil is probably the best memory aid ever invented. No one, not even the most experienced and perceptive reader, remembers everything—and let's face it, not everything that you read is worth remembering. Writing annotations as you read will lead you back to important points. And annotating helps you start analyzing a reading—long before you start writing an essay—rather than uncritically accepting what's on the page. If you are using an electronic version of this text, you can do the same with the highlight and annotate tools available in most e-readers.

There's yet another reason to annotate what you read: You can use the material you've identified as the starting point for your journal notes and essays, and since it doesn't take long to circle a word or jot a note in the margin, you can save a great deal of time in the long run. We suggest that you *not* use a highlighter. While using a highlighter is better than using nothing—it can at least help you mark key points—writing *words* in your book goes much further in helping you analyze what you read. We've seen entire pages bathed in fluorescent-yellow highlighter, and that's of doubtful use in identifying the important stuff. Of course, if you simply can't bring yourself to mark up your book, write on sticky notes instead and put those in the margins.

So as you read, circle key words, note transitions between ideas, jot definitions of unfamiliar terms (you can probably guess their meaning from the context or look them up later), underline phrases or terms to research on a search engine such as Google, write short summaries of important points, or simply note where you're confused or lost with a question mark or a *huh?!* In fact, figuring out exactly what parts you do and don't understand is one of the best ways to tackle a difficult reading. Frequently, the confusing bits turn out to be the most interesting—and sometimes the most important. Responding to what you read *as* you read will help you become a more active reader—and will ultimately help you become a stronger writer.

Signs of Life in the U.S.A. frequently asks you to respond to a reading selection in a *journal* or *reading log*, sometimes directly and sometimes indirectly, as in suggestions that you write a letter to the author of a selection. In doing so, you're taking a first step in articulating your response to the issues and to the author's presentation of them. In asking you to keep a journal or a reading log, your instructor will probably be less concerned with your writing style than with your comprehension of assigned readings and your thoughtful responses to them. Let's say you're asked to write your response to Jessica Hagedorn's "Asian Women in Film: No Joy, No Luck" in Chapter 4. You should first think through exactly what Hagedorn is saying—what her point is—by asking the questions listed on pages 22–23 and by reviewing your annotations. Then consider how you feel about her essay. If you agree with Hagedorn's contention that films perpetuate outmoded stereotypes of Asian women, why do you feel that way? Can you think of films Hagedorn does not mention that reflect the gendered patterns she observes? Or do you know of films that represent Asian female characters positively? Suppose you're irritated by Hagedorn's argument: Again, why do you feel that way? Your aim in jotting all this down is not to produce a draft of an essay. It's to play with your own ideas, see where they lead, and even just help you decide what your ideas are in the first place.

Prewriting Strategies

Before you start writing, you'll find it useful to spend some time generating your ideas freely and openly: Your goal at this point is to develop as many ideas as possible, even ones that you might not actually use in your essay. Writing instructors call this process *prewriting*, and it's a step you should take when writing on any subject in any class, not just in your writing class. This textbook includes many suggestions for how you can develop your ideas; even if your instructor doesn't require you to use all of them, you can try them on your own.

These strategies will work when you are asked to respond to a particular reading or image. Sometimes, though, you may be asked to write about a more general subject. Your instructor may ask you to brainstorm ideas or to freewrite in response to an issue. You can use both strategies in your journal or on your own as you start working on an essay. *Brainstorming* is simply amassing as many relevant (and even some irrelevant) ideas as possible. Let's say your instructor asks you to brainstorm a list of popular toys used by girls and boys in preparation for an essay about the gendered designs of children's toys. Try to list your thoughts freely, jotting down whatever comes to mind. Don't censor yourself at this point. That is, don't worry if something is really a game rather than a toy, or if both boys and girls play with it, or if it is really an adult toy. Later on you can throw out ideas that don't fit. What you'll be left with is a rich list of examples that you can then study and analyze. *Freewriting* works much the same way and is particularly useful when you're not sure how you feel about an issue. Sit down and just start writing or typing, and don't stop until you've written for at least ten or fifteen minutes. Let your ideas wander around your subject, working associatively, following their own path. As with brainstorming, you may produce some irrelevant ideas, but you may also arrive at a sharper picture of your beliefs.

If your instructor asks you to create your own topic, you might wonder, "Where should I start?" Suppose you need to analyze an aspect of the film industry but can't decide on a focus. Here, the Internet might help. You could explore a resource such as filmsite.org, a site divided into categories such as History, Genres, and Reviews. These categories can lead you to more specific links, such as "Film History by Decade" and "Film Reviews by Decade." With so many to choose from, you're bound to find something that interests you. In effect, you can go online to engage in *electronic brainstorming* about your topic.

One cautionary note: When going online to brainstorm, be sure to *evaluate the appropriateness of your sources* (see p. 60). Many sites are commercial and are therefore intended more to sell a product or image than to provide reliable information. In addition, since anyone with the technological know-how can set up a Web site, some sites amount to little more than personal expression and need to be evaluated for their reliability, accuracy, and authenticity. Scrutinize the sites you use carefully: Is the author an authority in the field? Does the site identify the author, at least by name and e-mail address? (Be wary of fully anonymous sites.) Does the site contain interesting and relevant links? If you find an advocacy site, one that openly advances a special interest, does the site's bias interfere with the accuracy of its information? Asking such questions can help ensure that your electronic brainstorming is fruitful and productive. If you are unsure of the validity of a site, you might want to check with your instructor.

You can also strengthen your argument if you consider the *history* of your subject. You might think this requires a lot of library research, but research may not be necessary if you are already familiar with the social and cultural history of your topic. If you know, for instance, that the baggy pants so popular among teens until recently were once ubiquitous among street-gang members, you know an important historical detail that goes a long way toward explaining their significance. Depending on your assignment, you might want to expand on your own historical knowledge and collect additional data about your topic, perhaps through surveys and interviews. If you're analyzing gendered patterns of courtship rituals, for instance, you could interview some people from different age groups, as well as both genders, to get a sense of how such patterns have evolved over time. The material you gather through such interviews will be raw data, and you'll want to do more than just "dump" the information into your essay. Instead, see this material as an original body of evidence that you'll sort through (you probably won't use every scrap of information), study, and interpret in its own right.

Not all prewriting activities need be solitary, of course. In fact, *Signs of Life* includes lots of suggestions that ask you to work with other students, either in your class or across campus. We suggest such *group work* because much academic work is collaborative and collegial. A scientist conducting research, for instance, often works with a team; in addition, he or she may present preliminary findings at colloquia or conferences and may call or e-mail a colleague at another school to try out some ideas. There's no reason you can't benefit from the social nature of academic thinking as well. But be aware that such in-class group work is by no means "busywork." The goal, rather, is to help you develop and shape your understanding of the issues and your attitudes toward them. If you're asked to study with three classmates how a product is packaged, for instance, you're starting to test Thomas Hine's thesis in "What's in a Package" (Chapter 1), seeing how it applies or doesn't apply and benefiting from your peers' insights. By discussing the package with your peers, you are articulating, perhaps for the first time, what it might mean and so are taking the first step toward writing a more formal analysis (especially if you receive feedback and comments from your class). Similarly, if you stage an in-class debate over whether multitasking is "healthy" or dangerous, you're amassing a storehouse of arguments, counterarguments, and evidence to consider when you write your own essay that either supports or refutes S. Craig Watkins's argument in "Fast Entertainment and Multitasking in an Always-On World" (Chapter 5). As with other prewriting strategies, you may not directly use every idea generated in conversation with your classmates, but that's OK. You should find yourself better able to sort through and articulate the ideas that you do find valuable.

Developing Strong Arguments about Popular Culture

We expect that students will write many different sorts of papers in response to the selections in this book. You may write personal experience narratives, semiotic analyses, opinion pieces, research papers, and many others. We'd like to focus here on writing analytic essays because the experience of analyzing popular culture may seem different from that of analyzing other subjects. Occasionally we've had students who feel reluctant to analyze popular culture because they think that analysis requires them to trash their subject, and they don't want to write a "negative" essay about what may be their favorite film or TV program. Or a few students may feel uncertain because "it's all subjective." Since most people have opinions about popular culture, they say, how can any one essay be stronger than another?

While these concerns are understandable, they needn't be an obstacle to writing a strong analytic paper — whether on popular culture or any other topic. To avoid overt subjectivity, you should begin by setting aside your own personal tastes when writing an analysis, not because your preferences are unimportant, but because you need to be aware of your own attitudes and observations about your topic. An analysis of, say, *The Big Bang Theory* is not the same as a paper that explains "why I like (or dislike) this TV program." Instead, an analysis would explain how it works, what cultural beliefs and viewpoints underlie it, what its significance is, and so forth. And such a paper would not necessarily be positive or negative; it would seek to explain *how* the elements of the show work together to have a particular effect on its audience. If your instructor asks you to write a critical analysis or a critical argument, he or she is requesting neither a hit job nor a celebration of your topic.

For most of your college essays, you will probably be asked to make sure that your paper has a clear *thesis*. A thesis statement lays out the argument you intend to make and provides a scope for your essay. If you think of your thesis as a road map that your paper will follow, you might find that it is easier to structure your paper. A thesis for an essay on popular culture should follow the usual guidelines for any academic essay: It should make a debatable, interesting assertion (as opposed to a statement of fact or a truism); it should be demonstrable through the presentation of specific evidence; it should have a clear focus and scope; and it should spark your readers' interest. Additionally, a strong thesis statement will help you overcome any anxieties you might have about writing a strong analysis, because a good thesis statement, rather than merely offering a simple opinion on your topic, also explains how you came to hold that opinion. The thesis statements in the sample papers that begin on page 34 are annotated to help you see how they function in academic writing.

When your paper has a strong thesis, subjectivity becomes even less of a problem. That's because your analysis should be grounded in concrete demonstration. You're not simply presenting a personal opinion about your subject; rather, you're presenting a central insight about its significance, and you need to demonstrate it with logical, specific evidence. It's that evidence that will take your essay out of the category of being "merely subjective." You should start with your own opinion, but you will want to add to it lots of support that shows the legitimacy of that opinion. Does that sound familiar? It should, because that's what you need to do in any analytic essay, no matter what your subject matter happens to be.

When writing about popular culture, students sometimes wonder what sort of evidence they should use to support their points. Your instructor will probably give you guidelines for each assignment, but we'll provide some suggestions here. Start with your subject itself. You'll find it's useful to view your subject — whether it's an ad, a film, or anything else — as a text that you can "read" closely. That's what you would do if you were asked to analyze a poem: You would read it carefully, studying individual words, images, rhythm, and so forth, and those details would support whatever claims you wanted to make about the poem. Read your pop culture subject with the same care. If your instructor asks you to analyze a television series, you should look at the details: What actors appear in the series, and what are their roles? What "story" does the program tell about its characters and the world in which they live? Is there anything missing from this world that you would expect to find? What are the *connotative* meanings behind the surface signs? Your answers to such questions could form the basis for the evidence that your essay needs.

Conducting a Semiotic Analysis

In an essay focused on a semiotic analysis, you can probe a wider range of questions about your subject that can yield even more specific evidence and arguments. You can start with some basic questions that we ask throughout the Chapter Introductions in this book, and which we summarize in the list below. Now let's apply these questions to an example, the TV series *House*, still popular and significant, even though it is now in reruns.

DENOTATIVE MEANINGS

What is a simple, literal description of your subject? You need to make sure you understand this before looking for "deeper meanings," because if you misunderstand the factual status of your subject, you will probably get derailed in your analysis. In the case of *House*, we find a story of a medical genius who, though he is his hospital's most successful diagnostician, is also

---

Questions for Conducting a Semiotic Analysis

- What is the **denotative** meaning of your subject? In other words, determine a factual definition of exactly what it is.
- What is your topic's **connotative** significance? To determine that, situate your subject in a system of related signs.
- What **associated** signs belong to that system?
- What **differences** do you see in those signs?
- What **abductive** explanation do you have for your observations? What is the most likely explanation for the patterns that you see?

---

e macmillanhighered.com/signsoflife
Need help editing for common grammar mistakes?
LearningCurve > Commas; Fragments; Run-ons and Comma Splices; Active and Passive Voice; Appropriate Language; Subject-Verb Agreement

rude, nasty, and practically dysfunctional in his personal life, suffering from an addiction to Vicodin and almost constant depression. The plots of *House* tend to exemplify the series's slogan, "Everybody lies," and often depict House's patients or their families as liars with dark secrets that they are concealing and that House eventually uncovers. Clearly, if we were to misidentify *House* as a documentary, we'd misconstrue it as a scathing political exposé of the U.S. medical system — but that doesn't feel right. *House* is no exposé.

CONNOTATIVE MEANINGS AND A SYSTEM OF RELATED SIGNS

After determining your subject's denotation, you must locate your subject within a larger system in order to determine its connotative meaning. Recall that a system is the network of related signs to which your topic belongs and that identifying the system helps to reveal its significance. This may sound hard to do, but it is through identifying a system that you can draw on your own vast knowledge of popular culture. So, in our analysis of *House*, we need to move from our denotative understanding of the series to its connotative significance. In order to make this move, we need to identify a system of related signs. In the case of *House*, this entails identifying programs with which it is similar. In other words, to what genre of television programming does *House* belong? What conventions, goals, and motifs do shows in this genre share? What is the history of the genre? *House*, of course, belongs to the medical drama genre, which is distinct from, say, situation comedy, even though *House* does have certain comic elements that would allow us to classify it as a medical *dramedy*. The history of TV medical drama includes such programs as *Dr. Kildare* and *Ben Casey* in the 1960s; *Marcus Welby, M.D.*, and *Quincy, M.E.*, in the 1970s; *St. Elsewhere* and *ER* in the 1980s and beyond; and *Grey's Anatomy* and *Nip/Tuck* in recent years. All these programs can be associated with *House* and testify to the enduring popularity of the genre. (Indeed, long before television, an old joke had it that the most certain formula to follow in writing a best seller was to write a book about Abraham Lincoln's doctor's dog.)

DIFFERENCES WITHIN THE SYSTEM

But while the associations between these television series demonstrate a popular interest in doctors and medical stories, there is still a striking difference to consider, a kind of dividing line marked by the series *St. Elsewhere*. Until *St. Elsewhere*, the main character in a medical series was a benevolent healer whose own personal life beyond the hospital was generally not a part of the story line (there were exceptions: Dr. Kildare once had a patient with whom he fell in love; Ben Casey had a somewhat edgy nature; and Jack Klugman's Quincy — a forensic pathologist whose mystery-solving abilities anticipate those of Gregory House — had plenty of attitude). But all in all, the physician protagonists of the earlier series maintained a general profile of almost superhuman benevolence; they were "official heroes," in Robert B. Ray's terms (see "The Thematic Paradigm," p. 450), caring for the innocent victims of disease.

St. Elsewhere changed that, and from that program onward (especially as developed by *ER*), the flaws in the lives and personalities of the main characters, the doctors, became much more prominent. The doctors were, in short, much more humanized — a shift in characterization that has led to the caustic, sometimes dysfunctional and lawbreaking, Dr. House.

ABDUCTIVE EXPLANATIONS

At this point, we are ready to start interpreting, seeking abductive explanations for the shift. We can begin with the construction of another system, this time looking at the larger context of other television genres. If we look at this system, we can find in situation comedies, crime series, Westerns, and many other genres a shift similar to the one in the history of medical dramas. The difference between the family sitcoms of the 1950s and 1960s and those of the 1980s and beyond is well known, taking us from the happy families of the Cleavers and the Nelsons to the dysfunctional Bundys and Griffins. Similarly, it is a long way from Dick Tracy and *Dragnet*'s Joe Friday to the callous cops of *The Wire*. And it is a long way from *Gunsmoke* to *Justified*. Many other such differences could be mentioned, but we'll move on to our abductive interpretation.

The post–*St. Elsewhere* medical drama reflects a broader trend in American entertainment away from squeaky-clean television protagonists to more "realistically" flawed ones, heroes who definitely have feet of clay. This trend reflects a cultural shift whose beginning can be found in the cultural revolution of the 1960s, when American mass culture began a long process of disillusionment. After the Vietnam War and Watergate, increasingly cynical Americans were no longer predisposed to believe in absolute human perfection, preferring a more "realistic" depiction of human beings with all their flaws visible.

Thus, we can now see *House* as part of a larger cultural trend in which the once-cherished, even revered, figure of the physician has been pulled off the pedestal and brought to earth along with everyone else. Heroes are still heroes (after all, Gregory House is just plain smarter than anyone else around him), but they are more like ordinary folks. They misbehave, get cranky, break rules. Even the victims of misfortune (patients in a medical drama) have been degraded, appearing no longer as the objects of our sympathy but as flawed people with dark secrets. *Everybody lies.* No one is innocent. To the disillusioned, *House*, with its all-too-human hero and cast, is an entertaining, if cynical, vision of the way things are — or at least of the way that large numbers of viewers think they are. Doctors (and cops, families, cowboys, and everyone else) have warts too, and, as a sort of anti–Marcus Welby, Gregory House entertains his audience by not being afraid to show his flaws to the world.

Reading Visual Images Actively

Signs of Life in the U.S.A. includes many visual images, in many cases with accompanying questions for analysis. In analyzing images, you will develop the ability to identify specific telling details and evidence — a talent useful no matter what your subject matter may be. Because the semiotic method lends itself especially well to visual analysis, it is an excellent means for honing this ability. Here are some questions to consider as you look at images.

Questions for Analyzing Images

- What is the **appearance of the image**? Is it black and white? Color? Glossy? Consider how the form in which the image is expressed affects its message. If an image is composed of primary colors, does it look fun and lively, for instance?

- What **kind of image** is it? Is it abstract, does it represent an actual person or place, or is it a combination of the two? If people are represented, who are they?

- Who is the intended **audience** for the image? Is it an artistic photograph or a commercial work, such as an advertisement? If it is an ad, to what kind of person is it directed? Where is the ad placed? If it is in a magazine, consider the audience for the publication.

- What **emotions** does the image convey? Overall, is it serious, sad, funny? Is that expression of emotion, in your opinion, intentional? What emotional associations do you have with the image?

- If the image includes more than one element, what is the most prominent element in the **composition**? A particular section? A logo? Any writing? A person or group of people? A product? How does each part contribute to the whole?

- Where does the image's **layout** lead your eye? Are you drawn to any specific part? What is the order in which you look at the various parts? Does any particular section immediately jump out?

- Does the image include **text**? If so, how do the image and the text relate to one another?

- Does the image call for a **response**? For instance, does it suggest that you purchase a product? If so, what claims does it make?

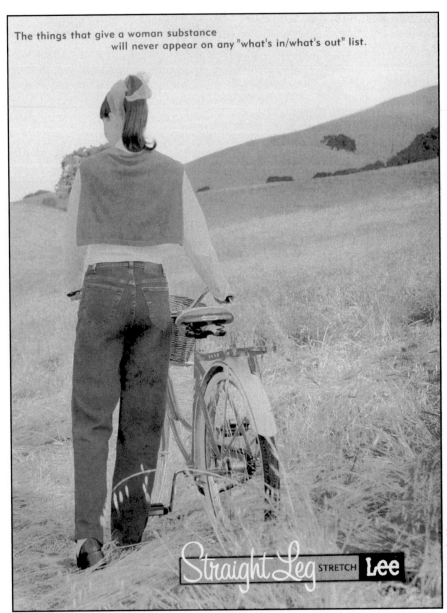

The things that give a woman substance will never appear on any "what's in/what's out" list.

Straight Leg STRETCH **Lee**

To see how we can apply these questions, let's look at a sample analysis of an advertisement for Lee jeans (see image on p. 32).

Appearance: Although this image is reproduced here in black and white, it originally appeared in color. The colors are muted, however, almost sepia-toned, and thus suggest an old-fashioned look.

Kind of image: This is a fairly realistic image, with a patina of rural nostalgia. A solitary woman, probably in her twenties or thirties, but perhaps older, is set against an empty natural expanse. She has a traditional hairstyle evocative of the 1950s or early 1960s and leads an old-fashioned bicycle with a wicker basket attached.

Audience: The intended audience for this jeans ad is most likely a woman in her late twenties or older. We see only the model's back, so she is faceless. That allows the viewer to project herself into the scene, and the nostalgic look suggests that the viewer could imagine herself at a younger time in her life. Note that the product is "stretch" jeans. There's no suggestion here, although it is often made in ads for other brands, that the jeans will enhance a woman's sexual appeal; rather, the claim is that the jeans are practical — and will fit a body beyond the teen years. Note the sensible hairstyle and shoes. For an interesting contrast, you might compare this ad to one for Diesel jeans.

Emotion: The woman's body language suggests individuality and determination; she's literally "going it alone." She's neither posing for nor aware of the viewer, suggesting that "what you see is what you get." And, perhaps, she doesn't particularly care what you think.

Composition and layout: The layout of the ad is carefully designed to lead your eye: The hill slopes down from top right toward middle left, and the bike draws your eye from bottom right to mid-left, with both lines converging on the product, the jeans. For easy readability, the text is included at the top against the blank sky.

Text: The message, "The things that give a woman substance will never appear on any 'what's in/what's out' list," suggests that Lee jeans are a product for women who aren't interested in following trends, but rather want a good, old-fashioned value — "substance," not frivolity.

Response: The manufacturer of Lee jeans would prefer, naturally, that the viewer of the ad buy the product. The viewer would identify with the woman wearing the jeans in the advertisement and be convinced that these practical (if not particularly cutting-edge) jeans would be a good purchase.

In sum, most fashion ads stress the friends (and often, mates) you will attract if you buy the product, but this ad presents "a road not taken," suggesting the American ideology of marching to the beat of a different drummer, the kind of old-fashioned individualism that brings to mind Robert Frost and Henry David Thoreau. The pastoral surroundings and the "old painting" effect echo artists such as Andrew Wyeth and Norman Rockwell. All these impressions connote lasting American values (rural, solid, middle American) that are meant to be associated with anti-trendiness and enduring qualities, such as individualism and practicality. And these impressions suggest the advertisers carefully and effectively kept the ad's semiotic messages in mind as they designed it.

Reading Essays about Popular Culture

In your writing course, it's likely that your instructor will ask you to work in groups with other students, perhaps reviewing each other's rough drafts. You'll find many benefits to this activity. Not only will you receive more feedback on your own in-progress work, but you will see other students' ideas and approaches to an assignment and develop an ability to evaluate academic writing. For the same reasons, we're including three sample student essays that satisfy assignments about popular culture. You may agree or disagree with the authors' views, and you might have responded to the assigned topics differently; that's fine. We've selected these essays because they differ in style, focus, and purpose and thus suggest different approaches to their assignments—approaches that might help you as you write your own essays about popular culture. We've annotated the essays to point out various argumentative, organizational, and rhetorical strategies. As you read the essays and the annotations, ask why the authors chose these strategies and how you might incorporate some of the same strategies into your own writing.

Essay 1

In this essay, Amy Lin of UCLA argues that the Barbie doll, and all its associated products and marketing, essentially is a means for engendering a consumerist ethos in young girls who are the toy's fans. To do so, Lin relies on a range of sources, including articles in *Signs of Life in the U.S.A.*, academic and journalistic sources, and a corporate Web site that presents the panoply of Barbie products. Notice that Lin does not treat toysrus.com as a source of unbiased information about the products (that would amount to taking promotional material at face value); rather, she analyzes the Web site as evidence for her larger argument about consumerism. As you read Lin's essay, study how she uses her sources and integrates them into her own discussion.

Barbie: Queen of Dolls and Consumerism

In my closet, a plastic bag contains five Barbie dolls. A cardboard box beside my nightstand holds yet another, and one more box contains a Ken doll. Under my bed we find my Barbies' traveling walk-in closet, equipped with a light-up vanity and foldout chair and desk. We also find Doctor Barbie along with the baby, sticker Band-Aids, and sounding stethoscope with which she came. Under my sister's bed are their furniture set, including sofas, loveseats, flower vases, and a coffee table. A Tupperware container holds Ken's pants, dress shirts, and special boots (whose spurs make patterns when rolled in ink) in addition to Barbie's excess clothing that did not fit in the walk-in closet. In a corner of my living room sits the special holiday edition Barbie, outfitted in a gown, fur stole, and holly headband.

Amy's introduction is a visual anecdote that illustrates her argument about consumption.

These plastic relics prove that, as a young girl, I, like many other females, fell into the waiting arms of the Mattel Corporation. Constantly feeding the public with newer, shinier toys, the Barbie enterprise illustrates America's propensity for consumerism. Upon close examination, Barbie products foster materialism in young females through both their overwhelmingly large selection and their ability to create a financially carefree world for children, sending the message that excessive consumption is acceptable. This consequently perpetuates the misassumption that "the American economy [is] an endlessly fertile continent whose boundaries never need be reached" (Shames 81) among the American youth.

Amy articulates her thesis and refers to Laurence Shames's article as a context.

Search the term "Barbie" at toysrus.com, and you will receive 286 items in return — more than enough to create a blur of pinkish-purple as you scroll down the Web page. The Barbie enterprise clearly embraces "the observation that 'no natural boundary seems to be set to the efforts of man'" (Shames 78). In other words, humankind is, in all ways, ambitious; people will keep creating, buying, and selling with the belief that these opportunities will always be available. This perfectly describes the mentality of those behind Barbie products, as new, but unnecessary, Barbie merchandise is put on shelves at an exorbitant rate. At toysrus.com, for example, a variety of four different mermaids, eleven fairies, and two "merfairies" — products from the "Fairytopia-Mermaidia" line — find their place among the search results (*Toys*). Instead of inventing

The corporate Web site is used not as a source of objective information but as evidence to support the thesis.

a more original or educational product, Mattel merges the mermaid world with the fairy world into "Fairytopia-Mermaidia," demonstrating the company's lack of innovation and care for its young consumers' development. Thus the corporation's main motivation reveals itself: profit. Another prime example found among the search results is the "Barbie: 12 Dancing Princesses Horse Carriage" (*Toys*), a more recent product in the Barbie family. The carriage, "in its original form, . . . can seat six princess dolls but . . . can expand to hold all 12 dolls at once" (*Toys*). The dolls, of course, do not come with it, forcing the child to buy at least one for the carriage to even be of any use. But that child will see the glorious picture of the carriage filled with all twelve dolls (which are inevitably on the box), and she will want to buy the remaining eleven. In addition, the product description states that the carriage "is inspired by the upcoming DVD release, Barbie in *The 12 Dancing Princesses*" (*Toys*). Essentially, one Mattel creation inspires another, meaning that the DVD's sole purpose is to give Mattel an excuse to create and market more useless merchandise.

Much of this, however, may have to do with branding, a strategy manufacturers utilize that ultimately results in "consumers transfer[ring] a favorable or unfavorable image from one product to others from the same brand" (Neuhaus and Taylor 419). In accordance with this strategy, all Barbie products must maintain a certain similarity so as not to "'confuse' potential customers . . . and thereby reduce demand for the products" (Sappington and Wernerfelt 280). This explains the redundancy found in much of Mattel's Barbie merchandise, since the sudden manufacturing of a radically different product could encourage the migration of consumers to another brand. But given that Barbie has become "the alpha doll" (Talbot 74) for girls in today's popular culture, young female consumers clearly associate only good things with Barbie. And who can blame them? Barbie has become a tradition handed down from mother to daughter or a rite of passage that most girls go through. In this way, excessive consumption and the effects of branding are handed down as well, as Barbie dolls are essentially their physical manifestations.

Amy moves to the larger marketing context.

With a company as driven to produce and sell products as Mattel, consumers can expect to find increasingly ridiculous items on toy store shelves. One such product found at toysrus.com is "Barbie and Tanner" (*Toys*), Tanner being Barbie's dog. The doll and dog come with brown pellets that function both as dog food and dog waste, a "special magnetic scooper[,] and trash can" (*Toys*). Upon telling any post-Barbie-phase female about this product, she will surely look amazed and ask, "Are you kidding me?" Unfortunately, Tanner's movable "mouth, ears, head and tail" (*Toys*) and "soft[,] . . . fuzzy" coat will most likely blind children to the product's absurdity, instead enchanting them into purchasing the product. Another particularly hilarious item is the "Barbie Collector Platinum Label Pink Grapefruit Obsession" (*Toys*). The doll wears a "pink, charmeuse mermaid gown with deep pink chiffon wedges sewn into the flared skirt and adorned with deep pink bands that end in bows under the bust and at the hip" (*Toys*). And "as a . . . special surprise, [the] doll's head is scented with the striking aroma of pink grapefruit" (*Toys*). Finally, the doll is described as "an ideal tribute to [the] delightful [grapefruit] flavor" (*Toys*). The consumer will find it difficult to keep a straight face as he or she reads through the description, as it essentially describes a doll dedicated to a scent. The doll's randomness shows Mattel's desperation for coming out with new products. Eager to make profit, Barbie's designers, it seems, make dolls according to whatever whim that happens to cross their minds.

In the quest to make profit by spreading the consumerist mindset, Barbie products even manage to commodify culture. Nowadays, Barbie dolls come in a variety of ethnicities. Take, for example, the "Diwali Festival Doll" from the "Barbie Dolls of the World" (*Toys*) line. Except for the traditional Indian apparel and dark hair, however, the doll could easily be mistaken for Caucasian. And what about Barbie's multiracial doll friends? They are reduced to mere accessories — disposable and only supplementary to Barbie, the truly important figure. Therefore, despite Mattel's attempts at identifying with a larger group of girls, an undeniable "aura of blondness still [clings] to the Mattel doll" (Talbot 82) because its attempts aim more toward creating a larger customer base than anything else.

But enough of dolls. Mattel has grown so large that it can expand its products beyond Barbie's mini-world. Consumers can easily find Barbie brand tennis shoes, rain boots, slippers, bicycles, and helmets. Many of Barbie's non-doll products even reflect the various fads among America's youth, such as video games, skateboards, scooters, guitars, and dance mats (in accordance with the

The paragraph includes a rich array of concrete, specific detail.

Amy develops her argument by considering the cultural and ethnic angle.

A quick, short transition moves the reader to a broader consideration of Mattel's promotion of materialism.

popularity of the game, Dance Dance Revolution). Anne Parducci, Mattel's senior VP of Barbie Marketing, claims Mattel does this because it "want[s] to make sure . . . [it] capture[s] girls in the many ways they are spending their time now and in the future," that it "want[s] Barbie to represent a lifestyle brand for girls, not just a brand of toys" (Edut). This phenomenon, however, can simply be seen as Mattel trying to "infiltrat[e] girls' lives everywhere they go" (Edut). Either way, Mattel's actions allow materialism to develop at an early age, especially since it makes the latest "it" items more accessible to children. Those behind Barbie figure that if children are going to buy into the latest trends anyway, they might as well buy them from Mattel.

Amy allows for a counter-argument but then refutes it.

Since Barbie products promote the attitude of keeping up with society's crazes, they create a carefree fantasy world for children, obscuring the fact that Mattel's motivation is making money. The company knows that if it enchants children, those children will in turn convince their parents to buy the products for them. The company also knows that commercials are its best opportunities to do this. One recent Mattel commercial advertises the "Let's Dance Genevieve" doll, a doll also inspired by *The 12 Dancing Princesses* DVD that interacts with its owner in three ways: the doll "can dance to music for the girl," "teach the girl dance moves by demonstrating and using speech prompts," and "follow along with the girl's dance moves using special bracelets and a shoe accessory" (*Toys*). Girls dressed in ballerina attire give overly joyous reactions to the doll's behaviors, making the doll seem remarkably advanced when, really, the doll can only raise its arms and legs. In addition, computer graphic scenes from the movie run seamlessly into scenes of the girls playing with the doll, and one of these girls is even transposed onto a clip of the movie. This blurs the lines of reality and fantasy, encouraging young viewers to think that if they own the doll, they, too, can feel like "dancing princesses," that somehow the doll can trans-port its owner into a fairy-tale world. In actuality, young females will likely tire of the doll within weeks. The commercial even resorts to flattery, describing the doll and its owner as "two beau-tiful dancers." Finally, the commercial ends with inspirational lyr-ics, singing, "You can shine." This sort of "vaguely girl-positive" advertising only "wrap[s] the Mattel message — buy our products now!" (Edut). Together, all these advertising elements add up to a highly desirable product among young girls.

Barbie undoubtedly increases the materialistic tendencies in children, specifically females, Barbie's target audience. After all, since "Barbie dolls need new clothes and accessories more often than boys' action figures do," "young girls learn . . . very early" to "assume consumer roles" (Katz). Interestingly, "Barbie was an early rebel against the domesticity that dominated the lives of baby-boom mothers," as she shows no "car[e] for babies or children" or "visible ties to parents" (Cross 773). But ironically, instead of "[teaching] girls to shed [such] female stereotypes," Barbie simply created a new stereotype for females — the shopaholic persona — because "she prompted [young girls] to associate the freedom of being an adult with carefree consumption" (Cross 774). So the overall effect of Barbie's presence in children's lives is increased expectations for material possessions. Or, in other words, Barbie products cause "catalog-induced anxiety," a condition that can occur "from [viewing] catalogs themselves or from other forms of public exposure of the lives of the rich or celebrated, . . . mak[ing] what a typical person possesses seem paltry, even if the person is one of the many . . . living well by objective standards" (Easterbrook 404, 405). Given that Barbie is a fictitious character, Mattel can make her as beautiful, hip, and rich as it pleases. But what happens when little girls begin comparing their lives to that of Barbie? They think, "If Barbie gets to have such amenities, so should I." And toys like the "Barbie Hot Tub Party Bus" (*Target*) do not help the situation. The product description reads that the bus contains "all the comforts of home like a flat screen TV, dinette table, and beds" (*Target*). Children will inevitably expect these luxuries that, for Barbie, are merely givens in her doll utopia, causing discontent when they discover they cannot have everything they want. It may even reach the point where, "as . . . more material things become available and fail to" satisfy children, "material abundance . . . [can] have the perverse effect of instilling unhappiness — because it will never be possible to have everything that economics can create" (Easterbrook 402).

For my long-forgotten Barbie dolls, as for those of many older females, the dream house has stopped growing. In fact, the house has been demolished, leaving my dolls homeless. But this does not

References to Gary Cross's article buttress the essay's argument.

Amy invokes Gregg Easterbrook as she explores the long-term implications of Mattel's promotion of consumerism.

Amy signals closure by coming full circle, returning to her opening anecdote.

mean that women have escaped the effects of years of Barbie play as they have temporarily escaped the clutches of Mattel. (I say temporarily because even if a woman has outgrown Barbie, Mattel will suck her back in through her daughters, nieces, goddaughters, and granddaughters.) Since Barbie preaches the admissibility of hyperconsumption to females at a young age, women, unsurprisingly, "engage in an estimated 80% of all consumer spending" (Katz). Women, conditioned from all those trips to the toy store looking for the perfect party dress for Barbie or the perfect convertible to take her to that party, still find themselves doing this — just on a larger scale — in shopping malls. But perhaps men's consumerism is catching up. The recent "proliferation of metrosexuals" signals a rise in "straight young men whose fashion and grooming tastes have crossed over into areas once reserved for feminine consumption" (St. John 177, 174). Mattel, too, takes part in this phenomenon through the "reintroduc[tion] [of] the Ken doll," which now possesses a "new metrosexual look" (Talbot 79). Well, one thing is certain: Mattel continues its expansive construction on Barbie's ever-costly dream mansion, and knows that millions of little girls will do the same.

By considering men's consumer habits and male dolls, Amy ends with a refreshing twist.

Works Cited

Cross, Gary. "Barbie, G.I. Joe, and Play in the 1960s." Maasik and Solomon 772–78.

Easterbrook, Gregg. "The Progress Paradox." Maasik and Solomon 400–407.

Edut, Ophira. "Barbie Girls Rule?" *Bitch: Feminist Response to Pop Culture* 31 Jan. 1999: 16. Print.

Katz, Phyllis A., and Margaret Katz. "Purchasing Power: Spending for Change." *Iris* 30 Apr. 2000: 36. Print.

Maasik, Sonia, and Jack Solomon, eds. *Signs of Life in the U.S.A.: Readings on Popular Culture for Writers.* 7th ed. Boston: Bedford, 2012. Print.

Neuhaus, Colin F., and James R. Taylor. "Variables Affecting Sales of Family-Branded Products." *Journal of Marketing Research* 9.4 (1972): 419–22. Print.

Sappington, David E. M., and Birger Wernerfelt. "To Brand or Not
to Brand? A Theoretical and Empirical Question." *Journal of
Business* 58.3 (1985): 279–93. Print.

Shames, Laurence. "The More Factor." Maasik and Solomon 76–82.

St. John, Warren. "Metrosexuals Come Out." Maasik and Solomon
174–77.

Talbot, Margaret. "Little Hotties: Barbie's New Rivals." *New Yorker*.
4 Dec. 2006: 74+. Print.

Target. Target Brands, Inc., 2006. Web. 14 Nov. 2006.

Toys "R" Us. Geoffrey LLC, 2006. Web. 14 Nov. 2006.

Essay 2

Exemplifying a semiotic approach, Rose Sorooshian, a student at California
State University, Northridge, explores the social and cultural conditions that
led *The Walking Dead* to become one of America's most popular TV programs.
The show became a hit not *despite* the difficult economic times in which it
aired, she concludes, but *because* of those troubled times. Here, Sorooshian
provides a fine reading of how a television program can be an articulate and
potent sign of its time.

The Walking 99 Percent: An Analysis of *The Walking Dead*
in the Context of the 2008 Recession

People have lost their homes and their jobs, and their standards of living are falling. People are fighting to survive, and these
catastrophic events are not their fault. Yet somehow these events
are affecting people more than they could possibly have imagined.
This description could be the premise of the popular television show
The Walking Dead, based on the series of graphic novels by the same
name. Set in Georgia, the show follows Sheriff Rick Grimes, his wife,
and their son, as well as a group of other survivors as they struggle
to stay alive and maintain their humanity in the midst of a zombie apocalypse. However, this description also matches a real-life
disaster that began in the United States in 2008 known as the Great
Recession. A report from a Pew Research Center Survey describes the
recent recession:

Of the 13 recessions that the American public has endured since the Great Depression of 1929–33, none has presented a more punishing combination of length, breadth and depth than this one. A new Pew Research survey finds that 30 months after it began, the Great Recession has led to a downsizing of Americans' expectations about their retirements and their children's future; a new frugality in their spending and borrowing habits; and a concern that it could take several years, at a minimum, for their house values and family finances to recover. (Taylor)

Rose locates The Walking Dead in the historical context of the Great Recession.

She poses a focusing question about the show's cultural significance.

Coming after a period of relatively stable economic times, the economic shock has created a great deal of fear and anger. And Americans are flocking to watch *The Walking Dead* in droves because they sense the parallels between the Great Recession and a zombie apocalypse. Though there have been cult-classic zombie movies in the past, never before has a zombie television show been so fervently embraced by such a widespread audience. What is the secret of its mainstream appeal, and what does the extreme popularity of *The Walking Dead* say about modern American society?

One reason this show is so popular among a diverse audience is that today's TV viewers feel a strong connection between the characters' attempts to live through a zombie apocalypse and their own attempts to cope with modern life and, especially, their recent economic struggles. The zombie apocalypse depicted in *The Walking Dead* shares many similarities with the economic recession that America has been suffering since 2008. Both events affected everyone in the country, and not just a particular group. During both, people lost homes, jobs, and a certain standard of living. People feel like they

Rose links the characters' struggles with Americans' economic woes.

are fighting just to survive and, most significantly, that this catastrophe is not their fault, is beyond their control, and is destroying their lives. Many feel that the government in some way caused it, should have prevented it, and should take responsibility for fixing it.

Another reason for *The Walking Dead*'s popularity is that it appeals to people who are highly critical of government entities such as politicians, the military, and government agencies. This mistrust is reflected in one of the ways the show departs from previous zombie movies. In most zombie movies, the protagonists' challenge is something like "hold on until morning." That is, they have a set amount of time they need to survive and then the government (the military) will save them. Or, sometimes the challenge is to arrive at a certain location where the government will take care of them. However, in *The Walking Dead*, no encounter with any government entity ends well. At the outset of the show, Rick is told that if he can make it to Atlanta, the CDC (Centers for Disease Control) has a base there that can help him. However, when he arrives, he finds the city overrun with zombies, and when Rick and his companions, including his wife and son, eventually do find the CDC compound, it quickly becomes clear that the government will not be rescuing anyone. All but one of the workers have either fled or committed suicide. The government has failed to devise a cure for the virus that is creating the zombies, and the building safety protocols almost kill off the main cast of characters. In the end, one of their group members and the last surviving CDC worker decide to stay behind in the gas explosion that destroys the building, killing themselves instead of continuing the struggle of living in the post-apocalyptic world. That indicates how completely hopeless people are feeling. In *The Walking Dead*, there is no magic cure, no government to come to their rescue, no military to save them. They are on their own. This parallel to the current economic environment is striking. People feel abandoned by and afraid of their own government, left to fend for themselves.

A comparison with other zombie movies points to a difference within the system.

Finally, the show's popularity spans across all demographics because it is set in a total fantasy world open to one's own interpretation. In other words, viewers can choose to think of the "bad guys," those responsible for the zombie apocalypse, as representing whomever they think are the bad guys in real life. As Leslie Savan states:

> Most of us watch because it's a terrific, suspenseful soap opera. But *TWD* also comes packed with a central metaphor — the zombie apocalypse — that can be used to explain just about every political point of view, whether right or left, pro-NRA or pro-gun control, small- or big-government, even pro-sequester or pro-stimulus.

The Walking Dead airs on AMC, a TV channel that also broadcasts two other top-rated dramas: *Mad Men* and *Breaking Bad*. On the surface, these three shows could hardly seem more different.

While *The Walking Dead* is a fairly standard horror show, *Mad Men* is a historical workplace drama set in the 1950s through 1960s in which most of the high-intensity moments come from whether or not an advertising deal will work out. And unlike both *Mad Men* and *The Walking Dead*, *Breaking Bad* is a modern-day reality show about a high school chemistry teacher who is diagnosed with terminal cancer and then begins dealing methamphetamine and becomes a drug lord. Although these three shows differ, they share the same attraction that makes them so popular today: All are chillingly realistic in their depiction of blood, guts, and a lot of naked skin. And this kind of realism is not exclusive to these three shows; most top television programs recently have followed this pattern, including comedies as well as dramas. *The Office, Parks and Recreation,* and *30 Rock* are three popular comedies that also present realistic portrayals of characters and situations. This becomes even more apparent in current fantasy and horror programs, including *The Walking Dead, Game of Thrones, Once upon a Time, Supernatural,* and *True Blood,* to name just a few. These shows tend to be very realistic in spite of their otherworldly concepts. Gone are the days of *Star Trek's* shiny view of the future in which everything is clean and silver and everyone wears a uniform. TV's fantasy worlds are no longer clean, fun, or nice. They are dirty, trying, harsh places where people are cruel and life is difficult. In other words, they are just like reality but with zombies and vampires. People living through extremely difficult times, worrying about losing their jobs and their homes, can identify with the fear that monsters are threatening them. It seems very real to them, and they want their shows to display the same nitty-gritty realism they face in their lives. Anything less would seem superficial and irrelevant.

This realism also applies to the characters. Most of the protagonists of previous decades were good, upstanding people: doctors, lawyers, fathers, and heroes. They were men, primarily, who did what they knew was right and stood for truth and justice. These days, however, those types of characters are viewed as old-fashioned, one-dimensional, and frankly silly. Instead, today's protagonists are flawed, sometimes immoral, characters, most of whom the average viewer would not want to meet. Viewers identify with complex characters with a lot of wiggle room in their moral structures, such as a serial killer with a conscience, murderers who are

Rose connects The Walking Dead *to other related TV programs.*

The focus narrows to an interpretation of the characters.

also great fathers, sheriffs who disregard the law, and vampires who love and protect. According to Stephen Garrett in "Why We Love TV's Antiheroes," "The heroes of today are radically different from those of two or three decades ago. They have evolved to represent a radically changed world" (319). Garrett goes on to state that in the past the difference between good and evil was clear, or, as he puts it, "There were never better baddies than the Nazis, and the causes, as well as the purposes, of the Second World War were crystal clear" (319). But now, Garrett explains, our wars are much less cut-and-dried. Conflicts now have "an element of moral ambiguity built into them" (319). Is it any wonder that, given such a change in our national moral compass, we would want television heroes who are likewise morally ambiguous? Gone are the days of the father character who comes home at five o'clock to pick up his pipe, listen to the problems of the wife and children, and lay down a simple solution. Gone are the days of the doctors who can cure all ills, the lawyers who always follow the law, and the police officers who adhere firmly to their moral codes. Characters now must exist in some kind of moral gray area, or else they will seem irrelevant to today's viewers. *The Walking Dead* fills that need quite well.

Zombies are a popular cultural phenomenon right now. *The Walking Dead*, *Warm Bodies*, plus countless zombie events such as zombie walks and runs in which large groups of people get together and dress as zombies, all point to a societal fascination with the concept of zombies. In fact, people seem interested in all kinds of undead beings. Vampires are, arguably, the most popular fantasy "creatures" right now, although contemporary vampires are no longer the monsters they once were. Vampires have become more human, more sympathetic, and much more sexy. Ever since another TV series, *Buffy the Vampire Slayer*, introduced the character of Angel as a sexy, brooding vampire with a soul, and with whom the title character, Buffy, was destined to fall in love, vampires have changed from bloodsucking monsters to bloodsucking heroes. As stated in *Signs of Life in the U.S.A.*, "To put it simply: Vampires are hot. From *True Blood* to *Twilight*, *The Vampire Diaries* to *The Gates*, contemporary popular culture is awash in vampire stories" (Maasik and Solomon 1). However, though vampires are still intensely popular, there appears to also be a continuing strong market for other types of supernatural monster drama, such as zombies.

Rose locates the show in the larger context of supernatural monster dramas.

The zombie movie has been a popular genre for decades, and the movie *Night of the Living Dead*, written and directed by George A. Romero, made zombie movies a staple of Hollywood. *The Walking Dead* has taken that popularity to a new level, however, because people facing their own fears and struggles seem to respond to the extremely realistic portrayal of the struggle of humans against zombies, who are, of course, a terrifying and perverted form of humans themselves. They reflect people's feelings of powerlessness and fear that they, their community, or their government will be "taken over" by evildoers. As Lee Roberts states, "The attraction of some to the zombie and the genre of films in which they appear represents an inner desire to place blame for society's misgivings on the establishment, i.e., big business, big government, etc., and use the zombie as the most logical outcome if the establishment were to be left unchecked by a complacent population" (Roberts).

Although *The Walking Dead*'s appeal may be that viewers strongly identify with characters who are fighting a battle against terrifying unknown forces, people who are insecure and fearful often cling to the known and even return to traditional behaviors and values. In a return to outdated gender roles, *The Walking Dead* portrays women as powerless and ineffective and men as strong and competent. Perhaps this indicates a desire on the part of the audience to go back to the 1950s, a more optimistic era when Americans had great hopes of increasing affluence and an always-increasing standard of living, but it also means a return to a time when women were weak and subservient to men.

She argues that the show appeals to traditional values and explains why.

In this show, what little power the women may have is frequently stripped away. In a show in which characters rely heavily on weapons, the women lack the training to use them, but the men are portrayed as fully competent with various weapons and prevent the women from obtaining or holding on to them. In the second season, one of the male characters, Dale, decides that it is no longer prudent for Andrea, a young woman, to carry a gun. Although Dale holds no real authority over her and the gun is legally hers, Andrea barely protests Dale's confiscation of the gun. In fact, the only real fight she gives is asking for Shane, another male character, to back her up. Shane sides with Dale, saying that until everyone is trained in the use of guns, the fewer they have "floating around camp," the better ("What Lies Ahead"). Andrea accepts this with little argument. So, in a traditional and patriarchal way, the men get to decide who has the weapons and the men generally carry the weapons and protect the women and children. For a show set in a contemporary setting, this is strikingly old-fashioned. In addition, females in the show are generally incompetent. Andrea, while still in possession of her gun, does not know how to clean it herself and, when attacked by a zombie, has the entire thing in pieces. Instead of successfully staying quiet and hidden, she attracts the zombie's attention and must rely on Dale's weapon in order to save herself. Lori often says things that are viewed by the other characters as weak or ignorant. When the group stumbles upon a veritable gold mine of supplies in the form of a pileup of old cars, Lori emotionally tries to persuade them not to use the supplies by saying "This is a graveyard" ("What Lies Ahead"). The others simply ignore her (female) sentimentality. When hiding from a group of zombies, it is Sophia, a young girl, not Carl, her male counterpart, who attracts the attention of two zombies and has to run off into the woods to hide. And then only the male characters go out to search for her.

Specific details support her claim about traditional values.

Overall, this show reinforces very strong, traditional gender roles. The women are soft-spoken, weak, and mothering. They do not carry weapons, they are ineffectual fighters, and they require almost constant protection by the men. They worry about clothes and hygiene in spite of the terrors surrounding them. The show goes so far as to show a group of women washing clothes and gossiping while a man looks on as protection. The men, on the other hand, are strong and capable. They carry guns and other weapons and can take care of themselves (and the women). They rarely require help from others and never from a woman. They are the doers—they come up with the plans and put them into action. The women are carried along in their wake. Without the men, the women would not last a day. Without the women, the men would have a much easier time surviving. In a time when many people feel somewhat uncertain about gender roles, the show roots itself securely in a more comfortable (for some, anyway) past.

Both the Great Depression and the Great Recession began after years of economic prosperity, and the 2008 recession was the worst economic downturn since the Great Depression. But the entertainment choices during the 1930s were very different from

Rose returns to history as her essay draws to a close.

those today. During the 1930s, Shirley Temple, a precocious child star, was the number one box office hit, and many found her movies to offer a temporary break from the misery and fear of the depressed economic state. "President Franklin Delano Roosevelt proclaimed that 'as long as our country has Shirley Temple, we will be all right'" ("Shirley Temple Black"). But now people seem to be looking for something else in their entertainment, immersing themselves in a terrifying zombie apocalypse. Why is this? Is it due to differences between the Great Depression and the Great Recession? According to National Public Radio, "Even though both events were momentous enough to earn the word 'great' as a modifier, they really are not comparable, according to recent research by economist Mark Vaughan, a fellow at the Weidenbaum Center on the Economy at Washington University in St. Louis" (qtd. in Geewax). Vaughn goes on to explain that the recent recession "pales in magnitude" with the Great Depression: "The Great Depression was painful in ways we can scarcely imagine now because we have grown so accustomed to having a government-funded safety net" (qtd. in Geewax).

In the 1930s, the public did not initially blame the government for the unemployment problem: This was prior to the passage of the Employment Act of 1946, which made the government responsible for maintaining high employment. In 2008, on the other hand, people felt betrayed and blamed the government and big business for the recession. During the Great Depression, people looked to entertainment as an escape from the frustrations of everyday life, while people today are, instead, looking for characters they can identify with as suffering victims being let down by the establishment and forced to take things into their own hands.

Rose encapsulates her answer to her opening question about the show's popularity.

The Walking Dead is a fairly well-written show with good acting and generally good special effects, and it tugs at emotional heartstrings and keeps the audience on the edge of their seats. But more than that, the show managed to come on the scene at just the perfect time when Americans were angry with government, angry with the establishment, and looking for a way to vent their frustrations. *The Walking Dead* is generic enough that all Americans can relate to it and, therefore, they can use it as a way to vicariously fight the recession without actually stepping out of their front doors.

Works Cited

Garrett, Stephen. "Why We Love TV's Antiheroes." Maasik and Solomon 318–21.

Geewax, Marilyn. "Did the Great Recession Bring Back the 1930s?" *NPR*. NPR, 11 July 2012. Web. 6 May 2013.

Maasik, Sonia, and Jack Solomon, eds. *Signs of Life in the U.S.A.: Readings on Popular Culture for Writers.* 7th ed. Boston: Bedford, 2012. Print.

Roberts, Lee. "Zombie Movie History: A Reference for Zombie Masters." *Best Horror Movies.* BestHorrorMovies.com, 2012. Web. 6 May 2013.

Savan, Leslie. "Whose Side Is *The Walking Dead* On?" *Nation.* The Nation, 7 Apr. 2013. Web. 6 May 2013.

"Shirley Temple Black." *The John F. Kennedy Center for the Performing Arts.* The John F. Kennedy Center for the Performing Arts, n.d. Web. 6 May 2013.

Taylor, Paul, ed. "How the Great Recession Has Changed Life in America." *Pew Research Social & Demographic Trends.* Pew Research Center, 30 June 2010. Web. 6 May 2013.

"*The Walking Dead* (Season 1)." *Wikipedia.* Wikimedia Foundation, 30 Apr. 2013. Web. 6 May 2013.

"What Lies Ahead." *The Walking Dead.* Dir. Ernest Dickerson and Gwyneth Horder-Payton. AMC. 16 Oct. 2011. Television.

Essay 3

In this essay, first-year UCLA student Ryan Kim explores the representation of Asians in film, focusing on *Gran Torino.* He notices that, at first glance, the film seems to depart from some typical ethnic stereotypes. However, using Michael Omi's "In Living Color: Race and American Culture" (p. 538) as a critical framework, Kim interprets *Gran Torino*'s representation of both Asians and whites, finding that the film ultimately reinforces conventional stereotypes. As you read Kim's essay, note his movement between "first glance" readings of the film and his deeper analysis based on Omi's essay.

A Reading of *Gran Torino*

Despite advancements made toward racial equality, racial discrimination still persists in America; as professor Michael Omi explains, "Film and television have been notorious in disseminating images of racial minorities which establish for audiences what these groups look like, how they behave, and in essence, 'who they are'" (629). In films, the Western genre has been especially harmful in its perpetuation of stereotypes, as in it, "the humanity of whites is contrasted with the brutality and treachery of nonwhites" and this notion of "white superiority" reveals certain "intriguing trends" (Omi 630). These trends are often contradictory and target many minority groups, including Asians. According to the documentary *Dragon Lady*, the stereotyping of Asians in film may have roots in historical events, but these portrayals can be inaccurate. The 2008 film *Gran Torino* attempts to combat these trends by providing a seemingly more accurate representation of the Hmong, a Southeast Asian ethnic group. However, the film's attempt at a realistic portrayal is undermined by the perpetuation of "the docile Asian" stereotype, double standards, insensitive motifs of white superiority, and the sexualization of Asian women commonly seen in older films.

Ryan articulates his thesis about the film's representation of Asians up front.

A brief overview of the film will highlight the most significant details for this analysis. *Gran Torino* follows the life of Walt Kowalski and his Hmong neighbors in a Michigan ghetto. Kowalski, a hardened "tough guy" veteran, is weighed down by his misdeeds during the Korean War, and he wrestles with the guilt. He is stern, traditional, and judgmental. Thao Vang Lor, Walt's next-door neighbor, is a fairly quiet and unconfident Hmong teenager. Both Walt and his family consider him somewhat womanly, as he is notably subordinate to his sister and mother. Unlike Thao, his older sister Sue is loud and confident, and is the first Hmong person toward whom Walt shows any goodwill. The film's main antagonists, Thao's gangster cousin, Spider, and his friend Smokie are brash, villainous, and relatively unintelligent. Throughout the movie, they bully Thao because he refuses to join their gang.

He provides a précis of the film, focusing on details relevant to his thesis.

The heart of the story begins after Thao fails to steal Walt's car during a gang initiation. As a form of apology, Thao is forced to work for Walt, who teaches Thao how to be a man, by forcing him to perform difficult yard work. Thao develops and grows more confident as the film progresses, finding a job and even asking a girl out on a date. However, he is constantly harassed by Spider and his gang, who do not appreciate him rejecting their invitations. Taking matters into his own hands, Walt pummels Smokie. In response, Smokie and Spider kidnap Sue, perform a drive-by shooting at the Vang Lor residence, and beat and rape Sue. Infuriated, Thao pushes Walt to seek vengeance with him. However, Walt locks Thao in his basement and goes to the gangster hangout unarmed. Knowing that his days were already numbered after receiving the results from his medical tests, Walt sacrifices himself to put the gangsters behind bars to protect Thao and Sue.

Gran Torino does differ from past films that made little distinction among Asian minorities by humanizing the Hmong as a unique group. After a large influx of new immigrants, many racial stereotypes were created, and the idea of "outsider" races was created (Omi 629). This insider-outsider mentality made differences between nonwhite ethnic groups somewhat irrelevant; as a result, many nonwhite ethnic groups were categorized together, particularly different Asian groups. Older films presented different Asian minorities as homogenous. Unlike those films, Gran Torino makes sure the audience is aware that the Hmong characters are "Hmong" and not simply "Asian." Additionally, it attempts to educate the audience about the Hmong's role in the Vietnam War. In a scene where Sue and Walt converse, Sue informs Walt that the Hmong fought with the United States in the war but were persecuted after the United States pulled out. This message from the filmmakers demonstrates an earnest attempt to avoid grouping Asians into one group as older films did.

Ryan locates Gran Torino within the context of other films that stereotype Asian characters.

The movie also attempts to subvert moral distinctions based on class. Walt considers himself superior to the Hmong, which showcases the perception of class based on race. Walt, a bigoted white man, considers himself more civilized than ethnic minorities. His offensive terms and jokes are indicative of this attitude, and he places himself higher on the social hierarchy. This distinction created between classes because of race exhibits a prevalent habit of the entertainment industry. As Michael Parenti illustrates, "The entertainment media present working people not only as unlettered and uncouth but also as less desirable and less moral than other

He extends
his argument
by consider-
ing class
difference.

people" (421). All of the Hmong in the film live in the ghetto and
are most likely poor. It is surprising, then, that the film depicts the
Hmong as more moral than Walt. Walt's unabashed racism contrasts
with Sue and Thao's attitude toward him, because they seem to
accept him regardless. But despite the film's efforts to present the
Hmong as a moral and unique ethnic group, *Gran Torino* ultimately
portrays old-Hollywood Asian stereotypes and harmful motifs.

Walt's blatantly racist epithets demonstrate the same
stereotypical portrayals of Asians and notions of white superiority
commonly seen in film. Walt's racism is an example of "overt racism," blatant examples of racial discrimination (Omi 627). As Omi
suggests, racial stereotypes "underscore white 'superiority' by reinforcing the traits, habits, and predispositions of nonwhites which
demonstrate their 'inferiority'" (630). Throughout the film, Walt
maliciously calls the Hmong "barbarians, chinks, gooks, and swamp
rats." Despite becoming close to Sue and Thao, Walt never ceases to
use his favorite racial slurs. This habit can be easily seen when he
interacts with Thao, purposely mispronouncing his name as "Toad"
and calling him a "zipperhead." While these epithets are designed
to be satirical and humorously mocking of bigots, they suggest that
Walt has more power and authority than the Hmong. The film does
nothing to counter this arrangement. Thao, as well as the other
Hmong, never seem to be offended, and they never retaliate. They
allow Walt to continue with his offensive mannerisms. The docility
of the Hmong perpetuates the stereotype that Asians are passive
and meek, and this stereotype is juxtaposed against Walt's ascen-
dency while "underscoring" his white superiority over them.

Ryan uses
Michael
Omi's article
to enhance
his analysis
of racial rep-
resentation.

In many older Hollywood films, white men would conquer territories in political turmoil, bring "order" to the region, and impart
their way of life onto the natives; *Gran Torino* privileges the same
Eurocentric worldview through Walt's protection of the Hmong.
Walt becomes a guardian to the broken Hmong community, as it
appears unable to resolve its own problems. Throughout the entire
film, Thao and Sue meet adversity and Walt resolves the problem. In
the beginning of the film, Walt prevents Thao from being abducted
by Spider. Later, he magically appears in time to save Sue from
being harassed and possibly kidnapped by African American thugs.
Walt is inevitably the one who sacrifices himself to lock up Spider,
Smokie, and the gangsters. It also appears that the Hmong need

Walt to perform even basic household tasks, as the entire neighborhood was in shambles until Walt steps in to fix it. Inferior because
of their inability to help themselves, the Hmong become a modern
parallel to the barbarians in the old Westerns. This further demonstrates that *Gran Torino* is cut from the same cloth as the other
Hollywood films.

The "good-bad variant" described by Omi is ever-present in
Gran Torino, demonstrating the film's failure to treat race progres-
sively. The "good-bad variant" is when a film attempts to compensate for negative racial stereotypes by providing a counterexample:
This attempt leads to the creation of a "good" racial character and
a "bad" one. Omi explains that such distinctions simply make the
"good" character "exist as a foil to underscore the intelligence,
courage, and virility of the white male hero" (631). At a cursory
glance, it seems the film is trying to subvert older stereotypes about
Asians by comparing Thao to the Hmong gangsters. Thao, one of
the "good characters," like the other Hmong, is initially passive
and noticeably nonthreatening. He perpetuates the stereotype that
Asians are docile and a "model minority." Ruthless and unforgiving,
the "bad Asians," Spider and Smokie, are dangerous "sinister criminals." The gangsters are much like the "barbarians" in Westerns.
Unlike the gangsters, Thao develops, eventually subverting the
docility stereotype by becoming more assertive and confident under
Walt's tutelage. *Gran Torino* appears to be adding another level of
dimension to the Hmong by providing differing and contradictory
images of them. Unfortunately, Thao is simply another "good character" acting as a foil to a white protagonist. He manages to discard
his old characteristics only with Walt's help, and even then, he is
simply embodying Walt's "white characteristics." By doing this, the
film inadvertently becomes another racially insensitive piece of
visual media, much like films before it.

Walt's tutelage of Thao also harkens back to older films
through the usage of masculine and feminine stereotypes. Hmong
men are mostly absent from the film, and when they do appear,
they seem unable to raise their own sons. Sue describes Hmong boys
as lacking in direction and being jail bound. Walt inevitably takes it
upon himself to teach Thao "how to be a man," specifically, a white
man. Thao performs feats of manual labor that "toughen him up"
and he learns about tool usage. Walt also teaches Thao how to "talk

*He again
extends his
discussion by
addressing
male gender
roles.*

like a real man" by taking him to his Italian barber. This "man talk" is an exchange of insults, racial slurs, and "manly" small talk. With these "masculine" skills under his belt, Thao finds a job at a construction site. This character shift links masculinity to being white, and Thao "becomes a man" when he learns how to be "white." Soon after, he develops the gumption to ask a girl out on a date. Before Thao becomes "white," he appears almost completely uninterested in girls. In fact, Walt had to lecture him for not taking initiative with Youa, the girl Thao eventually asks out. Thao only discovers success in his "masculine" endeavors by emulating Walt, revealing a notion of the superiority of white masculinity over Asian masculinity. Nothing in the movie challenges this. Sue even admits that Walt is Thao's biggest father figure, because her late father was "too traditional." Walt tells her that he is old-fashioned as well. Sue, however, argues, "But you're an American." Sue is admitting that traditional American values are better than Asian ones. In a racial context, the film depicts masculinity as being white.

He follows up with female gender roles.

The portrayal of Asian women in *Gran Torino* also reveals the film's link to older films. As Jessica Hagedorn explains, Asian women in film have been mostly "decorative, invisible, or one-dimensional" (403). Asian women were thus hypersexualized in old Hollywood, according to *Slaying the Dragon*, and the Hmong women in *Gran Torino* are just as one-dimensional as the Asian women in the films of old. For example, Youa as a character is very underdeveloped: She speaks very few lines, and her role is only to act as a stepping-stone for Thao's development as a man. In this way, Youa is defined as a goal rather than a person; this in turn subtly sexually objectifies her, as she becomes nothing more than an "object of desire" (Hagedorn 403). Although Sue does not obviously conform to any Asian stereotype, even she is sexualized. When she is harassed by the African American thugs, they explicitly sexualize her because of race, and they speak to her in extremely derogatory and lewd terms.

Ryan closes by lamenting Gran Torino's *representation of Asians.*

While *Gran Torino* was well-intentioned and was meant to bring a neglected and misunderstood ethnic group to the spotlight, it has merely perpetuated racially insensitive motifs and has spread racism further. It successfully avoids some of the mistakes of older films by humanizing the Hmong in giving them a distinct identity and moral high ground. However, the film uses or reinvents older motifs. The lack of initiative by the Hmong indicates a persistence of the docile Asian stereotype in the film. Additionally, the film entertains white superiority by using Thao as a foil for Walt, promoting "white" characteristics and ways of life, while Sue and Youa are sexualized—just as Asian women in film have been since old Hollywood. These stereotypes began with the initial contact of Western and Eastern cultures yet still persist today, despite the rich mixing of cultures that occurs across our modern society.

Works Cited

Hagedorn, Jessica. "Asian Women in Film: No Joy, No Luck." Maasik and Solomon 396–404.

Maasik, Sonia, and Jack Solomon, eds. *Signs of Life in the U.S.A.: Readings on Popular Culture for Writers.* 7th ed. Boston: Bedford, 2012. Print.

Omi, Michael. "In Living Color: Race and American Culture." Maasik and Solomon 625–35.

Parenti, Michael. "Class and Virtue." Maasik and Solomon 421–23.

Slaying the Dragon. Dir. Deborah Gee. Perf. Herb Wong. Asian Women United of California, 2011. DVD.

CONDUCTING RESEARCH AND CITING SOURCES

Your instructor may ask you to use secondary sources to support your analyses of popular culture. These sources may include a wide variety of published materials, from other essays (such as those featured in this book) to interviews you conduct to YouTube videos. When you write about popular culture, a host of sources are available to you to help lend weight to your arguments as well as help you develop fresh thinking about your topic.

The Internet age has afforded us innovative research opportunities, and with a wealth of information at your fingertips, it is up to you, the writer, to learn to determine which sources you should trust and which you should be suspicious of. As always, the library is a great place to begin. Research librarians continue to be excellent resources not only for finding sources for your papers, but for learning best practices for conducting research. It is more than likely that they are aware of resources at your disposal that you haven't considered, from academic databases like EBSCOhost to library catalogs to film and video archives.

The following selections offer additional help for conducting academically sound research online.

e macmillanhighered.com/signsoflife
Tutorials > Working with Sources > Do I Need to Cite This?

SCOTT JASCHIK

A Stand against Wikipedia

Increasingly, college faculty are concerned about the widespread use
of Wikipedia in student research and writing. The problem, as faculty
see it, is twofold. First, there is the problem of reliability. Wikipedia
does strive to provide reliable information, but given the wide-open
nature of the site—anyone can contribute—ensuring accuracy is not
really possible. This leads to student work that can disseminate misinformation. Second, even where Wikipedia is accurate (and it can
be an accurate source of information), it is, after all, an encyclopedia, and while encyclopedic sources may be suitable for background
information, students performing college-level research should seek
primary sources and academic-level secondary sources that they find
on their own. The following article from insidehighered.com surveys
the problems with Wikipedia as a research source as seen by college
faculty from a number of universities.

As Wikipedia has become more and more popular with students, some
professors have become increasingly concerned about the online, reader-
produced encyclopedia.

While plenty of professors have complained about the lack of accuracy or
completeness of entries, and some have discouraged or tried to bar students
from using it, the history department at Middlebury College is trying to take
a stronger, collective stand. It voted this month to bar students from citing
the Web site as a source in papers or other academic work. All faculty members will be telling students about the policy and explaining why material on
Wikipedia—while convenient—may not be trustworthy. "As educators, we
are in the business of reducing the dissemination of misinformation," said
Don Wyatt, chair of the department. "Even though Wikipedia may have some
value, particularly from the value of leading students to citable sources, it is
not itself an appropriate source for citation," he said.

The department made what Wyatt termed a consensus decision on the
issue after discussing problems professors were seeing as students cited incorrect information from Wikipedia in papers and on tests. In one instance,
Wyatt said, a professor noticed several students offering the same incorrect
information, from Wikipedia. There was some discussion in the department
of trying to ban students from using Wikipedia, but Wyatt said that didn't
seem appropriate. Many Wikipedia entries have good bibliographies, Wyatt
said. And any absolute ban would just be ignored. "There's the issue of freedom of access," he said. "And I'm not in the business of promulgating unen-
forceable edicts."

Wyatt said that the department did not specify punishments for citing Wikipedia, and that the primary purpose of the policy was to educate, not to be punitive. He said he doubted that a paper would be rejected for having a single Wikipedia footnote, but that students would be told that they shouldn't do so, and that multiple violations would result in reduced grades or even a failure. "The important point that we wish to communicate to all students taking courses and submitting work in our department in the future is that they cite Wikipedia at their peril," he said. He stressed that the objection of the department to Wikipedia wasn't its online nature, but its unedited nature, and he said students need to be taught to go for quality information, not just convenience.

The frustrations of Middlebury faculty members are by no means unique.   5 Last year, Alan Liu, a professor of English at the University of California at Santa Barbara, adopted a policy that Wikipedia "is not appropriate as the primary or sole reference for anything that is central to an argument, complex, or controversial." Liu said that it was too early to tell what impact his policy is having. In explaining his rationale — which he shared with an e-mail list — he wrote that he had "just read a paper about the relation between structuralism, deconstruction, and postmodernism in which every reference was to the Wikipedia articles on those topics with no awareness that there was any need to read a primary work or even a critical work."

Wikipedia officials agree — in part — with Middlebury's history department. "That's a sensible policy," Sandra Ordonez, a spokeswoman, said in an e-mail interview. "Wikipedia is the ideal place to start your research and get a global picture of a topic; however, it is not an authoritative source. In fact, we recommend that students check the facts they find in Wikipedia against other sources. Additionally, it is generally good research practice to cite an original source when writing a paper, or completing an exam. It's usually not advisable, particularly at the university level, to cite an encyclopedia." Ordonez acknowledged that, given the collaborative nature of Wikipedia writing and editing, "there is no guarantee an article is 100 percent correct," but she said that the site is shifting its focus from growth to improving quality, and that the site is a great resource for students. "Most articles are continually being edited and improved upon, and most contributors are real lovers of knowledge who have a real desire to improve the quality of a particular article," she said.

Experts on digital media said that the Middlebury history professors' reaction was understandable and reflects growing concern among faculty members about the accuracy of what students find online. But some worry that bans on citing Wikipedia may not deal with the underlying issues.

Roy Rosenzweig, director of the Center for History and New Media at George Mason University, did an analysis of the accuracy of Wikipedia for the *Journal of American History*, and he found that in many entries, Wikipedia was as accurate as or more accurate than more traditional encyclopedias. He said that the quality of material was inconsistent, and that biographical entries were generally well done, while more thematic entries were much less so. Like Ordonez, he said the real problem is one of college students using encyclopedias when they should be using more advanced sources. "College students shouldn't be citing encyclopedias in their papers," he said. "That's not what college is about. They either should be using primary sources or serious secondary sources."

In the world of college librarians, a major topic of late has been how to guide students in the right direction for research, when Wikipedia and similar sources are so easy. Some of those who have been involved in these discussions said that the Middlebury history department's action pointed to the need for more outreach to students. Lisa Hinchliffe, head of the undergraduate library and coordinator of information literacy at the University of Illinois at Urbana-Champaign, said that earlier generations of students were in fact taught when it was appropriate (or not) to consult an encyclopedia and why for many a paper they would never even cite a popular magazine or nonscholarly work. "But it was a relatively constrained landscape," and students didn't have easy access to anything equivalent to Wikipedia, she said. "It's not that students are being lazy today. It's a much more complex environment."

When she has taught, and spotted footnotes to sources that aren't appro-   10 priate, she's considered that "a teachable moment," Hinchliffe said. She said that she would be interested to see how Middlebury professors react when they get the first violations of their policy, and said she thought there could be positive discussions about why sources are or aren't good ones. That kind of teaching, she said, is important "and can be challenging."

Steven Bell, associate librarian for research and instructional services at Temple University, said of the Middlebury approach: "I applaud the effort for wanting to direct students to good quality resources," but he said he would go about it in a different way. "I understand what their concerns are. There's no question that [on Wikipedia and similar sites] some things are great and some things are questionable. Some of the pages could be by eighth graders," he said. "But to simply say 'don't use that one' might take students in the wrong direction from the perspective of information literacy."

Students face "an ocean of information" today, much of it of poor quality, so a better approach would be to teach students how to "triangulate" a source like Wikipedia, so they could use other sources to tell whether a given entry could be trusted. "I think our goal should be to equip students with the critical thinking skills to judge."

PATTI S. CARAVELLO

Judging Quality on the Web

When you conduct research on the Internet, you'll find a dizzying range of sources, from academic journals to government Web sites, from newspapers and popular magazines to blogs, wikis, and social networking and file-sharing sites. Having a plethora of sources at hand with just the click of a mouse has been a boon to research-ers in all fields. But the very democratic basis of the Internet that makes all this information so readily available creates a challenge, for it comes with no guarantees of quality control. Indeed, it is incumbent upon you, the researcher, to determine the reliability of the Web sources that you use. The following article from the UCLA Library's Web site, "Judging Quality on the Web," lists criteria that will allow you to evaluate the usefulness and reliability of Internet sources.

Even after refining a query in a search engine, a researcher often retrieves a huge number of Web sites. It is essential to know how to evaluate Web sites for the same reasons you would evaluate a periodical article or a book: *to ascertain whether you can rely on the information, to identify its inherent biases or limitations, and to see how or whether it fits into your overall research strategy.*

A good (useful, reliable) Web site:

1. Clearly states the author and/or organizational **source** of the information
   Your task:
   - Consider the qualifications, other works, and organizational affilia-tion of the author
   - Look up the organization which produced the Web site (if it's unfa-miliar) to identify its credentials, viewpoint, or agenda
   - If the source is an E-journal, discover whether it is refereed (re-viewed by scholars before it is accepted for publication)

2. Clearly states the **date** the material was written and the date the site was last revised
   Your task:
   - If the information is not current enough for your purposes or the date is not given, look elsewhere

3. Provides **accurate** data whose parameters are clearly defined
   Your task:
   - Compare the data found on the Web site with data found in other sources (encyclopedias, reference books, articles, etc.) for accuracy, completeness, recency
   - Ask a librarian about other important sources to check for this information

4. Provides the **type and level** of information you need
   Your task:
   - Decide whether the level of detail and comprehensiveness, the treatment of the topic (e.g., scholarly or popular), and the graphics or other features are acceptable
   - If the site does not provide the depth of coverage you need, look elsewhere

5. Keeps **bias** to a minimum, and clearly indicates point of view
   Your task:
   - Be aware that producing a Web page does not require the checking and review that publishing a scholarly book requires; you might have retrieved nothing but someone's personal opinion on the topic
   - Appealing graphics can distract you from noticing even overt bias, so heighten your skepticism and examine the evidence (source, date, accuracy, level, links)

6. Provides live **links** to related high-quality Web sites
   Your task:
   - Click on several of the links provided to see if they are active (or if they give an "error" message indicating the links are not being maintained) and to see if they are useful
   - Check to see if the criteria are stated for selecting the links

7. In the case of **commercial** sites, keeps advertising separate from content, and does not let advertisers determine content
   Your task:
   - Look at the Web address: Sites that are commercial have *.com* in their addresses and might have advertising or offer to sell something. The *.com* suffix is also found in news sites (e.g., newspapers, TV networks) and personal pages (sites created by individuals who

have purchased a domain name but who may or may not have a commercial or institutional affiliation)

8. Is clearly organized and **designed** for ease of use

    Your task:

    - Move around the page to see if its organization makes sense and it is easy to return to the top or to the sections you need
    - Decide whether the graphics enhance the content or detract from it

TRIP GABRIEL

For Students in Internet Age, No Shame in Copy and Paste

The Internet is an invaluable source for information about popular culture, both because of its instant accessibility and because of its ability to keep pace with the rapid turnover in popular fashions and trends in a way that print-technology publication never can. But, as is so often the case with the Internet, there is a downside to the matter. Because, as Trip Gabriel observes in this feature that originally appeared in the *New York Times*, "concepts of intellectual property, copyright, and originality are under assault in the unbridled exchange of online information," the result is a pandemic of inadvertent, and sometimes deliberate, plagiarism. Certainly in an era of group-oriented writing — as on Wikipedia — traditional notions of individual authorship are being deconstructed, which makes it all the more important that students learn in their writing classes what the conventions for documentation are and why they are still necessary. Trip Gabriel is a longtime reporter, and former Styles editor, at the *New York Times*.

At Rhode Island College, a freshman copied and pasted from a Web site's frequently asked questions page about homelessness — and did not think he needed to credit a source in his assignment because the page did not include author information.

At DePaul University, the tip-off to one student's copying was the purple shade of several paragraphs he had lifted from the Web; when confronted by a writing tutor his professor had sent him to, he was not defensive — he just wanted to know how to change purple text to black.

And at the University of Maryland, a student reprimanded for copying from Wikipedia in a paper on the Great Depression said he thought its entries — unsigned and collectively written — did not need to be credited since they counted, essentially, as common knowledge.

Professors used to deal with plagiarism by admonishing students to give credit to others and to follow the style guide for citations, and pretty much left it at that.

But these cases — typical ones, according to writing tutors and officials responsible for discipline at the three schools who described the plagiarism — suggest that many students simply do not grasp that using words they did not write is a serious misdeed.

It is a disconnect that is growing in the Internet age as concepts of intellectual property, copyright and originality are under assault in the unbridled exchange of online information, say educators who study plagiarism.

Digital technology makes copying and pasting easy, of course. But that is the least of it. The Internet may also be redefining how students — who came of age with music file-sharing, Wikipedia and Web-linking — understand the concept of authorship and the singularity of any text or image.

"Now we have a whole generation of students who've grown up with information that just seems to be hanging out there in cyberspace and doesn't seem to have an author," said Teresa Fishman, director of the Center for Academic Integrity at Clemson University. "It's possible to believe this information is just out there for anyone to take."

Professors who have studied plagiarism do not try to excuse it — many are champions of academic honesty on their campuses — but rather try to understand why it is so widespread.

In surveys from 2006 to 2010 by Donald L. McCabe, a co-founder of the Center for Academic Integrity and a business professor at Rutgers University, about 40 percent of 14,000 undergraduates admitted to copying a few sentences in written assignments.

Perhaps more significant, the number who believed that copying from the Web constitutes "serious cheating" is declining — to 29 percent on average in recent surveys from 34 percent earlier in the decade.

Sarah Brookover, a senior at the Rutgers campus in Camden, N.J., said many of her classmates blithely cut and paste without attribution.

"This generation has always existed in a world where media and intellectual property don't have the same gravity," said Ms. Brookover, who at 31 is older than most undergraduates. "When you're sitting at your computer, it's the same machine you've downloaded music with, possibly illegally, the same machine you streamed videos for free that showed on HBO last night."

Ms. Brookover, who works at the campus library, has pondered the differences between researching in the stacks and online. "Because you're not walking into a library, you're not physically holding the article, which takes you closer to 'this doesn't belong to me,'" she said. Online, "everything can belong to you really easily."

A University of Notre Dame anthropologist, Susan D. Blum, disturbed by   15 the high rates of reported plagiarism, set out to understand how students view authorship and the written word, or "texts" in Ms. Blum's academic language.

She conducted her ethnographic research among 234 Notre Dame undergraduates. "Today's students stand at the crossroads of a new way of conceiving texts and the people who create them and who quote them," she wrote last year in the book *My Word!: Plagiarism and College Culture*, published by Cornell University Press.

Ms. Blum argued that student writing exhibits some of the same qualities of pastiche that drive other creative endeavors today — TV shows that constantly reference other shows or rap music that samples from earlier songs.

In an interview, she said the idea of an author whose singular effort creates an original work is rooted in Enlightenment ideas of the individual. It is buttressed by the Western concept of intellectual property rights as secured by copyright law. But both traditions are being challenged.

"Our notion of authorship and originality was born, it flourished, and it may be waning," Ms. Blum said.

She contends that undergraduates are less interested in cultivating a   20 unique and authentic identity — as their 1960s counterparts were — than in trying on many different personas, which the Web enables with social networking.

"If you are not so worried about presenting yourself as absolutely unique, then it's O.K. if you say other people's words, it's O.K. if you say things you don't believe, it's O.K. if you write papers you couldn't care less about because they accomplish the task, which is turning something in and getting a grade," Ms. Blum said, voicing student attitudes. "And it's O.K. if you put words out there without getting any credit."

The notion that there might be a new model young person, who freely borrows from the vortex of information to mash up a new creative work, fueled a brief brouhaha earlier this year with Helene Hegemann, a German teenager whose best-selling novel about Berlin club life turned out to include passages lifted from others.

Instead of offering an abject apology, Ms. Hegemann insisted, "There's no such thing as originality anyway, just authenticity." A few critics rose to her defense, and the book remained a finalist for a fiction prize (but did not win).

That theory does not wash with Sarah Wilensky, a senior at Indiana University, who said that relaxing plagiarism standards "does not foster creativity, it fosters laziness."

"You're not coming up with new ideas if you're grabbing and mixing and   25 matching," said Ms. Wilensky, who took aim at Ms. Hegemann in a column in her student newspaper headlined "Generation Plagiarism."

"It may be increasingly accepted, but there are still plenty of creative people — authors and artists and scholars — who are doing original work," Ms. Wilensky said in an interview. "It's kind of an insult that that ideal is gone, and now we're left only to make collages of the work of previous generations."

In the view of Ms. Wilensky, whose writing skills earned her the role of informal editor of other students' papers in her freshman dorm, plagiarism has nothing to do with trendy academic theories.

The main reason it occurs, she said, is because students leave high school unprepared for the intellectual rigors of college writing.

"If you're taught how to closely read sources and synthesize them into your own original argument in middle and high school, you're not going to be tempted to plagiarize in college, and you certainly won't do so unknowingly," she said.

At the University of California, Davis, of the 196 plagiarism cases referred to the disciplinary office last year, a majority did not involve students ignorant of the need to credit the writing of others. 30

Many times, said Donald J. Dudley, who oversees the discipline office on the campus of 32,000, it was students who intentionally copied — knowing it was wrong — who were "unwilling to engage the writing process."

"Writing is difficult, and doing it well takes time and practice," he said.

And then there was a case that had nothing to do with a younger generation's evolving view of authorship. A student accused of plagiarism came to Mr. Dudley's office with her parents, and the father admitted that he was the one responsible for the plagiarism. The wife assured Mr. Dudley that it would not happen again.

Synthesizing and Citing Sources

One of the questions you might ask yourself as you write is, "How many sources do I need?" Your instructor may give you guidance, but questions of exactly when you need to employ the support of other authors is up to you. Synthesis in academic writing refers to the incorporation of sources into your writing. As you develop your arguments, you will want to look at your sources and consider how what they say interacts with your own opinions. Do you see any similarities between what you want to write and what your sources say, or will you be faced with the task of discussing how your sources don't see your topic the way you do? Think of your paper as a conversation between you and your sources. As you write, ask yourself where you and

macmillanhighered.com/signsoflife
LearningCurve > Working with Sources (MLA)
Tutorials > How to Cite an Article in MLA Style; How to Cite a Book in MLA Style; How to Cite a Database in MLA Style; How to Cite a Web Site in MLA Style

your sources agree and disagree, and make sure you account for this in your paper. You might want to ask yourself the following questions:

- Have I used my sources as evidence to support any claims I'm making?
- Have I considered any counterarguments?
- Have I taken care to characterize my sources in a way that is fair and accurate?
- When I have finished my draft, have I reconsidered my thesis in light of the source material I've used? Do I need to change my thesis to reflect any new discoveries I've made?

Finally, you will want to make sure you have properly documented any sources you use in your papers. When you write an essay and use another author's work — whether you use the author's exact words or paraphrase them — you need to cite that source for your readers. In most humanities courses, writers use the system of documentation developed by the Modern Language Association (MLA). This system indicates a source in two ways: (1) notations that briefly identify the sources in the body of your essay and (2) notations that give fuller bibliographic information about the sources at the end of your essay. The notations for some commonly used types of sources are illustrated in this chapter. For documenting other sources, consult a writing handbook or Joseph Gibaldi's *MLA Handbook for Writers of Research Papers*, Seventh Edition (New York: Modern Language Association of America, 2009).

In-Text Citations

In the body of your essay, you should signal to your reader that you've used a source and indicate, in parentheses, where your reader can find the source in your list of works cited. You don't need to repeat the author's name in both your writing and in the parenthetical note.

SOURCE WITH ONE AUTHOR

Patrick Goldstein asserts that "Talk radio has pumped up the volume of our public discourse and created a whole new political language — perhaps the prevailing political language" (16).

SOURCE WITH TWO OR THREE AUTHORS

Researchers have found it difficult to study biker subcultures because, as one team describes the problem, "it was too dangerous to take issue with outlaws on their own turf" (Hooper and Moore 368).

INDIRECT SOURCE

In discussing the baby mania trend, *Time* claimed, "Career women are opting for pregnancy and they are doing it in style" (qtd. in Faludi 106).

List of Works Cited

At the end of your essay, include a list of all the sources you have cited in parenthetical notations. This list, alphabetized by author, should provide full publication information for each source; you should indicate the date you accessed any online sources.

The first line of each entry should begin flush left. Subsequent lines should be indented half an inch (or five spaces) from the left margin. Double-space the entire list, both between and within entries.

Nonelectronic Sources

BOOK BY ONE AUTHOR

Weisman, Alan. *The World without Us.* New York: Dunne, 2007. Print.

BOOK BY TWO OR MORE AUTHORS

Collins, Ronald K. L., and David M. Skover. *The Death of Discourse.* New York: Westview, 1996. Print.

(Note that only the first author's name is reversed.)

WORK IN AN ANTHOLOGY

Corbett, Julia B. "A Faint Green Sell: Advertising and the Natural World." *Signs of Life in the U.S.A.: Readings on Popular Culture for Writers.* 7th ed. Ed. Sonia Maasik and Jack Solomon. Boston: Bedford, 2012. 227–45. Print.

ARTICLE IN A WEEKLY MAGAZINE

Lacayo, Richard. "How Does '80s Art Look Now?" *Time* 28 Mar. 2005: 58+. Print.

(A plus sign is used to indicate that the article is not printed on consecutive pages; otherwise, a page range should be given: *16–25*, for example.)

ARTICLE IN A MONTHLY MAGAZINE

Judd, Elizabeth. "After School." *Atlantic* June 2005: 118. Print.

ARTICLE IN A JOURNAL

Hooper, Columbus B., and Johnny Moore. "Women in Outlaw Motorcycle Gangs." *Journal of Contemporary Ethnography* 18.4 (1990): 363–87. Print.

PERSONAL INTERVIEW

Chese, Charlie. Personal interview. 28 Sept. 2014.

Electronic Sources

FILM OR DVD

Hachi: A Dog's Tale. Dir. Lasse Hallström. Perf. Richard Gere. Stage 6 Films, 2009.
   Film.
No Country for Old Men. Dir. Ethan and Joel Coen. 2007. Buena Vista Home
   Entertainment, 2008. DVD.

TELEVISION PROGRAM

"Collateral Damage." *CSI: Miami.* Perf. David Caruso. KBAK, Bakersfield. 4 May 2009.
   Television.

SOUND RECORDING

Adams, Ryan. *Cold Roses.* Lost Highway, 2005. MP3 file.

E-MAIL

Katt, Susie. "Interpreting the Mall." Message to the author. 29 Sept. 2014. E-mail.

ARTICLE IN AN ONLINE REFERENCE BOOK

"Gender." *Britannica Online.* Encyclopaedia Britannica, 22 Oct. 2013. Web. 30 May
   2014.

   (Note that the first date indicates when the information was posted; the
second indicates the date of access.)

ARTICLE IN AN ONLINE JOURNAL

Schaffer, Scott. "Disney and the Imagineering of Histories." *Postmodern Culture* 6.3
   (1996): n. pag. Web. 26 Aug. 2014.

ARTICLE IN AN ONLINE MAGAZINE

Rosenberg, Scott. "Don't Link or I'll Sue!" *Salon.* Salon Media Group, 12 Aug. 1999.
   Web. 13 Aug. 2014.

ONLINE BOOK

James, Henry. *The Bostonians.* London and New York, 1886. *The Henry James
   Scholar's Guide to Web Sites.* Aug. 1999. Web. 15 Oct. 2014.

ONLINE POEM

Frost, Robert. "The Road Not Taken." *Mountain Interval*. New York, 1915. *Project Bartleby Archive*. Ed. Steven van Leeuwen. Mar. 1995. Web. 13 Aug. 2014.

PROFESSIONAL WEB SITE

National Council of Teachers of English. *National Council of Teachers of English*. Jan. 2014. Web. 6 July 2014.

PERSONAL HOME PAGE

Stallman, Richard. Home page. Mar. 2008. Web. 4 Mar. 2014.

POSTING TO A DISCUSSION LIST

Diaz, Joanne. "Poetic Expressions." *Conference on College Composition and Communication*. NCTE, 29 Apr. 2006. Web. 4 July 2006.

ONLINE SCHOLARLY PROJECT

Barlow, Michael, ed. *Corpus Linguistics*. Rice U, Apr. 1998. Web. 13 Aug. 2010.

WORK FROM A DATABASE SERVICE

Cullather, Nick. "The Third Race." *Diplomatic History* 33.3 (2009): 507–12. *Academic OneFile*. Web. 1 May 2009.

YOUTUBE OR OTHER ONLINE VIDEO

"iTunes Version — Bed Intruder Song." UCLA Library. *YouTube*. YouTube, 2010. Web. 12 Feb. 2011.

PHOTOGRAPH OR WORK OF ART

Warhol, Andy. *Black Bean*. 1968. Whitney Museum of American Art. *whitney.org*. Web. 26 Aug. 2014.

AP Photo/Eugene Hoshiko

CONSUMING PASSIONS

The Culture of American Consumption

The CCI

The CCI is one of the most avidly watched broadcasts in America, and, no, it isn't a television crime series. Based on the monthly Consumer Confidence Survey, as issued by the Conference Board (a private, nonprofit organization that, in its own words, "is a global, independent business membership and research association working in the public interest"), the Consumer Confidence Index charts the mood of American consumers. When it goes up, the stock market goes up; when it goes down, the stock market goes down with it.

What does this have to do with popular culture? The short answer is "everything" because American popular culture is grounded in consumption, whether we are looking at the direct purchase of goods and services; the enjoyment of music, movies, and television; or simply the use of your iPhone or other digital devices and all that such devices offer you. That is why your Facebook profile, Tumblr microblog, Google searches, and Twitter account are free; it is why traditional network television and traditional radio are free as well. All such media are free because they are underwritten by advertising and marketing expenditures made by companies that want to sell you something. While movies, for their part, are usually not free, they themselves are commodities to be consumed through the purchase of tickets, DVDs, cable subscriptions, Netflix or Red Box accounts, and so on. Music, too, is a commodity, whether consumed via download, CD, or vinyl (yes, there has been a small resurgence of that most venerable of music technologies). In short, American popular culture is grounded in a consumer society, and that is why this chapter appears first in this book.

At the same time, people in consumer societies use their possessions to communicate with one another, which is to say that consumer goods aren't simply objects, they're **signs**—from the out-and-out status symbols whose purpose is to convey your place in the social hierarchy, to the clothes you wear, the music you listen to, and even the smartphone you choose to purchase. Like all signs, they get their meaning from the cultural **systems**, or **codes**, within which they appear, and their meanings can change as history reworks the systems that define them. To see how, let's look at a consumer trend that has been in fashion for a number of years now and looks to continue for a number of years more.

The Skinny on Skinny Jeans

Once again, it all begins with a *difference*: baggy versus skinny.

From the 1980s through the 1990s and into the early 2000s, baggy jeans were the jean fashion of choice for many young Americans, especially boys and men. That changed sometime early in the new millennium, when decidedly tight skinny jeans exploded into popularity for both men and women. In itself, such a difference would appear to be meaningless, but when systematically situated within the history of blue jeans and the meanings that jeans have conveyed over the years, this difference becomes significant—in fact, very complicatedly significant.

So let's look at some history. Blue jeans first appeared in the nineteenth century when Levi Strauss tailored durable denim cloth into trousers for workers in the California gold fields. As such, their **denotation** was simply the pants themselves. But given their use by men engaged in heavy manual labor, those trousers came to **connote**, or signify, "working-class clothing," with cowboys being the most glamorous of their wearers. By the 1950s, however, blue jeans began to bear an additional class significance as "casual wear" for middle-class Americans; but whether they connoted working-class or casual middle-class wear, blue jeans were still regarded as unsuitable for formal middle-class attire either in school or on the job.

But during the countercultural revolution of the 1960s, American baby boomers self-consciously adopted blue jeans as a kind of uniform in defiance of middle-class proscriptions, often wearing them as a sign of solidarity with the working class. Jeans became so identified with the counterculture that Charles Reich, in his popular 1970 book *The Greening of America*, argued that denim bell-bottoms were a symbol of the Age of Aquarius, signifying a free and freewheeling new generation.

Eventually, as happens so often in American consumer culture, what was once a symbol of defiance settled down into a simple fashion statement, and by the 1970s, blue jeans signified little more than "fashionable clothing." This opened the way for designer jeans, like Jordache and Chic, which were worn very tight by both men and women and were styled to enhance their sex appeal.

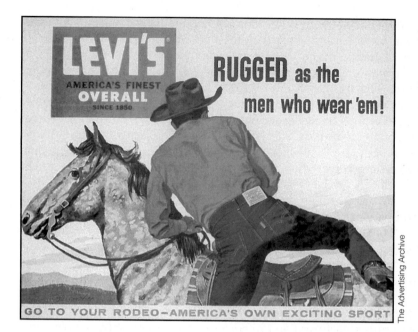

In the 1970s, however, blue jeans also assumed a new significance as members of some punk rock and New Wave bands introduced a new jeans alternative. The album jacket art for Blondie's record *Parallel Lines* provides a good illustration: The male band members all wear narrowly tailored black jeans that taper down tightly at the ankle. What is more, one member of the group wears bright red Converse sneakers, while another wears one black Converse sneaker and one red one. The look is "hipster" rather than sexy,

---

Discussing the Signs of Consumer Culture

On the board, list in categories the fashion styles worn by members of the class. Be sure to note details, such as styles of shoes, jewelry, backpacks, or sunglasses, as well as broader trends. Next, discuss what the clothing choices say about individuals. What messages are people sending about their personal identity? Do individual students agree with the class's interpretations of their clothing choices? Can any distinctions be made by gender, age, or ethnicity? Then discuss what the fashion styles worn by the whole class say: Is a group identity projected by class members?

recalling one of the Beat fashions of fifties-era bohemianism, and, as we shall see in a moment, has important resonances with today's skinny jeans trend.

Meanwhile, in the 1980s extravagantly oversized, or baggy, jeans entered into denim's history as part of the hip-hop scene. Taking the place of the loose sweats popular during the break-dancing era, baggy jeans were a signifier of the evolution of rap/hip-hop toward its gangsta incarnation. Part of a uniform that then included backward-facing ball caps and untied Nikes, baggy jeans were often worn "sagging." The gangsta-inflected fashion system within which baggy jeans signified soon was supplemented by a parallel, but different, system when white American youth adopted (or adapted) rap/hip-hop styles for themselves — as when skateboarders appropriated baggy jeans for their own use, and grunge fashion included an ensemble that combined Doc Martens with baggy cutoffs. This turn to oversized jeans among a diverse group of consumers created a national fashion system that endured for well over twenty years, signifying what can best be called "attitude" on the part of their wearers — until the whole thing simmered down into just another teen fashion without any real significance, as so often happens with fashions originally intended to be subversive.

All of which takes us to the present. In the early 2000s, the look that Blondie had resurrected from the 1950s came to be adopted by various post-punk, indie, and otherwise "alternative" bands. So skinny jeans entered the fashion system big time, assuming a new connotative significance, one very different from the "flower child" meanings of the patched-jeans sixties, the "grunge" inflections of the early nineties, and the "street gang" connotations of the baggy era. In short, skinny jeans became "hip," where hip meant "coffee shop–indie / alternative hipster." But just as baggy jeans came eventually to signify little more than "youth fashion item," so, too, have skinny jeans become so pervasive today that they have lost much of their "hipster" connotation and usually signify nothing more than "I'm wearing what everyone else is wearing."

Yet, not quite. Because, as you may have already noted for yourself, there is a racial component to the recent history of blue jeans that we have not addressed yet. That angle on the matter becomes quite obvious when you consider the racial connotations of "alternative" versus "hip-hop" culture. Alternative culture has a "white" association; hip-hop is a code of black America. These associations became quite obvious in 2009 when rappers New Boyz released a video called "You're a Jerk" — a single from their significantly titled album *Skinny Jeanz and a Mic*. Highlighting both skinny jeans and brightly colored sneakers, this video initially attracted some very angry commentary on YouTube. Since these comments aren't reprintable here, let's just say that along with the positive fan responses, in 2009 there were a lot of hostile accusations that the New Boyz were "murdering" hip-hop.

The crux of the matter goes back to those baggy jeans, which became such an enduring signifier of African American street culture. One may say that it was a question of authenticity, with "skinny rather than baggy" signifying to some black consumers a kind of fashion betrayal. Interviews with the members of New Boyz and other figures in the jerkin' scene in 2009 clearly indicate that they were quite aware of what they were doing, for while they retained many of the signifiers of hip-hop culture through their rapping, their wearing of baseball caps (though adjusted their own way), and their wearing of sagging skinny jeans, they explicitly distinguished themselves from the gangsta subculture, speaking to interviewers at the time of the "positive" attractions of elements such as entrepreneurialism. Given that their skinny jeans had their origins in such white-coded fashions as punk (significantly, a hairstyle seen among jerkers was called the "frohawk") and New Wave, the New Boyz were thus not only adopting a white-coded fashion statement but also reversing a certain trend in the history of American youth culture that usually features white youth adopting and adapting the signifiers of black youth. Hence the hostile reaction. Indeed, several years ago, one fan of skinny jeans remarked to a reporter that he swapped his skinny jeans for baggy ones before returning home in order to avoid getting into trouble in his neighborhood.

But that was then, and fashion history rolls on. A survey of the more recent YouTube comments accompanying the "New Boyz 'You're a Jerk' OFFICIAL Music Video HD Extended" version reveals that the whole matter has lost its sting. One commenter places it in the "distant" past ("my daddy use to always try to do this dance lols whole house be shakin"), while another simply says "wonderful." But still, one quietly unhappy holdover from the old days remarks: "I am still angry at them for introducing dudes to skinny pants . . . sigh," he (or she) writes. Black consumer or white, then, skinny jeans appear to have crossed over into a simple fashion statement, all (or at least most) passion spent.

Disposable Decades

When analyzing a consumer sign, you will often find yourself referring to particular decades (as we have above) in which certain popular fads and trends were prominent, because the decade in which a given style appears may be an essential key to the system that explains it. Have you ever wondered why American cultural trends seem to change with every decade, why it is so easy to speak of the sixties or the seventies or the eighties and immediately recognize the popular styles that dominated each decade? Have you ever looked at the style of a friend and thought, "Oh, she's so seventies"? Can you place platform shoes or bell-bottoms at the drop of a hat? A change in the calendar always seems to herald a change in style in a consuming culture. But why?

The decade-to-decade shift in America's pop cultural and consumer identity goes back a good number of years. It is still easy, for example, to distinguish F. Scott Fitzgerald's Jazz Age twenties from John Steinbeck's wrathful thirties. The fifties, an especially connotative decade, raise images of ducktail haircuts and poodle skirts, drive-in culture and Elvis, family sitcoms and white-bread innocence, while the sixties are remembered for acid rock, hippies, the student revolution, and back-to-the-land communes. We remember the seventies as a pop cultural era divided among disco, Nashville, and preppiedom, with John Travolta, truckers, and Skippy and Muffy as dominant pop icons. The boom-boom eighties gave us Wall Street glitz and the yuppie invasion. Indeed, each decade since World War I—which, not accidentally, happens to coincide roughly with the rise of modern advertising and mass production—seems to carry its own consumerist style.

It's no accident that the decade-to-decade shift in consumer styles coincides with the advent of modern advertising and mass production, because it was mass production that created a need for constant consumer turnover in the first place. Mass production, that is, promotes stylistic change because with so many products being produced, a market must be created to consume all of them, and this means constantly consuming *more*. To get consumers to keep buying all the new stuff, you have to convince them that the stuff they already have is passé. Why else do fashion designers completely change their lines each year? Why do car manufacturers annually change their color schemes and body shapes when the previous year's model seemed good enough? Why did the Apple iPhone 5c come out in so many colors? The new colors and designs aren't simply functional improvements (though they are marketed as such); they are inducements to go out and replace what you already have to avoid appearing out of fashion. Just think: If you could afford to buy any car or phone you want, what would it be? Would your choice a few years ago have been the same?

Mass production, then, creates consumer societies based on the constant creation of new products that are intended to be disposed of with the next product year. But something happened along the way to the establishment of our consumer culture: We began to value consumption more than production. Shoppers storm the doors as the Christmas shopping season begins earlier and earlier every year. Listen to the economic news: Consumption, not production, is relied upon to carry America out of its economic downturns. When Americans stop buying, our economy grinds to a halt. Consumption lies at the center of our

---

Exploring the Signs of Consumer Culture

"You are what you buy." In your journal, freewrite on the importance of consumer products in your life. How do you respond to being told your identity is equivalent to the products you buy? Do you resist the notion? Do you recall any instances when you have felt lost without a favorite object? How do you communicate your sense of self to others through objects, whether clothing, books, food, home decor, electronic goods, or something else?

economic system now, constituting some two-thirds of our economic activity, and the result has been a transformation in the very way we view ourselves.

A Tale of Two Cities

It has not always been thus in America, however. Once, Americans prided themselves on their productivity. In 1914, for example, the poet Carl Sandburg boasted of a Chicago that was "Hog Butcher for the World, / Tool maker, Stacker of Wheat, / Player with Railroads and the Nation's Freight Handler." One wonders what Sandburg would think of the place today. From the South Side east to the industrial suburb of Gary, Indiana, Chicago's once-proud mills and factories rust in the winter wind. At the Chicago Mercantile Exchange, trade today is in commodity futures, not commodities.

Meanwhile, a few hundred miles to the northwest, Bloomington, Minnesota, buzzes with excitement. For there stands the Mall of America, a colossus of consumption so large that it contains within its walls a seven-acre Nickelodeon Universe theme park, with lots of room to spare. You can find almost anything you want in the Mall of America, but most of what you will find won't have been manufactured in America. The proud tag "Made in the U.S.A." is an increasingly rare item.

It's a long way from Sandburg's Chicago to the Mall of America, a trip that traverses America's shift from a producer to a consumer economy. This shift is not simply economic; it is behind a cultural transformation that is shaping a new mythology in which we define ourselves, our hopes, and our desires.

Ask yourself right now what your own goals are in going to college. Do you envision a career in law, or medicine, or banking and finance? Do you want to be a teacher, an advertising executive, or a civil servant? Or maybe you are preparing for a career in an Internet-related field. If you've considered any of these careers, you are contemplating what are known as service jobs. While essential to society, none of them actually produces anything. If you've given thought to going into some facet of manufacturing, on the other hand, you are unusual because America offers increasingly fewer opportunities in that area and little prestige. The prestigious jobs are in law and medicine and in high-tech operations like Google and Facebook, a fact that is easy to take for granted. But ask yourself: Does it have to be so?

To live in a consumer culture is not simply a matter of shopping or career choice, however; it is also a matter of being. Often aligned with the preeminent American mythology of personal freedom, the freedom to consume *what* you want *whenever* you want it has become—thanks in large part to the advent of mobile digital technology—a defining value of modern American life: a human right, not a mere pleasure or convenience. You are what you buy, and what you buy fulfills what you are. And in case you forget this, a constant drumbeat of advertising and marketing schemes exhorts you to go out and buy something, replacing the freedom to march to the beat of a different drummer with the freedom to buy.

When the Going Gets Tough, the Tough Go Shopping

In a cultural system where our identities are displayed in the products we buy, it accordingly behooves us to pay close attention to what we consume and why. From the cars we drive to the clothes we wear, we are enmeshed in a web of consumption. As students, you are probably freer to choose the images you wish to project through the products you consume than most other demographic groups in America. This claim may sound paradoxical: After all, don't working adults have more money than starving students? Yes, generally. But the working world places severe restrictions on the choices employees can make in their clothing and grooming styles, and even automobile choice may be restricted (real estate agents, for example, can't escort their clients around town in Kia Souls). Corporate business wear, for all its variations, still revolves around a central core of necktied and dark-hued sobriety, regardless of the gender of the wearer. On campus, however, you can be pretty much whatever you want to be, which is why your own daily life provides you with a particularly rich field of consumer signs to read and decode.

So go to it. By the time you finish reading this book, a lot will have changed. Look around. Start reading the signs.

The Readings

As this chapter's lead-off essay, Laurence Shames's "The More Factor" offers a historical context for American consumer culture, relating America's frontier history to our ever-expanding desire for more goods and services. Anne

Reading Consumer Culture Online

Log on to one of the many home shopping networks or auction sites. You might try QVC (www.QVC.com), Shop at Home (www.shopathome .com), or eBay (www.ebay.com). Analyze both the products sold and the way they are marketed. Who is the target audience for the network you're studying, and what images and values are used to attract this market? How does the marketing compare with nonelectronic sales pitches, such as displays in shopping malls and magazines or TV advertising? Does the electronic medium affect your behavior as a consumer, or does the time pressure of an electronic auction affect your behavior as well? How do you account for any differences in electronic and traditional marketing strategies?

Norton and Malcolm Gladwell follow with a paired set of readings on the ways in which retailers seek to maximize sales by designing the shopping experience to influence consumers' buying behavior, with Norton providing semiotic analyses of shopping malls and mail-order catalogs and Gladwell reporting on the measures that brick-and-mortar-store managers take to encourage spending. Next, Jon Mooallem explores the world of self-storage facilities in an era when consumption is outstripping many Americans' ability to house all their stuff. Stephanie Clifford and Quentin Hardy's *Business Day* article reports on the ways in which even brick-and-mortar shops are now tracking customers' behavior by monitoring their smartphone signals, while Thomas Hine takes us into the low-tech world of packaging, revealing how a simple package can be a complex sign system used in the front lines of marketing. James A. Roberts's survey of status consumption and the paradox of diminishing returns provides a piquant counterpoint to Phyllis M. Japp and Debra K. Japp's rhetorical analysis of the "voluntary simplicity movement," a consumer phenomenon that manages to commodify the desire not to be addicted to consumption. Steve McKevitt then analyzes the ways in which technology and psychology come together in the consumer marketplace. The chapter concludes with Thomas Frank's revelation of how corporate America has turned consumption into a hip signifier of inauthentic rebellion: a "commodification of dissent."

LAURENCE SHAMES
The More Factor

A bumper sticker popular in the 1980s read, "Whoever dies with the most toys wins." In this selection from *The Hunger for More: Searching for Values in an Age of Greed* (1989), Laurence Shames shows how the great American hunger for more — more toys, more land, more opportunities — is an essential part of our history and character, stemming from the frontier era when the horizon alone seemed the only limit to American desire. The author of *The Big Time: The Harvard Business School's Most Successful Class and How It Shaped America* (1986) and the holder of a Harvard MBA, Shames is a journalist who has contributed to such publications as *Playboy*, *Vanity Fair*, *Manhattan, inc.*, and *Esquire*. He currently is working full-time on writing fiction and screenplays, with his most recent publications including *Florida Straits* (1992), *Sunburn* (1995), *Welcome to Paradise* (1999), *The Naked Detective* (2000), *Not Fade Away* (2003, with Peter Barton), and *Shot on Location* (2013).

1

Americans have always been optimists, and optimists have always liked to speculate. In Texas in the 1880s, the speculative instrument of choice was towns, and there is no tale more American than this.

What people would do was buy up enormous tracts of parched and vacant land, lay out a Main Street, nail together some wooden sidewalks, and start slapping up buildings. One of these buildings would be called the Grand Hotel and would have a saloon complete with swinging doors. Another might be dubbed the New Academy or the Opera House. The developers would erect a flagpole and name a church, and once the workmen had packed up and moved on, the towns would be as empty as the sky.

But no matter. The speculators, next, would hire people to pass out handbills in the Eastern and Midwestern cities, tracts limning the advantages of relocation to "the Athens of the South" or "the new plains Jerusalem." When persuasion failed, the builders might resort to bribery, paying people's moving costs and giving them houses, in exchange for nothing but a pledge to stay until a certain census was taken or a certain inspection made. Once the nose count was completed, people were free to move on, and there was in fact a contingent of folks who made their living by keeping a cabin on skids and dragging it for pay from one town to another.

📱 macmillanhighered.com/signsoflife
How does materialism affect us psychologically?
e-readings > **Gene Brockhoff**, *Shop 'til You Drop* [video]

80

The speculators' idea, of course, was to lure the railroad. If one could create a convincing semblance of a town, the railroad might come through it, and a real town would develop, making the speculators staggeringly rich. By these devices a man named Sanborn once owned Amarillo.[1]

But railroad tracks are narrow and the state of Texas is very, very wide. 5 For every Wichita Falls or Lubbock there were a dozen College Mounds or Belchervilles,[2] bleached, unpeopled burgs that receded quietly into the dust, taking with them large amounts of speculators' money.

Still, the speculators kept right on bucking the odds and depositing empty towns in the middle of nowhere. Why did they do it? Two reasons — reasons that might be said to summarize the central fact of American economic history and that go a fair way toward explaining what is perhaps the central strand of the national character.

The first reason was simply that the possible returns were so enormous as to partake of the surreal, to create a climate in which ordinary logic and prudence did not seem to apply. In a boom like that of real estate when the railroad barreled through, long shots that might pay one hundred thousand to one seemed worth a bet.

The second reason, more pertinent here, is that there was a presumption that America would *keep* on booming — if not forever, then at least longer than it made sense to worry about. There would always be another gold rush, another Homestead Act, another oil strike. The next generation would always ferret out opportunities that would be still more lavish than any that had gone before. America *was* those opportunities. This was an article not just of faith, but of strategy. You banked on the next windfall, you staked your hopes and even your self-esteem on it, and this led to a national turn of mind that might usefully be thought of as the habit of more.

A century, maybe two centuries, before anyone had heard the term *baby boomer*, much less *yuppie*, the habit of more had been instilled as the operative truth among the economically ambitious. The habit of more seemed to suggest that there was no such thing as getting wiped out in America. A fortune lost in Texas might be recouped in Colorado. Funds frittered away on grazing land where nothing grew might flood back in as silver. There was always a second chance, or always seemed to be, in this land where growth was destiny and where expansion and purpose were the same.

The key was the frontier, not just as a matter of acreage, but as idea. Vast, 10 varied, rough as rocks, America was the place where one never quite came to the end. Ben Franklin explained it to Europe even before the Revolutionary War had finished: America offered new chances to those "who, in their own

---

[1]For a fuller account of railroad-related land speculation in Texas, see F. Stanley, *Story of the Texas Panhandle Railroads* (Borger, Tex.: Hess Publishing Co., 1976).

[2]T. Lindsay Baker, *Ghost Towns of Texas* (Norman, Okla.: University of Oklahoma Press, 1986).

Countries, where all the Lands [were] fully occupied . . . could never [emerge] from the poor Condition wherein they were born."[3]

So central was this awareness of vacant space and its link to economic promise that Frederick Jackson Turner, the historian who set the tone for much of the twentieth century's understanding of the American past, would write that it was "not the constitution, but free land . . . [that] made the democratic type of society in America."[4] Good laws mattered; an accountable government mattered; ingenuity and hard work mattered. But those things were, so to speak, an overlay on the natural, geographic America that was simply *there*, and whose vast and beckoning possibilities seemed to generate the ambition and the sometimes reckless liberty that would fill it. First and foremost, it was open space that provided "the freedom of the individual to rise under conditions of social mobility."[5]

Open space generated not just ambition, but metaphor. As early as 1835, Tocqueville was extrapolating from the fact of America's emptiness to the observation that "no natural boundary seems to be set to the efforts of man."[6] Nor was any limit placed on what he might accomplish, since, in that heyday of the Protestant ethic, a person's rewards were taken to be quite strictly proportionate to his labors.

Frontier; opportunity; more. This has been the American trinity from the very start. The frontier was the backdrop and also the raw material for the streak of economic booms. The booms became the goad and also the justification for the myriad gambles and for Americans' famous optimism. The optimism, in turn, shaped the schemes and visions that were sometimes noble, sometimes appalling, always bold. The frontier, as reality and as symbol, is what has shaped the American way of doing things and the American sense of what's worth doing.

But there has been one further corollary to the legacy of the frontier, with its promise of ever-expanding opportunities: Given that the goal—a realistic goal for most of our history—was *more*, Americans have been somewhat backward in adopting values, hopes, ambitions that have to do with things *other than* more. In America, a sense of quality has lagged far behind a sense of scale. An ideal of contentment has yet to take root in soil traditionally more hospitable to an ideal of restless striving. The ethic of decency has been upstaged by the ethic of success. The concept of growth has been applied almost exclusively to things that can be measured, counted, weighed. And the hunger for those things that are unmeasurable but fine—the sorts of accomplishment that cannot be undone by circumstance or a shift in social fashion, the kind of serenity that cannot be shattered by tomorrow's headline—has gone largely unfulfilled, and even unacknowledged.

[3]Benjamin Franklin, "Information to Those Who Would Remove to America," in *The Autobiography and Other Writings* (New York: Penguin Books, 1986), 242.

[4]Frederick Jackson Turner, *The Frontier in American History* (Melbourne, Fla.: Krieger, 1976 [reprint of 1920 edition]), 293.

[5]Ibid., 266.

[6]Tocqueville, *Democracy in America*.

2

If the supply of more went on forever, perhaps that wouldn't matter very 15
much. Expansion could remain a goal unto itself, and would continue to
generate a value system based on bulk rather than on nuance, on quantities
of money rather than on quality of life, on "progress" itself rather than on
a sense of what the progress was for. But what if, over time, there was less
more to be had?

That is the essential situation of America today.

Let's keep things in proportion: The country is not running out of wealth,
drive, savvy, or opportunities. We are not facing imminent ruin, and neither
panic nor gloom is called for. But there have been ample indications over the
past two decades that we are running out of more.

Consider productivity growth — according to many economists, the single
most telling and least distortable gauge of changes in real wealth. From 1947
to 1965, productivity in the private sector (adjusted, as are all the following
figures, for inflation) was advancing, on average, by an annual 3.3 percent.
This means, simply, that each hour of work performed by a specimen American worker contributed 3.3 cents worth or more to every American dollar every year; whether we saved it or spent it, that increment went into a
national kitty of ever-enlarging aggregate wealth. Between 1965 and 1972,
however, the "more-factor" decreased to 2.4 percent a year, and from 1972
to 1977 it slipped further, to 1.6 percent. By the early 1980s, productivity
growth was at a virtual standstill, crawling along at 0.2 percent for the five
years ending in 1982.[7] Through the middle years of the 1980s, the numbers
rebounded somewhat — but by then the gains were being neutralized by the
gargantuan carrying costs on the national debt.[8]

Inevitably, this decline in the national stockpile of more held consequences for the individual wallet.[9] During the 1950s, Americans' average
hourly earnings were humping ahead at a gratifying 2.5 percent each year. By
the late seventies, that figure stood just where productivity growth had come
to stand, at a dispiriting 0.2 cents on the dollar. By the first half of the eighties, the Reagan "recovery" notwithstanding, real hourly wages were actually
moving backward — declining at an average annual rate of 0.3 percent.

Compounding the shortage of more was an unfortunate but crucial demo- 20
graphic fact. Real wealth was nearly ceasing to expand just at the moment

---

[7]These figures are taken from the Council of Economic Advisers, *Economic Report of the
President*, February 1984, 267.

[8]For a lucid and readable account of the meaning and implications of our reservoir
of red ink, see Lawrence Malkin, *The National Debt* (New York: Henry Holt and Co., 1987).
Through no fault of Malkin's, many of his numbers are already obsolete, but his explanation
of who owes what to whom, and what it means, remains sound and even entertaining in a
bleak sort of way.

[9]The figures in this paragraph and the next are from "The Average Guy Takes It on the
Chin," *New York Times*, 13 July 1986, sec. 3.

when the members of that unprecedented population bulge known as the baby boom were entering what should have been their peak years of income expansion. A working man or woman who was thirty years old in 1949 could expect to see his or her real earnings burgeon by 63 percent by age forty. In 1959, a thirty-year-old could still look forward to a gain of 49 percent by his or her fortieth birthday.

But what about the person who turned thirty in 1973? By the time that worker turned forty, his or her real earnings had shrunk by a percentage point. For all the blather about yuppies with their beach houses, BMWs, and radicchio salads, and even factoring in those isolated tens of thousands making ludicrous sums in consulting firms or on Wall Street, the fact is that between 1979 and 1983 real earnings of all Americans between the ages of twenty-five and thirty-four actually declined by 14 percent.[10] The *New York Times*, well before the stock market crash put the kibosh on eighties confidence, summed up the implications of this downturn by observing that "for millions of bread-winners, the American dream is becoming the impossible dream."[11]

Now, it is not our main purpose here to detail the ups and downs of the American economy. Our aim, rather, is to consider the effects of those ups and downs on people's goals, values, sense of their place in the world. What happens at that shadowy juncture where economic prospects meld with personal choice? What sorts of insights and adjustments are called for so that economic ups and downs can be dealt with gracefully?

Fact one in this connection is that, if America's supply of more is in fact diminishing, American values will have to shift and broaden to fill the gap where the expectation of almost automatic gains used to be. Something more durable will have to replace the fat but fragile bubble that had been getting frailer these past two decades and that finally popped—a tentative, partial pop—on October 19, 1987. A different sort of growth—ultimately, a growth in responsibility and happiness—will have to fulfill our need to believe that our possibilities are still expanding.

The transition to that new view of progress will take some fancy stepping, because, at least since the end of World War II, simple economic growth has stood, in the American psyche, as the best available substitute for the literal frontier. The economy has *been* the frontier. Instead of more space, we have had more money. Rather than measuring progress in terms of geographical expansion, we have measured it by expansion in our standard of living. Economics has become the metaphor on which we pin our hopes of open space and second chances.

The poignant part is that the literal frontier did not pass yesterday: it has not existed for a hundred years. But the frontier's promise has become so much a part of us that we have not been willing to let the concept die. We have kept the frontier mythology going by invocation, by allusion, by hype.

25

---

[10]See, for example, "The Year of the Yuppie," *Newsweek*, 31 December 1984, 16.
[11]"The Average Guy."

It is not a coincidence that John F. Kennedy dubbed his political program the New Frontier. It is not mere linguistic accident that makes us speak of Frontiers of Science or of psychedelic drugs as carrying one to Frontiers of Perception. We glorify fads and fashions by calling them Frontiers of Taste. Nuclear energy has been called the Last Frontier; solar energy has been called the Last Frontier. Outer space has been called the Last Frontier; the oceans have been called the Last Frontier. Even the suburbs, those blandest and least adventurous of places, have been wryly described as the crabgrass frontier.[12]

What made all these usages plausible was their being linked to the image of the American economy as an endlessly fertile continent whose boundaries never need be reached, a domain that could expand in perpetuity, a gigantic playing field that would never run out of room and on which the game would get forever bigger and more filled with action. This was the frontier that would not vanish.

It is worth noting that people in other countries (with the possible exception of that other America, Australia) do not talk about frontier this way. In Europe, and in most of Africa and Asia, "frontier" connotes, at worst, a place of barbed wire and men with rifles, and at best, a neutral junction where one changes currency while passing from one fixed system into another. Frontier, for most of the world's people, does not suggest growth, expanse, or opportunity.

For Americans, it does, and always has. This is one of the things that sets America apart from other places and makes American attitudes different from those of other people. It is why, from *Bonanza* to the Sierra Club, the notion or even the fantasy of empty horizons and untapped resources has always evoked in the American heart both passion and wistfulness. And it is why the fear that the economic frontier — our last, best version of the Wild West — may finally be passing creates in us not only money worries but also a crisis of morale and even of purpose.

3

It might seem strange to call the 1980s an era of nostalgia. The decade, after 30 all, has been more usually described in terms of coolness, pragmatism, and a blithe innocence of history. But the eighties, unawares, were nostalgic for frontiers; and the disappointment of that nostalgia had much to do with the time's greed, narrowness, and strange want of joy. The fear that the world may not be a big enough playground for the full exercise of one's energies and yearnings, and worse, the fear that the playground is being fenced off and will no longer expand — these are real worries and they have had consequences. The eighties were an object lesson in how people play the game when there is an awful and unspoken suspicion that the game is winding down.

[12]With the suburbs again taking on a sort of fascination, this phrase was resurrected as the title of a 1985 book — *Crabgrass Frontier: The Suburbanization of America*, by Kenneth T. Jackson (Oxford University Press).

It was ironic that the yuppies came to be so reviled for their vaunting ambition and outsized expectations, as if they'd invented the habit of more, when in fact they'd only inherited it the way a fetus picks up an addiction in the womb. The craving was there in the national bloodstream, a remnant of the frontier, and the baby boomers, described in childhood as "the luckiest generation,"[13] found themselves, as young adults, in the melancholy position of wrestling with a two-hundred-year dependency on a drug that was now in short supply.

True, the 1980s raised the clamor for more to new heights of shrillness, insistence, and general obnoxiousness, but this, it can be argued, was in the nature of a final binge, the storm before the calm. America, though fighting the perception every inch of the way, was coming to realize that it was not a preordained part of the natural order that one should be richer every year. If it happened, that was nice. But who had started the flimsy and pernicious rumor that it was normal?

READING THE TEXT

1. Summarize in a paragraph how, according to Shames, the frontier functions as a symbol of American consciousness.

2. What does Shames mean when he says, "Open space generated not just ambition, but metaphor" (para. 12)?

3. What connections does Shames make between America's frontier history and consumer behavior?

4. Why does Shames term the 1980s "an era of nostalgia" (para. 30)?

5. Characterize Shames's attitude toward the American desire for more. How does his tone reveal his personal views on his subject?

READING THE SIGNS

1. Shames asserts that Americans have been influenced by the frontier belief "that America would *keep* on booming" (para. 8). Do you feel that this belief continues to be influential into the twenty-first century? Write an essay arguing for your position.

2. Shames claims that, because of the desire for more, "the ethic of decency has been upstaged by the ethic of success" (para. 14). In class, form teams and debate the validity of Shames's claim.

3. **CONNECTING TEXTS**   Read or review Steve McKevitt's "Everything Now" (p. 143). Using Maslow's hierarchy of needs (p. 147), write an essay illustrating, refuting, or complicating the proposition that "the hunger for more" is driven by the fact that "our *needs* have been fulfilled and so, for the first time ever, we have an economy that is almost entirely devoted to the business of satisfying our *wants* instead" (para. 3).

4. In an essay, argue for or refute the proposition that the "hunger for more" that Shames describes is a universal human trait, not simply an American one.

[13]Thomas Hine, *Populuxe* (New York: Alfred A. Knopf, 1986), 15.

ANNE NORTON

The Signs of Shopping

Shopping malls are more than places to shop, just as mail-order catalogs are more than simple lists of goods. Both malls and catalogs are coded systems that not only encourage us to buy but, more profoundly, help us construct our very sense of identity, as in the J. Peterman catalog that "constructs the reader as a man of rugged outdoor interests, taste, and money." In this selection from *Republic of Signs* (1993), Anne Norton, a professor of political science at the University of Pennsylvania, analyzes the many ways in which malls, catalogs, and home shopping networks sell you what they want by telling you who you are. Norton's other books include *Alternative Americas* (1986), *Reflections on Political Identity* (1988), *Ninety-Five Theses on Politics, Culture, and Method* (2003), *Leo Strauss and the Politics of American Empire* (2004), and *On the Muslim Question* (2013).

Shopping at the Mall

The mall has been the subject of innumerable debates. Created out of the modernist impulse for planning and the centralization of public activity, the mall has become the distinguishing sign of suburban decentralization, springing up in unplanned profusion. Intended to restore something of the lost unity of city life to the suburbs, the mall has come to export styles and strategies to stores at the urban center. Deplored by modernists, it is regarded with affection only by their postmodern foes. Ruled more by their content than by their creators' avowed intent, the once sleek futurist shells have taken on a certain aura of postmodern playfulness and popular glitz.

The mall is a favorite subject for the laments of cultural conservatives and others critical of the culture of consumption. It is indisputably the cultural locus of commodity fetishism. It has been noticed, however, by others of a less condemnatory disposition that the mall has something of the mercado, or the agora, about it. It is both a place of meeting for the young and one of the rare places where young and old go together. People of different races and classes, different occupations, different levels of education meet there. As M. Pressdee and John Fiske note, however, though the mall appears to be a public place, it is not. Neither freedom of speech nor freedom of assembly is permitted there. Those who own and manage malls restrict what comes within their confines. Controversial displays, by stores or customers or the plethora of organizations and agencies that present themselves in the open spaces of the mall, are not permitted. These seemingly public spaces conceal a pervasive private authority.

The mall exercises its thorough and discreet authority not only in the regulation of behavior but in the constitution of our visible, inaudible, public discourse. It is the source of those commodities through which we speak of our identities, our opinions, our desires. It is a focus for the discussion of style among peripheral consumers. Adolescents, particularly female adolescents, are inclined to spend a good deal of time at the mall. They spend, indeed, more time than money. They acquire not simple commodities (they may come home with many, few, or none) but a well-developed sense of the significance of those commodities. In prowling the mall they embed themselves in a lexicon of American culture. They find themselves walking through a dictionary. Stores hang a variety of identities on their racks and mannequins. Their window displays provide elaborate scenarios conveying not only what the garment is but what the garment means.

A display in the window of Polo provides an embarrassment of semiotic riches. Everyone, from the architecture critic at the *New York Times* to kids in the hall of a Montana high school, knows what *Ralph Lauren* means. The polo mallet and the saddle, horses and dogs, the broad lawns of Newport, Kennebunkport, old photographs in silver frames, the evocation of age, of ancestry and Anglophilia, of indolence and the Ivy League, evoke the upper class. Indian blankets and buffalo plaids, cowboy hats and Western saddles, evoke a past distinct from England but nevertheless determinedly Anglo. The supposedly arcane and suspect arts of deconstruction are deployed easily, effortlessly, by the readers of these cultural texts.

Walking from one window to another, observing one another, shoppers, especially the astute and observant adolescents, acquire a facility with the language of commodities. They learn not only words but a grammar. Shop windows employ elements of sarcasm and irony, strategies of inversion and allusion. They provide models of elegant, economical, florid, and prosaic expression. They teach composition.

The practice of shopping is, however, more than instructive. It has long been the occasion for women to escape the confines of their homes and enjoy the companionship of other women. The construction of woman's role as one of provision for the needs of the family legitimated her exit. It provided an occasion for women to spend long stretches of time in the company of their friends, without the presence of their husbands. They could exchange information and reflections, ask advice, and receive support. As their daughters grew, they would be brought increasingly within this circle, included in shopping trips and lunches with their mothers. These would form, reproduce, and restructure communities of taste.

The construction of identity and the enjoyment of friendship outside the presence of men was thus effected through a practice that constructed women as consumers and subjected them to the conventions of the marketplace. Insofar as they were dependent on their husbands for money, they were dependent on their husbands for the means to the construction of their identities. They could not represent themselves through commodities without the funds men provided, nor could they, without money, participate in the community of women that was realized in "going shopping." Their identities were made contingent not only on the possession of property but on the recognition of dependence.

Insofar as shopping obliges dependent women to recognize their dependence, it also opens up the possibility of subversion.[1] The housewife who shops for pleasure takes time away from her husband, her family, and her house and claims it for herself. Constantly taught that social order and her private happiness depend on intercourse between men and women, she chooses the company of women instead. She engages with women in an activity marked as feminine, and she enjoys it. When she spends money, she exercises an authority over property that law and custom may deny her. If she has no resources independent of her husband, this may be the only authority over property she is able to exercise. When she buys things her husband does not approve — or does not know of — she further subverts an order that leaves control over property in her husband's hands.[2]

Her choice of feminine company and a feminine pursuit may involve additional subversions. As Fiske and Pressdee recognize, shopping without buying and shopping for bargains have a subversive quality. This is revealed, in a form that gives it additional significance, when a saleswoman leans forward and tells a shopper, "Don't buy that today, it will be on sale on Thursday." Here solidarity of gender (and often of class) overcome, however partially and briefly, the imperatives of the economic order.

Shoppers who look, as most shoppers do, for bargains, and salespeople who warn shoppers of impending sales, see choices between commodities as something other than the evidence and the exercise of freedom. They see covert direction and exploitation; they see the withholding of information and the manipulation of knowledge. They recognize that they are on enemy terrain and that their shopping can be, in Michel de Certeau's[3] term, a "guerrilla raid." This recognition in practice of the presence of coercion in choice challenges the liberal conflation of choice and consent.

Shopping at Home

Shopping is an activity that has overcome its geographic limits. One need no longer go to the store to shop. Direct mail catalogues, with their twenty-four-hour

[1]Nuanced and amusing accounts of shopping as subversion are provided in John Fiske's analyses of popular culture, particularly *Reading the Popular* (Boston: Unwin Hyman [now Routledge], 1989), pp. 13–42.

[2]See R. Bowlby, *Just Looking: Consumer Culture in Dreiser, Gissing, and Zola* (London: Methuen, 1985), p. 22, for another discussion and for an example of the recommendation of this strategy by Elizabeth Cady Stanton in the 1850s.

[3]**Michel de Certeau** (1925–1986) French social scientist and semiotician who played an important role in the development of contemporary cultural studies. –EDS.

phone numbers for ordering, permit people to shop where and when they please. An activity that once obliged one to go out into the public sphere, with its diverse array of semiotic messages, can now be done at home. An activity that once obliged one to be in company, if not in conversation, with one's compatriots can now be conducted in solitude.

The activity of catalogue shopping, and the pursuit of individuality, are not, however, wholly solitary. The catalogues invest their commodities with vivid historical and social references. The J. Peterman catalogue, for example, constructs the reader as a man of rugged outdoor interests, taste, and money.[4] He wears "The Owner's Hat" or "Hemingway's Cap," a leather flight jacket or the classic "Horseman's Duster," and various other garments identified with the military, athletes, and European imperialism. The copy for "The Owner's Hat" naturalizes class distinctions and, covertly, racism:

> Some of us work on the plantation.
> Some of us own the plantation.
> Facts are facts.
> This hat is for those who own the plantation.[5]

Gender roles are strictly delineated. The copy for a skirt captioned "Women's Legs" provides a striking instance of the construction of the gaze as male, of women as the object of the gaze:

> Just when you think you see something, a shape you think you recognize, it's gone and then it begins to return and then it's gone and of course you can't take your eyes off it.
>
> Yes, the long slow motion of women's legs. Whatever happened to those things at carnivals that blew air up into girls' skirts and you could spend hours watching.[6]

"You," of course, are male. There is also the lace blouse captioned "Mystery": "lace says yes at the same time it says no."[7] Finally, there are notes of imperialist nostalgia: the Shepherd's Hotel (Cairo) bathrobe and white pants for "the bush" and "the humid hell-holes of Bombay and Calcutta."[8]

---

[4] I have read several of these. I cite *The J. Peterman Company Owner's Manual No. 5*, from the J. Peterman Company, 2444 Palumbo Drive, Lexington, Ky. 40509.

[5] Ibid., p. 5. The hat is also identified with the Canal Zone, "successfully bidding at Beaulieu," intimidation, and LBOs. Quite a hat. It might be argued against my reading that the J. Peterman Company also offers the "Coal Miner's Bag" and a mailbag. However, since the descriptive points of reference on color and texture and experience for these bags are such things as the leather seats of Jaguars, and driving home in a Bentley, I feel fairly confident in my reading.

[6] Ibid., p. 3. See also pp. 15 and 17 for instances of women as the object of the male gaze. The identification of the gaze with male sexuality is unambiguous here as well.

[7] Ibid., p. 17.

[8] Ibid., pp. 7, 16, 20, 21, 37, and 50.

It may no longer be unforgivable to say that the British left a few good things behind in India and in Kenya, Singapore, Borneo, etc., not the least of which was their Englishness.[9]

As Paul Smith observes, in his reading of their catalogues, the Banana Republic has also made capital out of imperial nostalgia.[10]

The communities catalogues create are reinforced by shared mailing lists. The constructed identities are reified and elaborated in an array of semiotically related catalogues. One who orders a spade or a packet of seeds will be constructed as a gardener and receive a deluge of catalogues from plant and garden companies. The companies themselves may expand their commodities to appeal to different manifestations of the identities they respond to and construct. Smith and Hawken, a company that sells gardening supplies with an emphasis on aesthetics and environmental concern, puts out a catalogue in which a group of people diverse in age and in their ethnicity wear the marketed clothes while gardening, painting, or throwing pots. Williams-Sonoma presents its catalogue not as a catalogue of things for cooking but as "A Catalog for Cooks." The catalogue speaks not to need but to the construction of identity.

The Nature Company dedicates its spring 1990 catalogue "to trees," endorses Earth Day, and continues to link itself to the Nature Conservancy through posters and a program in which you buy a tree for a forest restoration project. Here, a not-for-profit agency is itself commodified, adding to the value of the commodities offered in the catalogue.[11] In this catalogue, consumption is not merely a means for the construction and representation of the self, it is also a means for political action. Several commodities are offered as "A Few Things You Can Do" to save the earth: a string shopping bag, a solar battery recharger, a home newspaper recycler. Socially conscious shopping is a liberal practice in every sense. It construes shopping as a form of election, in which one votes for good commodities or refuses one's vote to candidates whose practices are ethically suspect. In this respect, it reveals its adherence to the same ideological presuppositions that structure television's Home Shopping Network and other cable television sales shows.

Both politically informed purchasing and television sales conflate the free market and the electoral process. Dollars are identified with votes, purchases with endorsements. Both offer those who engage in them the possibility to "talk back" to manufacturers. In television sales shows this ability to talk back is both more thoroughly elaborated and more thoroughly exploited. Like the "elections" on MTV that invite viewers to vote for their favorite video by calling a number on their telephones, they permit those who watch to respond,

[9]Ibid., p. 20.

[10]Paul Smith, "Visiting the Banana Republic," in *Universal Abandon?* ed. Andrew Ross for *Social Text* (Minneapolis: University of Minnesota Press, 1988), pp. 128–48.

[11]*The Nature Company Catalog*, The Nature Company, P.O. Box 2310, Berkeley, Calif. 94702, Spring 1990. See pp. 1–2 and order form insert between pp. 18 and 19. Note also the entailed donation to Designs for Conservation on p. 18.

to speak, and to be heard by the television. Their votes, of course, cost money. On MTV, as in the stores, you can buy as much speech as you can afford. On the Home Shopping Network, the purchase of speech becomes complicated by multiple layers and inversions.

Each commodity is introduced. It is invested by the announcer with a number of desirable qualities. The value of these descriptions of the commodities is enhanced by the construction of the announcer as a mediator not only between the commodity and the consumer but between the salespeople and the consumer. The announcer is not, the format suggests, a salesperson (though of course the announcer is). He or she is an announcer, describing goods that others have offered for sale. Television claims to distinguish itself by making objects visible to the eyes, but it is largely through the ears that these commodities are constructed. The consumer, in purchasing the commodity, purchases the commodity, what the commodity signifies, and, as we say, "buys the salesperson's line." The consumer may also acquire the ability to speak on television. Each purchase is recorded and figures as a vote in a rough plebiscite, confirming the desirability of the object. Although the purchase figures are announced as if they were confirming votes, it is, of course, impossible to register one's rejection of the commodity. Certain consumers get a little more (or rather less) for their money. They are invited to explain the virtue of the commodity — and their purchase — to the announcer and the audience. The process of production, of both the consumers and that which they consume, continues in this apology for consumption.

The semiotic identification of consumption as an American activity, indeed, a patriotic one, is made with crude enthusiasm on the Home Shopping Network and other video sales shows. Red, white, and blue figure prominently in set designs and borders framing the television screen. The Home Shopping Network presents its authorities in an office conspicuously adorned with a picture of the Statue of Liberty.[12] Yet the messages that the Home Shopping Network sends its customers — that you can buy as much speech as you can afford, that you are recognized by others in accordance with your capacity to consume — do much to subvert the connection between capitalism and democracy on which this semiotic identification depends.

READING THE TEXT

1. What does Norton mean when she claims that the suburban shopping mall appears to be a public place but in fact is not?
2. What is Norton's interpretation of Ralph Lauren's Polo stores?
3. How is shopping a subversive activity for women, according to Norton?

[12]This moment from the Home Shopping Network was generously brought to my attention, on videotape, by Peter Bregman, a student in my American Studies class of fall 1988, at Princeton University.

4. How do mail-order catalogs create communities of shoppers, in Norton's view?

5. What are the political messages sent by the Home Shopping Network, as Norton sees them, and how are they communicated?

READING THE SIGNS

1. Visit a local shopping mall, and study the window displays, focusing on stores intended for one group of consumers (teenagers, for example, or children). Then write an essay in which you analyze how the displays convey what the stores' products "mean."

2. Bring a few product catalogs to class, and in small groups compare the kinds of consumer "constructed" by the cultural images and allusions in the catalogs. Do you note any patterns associated with gender, ethnicity, or age group? Report your group's interpretations to the whole class.

3. Interview five women of different age groups about their motivations and activities when they shop in a mall. Use your results as evidence in an essay in which you support, refute, or complicate Norton's assertion that shopping constitutes a subversive activity for women.

4. Watch an episode of the Home Shopping Network or a similar program, and write a semiotic analysis of the ways in which products are presented to consumers.

5. Select a single mail-order catalog, and write a detailed semiotic interpretation of the identity it constructs for its market.

6. Visit the Web site for a major chain store (for instance, www.urbanoutfitters.com), and study how the site "moves" the consumer through it. How does the site induce you to consume?

UNDERSTANDING SHOPPING

MALCOLM GLADWELL

The Science of Shopping

Ever wonder why the season's hottest new styles at stores like the Gap are usually displayed on the right at least fifteen paces in from the front entrance? It's because that's where shoppers are most likely to see them as they enter the store, gear down from the walking pace of a mall corridor, and adjust to the shop's spatial environment. Ever wonder how shop managers know this sort of thing? It's because, as Malcolm Gladwell reports here, they hire consultants like Paco Underhill, a "retail anthropologist" and "urban geographer" whose studies (often aided by hidden cameras) of shopping behavior have become valuable guides to store managers looking for the best ways to move the goods. Does this feel just a little Orwellian? Read on. A staff writer for the *New Yorker*, in which this selection first appeared, Gladwell has also written *The Tipping Point* (2000), *Blink: The Power of Thinking without Thinking* (2005), *Outliers: The Story of Success* (2008), *What the Dog Saw: And Other Adventures* (2009 compilation of *New Yorker* articles), and *David and Goliath* (2013).

Human beings walk the way they drive, which is to say that Americans tend to keep to the right when they stroll down shopping-mall concourses or city sidewalks. This is why in a well-designed airport travellers drifting toward their gate will always find the fast-food restaurants on their left and the gift shops on their right: people will readily cross a lane of pedestrian traffic to satisfy their hunger but rarely to make an impulse buy of a T-shirt or a magazine. This is also why Paco Underhill tells his retail clients to make sure that their window displays are canted, preferably to both sides but especially to the left, so that a potential shopper approaching the store on the inside of the sidewalk — the shopper, that is, with the least impeded view of the store window — can see the display from at least twenty-five feet away.

Of course, a lot depends on how fast the potential shopper is walking. Paco, in his previous life, as an urban geographer in Manhattan, spent a great deal of time thinking about walking speeds as he listened in on the great debates of the nineteen-seventies over whether the traffic lights in midtown should be timed to facilitate the movement of cars or to facilitate the movement of pedestrians and so break up the big platoons that move down Manhattan sidewalks. He knows that the faster you walk the more your peripheral vision narrows, so you become unable to pick up visual cues as quickly as someone who is just ambling along. He knows, too, that people who walk fast take a surprising amount of time to slow down — just as it takes a good stretch of road to change gears with a stick-shift automobile. On the basis of his research, Paco estimates the human downshift period to be anywhere from twelve to twenty-five feet, so if you own a store, he says, you never want to be next door to a bank: potential shoppers speed up when they walk past a bank (since there's nothing to look at), and by the time they slow down they've walked right past your business. The downshift factor also means that when potential shoppers enter a store it's going to take them from five to fifteen paces to adjust to the light and refocus and gear down from walking speed to shopping speed — particularly if they've just had to navigate a treacherous parking lot or hurry to make the light at Fifty-seventh and Fifth.

Paco calls that area inside the door the Decompression Zone, and something he tells clients over and over again is never, ever put anything of value in that zone — not shopping baskets or tie racks or big promotional displays — because no one is going to see it. Paco believes that, as a rule of thumb, customer interaction with any product or promotional display in the Decompression Zone will increase at least thirty percent once it's moved to the back edge of the zone, and even more if it's placed to the right, because another of the fundamental rules of how human beings shop is that upon entering a store — whether it's Nordstrom or K Mart, Tiffany or the Gap — the shopper invariably and reflexively turns to the right. Paco believes in the existence of the Invariant Right because he has actually verified it. He has put cameras in stores trained directly on the doorway, and if you go to his office, just above Union Square, where videocassettes and boxes of Super-eight film from all his work over the years are stacked in plastic Tupperware containers practically up to the ceiling, he can show you reel upon reel of grainy entryway video — customers striding in the door, downshifting, refocusing, and then, again and again, making that little half turn.

Paco Underhill is a tall man in his mid-forties, partly bald, with a neatly trimmed beard and an engaging, almost goofy manner. He wears baggy khakis and shirts open at the collar, and generally looks like the academic he might have been if he hadn't been captivated, twenty years ago, by the ideas of the urban anthropologist William Whyte. It was Whyte who pioneered the use of time-lapse photography as a tool of urban planning, putting cameras in parks and the plazas in front of office buildings in midtown Manhattan, in order to determine what distinguished a public space that worked from one that didn't. As a Columbia undergraduate, in 1974, Paco heard a lecture on Whyte's work and, he recalls, left the room "walking on air." He immediately read everything Whyte had written. He emptied his bank account to buy cameras and film and make his own home movie, about a pedestrian mall in Poughkeepsie. He took his "little exercise" to Whyte's advocacy group, the Project for Public Spaces, and was offered a job. Soon, however, it dawned on Paco that Whyte's ideas could be taken a step further — that the same techniques he used to establish why a plaza worked or didn't work could also be used to determine why a store worked or didn't work. Thus was born the field of retail anthropology, and, not long afterward, Paco founded Envirosell, which in just over fifteen years has counselled some of the most familiar names in American retailing, from Levi Strauss to Kinney, Starbucks, McDonald's, Blockbuster, Apple Computer, AT&T, and a number of upscale retailers that Paco would rather not name.

When Paco gets an assignment, he and his staff set up a series of video 5 cameras throughout the test store and then back the cameras up with Envirosell staffers — trackers, as they're known — armed with clipboards. Where the cameras go and how many trackers Paco deploys depends on exactly what the store wants to know about its shoppers. Typically, though, he might use six cameras and two or three trackers, and let the study run for two or three days, so that at the end he would have pages and pages of carefully annotated tracking sheets and anywhere from a hundred to five hundred hours of film. These days, given the expansion of his business, he might tape fifteen thousand hours in a year, and, given that he has been in operation since the late seventies, he now has well over a hundred thousand hours of tape in his library.

Even in the best of times, this would be a valuable archive. But today, with the retail business in crisis, it is a gold mine. The time per visit that the average American spends in a shopping mall was sixty-six minutes last year—down from seventy-two minutes in 1992—and is the lowest number ever recorded. The amount of selling space per American shopper is now more than double what it was in the mid-seventies, meaning that profit margins have never been narrower, and the costs of starting a retail business—and of failing—have never been higher. In the past few years, countless dazzling new retailing temples have been built along Fifth and Madison Avenues—Barneys, Calvin Klein, Armani, Valentino, Banana Republic, Prada, Chanel, NikeTown, and on and on—but it is an explosion of growth based on no more than a hunch, a hopeful multimillion-dollar gamble that the way to break through is to provide the shopper with spectacle and more spectacle. "The arrogance is gone," Millard Drexler, the president and C.E.O. of the Gap, told me. "Arrogance makes failure. Once you think you know the answer, it's almost always over." In such a competitive environment, retailers don't just want to know how shoppers behave in their stores. They *have* to know. And who better to ask than Paco Underhill, who in the past decade and a half has analyzed tens of thousands of hours of shopping videotape and, as a result, probably knows more about the strange habits and quirks of the species *Emptor americanus* than anyone else alive?

Paco is considered the originator, for example, of what is known in the trade as the butt-brush theory—or, as Paco calls it, more delicately, *le facteur bousculade*—which holds that the likelihood of a woman's being converted from a browser to a buyer is inversely proportional to the likelihood of her being brushed on her behind while she's examining merchandise. Touch—or brush or bump or jostle—a woman on the behind when she has stopped to look at an item, and she will bolt. Actually, calling this a theory is something of a misnomer, because Paco doesn't offer any explanation for why women react that way, aside from venturing that they are "more sensitive back there." It's really an observation, based on repeated and close analysis of his videotape library, that Paco has transformed into a retailing commandment: A women's product that requires extensive examination should never be placed in a narrow aisle.

Paco approaches the problem of the Invariant Right the same way. Some retail thinkers see this as a subject crying out for interpretation and speculation. The design guru Joseph Weishar, for example, argues, in his magisterial *Design for Effective Selling Space*, that the Invariant Right is a function of the fact that we "absorb and digest information in the left part of the brain" and "assimilate and logically use this information in the right half," the result being that we scan the store from left to right and then fix on an object to the right "essentially at a 45 degree angle from the point that we enter." When I asked Paco about this interpretation, he shrugged, and said he thought the reason was simply that most people are right-handed. Uncovering the fundamentals of "why" is clearly not a pursuit that engages him much. He is not a theoretician but an empiricist, and for him the important thing is that in amassing his huge library of in-store time-lapse photography he has gained enough hard evidence to know how often and under what circumstances the Invariant Right is expressed and how to take advantage of it.

What Paco likes are facts. They come tumbling out when he talks, and, because he speaks with a slight hesitation—lingering over the first syllable in, for example, "re-tail" or "de-sign"—he draws you in, and you find yourself truly hanging on his words. "We have reached a historic point in American history," he told me in our very first conversation. "Men, for the first time, have begun to buy their own underwear." He then paused to let the comment sink in, so that I could absorb its implications, before he elaborated: "Which means that we have to *totally* rethink the way we sell that product." In the parlance of Hollywood scriptwriters, the best endings must be surprising and yet inevitable; and the best of Paco's pronouncements take the same shape. It would never have occurred to me to wonder about the increasingly critical role played by touching—or, as Paco calls it, petting—clothes in the course of making the decision to buy them. But then I went to the Gap and to Banana Republic and saw people touching, and fondling and, one after another, buying shirts and sweaters laid out on big wooden tables, and what Paco told me—which was no doubt based on what he had seen on his videotapes—made perfect sense: that the reason the Gap and Banana Republic have tables is not merely that sweaters and shirts look better there, or that tables fit into the warm and relaxing residential feeling that the Gap and Banana Republic are trying to create in their stores, but that tables invite—indeed, symbolize—touching. "Where do we eat?" Paco asks. "We eat, we pick up food, on tables."

Paco produces for his clients a series of carefully detailed studies, totalling 10 forty to a hundred and fifty pages, filled with product-by-product breakdowns

Sports apparel for sale at a NikeTown store in Chicago.

and bright-colored charts and graphs. In one recent case, he was asked by a major clothing retailer to analyze the first of a new chain of stores that the firm planned to open. One of the things the client wanted to know was how successful the store was in drawing people into its depths, since the chances that shoppers will buy something are directly related to how long they spend shopping, and how long they spend shopping is directly related to how deep they get pulled into the store. For this reason, a supermarket will often put dairy products on one side, meat at the back, and fresh produce on the other side, so that the typical shopper can't just do a drive-by but has to make an entire circuit of the store, and be tempted by everything the supermarket has to offer. In the case of the new clothing store, Paco found that ninety-one percent of all shoppers penetrated as deep as what he called Zone 4, meaning more than three-quarters of the way in, well past the accessories and shirt racks and belts in the front, and little short of the far wall, with the changing rooms and the pants stacked on shelves. Paco regarded this as an extraordinary figure, particularly for a long, narrow store like this one, where it is not unusual for the rate of penetration past, say, Zone 3 to be under fifty percent. But that didn't mean the store was perfect — far from it. For Paco, all kinds of questions remained.

Purchasers, for example, spent an average of eleven minutes and twenty-seven seconds in the store, nonpurchasers two minutes and thirty-six seconds. It wasn't that the nonpurchasers just cruised in and out: in those two minutes and thirty-six seconds, they went deep into the store and examined an average of 3.42 items. So why didn't they buy? What, exactly, happened to cause some browsers to buy and other browsers to walk out the door?

Then, there was the issue of the number of products examined. The purchasers were looking at an average of 4.81 items but buying only 1.33 items. Paco found this statistic deeply disturbing. As the retail market grows more cutthroat, store owners have come to realize that it's all but impossible to increase the number of customers coming in, and have concentrated instead on getting the customers they do have to buy more. Paco thinks that if you can sell someone a pair of pants you must also be able to sell that person a belt, or a pair of socks, or a pair of underpants, or even do what the Gap does so well: sell a person a complete outfit. To Paco, the figure 1.33 suggested that the store was doing something very wrong, and one day when I visited him in his office he sat me down in front of one of his many VCRs to see how he looked for the 1.33 culprit.

It should be said that sitting next to Paco is a rather strange experience. "My mother says that I'm the best-paid spy in America," he told me. He laughed, but he wasn't entirely joking. As a child, Paco had a nearly debilitating stammer, and, he says, "since I was never that comfortable talking I always relied on my eyes to understand things." That much is obvious from the first moment you meet him: Paco is one of those people who looks right at you, soaking up every nuance and detail. It isn't a hostile gaze, because Paco isn't hostile at all. He has a big smile, and he'll call you "chief" and use your first name a lot and generally act as if he knew you well. But that's the awkward thing: He has looked at you so closely that you're sure he does know you well, and you, meanwhile, hardly know him at all.

This kind of asymmetry is even more pronounced when you watch his shopping videos with him, because every movement or gesture means some-thing to Paco—he has spent his adult life deconstructing the shopping experi-ence—but nothing to the outsider, or, at least, not at first. Paco had to keep stopping the video to get me to see things through his eyes before I began to understand. In one sequence, for example, a camera mounted high on the wall outside the changing rooms documented a man and a woman shopping for a pair of pants for what appeared to be their daughter, a girl in her midteens. The tapes are soundless, but the basic steps of the shopping dance are so familiar to Paco that, once I'd grasped the general idea, he was able to provide a running commentary on what was being said and thought. There is the girl emerging from the changing room wearing her first pair. There she is glancing at her reflection in the mirror, then turning to see herself from the back. There is the mother looking on. There is the father—or, as fathers are known in the trade, the "wallet carrier"—stepping forward and pulling up the jeans. There's the girl trying on another pair. There's the primp again. The twirl. The mother. The wallet carrier. And then again, with another pair. The full sequence lasted twenty minutes, and at the end came the take-home lesson, for which Paco called in one of his colleagues, Tom Moseman, who had supervised the project.

"This is a very critical moment," Tom, a young, intense man wearing 15 little round glasses, said, and he pulled up a chair next to mine. "She's saying, 'I don't know whether I should wear a belt.' Now here's the salesclerk. The girl says to him, 'I need a belt,' and he says, 'Take mine.' Now there he is taking her back to the full-length mirror."

A moment later, the girl returns, clearly happy with the purchase. She wants the jeans. The wallet carrier turns to her, and then gestures to the salesclerk. The wallet carrier is telling his daughter to give back the belt. The girl gives back the belt. Tom stops the tape. He's leaning forward now, a finger jabbing at the screen. Beside me, Paco is shaking his head. I don't get it—at least, not at first—and so Tom replays that last segment. The wallet carrier tells the girl to give back the belt. She gives back the belt. And then, finally, it dawns on me why this store has an average purchase number of only 1.33. "Don't you see?" Tom said. "*She wanted the belt.* A great opportunity to make an add-on sale . . . *lost!*"

Should we be afraid of Paco Underhill? One of the fundamental anxieties of the American consumer, after all, has always been that beneath the pleasure and the frivolity of the shopping experience runs an undercurrent of manip-ulation, and that anxiety has rarely seemed more justified than today. The practice of prying into the minds and habits of American consumers is now a multibillion-dollar business. Every time a product is pulled across a supermarket checkout scanner, information is recorded, assembled, and sold to a market-research firm for analysis. There are companies that put tiny cameras inside frozen-food cases in supermarket aisles; market-research firms that feed census data and behavioral statistics into algorithms and come out with complicated maps of the American consumer; anthropologists who sift through the garbage of carefully targeted households to analyze their true consumption patterns; and endless rounds of highly organized focus groups and questionnaire takers and phone surveyors. That some people are now tracking our every shopping move with video cameras seems in many respects the last straw: Paco's movies are, after all, creepy. They look like the surveillance videos taken during convenience-store holdups—hazy and soundless and slightly warped by the angle of the lens. When you watch them, you find yourself waiting for something bad to happen, for someone to shoplift or pull a gun on a cashier.

The more time you spend with Paco's videos, though, the less scary they seem. After an hour or so, it's no longer clear whether simply by watching people shop—and analyzing their every move—you can learn how to control them. The shopper that emerges from the videos is not pliable or manipulable. The screen shows people filtering in and out of stores, petting and moving on, abandoning their merchandise because checkout lines are too long, or leaving a store empty-handed because they couldn't fit their stroller into the aisle between two shirt racks. Paco's shoppers are fickle and headstrong, and are quite unwilling to buy anything unless conditions are perfect—unless the belt is presented at *exactly* the right moment. His theories of the butt-brush and petting and the Decompression Zone and the Invariant Right seek not to make shoppers conform to the desires of sellers but to make sellers conform to the desires of shoppers. What Paco is teaching his clients is a kind of slavish devotion to the shopper's every whim. He is teaching them humility.

READING THE TEXT

1. Summarize in your own words the ways that retailers use spatial design to affect the consumer's behavior and buying habits.

2. What is Gladwell's tone in this selection, and what does it reveal about his attitudes toward the retail industry's manipulation of customers?

3. What is the effect on the reader of Gladwell's description of Paco Underhill's background and physical appearance?

4. Why does Paco Underhill's mother say that he is "the best-paid spy in America" (para. 13)?

READING THE SIGNS

1. **CONNECTING TEXTS** Visit a local store or supermarket, and study the spatial design. How many of the design strategies that Gladwell describes do you observe, and how do they affect customers' behavior? Use your observations as the basis for an essay interpreting the store's spatial design. To develop your ideas further, consult Anne Norton's "The Signs of Shopping" (p. 87).

2. In class, form teams and debate the proposition that the surveillance of consumers by retail anthropologists is manipulative and unethical.

3. Visit the Web site of a major retailer (such as www.abercrombieandfitch.com or www.gap.com). How is the online "store" designed to encourage consuming behavior?

4. Write an essay in response to Gladwell's question "Should we be afraid of Paco Underhill?" (para. 17).

Credit Card Barbie

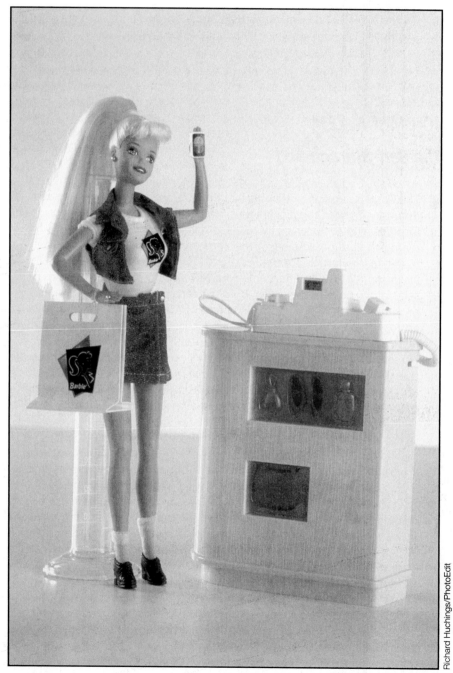

READING THE SIGNS

1. Why might girls enjoy playing with a Barbie who shops rather than engaging her in some other kind of activity?

2. Do you think that having Barbie use a credit card to purchase cosmetics has an effect on the girls who play with the doll? If so, what are those effects?

JON MOOALLEM
The Self-Storage Self

The Great Recession emptied a lot of homes as their owners were cast in to the abyss of foreclosure, but in doing so it filled a lot of storage facilities with the piles of things — some of them mere junk, some of them priceless possessions — that most of us accumulate in our lives. In this feature article for the *New York Times Magazine*, Jon Mooallem visits some of the ordinary folk who have found themselves needing self-storage units in the wake of broken careers, broken engagements, broken marriages, or simply disrupted lives. And the things they hold on to, paying sizable fees to store stuff that often appears to be little better than trash, may be surprising—until we remember that our possessions are an important measure of our lives. Jon Mooallem is a contributing writer for the *New York Times Magazine* and is the author of *Wild Ones: A Sometimes Dismaying, Weirdly Reassuring Story about Looking at People Looking at Animals in America* (2013).

Statewide Self Storage spreads out near Highway 4 in Antioch, Calif., a suburban community between San Francisco and Sacramento. It's a phalanx of long, low-slung buildings separated by wide driveways and lined with red doors. The complex houses 453 storage units and is wedged between a car dealership and a Costco.

It was the last afternoon in May, and the sun seared all the concrete and corrugated steel. Statewide's gate opened, and a man named Jimmy Sloan made for the far corner of the property. Sloan, who dresses and styles his hair like James Dean, is a part-owner of the Harley-Davidson repair shop nearby. He rolled open the door of a 10-by-30-foot unit, the largest Statewide offers. It was his ex-fiancée's but still leased under his name, and packed with, among other things, a particleboard shelving unit, some wicker items, a microwave oven, a box labeled "Mickey's Hornet Neon," a floor lamp, a television and a wooden child's bed standing on its end on a desk. It was hard to tell how deep the inventory went. "She hasn't seen most of this stuff in six years," Sloan said.

For five years, he stored most of it above the garage of his house. But he had to borrow on the house to keep the bike shop running, and last year, feeling in over his head, he opted to sell the house and downsize before he fell behind and risked foreclosure. "Pretty much got out of that house at zero — didn't make a penny on it," he told me with the kind of ascetic pride that wouldn't have made any sense before our economically crippled era. Sloan's fiancée insisted he rent a storage unit and move everything over the garage into it for her. So he did. Then they split up.

He kept paying the rent on the unit for almost a year — $217 every month. But Sloan finally lost his patience and told her: "You know, we're not even together anymore. This stuff's gotta go." Everything here, he told me, was worth less than what he had paid to store it. "Storage is always a bad investment, any way you look at it," he said. The rent was her responsibility now. But the former future Mrs. Jimmy Sloan never paid Statewide. By now, it seemed likely that the managers would end up auctioning off the contents of the unit in accordance with state law. That was fine with Jimmy Sloan. But he wanted to get in first and make sure that his late father's collection of hunting knives and die-cast toy tractors, which he'd lost track of, weren't mixed in there. And so, to regain access, he'd just walked into the office and paid Statewide what was owed: $460. He'd counted out the cash unresentfully, like a man retrieving his dog from a neighbor's house for the 10th or 11th time.

"That stuff is Happy Meal junk," he now said, pointing to a see-through 5 Rubbermaid bin in the storage unit's brickwork of boxes. It was full of brightly colored plastic toys and a pair of hot pink sunglasses that belonged to his ex-fiancée's children. "The kids broke it, played with it once. It wasn't even for Christmas," he said.

Sloan had not started rummaging for his dad's knife and tractor collections in earnest; he was still pecking at the concretion's surface, not tunneling into it. But already he'd found a Marilyn Monroe poster and a souvenir road sign for James Dean Boulevard and set them near the door. They were his, from his old living room. He had forgotten about them and wanted to take them home. Soon, he peeled back the top of a huge bin. Inside, I could see a VHS cassette of "American Pie" and a black-and-white toy football with the logo of the Oakland Raiders. "Look at that!" Sloan said suddenly. "A Raider football!" He put it next to the poster and the road sign. Apparently it, too, was just appealing enough to hang on to.

The Self Storage Association, a nonprofit trade group, estimates that since the onset of the recession, occupancies at storage facilities nationwide are down, on average, about 2 or 3 percent. It's not a cataclysmic drop but enough to disorient an industry that has always considered itself recession-resistant, if not outright recession-proof. But the collapsing economy created an opportunity, and in some cases an ultimatum, for Americans to reassess the raft of obligations and the loads of stuff we accumulated before things went wrong. We've been making difficult decisions, and for a lot of us, that has involved rolling up the door of a storage unit and carting property in or out. The storage industry's expansion in the first flush years of this decade was both enabled by, and helped enable, the extreme consumption that defined America then. The people coming through the gates now are defining who we will be when this turmoil is over.

The first modern self-storage facilities opened in the 1960s, and for two decades storage remained a low-profile industry, helping people muddle through what it terms "life events." For the most part, storage units were meant to temporarily absorb the possessions of those in transition: moving, marrying or divorcing, or dealing with a death in the family. And the late 20th century turned out to be a golden age of life events in America, with peaking divorce rates and a rush of second- and third-home buying. At the same time, the first baby boomers were left to face down the caches of heirlooms and clutter in their parents' basements.

Across America, from 2000 to 2005, upward of 3,000 self-storage facilities went up every year. Somehow, Americans managed to fill that brand-new empty space. It raises a simple question: where was all that stuff before? "A lot of it just comes down to the great American propensity toward accumulating stuff," [industry veteran Tom] Litton explained. Between 1970 and 2008, real disposable personal income per capita doubled, and by 2008 we were spending nearly all of it—all but 2.7 percent—each year. Meanwhile, the price of much of what we were buying plunged. Even by the early '90s, American families had, on average, twice as many possessions as they did 25 years earlier. By 2005, according to the Boston College sociologist Juliet B. Schor, the average consumer purchased one new piece of clothing every five and a half days.

Schor has been hacking intrepidly through the jumble of available data 10 quantifying the last decade's consumption spree. Between 1998 and 2005, she found, the number of vacuum cleaners coming into the country every year more than doubled. The number of toasters, ovens and coffeemakers tripled. A 2006 U.C.L.A. study found middle-class families in Los Angeles "battling a nearly universal overaccumulation of goods." Garages were clogged. Toys and outdoor furniture collected in the corners of backyards. "The home-goods storage crisis has reached almost epic proportions," the authors of the study wrote. A new kind of customer was being propelled, hands full, into self-storage.

Consider our national furniture habit. In an unpublished paper, Schor writes that "anecdotal evidence suggests an 'Ikea effect.'" We've spent more on furniture even as prices have dropped, thereby amassing more of it. The amount entering the United States from overseas doubled between 1998 and 2005, reaching some 650 million pieces a year. Comparing Schor's data with E.P.A. data on municipal solid waste shows that the rate at which we threw out old furniture rose about one-thirteenth as fast during roughly the same period. In other words, most of that new stuff—and any older furniture it displaced—is presumably still knocking around somewhere. In fact, some seven million American households now have at least one piece of furniture in their storage units. Furniture is the most commonly stored thing in America.

The marketing consultant Derek Naylor told me that people stockpile furniture while saving for bigger or second homes but then, in some cases, "they don't want to clutter up their new home with all the things they have in storage." So they buy new, nicer things and keep paying to store the old ones anyway. Clem Tang, a spokesman for Public Storage, explains: "You say, 'I paid $1,000 for this table a couple of years ago. I'm not getting rid of it, or selling it for 10 bucks at a garage sale. That's like throwing away $1,000.'" It's not a surprising response in a society replacing things at such an accelerated rate—this inability to see our last table as suddenly worthless, even though we've just been out shopping for a new one as though it were.

"My parents were Depression babies," Litton told me, "and what they taught me was, it's the accumulation of things that defines you as an American, and to throw anything away was being wasteful." The self-storage industry reconciles these opposing values: paying for storage is, paradoxically, thrifty. "That propensity toward consumption is what fueled the world's economy," Litton said. The self-storage industry almost had to expand; it grew along with the volume of container ships reaching our ports.

By 2007, a full 15 percent of customers told the Self Storage Association they were storing items that they "no longer need or want." It was the third-most-popular use for a unit and was projected to grow to 25 percent of renters the following year. The line between necessity and convenience—between temporary life event and permanent lifestyle—totally blurred. "There's a lot of junk stored in our properties," Ronald L. Havner Jr., Public Storage's chief executive, told a symposium in New York. But really, there's no way of knowing exactly who is still [storing their possessions], what they've got locked up and how they feel about it—and, more important, how those complicated feelings might change if the psychology of the American consumer is substantially reshaped in a recovery.

Tom Litton, for example, still keeps four storage units himself, at two facilities, all of them 10-by-30 units. I asked what's inside. "I have a canoe, I have a vending machine, I have a drill press," Litton began. His old lawn mower was in one. (He got a bigger, riding lawn mower when he bought a ranch in wine country.) "I've got some of my old clothes that I probably wouldn't wear anyway," he continued, and some trophies from college. "I also have some old cassette tapes that I produced." The cassettes are like audiobooks, he explained—tutorials on how to get into the storage industry and succeed. He made them before the storage-facility building boom ended a couple of years ago. "They didn't sell," Litton said, "so they're all in storage now." 15

One afternoon in late May, a woman slouched inside one of Statewide's narrow hallways, reorganizing the innards of her unit. She said her name was Elizabeth—no last name given, since, as she told me, "this is not a high-self-esteem moment." Most everything here belonged to Elizabeth's parents, who entered assisted living last year, and she needed to clear it out to cut expenses. She was keeping an eye out for particular family memorabilia, but otherwise it was a long, beleaguering purge. "Just stuff? Like my mother's kitchen stuff?" she told me. "Whatever."

Boxed haphazardly inside the closet-size space was, as she put it, 53 years of married life. An empty pill bottle and an egg carton lingered on the little bit of visible floor space. "I got rid of all the furniture," Elizabeth said, except her own drafting table, which, she pointed out, had wound up against the rear wall. She was an architect, accomplished but out of work ("Architecture is dead, dead, dead, dead," she explained) and was attacking this project with a conspicuously architect-ish methodology.

She had brought with her dozens of new, perfectly uniform white boxes, each bearing the Harry Potter logo in one of several colors. They lined the hallway behind her, still flattened. "When the books come out, there's just hundreds and hundreds of these boxes at every bookstore," she said. "I just went around and got them." She repacked and erected a tidy column of Harry Potter boxes in one corner of the unit. She turned a few others, tops folded inward, into a kind of bookshelf. "This was when *The Half-Blood Prince* came out," Elizabeth said. "They stack really nicely." She was going to transfer these boxes, full of the few things worth saving, into a storage unit she recently rented in a nearby town. That unit housed most of what Elizabeth owned. Forced to leave her parents' old house and unable to afford a place of her own, she had moved in with a friend about eight months ago. As far as the storage industry was concerned, then, all the contemporaneous chaos of Elizabeth's and her parents' lives ultimately amounted to a wash: one old unit was being vacated, one new one was being rented.

In fact, since last year, owners around the country have reported quickening rates of both move-outs and move-ins, making any occupancy rate — the industry's fundamental yardstick — feel kind of arbitrary, like the momentary averaging-out of a blur of activity, with no single, dominant trend (or maybe even logic) behind it. At Statewide, for example, those like Elizabeth renting smaller units — traditionally the backbone of the business — have been steadily leaving. "All I hear is, 'I can't afford it anymore,'" says Joe Dopart, who manages Statewide along with his daughter Amy and his wife, Evie, a retired schoolteacher. At the same time, though, Statewide's larger units — mostly empty for years — are now completely full. "Every single one, practically, has a foreclosure in it," Amy told me. Others were being rented by endangered businesses, like a coffee shop and a tea room whose owners were forced to shutter their storefronts in Antioch's struggling historic downtown and move everything into storage while they plotted their next moves.

The upshot, while this traffic runs both ways in the background, is that 20 Statewide has remained about 88 percent full — about two or three points lower than last summer, right in line with the national estimate. But that may obscure a more meaningful shift. By shaking up the composition of renters, and their reasons for renting, the recession could be quietly tilting the character of American storage closer to what it was originally: a pragmatic solution to a sudden loss of space, rather than a convenient way of dealing with, or putting off dealing with, an excess of stuff.

Of course, some people don't fit entirely into one category or the other. I found people who had been foreclosed on at most of the storage places I hung around at, and I met many more who were forced to walk away from places they were renting. Among them were two teenage brothers, Luis Jaramillo and Nikolas Aceves, in the city of Stockton, an hour from Sacramento, whose family was about to scatter to relatives' houses in surrounding towns. And Jason Williams, a 38-year-old father of three who was filling a unit with furniture before he and his family moved in with his stepmother.

On one of my first mornings at Statewide, Evie Dopart introduced me to Danielle Johnson, who worked at Dollar Tree and was also studying criminal justice. After her husband left to serve in Iraq, she couldn't afford the rent on their house in Oakland. So she locked everything but her clothes and schoolbooks in storage and moved in with her grandma. "It's O.K.," she assured me, "I'll get another one someday." She meant another house. That was a year ago. Her husband was now stationed in Kentucky, but if Johnson pulled out of school to join him, she would have to repay her student loans immediately and would end up with nothing. "Well," she told me, "I'm just going to finish, and I'll have my degree. He can wait." She seemed incapable of not putting a good face on the situation. "Actually," she told me and Evie, "it's kind of cool living with Grandma. Home-cooked meals are awesome, and no one makes them like Grandma does."

"Your family's Italian, right?" Evie asked.

"No, we're redneck, though," Johnson said with a big smile. "And I mean rednecks make some really good food. Gosh! My grandma's biscuits and gravy are screaming."

Virtually no one I asked, at any level of the business, took seriously the idea that this recession would produce a sea change in who uses self-storage and why. In an industry whose freewheeling success has been so closely tied to the evolving character and prosperity of our society, it can be hard to even talk about storage's future without getting philosophical or patriotic.

"I really think there's a spirit that things will turn around," Jim Chiswell, a Virginia-based consultant to the industry, told me. "I believe that my children—and both my children are proving it already—they're going to have more at the end of their lifetimes, and more success, than I've had. And so will their children. I don't believe the destiny of this country as a beacon of freedom and hope is over. And I believe there will be more growth, and more people wanting to have things and collect things." Tom Litton put it another way: "The good news is that your age group"—I'm 31—"has the same propensity for accumulating crap that I have. You guys got introduced to it in college, and you actually think you really need storage. You see storage the way that we all see cable and Internet access."

Maybe the recession really is making American consumers serious about scaling back, about decluttering and de-leveraging. But there are upward of 51,000 storage facilities across this country—more than seven times the number of Starbucks. Storage is part of our national infrastructure now. And all it is, is empty space: something Americans have always colonized and capitalized on in good times, and retreated into to regroup when things soured. It's tough to imagine a product more malleable to whatever turns our individual life stories take, wherever we're collectively heading.

But where are we now? Of all the storage units I toured, one sticks out as being most emblematic of this particular moment. It belonged to Terry Wallace, a 59-year-old veteran with white streaks in his hair and a broad, shaggy moustache who, when I stumbled across his 10-by-30 at a Storage PRO in Stockton, was sitting in a leather office chair, working at his desk under the open door, like a notary in a storefront. Some open mail and a Herman Wouk novel were pushed aside, and the desk was covered with stacks of quarters, the ones celebrating the 50 states. Wallace was sorting them, state by state, into empty prescription-pill bottles. "I've got 'em all," he said, astounded. "I've got all 50." Then he invited me in.

A folded-up Nordic Track leaned against the desk, and a bucket of fire axes sat behind him. (After serving as a helicopter mechanic in Vietnam, Wallace worked as a back-country firefighter in Yosemite.) But otherwise, the unit looked warehouselike. Stacked, labeled boxes stretched down either side of the deep, rectangular space with a snug but passable aisle between. This was everything Wallace owned, except the truck parked outside. A year ago, he was living in an apartment in Carson City, Nev., funneling the entire $1,200 he collected in retirement benefits and disability directly into his rent and alimony payments every month. "So I started doing a lot of credit-card stuff," he said. Soon he was $30,000 in debt.

Wallace hated living in a city anyway, "so because of my debt crisis and 30 my marriage crisis and everything, I moved everything into storage and I just live out of my truck," he told me, resting his hands on his gut. That was June 15, 2008. At first, he rented a second unit across the way and spent a few months sorting, giving away items he didn't need to an organization for homeless veterans. "You can call me homeless," he told me. "But I'm not goofing around. I've got money, but I just want to get this debt down."

It was like a cleansing: the storage unit cost about $200 a month. But aside from gas, truck payments and food (he had several boxes of meals-ready-to-eat stocked here), it was his only major expense. He had cut out rent, cable, phone and electricity, and purged all the unnecessary fees from his bank statements. For the last year, he had been camping a lot and driving around the West visiting ex-firefighter friends. He saw a woman in Antioch occasionally. "It's feeling good," he said, "and it's working. That's the thing: it's working. Debts are down to almost zippo right now." He figured he'd be done by Thanksgiving.

For a decade at least, storage has been a mechanism allowing Americans to live beyond our means. Wallace was using his unit as a center of gravity, to pull his financial life back within reach. He had even started saving, he told me, and was looking into a small condo in a suburb near Lake Tahoe. "It's not my style or anything," he said; he'd prefer something more secluded — bigger, and with land. "But I could do that." He missed sleeping in his own bed.

He also missed his music collection — and the books and rare coins he had collected. Also, his pins. "Little pins, like flag pins," he explained. "I've got veterans pins, and I've got Rose Parade pins, and pins that I got at fairs." He missed his stuff. "Hey," he said as I left. "I'll call you when I'm getting ready to load the truck."

READING THE TEXT

1. How does Mooallem's opening anecdote about repair-shop owner Jimmy Sloan's visit to his Statewide Self Storage unit set a tone for the rest of the selection?

2. According to Mooallem, how has the Great Recession affected the self-storage industry?

3. Synthesize in your own words the various reasons that customers rely upon self-storage facilities.

4. What does sociologist Juliet B. Schor mean by the "Ikea effect" (para. 11)?

5. What does storage industry consultant Tom Litton mean by saying young people have "the same propensity for accumulating crap that I have. . . . [They] see storage the way that we all see cable and Internet access" (para. 26)?

READING THE SIGNS

1. In a journal entry, contemplate your own and/or your family's possessions. If you needed to scale back what you own, how would you decide what to dispose of, keep, store, or sell? What would your choices indicate about your priorities and interests?

2. **CONNECTING TEXTS** Write an essay in which you evaluate the validity of Tom Litton's claim that "it's the accumulation of things that defines you as an American" (para. 13). To develop your ideas, consult Laurence Shames's "The More Factor" (p. 80) and the Introduction to Chapter 1, "Consuming Passions: The Culture of American Consumption" (p. 71).

3. **CONNECTING TEXTS** In "Everything Now" (p. 143), Steve McKevitt argues that our current consumption habits are "enormously wasteful: a huge and unnecessary drain on the world's dwindling natural resources" (para. 22). In an essay, write an argument that assesses the extent to which Americans' propensity for accumulating material objects contributed to that drain. Does storing items actually reduce the need to produce more, or does it serve to enable the production of more waste?

4. Despite the economic woes suffered by many of the people interviewed in this article, industry consultant Tom Litton remains confident about America's economic future. What is the basis of his confidence? Write an essay in which you demonstrate, refute, or modify his position.

STEPHANIE CLIFFORD AND QUENTIN HARDY

Attention, Shoppers: Store Is Tracking Your Cell

Between the scandal over the National Security Administration's global surveillance and the periodic flaps over Facebook's privacy policies, most people today are aware that their Internet activities are being monitored. But the news that we are being tracked via smartphone Wi-Fi signals when we are simply walking around while shopping in a brick-and-mortar store is something else again. As this report from the *New York Times* Business Day section by Stephanie Clifford and Quentin Hardy suggests, a lot of people aren't happy about it. "Way over the line," expresses one consumer in a post, ironically enough, to a Facebook account. Maybe that person is already receiving unsolicited ads for things that go over the line. Stephanie Clifford and Quentin Hardy are writers for the *New York Times*.

Like dozens of other brick-and-mortar retailers, Nordstrom wanted to learn more about its customers — how many came through the doors, how many were repeat visitors — the kind of information that e-commerce sites like Amazon have in spades. So last fall the company started testing new technology that allowed it to track customers' movements by following the Wi-Fi signals from their smartphones.

But when Nordstrom posted a sign telling customers it was tracking them, shoppers were unnerved. "We did hear some complaints," said Tara Darrow, a spokeswoman for the store. Nordstrom ended the experiment in May, she said, in part because of the comments.

Nordstrom's experiment is part of a movement by retailers to gather data about in-store shoppers' behavior and moods, using video surveillance and signals from their cellphones and apps to learn information as varied as their sex, how many minutes they spend in the candy aisle and how long they look at merchandise before buying it. All sorts of retailers — including national chains, like Family Dollar, Cabela's and Mothercare, a British company, and specialty stores like Benetton and Warby Parker — are testing these technologies and using them to decide on matters like changing store layouts and offering customized coupons.

But while consumers seem to have no problem with cookies, profiles and other online tools that let e-commerce sites know who they are and how they shop, some bristle at the physical version, at a time when government surveillance — of telephone calls, Internet activity and Postal Service deliveries — is front and center because of the leaks by Edward J. Snowden. "Way over the line," one consumer posted to Facebook in response to a local news story about Nordstrom's efforts at some of its stores. Nordstrom says the counts were made anonymous. Technology specialists, though, say the tracking is worrisome. "The idea that you're being stalked in a store is, I think, a bit creepy, as opposed to, it's only a cookie—they don't really know who I am," said Robert Plant, a computer information systems professor at the University of Miami School of Business Administration, noting that consumers can rarely control or have access to this data.

Some consumers wonder how the information is used. "The creepy thing 5 isn't the privacy violation, it's how much they can infer," said Bradley Voytek, a neuroscientist who had stopped in at Philz Coffee in Berkeley, Calif. Philz uses technology from Euclid Analytics, of Palo Alto, Calif., the company that worked on the Nordstrom experiment, to measure the signals between a smartphone and a Wi-Fi antenna to count how many people walk by a store and how many enter.

Still, physical retailers argue that they are doing nothing more than what is routinely done online. "Brick-and-mortar stores have been disadvantaged compared with online retailers, which get people's digital crumbs," said Guido Jouret, the head of Cisco's emerging technologies group, which supplies tracking cameras to stores. Why, Mr. Jouret asked, should physical stores not "be able to tell if someone who didn't buy was put off by prices, or was just coming in from the cold?" The companies that provide this technology offer a wide range of services.

One, RetailNext, uses video footage to study how shoppers navigate, determining, say, that men spend only one minute in the coat department, which may help a store streamline its men's outerwear layout. It also differentiates men from women, and children from adults. RetailNext, based in San Jose, Calif., adds data from shoppers' smartphones to deduce even more specific patterns. If a shopper's phone is set to look for Wi-Fi networks, a store that offers Wi-Fi can pinpoint where the shopper is in the store, within a 10-foot radius, even if the shopper does not connect to the network, said Tim Callan, RetailNext's chief marketing officer. The store can also recognize returning shoppers, because mobile devices send unique identification codes when they search for networks. That means stores can now tell how repeat customers behave and the average time between visits. RetailNext also uses data to map customers' paths; perhaps the shopper is 70 percent likely to go right immediately, or 14 percent likely to linger at a display, Mr. Callan said.

Brickstream uses video information to watch shoppers. The company, based near Atlanta, sells a $1,500 stereoscopic camera that separates adults from children, and counts people in different parts of a store to determine which aisles are popular and how many cash registers to open. "Watching where people go in a store is like watching how they looked at a second or third Web page" on an online retailer, said Ralph Crabtree, Brickstream's chief technical officer.

Cameras have become so sophisticated, with sharper lenses and data-processing, that companies can analyze what shoppers are looking at, and even what their mood is. For example, Realeyes, based in London, which analyzes facial cues for responses to online ads, monitors shoppers' so-called happiness levels in stores and their reactions at the register. Synqera, a start-up in St. Petersburg, Russia, is selling software for checkout devices or computers that tailors marketing messages to a customer's gender, age and mood, measured by facial recognition. "If you are an angry man of 30, and it is Friday evening, it may offer you a bottle of whiskey," said Ekaterina Savchenko, the company's head of marketing.

Nomi, of New York, uses Wi-Fi to track customers' behavior in a store, but goes one step further by matching a phone with an individual. When a shopper has volunteered some personal information, either by downloading a retailer's app or providing an e-mail address when using in-store Wi-Fi, Nomi pulls up a profile of that customer — the number of recent visits, what products that customer was looking at on the Web site last night, purchase history. The store then has access to that profile.   10

"I walk into Macy's, Macy's knows that I just entered the store, and they're able to give me a personalized recommendation through my phone the moment I enter the store," said Corey Capasso, Nomi's president. "It's literally bringing the Amazon experience into the store." Nomi then uses Wi-Fi signals to follow the customer throughout the store, adding to the information it maintains. "If I'm going and spending 20 minutes in the shoe section, that means I'm highly interested in buying a pair of shoes," Mr. Capasso said, and the store might send a coupon for sneakers.

If these methods seem intrusive, at least some consumers seem happy to trade privacy for deals. Placed, a company based in Seattle, has an app that asks consumers where they are in a store in exchange for cash and prepaid gift cards from Amazon and Google Play, among others. More than 500,000 people have downloaded the app since last August, said a company spokeswoman, Sarah Radwanick, providing information like gender, age and income, and agreeing to be tracked over GPS, Wi-Fi and cellular networks. Placed then sells the data to store owners, online retailers and app developers.

"I would just love it if a coupon pops up on my phone," said Linda Vertiieb, 30, a blogger in Philadelphia, who said that she was not aware of the tracking methods, but that the idea did not bother her. Stores are "trying to sell, so that makes sense," she said.

READING THE TEXT

1. Summarize in your own words the various strategies retailers use to track store customers electronically.

2. According to Clifford and Hardy, what use do stores make of the information gleaned by electronic tracking of shoppers?

3. What objections do technology experts voice to the electronic tracking of shoppers? What objections do consumers voice?

4. How do retailers defend the practice of tracking shoppers electronically?

5. What concerns does electronic tracking raise about personal privacy?

READING THE SIGNS

1. In your journal, reflect on whether you agree with Professor Robert Plant's claim that "the idea that you're being [electronically] stalked in a store is . . . a bit creepy" (para. 4).

2. In an argumentative essay, support, oppose, or complicate retailers' justification that store tracking simply levels the playing field with online retailers.

3. **CONNECTING TEXTS**   Both Malcolm Gladwell's "The Science of Shopping" (p. 93) and this selection describe ways in which retailers use surveillance strategies to learn more about consumers' behavior. Write an essay in which you evaluate the ethics of such strategies. To what extent do the techniques described in these essays cross an unwritten standard of acceptable intrusiveness? Are there ways in which the public can benefit from these techniques?

THOMAS HINE

What's in a Package

What's in a package? According to Thomas Hine, a great deal, perhaps even more than what is actually inside the package. From the cereal boxes you find in the supermarket to the perfume bottles sold at Tiffany's, the shape and design of the packages that contain just about every product we consume have been carefully calculated to stimulate consumption. Indeed, as Hine explains in this excerpt from *The Total Package: The Evolution and Secret Meanings of Boxes, Bottles, Cans, and Tubes* (1995), "for manufacturers, packaging is the crucial final payoff to a marketing campaign." A former architecture and design critic for the *Philadelphia Inquirer*, Hine has published *Populuxe* (1986), on American design and culture; *Facing Tomorrow* (1991), on past and current attitudes toward the future; *The Rise and Fall of the American Teenager: A New History of the American Adolescent Experience* (1999); *I Want That! How We All Became Shoppers* (2002); and *The Great Funk: Falling Apart and Coming Together (on a Shag Rug) in the Seventies* (2007).

When you put yourself behind a shopping cart, the world changes. You become an active consumer, and you are moving through environments — the supermarket, the discount store, the warehouse club, the home center — that have been made for you.

During the thirty minutes you spend on an average trip to the supermarket, about thirty thousand different products vie to win your attention and ultimately to make you believe in their promise. When the door opens, automatically, before you, you enter an arena where your emotions and your appetites are in play, and a walk down the aisle is an exercise in self-definition. Are you a good parent, a good provider? Do you have time to do all you think you should, and would you be interested in a shortcut? Are you worried about your health and that of those you love? Do you care about the environment? Do you appreciate the finer things in life? Is your life what you would like it to be? Are you enjoying what you've accomplished? Wouldn't you really like something chocolate?

Few experiences in contemporary life offer the visual intensity of a Safeway, a Krogers, a Pathmark, or a Piggly Wiggly. No marketplace in the world—not Marrakesh or Calcutta or Hong Kong—offers so many different goods with such focused salesmanship as your neighborhood supermarket, where you're exposed to a thousand different products a minute. No wonder it's tiring to shop.

There are, however, some major differences between the supermarket and a traditional marketplace. The cacophony of a traditional market has given way to programmed, innocuous music, punctuated by enthusiastically intoned commercials. A stroll through a traditional market offers an array of sensuous aromas; if you are conscious of smelling something in a super-market, there is a problem. The life and death matter of eating, expressed in traditional markets by the sale of vegetables with stems and roots and by hanging animal carcasses, is purged from the supermarket, where food is pro-cessed somewhere else, or at least trimmed out of sight.

But the most fundamental difference between a traditional market and the places through which you push your cart is that in a modern retail setting nearly all the selling is done without people. The product is totally dissociated from the personality of any particular person selling it—with the possible exception of those who appear in its advertising. The supermarket purges sociability, which slows down sales. It allows manufacturers to control the way they present their products to the world. It replaces people with packages. 5

Packages are an inescapable part of modern life. They are omnipresent and invisible, deplored and ignored. During most of your waking moments, there are one or more packages within your field of vision. Packages are so ubiquitous that they slip beneath conscious notice, though many packages are designed so that people will respond to them even if they're not paying attention.

Once you begin pushing the shopping cart, it matters little whether you are in a supermarket, a discount store, or a warehouse club. The impor-tant thing is that you are among packages: expressive packages intended to engage your emotions, ingenious packages that make a product useful, infor-mative packages that help you understand what you want and what you're getting. Historically, packages are what made self-service retailing possible, and in turn such stores increased the number and variety of items people buy. Now a world without packages is unimaginable.

Packages lead multiple lives. They preserve and protect, allowing people to make use of things that were produced far away, or a while ago. And they are potently expressive. They assure that an item arrives unspoiled, and they help those who use the item feel good about it.

We share our homes with hundreds of packages, mostly in the bathroom and kitchen, the most intimate, body-centered rooms of the house. Some packages — a perfume flacon, a ketchup bottle, a candy wrapper, a beer can — serve as permanent landmarks in people's lives that outlast homes, careers, or spouses. But packages embody change, not just in their age-old promise that their contents are new and improved, but in their attempt to respond to changing tastes and achieve new standards of convenience. Packages record changing hairstyles and changing lifestyles. Even social policy issues are reflected. Nearly unopenable tamperproof seals and other forms of closures testify to the fragility of the social contract, and the susceptibility of the great mass of people to the destructive acts of a very few. It was a mark of rising environmental consciousness when containers recently began to make a novel promise: "less packaging."

For manufacturers, packaging is the crucial final payoff to a marketing campaign. Sophisticated packaging is one of the chief ways people find the confidence to buy. It can also give a powerful image to products and commodities that are in themselves characterless. In many cases, the shopper has been prepared for the shopping experience by lush, colorful print advertisements, thirty-second television minidramas, radio jingles, and coupon promotions. But the package makes the final sales pitch, seals the commitment, and gets itself placed in the shopping cart. Advertising leads consumers into temptation. Packaging is the temptation. In many cases it is what makes the product possible. 10

But the package is also useful to the shopper. It is a tool for simplifying and speeding decisions. Packages promise, and usually deliver, predictability. One reason you don't think about packages is that you don't need to. The candy bar, the aspirin, the baking powder, or the beer in the old familiar package may, at times, be touted as new and improved, but it will rarely be very different.

You put the package into your cart, or not, usually without really having focused on the particular product or its many alternatives. But sometimes you do examine the package. You read the label carefully, looking at what the product promises, what it contains, what it warns. You might even look at the package itself and judge whether it will, for example, reseal to keep a product fresh. You might consider how a cosmetic container will look on your dressing table, or you might think about whether someone might have tampered with it or whether it can be easily recycled. The possibility of such scrutiny is one of the things that make each detail of the package so important.

The environment through which you push your shopping cart is extraordinary because of the amount of attention that has been paid to the packages that line the shelves. Most contemporary environments are landscapes of inattention. In housing developments, malls, highways, office buildings, even furniture, design ideas are few and spread very thin. At the supermarket, each box and jar, stand-up pouch and squeeze bottle, each can and bag and tube and spray has been very carefully considered. Designers have worked and reworked the design on their computers and tested mock-ups on the store shelves. Refinements are measured in millimeters.

All sorts of retail establishments have been redefined by packaging. Drugs and cosmetics were among the earliest packaged products, and most drugstores now resemble small supermarkets. Liquor makers use packaging to add a veneer of style to the intrinsic allure of intoxication, and some sell their bottle rather than the drink. It is no accident that vodka, the most characterless of spirits, has the highest-profile packages. The local gas station sells sandwiches and soft drinks rather than tires and motor oil, and in turn, automotive products have been attractively repackaged for sales at supermarkets, warehouse clubs, and home centers.

With its thousands of images and messages, the supermarket is as visu- 15 ally dense, if not as beautiful, as a Gothic cathedral. It is as complex and as predatory as a tropical rain forest. It is more than a person can possibly take in during an ordinary half-hour shopping trip. No wonder a significant percentage of people who need to wear eyeglasses don't wear them when they're shopping, and some researchers have spoken of the trancelike state that pushing a cart through this environment induces. The paradox here is that the visual intensity that overwhelms shoppers is precisely the thing that makes the design of packages so crucial. Just because you're not looking at a package doesn't mean you don't see it. Most of the time, you see far more than a container and a label. You see a personality, an attitude toward life, perhaps even a set of beliefs.

The shopper's encounter with the product on the shelf is, however, only the beginning of the emotional life cycle of the package. The package is very important in the moment when the shopper recognizes it either as an old friend or a new temptation. Once the product is brought home, the package seems to disappear, as the quality or usefulness of the product it contains becomes paramount. But in fact, many packages are still selling even at home, enticing those who have bought them to take them out of the cupboard, the closet, or the refrigerator and consume their contents. Then once the product has been used up, and the package is empty, it becomes suddenly visible once more. This time, though, it is trash that must be discarded or recycled. This instant of disposal is the time when people are most aware of packages. It is a negative moment, like the end of a love affair, and what's left seems to be a horrid waste.

The forces driving package design are not primarily aesthetic. Market researchers have conducted surveys of consumer wants and needs, and consultants have studied photographs of families' kitchen cupboards and medicine chests to get a sense of how products are used. Test subjects have been tied into pieces of heavy apparatus that measure their eye movement, their blood pressure or body temperature, when subjected to different packages. Psychologists get people to talk about the packages in order to get a sense of their innermost feelings about what they want. Government regulators and private health and safety advocates worry over package design and try to make it truthful. Stock-market analysts worry about how companies are managing their "brand equity," that combination of perceived value and consumer loyalty that is expressed in advertising but embodied in packaging. The retailer is paying attention to the packages in order to weed out the ones that don't sell or aren't sufficiently profitable. The use of supermarket scanners generates information on the profitability of every cubic inch of the store. Space on the supermarket shelf is some of the most valuable real estate in the world, and there are always plenty of new packaged products vying for display.

Packaging performs a series of disparate tasks. It protects its contents from contamination and spoilage. It makes it easier to transport and store goods. It provides uniform measuring of contents. By allowing brands to be created and standardized, it makes advertising meaningful and large-scale distribution possible. Special kinds of packages, with dispensing caps, sprays, and other convenience features, make products more usable. Packages serve as symbols both of their contents and of a way of life. And just as they can very powerfully communicate the satisfaction a product offers, they are equally potent symbols of wastefulness once the product is gone.

Most people use dozens of packages each day and discard hundreds of them each year. The growth of mandatory recycling programs has made people increasingly aware of packages, which account in the United States for about forty-three million tons, or just under 30 percent of all refuse discarded. While forty-three million tons of stuff is hardly insignificant, repeated surveys have shown that the public perceives that far more than 30 percent — indeed, nearly all — their garbage consists of packaging. This perception creates a political problem for the packaging industry, but it also demonstrates the power of packaging. It is symbolic. It creates an emotional relationship. Bones and wasted food (thirteen million tons), grass clippings and yard waste (thirty-one million tons), or even magazines and newspapers (fourteen million tons) do not feel as wasteful as empty vessels that once contained so much promise.

Packaging is a cultural phenomenon, which means that it works differently 20 in different cultures. The United States has been a good market for packages since it was first settled and has been an important innovator of packaging technology and culture. Moreover, American packaging is part of an international culture of modernity and consumption. At its deepest level, the culture of American packaging deals with the issue of surviving among strangers in a new world. This is an emotion with which anyone who has been touched by modernity can identify. In lives buffeted by change, people seek the safety and reassurance that packaged products offer. American packaging, which has always sought to appeal to large numbers of diverse people, travels better than that of most other cultures.

But the similar appearance of supermarkets throughout the world should not be interpreted as the evidence of a single, global consumer culture. In fact, most companies that do business internationally redesign their packages for each market. This is done partly to satisfy local regulations and adapt to available products and technologies. But the principal reason is that people in different places have different expectations and make different uses of packaging.

The United States and Japan, the world's two leading industrial powers, have almost opposite approaches to packaging. Japan's is far more elaborate than America's, and it is shaped by rituals of respect and centuries-old traditions of wrapping and presentation. Packaging is explicitly recognized as an expression of culture in Japan and largely ignored in America. Japanese packaging is designed to be appreciated; American packaging is calculated to be unthinkingly accepted.

Foods that only Japanese eat — even relatively humble ones like refrigerated prepared fish cakes — have wrappings that resemble handmade paper or leaves. Even modestly priced refrigerated fish cakes have beautiful wrappings in which traditional design accommodates a scannable bar code. Such products look Japanese and are unambiguously intended to do so. Products that are foreign, such as coffee, look foreign, even to the point of having only Roman lettering and no Japanese lettering on the can. American and European companies are sometimes able to sell their packages in Japan virtually unchanged, because their foreignness is part of their selling power. But Japanese exporters hire designers in each country to repackage their products. Americans — whose culture is defined not by refinements and distinctions but by inclusiveness — want to think about the product itself, not its cultural origins.

We speak glibly about global villages and international markets, but problems with packages reveal some unexpected cultural boundaries. Why are Canadians willing to drink milk out of flexible plastic pouches that fit into reusable plastic holders, while residents of the United States are believed to be so resistant to the idea that they have not even been given the opportunity to do so? Why do Japanese consumers prefer packages that contain two tennis balls and view the standard U.S. pack of three to be cheap and undesirable? Why do Germans insist on highly detailed technical specifications on packages of videotape, while Americans don't? Why do Swedes think that blue is masculine, while the Dutch see the color as feminine? The answers lie in unquestioned habits and deep-seated imagery, a culture of containing, adorning, and understanding that no sharp marketer can change overnight.

There is probably no other field in which designs that are almost a century 25 old — Wrigley's gum, Campbell's soup, Hershey's chocolate bar — remain in production only subtly changed and are understood to be extremely valuable corporate assets. Yet the culture of packaging, defined by what people are buying and selling every day, keeps evolving, and the role nostalgia plays is very small.

For example, the tall, glass Heinz ketchup bottle has helped define the American refrigerator skyline for most of the twentieth century (even though it is generally unnecessary to refrigerate ketchup). Moreover, it provides the tables of diners and coffee shops with a vertical accent and a token of hospitality, the same qualities projected by candles and vases of flowers in more upscale eateries. The bottle has remained a fixture of American life, even though it has always been a nuisance to pour the thick ketchup through the little hole. It seemed not to matter that you have to shake and shake the bottle, impotently, until far too much ketchup comes out in one great scarlet plop. Heinz experimented for years with wide-necked jars and other sorts of bottles, but they never caught on.

Then in 1992 a survey of consumers indicated that more Americans believed that the plastic squeeze bottle is a better package for ketchup than the glass bottle. The survey did not offer any explanations for this change of preference, which has been evolving for many years as older people for whom the tall bottle is an icon became a less important part of the sample. Could it be that the difficulty of using the tall bottle suddenly became evident to those born after 1960? Perhaps the tall bottle holds too little ketchup. There is a clear trend toward buying things in larger containers, in part because lightweight plastics have made them less costly for manufacturers to ship and easier for consumers to use. This has happened even as the number of people in an average American household has been getting smaller. But houses, like packages, have been getting larger. Culture moves in mysterious ways.

The tall ketchup bottle is still preferred by almost half of consumers, so it is not going to disappear anytime soon. And the squeeze bottle does contain visual echoes of the old bottle. It is certainly not a radical departure. In Japan, ketchup and mayonnaise are sold in cellophane-wrapped plastic bladders that would certainly send Americans into severe culture shock. Still, the tall bottle's loss of absolute authority is a significant change. And its ultimate disappearance would represent a larger change in most people's visual environment than would the razing of nearly any landmark building.

But although some package designs are pleasantly evocative of another time, and a few appear to be unchanging icons in a turbulent world, the reason they still exist is because they still work. Inertia has historically played a role in creating commercial icons. Until quite recently, it was time-consuming and expensive to make new printing plates or to vary the shape or material of a container. Now computerized graphics and rapidly developing technology in the package-manufacturing industries make a packaging change easier than in the past, and a lot cheaper to change than advertising, which seems a far more evanescent medium. There is no constituency of curators or preservationists to protect the endangered package. If a gum wrapper manages to survive nearly unchanged for ninety years, it's not because any expert has determined that it is an important cultural expression. Rather, it's because it still helps sell a lot of gum.

So far, we've been discussing packaging in its most literal sense: designed 30 containers that protect and promote products. Such containers have served as the models for larger types of packaging, such as chain restaurants, supermarkets, theme parks, and festival marketplaces. . . . Still, it is impossible to ignore a broader conception of packaging that is one of the preoccupations of our time. This concerns the ways in which people construct and present their personalities, the ways in which ideas are presented and diffused, the ways in which political candidates are selected and public policies formulated. We must all worry about packaging ourselves and everything we do, because we believe that nobody has time to really pay attention.

Packaging strives at once to offer excitement and reassurance. It promises something newer and better, but not necessarily different. When we talk about a tourist destination, or even a presidential contender, being packaged, that's not really a metaphor. The same projection of intensified ordinariness, the same combination of titillation and reassurance, are used for laundry detergents, theme parks, and candidates alike.

The imperative to package is unavoidable in a society in which people have been encouraged to see themselves as consumers not merely of toothpaste and automobiles, but of such imponderables as lifestyle, government, and health. The marketplace of ideas is not an agora, where people haggle, posture, clash, and come to terms with one another. Rather, it has become a supermarket, where values, aspirations, dreams, and predictions are presented with great sophistication. The individual can choose to buy them, or leave them on the shelf.

In such a packaged culture, the consumer seems to be king. But people cannot be consumers all the time. If nothing else, they must do something to earn the money that allows them to consume. This, in turn, pressures people to package themselves in order to survive. The early 1990s brought economic recession and shrinking opportunities to all the countries of the developed world. Like products fighting for their space on the shelf, individuals have had to re-create, or at least represent, themselves in order to seem both desirable and safe. Moreover, many jobs have been reconceived to depersonalize individuals and to make them part of a packaged service experience.

These phenomena have their own history. For decades, people have spoken of writing resumes in order to package themselves for a specific opportunity. Thomas J. Watson Jr., longtime chairman of IBM, justified his company's famously conservative and inflexible dress code—dark suits, white shirts, and rep ties for all male employees—as "self-packaging," analogous to the celebrated product design, corporate imagery, and packaging done for the company by Elliot Noyes and Paul Rand. You can question whether IBM's employees were packaging themselves or forced into a box by their employer. Still, anyone who has ever dressed for success was doing a packaging job.

Since the 1950s, there have been discussions of packaging a candidate 35 to respond to what voters are telling the pollsters who perform the same tasks as market researchers do for soap or shampoo. More recently, such discussions have dominated American political journalism. The packaged candidate, so he and his handlers hope, projects a message that, like a Diet Pepsi, is stimulating without being threatening. Like a Weight Watchers frozen dessert bar, the candidate's contradictions must be glazed over and, ultimately, comforting. Aspects of the candidate that are confusing or viewed as extraneous are removed, just as stems and sinew are removed from packaged foods. The package is intended to protect the candidate; dirt won't stick. The candidate is uncontaminated, though at a slight remove from the consumer-voter.

People profess to be troubled by this sort of packaging. When we say a person or an experience is "packaged," we are complaining of a sense of excessive calculation and a lack of authenticity. Such a fear of unreality is at least a century old; it arose along with industrialization and rapid communication. Now that the world is more competitive, and we all believe we have less time to consider things, the craft of being instantaneously appealing has taken on more and more importance. We might say, cynically, that the person who appears "packaged" simply doesn't have good packaging.

Still, the sense of uneasiness about encountering packaged people in a packaged world is real, and it shouldn't be dismissed. Indeed, it is a theme of contemporary life, equally evident in politics, entertainment, and the supermarket. Moreover, public uneasiness about the phenomenon of packaging is compounded by confusion over a loss of iconic packages and personalities.

Producers of packaged products have probably never been as nervous as they became during the first half of the 1990s. Many of the world's most famous brands were involved in the merger mania of the 1980s, which produced debt-ridden companies that couldn't afford to wait for results either from their managers or their marketing strategies. At the same time, the feeling was that it was far too risky to produce something really new. The characteristic response was the line extension — "dry" beer, "lite" mayonnaise, "ultra" detergent. New packages have been appearing at a rapid pace, only to be changed whenever a manager gets nervous or a retailer loses patience.

The same skittishness is evident in the projection of public personalities as the clear, if synthetic, images of a few decades ago have lost their sharpness and broken into a spectrum of weaker, reflected apparitions. Marilyn Monroe, for example, had an image that was, Jayne Mansfield notwithstanding, unique and well defined. She was luscious as a Hershey's bar, shapely as a Coke bottle. But in a world where Coke can be sugar free, caffeine free, and cherry flavored (and Pepsi can be clear!), just one image isn't enough for a superstar. Madonna is available as Marilyn or as a brunette, a Catholic schoolgirl, or a bondage devotee. Who knows what brand extension will come next? Likewise, John F. Kennedy and Elvis Presley had clear, carefully projected images. But Bill Clinton is defined largely by evoking memories of both. As our commercial civilization seems to have lost the power to amuse or convince us in new and exciting ways, formerly potent packages are recycled and devalued. That has left the door open for such phenomena as generic cigarettes, President's Choice cola, and H. Ross Perot.

This cultural and personal packaging both fascinates and infuriates. There ⁴⁰ is something liberating in its promise of aggressive self-creation, and something terrifying in its implication that everything must be subject to the ruthless discipline of the marketplace. People are at once passive consumers of their culture and aggressive packagers of themselves, which can be a stressful and lonely combination.

READING THE TEXT

1. How does Hine compare a supermarket with a traditional marketplace?
2. What does Hine mean when he asserts that modern retailing "replaces people with packages" (para. 5)?
3. How does packaging stimulate the desire to buy, according to Hine?
4. How do Americans' attitudes toward packaging compare with those of the Japanese, according to Hine?

READING THE SIGNS

1. Bring one product package to class; preferably, all students should bring items from a few similar product categories (personal hygiene, say, or bottled water). In class, give a brief presentation in which you interpret your package. After all the students have presented, compare the different messages the packages send to consumers.
2. Visit a popular retail store, such as Urban Outfitters or Victoria's Secret, and study the ways the store uses packaging to create, as Hine puts it, "a personality, an attitude toward life" (para. 15). Be thorough in your observations, studying everything from the store's bags to perfume or cologne packages to clothing labels. Use your findings as evidence for an essay in which you analyze the image the store creates for itself and its customers.
3. In your journal, write an entry in which you explore your motives for purchasing a product simply because you liked the package. What did you like about the package, and how did it contribute to your sense of identity?
4. Visit a store with an explicit political theme, such as the Body Shop or Whole Foods, and write a semiotic analysis of the packaging you see in the store.
5. Study the packages that are visible to a visitor to your home, and write an analysis of the messages those packages might send to the visitor.

JAMES A. ROBERTS

The Treadmill of Consumption

Once, "keeping up with the Joneses" was a neighborhood affair; now, thanks to modern mass media, it's a matter of "keeping up with the Kardashians" — that is, competing with the rich and famous in a never-ending spiral of status consumption. James A. Roberts's analysis of the compulsion to signify "social power through conspicuous consumption" is a sobering read for anyone who has ever gone into debt just to have a snazzier cell phone, like GoldVish's million-dollar white-gold and diamond offering. A professor of marketing at Baylor University, Roberts is the author of *Shiny Objects: Why We Spend Money We Don't Have in Search of Happiness We Can't Buy* (2011), from which this selection is taken.

Using material possessions to exhibit status is commonplace in today's consumer culture. We may not know our neighbors, but we feel compelled to make sure they know that we're people of value. As humans we rely on visual cues such as material possessions to convey our status to others and to ascertain the status of people we don't know. The quest for status symbols influences both kids and adults, although the objects we choose to display may differ with age. (Cell phones may be an exception that spans all age groups.)

For young people, cell phones are seen as necessities, not luxuries. A teen or even preteen without a cell phone feels set apart, on the outside looking in. This is in part because cell phones are a way to stay tightly connected with others (text messaging "blind," with cell phone in the pocket, is one of my favorites); however, cell phones are also important fashion statements and social props. For young people, cell phones are second only to cars as symbols of independence. Many teens see cell phones as an extension of their personality, and phone manufacturers and service providers, knowing this, give them many options to express their inner selves — ways to personalize their ringtone, change their "wallpaper," and customize their "skin," for example, as well as add many apps and accessories.

Adults, especially men, are also susceptible to the status appeal of cell phones. Researchers in the United Kingdom studied the use of cell phones after reading newspaper stories about nightclubs in South America that required patrons to check their phones at the door. Club managers found, the stories reported, that many checked phones were props — not working cell phones. To learn more about whether and how people were using their cell phones as social props, the researchers studied cell phone use in upscale pubs in the UK. What they found is most interesting: men and women used their cell phones in different manners. While women would leave their phone in their purse until they needed it, men were more likely to take their phone out of their pocket or briefcase and place it on the counter or table in view of all. Furthermore, like peacocks strutting with their plumage in full display to attract a mate, men spent more time tinkering with and displaying their phone when the number of men relative to women in the pub increased.[1]

As long as consumers attempt to signal their social power through conspicuous consumption, the levels required to make a visible statement of power will continue to rise. If person A buys a new car, person B has to buy a better car to compete; and then person A has to buy a boat as well—and so on. But once basic needs are met there's no additional happiness with additional purchases. The process of moving ahead materially without any real gain in satisfaction is often called "the treadmill of consumption." That treadmill is a barrier to raising your level of happiness, because it causes you to quickly adapt to good things by taking them for granted.

Research has shown that humans are very flexible. We tend to get used to new circumstances in our lives — including financial circumstances, both good and bad — and we make such mental shifts quickly. Economic gains or losses do give us pleasure or pain, but the effects wear off quickly. When our situation improves, having more money or possessions almost instantaneously becomes the new "normal." As our store of material possessions grows, so do our expectations.

Many researchers have likened this process to drug addiction, where the addict continually needs more and more of the drug of choice to achieve an equivalent "high." This means that acquiring more possessions doesn't take us any closer to happiness; it just speeds up the treadmill. I regret to say that there is a great deal of evidence supporting the existence — and potential harm — of the treadmill of consumption.

If the treadmill didn't exist, people with more possessions would be happier than those "less fortunate" souls who own less. But this simply isn't the case. The "less fortunate" are, for the most part, just as happy as those with more stuff. Big purchases and the piling up of material possessions hold little sway over happiness. Probably the most discouraging proof for this statement can be found in the study of lottery winners. An integral component of the shiny-objects ethos is quick riches. What better way to catapult yourself past your neighbors than to strike it rich with the lottery, right? If you foresee nothing but a lifetime of fun and sun for lottery winners, you're wrong. A study of twenty winners found that they were no happier a few years after their good fortune; in fact, some were even less happy than before they bought their winning ticket.[2] If the lottery can't pull us out of our current torpor, what hope is there for a raise at work, a flat-screen (plasma) television, an iPhone, or a new car (surely the new Lexus would be an exception)?

Consuming for Status

One important reason that consumers buy products is to satisfy social needs. Many of us spend a large proportion of our disposable income on so-called status items, and this trend is on the rise as we continue to embrace the shiny-objects ethos. "Wait a minute," some of you might be saying; "hasn't the current economic crisis stemmed the tide of status consumption?" My response to that question is that it never has in the past. Sure, we might mind our financial p's and q's during the actual crisis, but we have always returned to our profligate ways once we've navigated our way through the economic doldrums.

You need look no further back than the early 2000s, when the Internet bubble burst and the stock market tanked. It wasn't long until our spending picked up again, and with a renewed vengeance. That's precisely what brought us where we are today. Similar economic corrections in the 1970s, '80s, and '90s produced the same results: we tightened our financial belts only to loosen them when the clouds receded. It's really a lot like yo-yo dieting. Each time after we fall off the financial wagon we're a little worse off than the time before. Apparently as consumers we tend to suffer from short-term memory loss!

Pursuing materialistic ideals is a competitive and comparative process — hence the expression "keeping up with the Joneses." And today, with daily twenty-four/seven media coverage of the lifestyles of the rich and famous, our competition is no longer limited to our neighborhood. Bill and Melinda Gates and the sultan of Brunei have replaced Joe and Irma down the street as our points of reference. To achieve a position of social power or status, one must exceed this expanding community norm. Even the superrich aren't happy. There's always someone with a bigger home or fancier yacht — or, heaven forbid, a prettier wife. Yes, we even use other humans as chattel in our attempt to secure our position in the social hierarchy! The result of all this social posturing is no end to our wants and little improvement in our satisfaction, despite an ever-increasing consumption of goods. And Madison Avenue knows it: after price, status is the principal theme of most advertising.

Status consumption has been defined as "the motivational process by which individuals strive to improve their social standing through conspicuous consumption of consumer products that confer or symbolize status to the individual and to surrounding significant others."[3] It is our attempt as consumers to gain the respect, consideration, and envy from those around us. Status consumption is the heart and soul of the consumer culture, which revolves around our attempts to signal our comparative degree of social power through conspicuous consumption. If you don't buy into status consumption yourself, you certainly know people who do. They go by many names, but "social climbers" and "status seekers" will do for now. Climbers and seekers work to surround

Can You Hear Me Now?

I thought I had found the ultimate status symbol when I came across Motorola's new $2,000 Aura cell phone. The avant-garde Aura sports 700-plus individual components, a stainless-steel housing, and a front plate that takes the manufacturer a month to create. Add to this list the world's first handset with a circular display (great color and resolution!), a sixty-two-carat sapphire crystal lens, a multimedia player, stereo Bluetooth, and much, much more.

My amazement over Motorola's Aura was short-lived, however. I lost interest when I heard about the $1 million — yes, $1 million — cell phone from GoldVish (a Swiss company). The phone is made of eighteen-carat white gold and is covered with diamonds. Bluetooth? Of course. How about a two-gigabyte memory, eight-megapixel camera, MP3 player, worldwide FM radio, and e-mail access? Not to worry if a million is a bit rich for you: GoldVish has made available several other phones for around $25,000 — no doubt delivered in plain brown-paper packaging to avoid any embarrassment associated with buying a cheaper model.[4]

themselves with visible evidence of the superior rank they claim or aspire to. Most of us, to some degree, are concerned with our social status, and we try to make sure others are aware of it as well.

Status consumption began in the United States as a way for members of the upper crust to flaunt their wealth to each other. Over the past century the practice has trickled down to the lower rungs of the economic ladder. People are willing to go into debt to buy certain products and brands — let's say a $2,500 Jimmy Choo handbag — because these status symbols represent power in our consumer culture. Cars, for example, are an expensive but easy way to tell the world you've made it; there's no mistaking which are the most expensive. The problem is that nearly everyone else is upgrading to the latest model as well, so no real increase in status occurs — another example of the treadmill of consumption. Fortunately — note the irony there — our consumer culture, with its vast array of products, allows us many other opportunities to confer status upon ourselves. Media mogul Ted Turner put it this way: "Life is a game. Money is how we keep score."[5]

Status consumers are willing to pay premium prices for products that are perceived to convey status and prestige. A high-end Patek Philippe watch is a good example of a product that is — and is blatantly marketed as — a quintessential status symbol. One of Patek's advertising slogans is, "You never really own a Patek Philippe. You merely look after it for the next generation." Trust me; you're buying it for yourself. Despite the manufacturer's claims to the contrary, a Patek Philippe does not keep better time than the myriad of cheaper alternatives on the market; on the contrary, it serves primarily as an unambiguous symbol of status. To many people, owning a Patek signals that you've made it. To me, however, it sends the signal that you've forgone a golden opportunity to do good with the money spent so lavishly on a very expensive watch. It's a zero-sum game no matter how much money you make.

And, of course, Patek Philippe watches are only one of a myriad of examples I could use to document our preoccupation with status consumption. What about Lucky Jeans, bling (it's shiny), Hummer automobiles (maybe one of the more blatant cries for help), iPhones, fifty-two-inch plasma TVs, $3,000 Chihuahua lap dogs (think Paris Hilton), McMansions, expensive rims for your car tires, anything couture, Gulfstream jets, Abercrombie & Fitch and Hollister clothes (for teens and preteens) — even drinking water! No consumer product category has been left untouched. Even the most banal, everyday products have been branded — think $2,000 fountain pens.

Today, status is conveyed more often through ownership of status products   15 than through personal, occupational, or family reputation. This is particularly true in large, impersonal metropolitan areas, where people can no longer depend on their behavior or reputation to convey their status and position in society.

NOTES

[1]John E. Lycett and Robin I. M. Dunbar, "Mobile Phones as Lekking Devices among Human Males," *Human Nature* 11, no. 1 (2000): 93–104.

[2]Philip Brickman et al., "Lottery Winners and Accident Victims: Is Happiness Relative?" *Journal of Personality and Social Psychology* 36, no. 8 (1978): 917–27.

[3]Jacqueline Eastman et al., "The Relationship between Status Consumption and Materialism: A Cross Cultural Comparison of Chinese, Mexican, and American Students," *Journal of Marketing Theory and Practice*, Winter 1997, 52–66, 58.

[4]Darren Murph, "Motorola Intros Avant-Garde $2,000 Aura, Markets It Like a Rolex," October 21, 2008, www.endgadget.com, accessed October 21, 2008.

[5]Ted Turner quote, www.quotegarden.com, accessed November 15, 2009.

READING THE TEXT

1. Define in your own words what Roberts means by "the treadmill of consumption."

2. How have the mass media affected the desire for status symbols, according to Roberts?

3. What explanation does Roberts give for his claim that economic downturns have a minimal effect on the pursuit of material goods?

4. In your own words, explain Roberts's concept of the "shiny-objects ethos" (para. 7).

READING THE SIGNS

1. In your journal, explore what items count as status symbols in your own circle of friends (these do not need to be the sort of high-end items that Roberts
   mentions but could be particular brands of jeans, handbags, shoes, or electronic devices). What appeal do these items have for you? Does acquiring
   them make you happy? If so, how long does that feeling last? If not, why not?

2. **CONNECTING TEXTS**   Roberts assumes that the treadmill of consumption is irre-
   versible, that we will inevitably "continue to embrace the shiny-objects ethos"
   (para. 8). Discuss this assumption in class. If you agree, what evidence can
   you advance to support Roberts's claim? If you do not, what economic or
   social evidence can you find to refute his belief? Use the class discussion
   as a springboard for your own essay on this topic. To develop your ideas,
   you might consult Laurence Shames's "The More Factor" (p. 80) and Steve
   McKevitt's "Everything Now" (p. 143).

3. In what ways does television, especially reality TV programming, encourage
   the shiny-objects ethos? Select one show, such as *Keeping Up with the Kardashians*, and analyze the way in which it stimulates the desire to buy products that convey prestige and status.

PHYLLIS M. JAPP AND DEBRA K. JAPP

Purification through Simplification: Nature, the Good Life, and Consumer Culture

One of the greatest paradoxes of American culture is its simultaneous devotion to rampant consumerism and its celebration of rural
simplicity as the ideal model for "the good life." And as Phyllis M.
Japp and Debra K. Japp argue in this reading, these two contradictory impulses come together in the "voluntary simplicity movement." Selecting the Home and Garden network's reality TV series
The Good Life as an apt expression of the movement and subjecting
it to an in-depth rhetorical analysis, they find a similar theme in each
episode — people "who have left highly paid, highly stressed jobs in
the city and relocated to a more natural environment to live a simpler and therefore better life" — with a similar outcome: "Voluntary
simplicity . . . appears to reinforce dictates of simple living while
wrapped firmly within commodity culture, defining it primarily as a
psychological search for self-actualization in which nature becomes
a resource for purchase." Phyllis M. Japp was a professor emerita
in the Department of Communication Studies at the University of

Nebraska–Lincoln and was the coeditor, with Mark Meister, of *Enviropop: Studies in Environmental Rhetoric and Popular Culture* (2002), from which this essay is taken. Debra K. Japp is a professor of communications studies at St. Cloud State University.

The search for the good life is a major theme in human societies, from Aristotle to the present. In its current incarnation in late twentieth century America, the term represents dual and contradictory visions. Since the beginning of the nation, two major myths of the good life have developed simultaneously. The first is the belief in happiness and fulfillment through technology, the availability and acquisition of wealth and possessions, upward social mobility, and political influence. Existing alongside and countering this mythos has been the belief that happiness and fulfillment are found in a life of simplicity, one with the minimum of possessions, a life that does not seek wealth or influence but finds joy in connection to nature and service to others. As Shi (1985) notes, "From colonial days, the image of America as a spiritual commonwealth and a republic of virtue has survived alongside the more tantalizing vision of America as a cornucopia of economic opportunities and consumer delights" (p. 277). If these are the two poles in the definition of the good life, there have been many variations over the years, as each era has engaged the tension between having less and having more.

In times of prosperity and unchecked consumption, when it seems as if the "more is better" mentality has gained complete control, a growing sense of unease and guilt seems to draw the "less is more" rhetoric into focus and odes to a simpler mode of life appear.

In popular culture, the opposing visions of the good life are integrated into advertising, entertainment, and popular literature. For example, a Sears advertising campaign informs consumers that Sears stands ready to supply the "good life at a great price, guaranteed" as we view clothing, appliances, and other commodities supposedly essential to the quality of life. Alternately, the state of Nebraska's advertising slogan is "Nebraska — The Good Life," invoking visions of endless sky and bountiful prairies, a place where life is simple and nature revered. Note that however contradictory these visions are in many respects, nature in some form is necessary to their fulfillment. In the first version, nature must provide the resources utilized to manufacture the endless list of commodities now necessary to living the good life, the SUVs and fuel to run them, the lumber for bigger and bigger homes, the land that can be converted to golf courses and resorts where one can vacation in style. In the second version, nature is a spiritual and psychological resource, a retreat from the frantic pace of urban life, a reassurance in the healing powers of the earth. . . .

If the "more is better" mythos uses nature as raw material to develop and maintain the commodities necessary for the good life, the "less is more" mythos finds the real meaning of life in the human connection to natural environments.

Nature plays a central role in this vision of life. Shi (1985) observes: "Contact with nature, whether the virgin wilderness, the plowed field, or the Arcadian retreat, meant turning away from the artificiality of modern civilization to more abiding realities. God and goodness always seemed more accessible in the woods than in the city. Moreover, the countryside offered fresh air and a stimulus to strenuous activity" (p. 195). And Kenneth Burke (1984b) concurs: "The most basic support of all, the Earth, is perhaps the deepest source of reestablishment for bewildered sophisticates who, having lost all sense of a moral fountainhead, would restore themselves by contact with the 'telluric'" (p. 205).

While simple living has been a consistent theme since the beginning of the republic, it remains an abstraction that can be shaped to fit a variety of conditions and purposes. As Shi (1985) notes, "the precise meaning of the simple life has never been fixed"; rather, it has always been represented by "a shifting cluster of ideas, sentiments, and activities" (p. 3). Staple ingredients in the traditional recipe have included "a hostility toward luxury and a suspicion of riches, a reverence for nature and a preference for rural over urban ways of life and work, a desire for personal self-reliance through frugality and diligence, a nostalgia for the past and a skepticism toward the claims of modernity, conscientious rather than conspicuous consumption, and an aesthetic taste for the plain and functional" (Shi, 1985, p. 3). Thus the concept survives as both an "enduring myth" and as "an actual way of living" for at least a few citizens in each era (Shi, 1985, p. 279). In a technologically oriented commodity culture, we argue, this long-standing tradition of frugal living is transformed by an inescapable dependence on, and embrace of, products and services that have come to be defined as necessities of life. The reverence for nature is transformed into consumption as well, as the natural environment becomes yet another commodity, to be owned or appropriated as part of the simple lifestyle. Thus the rhetoric of simple living is inescapably infiltrated with the attitudes and orientations of consumption.

Burke and Environmental Rhetoric

Kenneth Burke looms as an important figure in many works on environmental rhetoric. He is well suited to be the patron theorist of environmental criticism for several reasons. First, Burke lived the life of an environmentalist, rejecting a life revolving around commodities for one closely in touch with the earth, the seasons, the rhythms of nature. Burks (1991) notes that Burke "seems to have despised consumerism and capitalism's promotion of it throughout his adult life" (p. 224). His lifestyle (Burke called himself an "agro-bohemian" with "Garden of Eden plumbing") testified to his rejection of consumer values and his need for engagement with nature (Burks, 1991, p. 224). Second, the environment is a theme that runs through his writings. Examples of the barnyard, the wren, the hapless fish with a faulty orientation, references to walking down the road, gardening, and the weather not only permeate his work but provided him inspiration to develop his critical perspective. Third, Burke's theory of symbolic action, his "tools" for deconstructing rhetoric, is ideal for discovering nuances in cultural artifacts. These tools are especially useful for the investigation of popular culture, for it is clear that what we desire, buy, eat, and wear, and where and how we choose to live are symbolic responses that articulate, support, and/or challenge the power structures of cultural institutions.

While Burke makes a number of specific references to the good life, the concept implicitly pervades his thought and energizes much of his terminology. Indeed, one could argue that a subtext of Burke's corpus could be the search for the good life, with attendant warnings about those motivational patterns that placed such in peril. Writing in the 1930s, Burke was traumatized by the Depression, by economic threats to the quality of life. By the 1960s he feared that nuclear war, the technology of destruction, could destroy all that we valued in life. He increasingly believed that environmental pollution, exacerbated and excused by consumer culture, stood poised to destroy any hope of a good life lived in tune with nature. Although he personally chose a life of simplicity, he was aware that the accumulation of possessions was the definition that most citizens embraced. Thus what is examined here, the cultural tension between the simple life of "less" and the commodified life of "more," is a tension also evident in Burke from *Counterstatement* (1968) to his last essays.

"Voluntary Simplicity": A Variation on *The Good Life*

A recent trend in contemporary popular culture is often termed "voluntary simplicity." This current variation on the theme of simple living is described in how-to books, films, television programming, and magazines. A recent bibliography of over 160 recent books, posted on a simple living Web site, includes such titles as *Circle of Simplicity: Return to the Good Life*, *101 Ways to Simplify Your Life*, *Six Weeks to a Simpler Life Style*, and *Skills for Simple Living*. Two simple living magazines have been recently launched, *Real Simple* and *Simplycity*. As *USA Today* observes in reviewing the magazines, "The simple life now comes with instructions" (Horovitz, 2000, p. 1A). Certainly there is much variation evident within this theme. Some advocate a complete lifestyle change and rejection of consumer values; others seek to downsize and de-stress within present circumstances. For still others, simplicity is a stylistic trend that determines which new home décor to purchase and what sort of vacation to take.

The vast amount of self-help literature surrounding this movement calls to mind Burke's (1973b) assertion that the people who consume such literature often have no intention of actually doing what is advocated. Reading is not the *prelude to*, but the *substitute for*, action; vicarious, armchair experience is less threatening than facing the decisions necessary for change

(Burke, 1973b, pp. 298–299). Certainly the widespread popularity of simple living ideas seems to have made little difference in the consumption styles of most of the population.

The theme of voluntary simplicity holds an especially powerful appeal for middle-class professionals torn between the need for more and the need for less as they try to manage the complexity of their lives. As with most calls for change, however, the desire for simple, painless maxims drives this massive quantity of literature. Irony abounds as self-styled experts in simplicity write books, circulate newspapers and magazines, develop Web sites, and travel the country presenting symposiums, consuming fuel and resources in the process, thereby reinforcing the importance of money, space, mobility, and other non-simple practices. The irony is reinforced as the media technology that has developed around the desire for wealth, that is the proliferation of materials, seminars, books, and guides advising people how to get rich, is now employed to help people simplify their lives. In the case study to follow, the television program *The Good Life* depends upon a complex media organization and a profusion of technology, including the equipment required to film a television series, although such is carefully kept out of camera range, rendering invisible its intrusion on the pristine natural settings in which the program is usually filmed.

Equally ironic is that this effort at simplicity must be *voluntary*, the result of a choice to renounce affluence and artificiality. The poor, who live lives of enforced rather than voluntary simplicity, are deprived of the moral value of such lives, voluntary simplicity being the prerogative of those "free to choose their standard of living" rather than the sordid poverty of those on the lower socioeconomic rungs of the hierarchy (Shi, 1985, p. 7). "Selective indulgence" is the theme of much of the current literature. As MonDesire (2000) notes, "The nostalgic urge for a simple life by and large emanates from people who've never had to duck a landlord on the first of the month, never had to wait in the rain for a packed city bus that rides on by, never had to slide the money for a half-gallon of milk under the narrow slot in a grocery store's bullet-proof window" (p. 19A).

Overall, the simple life appears dictated by personal needs and is framed almost entirely in the desire for fulfillment and personal growth. Converts do not renounce consumerism for religious reasons, for political dedication, or as a result of an environmental conscience. The quest is personal not political; secular rather than religious; self- instead of other-centered. As defined by the oxymoronic *Simple Life Corporation*, the concept means a journey, an awakening to self and one's inner needs, the removal of things that distract one from "finding" oneself, including not only possessions but activities, relationships, and duties. A *Cathy* cartoon strip neatly sums up the ironies. The script reads: "The simple life: Discard the day planner, disconnect call waiting, unplug the TV, cancel all subscriptions, say 'no' to invitations, clear closets and cupboards of everything but the bare essentials, and travel to a cool, quiet place that inspires possibility. The Mall" (Guisewite, 2000).

HGTV's *The Good Life*

A variety of texts could be used to exemplify the rhetoric of voluntary simplicity, for example, Internet Web sites, books, advice columns, sermons,
and instructional seminars, for it is the interaction of these aspects of popular culture that constructs and supports the ideologies of simple living. For
this essay, a Home and Garden network (HGTV) half-hour series entitled *The
Good Life* was chosen and the analysis included more than twenty episodes
aired over a period of two years. Although the stories vary — there are former lawyers, professors, journalists, models, executives, importers, even oil
riggers — they are all variations on a theme. All articulate a core vision of what
it means to live the good life. The stories, in fact, are strikingly similar despite
the assurance that the good life is different for every individual. In these dramatic presentations the cultural drama of "less is more" plays out against its
counter, "more is better." The stories are introduced as examples of people
("people just like you and me" the narrator assures us) who have left highly
paid, highly stressed jobs in the city and relocated to a more natural environment to live a simpler and therefore better life. The verbal and visual dramas
provide standard, mutually reinforcing formulas as viewers follow the stories
of people who have changed their lives, following their dreams to the good
life. Although viewers experience visual and verbal dramas simultaneously,
in this essay visual and verbal dramas are each considered first as a separate domain of meaning, and then considered together to point out how each
complements the other as they construct the meanings of *The Good Life*.

The Verbal Drama of *The Good Life*

The verbal drama of *The Good Life* is a classic example of Burke's dramatis-
tic process of guilt, repentance, and redemption. This well-known cycle of
cleansing, drawn from religious rhetoric, is appropriated by Burke as a critical
strategy for understanding how both social and personal change takes place
symbolically. In this drama, conflicts of motives construct hierarchies, which
in turn create various sorts of guilt. These shortcomings, when recognized,
require change or redemption. Burke argues this process as fundamental to
human communication. Thus in any situation, a critic can profitably look for
the guilt, that is, the shortcoming, inadequacy, inconsistency, need for closure,
that is the impetus for communicating. In the inevitable socioeconomic hierarchies, those with more are guilty of their excesses, those with less, of their lack
of prestige or attainments; and each must seek to be redeemed via explanation and justification. In any social structure characterized by hierarchies, says
Burke (1966), "Those 'Up' are guilty of not being 'Down,' those 'Down' are
certainly guilty of not being 'Up'" (p. 15). These are not necessarily conscious
emotions or explicit rhetorical strategies but are inherent motives or "patterns
of action" that drive explanations, justifications, comparisons, identifications,

divisions. In *The Good Life*, these implicit motives become an explicit motif or narrative form.

The Good Life features such salvation stories as its fundamental script. 15 Participants guilty of the sin of overwork at high-stress professions and refugees from frantic urban lifestyles repent of their erring ways and seek redemption. Nature is, as we will see, the primary agency of purification. Thus each episode of *The Good Life* turns on a conversion experience, as overworked suburbanites discover that something is missing in their lives and embrace change. At the root of their desires is a need for purification, through nature, from the guilt of consumerism. They repent, turn from their current way of life, and become new people, born again to a supposedly simpler existence, closer to nature, and implicitly, closer to God. Edye Ellis, the host and guru of the program, serves as an evangelist for this lifestyle change, exhorting others to follow in the footsteps of those whose conversion story was featured in this week's program. As with the self-help genre that infuses this portrayal, there is the "before and after" theme characteristic of any narrative of change (weight loss, addiction recovery, relational renewal, or political or religious conversions, to mention a few examples). The story each week follows the standard form of conversion testimony, from guilt to repentance to redemption.

Establishing guilt. The narrative begins with attention to the pathology of the participants' old way of life, by implication a "bad life." They describe their former lives as filled with stress, complexity, urban crowding, and long daily commutes, as they recount long hours on the job, mourn their disconnect from nature, and describe familial relationships in peril. The resulting self-diagnosis is described as a loss of self, identity, and meaning. They are no longer satisfied with the success they sought, the prestige gained, or the possessions accumulated by climbing the ladder to the top of their professions. "There must be something better" is the mantra of these seeking souls. For example, a former university dean tells of the day he discovered that he "had everything he wanted but didn't want anything he had" and vowed to quit his job and change his life.

Evincing repentance. The conversion always involves *risk* as well as renunciation. Penitents must pay the price by taking an economic or social risk, giving up something, either something *actual* (e.g., a high salary, social prestige) or *potential* (e.g., the chance for advancement). The "no pain, no gain" formula is reminiscent of the stories of risk-taking in pursuit of wealth. The definitions of risk, however, are comfortably middle class, attractive to those who know they can somehow recover what may be lost. Thus they risk investing their savings in a business, in a move from a familiar location, by leaving their circle of friends, by choosing to live in a smaller space, or by making do with fewer possessions in their quest for something better. Although there is an attempt to maintain suspense, risk remains little more than a minor and temporary challenge to their middle-class values and identities. For example, a former journalist risks his savings to open a bakery in a small town, a

Texas landscaper invests his life savings to convert a rural hotel to a bed-and-breakfast, a Chicago lawyer abandons his practice to open a restaurant.

Seeking redemption. Once willingness to risk is established, the redemptive moment of the narrative occurs, a turning point of almost mystical quality. Some penitents drive down a country road and find at the end a location where they are "meant to be." Or they may discover a small town and feel instantly as if they were born there. Almost always this redemptive moment involves some contact with the earth, or with nature in some form. This mystical moment is also a pivotal point at which penitents can surrender and embrace the salvation of the good life or draw back from the risk and remain doomed to its alternative. Following the muse involves, above all, the search for a location where a good life is possible. Few manage the conversion without some physical move, most frequently from urban to rural, large town to small town.

Thus, communion with nature is essential to the good life, whether from a cabin in the woods, a farm, the rural charm of a small town, or even a tranquil garden in a suburban backyard. Also essential to the conversion experience is a new occupation compatible with the conversion values. Work in some form is essential; few remain idle. Entrepreneurship is especially attractive, satisfying the yearning to be one's own boss, control one's own time. Artistry is likewise a key to the good life (writing, crafting, achieving creative fulfillment, and frequently making money from the endeavor). The new occupation or avocation often requires some contact with the earth, from growing one's own food to using natural products to make beautiful and artistic creations.

A constant redemptive theme is the search for ideal relationships, for people with whom one can live the good life. Some converts bring intact families in need of renewal via simplicity; some seek change because of broken relationships and look for new, like-minded friends and/or life partners. Problems in previous relationships are linked to the values and practices of the old life (to date we have seen no programs about those whose relationships have broken up as a result of converting to the simple life). The search for self is paramount, however. As the old life is stripped away, as old locations, occupations, and relationships are replaced, the unique authentic self of the convert is revealed, hidden below the artificiality of the old life. The needs that were ignored in the complexity of urban professional life can now thrive and grow. Hidden skills and talents are uncovered: a professor discovers he is an artist, a former model becomes a world-class chef, others find amazing abilities to sculpt, create music, take prize-winning photographs.

Bearing witness. The final turn of the salvation drama is the evangelical responsibility of the convert. All participants devoutly affirm that they are now living the good life, lives of "deep fulfillment" as one declares. To a person, they express no regrets or nostalgia for the life left behind. The gains are far greater than the losses, the satisfaction worth the risk. They encourage others to make the same choice, again emphasizing choice and reinforcing the voluntary nature of their life change. The host completes the narrative with an altar call for conversion as she addresses viewers directly: "You too can have the good life." Like these inspiring stories, renewal begins "one step at a time."

Nature's role as commodity is evident in the consumerist attitude of selecting and owning an appropriate natural setting or backdrop for living the simple life. Control of life choices remains central; the stories turn on the volunteerist motive. The centrality of voluntary choice is significant. It implies that what has been surrendered can, if desired, be reappropriated. Participants stress they could have continued, even succeeded, in their former circumstances but chose to change their lives, always for personal and relational reasons. Thus choice implies a way out if the rigors of simple living are too great and smoothes a path back into the former lifestyle. The factors that support the ability to choose simplicity (money, education, social class) are also the very attributes necessary to success in a consumer society; thus these important qualities remain the property of the individual, to be played out as desires dictate. The sense of entitlement or ownership of nature as well as the implicit dependence on the attributes of consumerism continue to reinforce the orientations of the "old life," undermining the claims of conversion to simplicity.

The Visual Drama of *The Good Life*

In this analysis of the visual drama of *The Good Life*, another dimension of Burke's dramatism is used, focusing on how various elements are presented visually as the substance or grounding of the good life. Burke's pentad is built upon the concept of substance, the symbolically constructed foundation or basis on which various aspects of the drama are played out. Burke (1973a) identifies five major orientations that compel the human drama — scene, act, agent, agency, and purpose (pp. 21–23). Humans use symbol systems to constitute their situations and contexts, their identities and differences, their shared pasts and futures, their needs, goals, desires. In the process, they construct compelling explanations of the human condition — narratives of human agency, of the constraining power of natural conditions, of being bound or liberated by ideas, of individual desire or cooperative action that overpowers restraints. Burke (1973a) argues that these orientations and the tensions among them, e.g. the struggle between the power of will (agent) and the power of situation (scene), are necessary to any well-rounded explanation of "what people are doing and why they are doing it" (p. xv). This perspective seems ideal for exploring the visual drama of *The Good Life* because of the overwhelming visual power of the physical settings as the essence or substance of the good life. We concentrate on the primacy of the scenic in the visualizations of the good life but the other terms are ever-present and inevitably accessed in understandings of the visual drama presented in the program.

Nature as scene. The visual drama powerfully constructs the scenic dimension of the good life, both the foundational substance that grounds this life and the context, that is, the physical spaces or places in which the good life can be lived. Nature is a major component of both the grounding and the setting of a good life. But this scene is not raw and unruly nature. It is a nature ordered, controlled, and structured into the perfect setting for the values and qualities of the good life. This nature of pristine mountains, meadows, streams, and oceans is a nature without heat, humidity, drought, cold, damp, mosquitoes, snakes, storms, or blight. Thus the camera pans over beautiful views, bountiful gardens, wildlife, forests, landscaped lawns, even occasional swimming pools and guest houses. Nature here is a visual feast, with shots carefully chosen to exclude power lines, cellular towers, jet contrails, litter, dams, encroaching urbanization, highways, and other visual blights from human development. Likewise the cameras, trucks, and other equipment necessary to filming are carefully kept out of camera range, as noted above, ignoring the irony that their presence destroys the very tranquility they are attempting to capture.

As the scene of the good life is visualized, it is done in true Burkean fashion by referencing what it "is not" in order to substantiate what it "is." Shots of the "old life" of stress and complexity, pollution and gridlock, are juxtaposed with those of the "new life." Nature thus is instantiated as both the substance that generates the good life and the setting or scene in which such a life is possible. (Of course, by implication, the scenes of the old life become places where a good life is not possible.)

Style as scene. There is another component to the scene, however, overlapping and extending the emphasis on nature. If the good life is grounded in nature, it is also rooted in the stylistic, an element necessary to separate the middle-class good life from the inadvertent and unavoidable simplicity of poverty and lower-class existence. Burke (1984b) defines style as a moral dimension of symbolizing that involves doing or being "right," that is, appropriate to the situation. It is "an elaborate set of prescriptions and proscriptions for 'doing the right thing' . . . a complex schema of what-goes-with-what carried through all the subtleties of manner and attitudes" (pp. 268–269). Those scenes and agents imbued with style determine the "correct" use of commodities. While most folks dress themselves, set their tables, and decorate their homes, to do so with style requires a knowledge of the nuances of social correctness as well as a flair for originality within the bounds of appropriateness. Thus style is an option for those with money and good taste, setting them apart from those who must take whatever is available at a price they can afford.

In *The Good Life*, nature as chief commodity must be stylized, made appropriate to the scene. Just as the natural beauty of the outdoors is configured into an aesthetic backdrop for the good life, the interiors of the simple but tasteful abodes are charmingly decorated with arts, crafts, and fabrics that utilize nature in elegant and artistic ways. Edye Ellis, the host of the program and the Martha Stewart of simple living, provides an enduring aura of taste, elegance, and aesthetic appeal. Cameras linger on Edye as she poses with flower arrangements, room décor, gardens, beautiful views, and tasteful accessories that embed style into the substance of the good life.

"Doing" nature with style: Constructing agents. Thus, these two components, nature and style, combine to produce the grounding for the good life. The scene, however, requires agents appropriate to that scene, generated by and imbued with its qualities. As Burke (1973a) explains: "It is a principle of drama that the nature of acts and agents should be consistent with the nature of the scene" (p. 3). As the verbal narrative stresses, converts to the good life must experience a rebirth, a reawakening of appreciation for nature and their own artistic abilities. The visual drama chronicles this rebirth. We see photos of the subjects as children, growing up, engaging as adults in the "bad life," juxtaposed with shots of new converts enjoying the good life. The visual connection between "what I was and what I am" constructs a new identity forged by their identification with the scene.

As noted above, converts to the good life almost always discover hidden artistic talents that can only now be developed. Abilities to paint, sculpt, photograph, decorate, or do crafts emerge as if by magic, as the substance of the good life draws these forth from participants. They thus possess the necessary style to be appropriate agents in the good life drama, style being a latent quality called forth by their participation in the scene. We often see participants actually constructing, physically and metaphorically, their placement in the new location. Often at the end of the program, the camera integrates agent and scene, as it lingers on converts engaged in the daily routines of the good life, for example, walking in the woods or by a lake, taking in a natural panorama from a deck, working in the garden, creating artistic objects from natural products, tastefully decorating their homes, or taking photographs of nature. The visual message is: "This is the good life and we now belong here, we have grown from and are now situated in this place, like the mountains and trees that surround us."

The snake in the garden: Commodity as agency. The visual drama has another 30 component, however, one that challenges and ultimately overpowers the Edenic visions of the good life, infusing both scene and agent with the values of commodity culture—advertising. According to Burke (1973a), agency is the manner or means by which action is possible (p. xv). Advertising thus is implicitly the agency or means by which a good life is possible. As with all television programming, advertising is a vital ingredient of the program, and becomes part of the visual flow of meaning. The viewer can validly assume that the products advertised are by implication those necessary for, or at least compatible with, the good life. Television programming constructs a flow of meaning, evoking "subtle associations between aspects of the show and the commodity" presented in the commercials (Budd, Craig, & Steinman, 1999, pp. 153–154). Thus as visuals of nature are juxtaposed with repeated ads for luxury automobiles, vacation cruises, and investment opportunities, the program implicitly argues that expensive commodities, consumed with style, are essential to the good life. In fact, these commodities and the wealth they imply are instantiated as

Speed Bump

the agency or means through which the good life is attained, making this a life framed by, surrounded by, and energized by consumer culture.

Style therefore is the essential quality that links nature and consumer culture. Living with nature appropriately requires style, just as style requires appreciation of the finest commodities that only money can purchase. The good life, then, uses consumption (with style) as agency to bridge the fundamental disjunction that has always rested at the heart of this culture's vision of the good life, the term that connects the "less is more" and "more is better" versions of the good life. As visualized in this program, the good life apparently means being able to drive up to your rural abode in your new Lexus, booking a Caribbean cruise from your rustic living room when you need a break from simplicity, and taking it for granted that you have a right to consume both nature and commodities as long as you do it with style.

Interaction of the Visual and Verbal Dramas of *The Good Life*

Obviously the verbal and visual dramas are interdependent, both needed to define the good life. If one considers the verbal narrative the dominant narrative — and that is only because our tools for dealing with words are more familiar — the visual narrative reduces and expands, abstracts and concretizes the verbal. Together the verbal and the visual dramas reside in the tensions between stability and change. If the verbal drama is the story of change, of agential choice shaping, molding, creating the desired environments for one's salvation, the visual drama privileges scenic power, as stable, enduring nature embraces the prodigal, restores those who dwell therein to the timeless serenity of the universe. The incompleteness of each makes space for the other; in their contradictions lies satisfactory completion.

The verbal drama of choice includes no admission that the lifestyle of consumption being renounced bears any responsibility for misuse of nature. The visual narrative presents a static, ever-stable natural beauty, for example, pristine mountains, streams, and meadows unaffected by human excess and mismanagement. As noted, nature is visual artwork, purchased and now possessed via the risks taken. In no sense is it an active entity. This visualization of nature energizes the verbal, temporal drama of human quest. The eternal ever-present backdrop of nature becomes an object of desire in the temporal formula, placed back in eternal timelessness at the end. Each narrative (spatial and temporal) supports and constrains the other. The visual reduces nature to an aesthetic that complements the verbal drama's definition of nature as a choice of lifestyle, implying that a beautiful environment exists to satisfy human desires but failing to assign any responsibility for preserving that environment.

HGTV's *The Good Life* is one example, among many, of current visions of simple living. It is particularly striking because it embeds so many values in one compact package and presents so many seemingly oppositional ideas in a coherent verbal and visual narrative; this version of the good life provides vicarious atonement, offers the chance to reform without serious sacrifice. Its pathology is that it allows no serious economic, social, or environmental issues to emerge. It reduces complex, potentially tragic consequences of policies and practices to matters of individual preference, stylistic choices, aesthetic visions. Here the good life is about following one's own dream, discovering one's inner self. It is individualized as the freedom to "do what I want, when I want," as a number of participants observe. There are no stories of failure, no acknowledgment of social responsibility, no sympathy for those who cannot choose. It maintains the myth of infinite possibility for all, defining simplicity not as a moral alternative or environmental necessity but as a trendy lifestyle, allowing the viewer to forget that only the fortunate few can choose to leave a mess they have helped to create and maintain for a flight to rural, unspoiled areas.

By implication, the good life takes place in select localities, in rural, 35 sparsely populated, attractive, and relatively unspoiled places such as the slopes of the Rockies, the foothills of the Appalachians, the ocean, lakefront, or bayou, in quaint New England towns, in other rural and unspoiled beauty spots of the nation. The visual component strengthens the aesthetic and grounds it in nature in ways the verbal cannot. Most examples presented in *The Good Life* require money, influence, and taste as the converts attempt to create a lifestyle of elegance and beauty in a new setting. Great emphasis is placed on improving communication in families and relationships; nature is the mystique that makes this possible. The work ethic is retained but relocated to include contact with nature. Each episode ends with an altar call, "You too can have the good life."

Thus, the good life utilizes natural environments as a stage-set for a lifestyle that continues to valorize commodity culture. Nature, in fact, is the foremost commodity; in order to live the good life it must be purchased, modified, and controlled. Nature and simplicity must be managed with the same skills and dedication that former professional careers were managed. As Burke (1973b) observes, the vision of the good life was built around the

> ideal of the "live-wire" salesman, with culture taken to mean the maximum purchase of manufactured commodities. . . . Out of books, out of delightful moments in one's personal life, out of sporadic voyages, out of *vacational* experiences as distinct from *vocational* ones, people got visions of a noncompetitive structure of living, a "good life" involving gentle surroundings, adequate physical outlets, the pursuit of knowledge, etc., and the very slogans of the commercial ethic assured them that they were "entitled" to all this. (p. 248)

Conclusion

Voluntary simplicity in 2002, then, appears to reinforce the dictates of simple living while wrapped firmly within commodity culture, defining it primarily as a psychological search for self-actualization in which nature becomes a resource for purchase. It calls us not to change our ways but to dabble in self-fulfillment, while continuing on our present course of overconsumption and self-indulgence. By reducing the issues to individual conversion experiences, there is no need for national repentance, for a brake on conspicuous and wasteful consumption of resources. As this example illustrates, the simple life discourse is framed in and contained by assumptions and connections to consumption. It is constructed in the language of a consumer society. It is not a call for change but a powerful endorsement of the status quo. The cultural myth of success, the "divine right" to consume the world's resources, the unwillingness to acknowledge that the environment is not merely a backdrop or stage-set for our consumption of goods and enactment of trendy lifestyles, makes many current odes to simplicity, the "less is more" narratives, merely alternate versions of the "more is better" stories.

One program from one genre of popular culture — television entertainment — says little except when, as with *The Good Life*, its assumptions and expectations are deeply embedded in American culture. The program draws from and reinforces the powers of consumerism and the inevitable subsuming of environmental concerns to consumerist values. When these same assumptions, expectations, and values are evident across various genres of popular culture, they become an uncritical and unconscious dimension of our cultural reality. Popular culture thus implicitly assures us that we are entitled to a good life, whether one of economic complexity or voluntary simplicity, and offers us nature for sale, an environment to be purchased and used in the search for personal fulfillment.

REFERENCES

Budd, M., Craig, S., & Steinman, C. (1999). *Consuming environments: Television and commercial culture*. New Brunswick, NJ: Rutgers University Press.
Burke, K. (1966). *Language as symbolic action*. Berkeley, CA: University of California Press.
Burke, K. (1973a). *Grammar of motives*. 2nd ed. Berkeley, CA: University of California Press.
Burke, K. (1973b). *Philosophy of literary form*. 3rd ed. Berkeley, CA: University of California Press.
Burke, K. (1984a). *Attitudes toward history*. 4th ed. Berkeley, CA: University of California Press.
Burke, K. (1984b). *Permanence and change*. 4th ed. Berkeley, CA: University of California Press.
Burks, D. (1991). Kenneth Burke: The agro-bohemian "Marxoid." *Communication Studies, 42,* 219–233.
Dudgeon, C. (Executive producer). *The Good Life*. Knoxville, TN: Home and Garden Television (HGTV). Retrieved from http://www.hgtv.com
Guisewite, C. (2000, June 24). *Cathy* [Cartoon]. *Omaha World Herald*.
Horovitz, B. (2000, June 1). Simplesells: Chic back-to-basics explosion carries hefty load of irony. *USA Today*, p.1A+.
MonDesire, D. (2000, June 9). How hard should we strive for simple life? *USA Today*, p. I9A.
Shi, D. E. (1985). *The simple life: Plain living and high thinking in American culture*. New York, NY: Oxford.

READING THE TEXT

1. What are the two major myths of the good life in American culture, according to Japp and Japp? What belief do Americans hold that contradicts the two major myths?

2. Summarize in your own words rhetorician Kenneth Burke's theory of symbolic action and how it applies to the HGTV program *The Good Life*.

3. How does American popular culture reflect, or mediate, the contradictory tendencies in Americans' views of the good life, according to the article?

4. What is the "voluntary simplicity movement," and how is it represented in *The Good Life*?

5. What are the "visual" and "verbal" dramas of *The Good Life*?

READING THE SIGNS

1. Visit a site such as TVrage.com or Hulu that archives TV programs, and watch a later episode of *The Good Life*. In an essay, analyze the narrative the episode tells about the featured participant. To what extent does it conform to the salvation formula that Japp and Japp claim is typical of the show? If it deviates, how does it do so, and what alternative narrative is created for the participant?

2. Analyze a magazine such as *Real Simple* or a TV program such as *Simple Living with Wanda Urbanska*. To what extent does your subject "reinforce the dictates of simple living while wrapped firmly within commodity culture." (para. 37)?

3. Read Jon Krakauer's *Into the Wild*, which narrates the ultimately fatal journey of Chris McCandless into the Alaska wilderness, and write an essay that analyzes the protagonist's experiment with "voluntary simplicity." Does he engage in a genuine rejection of material culture and embrace of nature or, as some critics have noted, does he turn living in nature into something of a self-indulgent competitive sport?

4. Write an analysis of the contradictions you find in green marketing campaigns that present the possession of consumer goods as ways to achieve the simple life. To develop your ideas, consult Julia B. Corbett's "A Faint Green Sell: Advertising and the Natural World" (p. 235).

5. Compare and contrast Japp and Japp's critique of the voluntary simplicity movement's use of nature with Thomas Frank's analysis of the countercultural pose of much current advertising (see "Commodify Your Dissent," p. 150). In what ways do the authors see nature and countercultural beliefs as being co-opted by consumer culture?

6. When describing the convention of "style as scene," Japp and Japp claim that "while most folks dress themselves, set their tables, and decorate their homes, to do so with style requires a knowledge of the nuances of social correctness as well as a flair for originality within the bounds of appropriateness" (para. 26). Analyze an issue of *Martha Stewart Living*. To what extent does the publication replicate Japp and Japp's indictment of media that simply present a visual drama of the good life?

STEVE McKEVITT

Everything Now

Paradoxically, although today people in developed societies have more consumer choices, 24/7 access to a global cornucopia of goods, and (thanks to generous credit availability) more sheer *stuff*, many report feelings of unhappiness, especially when it comes to the stress triggered by working to pay for all that stuff. But while work indeed contributes to that unhappiness, Steve McKevitt argues in this selection that much of it can be credited to massive marketing campaigns designed to convince us that if we only buy this product or that service, we will be happy. Combining psychology with the technological ability to bombard us around the clock with clever advertisements designed to convince us that our every *want* is actually a *need*, current marketing strategies keep us unhappy in order to move the goods. A marketing consultant and author whose books include *City Slackers* (2006) and *Everything Now* (2013, from where this selection comes), McKevitt is chairman of Golden, "an ideas agency."

> You can never get enough of what you don't need to make you happy.
> — ERIC HOFFER, philosopher and social writer

What do you want?

Whether you are looking for motor cars, mobile phones, holidays or simply what to have for lunch, the range of options available to you can be genuinely overwhelming. With nothing more than a broadband Internet connection, you can enjoy immediate and unfettered access to millions of books, newspapers and magazines; thousands of movies and TV shows and almost the entire canon of recorded music. Many lifetimes' worth of content, all of it available at the click of a mouse. Whatever it is you want, you can have it. Everything Now.

We are living through a time of endless choices and unlimited convenience. We now take for granted the ubiquity of goods and services that can be instantly accessed, but the 24/7 society we live in — where everything is available practically all the time — is a recent achievement. Everything Now did not happen by chance or overnight. It is the culmination of a deliberate and concerted 30-year drive to increase choice and convenience for everyone. Those of us lucky enough to be living in the developed world today are, on average, healthier, wealthier, longer lived and better educated than at any other point in history. Our *needs* have been fulfilled and so, for the first time ever, we have an economy that is almost entirely devoted to the business of satisfying our *wants* instead. The question is: with so much effort dedicated to giving us what we want, why aren't we happier or, at the very least, worrying less and enjoying life more? . . .

People do not buy technology, what they buy is functionality. Consumers do not purchase stereos, DVD players and mobile phones because they want the items for themselves, but because they want to listen to music, watch movies, and keep in touch with family and friends. The same is true of computers. But in this case there is much more functionality, so people end up buying computers for many different reasons—to work, play games, browse the Internet, edit movies, create magazines and so on. To do this they need to run software. To gain a competitive edge within a crowded market, software publishers were creating products crammed with features and optimised to run most effectively on the fastest machines available at the time of their release.

This was especially true for computer games, which, because of their rich graphics, placed the heaviest demands upon the hardware. If consumers wanted to derive the most functionality from the latest software—in the case of my games, experience the smoothest animation, highest resolution and most spectacular visuals—they would need the fastest computer, which would almost certainly contain one of [Intel's] microprocessors.

However, as Intel's business model demonstrated, it would only be the fastest computer for a maximum of three months. The pace of this process was so rapid that [Intel VP of Marketing] Manfred could be confident that even the best computer available today would not be able to cope with the latest software being published three years hence. The pursuit of functionality—our games—could be used to force consumers to invest in Intel's new technology. Intel was not only creating faster microprocessors, it was also creating the demand for them.

Intel may be a master of the art, but it is certainly not the only company in the business of inventing wants as well as products. Manfred is correct: wants are very different to needs. "Want versus Need" is one of the most basic concepts in economics. A need is something we have to have—like food, sleep or water. A want is something we would like to have—like a Big Mac, a Tempur mattress or a bottle of Evian. You might think that you cannot survive without your BlackBerry or your BMW, but you can. It might even be the case that you do need a phone to carry out your work and a car to get around in, but what brand it is and, to a large extent, what features it has are really just wants.

Needs are rational and permanent. We have always needed—and will always need—food, water and shelter. The solution may change, but the problem is always the same, you can't create new needs. Wants, on the other hand, are emotional, ephemeral and ever changing. Just because you want something today doesn't mean you will want it tomorrow, always want it, or ever want it again. For example, back in 1981, everybody wanted a Rubik's Cube, it was the world's most popular toy, but it is unlikely to ever repeat this feat in the future. This transience creates an opportunity for anyone who is trying to sell us something—whether that's a product, a service or even an idea—and they can invent wants for us as well as the means to assuage them.

In 1976, a year with one of the hottest summers on record, almost nobody drank bottled water in the UK (unless they went on holiday "abroad"); we spent less than £200,000 on just 3 million litres of the stuff. Today, each of us drinks an average of 33 litres per year, spending a total of £1.4 billion. We do this despite the fact that tap water is essentially an identical product that is as widely and freely available as it was in 1976.

Manufacturing wants for things like bottled water is what keeps us in ₁₀ a permanent state of dissatisfaction, because only by making us unhappy with what we have today is it possible to persuade us to pay for something that will make us happy tomorrow. In the case of bottled water, its success depended on us becoming dissatisfied with drinking tap water. The basis of this dissatisfaction is usually emotional rather than rational, it doesn't require hard evidence—all that is needed, perhaps, is promoting a notion that bottled water tastes better or using language to suggest it is somehow healthier than tap water. In Intel's case, the continual introduction of new microprocessors means that purchasing a new computer will only briefly appease the existing want for maximum functionality. Likewise, once upon a time, you may have yearned for an iPhone Mk1, but now, several upgrades later with that model nothing more than a distant memory, you've become dissatisfied with your current handset, and can't wait for the opportunity to forsake it for next year's version. It is simple and, as ever-increasing sales of bottled water, personal computers and mobile phones testifies, it has been extremely effective.

Maslow's Hierarchy of Needs is a theory of developmental psychology which describes the phases of human growth. It is often portrayed as a pyramid, with the biggest, most basic needs at the bottom (air, food, water), then safety issues (health, employment, property), moving up through relationships and esteem (achievement, confidence, respect), reaching self-actualisation at the top (morality, creativity and problem solving).

Maslow believed that these needs play a major role in motivating behaviours in Western societies where the individual is paramount. Basic biological, physiological and safety needs will always take priority over the need for respect or self-expression, but once they have been satisfied, the needs higher up the pyramid become increasingly important. As one set of needs is assuaged, focus moves to those on the next level up the pyramid. Everything Now is an extreme example of an individualistic society, hence our tendency is to be egocentric, focusing on the improvement of one's self and circumstances, with self-actualisation at the zenith.

For example, tackling obesity and associated issues of low self-esteem is a priority in the UK and USA, where food is cheap and plentiful, but in places where food is expensive and in short supply, these problems simply don't exist. There are few branches of Weight Watchers in the Third World and no need, at present, for Western governments to develop famine-relief strategies to feed their own people. . . .

Yes we are still innovating, but we are doing so in small steps, not the giant leaps we once were. [John] Smart makes a very interesting observation about the areas in which innovation is taking place:

> Certain types of innovation saturation might now appear to be occurring because our accelerating technological productivity is beginning to intersect with an effectively fixed number of human needs . . . We may observe that as the world develops and we all climb higher on Maslow's

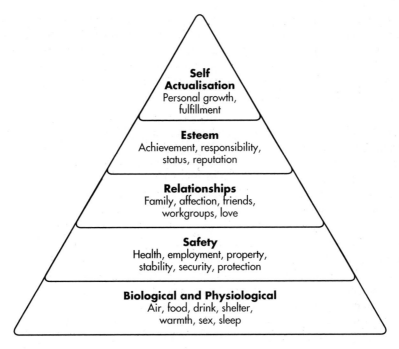

Figure 1. Maslow's Hierarchy of Needs

hierarchy of relatively fixed needs, those who already have sufficient housing, transportation, etc., are now pursuing innovations on the most abstract, virtual, and difficult-to-quantify levels, like social interaction, status, entertainment, and self-esteem.

It is because we don't really need anything anymore that the focus of inno- 15 vation has itself turned to addressing our wants instead. As Maslow demonstrates, once needs are taken care of, wants can be just as powerful drivers. This is all well and good if we know what it is that we want, but most of the time we don't. Nor do the things we want necessarily have to be good, either for ourselves or for the rest of society. Some people want to smoke, to take drugs or, as a more extreme example, to commit crimes. Needs require rational decision-making. However, the evidence is that decisions about wants are driven entirely by our emotions and these feelings can be so strong that they cause us to over-rule or simply ignore rational objections. This combination makes us highly suggestible: easily persuaded by things that engage our sympathies, willing to be told what it is that we want, and then to act upon that information, regard-less of the consequences. We should also consider that the people empathising with us—the ones engaging our sympathies and then telling us what it is that we want—are often trying to hawk us a solution as well.

You can find examples of this everywhere. Just look at an everyday product, like toothpaste. We need toothpaste to ensure our teeth and gums remain healthy. On average, people with healthy teeth live longer and tend to lead healthier lives than those who lose their teeth prematurely. Visit your local supermarket and you'll find around 120 different brands of toothpaste to choose from. Some promise fresher breath, others whiter teeth, others healthier gums. There will be brands for sensitive teeth, for people with fillings or cavities, there will be gels, pastes and powders, but despite this welter of options, each and every one will be virtually identical chemically; essentially the same thing, packaged and positioned in dozens of slightly different ways. The same is true whatever the category, from soap to soap operas. Scratch beneath the surface of Everything Now's apparently endless choice at any point and what you will find is hundreds of virtually identical products. Toothpaste is really just toothpaste.

Nobody needs to have 120 different varieties of intrinsically indistinguishable products like toothpaste or soap to choose from, and you may argue that nobody wants them either, but these "choices" are offered in a much more subtle way. Where once there was a category called soap, now there are soaps for dry skin, greasy skin, sensitive skin; there is strong soap, gentle soap; soap in a bar, in a bottle, in a jar or from a dispenser; liquid soap, foam soap, hard soap, scented soap, simple soap, plain soap, soft soap and soap on a rope. Now all you have to do is choose one.

Things can't go on like this. And that's not some liberal cri de coeur, I mean it literally: they can't. Whatever your views are on climate change, you have to at least concede that we are not going to be able to rely on fossil fuels forever. If we carry on at the current rate of consumption—some 85 million barrels of oil a day, burning through the fossil record at the rate of 20 million years, every year—then we're going to run out sooner rather than later. Well, I'm all for screwing in low-energy light bulbs, buying locally produced peas and only drinking European wine, if that's what it takes to save the planet, yet I can't help thinking that, in the face of the thousands of freight carriers that are making their way to these shores slowly, but inexorably, from China and India to deliver their precious cargoes of Christmas cracker gifts and trinkets, these Herculean efforts might not suffice!

And even if we do discover substantial new reserves of oil and gas to ensure we can be supplied with miniature screwdriver sets and mini playing cards for the next 200 years, there still aren't enough resources for everyone to live as wastefully as we do in the developed world. We are currently using 1.5 times the world's gross annual product every year, which requires us to draw on an inevitably limited and dwindling stockpile of natural resources to make up the shortfall. But even as we burn through 50 percent more than we produce, over-fishing, over-farming, over-watering and deforesting as we go, competition for these diminishing resources is increasing as the huge economies in Brazil, Russia, India and China (the so-called BRIC nations) and those in the rest of Southern Asia and South America become stronger. This means that even if those miniature screwdriver sets are still available, they're going to be a lot more expensive. And I do mean a lot more. Economists expect food prices to double in the next 20 years in real terms. Remember, this is the case even if we ignore climate change, which, I'll concede, is a bit like ignoring a herd of elephants in your living room. . . .

The world we live in today no longer needs either stone knappers or rocket-scientists. It requires people to work out how the music industry can make money from file sharing; how Sunday newspaper executives can convince new readers that 500,000 words of content is worth the price of a cup of coffee; how TV channels can survive without relying on advertising revenue. It needs marketers and creative thinkers who can persuade millions of other people that This Brand is exclusively for them, that the next version of this film/TV/video game franchise is really the best one ever, or that some website helps us get closer to the things we love. It needs people who can develop products that are slightly better than the previous version, who can identify tiny gaps in crowded markets, who can think up new ways to package, deliver or sell the same things. It needs people who can find innovative ways of managing finance, who can manipulate the money markets, exploit political boundaries and economic loopholes, who can persuade people to leverage their assets, or to liquidate, re-mortgage, plough-back or reinvest, or just to keep their capital moving. But most of all it needs people who can work out ways of getting all of the above to us as soon as we want it. And of course, we want it now.

Inventors are innovating as much now as they ever have, it's just that they are solving problems that won't necessarily be rewarded with patents. The inventors are busy doing other things. Not necessarily brilliant things either. For every iPad there is a Chicken Nugget—but both are, in their own way, elegant solutions to problems people didn't know that they had.

Everything Now is enormously wasteful: a huge and unnecessary drain on the world's dwindling natural resources. By skewing our motivation it has entirely displaced the process of innovation. This is the real cost of changing our focus to wants instead of needs. Everything Now is making it almost impossible for us to address any genuinely big problems we face in the long term. We are not just demand-led, but are busily creating the demands themselves. We have become so obsessed with inventing and meeting the wants of the individual in the short term that attention has become diverted from the real challenges of meeting fundamental human needs of the future: energy and food supply, changing climate, population growth and the sustainable use of natural resources.

SOURCES

Bott, David (Director of Innovation Programmes, UK Government Technology Strategy Board), "Challenge = Opportunity" The 9th Roberts Lecture, University of Sheffield, 18 October 2011
Davies, John, "Debt Facts and Figures July 2011," Credit Action, July 2011
Purdy, L., "The Dissatisfaction Syndrome," Publicis, May 2002

READING THE TEXT

1. Summarize in your own words the distinctions between "wants" and "needs," according to McKevitt.

2. What is the logic behind Maslow's hierarchy of needs?

3. How does the marketing of products such as computers and bottled water convince consumers that these items are "needs," not "wants," as McKevitt explains?

4. After describing the world of "Everything Now," McKenna says, "Things can't go on like this. . . . I mean it literally: they can't" (para. 18). Why does he believe this?

5. What effect has the wide variety of consumer choices had on the relative happiness of people today, according to McKevitt?

READING THE SIGNS

1. In your journal, write your own response to McKevitt's opening quotation from Eric Hoffer: "You can never get enough of what you don't need to make you happy."

2. In class, make a list of all the consumer products that you and your classmates need, and then a list of what you want. What differences, if any, are there between the lists? If you have difficulty categorizing a product as a need or a want, how do you explain that difficulty?

3. **CONNECTING TEXTS**   Using McKevitt's selection as a critical perspective, write an essay analyzing the results of the University of Maryland research study described in "Students Addicted to Social Media" (p. 403). Do you think the students reported on in that selection would categorize their electronic devices as needs or wants? Where would you locate those devices on Maslow's hierarchy of needs?

4. Study current advertisements (either print or online) for bottled water. Do today's ads reflect McKevitt's claim that "only by making us unhappy with what we have today is it possible to persuade us to pay for something that will make us happy tomorrow" (para. 10)?

THOMAS FRANK

Commodify Your Dissent

"Sometimes You Gotta Break the Rules." "This is different. Different is good." "The Line Has Been Crossed." "Resist the Usual." If you are guessing that these defiant declarations must come from the Che Guevara/Jack Kerouac Institute of World Revolution and Extreme Hipness, you're in for a surprise, because they are actually advertising slogans for such corporations as Burger King, Arby's, Toyota, Clash Clear Malt, and Young & Rubicam. Just why huge corporations are aping the language of the Beats and the 1960s counterculture is the centerpiece of Thomas Frank's thesis that the countercultural idea has become "an official aesthetic of consumer society." Commodifying the decades-long youth habit of dissenting against corporate America, corporate America has struck back by adopting the very attitudes that once meant revolution, Frank believes, thus turning to its own capitalist uses the postures of rebellion. Indeed, when Apple can persuade you to buy a computer because its guy is just plain *cooler* than some IBM nerd, there may be no way out. Frank is the author of *Commodify Your Dissent: Salvos from the Baffler* (with Matt Weiland, 1997), from which this selection is taken; *The Conquest of Cool: Business Culture, Counterculture, and the Rise of Hip Consumerism* (1998); *One Market under God: Extreme Capitalism, Market Populism, and the End of Economic Democracy* (2001); *What's the Matter with Kansas?: How Conservatives Won the Heart of America* (2005); *The Wrecking Crew: How Conservatives Rule* (2008); and *Pity the Billionaire: The Hard-Times Swindle and the Unlikely Comeback of the Right* (2012).

The public be damned! I work for my stockholders.
—WILLIAM H. VANDERBILT, 1879

Break the rules. Stand apart. Keep your head. Go with your heart.
—TV commercial for Vanderbilt perfume, 1994

Capitalism is changing, obviously and drastically. From the moneyed pages of the *Wall Street Journal* to TV commercials for airlines and photocopiers we hear every day about the new order's globe-spanning, cyber-accumulating ways. But our notion about what's wrong with American life and how the figures responsible are to be confronted haven't changed much in thirty years. Call it, for convenience, the "countercultural idea." It holds that the paramount ailment of our society is conformity, a malady that has variously been described as over-organization, bureaucracy, homogeneity, hierarchy, logocentrism, technocracy, the Combine, the Apollonian.[1] We all know what it is and what it does. It transforms humanity into "organization man," into "the man in the gray flannel suit." It is "Moloch[2] whose mind is pure machinery," the "incomprehensible prison" that consumes "brains and imagination." It is artifice, starched shirts, tailfins, carefully mowed lawns, and always, always, the consciousness of impending nuclear destruction. It is a stiff, militaristic order that seeks to suppress instinct, to forbid sex and pleasure, to deny basic human impulses and individuality, to enforce through a rigid uniformity a meaningless plastic consumerism.

As this half of the countercultural idea originated during the 1950s, it is appropriate that the evils of conformity are most conveniently summarized with images of 1950s suburban correctness. You know, that land of sedate

---

[1]**Apollonian** An allusion to the god Apollo, a term for rational consciousness. –EDS.
[2]**Moloch** An ancient idol to whom children were sacrificed, used by Allen Ginsberg as a symbol for industrial America in his poem "Howl." –EDS.

music, sexual repression, deference to authority, Red Scares, and smiling white people standing politely in line to go to church. Constantly appearing as a symbol of arch-backwardness in advertising and movies, it is an image we find easy to evoke.

The ways in which this system are to be resisted are equally well understood and agreed-upon. The Establishment demands homogeneity; we revolt by embracing diverse, individual lifestyles. It demands self-denial and rigid adherence to convention; we revolt through immediate gratification, instinct uninhibited, and liberation of the libido and the appetites. Few have put it more bluntly than Jerry Rubin did in 1970: "Amerika says: Don't! The yippies say: Do It!" The countercultural idea is hostile to any law and every establishment. "Whenever we see a rule, we must break it," Rubin continued. "Only by breaking rules do we discover who we are." Above all rebellion consists of a sort of Nietzschean antinomianism,[3] an automatic questioning of rules, a rejection of whatever social prescriptions we've happened to inherit. Just Do It is the whole of the law.

The patron saints of the countercultural idea are, of course, the Beats, whose frenzied style and merry alienation still maintain a powerful grip on the American imagination. Even forty years after the publication of *On the Road*, the works of Kerouac, Ginsberg, and Burroughs remain the sine qua non of dissidence, the model for aspiring poets, rock stars, or indeed anyone who feels vaguely artistic or alienated. That frenzied sensibility of pure experience, life on the edge, immediate gratification, and total freedom from moral restraint, which the Beats first propounded back in those heady days when suddenly everyone could have their own TV and powerful V-8, has stuck with us through all the intervening years and become something of a permanent American style. Go to any poetry reading and you can see a string of junior Kerouacs go through the routine, upsetting cultural hierarchies by pushing themselves to the limit, straining for that gorgeous moment of original vice when Allen Ginsberg first read "Howl" in 1955 and the patriarchs of our fantasies recoiled in shock. The Gap may have since claimed Ginsberg and *USA Today* may run feature stories about the brilliance of the beloved Kerouac, but the rebel race continues today regardless, with ever-heightening shit-references calculated to scare Jesse Helms, talk about sex and smack that is supposed to bring the electricity of real life, and ever-more determined defiance of the repressive rules and mores of the American 1950s — rules and mores that by now we know only from movies.

But one hardly has to go to a poetry reading to see the countercultural 5 idea acted out. Its frenzied ecstasies have long since become an official aesthetic of consumer society, a monotheme of mass as well as adversarial culture. Turn on the TV and there it is instantly: the unending drama of consumer unbound and in search of an ever-heightened good time, the inescapable rock 'n' roll soundtrack, dreadlocks and ponytails bounding into Taco Bells, a drunken, swinging-camera epiphany of tennis shoes, outlaw soda pops, and

---

[3]**Nietzschean antinomianism** An allusion to the German philosopher Friedrich Nietzsche's challenging of conventional Christian morality. –EDS.

mind-bending dandruff shampoos. Corporate America, it turns out, no longer speaks in the voice of oppressive order that it did when Ginsberg moaned in 1956 that *Time* magazine was

> always telling me about responsibility. Business-
> men are serious. Movie producers are serious.
> Everybody's serious but me.

Nobody wants you to think they're serious today, least of all Time Warner. On the contrary: the Culture Trust is now our leader in the Ginsbergian search for kicks upon kicks. Corporate America is not an oppressor but a sponsor of fun, provider of lifestyle accoutrements, facilitator of carnival, our slang-speaking partner in the quest for that ever-more apocalyptic orgasm. The countercultural idea has become capitalist orthodoxy, its hunger for transgression upon transgression now perfectly suited to an economic-cultural regime that runs on ever-faster cyclings of the new; its taste for self-fulfillment and its intolerance for the confines of tradition now permitting vast latitude in consuming practices and lifestyle experimentation.

Consumerism is no longer about "conformity" but about "difference." Advertising teaches us not in the ways of puritanical self-denial (a bizarre notion on the face of it), but in orgiastic, never-ending self-fulfillment. It counsels not rigid adherence to the tastes of the herd but vigilant and constantly updated individualism. We consume not to fit in, but to prove, on the surface at least, that we are rock 'n' roll rebels, each one of us as rule-breaking and hierarchy-defying as our heroes of the '60s, who now pitch cars, shoes, and beer. This imperative of endless difference is today the genius at the heart of American capitalism, an eternal fleeing from "sameness" that satiates our thirst for the New with such achievements of civilization as the infinite brands of identical cola, the myriad colors and irrepressible variety of the cigarette rack at 7-Eleven.

As existential rebellion has become a more or less official style of Information Age capitalism, so has the countercultural notion of a static, repressive Establishment grown hopelessly obsolete. However the basic impulses of the countercultural idea may have disturbed a nation lost in Cold War darkness, they are today in fundamental agreement with the basic tenets of Information Age business theory. . . .

Contemporary corporate fantasy imagines a world of ceaseless, turbulent change, of centers that ecstatically fail to hold, of joyous extinction for the craven gray-flannel creature of the past. Businessmen today decorate the walls of their offices not with portraits of President Eisenhower and emblems of suburban order, but with images of extreme athletic daring, with sayings about "diversity" and "empowerment" and "thinking outside the box." They theorize their world not in the bar car of the commuter train, but in weepy corporate retreats at which they beat their tom-toms and envision themselves as part of the great avant-garde tradition of edge-livers, risk-takers, and ass-kickers. Their world is a place not of sublimation and conformity, but of "leadership" and bold talk about defying the herd. And there is nothing this new enlightened

species of businessman despises more than "rules" and "reason." The prominent culture-warriors of the right may believe that the counterculture was capitalism's undoing, but the antinomian businessmen know better. "One of the
t-shirt slogans of the sixties read, 'Question authority,'" the authors of *Reengineering the Corporation* write. "Process owners might buy their reengineering
team members the nineties version: 'Question assumptions.'"

The new businessman quite naturally gravitates to the slogans and sensibility of the rebel sixties to express his understanding of the new Information World. He is led in what one magazine calls "the business revolution" by
the office-park subversives it hails as "business activists," "change agents," and
"corporate radicals." . . . In television commercials, through which the new
American businessman presents his visions and self-understanding to the public, perpetual revolution and the gospel of rule-breaking are the orthodoxy of
the day. You only need to watch for a few minutes before you see one of these
slogans and understand the grip of antinomianism over the corporate mind:

> Sometimes You Gotta Break the Rules — Burger King
> If You Don't Like the Rules, Change Them — WXRT-FM
> The Rules Have Changed — Dodge
> The Art of Changing — Swatch
> There's no one way to do it. — Levi's
> This is different. Different is good. — Arby's
> Just Different From the Rest — Special Export beer
> The Line Has Been Crossed: The Revolutionary New Supra — Toyota
> Resist the Usual — the slogan of both Clash Clear Malt and Young &
>   Rubicam
> Innovate Don't Imitate — Hugo Boss
> Chart Your Own Course — Navigator Cologne
> It separates you from the crowd — Vision Cologne

In most, the commercial message is driven home with the vanguard iconography of the rebel: screaming guitars, whirling cameras, and startled old timers
who, we predict, will become an increasingly indispensable prop as consumers require ever-greater assurances that, Yes! You are a rebel! Just look at how
offended they are! . . .

The structure and thinking of American business have changed enormously 10
in the years since our popular conceptions of its problems and abuses were
formulated. In the meantime the mad frothings and jolly apolitical revolt of
Beat, despite their vast popularity and insurgent air, have become powerless
against a new regime that, one suspects, few of Beat's present-day admirers
and practitioners feel any need to study or understand. Today that beautiful countercultural idea, endorsed now by everyone from the surviving Beats
to shampoo manufacturers, is more the official doctrine of corporate America than it is a program of resistance. What we understand as "dissent" does
not subvert, does not challenge, does not even question the cultural faiths of
Western business. What David Rieff wrote of the revolutionary pretensions

of multiculturalism is equally true of the countercultural idea: "The more one reads in academic multiculturalist journals and in business publications, and the more one contrasts the speeches of CEOs and the speeches of noted multiculturalist academics, the more one is struck by the similarities in the way they view the world." What's happened is not co-optation or appropriation, but a simple and direct confluence of interest.

READING THE TEXT

1. In your own words, define what Frank means by the terms "countercultural idea" (para. 1) and its commodification.

2. How does Frank explain the relationship between the countercultural idea and conformity?

3. How were the Beats early progenitors of today's countercultural ideas, according to Frank?

4. In what ways does Frank believe that modern business has co-opted the countercultural idea?

5. How do you characterize Frank's tone in this selection? Does his tone enhance or detract from the forcefulness of his argument?

READING THE SIGNS

1. Analyze some current advertising in a magazine, on the Internet, or on television, determining whether the advertisements employ the countercultural idea as a marketing ploy. Use your observations as the basis for an essay in which you assess whether the countercultural idea and the associated "iconography of the rebel" (para. 9) still prevail in advertising, as Frank suggests.

2. In class, brainstorm a list of today's cultural rebels, either marketing characters or real people such as actors or musicians, and discuss why these rebels are considered attractive to their intended audience. Use the class discussion as a springboard for your own essay in which you analyze how the status of cultural rebels is a sign of the mood of modern American culture.

3. Write an essay in which you agree, disagree, or modify Frank's contention that marketing no longer promotes conformity but, rather, promotes "never-ending self-fulfillment" and "constantly updated individualism" (para. 6).

4. Visit a youth-oriented store such as Urban Outfitters, and analyze its advertising, product displays, exterior design, and interior decor. Write an essay in which you gauge the extent to which the store uses the iconography of the rebel as a marketing strategy.

5. Study a current magazine focused on business or on modern technology, such as *Bloomberg BusinessWeek*, *Business 2.0*, or *Wired*. To what extent does the magazine exemplify Frank's claim that modern business eschews conformity and embraces rebellion and rule breaking? Alternatively, you might analyze some corporate Web sites, preferably several from companies in the same industry. Keep in mind that different industries may have very different corporate cultures; the values and ideals that dominate high tech, for instance, may differ dramatically from those in finance, entertainment, or social services.

YOUR CARD.
YOUR TOWN.

Mlife
mlife.com

ClearChannel

BROUGHT TO YOU B(U)Y

The Signs of Advertising

A Requiem for Vampires

It could have been a scene from a new TV vampire series. Gathered in a dark forest clearing with a blazing campfire, sexy young vampires party it up, dancing, flirting, climbing trees — you know, doing vampire things. The camera cuts to the interior of an Audi driven by a hip-looking undead party animal who's got the vampire equivalent of liquid refreshments in a cooler on the passenger seat. "The party's arrived," he smirks as he motors into the clearing, pulls out his case of Type O+, and approaches the welcoming crowd.

Now, before you throw down this book in disdain with the conviction that any reference to vampires is just so hopelessly out-of-date, hold on, because a semiotic reading of this television advertisement from Super Bowl XLVI will reveal that that is exactly the point. The ad works precisely on the assumption that its target audience is getting sick of vampires, and it calculates its effect on the "Gotcha!" with which it concludes.

That happens as Mr. Undead Party Animal of 2012 gets out of his Audi with the headlights still on. Immediately, as his friends turn to greet him, they are vaporized by his Audi's light beams. He gets it too. And so we come to the punch line. As the remnants of the vampires and their party gear burn up in the darkness, a message appears on the screen: "Daylight, now in a headlight. Audi LED headlights." This is followed by a hashtag: "#SoLongVampires." End of ad.

The ad, of course, is a joke. But in order to get the joke, you have to be in on its premise. That premise, as calculated by the team that created the ad, is that you are yourself young (late teens to late twenties), that you tweet

---

Discussing the Signs of Advertising

Bring to class a print ad from a newspaper, a magazine, or a commercial Web site and in small groups discuss your semiotic reading of it. Be sure to ask, "Why am I being shown this or being told that?" How do the characters in the ad function as signs? What sort of people don't appear as characters? What cultural myths are invoked in this ad? What relationship do you see between those myths and the intended audience of the publication? Which ads do your group members respond to positively, and why? Which ads doesn't your group like?

---

or at least understand the mechanics of Twitter, and, most importantly, that you know all about the *Twilight / Vampire Diaries* phenomenon and that you are getting sick of it. The whole gag about LED headlights being like daylight turns upon your knowledge that traditional vampires can't stand daylight, which is made funnier by your satisfaction in seeing a bunch of *Twilight*-style vampires getting offed. The hope is that you will connect this satisfaction with Audi automobiles and that the next time you are in the market for a car, you'll pick Audi accordingly.

And Here's the Pitch

The preceding analysis is intended to illustrate how advertisements, too, are **signs** of cultural desire and consciousness. Indeed, advertising is not just show-and-tell. In effect, it's a form of behavior modification, a psychological strategy designed not only to inform you about products but also to persuade you to buy them by making associations between the product and certain pleasurable experiences or emotions that may have nothing to do with the product at all — like sex, or a promise of social superiority, or a simple laugh. Indeed, in no other area of popular culture can we find a purer example of the deliberate movement from objective **denotation** (the pictorial image of a product that appears in an advertisement) to subjective **connotation** (the feeling that the advertiser wishes to associate with the product), thereby transforming *things* into signs.

No one knows for sure just how effective a given ad campaign might be in inducing consumer spending by turning objects into signs, but no one is taking any chances either, as the annual increase in advertising costs for the Super Bowl reveals: At last count a thirty-second spot cost as much as $4 million. And it is the promise of ever-increasing advertising revenues that has turned Google into the darling of Wall Street. As James B. Twitchell has written, America is indeed an "ad culture," a society saturated with advertising.

Exploring the Signs of Advertising

Select one of the products advertised in the "Portfolio of Advertisements" (in this chapter), and design in your journal an alternative ad for that product. Consider what different images or cast of characters you could include. What different **mythologies**—and thus different values—could you use to pitch this product? Then freewrite on the significance of your alternative ad. If you have any difficulty imagining an alternative image for the product, what does that say about the power of advertising to control our view of the world? What does your choice of imagery and cultural myths say about you?

The New Marketing

With all the advertising out there, it is getting harder for advertisers to get our attention, or keep it, so they are constantly experimenting with new ways of getting us to listen. For years now, advertisers who are out to snag the youth market have staged their TV ads as if they were music videos—complete with rapid jump cuts, rap or rock music, and dizzying montage effects—to grab the attention of their target audience and to cause their viewers to associate the product with the pleasures of music videos. Self-conscious irony is also a popular technique to overcome the ad-savvy sophistication of generations of consumers who have become skeptical of advertising ploys.

More recently, a marketing strategy known as "stealth advertising" has appeared in selected locations. For example, companies pay people to do things like sit in Starbucks and play a game on a smartphone; when someone takes an interest, they talk about how cool the game is, and ask others to take their photo with this really cool smartphone—and by the way, they say, isn't this a really cool smartphone? The trick here is to advertise a smartphone without having people actually know they're being marketed to—just what the ad doctor ordered for advertising-sick consumers.

Then there are those stealth ads that appear on such Web sites as BuzzFeed and Yahoo! Interspersed among the actual news headlines are news-sponsored "headlines" that are really advertisements in disguise: advotainment, if you will. By masking the ad in the form of the content for which you went to the Web site in the first place, such a marketing strategy updates for the digital era the television trick of turning commercials into, say, sitcoms to accompany actual sitcoms.

But most profoundly, those with products and services to sell are coming to rely on marketing strategies based on data mining (a polite term for on-line spying) rather than attention getting. That is, by purchasing information about our online behavior from such titans as Facebook and Google, would-be advertisers attempt to determine just which consumers would be most susceptible to their ads. If you post on your Facebook page that you are planning a long trip, for example, you will immediately find airline ads on your screen. If you conduct a Google search for watches, ads for watches suddenly appear.

Many people do not mind this sort of marketing surveillance and in fact regard it as a way of receiving relevant product information more efficiently than the traditional hit-or-miss advertising approach. For such consumers, the convenience offered by online data mining offsets its invasiveness. For others, especially after the revelation in 2013 of the scale of the National Security Administration's phone and Internet surveillance, the corporate invasion of their privacy is more alarming. Whatever your own personal take on the matter happens to be, there is no question that personal privacy has been a major casualty of a digital culture that is mostly underwritten by the advertising revenues that flow from data mining.

As the years pass and the national mood shifts with the tides of history, new advertising techniques will surely emerge. So look around and ask yourself, as you're bombarded with advertising, "Why am I being shown *that*, or being told *this*?" Or cast yourself as the director of an ad, asking yourself what you would do to pitch a product; then look at what the advertiser has done. Pay attention to the way an ad's imagery is organized, its precise denotation. Every detail counts. Why are these colors used, or why is the ad in black and white? Why are cute stuffed animals chosen to pitch toilet paper? What are those people doing in that perfume commercial? Why the cowboy hat in an ad for jeans? Look, too, for what the ad doesn't include: Is it missing a clear view of the product itself or an ethnically diverse cast of characters? In short, when interpreting an ad, transform it into a text, going beyond what it denotes to what it connotes — to what it is trying to insinuate or say.

The Semiotic Foundation

There is perhaps no better field for semiotic analysis than advertising, for ads work characteristically by substituting signs for things, and by reading those signs you can discover the values and desires that advertisers seek to exploit. It has long been recognized that advertisements substitute images of desire for the actual products, selling images of fun, popularity, or sheer celebrity — promising a gratifying association with the likes of LeBron James if you get your next burger from McDonald's. Automobile commercials, for their part, are notorious for selling not transportation but fantasies of power, prestige, and sexual potency.

By substituting desirable images for concrete needs, modern advertising seeks to transform desire into necessity. You need food, for example, but it takes an ad campaign to convince you through attractive images that you need a Big Mac. Your job may require you to have a car, but it's an ad that persuades you that a Land Rover is necessary for your happiness. If advertising worked otherwise, it would simply present you with a functional profile of a product and let you decide whether it will do the job.

From the early twentieth century, advertisers have seen their task as the transformation of desire into necessity. In the 1920s and 1930s, for example, advertisements created elaborate story lines designed to convince readers that they needed this mouthwash to attract a spouse or that caffeine-free breakfast drink to avoid trouble on the job. In such ads, products were made to appear not only desirable but absolutely necessary. Without them, your very survival as a socially competent being would be in question. Many ads still work this way, particularly "guilt" ads that prey on your insecurities and fears. Deodorants and mouthwashes still are pitched in such a fashion, playing on our fear of smelling bad in public. Can you think of any other products whose ads play on guilt or shame? Do you find them to be effective?

The Commodification of Desire

Associating a logically unrelated desire with an actual product (as in pitching beer through sexual come-ons) can be called the **commodification** of desire. In other words, desire itself becomes the product that the advertiser is selling. This marketing of desire was recognized as early as the 1950s in Vance Packard's *The Hidden Persuaders*. In that book, Packard points out that by the 1950s America was well along in its historic shift from a producing to a consuming economy. The implications for advertisers were enormous. Since the American economy was increasingly dependent on the constant growth of consumption, as discussed in the Introduction to Chapter 1, manufacturers had to find ways to convince people to consume ever more goods. So they turned to the advertising mavens on Madison Avenue, who responded with ads that persuaded consumers to replace perfectly serviceable products with "new and improved" substitutions within an overall economy of planned design obsolescence.

America's transformation from a producer to a consumer economy also explains why while advertising is a worldwide phenomenon, it is nowhere as prevalent as it is here. Open a copy of *Vogue*. It is essentially a catalog, where scarcely a page is without an ad. Indeed, advertisers themselves call this plethora of advertising "clutter" that they must creatively "cut through" each time they design a new ad campaign. The ubiquity of advertising in our lives points to an economy in which people are constantly pushed to buy, as opposed to economies like China's, which despite recent rises in consumer interest, continues to emphasize constant increases in production. And desire is what opens the wallet.

While the basic logic of advertising may be similar from era to era, the content of an ad, and hence its significance, differs as popular culture changes. This is why a thorough analysis of a specific advertisement should include a historical survey of ads by the same company (and even from competing companies) for the same product, examining the *differences* that point

---

Reading Advertising Online

Many viewers watch the Super Bowl as much for the commercials as for the football game; indeed, the Super Bowl ads now have their own pregame public-relations hype and, in many a media outlet, their own postgame analysis and ratings. Visit *Advertising Age*'s report on the most recent Super Bowl (www.adage.com), and study the ads and the commentary about them. What images and styles predominate, and what do the dominant patterns say about popular taste? What does the public's avid interest in Super Bowl ads say about the power of advertising and its role in American culture?

---

to significance. (The Internet has made this task much easier, as enormous archives of both print and television ads can be found on Web sites such as YouTube and vintageadbrowser.com; a simple ad search entry will produce all sorts of relevant images and information.)

Looking at ads from different eras reveals just what was preoccupying Americans at different times in their history. Advertising in the 1920s, for instance, focused especially on its market's desires for improved social status. Ads for elocution and vocabulary lessons appealed to working- and lower-middle-class consumers, who were invited to fantasize that buying the product or service could help them enter the middle class. Meanwhile, middle-class consumers were invited to compare their enjoyment of the sponsor's product with that of the upper-class models shown happily slurping the advertised coffee or purchasing the advertised vacuum cleaner. Of course, things haven't changed that much since the twenties. Can you think of any ads that use this strategy today? How often are glamorous celebrities called in to make you identify with their "enjoyment" of a product?

One particularly amusing ad from the 1920s played on America's fear of communism in the wake of the Bolshevik revolution in Russia. "Is your washroom breeding Bolsheviks?" asks a print ad from the Scott Paper Company. The ad's lengthy copy explains how your bathroom might be doing so: If your company restroom is stocked with inferior paper towels, it says, discontent will proliferate among your employees and lead to subversive activities. RCA Victor and Campbell's Soup, we are assured, are no such breeding grounds of subversion, thanks to their contracts with Scott. You, too, can fight the good fight against communism by buying Scott towels, the ad suggests.

Populism versus Elitism

American advertising tends to swing in a pendulum motion between the status-conscious ads that dominated the twenties and the more populist approach of decades like the seventies, when *The Waltons* was a top TV series and country music and truck-driving cowboys lent their popular appeal to Madison Avenue. This swing between elitist and populist approaches in advertising reflects a basic division within the American dream itself, a mythic promise that at once celebrates democratic equality and encourages you to rise above the crowd, to be better than anyone else. Sometimes Americans are more attracted to one side than to the other, but there is bound to be a shift back to the other side when the thrill wears off. Thus, the populist appeal of the seventies (even disco had a distinct working-class flavor: recall John Travolta's character in *Saturday Night Fever*) gave way to the elitist eighties, and advertising followed. Products such as Gallo varietal wines, once considered barely a step up from jug wine, courted an upscale market, while Michelob light beer promised its fans that they "could have it all." Status advertising was all the rage in that glitzy, go-for-the-gold decade.

The nineties brought in a different kind of advertising that was neither populist nor elitist but was characterized by a cutting, edgy humor. This humor was especially common in dot.com ads that typically addressed the sort of young, irreverent, and rather cocky souls who were the backbone of what was then called the "New Economy" and is now called "Web 1.0." More broadly, edgy advertising appealed to twentysomething consumers who were coveted by the marketers who made possible such youth-oriented TV networks as Fox and the WB. Raised in the *Saturday Night Live* era, such consumers were accustomed to cutting humor and were particularly receptive to anything that smacked of attitude, and in the race to get their attention, advertisers followed with attitude-laden advertising.

The new millennium has seen an increasing tendency of advertising that focuses on demographically targeted markets. Such *niche marketing* is not new, but it has been intensified both by the growth of digital media and by the number of subscription television sources that cater to an enormous variety of viewer categories. Once upon a time, TV advertisers had only three networks to choose from: ABC, CBS, and NBC (and their affiliated stations). In those days, television ads were constructed to appeal to a relatively undifferentiated (though primarily white and middle class) national audience. Today, with audiences identifying their tastes and even identities through their cable choices and online behavior, advertisers tailor their ads much more specifically, choosing images and strategies designed to appeal to particular demographics and even to particular individuals. This development appears to be breaking up America's "common culture" into an atomized one. What effect this change may be having on our society could prove to be one of the most important semiotic questions of all.

The Readings

Jack Solomon begins the chapter with a semiotic analysis of American advertising, highlighting the ways in which conflicting mythologies of populism and elitism are exploited to push the goods. A paired set of readings by James B.

Twitchell and Steve Craig follows, revealing the elaborate psychological pro-filing schemes by which marketers categorize potential consumers and the gender-coded formulas that can be found in television advertisements. Next, Jennifer L. Pozner lambastes the chauvinistic critics of the Dove "Campaign for Real Beauty," while Gloria Steinem's insider's view of what goes on be-hind the scenes at women's magazines provides an exposé of the often-cozy relationships between magazine content and advertisers' demands. Juliet B. Schor then surveys the ways in which marketers try to turn kids into cool cus-tomers — perhaps somewhat ahead of their actual years — and Joseph Turow explores the brave new world of market spying, explaining how digital tech-nology enables advertisers to target their ads by following you around on the Internet. Julia B. Corbett concludes the readings with a look at marketers who seek to cash in on the "lucrative market of 'green consumers.'" The chapter then presents a "Portfolio of Advertisements" for you to decode for yourself.

When You Come Home

165

READING THE SIGNS

1. The advertisement on page 165 tells a story. What is it? You might start with the title of the ad.

2. To whom is the ad directed? What emotions does it play on? Be sure to provide evidence for your answers. What are the "dearest possessions" the ad refers to?

3. This ad originally appeared in 1914. If you were to update it for a magazine today, what changes would you make? Why?

JACK SOLOMON
Masters of Desire: The Culture of American Advertising

When the background music in a TV or radio automobile commercial is classical, you can be pretty certain that the ad is pitching a Lexus or a Mercedes. When it's country western, it's probably for Dodge or Chevy. English accents are popular in Jaguar ads, while a good western twang sure helps move pickup trucks. Whenever advertisers make use of status-oriented or common-folk-oriented cultural cues, they are playing on one of America's most fundamental contradictions, as Jack Solomon explains in this cultural analysis of American advertising. The contradiction is between the simultaneous desire for social superiority (elitism) and social equality (populism) that lies at the heart of the American dream. And one way or another, it offers a good way to pitch a product. Solomon, a professor of English at California State University, Northridge, is the author of *The Signs of Our Time* (1988), from which this selection is taken, and *Discourse and Reference in the Nuclear Age* (1988). He is also coeditor with Sonia Maasik of both *California Dreams and Realities* (2005) and this textbook.

Amongst democratic nations, men easily attain a certain equality of condition; but they can never attain as much as they desire.
— ALEXIS DE TOCQUEVILLE

On May 10, 1831, a young French aristocrat named Alexis de Tocqueville arrived in New York City at the start of what would become one of the most famous visits to America in our history. He had come to observe firsthand the institutions of the freest, most egalitarian society of the age, but what he found was a paradox. For behind America's mythic promise of equal opportunity, Tocqueville discovered a desire for *unequal* social rewards, a ferocious competition for privilege and distinction. As he wrote in his monumental study, *Democracy in America*:

> When all privileges of birth and fortune are abolished, when all professions are accessible to all, and a man's own energies may place him at the top of any one of them, an easy and unbounded career seems open to his ambition. . . . But this is an erroneous notion, which is corrected by daily experience. [For when] men are nearly alike, and all follow the same track, it is very difficult for any one individual to walk quick and cleave a way through the same throng which surrounds and presses him.

Yet walking quick and cleaving a way is precisely what Americans dream of. We Americans dream of rising above the crowd, of attaining a social summit beyond the reach of ordinary citizens. And therein lies the paradox.

The American dream, in other words, has two faces: the one communally egalitarian and the other competitively elitist. This contradiction is no accident; it is fundamental to the structure of American society. Even as America's great myth of equality celebrates the virtues of mom, apple pie, and the girl or boy next door, it also lures us to achieve social distinction, to rise above the crowd and bask alone in the glory. This land is your land and this land is my land, Woody Guthrie's populist anthem tells us, but we keep trying to increase the "my" at the expense of the "your." Rather than fostering contentment, the American dream breeds desire, a longing for a greater share of the pie. It is as if our society were a vast high-school football game, with the bulk of the participants noisily rooting in the stands while, deep down, each of them is wishing he or she could be the star quarterback or head cheerleader.

For the semiotician, the contradictory nature of the American myth of equality is nowhere written so clearly as in the signs that American advertisers use to manipulate us into buying their wares. "Manipulate" is the word here, not "persuade"; for advertising campaigns are not sources of product information, they are exercises in behavior modification. Appealing to our subconscious emotions rather than to our conscious intellects, advertisements are designed to exploit the discontentments fostered by the American dream, the constant desire for social success and the material rewards that accompany it. America's consumer economy runs on desire, and advertising stokes the engines by transforming common objects — from peanut butter to political candidates — into signs of all the things that Americans covet most.

But by semiotically reading the signs that advertising agencies manufacture to stimulate consumption, we can plot the precise state of desire in the audiences to which they are addressed. Let's look at a representative sample of ads and what they say about the emotional climate of the country and the fast-changing trends of American life. Because ours is a highly diverse, pluralistic society, various advertisements may say different things depending on their intended audiences, but in every case they say something about America, about the status of our hopes, fears, desires, and beliefs.

We'll begin with two ad campaigns conducted by the same company that bear out Alexis de Tocqueville's observations about the contradictory nature of American society: General Motors' campaigns for its Cadillac and Chevrolet lines. First, consider an early magazine ad for the Cadillac Allanté. Appearing as a full-color, four-page insert in *Time*, the ad seems to say "I'm special—and so is this car" even before we've begun to read it. Rather than being printed on the ordinary, flimsy pages of the magazine, the Allanté spread appears on glossy coated stock. The unwritten message is that an extraordinary car deserves an extraordinary advertisement, and that both car and ad are aimed at an extraordinary consumer, or at least one who wishes to appear extraordinary compared to ordinary citizens.

Ads of this kind work by creating symbolic associations between their product and what the consumers to whom they are addressed most covet. It is significant, then, that this ad insists that the Allanté is virtually an Italian rather than an American car; as its copy runs, "Conceived and Commissioned by America's Luxury Car Leader—Cadillac" but "Designed and Handcrafted by Europe's Renowned Design Leader—Pininfarina, SpA, of Turin, Italy." This is not simply a piece of product information, it's a sign of the prestige that European luxury cars enjoy in today's automotive marketplace. Once the luxury car of choice for America's status drivers, Cadillac has fallen far behind its European competitors in the race for the prestige market. So the Allanté essentially represents Cadillac's decision, after years of resisting the trend toward European cars, to introduce its own European import—whose high cost is clearly printed on the last page of the ad. . . .

American companies manufacture status symbols because American consumers want them. As Alexis de Tocqueville recognized a century and a half ago, the competitive nature of democratic societies breeds a desire for social distinction, a yearning to rise above the crowd. But given the fact that those who do make it to the top in socially mobile societies have often risen from the lower ranks, they still look like everyone else. In the socially immobile societies of aristocratic Europe, generations of fixed social conditions produced subtle class signals. The accent of one's voice, the shape of one's nose, or even the set of one's chin immediately communicated social status. Aside from the nasal bray and uptilted head of the Boston Brahmin, Americans do not have any native sets of personal status signals. If it weren't for his Mercedes-Benz and Manhattan townhouse, the parvenu Wall Street millionaire often couldn't be distinguished from the man who tailors his suits. Hence, the demand for status symbols, for the objects that mark one off as a social success, is particularly strong in democratic nations—stronger even than in aristocratic societies, where the aristocrat so often looks and sounds different from everyone else.

Status symbols, then, are signs that identify their possessors' place in a social hierarchy, markers of rank and prestige. We can all think of any number of status symbols — Rolls-Royces, Beverly Hills mansions, even shar-pei puppies (whose rareness and expense has rocketed them beyond Russian wolfhounds as status pets and has even inspired whole lines of wrinkle-faced stuffed toys) — but how do we know that something *is* a status symbol? The explanation is quite simple: When an object (or puppy!) either costs a lot of money or requires influential connections to possess, anyone who possesses it must also possess the necessary means and influence to acquire it. The object itself really doesn't matter, since it ultimately disappears behind the presumed social potency of its owner. Semiotically, what matters is the signal it sends, its value as a sign of power. One traditional sign of social distinction is owning a country estate and enjoying the peace and privacy that attend it. Advertisements for Mercedes-Benz, Jaguar, and Audi automobiles thus frequently feature drivers motoring quietly along a country road, presumably on their way to or from their country houses.

Advertisers have been quick to exploit the status signals that belong to body language as well. As Hegel observed in the early nineteenth century, it is an ancient aristocratic prerogative to be seen by the lower orders without having to look at them in return. Tilting his chin high in the air and gazing down at the world under hooded eyelids, the aristocrat invites observation while refusing to look back. We can find such a pose exploited in an advertisement for Cadillac Seville in which we see an elegantly dressed woman out for a drive with her husband in their new Cadillac. If we look closely at the woman's body language, we can see her glance inwardly with a satisfied smile on her face but not outward toward the camera that represents our gaze. She is glad to be seen by us in her Seville, but she isn't interested in looking at *us*!

Ads that are aimed at a broader market take the opposite approach. If the American dream encourages the desire to "arrive," to vault above the mass, it also fosters a desire to be popular, to "belong." Populist commercials accordingly transform products into signs of belonging, utilizing such common icons as country music, small-town life, family picnics, and farmyards. All of these icons are incorporated in GM's Heartbeat of America campaign for its Chevrolet line. Unlike the Seville commercial, the faces in the Chevy ads look straight at us and smile. Dress is casual; the mood upbeat. Quick camera cuts take us from rustic to suburban to urban scenes, creating an American montage filmed from sea to shining sea. We all "belong" in a Chevy.

Where price alone doesn't determine the market for a product, advertisers can go either way. Both Johnnie Walker and Jack Daniel's are better-grade whiskies, but where a Johnnie Walker ad appeals to the buyer who wants a mark of aristocratic distinction in his liquor, a Jack Daniel's ad emphasizes the down-home, egalitarian folksiness of its product. Johnnie Walker associates itself with such conventional status symbols as sable coats, Rolls-Royces, and black gold; Jack Daniel's gives us a Good Ol' Boy in overalls. In fact, Jack Daniel's Good Ol' Boy is an icon of backwoods independence, recalling the days of the moonshiner and the Whisky Rebellion of 1794. Evoking emotions quite at odds with those stimulated in Johnnie Walker ads, the advertisers of Jack Daniel's transform their product into a sign of America's populist tradition. The fact that both ads successfully sell whisky is itself a sign of the dual nature of the American dream. . . .

Populist advertising is particularly effective in the face of foreign competition. When Americans feel threatened from the outside, they tend to circle the wagons and temporarily forget their class differences. In the face of the Japanese automotive "invasion," Chrysler runs populist commercials in which Lee Iacocca joins the simple folk who buy his cars as the jingle "Born in America" blares in the background. Seeking to capitalize on the popularity of Bruce Springsteen's *Born in the USA* album, these ads gloss over Springsteen's ironic lyrics in a vast display of flag-waving. Chevrolet's Heartbeat of America campaign attempts to woo American motorists away from Japanese automobiles by appealing to their patriotic sentiments.

The patriotic iconography of these campaigns also reflects the general cultural mood of the early to mid-1980s. After a period of national anguish in the wake of the Vietnam War and the Iran hostage crisis, America went on a patriotic binge. American athletic triumphs in the Lake Placid and Los Angeles Olympics introduced a sporting tone into the national celebration, often making international affairs appear like one great Olympiad in which America was always going for the gold. In response, advertisers began to do their own flag-waving.

The mood of advertising during this period was definitely upbeat. Even deodorant commercials, which traditionally work on our self-doubts and fears of social rejection, jumped on the bandwagon. In the guilty sixties, we had ads like the Ice Blue Secret campaign with its connotations of guilt and shame. In the feel-good Reagan eighties, Sure deodorant commercials featured images of triumphant Americans throwing up their arms in victory to reveal — no wet marks! Deodorant commercials once had the moral echo of Nathaniel Hawthorne's guilt-ridden *The Scarlet Letter*; in the early eighties they had all the moral subtlety of *Rocky IV*, reflecting the emotions of a Vietnam-weary nation eager to embrace the imagery of America Triumphant. . . .

Live the Fantasy

By reading the signs of American advertising, we can conclude that America 15 is a nation of fantasizers, often preferring the sign to the substance and easily enthralled by a veritable Fantasy Island of commercial illusions. Critics of Madison Avenue often complain that advertisers create consumer desire, but semioticians don't think the situation is that simple. Advertisers may shape consumer fantasies, but they need raw material to work with, the subconscious dreams and desires of the marketplace. As long as these desires remain unconscious, advertisers will be able to exploit them. But by bringing the fantasies to the surface, you can free yourself from advertising's often hypnotic grasp.

I can think of no company that has more successfully seized upon the subconscious fantasies of the American marketplace — indeed the world marketplace—than McDonald's. By no means the first nor the only ha. burger chain in the United States, McDonald's emerged victorious in the "burger wars" by transforming hamburgers into signs of all that was desirable in American life. Other chains like Wendy's, Burger King, and Jack-In-The-Box continue to advertise and sell widely, but no company approaches McDonald's transformation of itself into a symbol of American culture.

McDonald's success can be traced to the precision of its advertising. Instead of broadcasting a single "one-size-fits-all" campaign at a time, McDonald's pitches its burgers simultaneously at different age groups, different classes, even different races (Budweiser beer, incidentally, has succeeded in the same way). For children, there is the Ronald McDonald campaign, which presents a fantasy world that has little to do with hamburgers in any rational sense but a great deal to do with the emotional desires of kids. Ronald McDonald and his friends are signs that recall the Muppets, *Sesame Street*, the circus, toys, storybook illustrations, even *Alice in Wonderland*. Such signs do not signify hamburgers. Rather, they are displayed in order to prompt in the child's mind an automatic association of fantasy, fun, and McDonald's.

The same approach is taken in ads aimed at older audiences—teens, adults, and senior citizens. In the teen-oriented ads we may catch a fleeting glimpse of a hamburger or two, but what we are really shown is a teenage fantasy: groups of hip and happy adolescents singing, dancing, and cavorting together. Fearing loneliness more than anything else, adolescents quickly respond to the group appeal of such commercials. "Eat a Big Mac," these ads say, "and you won't be stuck home alone on Saturday night."

To appeal to an older and more sophisticated audience no longer so afraid of not belonging and more concerned with finding a place to go out to at night, McDonald's has designed the elaborate "Mac Tonight" commercials, which have for their backdrop a nightlit urban skyline and at their center a cabaret pianist with a moon-shaped head, a glad manner, and Blues Brothers shades. Such signs prompt an association of McDonald's with nightclubs and urban sophistication, persuading us that McDonald's is a place not only for breakfast or lunch but for dinner too, as if it were a popular off-Broadway nightspot, a place to see and be seen. Even the parody of Kurt Weill's "Mack the Knife" theme song that Mac the Pianist performs is a sign, a subtle signal to the sophisticated hamburger eater able to recognize the origin of the tune in Bertolt Brecht's *Threepenny Opera*.

For yet older customers, McDonald's has designed a commercial around 20 the fact that it employs a large number of retirees and seniors. In one such ad, we see an elderly man leaving his pretty little cottage early in the morning to start work as "the new kid" at McDonald's, and then we watch him during his first day on the job. Of course he is a great success, outdoing everyone else with his energy and efficiency, and he returns home in the evening to a loving wife and a happy home. One would almost think that the ad was a kind of moving "help wanted" sign (indeed, McDonald's *was* hiring elderly employees at the time), but it's really just directed at consumers. Older viewers can see themselves wanted and appreciated in the ad—and perhaps be distracted from the rationally uncomfortable fact that many senior citizens take such jobs because of financial need and thus may be unlikely to own the sort of home that one sees in the commercial. But realism isn't the point here. This is fantasyland, a dream world promising instant gratification no matter what the facts of the matter may be.

Practically the only fantasy that McDonald's doesn't exploit is the fantasy of sex. This is understandable, given McDonald's desire to present itself as a family restaurant. But everywhere else, sexual fantasies, which have always had an important place in American advertising, dominate the advertising scene. You expect sexual come-ons in ads for perfume or cosmetics or jewelry—after all, that's what they're selling—but for room deodorizers? In a magazine ad for Claire Burke home fragrances, for example, we see a well-dressed couple cavorting about their bedroom in what looks like a cheery preparation for sadomasochistic exercises. Jordache and Calvin Klein pitch blue jeans as props for teenage sexuality. The phallic appeal of automobiles, traditionally an implicit feature in automotive advertising, becomes quite explicit in a Dodge commercial that shifts back and forth from shots of a young man in an automobile to teasing glimpses of a woman—his date—as she dresses in her apartment.

The very language of today's advertisements is charged with sexuality. Products in the more innocent fifties were "new and improved," but everything in the eighties is "hot!"—as in "hot woman," or sexual heat. Cars are "hot." Movies are "hot." An ad for Valvoline pulses to the rhythm of a "heat wave, burning in my car." Sneakers get red hot in a magazine ad for Travel Fox athletic shoes in which we see male and female figures, clad only in Travel Fox shoes, apparently in the act of copulation—an ad that earned one of *Adweek*'s annual "badvertising" awards for shoddy advertising.

The sexual explicitness of contemporary advertising is a sign not so much of American sexual fantasies as of the lengths to which advertisers will go to get attention. Sex never fails as an attention-getter, and in a particularly competitive, and expensive, era for American marketing, advertisers like to bet on a sure thing. Ad people refer to the proliferation of TV, radio, newspaper, magazine, and billboard ads as "clutter," and nothing cuts through the clutter like sex.

By showing the flesh, advertisers work on the deepest, most coercive human emotions of all. Much sexual coercion in advertising, however, is a sign of a desperate need to make certain that clients are getting their money's worth. The appearance of advertisements that refer directly to the prefabricated fantasies of Hollywood is a sign of a different sort of desperation: a desperation for ideas. With the rapid turnover of advertising campaigns mandated by the need to cut through the "clutter," advertisers may be hard pressed for new ad concepts, and so they are more and more frequently turning to already-established models. In the early 1980s, for instance, Pepsi-Cola ran a series of ads broadly alluding to Steven Spielberg's *E.T.* In one such ad, we see a young boy, who, like the hero of *E.T.*, witnesses an extraterrestrial visit. The boy is led to a soft-drink machine where he pauses to drink a can of Pepsi as the spaceship he's spotted flies off into the universe. The relationship between the ad and the movie, accordingly, is a parasitical one, with the ad taking its life from the creative body of the film. . . .

Madison Avenue has also framed ad campaigns around the cultural 25 prestige of high-tech machinery. This is especially the case with sports cars, whose high-tech appeal is so powerful that some people apparently fantasize about *being* sports cars. At least, this is the conclusion one might draw from a Porsche commercial that asked its audience, "If you *were* a car, what kind of car would you be?" As a candy-red Porsche speeds along a rain-slick forest road, the ad's voice-over describes all the specifications you'd want to have if you *were* a sports car. "If you were a car," the commercial concludes, "you'd be a Porsche."

In his essay "Car Commercials and *Miami Vice*," Todd Gitlin explains the semiotic appeal of such ads as those in the Porsche campaign. Aired at the height of what may be called America's "myth of the entrepreneur," these commercials were aimed at young corporate managers who imaginatively identified with the "lone wolf" image of a Porsche speeding through the woods. Gitlin points out that such images cater to the fantasies of faceless corporate men who dream of entrepreneurial glory, of striking out on their own like John DeLorean and telling the boss to take his job and shove it. But as DeLorean's spectacular failure demonstrates, the life of the entrepreneur can be extremely risky. So rather than having to go it alone and take the risks that accompany entrepreneurial independence, the young executive can substitute fantasy for reality by climbing into his Porsche — or at least that's what Porsche's advertisers wanted him to believe.

But there is more at work in the Porsche ads than the fantasies of corporate America. Ever since Arthur C. Clarke and Stanley Kubrick teamed up to present us with HAL 9000, the demented computer of *2001: A Space Odyssey*, the American imagination has been obsessed with the melding of man and machine. First there was television's *Six Million Dollar Man*, and then movieland's *Star Wars*, *Blade Runner*, and *Robocop*, fantasy visions of a future dominated by machines. Androids haunt our imaginations as machines seize the initiative. *Time* magazine's "Man of the Year" for 1982 was a computer. Robot-built automobiles appeal to drivers who spend their days in front of computer screens — perhaps designing robots. When so much power and prestige is being given to high-tech machines, wouldn't you rather be a Porsche?

In short, the Porsche campaign is a sign of a new mythology that is emerging before our eyes, a myth of the machine, which is replacing the myth of the human. The iconic figure of the little tramp caught up in the cogs of industrial production in Charlie Chaplin's *Modern Times* signified a humanistic revulsion to the age of the machine. Human beings, such icons said, were superior to machines. Human values should come first in the moral order of things. But as Edith Milton suggests in her essay "The Track of the Mutant," we are now coming to believe that machines are superior to human beings, that mechanical nature is superior to human nature. Rather than being threatened by machines, we long to merge with them. *The Six Million Dollar Man* is one iconic figure in the new mythology; Harrison Ford's sexual coupling with an android is another. In such an age it should come as little wonder that computer-synthesized Max Headroom should be a commercial spokesman for Coca-Cola, or that Federal Express should design a series of TV ads featuring mechanical-looking human beings revolving around strange and powerful machines.

Fear and Trembling in the Marketplace

While advertisers play on and reflect back at us our fantasies about everything from fighter pilots to robots, they also play on darker imaginings. If dream and desire can be exploited in the quest for sales, so can nightmare and fear.

The nightmare equivalent of America's populist desire to "belong," for 30 example, is the fear of not belonging, of social rejection, of being different. Advertisements for dandruff shampoos, mouthwashes, deodorants, and laundry detergents ("Ring around the Collar!") accordingly exploit such fears, bullying us into consumption. Although ads of this type were still around in the 1980s, they were particularly common in the fifties and early sixties, reflecting a society still reeling from the witch-hunts of the McCarthy years. When any sort of social eccentricity or difference could result in a public denunciation and the loss of one's job or even liberty, Americans were keen to conform and be like everyone else. No one wanted to be "guilty" of smelling bad or of having a dirty collar.

"Guilt" ads characteristically work by creating narrative situations in which someone is "accused" of some social "transgression," pronounced guilty, and then offered the sponsor's product as a means of returning to "innocence." Such ads, in essence, are parodies of ancient religious rituals of guilt and atonement, whereby sinning humanity is offered salvation through the agency of priest and church. In the world of advertising, a product takes the place of the priest, but the logic is quite similar.

In commercials for Wisk detergent, for example, we witness the drama of a hapless housewife and her husband as they are mocked by the jeering voices of children shouting "Ring around the Collar!" "Oh, those dirty rings!" the housewife groans in despair. It's as if she and her husband were being stoned by an angry crowd. But there's hope, there's help, there's Wisk. Cleansing her soul of sin as well as her husband's, the housewife launders his shirts with Wisk, and behold, his collars are clean. Product salvation is only as far as the supermarket. . . .

If guilt looks backward in time to past transgressions, fear, like desire, faces forward, trembling before the future. In the late 1980s, a new kind of fear commercial appeared, one whose narrative played on the worries of young corporate managers struggling up the ladder of success. Representing the nightmare equivalent of the elitist desire to "arrive," ads of this sort created images of failure, story lines of corporate defeat. In one ad for Apple computers, for example, a group of junior executives sits around a table with the boss as he asks each executive how long it will take his or her department to complete some publishing jobs. "Two or three days," answers one nervous executive. "A week, on overtime," a tight-lipped woman responds. But one young up-and-comer can have everything ready tomorrow, today, or yesterday, because his department uses a Macintosh desktop publishing system. Guess who'll get the next promotion?

For other markets, there are other fears. If McDonald's presents senior citizens with bright fantasies of being useful and appreciated beyond retirement, companies like Secure Horizons dramatize senior citizens' fears of being caught short by a major illness. Running its ads in the wake of budgetary cuts in the Medicare system, Secure Horizons designed a series of commercials featuring a pleasant old man named Harry — who looks and sounds rather like Carroll O'Connor — who tells us the story of the scare he got during his wife's recent illness. Fearing that next time Medicare won't cover the bills, he has purchased supplemental health insurance from Secure Horizons and now securely tends his roof-top garden. . . .

The Future of an Illusion

There are some signs in the advertising world that Americans are getting fed 35 up with fantasy advertisements and want to hear some straight talk. Weary of extravagant product claims and irrelevant associations, consumers trained by years of advertising to distrust what they hear seem to be developing an immunity to commercials. At least, this is the semiotic message I read in the "new realism" advertisements of the eighties, ads that attempt to convince you that what you're seeing is the real thing, that the ad is giving you the straight dope, not advertising hype.

You can recognize the "new realism" by its camera techniques. The lighting is usually subdued to give the ad the effect of being filmed without studio lighting or special filters. The scene looks gray, as if the blinds were drawn. The camera shots are jerky and off-angle, often zooming in for sudden and unflattering close-ups, as if the cameraman were an amateur with a home video recorder. In a "realistic" ad for AT&T, for example, we are treated to a monologue by a plump stockbroker — his plumpness intended as a sign that he's for real and not just another actor — who tells us about the problems he's had with his phone system (not AT&T's) as the camera jerks around, generally filming him from below as if the photographer couldn't quite fit the equipment into the crammed office. "This is no fancy advertisement," the ad tries to convince us, "this is sincere."

An ad for Miller draft beer tries the same approach, re-creating the effect of an amateur videotape of a wedding celebration. Camera shots shift suddenly from group to group. The picture jumps. Bodies are poorly framed. The color is washed out. Like the beer it is pushing, the ad is supposed to strike us as being "as real as it gets."

Such ads reflect a desire for reality in the marketplace, a weariness with Madison Avenue illusions. But there's no illusion like the illusion of reality. Every special technique that advertisers use to create their "reality effects" is, in fact, more unrealistic than the techniques of "illusory" ads. The world, in reality, doesn't jump around when you look at it. It doesn't appear in subdued gray tones. Our eyes don't have zoom lenses, and we don't look at things with our heads cocked to one side. The irony of the "new realism" is that it is more unrealistic, more artificial, than the ordinary run of television advertising.

But don't expect any truly realistic ads in the future, because a realistic advertisement is a contradiction in terms. The logic of advertising is entirely semiotic: It substitutes signs for things, framed visions of consumer desire for the thing itself. The success of modern advertising, its penetration into every corner of American life, reflects a culture that has itself chosen illusion over reality. At a time when political candidates all have professional image-makers attached to their staffs, and the president of the United States can be an actor who once sold shirt collars, all the cultural signs are pointing to more illusions in our lives rather than fewer — a fecund breeding ground for the world of the advertiser.

Reading the Text

1. Describe in your own words the paradox of the American dream, as Solomon sees it.

2. In Solomon's view, why do status symbols work particularly well in manipulating American consumers?

3. Why, in Solomon's view, has McDonald's been so successful in its ad campaigns?

4. What is a "guilt" ad (para. 31), according to Solomon, and how does it affect consumers?

5. What relationship does Solomon find between the "new realism" (para. 35) of some ads and the paradoxes of the American dream?

Reading the Signs

1. **CONNECTING TEXTS**   The American political scene has changed since the late 1980s, when this essay was first published. Do you believe the contradiction between populism and elitism that Solomon describes still affects American advertising and media? In an analytic essay, argue your case. Be sure to discuss specific media examples. To develop your ideas, you might consult Thomas Frank's "Commodify Your Dissent" (p. 150).

2. **CONNECTING TEXTS**   In television advertising, the most coveted market is the eighteen to forty-nine age group, a cohort that often includes what James B. Twitchell ("What We Are to Advertisers," p. 177) describes as "experiencers"

and "strivers." To what extent do the TV ads you view display a populist or elitist ethos? Or do you find that the ads do not harbor class sensitivity? How do you explain your observations?

3. Bring to class a general-interest magazine (such as *People* or *O: The Oprah Magazine*), and in small groups study the advertising. Do the ads tend to have an elitist or a populist appeal? What relationship do you see between the appeal you identify and the magazine's target readership? Present your group's findings to the class.

4. In class, brainstorm a list of status symbols common in advertising today. Then discuss what groups they appeal to and why. Can you detect any patterns based on gender, ethnicity, or age?

5. Visit your college library, and locate an issue of a popular magazine from earlier decades, such as the 1930s or 1940s. Then write an essay in which you compare and contrast the advertising found in the early issue with that in a current issue of the same publication. What similarities and differences do you find in the myths underlying the advertising, and what is the significance of these similarities and differences?

CREATING CONSUMERS

JAMES B. TWITCHELL
What We Are to Advertisers

Are you a "believer" or a "striver," an "achiever" or a "struggler," an "experiencer" or a "maker"? Or do you have no idea what we're talking about? If you don't, James Twitchell explains it all to you in this selection in which the psychological profiling schemes of American advertising are laid bare. For like it or not, advertisers have, or think they have, your number, and they will pitch their products according to the personality profile they have concocted for you. And the really spooky thing is that they're often right. A prolific writer on American advertising and culture, Twitchell's books include *Adcult USA: The Triumph of Advertising in American Culture* (1996); *Twenty Ads That Shook the World* (2000); *Living It Up: Our Love Affair with Luxury* (2002); *Lead Us into Temptation: The Triumph of American Materialism* (1999), from which this selection is taken; and *Branded Nation* (2004). His most recent book is *Look Away Dixieland* (2011).

Mass production means mass marketing, and mass marketing means the creation of mass stereotypes. Like objects on shelves, we too cluster in groups. We find meaning together. As we mature, we move from shelf to shelf, from aisle to aisle, zip code to zip code, from lifestyle to lifestyle, between what the historian Daniel Boorstin calls "consumption communities." Finally, as full-grown consumers, we stabilize in our buying, and hence meaning-making, patterns. Advertisers soon lose interest in us not just because we stop buying but because we have stopped changing brands.

The object of advertising is not just to brand parity objects but also to brand consumers as they move through these various communities. To explain his job, Rosser Reeves, the master of hard-sell advertising like the old Anacin ads, used to hold up two quarters and claim his job was to make you believe they were different, and, more importantly, that one was better than the other. Hence, at the macro level the task of advertising is to convince different sets of consumers — target groups — that the quarter they observe is somehow different in meaning and value than the same quarter seen by their across-the-tracks neighbors.

In adspeak, this is called *positioning*. "I could have positioned Dove as a detergent bar for men with dirty hands," David Ogilvy famously said, "but I chose to position it as a toilet bar for women with dry skin." Easy to say, hard to do. But if Anheuser-Busch wants to maximize its sales, the soccer mom driving the shiny Chevy Suburban must feel she drinks a different Budweiser than the roustabout in the rusted-out Chevy pickup.[1]

The study of audiences goes by any number of names: psychographics, ethnographics, macrosegmentation, to name a few, but they are all based on the ineluctable principle that birds of a feather flock together. The object of much consumer research is not to try to twist their feathers so that they will flock to your product, but to position your product in such a place that they will have to fly by it and perhaps stop to roost. After roosting, they will eventually think that this is a part of their flyway and return to it again and again.

Since different products have different meanings to different audiences,   5 segmentation studies are crucial. Although agencies have their own systems for naming these groups and their lifestyles, the current supplier of much raw data about them is a not-for-profit organization, the Stanford Research Institute (SRI).

---

[1]Cigarette companies were the first to find this out in the 1930s, much to their amazement. Blindfolded smokers couldn't tell what brand they were smoking. Instead of making cigarettes with different tastes, it was easier to make different advertising claims to different audiences. Cigarettes are hardly unique. Ask beer drinkers why they prefer a particular brand and invariably they tell you: "It's the taste," "This goes down well," "This is light and refreshing," "This is rich and smooth." They will say this about a beer that has been described as their brand, but is not. Anheuser-Busch, for instance, spent three dollars per barrel in 1980 to market a barrel of beer; now they spend nine dollars. Since the cost to reach a thousand television households has doubled at the same time the audience has segmented (thanks to cable), why not go after a particular market segment by tailoring ads emphasizing, in different degrees, the Clydesdales, Ed McMahon, Beechwood aging, the red and white can, dates certifying freshness, the spotted dog, the Eagle, as well as "the crisp, clean taste." While you cannot be all things to all people, the object of advertising is to be as many things to as many segments as possible. The ultimate object is to convince as many segments as possible that "This Bud's for you" is a sincere statement.

The "psychographic" system of SRI is called acronomically VALS (now VALS2+), short for Values and Lifestyle System. Essentially this schematic is based on the common-sense view that consumers are motivated "to acquire products, services, and experiences that provide satisfaction and give shape, substance, and character to their identities" in bundles. The more "resources" (namely money, but also health, self-confidence, and energy) each group has, the more likely they will buy "products, services, and experiences" of the group they associate with. But resources are not the only determinant. Customers are also motivated by such ineffables as principles, status, and action. When SRI describes these various audiences, they peel apart like this (I have provided them an appropriate car to show their differences):

- Actualizers: These people at the top of the pyramid are the ideal of everyone but advertisers. They have "it" already, or will soon. They are sophisticated, take-charge people interested in independence and character. They don't need new things; in fact, they already have their things. If not, they already know what "the finer things" are and won't be told. They don't need a new car, but if they do they'll read *Consumer Reports*. They do not need a hood ornament on their car.

- Fulfilled: Here are mature, satisfied, comfortable souls who support the status quo in almost every way. Often they are literally or figuratively retired. They value functionality, durability, and practicality. They drive something called a "town car," which is made by all the big three automakers.

- Believers: As the word expresses, these people support traditional codes of family, church, and community, wearing good Republican cloth coats. As consumers they are predictable, favoring American products and recognizable brands. They regularly attend church and Walmart, and they are transported there in their mid-range automobile like an Oldsmobile. Whether Oldsmobile likes it or not, they do indeed drive "your father's Oldsmobile."

Moving from principle-oriented consumers who look inside to status-driven consumers who look out to others, we find the Achievers and Strivers.

- Achievers: If consumerism has an ideal, here it is. Bingo! Wedded to their jobs as a source of duty, reward, and prestige, these are the people who not only favor the establishment but are the establishment. They like the concept of prestige. Not only are they successful, they demonstrate their success by buying such objects as prestigious cars to show it. They like hood ornaments. They see no contradiction in driving a Land Rover in Manhattan.

- Strivers: A young Striver is fine; he will possibly mature into an Achiever. But an old Striver can be nasty; he may well be bitter. Since they are unsure of themselves, they are eager to be branded as long as the brand is elevating. Money defines success and they don't have enough of it.

Being a yuppie is fine as long as the prospect of upward mobility is possible. Strivers like foreign cars even if it means only leasing a BMW.

[And then there] are those driven less by the outside world but by their desire to participate, to be part of a wider world.

- Experiencers: Here is life on the edge—enthusiastic, impulsive, and even reckless. Their energy finds expression in sports, social events, and "doing something." Politically and personally uncommitted, experiencers are an advertiser's dream come true as they see consumption as fulfillment and are willing to spend a high percent of their disposable income to attain it. When you wonder about who could possibly care how fast a car will accelerate from zero to sixty m.p.h., they care.

- Makers: Here is the practical side of Experiencers; they like to build things and they experience the world by working on it. Conservative, suspicious, respectful, they like to do things in and to their homes, like adding a room, canning vegetables, or changing the oil in their pickup trucks.

- Strugglers: Like Actualizers, these people are outside the pale of materialism not by choice, but by low income. Strugglers are chronically poor. Their repertoire of things is limited not because they already have it all, but because they have so little. Although they clip coupons like Actualizers, theirs are from the newspaper. Their transportation is usually public, if any. They are the invisible millions.

As one might imagine, these are very fluid categories, and we may move through as many as three of them in our lifetimes. For instance, between ages 18 and 24 most people (61 percent) are Experiencers in desire or deed, while less than 1 percent are Fulfilled. Between ages 55 and 64, however, the Actualizers, Fulfilled, and Strugglers claim about 15 percent of the population each, while the Believers have settled out at about a fifth. The Achievers, Strivers, and Makers fill about 10 percent apiece, and the remaining 2 percent are Experiencers. The numbers can be broken down at every stage allowing for marital status, education, household size, dependent children, home ownership, household income, and occupation. More interesting still is the ability to accurately predict the appearance of certain goods in each grouping. SRI sells data on precisely who buys single-lens reflex cameras, who owns a laptop computer, who drinks herbal tea, who phones before five o'clock, who reads the *Reader's Digest*, and who watches *Beavis and Butthead*.

When one realizes the fabulous expense of communicating meaning for a product, the simple-mindedness of a system like VALS2+ becomes less risible. When you are spending millions of dollars for a few points of market share for your otherwise indistinguishable product, the idea that you might be able to attract the owners of socket wrenches by shifting ad content around just a bit makes sense. Once you realize that in taste tests consumers cannot tell one brand of cigarettes from another—including their own—nor distinguish such products as soap, gasoline, cola, beer, or what-have-you, it is clear that the product must be overlooked and the audience isolated and sold.

READING THE TEXT

1. What do marketers mean by "positioning" (para. 3), and why is it an important strategy to them?
2. What does the acronym VALS stand for, and what is the logic behind this system?
3. Why do marketers believe that the "product must be overlooked and the audience isolated and sold" (para. 8), according to Twitchell?
4. Why does Twitchell explain that the VALS2 categories are "fluid" (para. 7)?

READING THE SIGNS

1. Write a journal entry in which you identify where you fit in the VALS2 system. Conversely, explain why none of the categories describe you. What is your attitude toward being stereotyped by marketers?
2. In class, discuss whether the categories of consumers defined by the VALS2 paradigm are an accurate predictor of consumer behavior. Use the discussion as the basis of an essay in which you argue for or against the proposition that stereotyping consumer lifestyles is an effective way of marketing goods and services.
3. Study the VALS2 paradigm in terms of the values it presumes. To what extent does it presume traditionally American values such as individualism? Use your analysis to formulate an argument about whether this marketing tool is an essentially American phenomenon.
4. Using the VALS2 paradigm, analyze the consumption habits of the interviewees described in Jon Mooallem's "The Self-Storage Self" (p. 102). Do they fit neatly into the paradigm, or do their patterns of consumption call for a revision of it? Use your findings as the basis of an essay in which you assess the usefulness of the paradigm.
5. **CONNECTING TEXTS** Twitchell, Stephanie Clifford and Quentin Hardy ("Attention, Shoppers: Store Is Tracking Your Cell," p. 110), and Malcolm Gladwell ("The Science of Shopping," p. 93) all describe marketing research strategies. Read these selections, and write an argument that supports, opposes, or modifies the proposition that marketers have misappropriated research techniques for manipulative and therefore ethically questionable purposes.

STEVE CRAIG

Men's Men and Women's Women

Men and women both drink beer, but you wouldn't guess that from the television ads that pitch beer as a guy beverage and associate beer drinking with such guy things as fishing trips, bars, and babes. Conversely, both men and women can find themselves a few pounds overweight, but you wouldn't know that from the ads, which almost always feature women, as they are intended to appeal to women dieters. In this selection, Steve Craig provides a step-by-step analysis of four TV commercials, showing how advertisers carefully craft their ads to appeal, respectively, to male and female consumers. A professor in the department of radio, television, and film at the University of North Texas, Craig has written widely on television, radio history, and gender and media. His most recent book is *Out of the Dark: A History of Radio and Rural America* (2009).

Gender and the Economics of Television Advertising

The economic structure of the television industry has a direct effect on the placement and content of all television programs and commercials. Large advertisers and their agencies have evolved the pseudo-scientific method of time purchasing based on demographics, with the age and sex of the consumer generally considered to be the most important predictors of purchasing behavior. Computers make it easy to match market research on product buying patterns with audience research on television viewing habits. Experience, research, and intuition thus yield a demographic (and even psychographic) profile of the "target audience." Advertisers can then concentrate their budgets on those programs which the target audience is most likely to view. The most economical advertising buys are those in which the target audience is most concentrated (thus, the less "waste" audience the advertiser must purchase) (Barnouw, 1978; Gitlin, 1983; Jhally, 1987).

Good examples of this demographic targeting can be seen by contrasting the ads seen on daytime television, aimed at women at home, with those on weekend sports telecasts. Ads for disposable diapers are virtually never

[e] macmillanhighered.com/signsoflife

Are the overt gender codes in classic TV advertising still evident today?
e-readings > **Ford**, *Two-Ford Freedom* [TV commercial]

seen during a football game any more than commercials for beer are seen during soap operas. True, advertisers of some products simply wish to have their commercials seen by the largest number of consumers at the lowest cost without regard to age, sex, or other demographic descriptors, but most consider this approach far too inefficient for the majority of products.

A general rule of thumb in television advertising, then, is that daytime is the best time to reach the woman who works at home. Especially important to advertisers among this group is the young mother with children. Older women, who also make up a significant proportion of the daytime audience, are generally considered less important by many advertisers in the belief that they spend far less money on consumer goods than young mothers.

Prime time (the evening hours) is considered a good time to reach women who work away from home, but since large numbers of men are also in the audience, it can also be a good time to advertise products with wider target audiences. Weekend sports periods (and, in season, "Monday Night Football") are the only time of the week when men outnumber women in the television audience, and therefore, become the optimum time for advertising products and services aimed at men.

Gendered Television, Gendered Commercials

In his book *Television Culture* (1987, Chs. 10, 11), John Fiske discusses "gen- 5 dered television," explaining that the television industry successfully designs some programs for men and others for women. Clearly, program producers and schedulers must consider the target audience needs of their clients (the advertisers) in creating a television program lineup. The gendering of programming allows the industry to provide the proper audience for advertisers by constructing shows pleasurable for the target audience to watch, and one aspect of this construction is in the gender portrayals of characters.

Fiske provides the following example:

> Women's view of masculinity, as evidenced in soap operas, differs markedly from that produced for the masculine audience. The "good" male in the daytime soaps is caring, nurturing, and verbal. He is prone to making comments like "I don't care about material wealth or professional success, all I care about is us and our relationship." He will talk about feelings and people and rarely express his masculinity in direct action. Of course, he is still decisive, he still has masculine power, but that power is given a "feminine" inflection. . . . The "macho" characteristics of goal centeredness, assertiveness, and the morality of the strongest that identify the hero in masculine television, tend here to be characteristics of the villain. (p. 186)

But if the programming manipulates gender portrayals to please the audience, then surely so must the commercials that are the programs' reason for being. My previous research (Craig, 1990) supports the argument that advertisers

also structure the gender images in their commercials to match the expectations and fantasies of their intended audience. Thus, commercials portraying
adult women with children were nearly four times more likely to appear during
daytime soap operas than during weekend sports (p. 50). Daytime advertisers
exploit the image of women as mothers to sell products to mothers. Likewise,
during the weekend sports broadcasts, only 18% of the primary male characters
were shown at home, while during the daytime ads, 40% of them were (p. 42).
For the woman at home, men are far more likely to be portrayed as being around
the house than they are in commercials aimed at men on weekends.

Gendered commercials, like gendered programs, are designed to give
pleasure to the target audience, since it is the association of the product with
a pleasurable experience that forms the basis for much American television
advertising. Yet patriarchy conditions males and females to seek their pleasure
differently. Advertisers therefore portray different images to men and women in
order to exploit the different deep-seated motivations and anxieties connected
to gender identity. I would now like to turn to a close analysis of four television
commercials to illustrate some of these differing portrayals. Variations in how
men and women are portrayed are especially apparent when comparing weekend and daytime commercials, since ads during these day parts almost completely focus on a target audience of men or women respectively.

Analysis of Four Commercials

In order to illustrate the variation of gender portrayal, I have chosen four commercials. Each was selected to provide an example of how men and women
are portrayed to themselves and to the other sex. The image of men and
women in commercials aired during weekend sports telecasts I call "Men's
Men" and "Men's Women." The portrayals of men and women in commercials aimed at women at home during the daytime hours I call "Women's
Men" and "Women's Women." Although there are certainly commercials
aired during these day parts that do not fit neatly into these categories, and
even a few that might be considered to be counter-stereotypical in their gender portrayals, the commercials and images I have chosen to analyze are
fairly typical and were chosen to permit a closer look at the practices revealed
in my earlier content analysis. Further, I acknowledge that the readings of
these commercials are my own. Others may well read them differently.

Men's Men

I would first like to consider two commercials originally broadcast during 10
weekend sports and clearly aimed at men. (These and the other commercials
I will discuss were broadcast on at least one of the three major networks. I
recorded them for analysis during January 1990.)

COMMERCIAL 1: ACURA INTEGRA (:30)

MUSIC: Light rock guitar music runs throughout. Tropical elements (e.g., a steel drum) are added later.

A young, white, blond, bespectacled male wearing a plain sweatshirt is shown cleaning out the interior of a car. He finds an old photograph of himself and two male companions (all are young, slender, and white) posing with a trophy-sized sailfish. He smiles. Dissolve to what appears to be a flashback of the fishing trip. The three men are now seen driving down the highway in the car (we now see that it is a new black Acura Integra) in a Florida-like landscape. We see a montage of close-ups of the three men inside the car, then a view out the car window of what looks to be the Miami skyline.

ANNOUNCER (male): "When you think about all the satisfaction you get out of going places . . . why would you want to take anything less . . ."

Dissolve to a silhouette shot of a young woman in a bathing suit walking along the beach at sunset.

ANNOUNCER: ". . . than America's most satisfying car?"

On this last line, the three young men are seen in silhouette knee-deep in the water at the same beach, apparently watching the woman pass. One of the men drops to his knees and throws his arms up in mock supplication. A montage of shots of the three men follows, shots of a deep-sea fishing boat intercut with shots of the first man washing the car. The montage ends with the three posing with the trophy sailfish. The screen flashes and freezes and becomes the still photo seen at the first shot of the commercial. The final shot shows a long shot of the car, freshly washed. The first man, dressed as in the first shot, gives the car a final polish and walks away. The words "Acura" and "Precision Crafted Performance" are superimposed over the final shot.

ANNOUNCER: "The Acura Integra."

This ad, which ran during a weekend sports telecast, has a number of features that makes it typical of many other commercials aimed at men. First, it is for an automobile. My previous research found that 29% of the network commercials telecast in the weekend time period were for cars and other automotive products (compared to only 1% during the daytime sample) (Craig, 1990, p. 36). In our culture, automobiles are largely the male's province, and men are seen by the automotive industry as the primary decision makers when it comes to purchases. Further, cars are frequently offered as a means of freedom (literally so in this ad), and escapism is an important component in many weekend ads (only 16% of weekend ads are set at home compared to 41% of daytime ads) (p. 43).

Second, with the exception of a brief silhouette of the woman on the beach, there are no women in this commercial. Camaraderie in all-male or nearly all-male groupings is a staple of weekend commercials, especially those for automobiles and beer. Again, my earlier research indicates that fully one-third of weekend commercials have an all-adult male cast (but only 20% of daytime commercials have an all-adult female cast) (p. 36).

The escapism and male camaraderie promised in this commercial are simply an extension of the escapism and camaraderie men enjoy when they watch (and vicariously participate in) weekend sports on television. Messner (1987) suggests that one reason for the popularity of sports with men is that it offers them a chance to escape from the growing ambiguity of masculinity in daily life.

> Both on a personal/existential level for athletes and on a symbolic/ideological level for spectators and fans, sport has become one of the "last bastions" of male power and superiority over — and separation from — the "feminization" of society. The rise of football as "America's number-one game" is likely the result of the comforting *clarity* it provides between the polarities of traditional male power, strength, and violence and the contemporary fears of social feminization. (p. 54)

The Acura commercial acts to reinforce male fantasies in an environment of clear masculinity and male domination. Men's men are frequently portrayed as men without women. The presence of women in the commercials might serve to threaten men's men with confusing uncertainty about the nature of masculinity in a sexist, but changing, society (Fiske, 1987, pp. 202–209, offers an extended psychoanalytic explanation of the absence of women in masculine television). On the other hand, the absence of women must *not* suggest homosexuality. Men's men are clearly heterosexual. To discourage any suspicions, the Acura ad portrays three (rather than two) men vacationing together.

It is also at least partly for this reason that the single quick shot in which the woman *does* appear in this commercial is important. She is nothing more than an anonymous object of desire (indeed, in silhouette, we cannot even see her face), but her presence both affirms the heterosexuality of the group while at the same time hinting that attaining sexual fulfillment will be made easier by the possession of the car. Men's men have the unchallenged freedom of a fantasized masculinity — to travel, to be free from commitment, to seek adventure.

Men's Women

COMMERCIAL 2: MILLER BEER (:30)

> We see the interior of a cheap roadside cafe. It is lit with an almost blinding sunlight streaming in the windows. A young couple sits in a far booth holding hands. A young, blond waitress is crossing the room. A silent jukebox sits in the foreground. At first we hear only natural sounds. We cut to a close-up from a low angle from outside the cafe of male legs as they enter the cafe. The legs are clad in blue jeans and cowboy boots.

As the man enters, we cut to a close-up of the blond waitress looking up to see the man. We see a close-up of the man's body as he passes the silent jukebox. As if by magic, the jukebox begins to play the rhythm and blues number "I Put a Spell on You." We see the couple that was holding hands turn in surprise. The man in the booth's face is unlit and we can see no features, but the woman is young with long blond hair. She looks surprised and pulls her hand away from the man's. We cut to an extreme close-up of the waitress's face. It is covered with sweat. As she watches the man pass, a smile appears on her face. She comes over to take the man's order. The camera takes the man's point of view.

MAN: "Miller Genuine Draft."
WAITRESS: "I was hopin' you'd say that."

We see a shot of a refrigerator door opening. The refrigerator is filled with sweating, backlit bottles of Miller beer. We then see a close-up of the man holding a bottle and opening it magically with a flick of his thumb (no opener). A montage of shots of the product amid blowing snow follows this. The sounds of a blizzard are heard.

ANNOUNCER: "Cold filtered. Never heat pasteurized. Miller Genuine Draft. For those who discover this real draft taste . . . the world is a *very* cool place."

On this last line we see close-ups of the woman in the booth and the waitress. Wind is blowing snow in their faces and they are luxuriating in the coolness. The waitress suddenly looks at the camera with shocked disappointment. We cut to an empty seat with the man's empty beer bottle rocking on the table. The music, snow, and wind end abruptly. We see the man's back as he exits the cafe. The final shot is of the waitress, elbow propped on the counter, looking after the man. The words "Tap into the Cold" are superimposed.

When women do appear in men's commercials, they seldom challenge the primary masculine fantasy. Men's women are portrayed as physically attractive, slim, and usually young and white, frequently blond, and almost always dressed in revealing clothing. Since most men's commercials are set in locations away from home, most men's women appear outside the home, and only infrequently are they portrayed as wives. There are almost always hints of sexual availability in men's women, but this is seldom played out explicitly. Although the sexual objectification of women characters in these ads is often quite subtle, my previous content analysis suggests that it is far more common in weekend than in daytime ads (Craig, 1990, p. 34). Men's women are also frequently portrayed as admirers (and at times, almost voyeurs), generally approving of some aspect of product use (the car he drives, the beer he drinks, the credit card he uses).

In these respects, the Miller ad is quite typical. What might have been a simple commercial about a man ordering and drinking a beer becomes an elaborate sexual fantasy, in many respects constructed like a porn film. The attractive, eager waitress is mystically drawn to the man who relieves her bored frustrations with an orgasmic chug-a-lug. She is "hot" while he (and the beer) is "*very* cool." But once he's satisfied, he's gone. He's too cool for conversation or commitment. We never see the man's face, but rather are invited, through the use of the point-of-view shot, to become a participant in the mystic fantasy.

There is, of course, considerable tongue-in-cheek intent in this ad. Males know that the idea of anonymous women lusting after them, eager for sex without commitment, is fantasy. But for many men, it is pleasurable fantasy, and common enough in weekend commercials. The main point is that the product has been connected, however briefly, with the pleasure of this fantasy. The physical pleasure of consuming alcohol (and specifically cold Miller beer) is tied to the pleasurable imaginings of a narrative extended beyond that which is explicitly seen.

One industry executive has explained this advertising technique. Noting the need for "an imaginary and motivating value" in ads, Nicolas (1988) argues that:

> Beyond the principle of utility, it becomes more and more important to associate a principle of pleasure to the value. The useful must be linked to the beautiful, the rational to the imaginary, the indispensable to the superfluous. . . . It is imperative that the image be seductive. (p. 7)

Although some research has documented changes in gender portrayals in 20 television advertising over the past few years (e.g., Bretl & Cantor, 1988; Ferrante et al., 1988), such conclusions are based on across-the-schedule studies or of prime time rather than of specifically gendered day parts. While avoiding portraying women as blatant sex objects is doubtless good business in daytime or prime time, it would almost certainly inhibit male fantasies such as this one, commonly seen during weekend sports. The man's woman continues to be portrayed according to the rules of the patriarchy.

The next two commercials were originally aired during daytime soap operas. They represent Madison Avenue's portrayal of women and men designed for women.

Women's Women

COMMERCIAL 3: WEIGHT WATCHERS (:30)

> The opening shot is a quick pan from toe to head of a young, thin, white woman with dark hair. She is dressed in a revealing red bathing suit and appears to be reclining on the edge of a pool. Her head is propped up with a pillow. She is wearing sunglasses and smiling.

> ANNOUNCER (woman, voice-over): "I hate diets . . . but I lost weight fast with Weight Watchers' new program."

We see the same woman sitting at a dining table in a home kitchen eating a meal. She is wearing a red dress. The camera weaves, and we briefly glimpse a man and two small children also at the table. Another close-up of the woman's body at the pool. This time the camera frames her waist.

ANNOUNCER: "And I *hate* starving myself."

We see the same family group eating pizza at a restaurant. More close-ups of the woman's body at poolside.

ANNOUNCER: "But with their new 'fast and flexible' program I don't have to."

Shot of the woman dancing with the man, followed by a montage of more shots of the family at dinner and close-ups of the woman at poolside.

ANNOUNCER: "A new food plan lets me live the way I want . . . eat with my family and friends, still have fun."

Close-up shot of balance scales. A woman's hand is moving the balance weight downward.

ANNOUNCER: "And in no time . . . *here I am!*"

Shot of the woman on the scales. She raises her hands as if in triumph. The identical shot is repeated three times.

ANNOUNCER: "Now there's only one thing I hate . . . not joining Weight Watchers sooner."

As this last line is spoken, we see a close-up of the woman at the pool. She removes her sunglasses. The man's head comes into the frame from the side and kisses her on the forehead.

This commercial portrays the woman's woman. Her need is a common one in women's commercials produced by a patriarchal society — the desire to attain and maintain her physical attractiveness. Indeed, my previous research indicates that fully 44% of the daytime ads sampled were for products relating to the body (compared with only 15% of the ads during weekend sports). In this ad, her desire for an attractive body is explicitly tied to her family. She is portrayed with a husband, small children, and a nice home. It is her husband with whom she dances and who expresses approval with a kiss. Her need for an attractive body is her need to maintain her husband's interest and maintain her family's unity and security. As Coward (1985) has written:

> Most women know to their cost that appearance is perhaps the crucial way by which men form opinions of women. For that reason, feelings about self-image get mixed up with feelings about security and comfort. . . . It sometimes appears to women that the whole possibility of being loved and comforted hangs on how their appearance will be received. (p. 78)

But dieting is a difficult form of self-deprivation, and she "hates" doing it. Implicit also is her hatred of her own "overweight" body—a body that no longer measures up to the idealized woman promoted by the patriarchy (and seen in the commercial). As Coward explains:

> . . . advertisements, health and beauty advice, fashion tips are effective precisely because somewhere, perhaps even subconsciously, an anxiety, rather than a pleasurable identification [with the idealized body], is awakened. (p. 80)

Weight Watchers promises to alleviate the pain of dieting at the same time it relieves (or perhaps delays) the anxiety of being "overweight." She can diet and "still have fun."

A related aspect is this ad's use of a female announcer. The copy is written in the first person, but we never see the model speaking in direct address. We get the impression that we are eavesdropping on her thoughts—being invited to identify with her—rather than hearing a sales pitch from a third person. My earlier research confirmed the findings of other content analyses that female voice-overs are relatively uncommon in commercials. My findings, however, indicated that while only 3% of the voice-overs during weekend sports were by women announcers, 16% of those during daytime were. Further, 60% of the women announcers during daytime were heard in commercials for body-related products (Craig, 1990, p. 52). 25

Women's Men

COMMERCIAL 4: SECRET DEODORANT (:30)

We open on a wide shot of a sailing yacht at anchor. It is sunrise and a woman is on deck. She descends into the cabin. Cut to a close-up of the woman as she enters the cabin.

WOMAN: "Four bells. Rise and shine!"

A man is seen in a bunk inside the cabin. He has just awakened. Both he and the woman are now seen to be young and white. She is thin and has bobbed hair. He is muscular and unshaven (and a Bruce Willis look-alike).

MUSIC: Fusion jazz instrumental (UNDER).
MAN (painfully): "Ohhhh . . . I can't move."
WOMAN: "Ohhhhh. I took a swim—breakfast is on—I had a shower. Now it's *your turn.*"

As she says this, she crosses the cabin and places a container of Secret deodorant on a shelf above the man. The man leans up on one elbow then falls back into bed with a groan.

MAN: "Ahhh, I can't."

She pulls him back to a sitting position then sits down herself, cradling him in her arms.

WOMAN: "Come onnn. You only changed *one* sail yesterday."
MAN (playfully): "Yeah, but it was a *big* sail."

Close-up of the couple. He is now positioned in the bed sitting with his back to her. He leans his head back on her shoulder.

WOMAN: "Didn't you know sailing's a sport? You know . . . an active thing."
MAN: "I just don't get it. . . . You're so together already. . . . Um. You smell great."
WOMAN: "Must be my Secret."

She looks at the container of Secret on the shelf. The man reaches over and picks it up. Close-up of the Secret with the words "Sporty Clean Scent" visible on the container.

MAN: "Sporty clean?"
WOMAN: "It's new."
MAN: "Sounds like something I could use."
WOMAN: "Unnnnn . . . I don't think so. I got it for me."

She takes the container from him and stands up and moves away. He stands up behind her and holds her from behind.

WOMAN: "For these close quarters . . . ?"
MAN: "Well, close is good."

He begins to kiss her cheek.

WOMAN: "I thought you said you couldn't move."

She turns to face him.

MAN: "I was saving my strength?"
WOMAN: "Mmmm."

We dissolve to a close-up of the product on the shelf.

ANNOUNCER (woman): "New Sporty Clean Secret. Strong enough for a man, but pH-balanced for an active woman."

This commercial portrays the woman's man. He's good looking, sensitive, romantic, and he appreciates her. What's more, they are alone in an exotic location where he proceeds to seduce her. In short, this commercial is a 30-second romance novel. She may be today's woman, be "so together," and she may be in control, but she still wants him to initiate the love-making. Her man is strong, active, and probably wealthy enough to own or rent a yacht. (Of course, a more liberated reading would have her as the owner of the yacht, or at least sharing expenses.) Yet he is also vulnerable. At first she mothers him, holding him in a Pietà-like embrace and cooing over his sore muscles. Then he catches her scent — her Secret — and the chase is on.

As in the Weight Watchers commercial, it is the woman's body that is portrayed as the source of the man's attraction, and it is only through maintaining that attraction that she can successfully negotiate the relationship. Although at one level the Secret woman is portrayed as a "new woman"—active, "sporty," self-assured, worthy of her own deodorant—she still must rely on special (even "Secret") products to make her body attractive. More to the point, she still must rely on her body to attract a man and fulfill the fantasy of security and family. After all, she is still mothering and cooking breakfast.

Once again, the product is the source of promised fantasy fulfillment—not only sexual fulfillment, but also the security of a caring relationship, one that allows her to be liberated, but not too liberated. Unlike the women of the Acura and Miller's commercials who remained anonymous objects of desire, the men of the Weight Watchers and Secret commercials are intimates who are clearly portrayed as having relationships that will exist long after the commercial is over.

Conclusion

Gender images in television commercials provide an especially intriguing field of study. The ads are carefully crafted bundles of images, frequently designed to associate the product with feelings of pleasure stemming from deep-seated fantasies and anxieties. Advertisers seem quite willing to manipulate these fantasies and exploit our anxieties, especially those concerning our gender identities, to sell products. What's more, they seem to have no compunction about capitalizing on dehumanizing gender stereotypes to seek these ends.

A threat to patriarchy is an economic threat, not only to men who may fear they will have their jobs taken by women, but also in a more fundamental way. Entire industries (automotive, cosmetics, fashion) are predicated on the assumption that men and women will continue behaving according to their stereotypes. Commercials for women therefore act to reinforce patriarchy and to co-opt any reactionary ideology into it. Commercials for men need only reinforce masculinity under patriarchy and, at most, offer men help in coping with a life plagued by women of raised conscience. Betty Friedan's comments of 1963 are still valid. Those "deceptively simple, clever, outrageous ads and commercials" (p. 270) she wrote of are still with us. If anything, they have become more subtle and insidious. The escape from their snare is through a better understanding of gender and the role of mass culture in defining it.

WORKS CITED

Barnouw, E. (1978). *The sponsor*. New York, NY: Oxford.
Bretl, D. J., & Cantor, J. (1988). The portrayal of men and women in U.S. television commercials: A recent content analysis and trends over 15 years. *Sex Roles, 18*(9/10), 595–609.
Coward, R. (1985). *Female desires: How they are sought, bought and packaged*. New York, NY: Grove.

Craig, S. (1990, December). *A content analysis comparing gender images in network television commercials aired in daytime, evening, and weekend telecasts.* (ERIC Document Reproduction Service Number ED329217)

Ferrante, C., Haynes, A., & Kingsley, S. (1988). Image of women in television advertising. *Journal of Broadcasting & Electronic Media, 32*(2), 231–237.

Fiske, J. (1987). *Television culture.* New York, NY: Methuen.

Friedan, B. (1963). *The feminine mystique.* New York, NY: Dell.

Gitlin, T. (1983). *Inside prime time.* New York, NY: Pantheon.

Jhally, S. (1987). *The codes of advertising: Fetishism and the political economy of meaning in the consumer society.* New York, NY: St. Martin's.

Messner, M. (1987). Male identity in the life course of the jock. In M. Kimmel (Ed.), *Changing men* (pp. 53–67). Newbury Park, CA: Sage.

Nicolas, P. (1988). From value to love. *Journal of Advertising Research, 28,* 7–8.

READING THE TEXT

1. How, according to John Fiske, is television programming gendered?

2. Why is male camaraderie such a common motif in "men's men" advertising, according to Craig?

3. What roles do women tend to play in the two types of commercials aimed at men? What roles do men tend to play in the two types of commercials aimed at women?

4. Why does Craig believe that "a threat to patriarchy is an economic threat" (para. 30)?

READING THE SIGNS

1. In class, discuss whether you agree with Craig's interpretations of the four commercials that he describes. If you disagree, what alternative analysis do you propose?

2. The four commercials Craig analyzes aired in 1990. View some current commercials broadcast during daytime and sports programs. Use your observations as the basis for an argument about whether the gendered patterns in advertising that Craig outlines exist today. If the patterns persist, what implications do they have for the tenacity of gender codes? If you see differences, how can you account for them?

3. Write an essay in which you support, refute, or modify Craig's belief that gendered advertising of the sort he describes is "dehumanizing" (para. 29).

4. Watch TV programs that are not overtly geared toward one gender, such as prime-time scripted drama or network news. To what extent does the advertising that accompanies these shows fit Craig's four categories of gender portrayal? How do you account for your findings?

5. **CONNECTING TEXTS**   Enter the debate over the origins of gender identity: Is it primarily biologically determined or largely socially constructed? Write an essay in which you advance your position; you can develop your ideas by consulting Aaron Devor's "Gender Role Behaviors and Attitudes" (p. 504) and Deborah Blum's "The Gender Blur: Where Does Biology End and Society Take Over?" (p. 511).

JENNIFER L. POZNER

Dove's "Real Beauty" Backlash

It sounds almost like the Macy's Santa Claus advising shoppers to look for something at Gimbel's in *Miracle on 34th Street*, but there you have it: Dove's "Campaign for Real Beauty" is actually telling ordinary girls and women to feel good about themselves. And, for the most part, Jennifer L. Pozner is rather glad it is, even if the Dove ads are still aimed at selling beauty products according to the implicit philosophy that "cellulite is unsightly, women's natural aging process is shameful, and flabby thighs are flawed and must be fixed." No, what angers Pozner are the male media figures who have voiced dismay at Dove's display of women with realistic figures and faces, some of whom dare to be middle-aged. Indeed, for Pozner, it is the commentary of such men that makes the Dove campaign so necessary in the first place. Pozner is executive director of Women In Media & News, and her media criticism has appeared in many national publications.

When it comes to Madison Avenue misogyny, usually it's the ad that's objectionable (hello, *Advertising Week*!), rather than the product itself.

The opposite is true in the latest incarnation of Dove's "Campaign for Real Beauty," which poses a bevy of full-figured babes in bras and boyshorts on billboards throughout New York, Chicago, D.C., L.A., and other top urban markets . . . just in time for the rollout of their new line of "firming cremes."

If the same smiling size sixes (and eights, and tens) were hawking hair dye or shilling for soap, the campaign would be revolutionary — but despite the company's continued and commendable intent to expand notions of female beauty to include the non-skinny and non-white, Dove's attempts are profoundly limited by a product line that comes with its own underlying philosophy: cellulite is unsightly, women's natural aging process is shameful, and flabby thighs are flawed and must be fixed . . . oh, so conveniently by Dove's newest lotion.

The feel-good "women are ok at whatever size" message is hopelessly hampered by the underlying attempt to get us to spend, spend, spend to "correct" those pesky "problem areas" advertisers have always told us to hate about our bodies. As Salon.com's Rebecca Traister put it, the message is "love your ass but not the fat on it."

Yet even though Dove's "Real Beauty" ads play to and subtly reinforce the 5 stereotypes they claim to be exposing, it's impossible not to feel inspired by the sight of these attractive, healthy women smiling playfully at us from their places of billboard honor, their voluptuous curves all the more luscious alongside the bags-of-bones in competitors' campaigns.

AP Photo/Nam Y. Huh

Gina Crisanti was featured in Dove's campaign.

Unless, of course, you're *Chicago Sun Times* columnist Richard Roeper, who reacted to Dove's "chunky women" with the sort of fear and loathing he should reserve for the cheesy Hollywood schlock he regularly "thumbs up" during his Ebert & Roeper film reviews. "I find these Dove ads a little unsettling. If I want to see plump gals baring too much skin, I'll go to Taste of Chicago, OK?," Roeper ranted, saying that while he knows he should probably praise Dove for breaking away from airbrushed, impossible-to-achieve, youth-obsessed ad imagery, he much prefers to bitch and moan. "When we're talking women in their underwear on billboards outside my living room windows, give me the fantasy babes, please. If that makes me sound superficial, shallow and sexist — well yes, I'm a man."

Unsettling? Try Roeper's implication that all men are just naturally sexist — and that a man who wears gender-based bigotry as a badge of pride has some of the most power in the media to determine which films succeed and which fail. (Remember Roeper's admission next time his thumb goes way up for a flick whose humor rarely rises above cheap gags about sperm as hair gel, or when he pans a promising movie centered around strong female characters.)

Dozens of major media outlets jumped on Roeper's comments as an excuse to run insulting headlines such as "Fab or Flab," with stories exploring the "controversy" over whether Dove's ads are, as *People* put it, "the best thing to happen to advertising since the free sample, or an eyesore of outsize proportions."

The tone of this debate turned nasty, quickly, with women's self-esteem in one camp and men's fragile eyes in another as typified by a second *Sun Times* writer's comments that these "disturbing" and "frightening" women should "put on clothes (please, really)" because "ads should be about the beautiful people. They should include the unrealistic, the ideal or the unattainable look for which so many people strive." Besides, wrote Lucio Guerrero, "the only time I want to see a thigh that big is in a bucket with bread crumbs on it."

From there, print and broadcast outlets featured a stream of man-on-   10
the-street interviews begging Madison Avenue to bring back the starvation-saturated, silicone-enhanced sweeties they'd come to expect seeing on their commutes to work, echoing Guerrero's mean-spirited musings.

Some masked their aesthetic objections under the guise of health concerns: "At the risk of sounding politically incorrect," Bill Zwecker, the balding, paunchy, middle-aged anchor of CBS's local newscast in Chicago, weighed in on his CBS blog, "In this day and age, when we are facing a huge obesity problem in this country, we don't need to encourage anyone—women OR men—to think it's okay to be out of shape." Perhaps this line of attack would have been more convincing if the women in the ads were unhealthily over-weight (they're actually smaller-sized than the average American woman), or if Zwecker was a little more *GQ* and a little less *Couch Potato Quarterly*.

Certainly, these men so quick to demonize "the Dove girls" show no understanding that those "fantasy babes" of traditional ads have a profoundly negative impact on the health of girls and women in America. Advertising has never glorified obesity (though that problem is arguably a byproduct of McDonald's, M&Ms, and other junk food ads), but the industry has equated starvation and drug addiction with women's beauty and value for decades.

The "real beauty" backlash underscores just how necessary Dove's campaign is—however hypocritical the product they're selling may be. What's "unsettling" is not that Roeper, Guerrero, and Zwecker might have to look at empowerment-infused ads targeted to female consumers—it's that men with power positions in the media still think it's acceptable to demand that women be displayed only in the hyper-objectifying images they feel is somehow their due.

READING THE TEXT

1. Why does Pozner believe that Dove's "Real Beauty" ads "reinforce the stereo-types they claim to be exposing" (para. 5)?

2. In Pozner's view, what is the basis of the objections that Richard Roeper and some other male commentators have to the Dove "Campaign for Real Beauty"?

3. Characterize Pozner's tone in this selection, particularly in her comments regarding male critics of Dove's ads. What effect does it have on your response to her essay?

READING THE SIGNS

1. In a creative journal assignment, assume the perspective of one of the Dove "Real Beauty" models, and write a letter in response to Richard Roeper's complaints about the Dove ads.

2. Write an argumentative essay that validates, rejects, or complicates Pozner's claim that "the 'real beauty' backlash underscores just how necessary Dove's campaign is — however hypocritical the product they're selling may be" (para. 13).

3. Write an essay evaluating Richard Roeper's response to the Dove ad campaign. Do you find his response "unsettling" (para. 7), as Pozner sees it, or do you find it simply honest?

4. Write an essay arguing whether ad campaigns such as Dove's "Real Beauty" and Nike's "My Butt Is Big" are indeed revolutionary or are simply a new twist on advertising's tendency to objectify women's bodies.

5. Since Pozner wrote her essay, Dove has embarked on a series of "Real Beauty Sketches," an experiment in which forensic artist Gil Zamora first draws a sight-unseen woman based on her own self-description and then draws the same woman based on a stranger's description of her. The goal of this experiment is to show women that they are "more beautiful" than they assume. Watch some of these sketches on YouTube, and then write an essay in which you critique the videos. How do you think Pozner would respond to them? Do you believe that they are problematic, as she considered the original "Real Beauty" ad campaign to be?

GLORIA STEINEM

Sex, Lies, and Advertising

One of the best-known icons of the women's movement, Gloria Steinem has been a leader in transforming the image of women in America. As a cofounder of *Ms.* magazine, in which this selection first appeared, Steinem has provided a forum for women's voices for more than forty years, but as her article explains, it has not been easy to keep this forum going. A commercial publication requires commercials, and the needs of advertisers do not always mesh nicely with the goals of a magazine like *Ms.* Steinem ruefully reveals the compromises *Ms.* magazine had to make over the years to satisfy its advertising clients, compromises that came to an end only when *Ms.* ceased to take ads. Steinem's publications include *Revolution from Within* (1992), a personal exploration of the power of self-esteem; *Moving beyond Words* (1994); *Outrageous Acts and Everyday Rebellions* (2nd ed., 1995), and *Doing Sixty & Seventy* (2006). Currently a consulting editor for *Ms.*, Steinem continues to combine her passion for writing and activism as an unflagging voice in American feminism.

Goodbye to cigarette ads where poems should be.
Goodbye to celebrity covers and too little space.
Goodbye to cleaning up language so *Ms.* advertisers won't be boycotted
   by the Moral Majority.
In fact, goodbye to advertisers *and* the Moral Majority.
Goodbye to short articles and short thinking.
Goodbye to "post-feminism" from people who never say "post-democracy."
Goodbye to national boundaries and hello to the world.
Welcome to the magazine of the post-patriarchal age.
The turn of the century is *our turn*!

That was my celebratory mood in the summer of 1990 when I finished the original version of the exposé you are about to read. I felt as if I'd been released from a personal, portable Bastille. At least I'd put on paper the ad policies that had been punishing *Ms.* for all the years of its nonconforming life and still were turning more conventional media, especially (but not only) those directed at women, into a dumping ground for fluff.

Those goodbyes were part of a letter inviting readers to try a new, ad-free version of *Ms.* and were also a homage to "Goodbye to All That," a witty and lethal essay in which Robin Morgan bade farewell to the pre-feminist male Left of twenty years before. It seemed the right tone for the birth of a brand-new, reader-supported, more international form of *Ms.*, which Robin was heading as editor-in-chief, and I was serving as consulting editor. Besides, I had a very personal kind of mantra running through my head: *I'll never have to sell another ad as long as I live.*

So I sent the letter off, watched the premiere issue containing my exposé go to press, and then began to have second thoughts: Were ad policies too much of an "inside" concern? Did women readers already know that magazines directed at them were filled with editorial extensions of ads—and not care? Had this deceptive system been in place too long for anyone to have faith in changing it? In other words: Would anybody give a damn?

After almost four years of listening to responses and watching the ripples spread out from this pebble cast upon the waters, I can tell you that, yes, readers do care; and no, most of them were not aware of advertising's control over the words and images around it. Though most people in the publishing industry think this is a practice too deeply embedded ever to be uprooted, a lot of readers are willing to give it a try—even though that's likely to mean paying more for their publications. In any case, as they point out, understanding the nitty-gritty of ad influence has two immediate uses. It strengthens healthy skepticism about what we read, and it keeps us from assuming that other women must want this glamorous, saccharine, unrealistic stuff.

Perhaps that's the worst punishment ad influence has inflicted upon us. It's made us feel contemptuous of other women. We know we don't need those endless little editorial diagrams of where to put our lipstick or blush — we don't identify with all those airbrushed photos of skeletal women with everything about them credited, *even their perfume* (can you imagine a man's photo airbrushed to perfection, with his shaving lotion credited?) — but we assume there must be women out there somewhere who *do* love it; otherwise, why would it be there?

Well, many don't. Given the sameness of women's magazines resulting from the demands made by makers of women's products that advertise in all of them, we probably don't know yet what a wide variety of women readers want. In any case, we do know it's the advertisers who are determining what women are getting now.

The first wave of response to this exposé came not from readers but from writers and editors for other women's magazines. They phoned to say the pall cast by anticipated or real advertising demands was even more widespread than rebellious *Ms.* had been allowed to know. They told me how brave I was to "burn my bridges" (no critic of advertising would ever be hired as an editor of any of the women's magazines, they said) and generally treated me as if I'd written about organized crime instead of practices that may be unethical but are perfectly legal. After making me promise not to use their names, they offered enough additional horror stories to fill a book, a movie, and maybe a television series. Here is a typical one: when the freelance author of an article on moisturizers observed in print that such products might be less necessary for young women — whose skin tends to be not dry but oily — the article's editor was called on the carpet and denounced by her bosses as "anti-moisturizer." Or how about this: the film critic for a women's magazine asked its top editor, a woman who makes millions for her parent company, whether movies could finally be reviewed critically, since she had so much clout. No, said the editor; if you can't praise a movie, just don't include it; otherwise we'll jeopardize our movie ads. This may sound like surrealism in everyday life, or like our grandmothers advising, "If you can't say something nice, don't say anything," but such are the forces that control much of our information.

I got few negative responses from insiders, but the ones I did get were bitter. Two editors at women's magazines felt I had demeaned them by writing the article. They loved their work, they said, and didn't feel restricted by ads at all. So I would like to make clear in advance that my purpose was and is to change the system, not to blame the people struggling within it. As someone who has written for most women's magazines, I know that many editors work hard to get worthwhile articles into the few pages left over after providing all the "complementary copy" (that is, articles related to and supportive of advertised products). I also know there are editors who sincerely want exactly what the advertisers want, which is why they're so good at their jobs.

Nonetheless, criticizing this ad-dominant system is no different from criticizing male-dominant marriage. Both institutions make some people happy, and both seem free as long as your wishes happen to fall within their traditional boundaries. But just as making more equal marital laws alleviates the suffering of many, breaking the link between editorial and advertising will help all media become more honest and diverse.

A second wave of reaction came from advertising executives who were asked to respond by reporters. They attributed all problems to *Ms.* We must have been too controversial or otherwise inappropriate for ads. I saw no stories that asked the next questions: Why had non-women's companies from Johnson & Johnson to IBM found our "controversial" pages fine for their ads? Why did desirable and otherwise unreachable customers read something so "inappropriate"? What were ad policies doing to *other* women's media? To continue my marriage parallel, however, I should note that these executives seemed only mildly annoyed. Just as many women are more dependent than men on the institution of marriage and so are more threatened and angry when it's questioned, editors of women's magazines tended to be more upset than advertisers when questioned about their alliance. . . .

Then came the third wave — reader letters which were smart, thought- 10 ful, innovative, and numbered in the hundreds. Their dominant themes were anger and relief: relief because those vast uncritical oceans of food/fashion/ beauty articles in other women's magazines weren't necessarily what women

Gloria Steinem (left) and Patricia Carbine cofounded *Ms.* magazine.

Angel Franco/New York Times Co./Getty Images

wanted after all, and also relief because *Ms.* wasn't going to take ads anymore, even those that were accompanied by fewer editorial demands; anger because consumer information, diverse articles, essays, fiction, and poetry could have used the space instead of all those oceans of articles about ad categories that had taken up most of women's magazines for years. . . .

Last and most rewarding was the response that started in the fall. Teachers of journalism, advertising, communications, women's studies, and other contemporary courses asked permission to reprint the exposé as a supplementary text. That's another reason why I've restored cuts, updated information, and added new examples — including this introduction. Getting subversive ideas into classrooms could change the next generation running the media.

The following pages are mostly about women's magazines, but that doesn't mean other media are immune.

Sex, Lies, and Advertising

Toward the end of the 1980s, when glasnost was beginning and *Ms.* magazine seemed to be ending, I was invited to a press lunch for a Soviet official. He entertained us with anecdotes about the new problems of democracy in his country; for instance, local Communist leaders who were being criticized by their own media for the first time, and were angry.

"So I'll have to ask my American friends," he finished pointedly, "how more subtly to control the press."

In the silence that followed, I said: "Advertising."   15

The reporters laughed, but later one of them took me aside angrily: How dare I suggest that freedom of the press was limited in this country? How dare I imply that *his* newsmagazine could be influenced by ads?

I explained that I wasn't trying to lay blame, but to point out advertising's media-wide influence. We can all recite examples of "soft" cover stories that newsmagazines use to sell ads, and self-censorship in articles that should have taken advertised products to task for, say, safety or pollution. Even television news goes "soft" in ratings wars, and other TV shows don't get on the air without advertiser support. But I really had been thinking about women's magazines. There, it isn't just a little content that's designed to attract ads; it's almost all of it. That's why advertisers — not readers — had always been the problem for *Ms.* As the only women's magazine that didn't offer what the ad world euphemistically describes as "supportive editorial atmosphere" or "complementary copy" (for instance, articles that praise food/fashion/beauty subjects in order to "support" and "complement" food/fashion/beauty ads), *Ms.* could never attract enough ads to break even.

"Oh, *women's* magazines," the journalist said with contempt. "Everybody knows they're catalogs — but who cares? They have nothing to do with journalism."

———

I can't tell you how many times I've had this argument since I started writing for magazines in the early 1960s, and especially since the current women's movement began. Except as moneymaking machines—"cash cows," as they are so elegantly called in the trade—women's magazines are usually placed beyond the realm of serious consideration. Though societal changes being forged by women have been called more far-reaching than the industrial revolution by such nonfeminist sources as the *Wall Street Journal*—and though women's magazine editors often try hard to reflect these changes in the few pages left after all the ad-related subjects are covered—the magazines serving the female half of this country are still far below the journalistic and ethical standards of news and general-interest counterparts. Most depressing of all, this fact is so taken for granted that it doesn't even rate as an exposé.

For instance: If *Time* and *Newsweek*, in order to get automotive and GM ads, had to lavish editorial praise on cars and credit photographs in which newsmakers were driving, say, a Buick from General Motors, there would be a scandal—maybe even a criminal investigation. When women's magazines from *Seventeen* to *Lear's* publish articles lavishing praise on beauty and fashion products, and credit in text, the cover, and other supposedly editorial photographs a particular makeup from Revlon or a dress from Calvin Klein because those companies also advertise, it's just business as usual. 20

When *Ms.* began, we didn't consider *not* taking ads. The most important reason was to keep the price of a feminist magazine low enough for most women to afford. But the second and almost equal reason was to provide a forum where women and advertisers could talk to each other and experiment with nonstereotyped, informative, imaginative ads. After all, advertising was (and is) as potent a source of information in this country as news or TV or movies. It's where we get not only a big part of our information but also images that shape our dreams.

We decided to proceed in two stages. First, we would convince makers of "people products" that their ads should be placed in a women's magazine: cars, credit cards, insurance, sound equipment, financial services—everything that's used by both men and women but was then advertised only to men. Since those advertisers were accustomed to the division between editorial pages and ads that news and general-interest magazines at least try to maintain, such products would allow our editorial content to be free and diverse. Furthermore, if *Ms.* could prove that women were important purchasers of "people products," just as men were, those advertisers would support other women's magazines, too, and subsidize some pages for articles about something other than the hothouse worlds of food/fashion/beauty. Only in the second phase would we add examples of the best ads for whatever traditional "women's products" (clothes, shampoo, fragrance, food, and so on) that subscriber surveys showed *Ms.* readers actually used. But we would ask those advertisers to come in *without* the usual quid pro quo of editorial features praising their product area; that is, the dreaded "complementary copy."

From the beginning, we knew the second step might be even harder than the first. Clothing advertisers like to be surrounded by editorial fashion spreads (preferably ones that credit their particular labels and designers); food advertisers have always expected women's magazines to publish recipes and articles on entertaining (preferably ones that require their products); and shampoo, fragrance, and beauty products in general insist on positive editorial coverage of beauty aids—a "beauty atmosphere," as they put it—plus photo credits for particular products and nothing too depressing; no bad news. That's why women's magazines look the way they do: saccharine, smiley-faced, and product-heavy, with even serious articles presented in a slick and sanitized way.

But if *Ms.* could break this link between ads and editorial content, then we should add "women's products" too. For one thing, publishing ads only for gender-neutral products would give the impression that women have to become "like men" in order to succeed (an impression that *Ms.* ad pages sometimes *did* give when we were still in the first stage). For another, presenting a full circle of products that readers actually need and use would allow us to select the best examples of each category and keep ads from being lost in a sea of similar products. By being part of this realistic but unprecedented mix, products formerly advertised only to men would reach a growth market of women, and good ads for women's products would have a new visibility.

Given the intelligence and leadership of *Ms.* readers, both kinds of products would have unique access to a universe of smart consultants whose response would help them create more effective ads for other media too. Aside from the advertisers themselves, there's nobody who cares as much about the imagery in advertising as those who find themselves stereotyped or rendered invisible by it. And they often have great suggestions for making it better.

As you can see, we had all our energy, optimism, and arguments in good working order.

I thought at the time that our main problem would be getting ads with good "creative," as the imagery and text are collectively known. That was where the women's movement had been focusing its efforts, for instance, the National Organization for Women's awards to the best ads, and its "Barefoot and Pregnant" awards for the worst. Needless to say, there were plenty of candidates for the second group. Carmakers were still draping blondes in evening gowns over the hoods like ornaments that could be bought with the car (thus also making clear that car ads weren't directed at women). Even in ads for products that only women used, the authority figures were almost always male, and voice-overs for women's products on television were usually male too. Sadistic, he-man campaigns were winning industry praise; for example, *Advertising Age* hailed the infamous Silva Thin cigarette theme, "How to Get a Woman's Attention: Ignore Her," as "brilliant." Even in medical journals, ads for tranquilizers showed depressed housewives standing next to piles of dirty dishes and promised to get them back to work. As for women's magazines, they seemed to have few guidelines, at least none that excluded even the ads for the fraudulent breast-enlargement or thigh-thinning products for which their back pages were famous.

Obviously, *Ms.* would have to avoid such offensive imagery and seek out the best ads, but this didn't seem impossible. The *New Yorker* had been screening ads for aesthetic reasons for years, a practice that advertisers accepted at the time. *Ebony* and *Essence* were asking for ads with positive black images, and though their struggle was hard, their requests weren't seen as unreasonable. . . .

Let me take you through some of our experiences — greatly condensed, but just as they happened. In fact, if you poured water on any one of these, it would become a novel:

• Cheered on by early support from Volkswagen and one or two other car 30 companies, we finally scrape together time and money to put on a major reception in Detroit. U.S. carmakers firmly believe that women choose the upholstery color, not the car, but we are armed with statistics and reader mail to prove the contrary: A car is an important purchase for women, one that is such a symbol of mobility and freedom that many women will spend a greater percentage of income for a car than will counterpart men.

But almost nobody comes. We are left with many pounds of shrimp on the table, and quite a lot of egg on our face. Assuming this near-total boy-cott is partly because there was a baseball pennant play-off the same day, we blame ourselves for not foreseeing the problem. Executives go out of their way to explain that they wouldn't have come anyway. It's a dramatic begin-ning for ten years of knocking on resistant or hostile doors, presenting endless documentation of women as car buyers, and hiring a full-time saleswoman in Detroit — all necessary before *Ms.* gets any real results.

This long saga has a semi-happy ending: Foreign carmakers understood better than Detroit that women buy cars, and advertised in *Ms.*; also years of research on the women's market plus door-knocking began to pay off. Even-tually, cars became one of our top sources of ad revenue. Even Detroit began to take the women's market seriously enough to put car ads in other women's magazines too, thus freeing a few more of their pages from the food/fashion/beauty hothouse.

But long after figures showed that a third, even half, of many car mod-els were being bought by women, U.S. makers continued to be uncomfort-able addressing female buyers. Unlike many foreign carmakers, Detroit never quite learned the secret of creating intelligent ads that exclude no one and then placing them in media that overcome past exclusion. Just as an African American reader may feel more invited by a resort that placed an ad in *Ebony* or *Essence*, even though the same ad appeared in *Newsweek*, women of all races may need to see ads for cars, computers, and other historically "mascu-line" products in media that are clearly directed at them. Once inclusive ads are well placed, however, there's interest and even gratitude from women. *Ms.* readers were so delighted to be addressed as intelligent consumers by a routine Honda ad with text about rack-and-pinion steering, for example, that they sent fan mail. But even now, Detroit continues to ask: "Should we make special ads for women?" That's probably one reason why foreign cars still have a greater share of the women's market in the United States than of the men's.

• In the *Ms.* Gazette, we do a brief report on a congressional hearing into coal tar derivatives used in hair dyes that are absorbed through the skin and may be carcinogenic. This seems like news of importance: Newspapers and newsmagazines are reporting it too. But Clairol, a Bristol-Myers subsidiary that makes dozens of products, a few of which have just come into our pages as ads *without* the usual quid pro quo of articles on hair and beauty, is outraged. Not at newspapers or newsmagazines, just at us. It's bad enough that *Ms.* is the only women's magazine refusing to provide "supportive editorial" praising beauty products, but to criticize one of their product categories on top of it, however generically or even accurately — well, *that* is going too far.

We offer to publish a letter from Clairol telling its side of the story. In an 35 excess of solicitousness, we even put this letter in the Gazette, not in Letters to the Editors, where it belongs. Eventually, Clairol even changes its hair-coloring formula, apparently in response to those same hearings. But in spite of surveys that show *Ms.* readers to be active women who use more of almost everything Clairol makes than do the readers of other women's magazines, *Ms.* gets almost no ads for those dozens of products for the rest of its natural life.

• Women of color read *Ms.* in disproportionate numbers. This is a source of pride to *Ms.* staffers, who are also more racially representative than the editors of other women's magazines (which may include some beautiful black models but almost no black decisionmakers; Pat Carbine hired the first black editor at *McCall's*, but she left when Pat did). Nonetheless, the reality of *Ms.*'s staff and readership is obscured by ads filled with enough white women to make the casual reader assume *Ms.* is directed at only one part of the population, no matter what the editorial content is.

In fact, those few ads we are able to get that feature women of color — for instance, one made by Max Factor for *Essence* and *Ebony* that Linda Wachner gives us while she is president of Max Factor — are greeted with praise and relief by white readers, too, and make us feel that more inclusive ads should win out in the long run. But there are pathetically few such images. Advertising "creative" also excludes women who are not young, not thin, not conventionally pretty, well-to-do, able-bodied, or heterosexual — which is a hell of a lot of women.

• Our intrepid saleswomen set out early to attract ads for the product category known as consumer electronics: sound equipment, computers, calculators, VCRs, and the like. We know that *Ms.* readers are determined to be part of this technological revolution, not to be left out as women have been in the past. We also know from surveys that readers are buying this kind of stuff in numbers as high as those of readers of magazines like *Playboy* and the "male 18 to 34" market, prime targets of the industry. Moreover, unlike traditional women's products that our readers buy but don't want to read articles about, these are subjects they like to see demystified in our pages. There actually *is* a supportive editorial atmosphere.

"But women don't understand technology," say ad and electronics executives at the end of our presentations. "Maybe not," we respond, "but neither do men — and we all buy it."

"If women *do* buy it," counter the decisionmakers, "it's because they're 40 asking their husbands and boyfriends what to buy first." We produce letters from *Ms.* readers saying how turned off they are when salesmen say things like "Let me know when your husband can come in."

Then the argument turns to why there aren't more women's names sent back on warranties (those much-contested certificates promising repair or replacement if anything goes wrong). We explain that the husband's name may be on the warranty, even if the wife made the purchase. But it's also true that women are experienced enough as consumers to know that such promises are valid only if the item is returned in its original box at midnight in Hong Kong. Sure enough, when we check out hair dryers, curling irons, and other stuff women clearly buy, women don't return those warranties very often either. It isn't the women who are the problem, it's the meaningless warranties.

After several years of this, we get a few ads from companies like JVC and Pioneer for compact sound systems — on the grounds that women can understand compacts, but not sophisticated components. Harry Elias, vice president of JVC, is actually trying to convince his Japanese bosses that there is something called a woman's market. At his invitation, I find myself speaking at trade shows in Chicago and Las Vegas trying to persuade JVC dealers that electronics showrooms don't have to be locker rooms. But as becomes apparent, however, the trade shows are part of the problem. In Las Vegas, the only women working at technology displays are seminude models serving champagne. In Chicago, the big attraction is Marilyn Chambers, a porn star who followed Linda Lovelace of *Deep Throat* fame as Chuck Traynor's captive and/or employee, whose pornographic movies are being used to demonstrate VCRs.

In the end, we get ads for a car stereo now and then, but no VCRs; a welcome breakthrough of some IBM personal computers, but no Apple or no Japanese-made ones. Furthermore, we notice that *Working Woman* and *Savvy*, which are focused on office work, don't benefit as much as they should from ads for office equipment either. . . .

• Then there is the great toy train adventure. Because *Ms.* gets letters from little girls who love toy trains and ask our help in changing ads and box-top photos that show only little boys, we try to talk to Lionel and to get their ads.

It turns out that Lionel executives *have* been concerned about little girls. They made a pink train and couldn't understand why it didn't sell.

Eventually, Lionel bows to this consumer pressure by switching to a photo- 45 graph of a boy *and* a girl — but only on some box tops. If trains are associated with little girls, Lionel executives believe, they will be devalued in the eyes of little boys. Needless to say, *Ms.* gets no train ads. If even 20 percent of little girls wanted trains, they would be a huge growth market, but this remains unexplored. In the many toy stores where displays are still gender divided, the "soft" stuff, even modeling clay, stays on the girls' side, while the "hard" stuff, especially rockets and trains, is displayed for boys — thus depriving both. By 1986, Lionel is put up for sale.

We don't have much luck with other kinds of toys either. A *Ms.* department, Stories for Free Children, edited by Letty Cottin Pogrebin, makes us one of the very few magazines with a regular feature for children. A larger proportion of *Ms.* readers have preschool children than do the readers of any other women's magazine. Nonetheless, the industry can't seem to believe that feminists care about children — much less have them.

• When *Ms.* began, the staff decided not to accept ads for feminine hygiene sprays and cigarettes on the same basis: They are damaging to many women's health but carry no appropriate warnings. We don't think we should tell our readers what to do — if marijuana were legal, for instance, we would carry ads for it along with those for beer and wine — but we should provide facts so readers can decide for themselves. Since we've received letters saying that feminine sprays actually kill cockroaches and take the rust off metal, we give up on those. But antismoking groups have been pressuring for health warnings on cigarette ads as well as packages, so we decide we will accept advertising if the tobacco industry complies.

Philip Morris is among the first to do so. One of its brands, Virginia Slims, is also sponsoring women's tennis tournaments and women's public opinion polls that are historic "firsts." On the other hand, the Virginia Slims theme, "You've come a long way, baby," has more than a "baby" problem. It gives the impression that for women, smoking is a sign of progress.

We explain to the Philip Morris people that this slogan won't do well in our pages. They are convinced that its success with *some* women means it will work with *all* women. No amount of saying that we, like men, are a segmented market, that we don't all think alike, does any good. Finally, we agree to publish a small ad for a Virginia Slims calendar as a test, and to abide by the response of our readers.

The letters from readers are both critical and smart. For instance: Would 50 you show a photo of a black man picking cotton next to one of an African American man in a Cardin suit, and symbolize progress from slavery to civil rights by smoking? Of course not. So why do it for women? But instead of honoring test results, the executives seem angry to have been proved wrong.

We refuse Virginia Slims ads, thus annoying tennis players like Billie Jean King as well as incurring a new level of wrath: Philip Morris takes away ads for *all* its many products, costing *Ms.* about $250,000 in the first year. After five years, the damage is so great we can no longer keep track.

Occasionally, a new set of Philip Morris executives listens to *Ms.* saleswomen, or laughs when Pat Carbine points out that even Nixon got pardoned. I also appeal directly to the chairman of the board, who agrees it is unfair, sends me to another executive — and *he* says no. Because we won't take Virginia Slims, not one other Philip Morris product returns to our pages for the next sixteen years.

Gradually, we also realize our naïveté in thinking we could refuse all cigarette ads, with or without a health warning. They became a disproportionate source of revenue for print media the moment television banned them, and few magazines can compete or survive without them; certainly not *Ms.*, which lacks the support of so many other categories. Though cigarette ads actually inhibit editorial freedom less than ads for food, fashion, and the like — cigarette companies want only to be distant from coverage on the dangers of smoking, and don't require affirmative praise or photo credits of their product — it is still a growing source of sorrow that they are there at all. By the 1980s, when statistics show that women's rate of lung cancer is approaching men's, the necessity of taking cigarette ads has become a kind of prison.

Though I never manage to feel kindly toward groups that protest our ads and pay no attention to magazines and newspapers that can turn them down and still keep their doors open — and though *Ms.* continues to publish new facts about smoking, such as its dangers during pregnancy — I long for the demise of the whole tobacco-related industry. . . .

- General Mills, Pillsbury, Carnation, Del Monte, Dole, Kraft, Stouffer, Hormel, Nabisco: You name the food giant, we try to get its ads. But no matter how desirable the *Ms.* readership, our lack of editorial recipes and traditional homemaking articles proves lethal.

We explain that women flooding into the paid labor force have changed the way this country eats; certainly, the boom in convenience foods proves that. We also explain that placing food ads *only* next to recipes and how-to-entertain articles is actually a negative for many women. It associates food with work — in a way that says only women have to cook — or with guilt over *not* cooking and entertaining. Why not advertise food in diverse media that don't always include recipes (thus reaching more men, who have become a third of all supermarket shoppers anyway) and add the recipe interest with specialty magazines like *Gourmet* (a third of whose readers are men)? 55

These arguments elicit intellectual interest but no ads. No advertising executive wants to be the first to say to a powerful client, "Guess what, I *didn't* get you complementary copy." Except for an occasional hard-won ad for instant coffee, diet drinks, yogurt, or such extras as avocados and almonds, the whole category of food, a mainstay of the publishing industry, remains unavailable to us. Period. . . .

• By the end of 1986, magazine production costs have skyrocketed and postal rates have increased 400 percent. Ad income is flat for the whole magazine industry. The result is more competition, with other magazines offering such "extras" as free golf trips for advertisers or programs for "sampling" their products at parties and other events arranged by the magazine for desirable consumers. We try to compete with the latter by "sampling" at what we certainly have enough of: movement benefits. Thus, little fragrance bottles turn up next to the dinner plates of California women lawyers (who are delighted), or wine samples lower the costs at a reception for political women. A good organizing tactic comes out of this. We hold feminist seminars in shopping centers. They may be to the women's movement what churches were to the civil rights movement in the South — that is, *where people are.* Anyway, shopping center seminars are a great success. Too great. We have to stop doing them in Bloomingdale's up and down the East Coast, because meeting space in the stores is too limited, and too many women are left lined up outside stores. We go on giving out fancy little liquor bottles at store openings, which makes the advertisers happy — but not us.

Mostly, however, we can't compete in this game of "value-added" (the code word for giving the advertisers extras in return for their ads). Neither can many of the other independent magazines. Deep-pocketed corporate parents can offer such extras as reduced rates for ad schedules in a group of magazines, free tie-in spots on radio stations they also own, or vacation junkets on corporate planes.

Meanwhile, higher costs and lowered income have caused the *Ms.* 60/40 preponderance of edit over ads — something we promised to readers — to become 50/50: still a lot better than most women's magazines' goals of 30/70, but not good enough. Children's stories, most poetry, and some fiction are casualties of reduced space. In order to get variety into more limited pages, the length (and sometimes the depth) of articles suffers. Though we don't solicit or accept ads that would look like a parody in our pages, we get so worn down that some slip through. Moreover, we always have the problem of working just as hard to get a single ad as another magazine might for a whole year's schedule of ads.

Still, readers keep right on performing miracles. Though we haven't been 60 able to afford a subscription mailing in two years, they maintain our guaranteed circulation of 450,000 by word of mouth. Some of them also help to make up the advertising deficit by giving *Ms.* a birthday present of $15 on its fifteenth anniversary, or contributing $1,000 for a lifetime subscription — even those who can ill afford it.

What's almost as angering as these struggles, however, is the way the media report them. Our financial problems are attributed to lack of reader interest, not an advertising double standard. In the Reagan–Bush era, when "feminism-is-dead" becomes one key on the typewriter, our problems are used to prepare a grave for the whole movement. Clearly, the myth that advertisers go where the readers are — thus, if we had readers, we would have advertisers — is deeply embedded. Even industry reporters rarely mention the editorial demands made by ads for women's products, and if they do, they assume advertisers must be right and *Ms.* must be wrong; we must be too controversial, outrageous, even scatalogical to support. In fact, there's nothing in our pages that couldn't be published in *Time, Esquire,* or *Rolling Stone* — providing those magazines devoted major space to women — but the media myth often wins out. Though comparable magazines our size (say, *Vanity Fair* or the *Atlantic*) are losing more money in a single year than *Ms.* has lost in sixteen years, *Ms.* is held to a different standard. No matter how much never-to-be-recovered cash is poured into starting a magazine or keeping it going, appearances seem to be all that matter. (Which is why we haven't been able to explain our fragile state in public. Nothing causes ad flight like the smell of nonsuccess.)

My healthy response is anger, but my not-so-healthy one is depression, worry, and an obsession with finding one more rescue. There is hardly a night when I don't wake up with sweaty palms and pounding heart, scared that we won't be able to pay the printer or the post office; scared most of all that closing our doors will be blamed on a lack of readers and thus the movement, instead of the real cause. ("Feminism couldn't even support one magazine," I can hear them saying.)

We're all being flattened by a velvet steamroller. The only difference is that at *Ms.*, we keep standing up again.

Do you think, as I once did, that advertisers make decisions based on rational and uniform criteria? Well, think again. There is clearly a double standard. The same food companies that insist on recipes in women's magazines place ads in *People* where there are no recipes. Cosmetics companies support the *New Yorker*, which has no regular beauty columns, and newspaper pages that have no "beauty atmosphere."

Meanwhile, advertisers' control over the editorial content of women's magazines has become so institutionalized that it is sometimes written into "insertion orders" or dictated to ad salespeople as official policy — whether by the agency, the client, or both. The following are orders given to women's magazines effective in 1990. Try to imagine them being applied to *Time* or *Newsweek.* 65

• Dow's Cleaning Products stipulated that ads for its Vivid and Spray 'n' Wash products should be adjacent to "children or fashion editorial"; ads for Bathroom Cleaner should be next to "home furnishing/family" features; with similar requirements for other brands. "If a magazine fails for $1/2$ the brands or more," the Dow order warned, "it will be omitted from further consideration."

• Bristol-Myers, the parent of Clairol, Windex, Drano, Bufferin, and much more, stipulated that ads be placed next to "a full page of compatible editorial."

• S. C. Johnson & Son, makers of Johnson Wax, lawn and laundry products, insect sprays, hair sprays, and so on, insisted that its ads "*should not be opposite extremely controversial features or material antithetical to the nature/copy of the advertised product.*" (Italics theirs.)

• Maidenform, manufacturer of bras and other women's apparel, left a blank for the particular product and stated in its instructions: "The creative concept of the _____ campaign, and the very nature of the product itself, appeal to the positive emotions of the reader/consumer. Therefore, it is imperative that all editorial adjacencies reflect that same positive tone. The editorial must not be negative in content or lend itself contrary to the _____ product imagery/message (e.g., *editorial relating to illness, disillusionment, large size fashion, etc.*)." (Italics mine.)

• The De Beers diamond company, a big seller of engagement rings, pro- 70 hibited magazines from placing its ads with "adjacencies to hard news or anti-love/romance themed editorial."

• Kraft/General Foods, a giant with many brands, sent this message with an Instant Pudding ad: "urgently request upbeat parent/child activity editorial, mandatory positioning requirements — opposite full page of positive editorial — right hand page essential for creative — minimum 6 page competitive separation (i.e., all sugar based or sugar free gelatins, puddings, mousses, creames [sic] and pie filling) — Do not back with clippable material. Avoid: controversial/negative topics and any narrow targeted subjects."

• An American Tobacco Company order for a Misty Slims ad noted that the U.S. government warning must be included, but also that there must be: "no adjacency to editorial relating to health, medicine, religion, or death."

• Lorillard's Newport cigarette ad came with similar instructions, plus: "Please be aware that the Nicotine Patch products are competitors. The minimum six page separation is required."

Quite apart from anything else, you can imagine the logistical nightmare this creates when putting a women's magazine together, but the greatest casualty is editorial freedom. Though the ratio of advertising to editorial pages in women's magazines is only about 5 percent more than in *Time* or *Newsweek*, that nothing-to-read feeling comes from all the supposedly editorial pages that are extensions of ads. To find out what we're really getting when we pay our money, I picked up a variety of women's magazines for February 1994, and counted the number of pages in each one (even including table of contents, letters to the editors, horoscopes, and the like) that were not ads and/or copy complementary to ads. Then I compared that number to the total pages. Out of 184 pages, *McCall's* had 49 that were nonad or ad-related. Of 202, *Elle* gave readers 48. *Seventeen* provided its young readers with only 51 nonad or ad-related pages out of 226. *Vogue* had 62 out of 292. *Mirabella* offered readers 45 pages out of a total of 158. *Good Housekeeping* came out on top, though only at about a third, with 60 out of 176 pages. *Martha Stewart Living* offered the least. Even counting her letter to readers, a page devoted to her personal calendar, and another one to a turnip, only 7 out of 136 pages had no ads, products, or product mentions. . . .

Within the supposedly editorial text itself, praise for advertisers' products 75 has become so ritualized that fields like "beauty writing" have been invented. One of its practitioners explained to me seriously that "It's a difficult art. How many new adjectives can you find? How much greater can you make a lipstick sound? The FDA restricts what companies can say on labels, but we create illusion. And ad agencies are on the phone all the time pushing you to get their product in. A lot of them keep the business based on how many editorial clippings they produce every month. The worst are products [whose manufacturers have] their own name involved. It's all ego."

Often, editorial becomes one giant ad. An issue of *Lear's* featured an elegant woman executive on the cover. On the contents page, we learn she is wearing Guerlain makeup and Samsara, a new fragrance by Guerlain. Inside, there just happen to be full-page ads for Samsara, plus a Guerlain antiwrinkle skin cream. In the article about the cover subject, we discover she is Guerlain's director of public relations and is responsible for launching, you guessed it, the new Samsara. . . .

When the *Columbia Journalism Review* cited this example in one of the few articles to include women's magazines in a critique of ad influence, Frances Lear, editor of *Lear's*, was quoted at first saying this was a mistake, and then shifting to the defense that "this kind of thing is done all the time."

She's right. Here's an example with a few more turns of the screw. Martha Stewart, *Family Circle*'s contributing editor, was also "lifestyle and entertaining consultant" for Kmart, the retail chain, which helped to underwrite the renovation of Stewart's country house, using Kmart products; *Family Circle* covered the process in three articles not marked as ads; Kmart bought $4 million worth of ad pages in *Family Circle*, including "advertorials" to introduce a line of Martha Stewart products to be distributed by Kmart; and finally, the "advertorials," which at least are marked and only *look* like editorial pages, were reproduced and distributed in Kmart stores, thus publicizing *Family Circle* (owned by the New York Times Company, which would be unlikely to do this kind of thing in its own news pages) to Kmart customers. This was so lucrative that Martha Stewart now has her own magazine, *Martha Stewart Living* (owned by Time Warner), complete with a television version. Both offer a happy world of cooking, entertaining, and decorating in which nothing critical or negative ever seems to happen.

I don't mean to be a spoilsport, but there are many articles we're very unlikely to get from that or any other women's magazine dependent on food ads. According to Senator Howard Metzenbaum of Ohio, more than half of the chickens we eat (from ConAgra, Tyson, Perdue, and other companies) are contaminated with dangerous bacteria; yet labels haven't yet begun to tell us to scrub the meat and everything it touches—which is our best chance of not getting sick. Nor are we likely to learn about the frequent working conditions of this mostly female work force, standing in water, cutting chickens apart with such repetitive speed that carpal tunnel syndrome is an occupational hazard. Then there's Dole Food, often cited as a company that keeps women in low-level jobs and a target of a lawsuit by Costa Rican workers who were sterilized by contact with pesticides used by Dole—even though Dole must have known these pesticides had been banned in the United States.

The consumerist reporting we're missing sometimes sounds familiar. Remember the *Ms.* episode with Clairol and the article about potential carcinogens in hair dye? Well, a similar saga took place with L'Oréal and *Mademoiselle* in 1992, according to an editor at Condé Nast. Now, editors there are supposed to warn publishers of any criticism in advance, a requirement that might well have a chilling effect.

Other penalties are increasing. As older readers will remember, women's magazines used to be a place where new young poets and short story writers could be published. Now, that's very rare. It isn't that advertisers of women's products dislike poetry or fiction, it's just that they pay to be adjacent to articles and features more directly compatible with their products.

Sometimes, advertisers invade editorial pages—literally—by plunging odd-shaped ads into the text, no matter how that increases the difficulty of reading. When Ellen Levine was editor of *Woman's Day*, for instance, a magazine originally founded by a supermarket chain, she admitted, "The day the copy had to rag around a chicken leg was not a happy one."

The question of ad positioning is also decided by important advertisers, a rule that's ignored at a magazine's peril. When Revlon wasn't given the place of the first beauty ad in one Hearst magazine, for instance, it pulled its ads from *all* Hearst magazines. In 1990 Ruth Whitney, editor in chief of *Glamour*, attributed some of this pushiness to "ad agencies wanting to prove to a client that they've squeezed the last drop of blood out of a magazine." She was also "sick and tired of hearing that women's magazines are controlled by cigarette ads." Relatively speaking, she was right. To be as controlling as most advertisers of women's products, tobacco companies would have to demand articles in flat-out praise of smoking, and editorial photos of models smoking a credited brand. As it is, they ask only to be forewarned so they don't advertise in the same issue with an article about the dangers of smoking. But for a magazine like *Essence*, the only national magazine for African American women, even taking them out of one issue may be financially difficult, because other advertisers might neglect its readers. In 1993, a group called Women and Girls Against Tobacco, funded by the California Department of Health Services, prepared an ad headlined "Cigarettes Made Them History." It pictured three black singers — Mary Wells, Eddie Kendricks, and Sarah Vaughan — who died of tobacco-related diseases. *Essence* president Clarence Smith didn't turn the ad down, but he didn't accept it either. When I talked with him in 1994, he said with pain, "the black female market just isn't considered at parity with the white female market; there are too many other categories we don't get." That's in spite of the fact that *Essence* does all the traditional food-fashion-beauty editorial expected by advertisers. According to California statistics, African American women are more addicted to smoking than the female population at large, with all the attendant health problems.

Alexandra Penney, editor of *Self* magazine, feels she has been able to include smoking facts in health articles by warning cigarette advertisers in advance (though smoking is still being advertised in this fitness magazine). On the other hand, up to this writing in 1994, no advertiser has been willing to appear opposite a single-page feature called "Outrage," which is reserved for important controversies, and is very popular with readers. Another women's magazine publisher told me that to this day Campbell's Soup refuses to advertise because of an article that unfavorably compared the nutritional value of canned food to that of fresh food — fifteen years ago.

I don't mean to imply that the editors I quote here share my objections to ad demands and/or expectations. Many assume that the women's magazines at which they work have to be the way they are. Others are justifiably proud of getting an independent article in under the advertising radar, for instance, articles on family violence in *Family Circle* or a series on child sexual abuse and the family courts in *McCall's*. A few insist they would publish exactly the same editorial, even if there were no ads. But it's also true that it's hard to be honest while you're still in the job. "Most of the pressure came in the form of direct product mentions," explained Sey Chassler, who was editor in chief of *Redbook* from the sixties to the eighties and is now out of the game. "We got threats from the big guys, the Revlons, blackmail threats. They wouldn't run ads unless we credited them."

What could women's magazines be like if they were as editorially free as good books? as realistic as the best newspaper articles? as creative as poetry and films? as diverse as women's lives? What if we as women — who are psychic immigrants in a public world rarely constructed by or for us — had the same kind of watchful, smart, supportive publications on our side that other immigrant groups have often had?

We'll find out only if we take the media directed at us seriously. If readers were to act in concert in large numbers for a few years to change the traditional practices of *all* women's magazines and the marketing of *all* women's products, we could do it. After all, they depend on our consumer dollars — money we now are more likely to control. If we include all the shopping we do for families and spouses, women make 85 percent of purchases at point of sale. You and I could:

- refuse to buy products whose ads have clearly dictated their surroundings, and write to tell the manufacturers why;

- write to editors and publishers (with copies to advertisers) to tell them that we're willing to pay *more* for magazines with editorial independence, but will *not* continue to pay for those that are editorial extensions of ads;

- write to advertisers (with copies to editors and publishers) to tell them that we want fiction, political reporting, consumer reporting, strong opinion, humor, and health coverage that doesn't pull punches, praising them when their ads support this, and criticizing them when they don't;

- put as much energy and protest into breaking advertising's control over what's around it as we put into changing the images within it or protesting harmful products like cigarettes;

- support only those women's magazines and products that take us seriously as readers and consumers;

- investigate new laws and regulations to support freedom from advertising influence. The Center for the Study of Commercialism, a group founded in 1990 to educate and advocate against "ubiquitous product marketing," recommends whistle-blower laws that protect any members of the media who disclose advertiser and other commercial conflicts of interest, laws that require advertiser influence to be disclosed, Federal Trade Commission involvement, and denial of income tax exemptions for advertising that isn't clearly identified — as well as conferences, citizen watchdog groups, and a national clearinghouse where examples of private censorship can be reported.

Those of us in the magazine world can also use this carrot-and-stick technique. The stick: If magazines were a regulated medium like television, the editorial quid pro quo demanded by advertising would be against the rules of the FCC, and payola and extortion would be penalized. As it is, there are potential illegalities to pursue. For example: A magazine's postal rates are determined by the ratio of ad pages to editorial pages, with the ads being charged at a higher rate than the editorial. Counting up all the pages that are *really* ads could make an interesting legal action. There could be consumer fraud cases lurking in subscriptions that are solicited for a magazine but deliver a catalog.

The carrot is just as important. In twenty years, for instance, I've found no independent, nonproprietary research showing that an ad for, say, fragrance is any more effective placed next to an article about fragrance than it would be when placed next to a good piece of fiction or reporting. As we've seen, there are studies showing that the greatest factor in determining an ad's effectiveness is the credibility and independence of its surroundings. An airtight wall between ads and edit would also shield corporations and agencies from pressures from both ends of the political spectrum and from dozens of pressure groups. Editors would be the only ones responsible for editorial content — which is exactly as it should be.

Unfortunately, few agencies or clients hear such arguments. Editors often   90
maintain the artificial purity of refusing to talk to the people who actually control their lives. Instead, advertisers see salespeople who know little about editorial, are trained in business as usual, and are usually paid on commission. To
take on special controversy editors might also band together. That happened
once when all the major women's magazines did articles in the same month on
the Equal Rights Amendment. It could happen again — and regularly.

Meanwhile, we seem to have a system in which everybody is losing. The
reader loses diversity, strong opinion, honest information, access to the arts,
and much more. The editor loses pride of work, independence, and freedom
from worry about what brand names or other critical words some sincere
freelancer is going to come up with. The advertiser loses credibility right
along with the ad's surroundings, and gets more and more lost in a sea of
similar ads and interchangeable media.

But that's also the good news. Because where there is mutual interest,
there is the beginning of change.

If you need one more motive for making it, consider the impact of U.S.
media on the rest of the world. The ad policies we tolerate here are invading
the lives of women in other cultures — through both the content of U.S. media
and the ad practices of multinational corporations imposed on other countries. Look at our women's magazines. Is this what we want to export?

Should *Ms.* have started out with no advertising in the first place? The odd
thing is that, in retrospect, I think the struggle was worth it. For all those years,
dozens of feminist organizers disguised as *Ms.* ad saleswomen took their
courage, research, slide shows, humor, ingenuity, and fresh point of view into
every advertising agency, client office, and lion's den in cities where advertising is sold. Not only were sixteen years of *Ms.* sustained in this way, with all
the changeful words on those thousands of pages, but some of the advertising
industry was affected in its imagery, its practices, and its understanding of the
female half of the country. Those dozens of women themselves were affected,
for they learned the art of changing a structure from both within and without,
and are now rising in crucial publishing positions where women have never
been. *Ms.* also helped to open nontraditional categories of ads for women's
magazines, thus giving them a little more freedom — not to mention making
their changes look reasonable by comparison.

But the world of advertising has a way of reminding us how far there is   95
to go.

Three years ago, as I was finishing this exposé in its first version, I got a
call from a writer for *Elle.* She was doing an article on where women parted
their hair: Why, she wanted to know, did I part mine in the middle?

It was all so familiar. I could imagine this writer trying to make something
out of a nothing assignment. A long-suffering editor laboring to think of new
ways to attract ads for shampoo, conditioner, hair dryers, and the like. Readers
assuming that other women must want this stuff.

As I was working on this version, I got a letter from Revlon of the sort we disregarded when we took ads. Now, I could appreciate it as a reminder of how much we had to disregard:

> We are delighted to confirm that Lauren Hutton is now under contract to Revlon.
>
> We are very much in favor of her appearing in as much editorial as possible, but it's important that your publication avoid any mention of competitive color cosmetics, beauty treatment, hair care or sun care products in editorial or editorial credits in which she appears.
>
> We would be very appreciative if all concerned are made aware of this.

I could imagine the whole chain of women — Lauren Hutton, preferring to be in the Africa that is her passion; the ad executive who signed the letter, only doing her job; the millions of women readers who would see the resulting artificial images; all of us missing sources of information, insight, creativity, humor, anger, investigation, poetry, confession, outrage, learning, and perhaps most important, a sense of connection to each other; and a gloriously diverse world being flattened by a velvet steamroller.

I ask you: Can't we do better than this?   100

READING THE TEXT

1. What does Steinem mean by "complementary copy" (para. 17) and "advertorials" (para. 78)?

2. Summarize the relationship Steinem sees between editorial content and advertising in women's magazines.

3. In Steinem's view, what messages about gender roles does complementary copy send readers of women's magazines?

4. What is the history of response to this article since its initial publication in 1990, according to Steinem?

READING THE SIGNS

1. In your journal, explore whether you believe advertisers infringe on freedom of the press.

2. Steinem asserts that virtually all content in women's magazines is a disguised form of advertising. Test her hypothesis in a detailed analysis of a single issue of a magazine such as *Cosmopolitan* or *Elle*. Do you find instances of complementary copy and advertorials? How do you react as a potential reader of such magazines?

3. Explore whether Steinem's argument holds for men's magazines such as *Maxim* or *GQ*. If you identify differences, how might they be based on different assumptions about gender roles?

4. Bring a favorite magazine to class, and compare it with those chosen by other students. In small groups, study the relationship between ads and articles.

What magazines have the most complementary copy? How can you account for your findings?

5. Steinem asks, "What could women's magazines be like if they were as editorially free as good books?" (para. 86). In a creative essay, write your own response to this question, presenting evidence to support your thesis. If you prefer, you could focus on another type of magazine, such as a young men's publication like *Maxim*, which also links advertising with editorial content.

JULIET B. SCHOR
Selling to Children: The Marketing of Cool

Being cool isn't just an attitude — it's a consumer lifestyle. As Juliet B. Schor describes the situation in this selection from her book *Born to Buy*, the marketing of edgy, sexy, violent, and subversive images of coolness has moved from teen and young-adult advertising to children's advertising. Closely related to what Thomas Frank calls the "commodification of dissent," cool marketing to kids has created a "giant feedback loop," whereby advertisers study youth behavior to see what kids respond to, while the kids study advertisements to see what's cool and what's not. A professor of sociology at Boston College, Schor is the author of numerous books on American consumption, including *The Overworked American: The Unexpected Decline of Leisure* (1993); *The Overspent American: Why We Want What We Don't Need* (1999); *Born to Buy: The Commercialized Child and the New Consumer Culture* (2005); and *True Wealth: How and Why Millions of Americans Are Creating a Time-Rich, Ecologically Light, Small-Scale, High-Satisfaction Economy* (2011).

The Marketing of Cool

Cool has been around for decades. Back in the fifties, there were cool cats and hipsters. In the sixties, hippies and the Beatles were cool. But in those days, cool was only one of many acceptable personal styles. Now it's revered as a universal quality — something every product tries to be and every kid needs to have.[1] Marketers have defined cool as the key to social success, as what matters for determining who belongs, who's popular, and who gets accepted by peers. While there is no doubt that the desire for social acceptance is a central theme of growing up, marketers have elevated it to the sine qua non of children's psyches. The promotion of cool is a good example of how the practices of marketing to teens, for whom social acceptance is even more important, have filtered down to the children's sphere. In a recent survey of 4,002 kids in grades 4 through 8, 66 percent reported that cool defines them.[2] Part of why is that cool has become *the* dominant theme of children's marketing.

Part of the genius of cool is its versatility. Cool isn't only about not being a dork. Cool takes on many incarnations. It can incorporate dork and jock, if necessary. It can be driven by neon or primary colors; it's retro or futuristic, techno or natural. Today, Target is cool. Yesterday it was the Gap. Good-bye Barney. Hello Kitty. By the time you read these words, today's cool will not be. But although cool is hard to pin down, in practice it centers on some recurring themes, and these themes are relentlessly pushed by marketers in the conception and design of products, packaging, marketing, and advertising. At every step, these principles apply.

One theme is that cool is socially exclusive, that is, expensive. In an earlier era, cheap stuff dominated kids' consumer worlds, mainly because they didn't have much money. They bought penny candy, plastic toys, and cheap thrills. In those days, the functional aspects of products were paramount, such as the fact that the toy is fun to play with or the candy tastes good. Social symbolism and status weren't wholly absent, but they were far less important. Now that kids have access to so much more money, status and its underlying values of inequality and exclusion have settled at the heart of the kid consumer culture. Branding expert Martin Lindstrom reports that for tweens, the brand took over from function as the main attraction of products in the 1990s.[3] From video games, to apparel, to that ubiquitous symbol of status, the athletic shoe, kids' products have upscaled, in the process becoming both more unaffordable and more desirable. Gene Del Vecchio, former Ogilvy and Mather executive and author of *Creating Ever-Cool: A Marketer's Guide to a Kid's Heart*, is more candid than most others about the exclusionary nature of cool: "Part of cool is having something that others do not. That makes a kid feel special. It is also the spark that drives kids to find the next cool item."[4] When Reebok introduced its computerized Traxtar shoe, it was banking on a message of "superiority" ("I have Traxtar and you don't"), according to the people who designed the program.[5] The shoe became the top seller in its category, a notable accomplishment given its significantly higher price. Marketers convey the view that wealth and aspiration to wealth are cool. Material excess, having lots of money, career achievement, and a lifestyle to go with it are all highly valued in the marketing world's definition of what's hot and what's not. Living modestly means living like a loser.

Cool is also associated with being older than one's age.[6] Marketers and advertisers take this common desire of kids and play into it in a variety of ways. They put a few older kids in ads that are targeted to younger kids. They have young kids in ads morph into older kids or into adults. They use adult celebrity endorsers for products or brands that kids buy. They depict fantasy worlds in which a young kid sees himself or herself grown up. Cool is also associated with an antiadult sensibility, as ads portray kids with attitude, outwitting their teachers and tricking their parents. Finally, cool is about the taboo, the dangerous, the forbidden other. Among advertisers, *edgy* has been and remains the adjective of the moment — not "over the edge," because that is too dangerous, but "at the edge," "pushing the edge."

Edgy style has associations with rap and hip-hop, with "street" and Afri- 5
can American culture. In the 1990s, ads aimed at white, middle-class Americans began to be filmed in inner-city neighborhoods with young black men as the stars. The ads made subtle connections to violence, drugs, criminality, and sexuality — the distorted and stereotypical images of young black men that have pervaded the mainstream media. As Harvard University's Douglas Holt wrote in 1999 in a paper we coauthored, "Street has proven to be a potent commodity because its aesthetic offers an authentic threatening edginess that is very attractive both to white suburban kids who perpetually recreate radical youth culture in relation to their parents' conservative views about the ghetto, and to urban cultural elites for whom it becomes a form of cosmopolitan radical chic. . . . We now have the commodification of a virulent, dangerous 'other' lifestyle. . . . Gangsta."[7]

The story of how street came to be at the core of consumer marketing began more than thirty years ago. Chroniclers of the marketing of "ghetto" point to the practices of athletic shoe companies, starting with Converse in the late 1960s and, more recently, Nike and its competitors. The shoe manufacturers intentionally associated their product with African American athletes, giving free shoes to coaches in the inner cities, targeting inner-city consumers in their research, attaching their brand to street athletics and sociability.[8] They also developed a practice dubbed "bro-ing" by industry insiders, that is, going to the streets to ask the brothers which designs deserve the moniker of cool. Apparel companies, beginning with Tommy Hilfiger, became active in this world, giving rap stars and other prominent tastemakers free samples of their latest styles.[9] While the connection to inner-city life may sound like a contradiction with the idea that cool is exclusive and upscale, it is partially resolved by the fact that many of the inner-city ambassadors of products are wealthy, conspicuous consumers such as rap stars and athletes driving fancy cars and living luxurious lifestyles.

Eventually soft drink companies, candy manufacturers, culture producers, and many others that sell products to teens and kids would be on the street, trying desperately to get some of that ineluctable cool to rub off on their brand. As advertiser Paul Kurnit explains, "What's going on in white America today is [that] the inner city is very much a Gold Standard. We've got lots of white kids who are walking around, emulating black lifestyle."[10] Of course, mere association with ghetto style is not a guarantee of success. Some campaigns have been flat-footed with their mimicry. Others lack basic credibility, such as preppy tennis shoe K-Swiss, which tried to position itself as a street brand. The brands that have been skilled at this approach are those with images that are more plausibly and authentically connected to it.

Although many aspects of African American culture have had a long historical association with cool such as jazz and sartorial styles, as well as a legacy of contributions to popular culture, what's happening now is unique. Never before have inner-city styles and cultural practices been such a dominant influence on, even a primary definer of, popular culture. The process is also no longer one of mainstreaming, in which a cultural innovation from the margins is incorporated into the larger culture. Rather, in the words of Douglas Holt again, "It is now the local, authentic qualities of Street culture that sell. Instead of black cultural products denuded of their social context, it is now primarily the context itself — the neighborhood, the pain of being poor, the alienation experienced by black kids. These are the commodifiable assets." The other new development is the role of large corporations in the movement of styles and cultural forms from the ghetto to the suburb. The process no longer develops through an organic movement as it once did. Instead, cool hunters manage the process of cultural transmission. Another novel aspect is the evolution of a back-and-forth dynamic between the companies and the grass roots, with cool-hunting and street marketing creating what media critics have called a feedback loop.

The feedback loop is a sharp departure from decades past, when consumers blindly followed where advertisers led. In Holt's words, marketers once possessed a monopoly on "cultural authority," in which they set the tone and agenda, and consumers eagerly looked to them to learn what to wear, eat, drive, and value.[11] That cultural authority has virtually disappeared. Its demise can be traced to the backlash against advertising that originally emerged in the 1950s with the popularity of books such as John Kenneth Galbraith's *The Affluent Society* and Vance Packard's *The Hidden Persuaders*.[12] By the 1960s, some of the most successful marketers were those who took their cues from consumers. Since, then, advertisers have increasingly attempted to figure out what people already value and let those findings direct ads. With youth, the process has gone a step further, because they know the advertisers are relying on them, and consciously play to their influence. That's the feedback idea, which has been identified by observers such as Douglas Kellner, Holt, and Douglas Rushkoff. As Rushkoff explains, in a plea to the industry: "It's turned into a giant feedback loop: you watch kids to find out what trend is 'in,' but the kids are watching you watching them in order to figure out how to act. They are exhibitionists, aware of corporate America's fascination with their every move, and delighting in your obsession with their tastes."[13] Although there's a democratic veneer to the feedback loop, that perspective obscures the fact that giant businesses orchestrate, control, and profit from the process. Furthermore, kids are increasingly pulling outrageous and even dangerous stunts to get themselves noticed by the great big marketing machine.

Originally, the marketing of edgy was a teen and young adult development.   10
Now it too has trickled down to the children's market, though with some adjustments. Kid advertisers had to become far more discriminating, screening

out what had become an anything-goes ethic. By way of illustration, consider the heroin-chic fashion photography of the mid-1990s, At that time cool hunters routinely included drugs, including hard ones, on their lists of what's hot and what's not. As one now-famous accounting from a cool-hunter publication that appeared in the *New Yorker* had it: "In San Francisco it's Nike, heroin, and reggae; in Chicago, Jungle music, Tag watches, and drugs."[14] Similarly, in kids' ads, violent images are more restricted, although this is less the case in movie ads, video games, and on the Web. The situation is similar with sexuality, exploitative racial imagery, and certain antisocial themes, all of which are prominent in cultural forms for teens and young adults. While going edgy can almost guarantee cool, it can also jeopardize a brand that depends on maintaining its wholesome image. Advertisers calibrate the degree of edginess and strive to go as far as, but not beyond what, a brand's image can tolerate.

Kids Rule: Nickelodeon and the Antiadult Bias

What else is cool? Based on what's selling in consumer culture, one would have to say that kids are cool and adults are not. Fair enough. Our country has a venerable history of generational conflict and youth rebellion. But marketers have perverted those worthy sentiments to create a sophisticated and powerful "antiadultism" within the commercial world.[15]

   This trend also has a history. Advertising agencies have been co-opting youth rebellion for years, beginning with Bill Bernbach's embrace of the counterculture in Volkswagen ads in the 1960s, a development insightfully chronicled in Thomas Frank's *The Conquest of Cool*. More recently, the entity most responsible for the commercial exploitation of youth rebellion has been Viacom. The trend began with MTV and its teen audience, as the enormously popular network capitalized on teen desires to separate from and rebel against their parents.[16] MTV allowed teens to immerse themselves in an increasingly separate culture, with its own fashions, language, and attitudes. Over time, some of that sensibility has trickled down to Nickelodeon's younger target.

   Nickelodeon was founded in 1979 as a cable network, but it has since become a transcendent brand identity, selling a wide array of products and a relationship with kids. Nickelodeon would eventually dominate children's media. Nickelodeon's audience outpaces all other kid-oriented networks by a wide margin. At 80 percent, its household penetration tops the children's cable networks.[17] As I write these words, it is enjoying its best ratings year ever, surging far above the competition. The Nickelodeon Web site is the number one children's online destination. Its magazines boast 1.1 million subscribers and 6.3 million readers.[18] Nickelodeon is shown in 158 countries. Incredibly enough, given its limited demographic target, Nickelodeon has become one of the nation's most profitable networks.[19] In the process, it has remade children's programming and advertising.

Early on, Nickelodeon earned a reputation for offering quality shows. Its graphics were visually arresting, and the content was fresh. In comparison to the tired world of program-length commercials, that is, shows whose primary purpose is to sell products, Nickelodeon's offerings stood out. The network has also benefited from its recognition that children are a diverse group in terms of race and ethnicity, family type, and age. On the revenue side, Nickelodeon has made hay with the insight that children are a major influence market for parental purchases. A senior executive explained their stance: "The whole premise of our company was founded on serving kids, and what we've found is that when you do good things for kids, it happens to be good for business."[20]

The secret of Nickelodeon's success is its core philosophy: *kids rule.* In everything that they do, Nickelodeon tries to take the child's perspective. The network has positioned itself as kids' best friend, on their side in an often-hostile environment. Donna Sabino, director for research and development at Nickelodeon's Magazine Group, explained the thinking to me: "It's hard to be a kid in an adult world. The adult world doesn't respect kids. Everywhere else adults rule; at Nick kids rule."[21] The Nickelodeon worldview is that childhood has gotten tough. "Kids are experiencing increased pressure for achievement and activity. They don't have enough time for homework, they're overscheduled." Nickelodeon gives them what they need: "funny, happy, empowering." There are thirteen criteria a program must have to pass muster at the network, including good quality, a kid-centered message, humor, and edgy visual design. In theory, these are good criteria. But in practice, when kid-centric and edgy come together, what often results is attitude — an antiauthoritarian us-versus-them sensibility that pervades the brand.

Nickelodeon is not unique in its positioning. The world of children's marketing is filled with variants of the us-versus-them message. A prominent example is the soft drink Sprite, one of the most successful youth culture brands.[22] One witty Sprite ad depicted an adolescent boy and his parents on a road trip. The parents are in the front seat singing "Polly wolly doodle all the day," the epitome of unnerving uncool. He's in the back, banging his head on the car window in frustration, the ignominy of being stuck with these two losers too much to bear. "Need a CD player?" the ad asks.

A Fruit-to-Go online promotion tells kids that "when it comes to fashion class, your principal is a flunkie." A spot for Sour Brite Crawlers has a group of tween boys in an elevator going into gross detail about how they eat this gummy worm candy, eventually sickening the adults and forcing them to flee. The creators of the spot consider it "a great example . . . where tweens demonstrate their superiority of the situation with control over the adults."[23]

Adults also enforce a repressive and joyless world, in contrast to what kids and products do when they're left in peace. Consider a well-known Starburst classroom commercial. As the nerdy teacher writes on the board, kids open the candy, and the scene erupts into a riotous party. When the teacher faces the class again, all is quiet, controlled, and dull. The dynamic repeats itself, as the commercial makes the point that the kid world, courtesy of the candy, is a blast. The adult world, by contrast, is drab, regimented, BORRRR-inggg.

A study of 200 video game ads produced between 1989 and 1999 revealed a similar approach. Researchers Stephen Kline and Greig de Peuter report themes of boy empowerment through "oedipal rebellion" and rejection of home environments depicted as boring suburban spaces. "Nintendo ads," they write, "often construct the gamer as under siege by the adultified world while promising the young male gamers 'empowerment' and 'control' in an unlimited virtual world."[24] This attitude pervades the company's marketing strategy as well. As one Nintendo marketer explained, "We don't market to parents. . . . We market to our target group, which is teens and tweens. . . . The parental seal of approval, while it is something that we like, it is not something that we actively encourage in our marketing because that might say to the kids that we're boring."[25]

A related theme in some kid advertising is to promote behavior that is annoying, antisocial, or mischievous. There's usually a playful quality to these spots, as in the various ads involving stealing candy at the movies. Julie Halpin of the Gepetto Group explains the strategy they used for Kids Foot Locker: "We wanted to be able to show them the empowerment they could have with the shoes. . . . What's really fun about a new pair of sneakers is a lot of the things that kids do that are really mischievous: squeaking on the floor, giving each other flat tires, writing little messages underneath. . . . Sales during the advertising period were about 34 percent higher than they were the previous year."[26]

Industry insiders and outsiders confirm the antiadultism in much of today's youth advertising. As one marketer explained to me: "Advertisers have kicked the parents out. They make fun of the parents. . . . We inserted the product in the secret kid world. . . . [It's] secret, dangerous, kid only."[27] Media critic Mark Crispin Miller makes a similar point: "It's part of the official advertising worldview that your parents are creeps, teachers are nerds and idiots, authority figures are laughable, nobody can really understand kids except the corporate sponsor. That huge authority has, interestingly enough, emerged as the sort of tacit superhero of consumer culture. That's the coolest entity of all."[28]

Similar trends can be found in programming. Journalist Bernice Kanner notes that "television dads—and to a lesser extent moms—once portrayed as loving and wise are now depicted as neglectful, incompetent, abusive or invisible. Parenthood, once presented as the source of supreme satisfaction on TV, is now largely ignored or debased." It's "parents as nincompoops."[29] After 9/11, Holly Gross, then of Saatchi and Saatchi kid Connection, counseled companies that although "families *are* reconnecting and kids and parents *do* wish for more time together . . . that doesn't mean the tender moments must be shared in *your* marketing communication . . . some parents are just *sooooo* embarrassing." She advises going "parent-free" to market to tweens.[30]

Marketers defend themselves against charges of antiadultism by arguing that they are promoting kid empowerment. Social conservatives, however, see treachery in the ridicule of adults. Wherever one comes down on this debate, it's important to recognize the nature of the corporate message: kids and products are aligned together in a really great, fun place, while parents, teachers, and other adults inhabit an oppressive, drab, and joyless world. The lesson to kids is that it's the product, not your parent, who's really on your side.

Age Compression

One of the hottest trends in youth marketing is age compression — the practice of taking products and marketing messages originally designed for older kids and targeting them to younger ones. Age compression includes offering teen products and genres, pitching gratuitous violence to the twelve-and-under crowd, cultivating brand preferences for items that were previously unbranded among younger kids, and developing creative alcohol and tobacco advertising that is not officially targeted to them but is widely seen and greatly loved by children. "By eight or nine they want 'N Sync," explained one tweening expert to me, in the days before that band was eclipsed by Justin Timberlake, Pink, and others.

Age compression is a sprawling trend. It can be seen in the import of tele- 25 vision programming specifically designed for one year olds, which occurred, ironically, with Public Broadcasting's *Teletubbies*. It includes the marketing of designer clothes to kindergarteners and first graders. It's the deliberate targeting of R-rated movies to kids as young as age nine, a practice the major movie studios were called on the carpet for by the Clinton administration in 2000. It's being driven by the recognition that many children nationwide are watching MTV and other teen and adult programming. One of my favorite MTV anecdotes comes from a third-grade teacher in Weston, Massachusetts, who reported that she started her social studies unit on Mexico by asking the class what they knew about the country. Six or seven raised their hands and answered, "That's the place where MTV's Spring Break takes place!" For those who haven't seen it, the program glorifies heavy partying, what it calls "bootylicious girls," erotic dancing, wet T-shirt contests, and binge drinking.

Nowhere is age compression more evident than among the eight- to twelve-year-old target. Originally a strategy for selling to ten- to thirteen-year-olds, children as young as six are being targeting for tweening. And what is that exactly? Tweens are "in-between" teens and children, and tweening consists mainly of bringing teen products and entertainment to ever-younger audiences. If you're wondering why your daughter came home from kindergarten one day singing the words to a Britney Spears or Jennifer Lopez song, the answer is that she got tweened. Tween marketing has become a major focus of the industry, with its own conferences, research tools, databases, books, and specialty firms. Part of why tweening is so lucrative is that it involves bringing new, more expensive products to this younger group. It's working because tweens have growing purchasing power and influence with parents. The more the tween consumer world comes to resemble the teen world, with its comprehensive branding strategies and intense levels of consumer immersion, the more money there is to be made.[31]

NOTES

[1]For a now-classic account of cool-hunting, see Gladwell (1997), reprinted in Schor and Holt (2000).

[2]A recent survey in which 66 percent of kids say cool defines them is from the KidID survey of JustKid Inc. Data provided to the author and presented by Wynne Tyree at KidPower 2002.

[3]On the shift from function to brand as the main attraction, see Lindstrom (2003), p. 82.

[4]Gene Del Vecchio quote "part of cool" is from Del Vecchio (1997), p. 121.

[5]On Traxtar marketing and its success, see Siegel et al. (2001), pp. 179–190.

[6]On kids wanting to be older than they are, this is what Paul Kurnit had to say in our interview: "Emulation and aspiration work up, but only to a certain point. So if you capture six to eleven year olds, your bull's-eye is probably the eleven year old boy. . . . If you're looking for the eleven year old boy you're probably in a commercial casting a twelve or thirteen year old boy."

[7]Douglas Holt quote on street as a potent commodity is from Holt and Schor (1998).

[8]On sneaker marketing in the inner city, see Vanderbilt (1998), ch. 1.

[9]On Hilfiger, see Smith (1997) and Spiegler (1997).

[10]Paul Kurnit quote from his interview with O'Barr (2001).

[11]On the cultural authority of marketers, see Holt (2002).

[12]On these issues, see Kellner (1998), Holt (2002), and Frank (1997) on the backlash against advertisers and the subsequent marketing of cool.

[13]The feedback loop is explored in the PBS special *Merchants of Cool*, available online at pbs.org/frontline/shows/cool/. Douglas Rushkoff quote from his essay "The Pursuit of Cool: Introduction to Anti-Hyper-Consumerism," available online at http://www.rushkoff.com/essay/sportswearinternational.html.

[14]On cool-hunters' lists of what's hot and what's not, see Gladwell (1997), from which these items are drawn.

[15]For an early recognition of the rise of antiadultism, see Nader (1996).

[16]On the sale of youth rebellion to teens, see Nader (1996), ch. 4 and conclusion.

[17]Nickelodeon's ratings are from *Kidscreen* magazine (2002), p. 33. On weekdays in 2002, Nickelodeon commanded a 2.7 audience share, a full point above the Cartoon Network; on Saturday mornings, its 4.2 share was 1.2 points higher than the number two.

[18]The 1.1 million subscribers and 6.3 million readers from June 2003 data provided by Donna Sabino to the author.

[19]On Nickelodeon's profitability, see Carter (2002). MTV Networks, to which Nickelodeon belongs, earned more than $3 billion in revenue in 2002. The statistic of 158 countries is also from this source.

[20]"Whole premise of our company" quote by Lisa Judson, senior vice president of programming and executive creative director, cited in Hood (2000).

[21]Sabino quote beginning "It's hard to be a kid" and thirteen criteria from interview with the author, July 2001.

[22]On Sprite's success positioning itself as a youth brand, see *Merchants of Cool*, program 1911, *Frontline*. Available at www.pbs.org/wgbh/pages/frontline/shows/cool/etc/script.html.

[23]The Sour Brite Crawlers example is from Siegel et al. (2001), p. 61.

[24]"Nintendo ads" from Kline and de Peuter (2002), p. 265.

[25]Nintendo marketer quote on targeting kids directly is from Kline and de Peuter (2002), p. 266.

[26]Halpin quote from an interview with her at Reveries, available online at http://www.reveries.com/reverb/kids_marketing/halpin/index.html.

[27]"Advertisers have kicked the parents out" quote from Mary Prescott (pseudonym), interview with the author, July 2001.

[28]Crispin Miller quote from *Merchants of Cool* transcript, cited above.

[29]Television dads quote from Kanner (2002), p. 45, and parents as nincompoops on p. 56. See also Hymowitz (1999), ch. 4, for a discussion of antifamilial attitudes in television.

[30]Holly Gross quote from Gross (2002b).

[31]On the idea of the tween and its evolution from earlier categories of sub- and preteen, see Cook and Kaiser (2003).

READING THE TEXT

1. Explain in your own words what constitutes "cool" in children's advertising, according to Schor.

2. How has "street" culture influenced consumer marketing, as Schor explains it?

3. What does researcher Douglas Holt mean by his claim that "the neighborhood, the pain of being poor, the alienation experienced by black kids . . . are the commodifiable assets" (para. 8) exploited in advertising?

4. What does the term "age compression" (para. 24) mean, in your own words?

READING THE SIGNS

1. Perform a semiotic analysis of an advertisement from any medium directed at children. What signifiers in the ad are especially addressed to children? To what extent do you see evidence of "cool marketing"? Consider such details as colors, music, voice track, the implied narrative of the ad, and its characters and their appearance.

2. Conduct an in-class debate over whether advertising to young people should be more strictly regulated. To develop support for your team's position, watch some TV programs aimed at children or teens and the advertising that accompanies them.

3. **CONNECTING TEXTS**   Read or reread James B. Twitchell's "What We Are to Advertisers" (p. 177), and write an essay in which you analyze whether Twitchell's assertion that "mass marketing means the creation of mass stereotypes" (para. 1) applies to child or tween consumers.

4. Using Thomas Frank's perspective in "Commodify Your Dissent" (p. 150) as a critical framework, analyze a suite of ads aimed at tweens and discuss the to extent to which the ads "commodify" coolness and edginess. Ads that promote popular clothing, such as jeans, can be especially rich objects of analysis.

JOSEPH TUROW

The Daily You: How the New Advertising Industry Is Defining Your Identity and Your Worth

It's called "data mining": the practice by which such digital media giants as Google and Facebook track every move by Internet users and sell that information to marketers who use it to construct advertisements that are tailor-made for their recipients. In this selection from his book *The Daily You*, Joseph Turow describes how this world of digital profiling and personalized marketing works. If his revelation "creeps you out," Turow explains, you are not alone. The Robert Lewis Shayon Professor of Communication at the University of Pennsylvania's Annenberg School, Turow is the author of many books, most recently *Playing Doctor: Television, Storytelling, and Medical Power* (2010); *Media Today: An Introduction to Mass Communication* (2011); and *The Daily You: How the New Advertising Industry Is Defining Your Identity and Your Worth* (2013).

At the start of the twenty-first century, the advertising industry is guiding one of history's most massive stealth efforts in social profiling. At this point you may hardly notice the results of this trend. You may find you're getting better or worse discounts on products than your friends. You may notice that some ads seem to follow you around the internet. Every once in a while a website may ask you if you like a particular ad you just received. Or perhaps your cell phone has told you that you will be rewarded if you eat in a nearby restaurant where, by the way, two of your friends are hanging out this very minute.

You may actually like some of these intrusions. You may feel that they pale before the digital power you now have. After all, your ability to create blogs, collaborate with others to distribute videos online, and say what you want on Facebook (carefully using its privacy settings) seems only to confirm what marketers and even many academics are telling us: that consumers are captains of their own new-media ships.

But look beneath the surface, and a different picture emerges. We're at the start of a revolution in the ways marketers and media intrude in — and shape — our lives. Every day most if not all Americans who use the internet, along with hundreds of millions of other users from all over the planet, are being quietly peeked at, poked, analyzed, and tagged as they move through the online world. Governments undoubtedly conduct a good deal of snooping, more in some parts of the world than in others. But in North America, Europe, and many other places, companies that work for marketers have taken the lead in secretly slicing and dicing the actions and backgrounds of

Portfolio of Advertisements

READING THE SIGNS

Consider these questions as you analyze the advertisements on the following pages.

1. This ad for the Bose Sound-Link Mini speaker reflects a change in the way that people listen to music. What is that change, and how is Bose responding to it through this ad?

2. This ad for Buffalo Exchange promotes an attitude as well as a lifestyle. What is that attitude, and how does it reflect what Thomas Frank calls the "commodification of dissent"?

3. An ad for a trade organization rather than a particular brand, this pitch for California Walnuts is intended to resemble a certain kind of movie poster. What is the kind of movie alluded to here, and why do you think it was chosen to spearhead this campaign?

4. The United States of America broke away from Britain and its royalist government in 1776, but this ad for Johnson's baby products is cast as an homage to the birth of a child to an heir to the British throne. Why do you think the creators of this ad presumed that such an approach would appeal to American consumers?

5. This ad for Playdead's video game Limbo contains a typical image from the game itself but otherwise very little information as to what the product being advertised is. What is the ad designer taking for granted about the audience for this ad? How might a fan of the game respond differently to the ad than someone unfamiliar with it?

6. This ad for Sanuk sandals contains numerous images, most of which are not of sandals. What are those images, and what do they say about the presumed lifestyles and desires of the target market for the product?

7. This ad contains a mixture of populist and elitist appeals. What are those appeals, and how do they combine to sell watches?

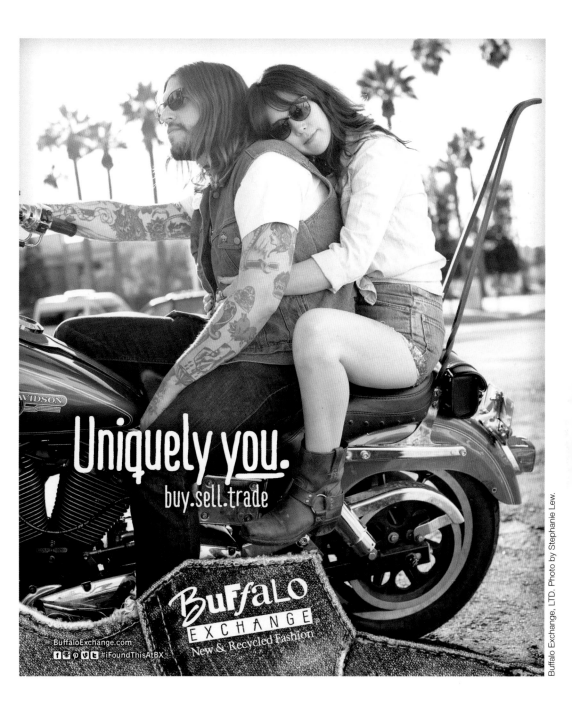

Uniquely you.
buy.sell.trade

BuFFaLO
EXCHANGE
New & Recycled Fashion

BuffaloExchange.com
#iFoundThisAtBX

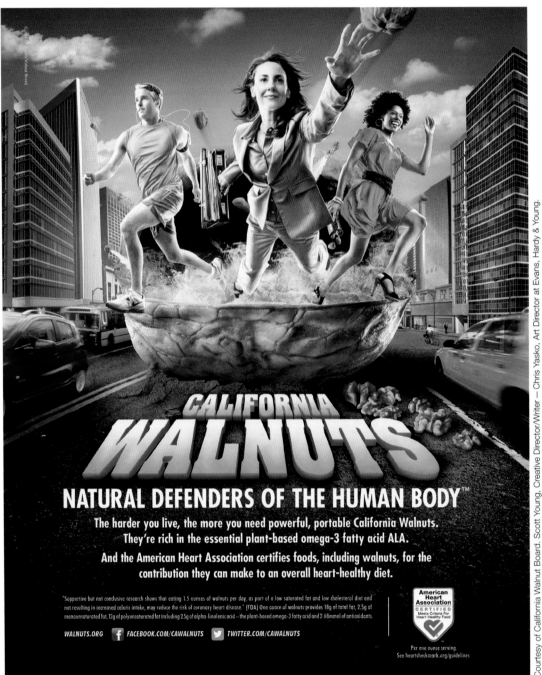

CALIFORNIA WALNUTS

NATURAL DEFENDERS OF THE HUMAN BODY™

The harder you live, the more you need powerful, portable California Walnuts.
They're rich in the essential plant-based omega-3 fatty acid ALA.

And the American Heart Association certifies foods, including walnuts, for the
contribution they can make to an overall heart-healthy diet.

"Supportive but not conclusive research shows that eating 1.5 ounces of walnuts per day, as part of a low saturated fat and low cholesterol diet and
not resulting in increased caloric intake, may reduce the risk of coronary heart disease." (FDA) One ounce of walnuts provides 18g of total fat, 2.5g of
monounsaturated fat, 13g of polyunsaturated fat including 2.5g of alpha-linolenic acid — the plant-based omega-3 fatty acid and 3.68mmol of antioxidants.

American Heart Association CERTIFIED Meets Criteria For Heart-Healthy Food

WALNUTS.ORG FACEBOOK.COM/CAWALNUTS TWITTER.COM/CAWALNUTS

Per one ounce serving.
See heartcheckmark.org/guidelines

A parent's love is the same the world over.

Congratulations from our humble family to your royal one.

Johnson's baby

Johnson and Johnson

LIMBO
On iPad and iPhone

SANDALS ARE FOR: <u>LAUGHTER, LOVE AND LATE NIGHTS</u>.

YOGA MAT SANDALS

THE LONG TRADITION OF DETROIT WATCHMAKING HAS JUST BEGUN.

WATCHES WILL BE MADE IN DETROIT FOR DECADES TO COME, BUT WE WILL NEVER MAKE THIS ONE AGAIN. RESERVE **THE RUNWELL**, AN EXTREMELY LIMITED SINGLE EDITION OF THE FIRST HANDMADE WATCH FROM THE MOTOR CITY.

SHINOLA.COM

SHINOLA
DETROIT

Where American is made.™

Some ppl may like being intruded about but should they beneath the surface and different surfaces

huge populations on a virtually minute-by-minute basis. Their goal is to find out how to activate individuals' buying impulses so they can sell us stuff more efficiently than ever before. But their work has broader social and cultural consequences as well. It is destroying traditional publishing ethics by forcing media outlets to adapt their editorial content to advertisers' public-relations needs and slice-and-dice demands. And it is performing a highly controversial form of social profiling and discrimination by customizing our media content on the basis of marketing reputations we don't even know we have.

Consider a fictional middle class family of two parents with three children who eat out a lot in fast-food restaurants. After a while the parents receive a continual flow of fast-food restaurant coupons. Data suggest the parents, let's call them Larry and Rhonda, will consistently spend far more than the coupons' value. Additional statistical evaluations of parents' activities and discussions online and off may suggest that Larry and Rhonda and their children tend toward being overweight. The data, in turn, result in a small torrent of messages by marketers and publishers seeking to exploit these weight issues to increase attention or sales. Videos about dealing with overweight children, produced by a new type of company called content farms, begin to show up on parenting websites Rhonda frequents. When Larry goes online, he routinely receives articles about how fitness chains emphasize weight loss around the holidays. Ads for fitness firms and diet pills typically show up on the pages with those articles. One of Larry and Rhonda's sons, who is fifteen years old, is happy to find a text message on his phone that invites him to use a discount at an ice cream chain not too far from his house. One of their daughters, by contrast, is mortified when she receives texts inviting her to a diet program and an ad on her Facebook page inviting her to a clothing store for hip, oversized women. What's more, people keep sending her Twitter messages about weight loss. In the meantime, both Larry and Rhonda are getting ads from check-cashing services and payday-loan companies. And Larry notices sourly on auto sites he visits that the main articles on the home page and the ads throughout feature entry-level and used models. His bitterness only becomes more acute when he describes to his boss the down-market Web he has been seeing lately. Quite surprised, she tells him she has been to the same auto sites recently and has just the opposite impression: many of the articles are about the latest German cars, and one home-page ad even offered her a gift for test-driving one at a dealer near her home.

This scenario of individual and household profiling and media customization is quite possible today. Websites, advertisers, and a panoply of other companies are continuously assessing the activities, intentions, and backgrounds of virtually everyone online; even our social relationships and comments are being carefully and continuously analyzed. In broader and broader ways, computer-generated conclusions about who we are affect the media content — the streams of commercial messages, discount offers, information, news, and entertainment — each of us confronts. Over the next few decades the business logic that drives these tailored activities will transform the ways we see ourselves, those around us, and the world at large. Governments too may be able to use marketers' technology and data to influence what we see and hear.

From this vantage point, the rhetoric of consumer power begins to lose credibility. In its place is a rhetoric of esoteric technological and statistical knowledge that supports the practice of social discrimination through profiling. We may note its outcomes only once in a while, and we may shrug when we do because it seems trivial—just a few ads, after all. But unless we try to understand how this profiling or reputation-making process works and what it means for the long term, our children and grandchildren will bear the full brunt of its prejudicial force.

The best way to enter this new world is to focus on its central driving force: the advertising industry's media-buying system. Media buying involves planning and purchasing space or time for advertising on outlets as diverse as billboards, radio, websites, mobile phones, and newspapers. For decades, media buying was a backwater, a service wing of advertising agencies that was known for having the lowest-paying jobs on Madison Avenue and for filling those jobs with female liberal arts majors fresh out of college. But that has all changed. The past twenty years have seen the rise of "media agencies" that are no longer part of ad agencies, though they may both be owned by the same parent company. Along with a wide array of satellite companies that feed them technology and data, media agencies have become magnets for well-remunerated software engineers and financial statisticians of both sexes.

In the United States alone, media-buying agencies wield more than $170 billion of their clients' campaign funds; they use these funds to purchase space and time on media they think will advance their clients' marketing aims. But in the process they are doing much more. With the money as leverage, they are guiding the media system toward nothing less than new ways of thinking about and evaluating audience members and defining what counts as a successful attempt to reach them. Traditionally, marketers have used media such as newspapers, magazines, radio, billboards, and television to reach out to segments of the population through commercial messages. These advertisers typically learned about audience segments from survey companies that polled representative portions of the population via a variety of methods, including panel research. A less prestigious direct-marketing business has involved contacting individuals by mail or phone. Firms have rented lists of public data or purchase information that suggests who might be likely customers.

The emerging new world is dramatically different. The distinction between reaching out to audiences via mass media and by direct-response methods is disappearing. Advertisers in the digital space expect all media firms to deliver to them particular types of individuals—and, increasingly, *particular* individuals—by leveraging a detailed knowledge about them and their behaviors that was unheard of even a few years ago. The new advertising strategy involves drawing as specific a picture as possible of a person based in large part on measurable physical acts such as clicks, swipes, mouseovers, and even voice commands. The strategy uses new digital tracking tools like cookies and beacons as well as new organizations with names like BlueKai, Rapleaf, Invidi, and eXelate. These companies track people on websites and across websites in an effort to learn what they do, what they care about, and who their friends are. Firms that exchange the information often do ensure that the targets' names and postal addresses remain anonymous — but not before they add specific demographic data and lifestyle information. For example:

- Rapleaf is a firm that claims on its website to help marketers "customize your customers' experience." To do that, it gleans data from individual users of blogs, internet forums, and social networks. It uses ad exchanges to sell the ability to reach those people. Rapleaf says it has "data on 900+ million records, 400+ million consumers, [and] 52+ billion friend connections." Advertisers are particularly aware of the firm's ability to predict the reliability of individuals (for example, the likelihood they will pay their mortgage) based on Rapleaf's research on the trustworthiness of the people in those individuals' social networks.

- A company called Next Jump runs employee discount and reward programs for about one-third of U.S. corporate employees. It gets personal information about all of them from the human relations departments of the companies and supplements that information with transactional data from the manufacturers it deals with as well as from credit companies. Armed with this combination of information, Next Jump can predict what people want and what they will pay for. It also generates a "UserRank" score for every employee based on how many purchases a person has made and how much he or she has spent. That score plays an important role in determining which employee gets what product e-mail offers and at what price.

- A firm called The Daily Me already sells an ad and news personalization technology to online periodicals. If a *Boston Globe* reader who reads a lot of soccer sports news visits a *Dallas Morning News* site, the Daily Me's technology tells the *Dallas Morning News* to serve him soccer stories. Moreover, when an ad is served along with the story, its text and photos are instantly configured so as to include soccer terms and photos as part of the advertising pitch. A basketball fan receiving an ad for the same product will get language and photos that call out to people with hoop interests.

These specific operations may not be in business a few years from now. ₁₀ In the new media-buying environment, companies come and go amid furious competition. The logic propelling them and more established firms forward, though, is consistent: the future belongs to marketers and media firms — *publishers*, in current terminology — that learn how to find and keep the most valuable customers by surrounding them with the most persuasive media materials. Special online advertising exchanges, owned by Google, Yahoo!, Microsoft, Interpublic, and other major players, allow publishers to auction and media agencies to "buy" individuals with particular characteristics, often in real time. That is, it is now possible to buy the right to deliver an ad to a person with specific characteristics at the precise moment that that person loads a Web page. In fact, through an activity called cookie matching, . . . an advertiser can actually bid for the right to reach an individual whom the advertiser knows from previous contacts and is now tracking around the Web. Moreover, the technology keeps changing. Because consumers delete Web cookies and marketers find cookies difficult to use with mobile devices, technology companies have developed methods to "fingerprint" devices permanently and allow for persistent personalization across many media platforms.

The significance of tailored commercial messages and offers goes far beyond whether or not the targeted persons buy the products. Advertisements and discounts are status signals: they alert people as to their social position. If you consistently get ads for low-priced cars, regional vacations, fast-food restaurants, and other products that reflect a lower-class status, your sense of the world's opportunities may be narrower than that of someone who is feted with ads for national or international trips and luxury products. Moreover, if like Larry and Rhonda you happen to know that your colleague is receiving more ads for the luxury products than you are, and more and better discounts to boot, you may worry that you are falling behind in society's estimation of your worth.

In fact, the ads may signal your opportunities actually *are* narrowed if marketers and publishers decide that the data points — profiles — about you across the internet position you in a segment of the population that is relatively less desirable to marketers because of income, age, past-purchase behavior, geographical location, or other reasons. Turning individual profiles into individual evaluations is what happens when a profile becomes a reputation. Today individual marketers still make most of the decisions about which particular persons matter to them, and about how much they matter. But that is beginning to change as certain publishers and data providers — Rapleaf and Next Jump, for example — allow their calculations of value to help advertisers make targeting decisions. In the future, these calculations of our marketing value, both broadly and for particular products, may become routine parts of the information exchanged about people throughout the media system.

The tailoring of news and entertainment is less advanced, but it is clearly under way. Technologies developed for personalized advertising and coupons point to possibilities for targeting individuals with personalized news and entertainment. Not only is this already happening, the logic of doing that is becoming more urgent to advertisers and publishers. Advertisers operate on the assumption that, on the internet as in traditional media, commercial messages that parade as soft (or "human interest") news and entertainment are more persuasive than straightforward ads. Publishers know this too, and in the heat of a terrible economic downturn even the most traditional ones have begun to compromise long-standing professional norms about the separation of advertising and editorial matter. And in fact many of the new online publishers — companies, such as Demand Media, that turn out thousands of text and video pieces a day—never really bought into the old-world ideas about editorial integrity anyway. What this means is that we are entering a world of intensively customized content, a world in which publishers and even marketers will package personalized advertisements with soft news or entertainment that is tailored to fit both the selling needs of the ads and the reputation of the particular individual.

The rise of digital profiling and personalization has spawned a new industrial jargon that reflects potentially grave social divisions and privacy issues. Marketers divide people into *targets* and *waste*. They also use words like *anonymous* and *personal* in unrecognizable ways that distort and drain them of their traditional meanings. If a company can follow your behavior in the digital environment—an environment that potentially includes your mobile phone and television set—its claim that you are "anonymous" is meaningless. That is particularly true when firms intermittently add off-line information such as shopping patterns and the value of your house to their online data and then simply strip the name and address to make it "anonymous." It matters little if your name is John Smith, Yesh Mispar, or 3211466. The persistence of information about you will lead firms to act based on what they know, share, and care about you, whether you know it is happening or not.

All these developments may sound more than a little unsettling; *creeped out* is a phrase people often use when they learn about them. National surveys I have conducted over the past decade consistently suggest that although people know companies are using their data and do worry about it, their understanding of exactly how the data are being used is severely lacking. That of course shouldn't be surprising. People today lead busy, even harried, lives. Keeping up with the complex and changing particulars of data mining is simply not something most of us have the time or ability to do. There are many great things about the new media environment. But when companies track people without their knowledge, sell their data without letting them know what they are doing or securing their permission, and then use those data to decide which of those people are targets or waste, we have a serious social problem. The precise implications of this problem are not yet clear. If it's allowed to persist, and people begin to realize how the advertising industry segregates them from and pits them against others in the ads they get, the discounts they receive, the TV-viewing suggestions and news stories they confront, and even the offers they receive in the supermarket, they may begin to suffer the effects of discrimination. They will likely learn to distrust the companies that have put them in this situation, and they may well be incensed at the government that has not helped to prevent it. A comparison to the financial industry is apt. Here was an industry engaged in a whole spectrum of arcane practices that were not at all transparent to consumers or regulators but that had serious negative impact on our lives. It would be deeply unfortunate if the advertising system followed the same trajectory.

Despite valiant efforts on the part of advocacy groups and some federal and state officials, neither government rulings nor industry self-regulation has set policies that will address these issues before they become major sources of widespread social distress. Part of the reason for the lack of action may be that neither citizens nor politicians recognize how deeply embedded in American life these privacy-breaching and social-profiling activities are. Few individuals outside advertising know about the power of the new media-buying system: its capacity to determine not only what media firms do but how we see our-selves and others. They don't know that that system is working to attach mar-keting labels to us based on the clicks we make, the conversations we have, and the friendships we enjoy on websites, mobile devices, iPads, supermarket carts, and even television sets. They don't know that the new system is forcing many media firms to sell their souls for ad money while they serve us commer-cial messages, discounts, and, increasingly, news and entertainment based on our marketing labels. They don't realize that the wide sharing of data suggests that in the future marketers and media firms may find it useful to place us into personalized "reputation silos" that surround us with worldviews and rewards based on labels marketers have created reflecting our value to them. Without this knowledge, it is hard to even begin to have broad-based serious discussions about what society and industry should do about this sobering new world: into the twenty-first century the media-buying system's strategy of social discrim-ination will increasingly define how we as individuals relate to society—not only how much we pay but what we see and when and how we see it.

READING THE TEXT

1. In your own words, describe how digital media agencies' methods to ascer-tain consumer behavior differ from traditional consumer research strategies used at least twenty years ago.
2. Describe in a paragraph what Turow means by the "advertising industry's media-buying system" (para. 7).
3. According to this selection, how are digitally obtained profiles of individuals and households translated into personalized advertising?
4. Make a list of the advantages and problems of digital marketing strategies.
5. What assumptions does Turow make about his readers' likely responses to his indictment of the digital mining of personal information? How do those assumptions shape your response to his argument?

READING THE SIGNS

1. Write a letter to the hypothetical couple Larry and Rhonda, whom Turow describes as being surprised and bitter about the precise profiling of their household by media marketers. Can you offer any suggestions about how to avoid being so profiled? To develop ideas about possible strategies, consult Gloria Steinem's "Sex, Lies, and Advertising" (p. 197).
2. In class, hold a debate on whether marketers' mining of personal information and creation of specific consumer profiles are advantageous or problematic

for the consumer (do not consider whether this strategy benefits the marketers or their clients). For the former position, your argument might focus on the advantages of customized "content"; for the latter, your argument might focus on the creation of social distinctions and/or privacy concerns. After the debate, write an essay in which you advance your own argument about this question.

3. As Turow explains, the majority of consumers do not realize that their Internet activities are mined for commercial reasons. Write an essay in which you support, oppose, or complicate the proposition that for-profit data miners such as Google should pay, in money or services, users whom they monitor for information that they then sell.

4. In an essay, analyze semiotically the Web site of one of the data-tracking companies that Turow mentions, such as Rapleaf or Next Jump, or the Web site of an online advertising exchange such as those owned by Google and Yahoo! What signs appear on the Web site (especially the home page) that indicate whose interests the company serves?

5. In his conclusion, Turow expresses a desire for "broad-based serious discussions about what society and industry should do about this sobering new world." He continues, "Into the twenty-first century the media-buying system's strategy of social discrimination will increasingly define how we as individuals relate to society — not only how much we pay but what we see and when and how we see it" (para. 16). Write an essay in which you respond to Turow's remarks.

JULIA B. CORBETT

A Faint Green Sell: Advertising and the Natural World

Though "green" marketing and advertising is not as prevalent today as it was in the 1980s and 1990s, advertisers still exploit natural imagery to move the goods. Believing, however, that "the business of advertising is fundamentally 'brown'" and that "therefore the idea of advertising being 'green' and capable of supporting environmental values is an oxymoron," Julia B. Corbett sets out to analyze and categorize the ways in which advertising exploits nature, from treating it as a commodity to presenting nature as something that exists solely for the pleasure of human beings. All these strategies, Corbett concludes, perpetuate "an anthropocentric, narcissistic relationship" with the natural world. In other words, beautiful mountain ad backgrounds do not mean that you should go out and buy an SUV. Julia B. Corbett is a professor of communication at the University of Utah.

In the 1980s, advertisers discovered the environment. When a revitalized environmental movement helped establish environmentalism as a legitimate, mainstream public goal (Luke, 1993), corporate America quickly capitalized on a lucrative market of "green consumers" (Ottman, 1993; Zinkham & Carlson, 1995). Marketers not only could create new products and services, they could also reposition existing ones to appear more environmentally friendly. What resulted was a flood of advertisements that focused on green product attributes, touting products as recyclable and biodegradable and claiming them good or safe for the environment. Increases in this genre were remarkable, with green print ads increasing 430% and green television ads increasing 367% between 1989 and 1990 (Ottman, 1993). The total number of products claiming green attributes doubled in 1990 to 11.4% from the previous year ("Selling green," 1991).

Virtually all of the existing research on so-called green advertising was conducted during this boom. Green advertising was defined by researchers as product ads touting environmental benefits or corporate green-image ads (Banerjee, Gulas, & Iyer, 1995; Shrum, McCarty, & Lowrey, 1995). Researchers also targeted and segmented green consumers (Ottman, 1993) and tested their motivations (Luke, 1993). Green appeals were categorized (Iyer & Banerjee, 1993; Obermiller, 1995; Schuhwerk & Lefkoff-Hagius, 1995) and consumer response to green ads analyzed (Mayer, Scammon, & Zick, 1993; Thorson, Page, & Moore, 1995).

By the late 1990s, advertisers announced the end of the green-ad boom. *Advertising Age* reported that as the country headed into the thirtieth anniversary of Earth Day, green positioning had become more than just a non-issue — it was almost an anti-issue (Neff, 2000). Marketers were launching a whole new class of disposable products from plastic storage containers to dust mops. There was a perceived decline in controversy over anti-green products such as disposable diapers, toxic batteries, and gas-guzzling SUVs (sport utility vehicles). In addition, only 5% of new products made claims about recyclability or recycled content, and the explosion of e-tailing added boxes, styrofoam peanuts, and air-puffed plastic bags to the waste stream. Green product ads in prime-time television, which never amounted to more than a blip, virtually disappeared by 1995, reflecting "the television tendency to get off the environmental bandwagon after it had lost its trendiness" (Shanahan & McComas, 1999, p. 108).

But Shanahan and McComas noted that their study — like virtually all research published during the green-ad boom — did not consider the most prevalent use of the environment in advertising: when nature functions as a rhetorically useful backdrop or stage. Using nature merely as a backdrop — whether in the form of wild animals, mountain vistas, or sparkling rivers — is the most common use of the natural world in advertisements. For all but the most critical message consumers, the environment blends into the background. We know that an advertisement for a car shows the vehicle outdoors and that ads for allergy medications feature flowers and "weeds." The environment per se is not for sale, but advertisers are depending on qualities and features of the non-human world (and our relationship to it) to help in the selling message. When the natural world is so depicted, it becomes a convenient, culturally relevant tool to which meanings can be attached for the purpose of selling goods and services. Although this intentional but seemingly casual use of the environment in advertising is by far the most common, it is the least studied by researchers.

Nature-as-backdrop ads also are notable for their enduring quality. 5 Although the number of ads that focus on product attributes such as "recyclable" may shift with marketing trends and political winds, nature has been used as a backdrop virtually since the dawn of advertising. The natural world was depicted in early automobile ads ("see the USA in your Chevrolet") and Hamms Beer commercials ("from the land of sky-blue water") and continues to be a prominent feature in the advertising landscape. Nature-as-backdrop ads, therefore, provide an important record of the position of the natural world in our cultural environment and, as such, deserve scrutiny.

Advertisements are a special form of discourse because they include visual signals and language fragments (either oral or written) that work together to create messages that go beyond the ability of either individually. This essay undertakes a critical analysis of the symbolic communicative discourse of advertising, viewing nature-as-backdrop ads as cultural icons of environmental values embedded in our social system. When ads present the environment with distorted, inauthentic, or exaggerated discourse, that discourse has the potential to foster inauthentic relationships to nature and influences the way we perceive our environment and its value to us.

Schudson (1989) argued that ads have special cultural power. In addition to being repetitive and ubiquitous, ads reinforce messages from primary institutions in the social system, provide dissonance to countering messages, and generally support the capitalistic structure that the advertising industry was created to support. This essay will discuss how the ad industry developed, how ads work on us, and how ads portray the natural world. It will argue, according to environmental theories such as deep ecology (Bullis, 1996; Naess, 1973), that the "green" in advertising is extremely faint by examining and developing six related concepts:

1. The business of advertising is fundamentally "brown"; therefore, the idea of advertising being "green" and capable of supporting environmental values is an oxymoron.
2. Advertising commodifies the natural world and attaches material value to non-material goods, treating natural resources as private and possessible, not public and intrinsic.
3. Nature-as-backdrop ads portray an anthropocentric, narcissistic relationship to the biotic community and focus on the environment's utility and benefit to humans.
4. Advertising idealizes the natural world and presents a simplified, distorted picture of nature as sublime, simple, and unproblematic.

5. The depiction of nature in advertising disconnects and estranges us from what is valued, yet at the same time we are encouraged to reconnect through products, creating a circular consumption.
6. As a ubiquitous form of pop culture, advertising reinforces consonant messages in the social system and provides strong dissonance to oppositional or alternative messages.

The "Brown" Business of Advertising

1. The business of advertising is fundamentally "brown"; therefore, the idea of advertising being "green" and capable of supporting environmental values is an oxymoron.

Advertisements are nothing new to this century or even previous ones. There are plentiful examples in literature, including the works of Shakespeare, that peddlers have long enticed buyers by advertising (in print or orally) a good's attributes and associated meanings. After World War II, however, advertising found a firm place in the worldview of Americans. According to Luke (1993), after 1945, corporate capital, big government, and professional experts pushed practices of a throw-away affluent society onto consumers as a purposeful political strategy to sustain economic growth, forestall mass discontent, and empower scientific authority. Concern for the environment was lacking in the postwar prosperity boom, at least until the mid-1960s when Rachel Carson sounded the alarm over chemicals and the modern-day environmental movement was born (Corbett, 2001).

To help alert consumers to new mass-produced goods, a new type of ¹⁰ show called the "soap opera" was created for the relatively recent phenomenon of television. These daytime dramas were created for the sole purpose of delivering an audience of homemakers to eager manufacturers of household products, including soap. Advertisers realized that advertising on soap operas would help to establish branding, or creating differing values for what are essentially common, interchangeable goods such as soap.

Essentially, advertising was viewed as part of the fuel that would help keep a capitalist economy burning. Capitalism is a market system that measures its success by constant growth (such as the gross national product and housing starts), a system that many environmentalists recognize as ultimately unsustainable. You might even say that advertising developed as the culture that would help solve what some economists view as the central problem of capitalism: the distribution of surplus goods (Twitchell, 1996). Schudson (1989) concluded, "Advertising is capitalism's way of saying 'I love you' to itself." In a capitalist economy, advertising is a vital handmaiden to consumption and materialism. In the words of the author of *Adcult*, Americans "are not too materialistic. We are not materialistic enough" (Twitchell, 1996, p. 11).

The development of mass media, particularly radio and television, played an important role in delivering audiences to advertisers. By the mid-1980s, half of U.S. homes had cable, and the burgeoning number of channels allowed advertisers to target more specific audience segments. Advertisers and media programmers engage in a dance to fill each other's needs, each having a vested interest in constructing certain versions of the world and not others. According to Turow (1999), "the ad industry affects not just the content of its own campaigns but the very structure and content of the rest of the media system" (p. 194). At the same time, media develop formats and tones for their outlets and programming deemed to be most acceptable to the audiences that they hope marketers find most attractive. What this means for programming is that the upscale twenty-something audience — the most appealing segment to advertisers — will find itself represented in more media outlets than older men and women to whom only a small number of highly targeted formats are aimed. According to researchers of the green marketing boom, the segments of the population most committed to the environment do not belong to this twenty-something group (Ottman, 1993).

It is precisely the ability of advertisers and media programmers to tell some stories and not others that gives these entities power. "When people read a magazine, watch a TV show, or use any other ad-sponsored medium, they are entering a world that was constructed as a result of close cooperation between advertisers and media firms" (Turow, 1999, p. 16). Because all media provide people with insights into parts of the world with which they have little direct contact, media representations of the natural world to a largely urbanized population are highly significant. They show us, over and over again, where we belong in the world and how we should treat it. Yet, representations of the natural world are crafted for the sole purpose of selling certain audiences to advertisers.

The close cooperation between advertisers and media firms is understandable given advertising's financial support of media. For newspapers and some magazines, at least 50% of their revenue is from advertising; ad support approaches 100% for much of radio and television. By some estimates, advertisers spent $27 billion on support to television, $9 billion on radio, $46 billion on daily newspapers, and about $7 billion on consumer magazines (Turow, 1999, p. 13).

Given advertising's purpose of selling audiences to advertisers, is it even 15 possible for any form of advertising — whether product ads or nature-as-backdrop ads — to be "green"? Dadd and Carothers (1991) maintained that a truly green economy would require all products to be audited and analyzed from cradle to grave for their environmental effects. Effects could include the resources used and pollution generated in the product's manufacture, energy used to produce and transport the product, the product's role in the economic and social health of the country of origin, investment plans of the company, and final disposal of product.

Applying this standard at the most basic level connotes it is an oxymoron to label marginally useful or necessary products (and the ads that promote them) as "green" or somehow good for the environment. Can an advertisement that encourages consumption of a product (or patronage of a company that produces the product) ever be green with a capital G? In his attempt to reconcile a brown industry with green ideals, Kilbourne (1995) identified three levels of green in advertisements. But even at the lowest level (defined as ads promoting a small "techno-fix" such as biodegradability) the message is still that "consuming is good, more is better, and the ecological cost is minimal" (p. 15). If an ad recognizes finite resources, it nevertheless views the environment purely as a resource, not as possessing intrinsic, non-economic value. Kilbourne concluded that from a purely ecological position, a truly Green ad is indeed an oxymoron: "the only Green product is the one that is not produced" (p. 16). Other researchers have likewise tried to categorize the green in advertisements (Banerjee et al., 1995). Adapting the deep and shallow ecology concepts of Naess (1973) to advertisements, they concluded that very few ads were "deep" — 2% of television and 9% of print — defined by the researchers as discussing environmental issues in depth and mentioning actions requiring more commitment.

However, these attempts to make advertising fit a green framework simply illustrate how ideologically opposed advertising and environmental values are. Because advertising is the workhorse of capitalism and supports continually increased production, it is ideologically contrary to environmentalism, which recognizes that ever-increasing growth and consumption are inherently unsustainable. It matters not whether an ad boasts of recyclability or quietly features pristine mountain meadows in the background; the basic business of advertising is brown. Perhaps the only truly Green product is not only one not produced, but also one not advertised.

Nature as Commodity

2. Advertising commodifies the natural world and attaches material value to non-material goods, treating natural resources as private and ownable, not public and intrinsic.

Have you ever viewed a single advertisement and then rushed out to buy that product? Probably not. That is not the way that advertising generally works on us, especially not for national consumer goods. Advertising scholars argue that ads cannot create, invent, or even satisfy our desires; instead, ads channel and express current desires with the hope of exploiting them.

You may disagree that ads cannot create desires, particularly if you have ever found yourself yearning for a product that six months ago you did not know existed or that you "needed." But even if ads do not greatly corrupt our immediate buying habits, they can gradually shape our values by becoming our social guides for what is important and valued. According to Benton (1995), advertising displays values and signals to people what our culture thinks is important. Advertising is not capable of inventing social values, but it does a masterful job at usurping and exploiting certain values and not others. The prominent (though not monopolistic) role of advertising in the symbolic marketplace is what gives advertising "a special cultural power" (Schudson, 1989). In the words of one scholar, "Advertising is simply one of a number of attempts to load objects with meaning . . . it is an ongoing conversation within a culture about the meaning of objects" (Twitchell, 1996, p. 13).

The rhetorical challenge for an advertiser, then, is to load one product (even though numerous similar ones exist) with sufficient meaning so that the product appears able to express a desire. The natural world is full of cultural meaning with which to associate products, thereby attaching commodity value to qualities that are impossible to own. By borrowing and adapting well-known, stereotypical portrayals of nature, advertising is able to associate water with freshness and purity and weather as fraught with danger. If, for example, an ad wants to attach the value of "safety" to one particular car, it might demonstrate the car's ability to dodge "dangerous" elements of nature, such as falling rocks. On the other hand, if the ad wants to convey a truck's durability, it could just as easily attach a very different meaning to the same resource and say the truck is "like a rock." Neither product guarantees that you can buy safety or durability; both product ads merely expressed a consumer desire for them by associating a non-material good with a material one.

Animals in particular provide cultural shorthand for advertising. Animals, as popular symbols of the nonhuman environment, are a way for advertisers to link the perceived "personality" and stereotyped cultural value of the animal to the product (Phillips, 1996). In car advertising alone, ads compare vehicles to rams, eagles, wolves, cougars, falcons, and panthers. Some ads go so far as to portray the vehicle as an animal itself. An individual needs no direct experience with untamed environs to know what an eagle or cougar represents and is valued for.

The portrayal of animals in advertising need not be authentic or realistic for us to ascertain the value they represent. In a television commercial, two raccoons are peering inside a brightly lit living room window, "singing" a song from *My Fair Lady.* As the camera moves beyond the raccoons into the living room — where it appears the residents are not home — it focuses on the rocker-recliner. The raccoons sing, "All I want is a room somewhere, far away from the cold night air. Warm hands, warm feet . . ."

In this ad, the rocker-recliner you are enticed to buy has no direct or obvious connection to the natural world, but animals are very much part of the overall persuasive message. We are able to overlook the anthropomorphized singing raccoons because we have enough shared cultural meaning about raccoons and their behavior. We can decipher that these cute, mischievous "bandits" would like to "break in" to this warm room far away from the cold night air and maybe even snooze in that rocker. The intrinsic value of raccoons as a species has been usurped and exploited to demonstrate the comfort and desirability of a certain brand of chair.

Even if the original function of advertising was to market simple products 25 such as soap, advertising now functions to market feelings, sensations, and lifestyles. According to advertisers, the consumption of an object often has more to do with its meaning than with its actual use (Twitchell, 1996). Discrete objects — whether cold medicine or fabric softener — are easier to sell if they are associated with social and personal meaning. The purpose of an ad is not to stress that the product functions properly, but that consumption of it will cure problems (Lasch, 1978), whether loneliness, aging, or even a desire to connect with the natural world. Advertising channels our psychological needs and ambitions into consumptive behaviors (Pollay, 1989). Price (1996) concluded that the success of the store The Nature Company depends "not so much [on] what nature is as what nature means to us" (p. 189).

Take for example a series of print and television ads for a particular SUV that labeled the vehicle as "the answering machine for the call of the wild." The print version tells us that "nature calls out for us" but with the vehicle's leather-trimmed seats, "civilization's never very far away." In television versions, we see the vehicle traveling over rugged terrain (but not the woman driving it) while an answering machine plays numerous messages from a worried mother and boyfriend to the woman who has escaped into the wild.

These ads do not focus on all the ways that this vehicle is superior to all the other very similar SUVs out there. The ads give us no reason to believe that the repair record, safety rating, price, or other important product attributes are somehow superior. Instead, these ads are selling meanings and values associated with the natural world. This product will reconnect you with "the wild," which appears to be missing in your life, and it will help you escape from your troubles and relationships. A rugged environment (yet one somehow made safer and more civilized by this SUV) is portrayed as the best place to find peace and this vehicle will take you there. (An ad for a very different type of product used the same slogan in a different way: "Radio Shack is answering the call of the wild with two-way personal radios." In the ad, "renowned wildlife expert" Jim Fowler uses the radio in a remote-looking location. "No matter where the wild calls you, you'll be ready to answer.")

Some scholars insist that advertising appeals primarily to personal dissatisfactions in our lives and insecurities over the ways and pace in which we live, not to our personal needs. In doing so, ads are carriers of anxiety that serve only to alienate us further (Lasch, 1978). In the SUV ads, the driver is not portrayed as using the vehicle for personal need, but for escape from relationship problems to an environment that is depicted as being free of all problems.

The rhetorical argument of commodification leads us to believe that we can solve problems and dissatisfactions with a purchase. We buy the peace and escape — represented by the wilderness and promised by the product — even though the product is incapable of fulfilling that promise. The intent of advertising, says Pollay (1989), is to preoccupy society with material concerns and to see goods as a path to happiness and a solution to problems (which is very brown thinking). In many of the appeals of nature-as-backdrop ads, the advertisements attempt to associate material goods with nonmaterial qualities that have disappeared from many people's lives, qualities such as solitude, wilderness, lush landscapes, free-flowing water, and clean air. In a print ad for L.L. Bean, we see a man wading across calm, milky blue waters to a small sailboat in early morning light. The caption reads, "Don't mistake a street address for where you actually live." Apparently this man cannot "live" in his everyday life — which we assume takes place in a far less serene setting — but must leave it to achieve qualities it lacks. Yet another SUV ad promises, "Escape. Serenity. Relaxation." Pristine mountain vistas and sparkling waters (usually devoid of people) allow us to romanticize about a life lost or connections broken. When such adventures are tied in such a way to products, that connection materializes a way of experiencing the natural world.

Commodification of what are essentially public resources — like milky 30 blue waters — encourages us to think of resources as private and possessible. Ads may invoke public values of family, friendship, and a common planet as part of their message, but these values are put to work to sell private goods, a very capitalist principle. The satisfaction derived from these goods, even those that appear inherently collective such as water, is depicted as invariably private. This encourages "the promotion of a social order in which people are encouraged to think of themselves and their private worlds" (Schudson, 1989, p. 83), a very anthropocentric and narcissistic perspective. The environment, in many respects, doesn't function well as private space.

For the Pleasure of Humans

3. Nature-as-backdrop ads portray an anthropocentric, narcissistic relationship to the biotic community and focus on the environment's utility and benefit to humans.

Another common feature in advertising appeals that utilize the natural world is self-absorption and narcissism. The word derives from Narcissus, a youth in Greek mythology who fell in love with his own reflection in a pool. The way in which advertising portrays this universal emotional type is as self-absorbed, self-righteous, and dependent on momentary pleasures of assertion. Narcissism in advertising often takes the form of outdoor adventure, as in this print ad: Two pickup trucks are parked on an expansive, rolling sand dune. In the open bed of each truck, a young man in a wet suit appears to be wind-surfing — through the manipulation of computer graphics. Water splashes around them in the air and onto the sand. The caption says the trucks are "built fun tough" and have "gallons of attitude." Of course we know this picture to be fake (although a similar juxtaposition of desert and water exists in human-made Lake Powell), but the picture tells us that these men are in it for the fun, for the adventure.

A narcissist is most concerned with pleasing himself or herself at the expense of others, and if we extend the analogy, at the expense of the environment. In terms of environmental ideology, a narcissist would be anthropocentric, believing that his or her own outdoor pleasure comes before that of other species and their needs. Ads that show people "conquering" natural elements are expressing me-first anthropocentrism. According to Lasch (1978), our culture is marked by an exaggerated form of self-awareness and mass narcissism, finely attuned (with the help of advertising) to the many demands of the narcissistic self.

Another example is a television ad that shows a young boy working through the pages of a puzzle book. He reads aloud, "Help the knight reach the castle," and with his crayon follows the winding path safely past the dragon to the castle. On the next page he reads, "Help the Jeep Wrangler reach the fishing hole." "Hmm," he says, grins, and makes a noise like a truck revving up. He draws a line straight across the puzzle book landscape, across two mountain ranges, a deep valley, and a patch of quicksand, ignoring the cleared path. As he smiles smugly, the announcer tells us that a Jeep is "more fun than you imagine."

Yet another truck commercial begins in a deserted mountain valley at 35 twilight. Next, a gigantic booted foot with a spur crashes to the ground, reverberating all in sight. We then see that the foot belongs to a cowboy the size of Paul Bunyan. The message is that the human is essentially larger than life, dominating the entire landscape and all within it, as Bunyan did. Such exaggerated domination intentionally positions humans at the top of a pyramid, instead of belonging equally to a biotic community.

Nature as Sublime

4. Nature-as-backdrop ads idealize the natural world and present a simplified, distorted picture of nature as sublime, simple, and unproblematic.

As much as ads intentionally distort reality (in images such as windsurfing in a truck or singing raccoons), they also present reality as it should be, a reality that is worth desiring and emulating (and owning). If you have backpacked or camped, you know that slapping mosquitoes, getting dirty, getting wet, and sweating are often part of the package. Such a real outdoor experience is unlikely to be depicted in advertisements (unless the product is for something like insect repellent). Instead, ads subordinate reality to a romanticized past, present, or even future. "Real" in advertising is a cultural construct: "The makers of commercials do not want what is real but what will seem real on film. Artificial rain is better than 'God's rain' because it shows up better on film or tape" (Schudson, 1989, p. 79). Advertisers do not intend to capture life as it really is, but intend instead to portray the "ideal" life and to present as normal and everyday what are actually relatively rare moments, such as a phenomenal sunset or a mosquito-less lake.

A great many nature-as-backdrop ads present the natural world as sublime, a noble place inspiring awe and admiration. As an exercise, my students draw their interpretation of a sublime place in nature, and invariably, similar elements appear in their pictures: snow-capped mountain peaks towering above pine trees and a grassy or flower-filled meadow, through which a clear creek or river flows. Sometimes, large mammals such as deer graze in the meadow. Humans are rarely present.

According to Oravec (1996), the sublime is a literary and artistic convention that uses a prescribed form of language and pictorial elements to describe nature, and that in turn encourages a specific pattern of responses to nature. Artistically, sublime representations can include blurring, exaggeration of detail, and compositional elements such as a foreground, middle ground, and frame. Settings are frequently pastoral or wild with varying amounts of human presence. There is a self-reflexive nature to the positioning, with the observer feeling both within a scene and also outside it, viewing the scene (and reflexively, the self) from a higher or more distant (and morally outstanding) perspective.

Oravec (1996) has called the sublime the founding trope in the rhetoric 40 of environmentalism: "Sublimity has remained a touchstone or grounding for our public conception of nature and, through nature, of the environment" (p. 68). As a conventional linguistic device, the sublime represents and encodes our understanding of the natural world. Because the sublime is associated with what is "natural," "the sublime connotes an authenticity and originality that is part of its very meaning; yet like rhetoric itself, it has a long-standing reputation for exaggeration and even falsehood" (p. 69).

The sublime is as much a part of advertising as it is of the artistic and literary realms. Advertising presents the natural world as pristine, simple, and not endangered, yet depictions are always contrived and often created. What appears as real rain is artificial, what looks like a natural wildlife encounter is contrived, and what appears entirely natural was created with computer animation and digital manipulation. The artificial seamlessly approximates the real in the sublime world of advertising.

Numerous vacation advertisements depict people in sublime settings, such as thin and tan couples on pristine white sand beaches, or peacefully cruising under sunny skies amid glaciers and whales. Vacationers in this idealized world never encounter anything other than perfect environmental conditions and enjoy these sublime locations unfettered by crowds.

A host of pharmaceutical ads likewise enlist nature backdrops as rhetoric for the sublime. One ad for an arthritis medication takes place in a pastoral setting assumed to be a park. The sun is shining, the park is empty except for the actors, there is no litter or noise, and even the dogs are exceedingly friendly and behaved. In another ad for what is presumed to be a mood-enhancer, a woman strolls slowly along a pristine, deserted beach in soft light, a contented smile on her face. In these instances, the sublime backdrop doubly represents the sublime state the person will achieve upon taking the medication. Many of these ads rely so heavily on the power of sublime meaning that the actual purpose of the drug is not stated, only assumed.

Other commercials depict the sublime after a product has changed problematic nature into idealized nature. Numerous ads for lawn care products and allergy medications first portray nature in a state of chaos or war, needing to be tamed and brought under control. One television ad for lawn chemicals showed a small army of men and supplies descending from the sky to tame and tackle nature. Some allergy commercials depict the flowers and weeds physically attacking people. But ah, after the product is introduced, unproblematic and peaceful nature returns.

When humans are introduced into sublime scenes, their representation is also idealized. Just as nature is presented as reality-as-it-should-be, people are presented as-they-should-be in a limited number of social roles. Therefore, people in ads are primarily attractive, young or middle-aged, vibrant, and thin, or they are celebrities with those qualities. The environments in which they live, whether inside or outside, are also limited to idealized conditions; no one has dirty houses or unkempt lawns, and no one travels through dirty city streets, encounters polluted rivers, or finds abused landscapes. In the world of advertising, there are no poor people, sick people, or unattractive people, and sometimes there are no people at all. For example, most car ads do not show anyone actually driving the vehicle through the tinted windows, and you hear only the disembodied voice of the announcer. The social roles played by advertising actors are easily identifiable — the businessperson, the grandmother, the teenager — but the actors are anonymous as individual people and portray only social roles tailored to specific demographic categories. The flat, abstract, idealized, and sometimes anonymous world of advertising "is part of a deliberate effort to connect specific products in people's imagination with certain demographic groupings or needs or occasions" (Schudson, 1989, p. 77).

Of course you recognize pieces of this idealized presentation of people and their environments, just as you recognize the utterly impossible pieces — a car parked on an inaccessible cliff or polar bears drinking Coke. We are not stupefied by a natural world that is unrealistic and idealized in advertising: in fact, we expect it.

A Natural Disconnect

5. The depiction of nature in advertising disconnects and estranges us from what is valued, and we attempt to reconnect through products, creating a circular consumption.

Some critics believe that advertising may be more powerful the less people believe it and the less it is acknowledged. According to Schudson (1989), ads do not ask to be taken literally and do not mean what they say, but "this may be the very center of their power" (p. 87). While we are being exposed to those 3,000 ads a day, we may carry an illusion of detachment and think them trivial and unimportant. According to some theories, though, it is very possible to "learn" without active involvement, a so-called sleeper effect. This myth of immunity from an ad's persuasion may do more to

protect our self-respect than help us comprehend the subtleties and implications of their influence (Pollay, 1989). Although we may not think an ad
speaks to us, its slogan may suddenly pop into our vocabulary — just do it, it
does a body good, got milk? We may be unaware and uninvolved in front of
the television, but the message of the ad may prove important at purchase
time. According to Pollay (1989), advertising does more than merely stimulate
wants; it plays a subtle role in changing habits.

Take the habit of drying your clothes, an activity that for many people
throughout the world involves pinning clothes to a line in the backyard or
between buildings. When I was a girl, I loved sliding between clean sheets
dried outside on the clothesline and drinking in the smell. How do many
people get that same outside-smell nowadays? They get it with detergents
and fabric softeners with names like "mountain air" and "springtime fresh"
or with similarly scented dryer sheets. Although perceived convenience and
affordable dryers no doubt helped change our clothes-drying habits, where
did we learn to associate the smell of outdoors with purchased products?
Advertising.

The message in these product ads is that the artificial smell is some- 50
how easier or superior or even just equivalent to the real smell in the natural
world. It not only commodifies something of value from the natural world,
it gradually disconnects us from that thing of value. The more successfully
ads teach us to associate natural qualities such as fresh air with products,
the more disconnected we become from what was originally valued. The
more estranged from the original thing of value, the more we may attempt
to reconnect through products that promise an easy replacement. When we
become so estranged from the natural world that we attempt to reconnect
through products, a circular consumptive pattern is created — which supports
the capitalist economy that advertising was created to support. If advertising
tells us that non-saleable qualities of the outdoors such as fresh air and natural smells are easy to bring inside, need we worry about the condition of the
real world?

Just as advertising can change habits, it can help create rituals and taboos.
A good example of a taboo largely created by advertising is litter. Through
national advertising campaigns begun decades ago, litter was labeled as an
environmental no-no. While cleaning up litter makes for a visually appealing
environment, the automobiles from which the trash is generally tossed cause
far more environmental harm than almost all types of litter.

Advertising also works to create rituals. A ritual is created when we
make inert, prosaic objects meaningful and give them symbolic significance.
Mistletoe means little to us as a parasitic evergreen, but it is loaded with significance as a holiday ritual about kissing. Whales mean more to us as communicative, spiritual symbols of the deep than for their inherent value and
place in ocean ecosystems. Price (1996) concluded that Native American
fetishes and baskets, which have been ritualized by nonnative populations
(and appropriated by advertising), "associate nature nearly interchangeably

with indigenous peoples" (p. 189). In a similar way, once a species or animal has been so ritualized, it precludes a more complete and accurate knowing of it and disconnects us.

Advertising, directly and subtly, idealizes and materializes a way of experiencing the world, including the natural world. It promotes products as the simple solutions to complex dilemmas by tapping into our dissatisfactions and desires. If you feel disconnected to the natural world, you can "solve" that with mountain-scented laundry products, bear fetishes, and whale audiotapes, but these purchases only increase the estrangement. If you need to escape modern life yet want to feel safe and civilized while doing so, you can simply solve that by taking a rugged SUV into the wilderness.

Yet environmental dilemmas are anything but simple, and wilderness is a good example. A print ad features a four-wheel-drive car crossing a sparkling, boulder-strewn stream and announces, "Coming soon to a wilderness near you." In this idealized portrayal, there is no mud being stirred up from the bottom of the stream, no dirt of any kind on the car, and of course, there is no visible driver. But in addition, "wilderness" is a rare commodity that rarely exists "near you," and by its very definition, includes few people and even fewer developed signs of people. In wilderness with a capital W, cars and all motorized equipment are forbidden. Setting aside an area as wilderness involves contentious negotiations and land-use trade-offs. But whether formally designated or not, experiencing wilderness is not the simple matter of materialization and driving a certain kind of car.

Another example of advertising portraying a complex environmental 55 issue as simple and uncomplicated is the depiction of water. We see it babbling down brooks in beverage commercials, refreshing someone in a soap commercial, quenching thirst in ads for water filters and bottled water. Pure, clean, healthy—but simple? More than half the world's rivers are drying up or are polluted. Agricultural chemicals have seeped into many U.S. underground aquifers. Oil, gas, and a host of herbicides and pesticides wash off streets and lawns into waterways. Political and legal fights are waged over dams, diversions, and water rights. A host of bacterial contaminants have threatened water supplies and public health in major U.S. cities, and traces of antibiotics and other prescription drugs have been detected in some municipal water supplies. Clean water is definitely not a simple environmental issue.

Advertising Does Not Stand Alone

6. *As a ubiquitous form of popular culture, advertising reinforces consonant messages in the social system and provides strong dissonance to oppositional or alternative messages.*

For any societal element to wield power, it must exist in concert with other social institutions in a way that is mutually reinforcing. Advertising is layered on top of other cultural elements and bound up with other institutions, from entertainment and popular culture to corporate America and manufacturing. Each element is heteroglossic, continually leaking into other sectors, with advertising slogans showing up in both casual conversation and political speeches. The very ubiquitousness of advertising — extending beyond regular media buys to include placing products in movies, sponsoring sporting events, and the full-length infomercial — ensures its power and influence in numerous places and institutions.

For an example of this interwoven character of advertising and consumption with other elements of society, consider plastics recycling. We routinely see ads touting how certain products are recyclable or made from recycled items. Currently, the plastics industry is running an advertising campaign that reminds us of all the wonderful ways that plastic contributes to our lives. That means that multiple corporate public relations departments and public relations agencies are involved in getting mileage from the recycling issue. Public relations and advertising personnel have regular contact with media people in both the advertising and editorial sides, and the boundaries between news and advertising functions are becoming increasingly blurred (Stauber & Rampton, 1995). Meanwhile, giant corporate conglomerates have become the norm, putting journalists under the same corporate roof as advertisers and the very companies they attempt to scrutinize. For example, if a television station is owned by General Electric and is also receiving thousands of dollars in revenue from an ad campaign about the value of plastics, there is dissonance — whether acknowledged or not— for those TV reporters covering a story about environmental impacts and energy used to recycle plastic.

The hallowed halls of education are not immune from commercial messages, including those about plastic. Captive youngsters are a tempting market: more than 43 million kids attend schools and even elementary-age children exert tremendous spending power, about $15 billion a year (McNeal, 1994). Ads cover school buses, book covers, and scoreboards, and corporate flags fly next to school flags. The Polystyrene Packaging Council, like other corporations, has supplied "supplemental educational materials" free of charge to K–12 classrooms. Their "Plastics and the Environment" lesson teaches that plastics are great and easily recycled, even though most plastics are not recyclable for lack of markets. Consumers Union evaluated this lesson as "highly commercial and incomplete with strong bias . . . [T]he disadvantages of plastics . . . are not covered" (Zillions, 1995, p. 46). Another critic noted that when teachers use such materials, "American students are introduced to environmental issues as they use materials supplied by corporations who pollute the soil, air, and water" (Molnar, 1995, p. 70).

Beyond communication and education, legal sectors also get involved 60 in advertising claims about recycled and recyclable plastic, and politicians know it is wise to support recycling as a generalized issue. Some municipalities sponsor curbside pick-up programs for plastic, and trash haulers and manufacturers run businesses dependent on recycling plastics. Recycling plastics not only creates new business opportunities, it also is philosophically consistent with a capitalist economy that is based on ever-increasing consumption. After all, the message of recycling is not to reduce or avoid consumption but essentially to consume something again. According to one critic in *Harper's*, oftentimes the new product created from recycled plastics is "the perfect metaphor for everything that's wrong with the idea of recycling plastics. It's ugly as sin, the world doesn't need it, and it's disposable" (Gutin, 1992, p. 56).

The vested interest of so many powerful social institutions makes it that much harder to separate the influence of one from another — such as advertising from news media — and to effect significant social change. It also makes the ubiquitous, repetitive messages of advertising reinforced and in a sense replicated, free of charge. Individuals or groups with oppositional messages about plastics would have to contend with what seems a united front about the place, if not the value, of plastic.

Working Together

Obviously, the six concepts presented here work in concert. Here is one final example of an ad that considers them together.

First, the visual of this television ad: A waterfall flows over the driver's seat of a car and a tiny kayaker (in relation to the size of the car seat) spills down the face of the falls. The scene quickly shifts to the kayaker (full-sized now and paddling away from us) amid glaciers. The next scene takes us into the car's back cargo area — still covered with water — and two orca whales breach in front of the kayaker, who pauses mid-stroke. (In all of these shots, we have never seen the kayaker's face; when he paddles away, his head is covered in a fur-lined parka that looks "native.") The next shot is a close-up of a paddle dipping into water shimmering with the colors of sunset and above the words "Discover Chevy Tahoe." The last scene shows the unoccupied vehicle parked on the edge of a stream in front of snow-covered mountain peaks. The accompanying audio includes Native American–sounding drum beats and a mixed chorus singing a chant-like, non-English song. Over this music, we hear the voice of a male announcer who quotes a passage from John Muir about how a person needs silence to get into the heart of the wilderness away from dust, hotels, baggage, and chatter.

The meanings that these elements convey to us are multiple. Peace, serenity, at-oneness with nature, and a return to a simple yet sublime "native" existence are part of the promise of this vehicle. Native drums, whales, glaciers, paddling through still waters, and even the deep ecologist Muir are powerful, idealized, and ritualized symbols that are employed to market a feeling and a sensation. The seamless juxtaposition of scene both inside and outside the vehicle conveys that nature is transported effortlessly for you to experience these things directly, without leaving the safety and luxury of your car. The vehicle is the commodity to aid your escape to this sublime place, a place depicted as real yet entirely contrived, with kayakers spilling over car seats. The entire promise is one of self-gratification, helping the driver/kayaker travel to this idealized wilderness. Yet, if you truly want to heed John Muir's advice, silence is needed to get into the heart of the wilderness, not a noisy car. Hence if you buy into (pun intended) the vehicle being the solution (and not existing instead in your own life or soul), the result is further estrangement from the very thing desired and valued. Advertising, as a primary support system for a capitalist economy, can only transfer meaning and express latent desires — not deliver on any of these promises.

REFERENCES

Banerjee, S., Gulas, C. S., & Iyer, E. (1995). Shades of green: A multidimensional analysis of environmental advertising. *Journal of Advertising, 24,* 21–32.

Benton, L. M. (1995). Selling the natural or selling out? Exploring environmental merchandising. *Environmental Ethics, 17,* 3–22.

Bullis, C. (1996). Retalking environmental discourses from a feminist perspective: The radical potential of ecofeminism. In J. G. Cantrill & C. L. Oravec (Eds.), *The symbolic earth: Discourse and our creation of the environment* (pp. 123–148). Lexington, KY: University Press of Kentucky.

Corbett, J. B. (2001). Women, scientists, agitators: Magazine portrayal of Rachel Carson and Theo Colborn. *Journal of Communication, 51,* 720–749.

Dadd, D. L., & Carothers, A. (1991). A bill of goods? Green consuming in perspective. In C. Plant & J. Plant (Eds.), *Green business: Hope or hoax?* Philadelphia, PA: New Society Publishers (pp. 11–29).

Fink, E. (1990). Biodegradable diapers are not enough in days like these: A critique of commodity environmentalism. *EcoSocialist Review, 4.*

Gutin, J. (1992, March–April). Plastics-a-go-go. *Harper's, 17,* 56–59.

Iyer, E., & Banerjee, B. (1993). Anatomy of green advertising. *Advances in Consumer Research, 20,* 484–501.

Kilbourne, W. E. (1995). Green advertising: Salvation or oxymoron? *Journal of Advertising, 24,* 7–20.

Lasch, C. (1978). *The culture of narcissism.* New York, NY: W. W. Norton.

Luke, T. W. (1993). Green consumerism: Ecology and the ruse of recycling. In J. Bennett & W. Chaloupka (Eds.), *In the nature of things: Languages, politics and the environment* (pp. 154–172). Minneapolis, MN: University of Minnesota Press.

Mayer, R. N., Scammon, D. L., & Zick, C. D. (1993). Poisoning the well: Do environmental claims strain consumer credulity? *Advances in Consumer Research, 20,* 698–703.

McNeal, J. U. (1994, February 7). Billions at stake in growing kids market. *Discount Store News, 41.*

Molnar, A. (1995). Schooled for profit. *Educational Leadership, 53,* 70–71.

Naess, A. (1973). The shallow and the deep, long-range ecology movement: A summary. *Inquiry, 16,* 95–100.

Neff, J. (2000, April 10). It's not trendy being green. *Advertising Age, 16.*

Obermiller, C. (1995). The baby is sick / the baby is well: A test of environmental communication appeals. *Journal of Advertising, 24,* 55–70.

Oravec, C. L. (1996). To stand outside oneself: The sublime in the discourse of natural scenery. In J. G. Cantrill & C. L. Oravec (Eds.), *The symbolic earth: Discourse and our creation of the environnment* (pp. 58–75). Lexington, KY: University Press of Kentucky.

Ottman, J. A. (1993). *Green marketing: Challenges and opportunities for the new marketing age.* Lincolnwood, IL: NTC Business Books.

Phillips, B. J. (1996). Advertising and the cultural meaning of animals. *Advances in Consumer Research, 23,* 354–360.

Pollay, R. W. (1989). The distorted mirror: Reflections on the unintended consequences of advertising. In R. Hovland & G. B. Wilcox (Eds.), *Advertising in society* (pp. 437–476). Lincolnwood, IL: NTC Business Books.

Price, J. (1996). Looking for nature at the mall: A field guide to the Nature Company. In W. Cronon (Ed.), *Uncommon ground: Rethinking the human place in nature,* (pp. 186–203). New York, NY: W. W. Norton.

Schudson, M. (1989). Advertising as capitalist realism. In R. Hovland & G. B. Wilcox (Eds.), *Advertising in society* (pp. 73–98). Lincolnwood, IL: NTC Business Books.

Schuhwerk, M. E., & Lefkoff-Hagius, R. (1995). Green or non-green? Does type of appeal matter when advertising a green product? *Journal of Advertising, 24,* 45–54.

Selling green. (1991, October). *Consumer Reports, 56,* 687–692.

Shanahan, J., & McComas, K. (1999). *Nature stories: Depictions of the environment and their effects.* Cresskill, NJ: Hampton Press.

Shrum, L. J., McCarty, J. A., & Lowrey, T. M. (1995). Buyer characteristics of the green consumer and their implications for advertising strategy. *Journal of Advertising, 24,* 71–82.

Stauber, J., & Rampton, S. (1995). *Toxic sludge is good for you! Lies, damn lies, and the public relations industry.* Monroe, ME: Common Courage Press.

Thorson, E., Page, T., & Moore, J. (1995). Consumer response to four categories of "green" television commercials. *Advances in Consumer Research, 22,* 243–250.

Turow, J. (1999). *Breaking up America: Advertisers and the new media world.* Chicago, IL: University of Chicago Press.

Twitchell, J. B. (1996). *Adcult USA: The triumph of advertising in American culture.* New York, NY: Columbia University Press.

Zillions: For Kids from Consumer Reports (1995). *Captive kids: Commercial pressures on kids at school.* New York, NY: Consumers Union Education Services.

Zinkham, G. M., & Carlson, L. (1995). Green advertising and the reluctant consumer. *Journal of Advertising, 24,* 1–6.

READING THE TEXT

1. Define in your own words "nature-as-backdrop" ads.

2. How, according to Corbett, did advertising become "part of the fuel that would help keep a capitalist economy burning" (para. 11)?

3. Why does Corbett claim, "commodification of what are essentially public resources — like milky blue waters — encourages us to think of resources as private and possessible" (para. 30)? Why does she think such commodification is problematic?

4. In your own words, define the term "sublime."

5. How can some ads using nature as a backdrop be considered to reflect our narcissism?

6. Why does Corbett have concerns regarding ad campaigns for plastics recycling, which is usually considered an environmentally conscious venture?

READING THE SIGNS

1. In an essay, write your own argument in response to Corbett's speculative question: "Is it even possible for any form of advertising—whether product ads or nature-as-backdrop ads—to be 'green'?" (para. 15).

2. Study some travel magazines, focusing on the advertising. To what extent is nature presented as "sublime" or as a backdrop? Use your observations to demonstrate, refute, or complicate the contention that presenting nature as "unproblematic" can have a dangerous effect on our environmental consciousness.

3. Select a single ad that uses nature as a backdrop, and conduct an in-depth analysis of it. As a critical framework, use the six reasons advertising can be "faint green" that Corbett outlines on pages 238–50.

4. Adopting the perspective of Laurence Shames ("The More Factor," p. 80), write an essay in which you argue whether the "faint green" advertising Corbett describes is an expression of the American desire for "more."

5. Corbett asserts that "attempts to make advertising fit a green framework simply illustrate how ideologically opposed advertising and environmental values are" (para. 17). In class, form teams and debate this assertion. Use the debate as a jumping-off point for your own essay in which you explore your own response.

6. Study advertisements for companies that produce oil, plastics, or chemicals. Do they use nature as a backdrop, as Corbett describes, or is nature presented in a different way? Use your observations to describe and critique the techniques such companies use to present a positive public image. As an alternative, do the same with automobile advertising, focusing on ads for SUVs (you might study a magazine such as *Car and Driver* or consult promotional material on auto companies' Web sites). Or study advertising that promotes alternative-fuel vehicles, such as the Prius, Volt, or Leaf.

VITAMEATAVEGAMIN
FOR HEALTH

VIDEO DREAMS

Television and Cultural Forms

The Walking Dead, Westerns, and the New Westerns

Forget the zombies for a moment and look at the basic setup. Against the backdrop of a lawless wilderness infested with savage killers who can leap to the attack at any moment, *The Walking Dead* centers on a small group of armed men and women as they struggle to survive in a postapocalyptic state of nature. Carrying guns, swords, and bows, they are unrestrained by any regulations in the possession of their weapons and are fully justified by their circumstances in using them whenever they need to.

Jump now to Westeros, the fictional setting of *Game of Thrones*. Here, too, armed men and women inhabit a nearly lawless landscape, with sudden violence a constant presence in their lives, and savage White Walkers (or Others) waiting mysteriously over the border at the far frontier, threatening the outbreak of even-greater mayhem in an ever-violent world.

It would seem to be a big jump between the futuristic *Walking Dead* and the Tolkienesque world of *Game of Thrones*, but these two wildly popular television series share a common significance; namely, a fundamental similarity to the Western, a now more or less defunct television genre that also features armed characters perpetually fighting it out in a lawless frontier. This similarity suggests a potential semiotic **system**, whose **associations** and **differences** can lead us to some cultural insights.

To determine the significance of what are called "the new Westerns," we can begin, as is usually the case with a semiotic analysis, with a survey of the history of the genre to which they belong. One of America's most popular narratives from the latter part of the nineteenth century (when it was consumed in the form of dime novels, newspaper features, and Western-themed circuses) through the middle of the twentieth (when it inspired a nearly endless stream of radio programs, TV series, and feature films), the Western originally reflected Americans' pride in their frontier history. The genre was a celebration of the pioneers, settlers, cowboys, and gunslinging lawmen who, as people used to say, "won the West." Like medieval knights in armor, the Western's armed men on horseback were the heroes of a national mythology, legendary outliers of a rapidly expanding nation.

This all changed in the later 1960s and the 1970s, when the historical distortions of the Western became all too clear — when, that is to say, winning the West came to be seen as a genocidal injustice to the native peoples who paid the price for American expansion, and former heroes like Wyatt Earp were revealed to be little more than bullies no better (and perhaps worse) than their victims. This difference in perception produced a new Western, a rewriting of the script that replaced the likes of Ben Cartwright of *Bonanza* with a revisionary George Armstrong Custer in movies like *Little Big Man* (1970), which retold the battles of Wounded Knee and the Little Big Horn from the Native American point of view.

At the same time, the Western's inherent violence was revisited in different ways. On the one hand, Westerns like Sam Peckinpah's *The Wild Bunch* turned that violence into a metaphor for the upheavals of the sixties, essentially critiquing, not celebrating it. On the other hand, a post–Vietnam War reaction against violent gunplay resulted in pacified Westerns like *Little House on the Prairie* and, years later as the genre was sputtering out, *Dr. Quinn, Medicine Woman*. By the new millennium, the television Western was pretty much finished, with *Deadwood* — a highly unflattering look at the fighters who won the West — standing as the last gasp of a genre that no longer appealed to the imagination of an audience who had become more diverse than the traditional Western's fundamentally WASP viewers and had become less interested in the frontier history that spawned the genre.

But science fiction narratives like the short-lived *Terra Nova* and the soon-to-be-sequelized *Avatar* reveal that the Western did not so much vanish as evolve to suit newer tastes and ideologies. Like the revisionary Western *Dances with Wolves*, *Avatar* reverses the traditional narrative by making the Na'vi the heroes and the Resources Development Administration (an obvious metaphor for the Euro-American conquest of the New World) the villains. It's good versus evil, but this time it's not the cavalry that comes to the rescue against the "Indians"; it's nature itself rising against an evil civilization.

This all returns us to *The Walking Dead* and *Game of Thrones*. If *Avatar* is a Western turned upside down, *The Walking Dead* and *Game of Thrones* are Westerns turned inside out. Here the frontier is a moral as well as a physical wilderness, and the battle between good and evil has devolved into little more than a messy struggle for survival. *The Walking Dead*, particularly, feels like a kind of National Rifle Association fantasy, in which constantly carrying, and using, weapons without restriction is not only necessary but justified. We can

A promotional poster for *The Walking Dead*.

further detect a vicarious wish fulfillment at work, through which audiences can imagine themselves living in a perilous world where they can fight back, with a wild freedom, against the forces that threaten and oppress them.

Such fantasies appeal to a society suffering from an apparently eternal threat of terroristic violence (zombies make good metaphors for ruthless terrorists) and economic malaise. As individuals we may feel helpless in the face of such forces, but as audiences we can find in the new Westerns an imaginary freedom to resist, while at the same time being reassured that everyone else is as badly off as we are. Thus, the new Westerns can be taken as a **sign**, a signifier of a society in distress.

Writing about Television

We begin this chapter with a brief semiotic analysis to show how you can look at television programs in the same way that you can look at any cultural phenomenon: as a series of signs, signifiers of the society that consumes them. But while you might find writing about television familiar from high school assignments in which you were asked to write about a favorite program — perhaps in a summary-writing exercise, a descriptive essay, or an opinion piece on why a particular program is your favorite show — writing semiotic interpretations of TV shows is a different task. Although you still need to rely on your skills in description and summary in writing semiotic analyses of TV, you should put aside your personal opinions of a show (that is, whether you like it or not) to construct interpretive arguments about its cultural significance.

Television offers an especially rich field of possible writing topics, ranging from a historical analysis of a whole category, or genre, of TV programming (as we briefly presented above with respect to the Western) or of a general trend, to an interpretation of a single TV show episode. Whatever approach to television you take, you will probably need to do some research. No one can be expected to know about all the television programs (from both the past and the present) that can be associated with and differentiated from any particular show that you are analyzing, so you should plan to find reliable sources to help you contextualize whatever program you are interpreting.

From Symbols to Icons

When writing about TV, keep in mind that the ubiquity of televised (or digitized) images in our lives represents a shift from one kind of sign system to another. As Marshall McLuhan pointed out over fifty years ago in *The Gutenberg Galaxy* (1962), Western culture since the fifteenth century has defined itself around the printed word — the linear text that reads from left to right and top to bottom. The printed word, in the terminology of the American founder of semiotics, Charles Sanders Peirce, is a **symbolic sign**, one whose meaning is entirely arbitrary or conventional. A symbolic sign means what it does because those who use it have decided so. Words don't look like what they mean. Their significance is entirely abstract.

Not so with a visual image, which does resemble its object and is not entirely arbitrary. Although a photograph is not literally the thing it depicts and may reflect a good deal of staging and manipulation by the photographer, we often respond to it as if it were an innocent reflection of the world. Peirce called such signs "icons," referring by this term to any sign that resembles what it means. The way you interpret an **icon**, then, differs from the way you interpret a symbol or word. The interpretation of words involves your cognitive capabilities; the viewing of icons is far more sensuous, more a matter of vision than cognition. The shift from a civilization governed by the paradigm of the book to one dominated by the image accordingly involves a shift in the way we "read" our world, as the symbolic field of the printed page yields to the iconic field of the screen.

The shift from a symbolic, or word-centered, world to an iconic universe filled with visual images carries profound cultural implications. For while we *can* read visual images actively and cognitively (which, of course, is the whole point of this book), the sheer visibility of icons tempts us to receive them uncritically and passively. Icons look so much like the realities they refer to that it is easy to forget that icons, too, are signs: images that people construct to carry ideological meanings.

The Kids Aren't All Right

Consider, for example, the image of the American family as presented in the classic situation comedies of the 1950s to 1960s. White, suburban, and middle class, these families signified an American ideal that glorified patriarchal authority. Even *I Love Lucy*, a sitcom showcasing Lucille Ball, reinforced masculine privilege through such plotlines as Lucy's attempt to market her own line of "Vitameatavegamin" dietary supplements, an endeavor which, the show implied, was predestined to end in disaster due to female business incompetence. The advent of such "dysfunctional" family sitcoms as *Married with Children*, which undermined *male* authority and competence, thus signified a profound difference, a rejection of the old patriarchal values.

By the turn of the new millennium, this ideological shift had produced such popular series as *Desperate Housewives*, a program that not only adopted a matriarchal rather than patriarchal point of view but also helped to create a new television genre — the "dramedy" — which is neither a comedy nor a drama but is instead a hybrid of the two. And while the show is now in syndication and is no longer producing new episodes, a close look at one of its episodes can reveal just how subversive a TV program can be.

When studying a single episode of a television program, you should consider every potentially significant detail in it — from the appearance and nature of the characters to the settings, plotlines, and dialogue. And as with all semiotic analyses, you should suspend your personal opinions — that is, whether you like a show or not. What you are working toward is a critical analysis, what you think a program's underlying cultural significance may be. This process can also differ from describing what you think the show's explicit

Discussing the Signs of Television

In class, choose a current television program, and have the entire class watch the same episode (either individually as "homework" or together in class). Interpret the episode semiotically. What values and cultural myths does the show project? What do the commercials broadcast during the show say about its presumed audience? Go beyond the episode's surface appeal or "message" to look at the particular images it uses to tell its story, always asking, "What is this program *really* saying?"

message is. Many programs present overt messages, or morals, but what you are looking for is the message beyond the message, so to speak — the implicit, often contradictory, signals the show is sending.

A clear example of this type of double message can be found in "My Heart Belongs to Daddy" (Episode 204 of *Desperate Housewives*). We chose this episode because of its especially sly way of undercutting its own apparently conservative "moral" with a subtle, but powerful, counterpoint. Concluding with a voice-over in which the show's ghostly narrator, Mary Alice, comments on the good things that happen when families have good fathers present, the episode appears to extol the old-fashioned patriarchal vision of the family. But a close reading of the plot reveals something quite different indeed.

You can find a recap of "My Heart Belongs to Daddy" at www.televisionwith outpity.com/show/desperate-housewives/my-heart-belongs-to-daddy/18/. Given the soap-operatic nature of a dramedy like *Desperate Housewives* — the way that any single episode is intertwined with past episodes and never achieves closure in itself — you should research the backstory of a series of this kind before attempting an analysis, as we did prior to our own analysis. But rather than attempting to summarize the highly involved situation in which this particular episode is entwined, we shall treat it as a largely stand-alone story, focusing on three different subplots featuring the behavior of young boys.

These subplots center on the characters of Lynette, Susan, and Bree. Lynette has recently returned to her job in the corporate world because her husband lost *his* job, and she is unhappy about missing time with her young son Parker. Unmarried Susan, for her part, is pursuing a romantic relationship with Mike, who happens to be the secret father of Zach, a homicidal teenage runaway. Zach is looking for Paul, his presumptive father, who has gone missing for reasons of his own. Meanwhile, widow Bree is dating George, and her son Andrew highly resents the relationship since it is so soon after his father's death. Got all that? The show's fans will be aware of the excessively complicated story line that has taken the series to this point, but this will do for our purposes.

Let's begin with Lynette. She isn't simply unhappy; she is driven to tears by Parker's behavior in response to her absence. He has invented an "imaginary friend" whom he calls Mrs. Mulberry and who is embodied in a black umbrella (obviously inspired by *Mary Poppins*) that he carries with him everywhere and insists on sleeping with. When his mother comes in to kiss him good night, Parker rejects her while expressing his deep affection for Mrs. Mulberry. The situation could make us very sympathetic for a child who is going through severe separation anxiety, but he is really nasty about the whole matter. Not only does he callously reject Lynette's sincere attempts to connect with him, but he uses the umbrella to assault his teacher at school, an event that leads to Lynette's having to visit the school principal.

Lynette surreptitiously tosses the umbrella into the trash, but the next morning the trash collector accidentally drops the umbrella in the street. When Lynette comes out shortly thereafter to take Parker (who is protesting that he can't leave until he finds Mrs. Mulberry) to school, she tells him that Mrs. Mulberry has gone on to help another child, but at this moment they both see the umbrella lying in the street. An expression of joy crosses Parker's face, soon to be replaced by one of horror when a car drives by and flattens the umbrella. Lynette looks relieved, as Parker finally turns to his mother for comfort. She's gotten him back, and she's back in control.

Meanwhile, Bree has invited George over for dinner, and Andrew, trying to disgust George and drive him away from his mother, starts telling him about the noises his mother makes during sex. Bree, who is in the kitchen, doesn't hear this, and when George erupts in anger, he is the one who looks bad to Bree as Andrew smirkingly looks on. The audience, however, can see clearly that Bree is being duped. George gets his revenge at a swim meet, carefully planning things so that just at the beginning of Andrew's race, Andrew will look up into the stands to see Bree rapturously kissing George. Andrew jumps out of the pool, runs into the stands, and begins to slug George. Bree erupts at Andrew, to George's great satisfaction. Andrew is subsequently packed off to a camp for troublesome children, and his mother is firmly in control at the end of the episode.

Finally, Susan, who has located the missing Zach, is on the verge of helping him find his "father," Paul, when Zach brings up his continuing romantic feelings for Susan's daughter, Julie. A homicidal near-maniac with a track record of threatening people with guns, Zach is not exactly any mother's idea of a good suitor for her daughter. Susan changes her mind about helping Zach and instead tricks him into leaving the state. As with Parker's shock and Andrew's comeuppance, the situation is presented in such a manner that the audience's sympathy is likely to be with the woman, not the boy. Susan skillfully controls the situation.

To determine a semiotic significance for these details, we need to keep in mind the program's target audience and what is likely to entertain that audience. Remember, commercial television exists to entertain, and analyzing what makes it entertaining is what leads us to its significance. In the case of *Desperate Housewives*, the target audience predominantly consists of women, often mothers, who can especially identify with the parenting difficulties of the women depicted in the program. An episode packed with conflicts with misbehaving boys who have taken control of various situations but who all get a put-down in the end **abductively** points to an existing frustration in the mothers who watch it. The entertainment value lies in the catharsis such viewers may feel in seeing the boys "punished." Now, none of the boys suffers any physical harm (mothers would not be entertained by *that*); the punishment lies in a restoration of maternal power. In each case, the boy's comeuppance leaves the woman in control after she had lost her authority for a while. Evidently, a significant number of American women are feeling such desperation, or the scriptwriters would not have exploited it. Commercial TV exists to attract its audience, not repel it, and *Desperate Housewives* is not a show for young boys.

This episode of *Desperate Housewives* thus sends a signal beyond the explicit message. Recall that the explicit message is, in effect, patriarchal, a declaration of the need for good and strong fathers. But the underlying message, somewhat contradictorily, is matriarchal, presenting the cathartic triumph of women over young males. The potentially subversive significance of this counter-message is masked by Mary Alice's voice-over, which makes the episode appear completely conventional and thus avoids the sort of controversy that could sink a prime-time series. But it is that unconventional, subtle counter-signal in the plot that may account for much of the success of *Desperate Housewives*, an indicator that there are a good many desperate women eager to see their frustrations sympathetically dramatized.

The Flow

Whatever show you choose to analyze, remember why it is on TV in the first place: Television, whether network or cable, is there to make money. It is a major part of our consumer culture, and most of what appears on TV is there because advertisers who want to reach their intended markets sponsor it. The shows that command the highest share of viewers, accordingly, command the highest advertising rates. Producers want their viewers to connect emotionally with their programs — and a main strategy for encouraging this connection involves satisfying viewer fantasies. This is especially striking in teen-addressed shows that feature fashion-model-glamorous actors (often in their twenties) playing adolescents in the awkward years, but it is also true for adult-addressed shows, which invite their viewers to identify with high-status professionals like doctors (*Grey's Anatomy*) and lawyers (*The Good Wife*). Identifying with their favorite characters, viewers will identify with the products they see advertised on the shows — and buy them (or so television sponsors hope).

For this reason, the advertising that accompanies the show is one of the most revealing features in a television program analysis. By paying attention to the ads, you can learn much about the intended audience. Why is the nightly news often sponsored by over-the-counter painkillers? Why is daytime TV, especially in the morning, typically accompanied by ads for vocational training schools? Why are youth-oriented prime-time shows filled with fast-food commercials, while family programs have a lot of car ads?

Your analysis of a single episode of a television program can also usefully include a survey of where the show fits in what cultural studies pioneer Raymond Williams called the "flow" of an evening's TV schedule. Flow refers to the sequence of TV programs and advertisements, from, say, the 5:00 news, through the pre-prime-time 7:00 to 8:00 slot, through prime time and on through to the 11:00 news and the late-night talk shows. What precedes your program? What follows? Can you determine the strategy behind your show's scheduling?

Exploring the Signs of Television: Viewing Habits

In your journal, explore your television-viewing habits and how the way you have watched TV has changed over time. When and why do you usually watch television? Have you transitioned from watching shows with your family or friends to watching them alone on a computer? Do you watch shows when they are broadcast, or do you watch them via Netflix, Hulu, or DVR on your own time? Do you think of watching television as a social activity? If so, write about how the diverse technical options for watching television have complicated this notion. If not, what place does watching television occupy in your life?

Reality Bites

No overview of modern television can be complete without a look at reality TV (RTV), and as with any semiotic analysis, some history is essential. One might say that reality television began in 1948 with Allen Funt's *Candid Camera*, which featured the filming of real people (who didn't know they were on camera) as they reacted to annoying situations concocted by the show's creators. The show's attraction lay in the humor viewers could enjoy by watching other people get into minor jams. There is a name for this kind of humor that comes from psychoanalytic theory: schadenfreude, or taking pleasure in the misfortunes of others, as when we laugh at someone slipping on a banana peel. And we shall see that this appeal from the early days of reality TV is very much a part of the genre's popularity today.

After *Candid Camera* came the 1970s PBS series *An American Family*. In this program, a camera crew moved in with a suburban family named the Louds and filmed them in their day-to-day lives. The Louds were not contestants and there were no prizes to be won. The program was conceived as an experiment in cinema verité to see if it was possible for television to be authentically realistic. The experiment was a bit of a failure, however, as the Loud family members began to act out for the camera. The result was the eventual dissolution of the Louds as a family unit and a general uneasiness about such experiments.

The next and probably most crucial step was when MTV launched *The Real World* in 1992. Like *An American Family*, *The Real World* (and similar programs like *Big Brother*) attempts to be realistic, with its constant camera recording a group of people living in the same house. Unlike *An American Family*, however, *The Real World* is a fantasy that caters to young-adult viewers, who can imagine themselves living in glamorous circumstances and vicariously enjoy the experience of becoming instant TV stars. That there is a certain tampering with reality in *The Real World*, a deliberate selection of participants based upon their appearance and how they can be cast into often-contrived romances as well as conflicts, constitutes a contradiction that differentiates *The Real World* from *An American Family* and leads us to the dawning of the reality revolution.

The astounding success of the inaugural versions of *Who Wants to Marry a Multi-Millionaire?* and *Survivor* established reality TV's full coming-of-age. In both programs, we can see strong traces of what made their pioneering predecessors popular. But through their introduction of a game show element, complete with contestants competing for huge cash prizes, a whole new dimension was added with new layers of significance in an even more **overdetermined** fashion. Reality programs that include a game show dimension offer their viewers the vicarious chance to imagine themselves as being in the shoes of the contestants (after all, anyone in principle can get on a game show) and winning lots of money. There is an element of schadenfreude here as well, if viewers take pleasure in watching the losers in game show competitions. But by adding the real-life element of marriage to the mix, *Who Wants to Marry a Multi-Millionaire?* (and its descendants) has brought an extra dimension of humiliation, not to mention voyeurism, to the genre. It's one thing to be caught on camera during the emotional upheaval of competing for large cash prizes, but it is quite another to be in an erotic competition, and lose, with millions watching you.

While game shows usually feature some sort of competition among the contestants, the *Survivor* series takes such competition to a new level by compelling its contestants to engage in backstabbing conspiracies as they claw their way to the top. (The 2006 season even introduced an element of racial conflict by forming tribes according to race.) It isn't enough for tribe to compete against tribe; there has to be intratribal backbiting and betrayal as well. Such a subtext constitutes a kind of grotesque parody of American capitalism itself, in which the cutthroat competition of the workplace is moved to the wilderness. Not to miss out on a good thing, RTV brought it all back to the office with *The Apprentice*, a show that makes capitalist competition its major theme, while echoing the talent show elements of *American Idol*. Indeed, so successful was the formula that *The Apprentice* would be joined for a while by *My Big Fat Obnoxious Boss*, which really turned the evils of life under capitalism into schadenfreude-laden entertainment.

Voyeurism. Schadenfreude. Dog-eat-dog capitalist competitiveness. Conspicuous consumption. RTV's formula seems to appeal to some of the most primitive and socially disruptive of human instincts, violating taboos in the name of profits (for an example of *real* taboo tweaking, consider the *Jackass* franchise). Indeed, after one of the *Survivor: The Australian Outback* contestants was seriously burned by a fire, commentators wondered whether future installments would have to include the death of a contestant to satisfy their viewers' ever-greater desire for mayhem. But while there has been no such event (to date), reality TV continues to grow, covering every imaginable possible topic (storage container speculation, anyone?). Combining disdain with desire, RTV invites viewers to fantasize that they, too, can effortlessly become rich or famous or beautiful, while sneering at those who—like the people of *Jersey Shore* and *Here Comes Honey Boo Boo*—are put on TV so their audiences can feel better about themselves by feeling superior to them. We've come a long way from the "I'm OK. You're OK." era. Today, it's more like "I'm not OK. You're an idiot."

Real Populists of the U.S.A.

Among the more recent varieties of reality television are programs that focus on fundamentally working-class occupations (*America's Toughest Jobs*, *Ice Road Truckers*, *Deadliest Catch*, and so on). Such programs, with their claim that viewers are being shown what life is like for ordinary working-class people, introduce yet another layer of significance to RTV that can best be explained in relation to the contradictory **mythologies** of American populism and elitism.

America's populist tradition celebrates the common citizen, the ordinary man or woman on the street, "Joe Six-Pack." These are the heroes of our democratic tradition and institutions. Programs like *America's Toughest Jobs* embrace this vision, inviting their viewers to identify with, and celebrate, ordinary people. It is highly significant, however, that *America's Toughest Jobs* lasted only one season, while elitist RTV programs that focus on the lives of wealthy families like the Kardashians or those that appear in one *Real Housewives of . . .* franchise or another seem to go on forever. Ask yourself what the appeal of such shows to their largely nonaffluent audiences might be. What signs do you see that their characters' lives are happy or unhappy, and what are they happy or unhappy about? What fantasies about being a mom at home do these shows encourage? Use your semiotic tool kit to extend the discussion we've started here, not only about these sorts of programs but about any TV show your instructor asks you to analyze.

The Medium Is the Message

In short, there are a myriad of RTV formulas to suit a highly segmented, niche-marketed audience, with a seemingly limitless appetite for programs that appeal to their particular fantasies, desires, interests, and even irritations. But perhaps all reality programming shares a fundamental common denominator that links it to the newer digital technologies that are now reshaping the American consciousness. This is the way that RTV offers ordinary people the chance to enjoy extraordinary media fame and exposure, or, conversely but in a similar fashion, offers at least the illusion of access to the lives of the truly famous. That is, whether you are auditioning for *American Idol* (at virtually impossible odds, of course) or viewing a program like *Duck Dynasty* or voting

---

Reading about TV Online

The Internet has given rise to a number of popular sites for TV criticism and community discussion, including tvworthwatching.com. Using a search engine, find a forum devoted to your favorite TV show and take notes on how the community of fans interacts. What about the show you've chosen most interests fans? What topics are most popular, or most contested? Does the conversation stick to television, or does it veer into discussions of users' personal lives? Are you drawn to participate? Using the forum as a microcosm, reflect on how television might be considered a social adhesive. How do the fans of TV shows use the Web to bond over the show and with one another?

---

on *Dancing with the Stars*, you are touching the big grid of a media-saturated and media-fascinated society. So, too, does your own Twitter feed (or YouTube account, Facebook page, or whatever) give you a place, however small, in a global media environment, even as it allows you to read celebrity tweets (or Facebook pages) and, perhaps, be tweeted back to.

Two sides of the same coin, RTV and social networking are signifiers of the full maturity of the age of **mass media**, an era in which nothing seems to matter unless it can be publicized and broadcast, and fame by any means trumps all other values. With the celebrity as the defining identity for our **mass culture**, both television and the social media made possible by the new technology are shaping a culture in which celebrity access seems to be open to all. Andy Warhol once quipped that in the future everyone would be famous for fifteen minutes, but while that fifteen minutes is still an unrealistic goal for the vast majority of us, reality television, along with its digital cousins, signifies a world where personal publicity or sheer notoriety is not only a means to an end but the end itself, the goal of goals.

The Readings

We begin the readings in this chapter with Nick Serpe's trenchant analysis of such reality television programs as *Repo Games*, *Pawn Stars*, and *Storage Wars*, in which he explores the depths to which RTV will go in a bad economy in order to make money. Claire Miye Stanford and Michelle Dean follow with a paired set of readings that take us to the country, with Stanford analyzing the feminist dimensions of ABC's *Nashville* and Dean critiquing *Here Comes Honey Boo Boo*'s exploitation of that old American stereotype: the redneck hillbilly. Next, Carl Matheson looks at *The Simpsons* — one of TV's longest-running institutions — and explores what happens when self-conscious irony overrides just about everything else that the show may represent, while Natasha Simons unravels the political significance of *Mad Men*, a show that looks quite different depending upon the ideology of the viewer. Jane Hu's nuanced analysis of sex, class, eating, and economics in *Girls* brings out the ambivalences of millennialist life in an era of reduced expectations, and Willa Paskin follows with a critique of the contradictions in *Devious Maids*, a program that at once skewers and celebrates the American dream. Neal Gabler concludes the chapter with his suggestion that having contributed to the atomization of American society, "TV has learned how to compensate for the increasing alienation it seems to induce" by filling its schedule with shows saturated with inauthentic "flocks" of friends and family relationships.

NICK SERPE

Reality Pawns: The New Money TV

> When the going gets tough, reality TV gets nasty. Such is the conclu-
> sion that Nick Serpe draws in this review of such RTV shows as *Repo
> Games*, "one of the vilest reality shows in the history of American
> television," as Serpe puts it. Pulling no punches, Serpe explores the
> ways in which the Great Recession has been exploited by RTV pro-
> ducers who have found that debt and down-and-outedness make for
> entertaining fare in such programs as *Pawn Stars* and *Storage Wars*,
> gritty shows that, like *Repo Games*, reap profits out of other people's
> losses. Nick Serpe is the online editor of *Dissent: A Quarterly of Poli-
> tics and Culture*, from which this selection is taken.

Repo Games, one of the vilest reality shows in the history of American television, premiered on Spike in 2011 with no fanfare and a simple premise,
delivered in a voiceover intro: "Nobody wants to meet the repo man. But
when this repo man comes, you'll get the chance to ditch those late notices
for good." A little more than a minute later, we see a man built like a professional wrestler pull up in front of a woman's house, along with a camera crew
that rushes into her driveway like a SWAT team. The owner's "REPO REPORT"
then flashes across the screen: "Name: Wallace. Age: 44, Vehicle: '96 Dodge
Caravan. Intel: Her weave alone will whoop your ass." Heavy metal plays in
the background. A tow truck backs in under the van, which Wallace does not
appreciate, and then the wrestler, co-host Tom DeTone, proceeds to describe
the situation in which Wallace now finds herself: Tom is going to repo her car,
but if she can answer three of five trivia questions right, the car will be hers,
and fully paid off. The tow rig lifts the back of the car when she gets answers
wrong and brings it down when she gets them right. With six family members watching on, Wallace prevails. She dances with Tom and then boasts in
the post-game interview, "I ain't going to even fucking look for a job now."

The next contestant, a skinny, shirtless stoner living at his mom's, has a
similar message when he wins: "Guess what I learned, America: if you don't
pay your bill, somebody else will."

The last contestant, a woebegone fifty-eight-year-old man, grovels when
he loses: "Even though I lost, you guys gave me an opportunity to save my car
and I appreciate that, because in this time and age not many people would
even do that." Tom responds, "Wish you all the best, John, and I wish I could
pay off everybody's car. It's just not possible."

Even in "this time and age" — years into a hollow economic recovery built
atop an already hollowed-out economy, more than a decade after the ascen-
dance of American reality television — and even given the very low bar of

taste set by Spike, I expected to find some online traces of outrage at the cruelty, exploitation, and heavy-handed stereotypes on display in *Repo Games*. All I could find was a commentary in the *American Thinker*, a conservative website, speculating that "the numerous stupid and vulgar contestants" on the show were typical Obama voters. In depicting these people seemingly cast from a Tea Partier's nightmare—the lazy welfare queen, the languid video-gamer mooching off the 'rents, the emasculated, aging white man who "never should've gotten this far"—the show "inadvertently [veered] from goofy entertainment into trenchant social commentary."

Reality television, though almost never considered serious, was seriously considered in its early days, and the attention was mostly negative. Some early precursors, such as MTV's *The Real World* (1992–present), which brought a group of young strangers together under one roof for a few months, earned begrudging respect for their occasionally frank depictions of stigmatized subjects. But the ethical tone and artistic qualities of reality TV seemed to be set by *Who Wants to Marry a Multi-Millionaire?*, a one-night special aired on Fox in February 2000. *Multi-Millionaire* was like a beauty pageant that collided with a high-stakes *Dating Game*: women were paraded on stage for a rich man, seen only in silhouette, who would pick a lucky winner and marry her right then and there. The National Organization of Women denounced the show, as did the bride in numerous interviews. (It turns out that a restraining order had been filed against the man by a former girlfriend, not to mention that he wasn't that rich after all.) The marriage was annulled in April. By the summer, American versions of *Survivor* and *Big Brother*, both European imports, had premiered and won huge audiences. These series featured "normal" people, competing for prizes and for their fifteen minutes of fame. They set the standards—confessional interviews, fierce competition, oblivious narcissism, casting designed to foster conflict, semi-scripted scenes—that would define the genre.

Critics worried about what had opened the reality TV floodgates. Perhaps it was the seductive intimation that anyone could be (briefly) famous—and that the skeptical audience probably deserved it more than the charmless cutthroats who auditioned successfully. Perhaps the viewing public was growing so detached, so impatient with clichés and inured to fictional cruelty, that they hungered for something realer. Maybe we'd watched so much television that we were all acting like TV characters anyway; someone just had to put the cameras in front of us. Or was the rest of TV already so bad that anything novel was welcome?

If you were reading the tea leaves of popular taste, you would find a lot to get upset about. But focusing only on viewers reinforces the idea that TV programming is driven by what consumers want. There's no doubt that reality TV would have remained a very marginal phenomenon without a willing audience, but it wouldn't have spread the way it did—with proliferating subgenres colonizing the whole TV landscape—were it not for the economics of producing these shows. According to Charles B. Slocum, assistant executive director of the Writers Guild of America, West:

In virtually every line of the production budget, reality-based programming is cheaper than traditional programming. Not as much equipment is needed, and it's cheaper. There is a smaller crew. There are fewer paid performers. There are fewer sets. The economic role of reality-based programming is to permit a network to cost-average down the price of programming across the entire primetime schedule.

And, as a strike this spring by writers on the show *Fashion Police* brought to public attention, reality writers are predominantly nonunionized, with wages and benefits that reflect this fact. Even if entertainment execs weren't terrified of the Internet pushing down their bottom lines, cheap and titillating programming was a no-brainer.

The cultural panic over reality programming faded as the genre became a permanent and profitable TV fixture. In the meantime, a relatively small group of intelligent and well-crafted television dramas, from *The Sopranos* to *Breaking Bad*, became critical darlings, arguably marking the first time the medium has surpassed mainstream American cinema as an art form.

As a result, more recent developments in reality TV, including some of the most popular cable shows of the last five years, have attracted less attention. Critics have taken note of the rise of so-called blue-collar TV—where "blue collar" means burly fishermen (*Deadliest Catch*) and loggers (*Ax Men*) risking their lives to take care of their families—and the related "redneck" subgenre, featuring, for example, Cajuns with thick accents hunting swamp alligators (*Swamp People*). *Repo Games* also follows people doing their jobs—the co-hosts are supposedly both actual repo men—but it is part of a different phenomenon: the money-crazed, market-idealizing reality show, immersed in a funhouse version of the culture of debt and credit.

Although consumer debt was holding the American economy together for [10] decades before the recession laid it bare, these shows are a distinctly post-recession phenomenon. They thrive on foreclosed property and unpaid bills; they promote a bargain-basement ethos where everything has a price, and where discovering and comparing those prices is a source of pleasure. These shows are competitive in the way that much reality TV is, but the competitions are embedded in actual economic practice. These shows are the popular idea of the free market, writ small.

Two shows define this subgenre more than any other: *Pawn Stars*, which premiered on the History Channel in the summer of 2009, and A&E's *Storage Wars*, launched in December 2010. These remarkably formulaic programs set viewing records on their respective channels and inspired cable TV execs to run dozens of imitators.

Pawn Stars depicts the goings-on at a Las Vegas pawn shop that caters both to people making ends meet at the end of the month and to habitual gamblers. Most of the store's transactions are pawns, offered at the industry's typically high interest rates. Most of the customers depicted on the show, however, resemble the people who bring heirlooms to *Antiques Roadshow*, if slightly gruffer. And most of the transactions depicted are sales and purchases, not loans. (The producers defend the absence of the typical pawn customer by appealing to the unique character of this pawn shop, to the repeat customers' desire for privacy, and to audience sensibilities.)

In its structure, *Pawn Stars* is in fact a lot like *Antiques Roadshow*, the old PBS standby. Both ride on the fantasy that treasure might be lurking in anyone's attic. But the differences between *Roadshow* and what History Channel executives are calling "artifactual entertainment" are telling. The pawn shop setting (unlike *Roadshow*'s convention hall set-up) tells us that we're here for business, and lends the show at least the pretense of documentary. The PBS series features dozens of experts in various fields, while on *Pawn Stars* the assessors are mainly in the family business: Richard Harrison the patriarch, his son Rick (the show's star), Rick's son Corey, and Corey's friend Austin "Chumlee" Russell. They sometimes call on specialist "friends" in town to assess or restore particular items, and they frequently go to shooting ranges to test antique weapons, such as a nineteenth-century cannon shown on the first episode. *Pawn Stars* also attempts to signify youthfulness (successfully, as evidenced by its high under-thirty-five viewer ratings) with generic hard-rock interludes and souped-up graphics.

Despite its alleged factual and historical content, *Pawn Stars* is character driven. The Harrisons and Chumlee bicker and mock each other more or less constantly, in scenes that seem scripted to varying extents. The arguments are presented as a tough-guy façade covering a warm, family-friendly core. These men make their living by driving down what their customers ask for, but they have to put food on their tables, too, and pay all those employees we don't see on camera. Their homespun manner, their fascination with historical artifacts and the moment of discovery, the fact that we don't see their private homes (a very rare sight in the entire subgenre) or any truly desperate clientele — all of it makes the pawn biz seem like an honest one: usury with a human face. There aren't any complex debt vehicles or international price-fixing scandals at this lender, and the simple profit calculus is literally shown on screen: projected sale price minus purchase price equals projected profit. When the Harrisons and their staff won the National Pawnbrokers Association "Pawnbroker of the Year" award in 2010, the organization claimed they had improved the public image of pawn shops more in one year than the NPA's publicity team had over decades.

On *Storage Wars*, naked economic warfare takes a more central role, but the family unit and flights of whimsy intervene to prevent the characters from looking like complete sociopaths. The show features a husband and wife duo who auction off storage units whose owners are delinquent in their payments. Various characters who want to resell the contents try to intimidate and frustrate each other as they compete for the units. The winners dig through their lockers and assign unverified prices to the items inside. On the first season, there's Dave, a brash man with a secondhand business big enough that he brings a team of men with him to carry off his hauls; Jarrod and Brandi, another husband-and-wife pair, who run a struggling consignment shop; Barry, a dilettante collector who employs various outlandish tricks (for instance, using a little person on stilts) to gain advantage; and Darrell, a perpetually sunburned and doltish man who, along with his son, is on the hunt for the "wow factor." One participant warns that "once we get through those gates, there is [sic] no friends, and there is no professional courtesy. It's every man for himself, and may the best man win," and at the end of each episode, the day's winner is declared according to self-reported profits. But despite the fierce bidding, the show's tone is light-hearted, even ironic.

Pawn Stars and *Storage Wars* launched an entire subgenre, with various epigones on cable channels including TLC, Lifetime, Discovery, Travel, Spike, and of course History and A&E. There are direct franchise spin-offs, such as *Cajun Pawn Stars* and *Storage Wars: Texas*, related shows such as *American Restoration* (which features an antique restorer frequently consulted on *Pawn Stars*), and a host of imitators. On *American Pickers*, two friends travel around the country dropping in on old farmers and hoarders to make on-the-spot deals on salvaged antiques. On *Barter Kings*, the hosts do away with cash altogether, transforming a small and inexpensive item into something grand through a series of in-kind trades with people they meet through Craigslist. Other shows transplant the auction idea into other settings, like *Baggage Battles* (unclaimed luggage at airports), *Container Wars* (unclaimed commercial shipping containers), *Texas Car Wars* (semi-junked hotrods), and *Flip Men* and *Property Wars* (foreclosed houses). On *Picker Sisters* and *Pawn Queens*, there are women.

One of the most notable of the debt-and-credit reality TV shows released in the wake of *Pawn Stars* and *Storage Wars* is *Hardcore Pawn*, truTV's most popular show and the inspiration for its own spin-offs, such as *Hardcore Pawn: Chicago* and the deranged *Combat Pawn*. Although it is clearly an attempt to cash in on the popularity of *Pawn Stars*, the show's producers and writers have set out to differentiate themselves from their relatively staid predecessor. Like the other shows in the subgenre, *Hardcore Pawn* extols the small-business owner, depends on a familial cast to drive the action ("We disagree more than regular employees, but we have each other's back"), and is full of scripted scenes that strain credulity. But *Hardcore Pawn* trades on its grit and volatility. The Harrisons appear to make money by playing with toys, while the Golds have captured the pugilistic atmosphere of *The Jerry Springer Show*, replete with bleeped-out cursing, fights broken up by large security guards, and a stripper pole (all on the first episode).

Despite the obvious fakery, the Detroit pawn shop owned by Les Gold, a third-generation pawnbroker working with his children Seth and Ashley, appears to have real customers who are about as happy as you would expect customers at a pawn shop — let alone a pawn shop in Detroit — to be. And as Les proudly states, "We don't call the experts, we are the experts." The customers lie and get lied to, and they are indeed desperate. "We're not *Antiques Roadshow*," Les told an interviewer, claiming *Hardcore Pawn* shows "how the *other* other half lives," a reverse image *Lifestyles of the Rich and Famous*. (David Paulin, author of the *American Thinker* commentary, explicitly draws a comparison between the people on *Repo Games* and the poor depicted in Michael Harrington's *The Other America*, all of whom he sees as suffering more from a lack of middle-class values than a lack of money.) "The draw that truTV has really focused on was the reality of what goes on in a real pawn shop with real people,"* Gold told an interviewer for the *Detroit Free Press*. Again, its claim to depicting real life is laughable. But the show might actually present what the typical petit bourgeois believes is typical of the working poor, either jocular deference or outrageous hijinks.

Watched in close succession, these cash-crazed shows reveal a number of common tropes. They portray an unforgiving social landscape, where taking risks at others' expense is the way to get ahead. They recommend crude psychological techniques for closing the sale: trick your auction competition into dropping too much money on a bad unit, encourage people selling their goods to name a price before you do, leverage their personal problems to encourage a less-than-ideal trade, and never be afraid to get the better deal. They rely on family and childhood friends to provide some centripetal moral force and invoke "the economy" and "the times" to explain why people are willing to do what they do. They express awe in the face of old, undiscovered, and abandoned riches, and nostalgia for a simpler capitalism. And beneath the veneer of small-town, small-business, conservative ethics, you can find the preening personalities, petty feuds, platitudes, and falsities that have characterized the bulk of reality television.

Some of the suspicious scenes are obvious and expected. Struggling 20 actors are cast into the parts of longtime assistants to the experts; the first "reveal" of a locked-up, foreclosed house begins with a camera already inside; a piece of dialogue is filled with zingers that could only have been written beforehand; transactions that could have taken place online are dramatized on location; shop owners implement harebrained schemes to squeeze a couple extra bucks.

But a lawsuit issued last fall by Dave Hester, possibly the most despised character on *Storage Wars*, after he was fired, charged that producers "salted" storage lockers with rare, expensive, and antique items before they went on the block. Allegedly, some of the items already belonged to the winner before

---

*truTV's motto is "Not Reality. Actuality," and its reality programming is consistently a couple of steps beyond credibility; some of its shows, including another repo show, *Operation Repo*, are filmed like reality shows but feature completely reconstructed scenes. The trajectory of truTV, which used to be Court TV (spell "court" backward, drop the "oc," and you get something like the truth), mirrors a number of other cable channels. The History Channel has dropped its standard historical content in favor of reality fare and picked up a slogan to reflect the change: "History: Made Every Day." TLC, which used to stand for "The Learning Channel," now stands for "TLC," and A&E (previously "Arts & Entertainment") is now just "A&E," presenting "Real Life. Drama."

the sale, and at other times goods were supplied by a large Los Angeles antiques store. The auctions themselves, Hester claims, were often staged, with producers giving extra money to contestants they wanted to win a particular locker. Parts of the far-reaching suit (as of this writing) have been dismissed by the Los Angeles Superior Court, and A&E denies his allegations. But given the unbelievable rate at which bidders find unbelievable items on the show, it's hard to believe that Hester is just making it up. Some committed, online amateur sleuths (like the person behind www.storagewarsisfake.com) have made a cause of finding inconsistencies in this show and other reality-cash programs that back up his claims.

One of the biggest revelations in the lawsuit was an incidental one: at the time the suit was issued, Hester was earning $25,000 per episode, plus numerous bonuses. The real cash was never in buying abandoned storage units, but in making the auctions an exciting venue of social conflict for TV. On online message boards, people claiming to have attended these auctions in the past write that they have given up: huge crowds now show up and lose lots of money in the elusive pursuit of the baseball card collections, rare coins, celebrity memorabilia, and bizarre antiques that frequently pop up on *Storage Wars* and its competitor shows. Others have reported their disappointment upon visiting the Harrisons' pawn shop in Las Vegas, where the main business now appears to be selling *Pawn Stars* tchotchkes.

This isn't to deny that the market in buying foreclosed properties, and in pawning and selling secondhand goods, has boomed in the post-recession years. As Richard Harrison told the *Las Vegas Sun*, "[Y]ou have to understand that 17 to 20 percent of people in the United States don't have an active checking account or any bank affiliation, and this is a place where they can get a loan." The same arguments are made by the booming payday loan industry and others in the quick-cash credit business. They can get away with charging usurious rates—what scholars have called "the cost of being poor"—because they satisfy a need that other institutions, from banks to employers to government programs, aren't meeting.

Are these shows also satisfying a need? Busted-economy reality TV wouldn't exist if it weren't cheap to make, and it may be popular for any number of the scary-seeming reasons that reality TV in general is popular. But it also seems like a coming out for a number of predatory business practices that seem refreshingly frank in the wake of a financial crisis that people are told is too complicated for them to understand. For an audience primed on the language of individual bootstrapping and grave threats to the free market, these shows may seem practically heartwarming.

Rick Harrison made his politics explicit in recent months. In an interview on the *Mark Levin Show*, a program hosted by one of the most popular right-wing radiomen this side of Rush Limbaugh, Harrison assailed the state for not granting him a permit to film a *Pawn Stars* segment on government land (they blamed, falsely, he believed, the sequester for the permit denial) and attacked Obamacare for hurting employers. After beginning to make an interesting if ill-informed point about how small banks were treated poorly by the Obama administration while the big banks were bailed out, Harrison revealed a simpler, more sinister endgame: "We have the government that's down on business, down on business, people with money. I know someone else who did that. His name was Lenin. I mean he blamed the banks, aka the Jews, he blamed the intelligentsia. Let's reeducate everybody."

This sort of statement is a commonplace in right-wing U.S. politics, and, along with Rick Santelli's infamous screed against "loser" homeowners who couldn't keep up with their mortgages, constitutes the worldview of the Tea Party Right: the beleaguered middle against the underclass and its elite allies. But coming from the *Pawn Stars* star, the statement brought to mind an exchange from the film *Repo Man*, Alex Cox's 1984 punk classic. Bud, played by Harry Dean Stanton, tells his repo trainee Otto (Emilio Estevez), "Credit is a sacred trust, it's what our free society is founded on. Do you think they give a damn about their bills in Russia?"

> OTTO: They don't pay bills in Russia, it's all free.
> BUD: All free? Free my ass. What are you, a fuckin' commie? Huh?
> OTTO: No, I ain't no commie.
> BUD: Well, you better not be. I don't want no commies in my car. No Christians either.

These shows and the seedy corner of the economy they depict aren't just about winners and losers, but strivers and failures, the bold and the broken. In this universe, there are simply some people on the right side of the asymmetrical information divide, and others born to be conned. And there is no mutual aid without interest.

READING THE TEXT

1. What reasons does Serpe provide to support his claim that the growth of reality TV was largely *not* audience driven?

2. Summarize in your own words the history of reality TV, as Serpe presents it.

3. What is the appeal of *Pawn Stars* and *Storage Wars*, according to Serpe?

4. What connection does Serpe see between "busted-economy reality TV" (para. 24) and right-wing politics in America, especially the Tea Party variety?

5. How do producers of shows like *Storage Wars* manipulate events to make the program more entertaining and less realistic, according to Serpe?

READING THE SIGNS

1. In class, discuss the tone of Serpe's article. To what extent does that tone enhance or reduce its effectiveness?

2. Watch one of the programs that Serpe discusses, and conduct your own analysis of it. Does the show use any of the "common tropes" (para. 19) that Serpe mentions? Is it a "funhouse version of the culture of debt and credit" (para. 9)?

3. Write an essay in which you support, refute, or complicate Serpe's link between right-wing politics and the popularity of "debt-and-credit" reality TV shows.

4. In the 1950s, the show *Queen for a Day* also focused on people in economic distress. Research *Queen for a Day*, and write an analysis comparing it to a program like *Repo Games*. In what way are the shows similar? How do you account for any differences?

5. **CONNECTING TEXTS** Read Jon Mooallem's "The Self-Storage Self" (p. 102), and compare the real-life lives of self-storage users with the lives of those depicted on reality TV programs like *Storage Wars*. Use your comparison as the basis for an essay in which you argue for the appropriateness of the word "reality" in RTV.

SOUTHERN WOMAN

CLAIRE MIYE STANFORD

You've Got the Wrong Song: Nashville *and Country Music Feminism*

Ever since Tammy Wynette counseled women to "Stand By Your Man" no matter what abuse he dishes out, country music has hardly been noteworthy for its feminist spirit. Such a background makes the country music–themed series *Nashville* all the more remarkable, Claire Miye Stanford argues in her review of the program, which she regards as "one of the most feminist television shows on television." In fact, for Stanford, *Nashville* resists simple political categorization and instead mixes femininity and feminism in the Dolly Parton tradition. Claire Miye Stanford is a freelance writer who has written for *The Millions, The Rumpus, Good,* and the *Los Angeles Review of Books,* in which this reading first appeared.

Both femininity and feminism have become harder and harder to define in 2013. In regard to the first, there are as many examples of femininity in the world as there are people (not just biological women) who embody them. As for the second, the term "feminism" is now so loaded with meaning, confusion, and incorrect associations that it has become all too common, especially among young women, to disavow the term entirely.

Into this complex terminology, enter Rayna James (Connie Britton) and Juliette Barnes (Hayden Panettiere), the lead characters of ABC's *Nashville*, created by former Nashville resident Callie Khouri. Khouri is a film veteran who wrote 1991's *Thelma & Louise,* a feminist classic that also won her the Academy Award for best original screenplay (typically a heavily male-dominated category). In its first season, the show has explored what it means to be both feminine and feminist in the world of country music and television.

Ultimately, any female-driven television show has to contend with these two concepts—whether that treatment is overt or more indirect, if only because every female-driven show will ultimately contend with the characters' love lives and how they interact with men (since their romantic interests are, almost always, male). But what stands out about *Nashville*, among all female-driven television shows, is that it places these omnipresent questions in unique contexts: professional, rather than personal, in the frame of a highly gendered genre, industry, city, and region.

But can a show that is so ostensibly interested in the "feminine"—in sexual and romantic relationships, in motherhood and daughterhood, in short skirts and spangly tops and big hair—also be feminist? That same question has been asked time and time again about country music itself, long considered a bastion of heteronormative, gendered songs about pick-up trucks. Historically, most feminist ire lands squarely on the shoulders of country music legend Tammy Wynette, and her biggest hit, 1968's "Stand By Your Man," in which Wynette advises the listener to forgive your man and, for that matter, to be "proud" of him, even when he's off having "good times / doing things that you don't understand." Whether these things that "you don't understand" are cheating, boozing, gambling, or other unsavory activities is not entirely clear, but still, Wynette counsels the listener to stand by him "'cause after all he's just a man"; in other words, he can't help it, it's in his Man Nature to mistreat you.

There are countless other songs, less famous than Wynette's, with the 5 same degrading message, but critics keep circling back to "Stand By Your Man" as a kind of shorthand for anti-feminist doctrine in country music, and, to a greater extent, life in general. In 1992, Hillary Clinton referred to the song when responding to allegations of then-presidential-hopeful Bill's extramarital affairs. "I'm not sitting here some little woman standing by my man like Tammy Wynette," she said in a *60 Minutes* interview. (In a whole other layer of feminist rhetoric, Clinton was pressured into apologizing to Wynette only days later by legions of country music fans who said it was an unfair comparison.)

Still, plenty of female country musicians have serious feminist chops, using their lyrics to take on political feminist issues from birth control and abortion to equal pay and spousal abuse. Loretta Lynn's 1975 song, "The Pill," is the first major song to mention oral contraceptives; more recently, Neko Case's 2002 song, "Pretty Girls," examines the judgment that comes with abortion. Other songs—about disappointment in marriage and motherhood, about not being slut-shamed for wearing a short skirt, about hitting your cheating husband upside the head with a cast-iron skillet—are not as overtly political, but still deal with realities of female experience head-on, without conforming to gender norms or social conventions.

Of all female country musicians, Dolly Parton presents the most interesting example of the tension that exists between femininity and feminism.

Her 1980 classic hit, "9 to 5," is set to a catchy beat but makes a political point about being an ambitious woman in a discriminatory workplace. Lesser known, her 1968 song "Just Because I'm a Woman" took on sexual hypocrisy and double standards way before "slut-shaming" was even an established phrase. But these days, Parton is often discounted as an artist — and as a feminist — made into a punch line about breast implants and plastic surgery; even when she is held up as a feminist icon, the argument often comes with a tone of questioning surprise and an acknowledgment that her big hair, big breasts, and tiny waist make her a less-than-obvious feminist heroine.

In their music on the show, both Rayna and Juliette fall firmly in the Dolly Parton camp of female country music star; while their songs are not overtly political or feminist — no abortion or birth control talk here — they are very much about women standing on their own, standing up for themselves, and being respected. Juliette's hits include "Telescope," which warns a cheating lover that she knows full well what he's up to; "Boys and Buses," advising that chasing after boys is a waste of time; and "Undermine," a heartfelt ballad about how it's harder — but more worthwhile — to achieve something on your own than to undermine someone else. Rayna's songs, tinged with more experience, are more downcast, but they, too, advocate for standing one's ground: "Buried Under" tells the story of a woman grappling with finding out her lover's long-buried secrets; in "No One Will Ever Love You," the singer insists that her love is the best love the listener will ever find, and he should accept it.

Of all *Nashville*'s songs, the song that Juliette and Rayna fictionally "co-wrote" does the most to situate them within the world of women in country music. Titled "Wrong Song," the song is a fiery duet, addressed to a lying, cheating man, and in classic Rayna/Juliette fashion, it stands up for the woman, saying that she won't stand for that. But "Wrong Song" goes a step further than the usual woman-power advocacy, adding a meta-layer of commentary on country music (and music in general), turning the song into a defiant take on expectations for country music and female narratives in general. The song begins with a series of conditional ifs, setting up the typical country-song scenario — man drinks too much, does foolish thing, woman misses him and forgives him:

> If you think you're gonna hear
> how much I miss you
> If you're needing to feel better 'bout yourself
> If you're waiting to hear me
> say I forgive you
> 'Cause tequila turned you into someone else

The song then slows down, ever so slightly, as it winds up to the chorus, meanwhile deploying the Tammy Wynette shorthand for the disempowered woman, the country music stereotype who stands by her man no matter what he does:

> If you're looking for one more chance
> A little stand by your man

And then there comes the booming chorus, both women's voices coming together for the coup de grace, calling out all those songs before it for so easily forgiving wayward men, and also calling out the listener himself for expecting that they would forgive him, just because they are country music singers, just because they are ladies. If you think you're getting the stereotypical female narrative of passivity and forgiveness (à la "Stand By Your Man"), they tell the listener, then you've got the wrong song and the wrong girl:

> You've got the wrong song
> Coming through your speakers
> This one's about a liar and a cheater
> Who didn't know what he had
> 'till it was gone
> You've got the wrong girl
> Cause I've got your number
> I don't know what kind of spell
> you think I'm under
> This ain't a feel-good,
> 'Everything's fine' sing-along
> You've got the wrong song

This song, this performance, is the epitome of *Nashville* womanhood: active, empowered, and take-charge. But this song is more than just a statement on behalf of the characters. In one catchy chorus, it takes on the music industry and its demands on female artists, and then goes a step further by putting that examination on television, a similar crucible of issues concerning money, sexuality, female image, and power.

As characters, Rayna and Juliette are strong women, still rare on televi- 10 sion, but not impossible to find. As a show, though, *Nashville* — in its unapologetically pure focus on female characters, its self-aware examination of the struggles of female artists, and its critique of male-dominated industries — is one of the most feminist television shows on television.

Still, neither Rayna nor Juliette is a feminist, or, at least, we've never heard them say that they are. *Nashville* has never dropped the F-bomb, surely afraid of alienating part of its audience. As the show goes on, however, and as both Rayna and Juliette give more and more fictional interviews to television talk shows and magazines, the absence of the word "feminist" becomes a more glaring omission; after all, media love to ask women to define themselves in terms of feminism, especially strong, powerful women.

But that kind of definitive stance — feminist or not feminist — doesn't interest *Nashville*. The show is focused on individual characters rather than overarching labels, in showing how strong, powerful women live their strong, powerful lives. There are men on *Nashville*, too, but they are pretty much ineffectual; any success they have comes, directly or indirectly, as a result of their partnerships with the show's various women. Indeed, every woman on the show — not just Rayna and Juliette — is portrayed as a strong woman; they may have their faults, but all of them, from up-and-comer Scarlett O'Connor to Rayna's sister Tandy to more minor characters like the managers and political wives, have ambition, drive, and agency, as well as a self-possessed dignity that leaves no question about who is in control.

There is only one notable exception to this otherwise consistently empowered cast of female characters: the needy, conniving, and man-reliant Peggy Kenter, who has an affair with Rayna's husband and leaks Rayna's subsequent divorce to the tabloids. In both her demeanor and her actions, Peggy appears like a caricature of a helpless female, as if a reminder of all the ghosts of stereotypical soapy female characters past. Peggy is also notably the only character whose situation is presented without a trace of compassion; the show, it would seem, has no sympathy for a woman like Peggy — a woman who belongs in a different kind of world, on a different kind of show.

In fact, even though *Nashville* is billed as a primetime soap, it is much better described as a workplace drama, where the workplace is the country music mainstage. Along with reproductive rights, women's advancement and equal treatment in the workplace is one of the last — and most persistent — issues for feminism, a fact that makes *Nashville*'s portrait of this very particular workplace all the more interesting from a feminist point of view.

As in a workplace drama, we see the way the women express themselves 15 in front of others, but we also see what happens when the stage curtain is pulled back, and how that empowerment translates to both their personal lives and their behind-the-scenes business decisions. And it's in this offstage life that the show truly uses Rayna and Juliette to explore questions of feminism, especially when it looks at the challenges a woman faces when she insists on being in control of her own life.

These challenges are different for Rayna and Juliette, who are at distinct stages in both their career and personal life. For Rayna, married with two daughters, they manifest as a question of how to balance her career ambitions with being a good ("good") mother, daughter, and wife (and eventually ex-wife). Rayna never feels guilty about any of the decisions she makes related to her career; she misses her daughters when she is on the road, but she does not feel guilty or ashamed that she has left them with their (very loving) father. On the flipside, when her father has a heart attack, she flies back to Nashville immediately and says she might have to cancel that night's concert, but those decisions are made without agony, without any drama over where to put family and where to put career. This departure from female guilt over the intersection of professional and domestic priorities is refreshing.

Rayna also faces the challenge of how to stay relevant as a female artist and performer in her forties, an age our society deems over the hill. Again, the show defies the stereotypical storyline — one that might end in a middle-age crisis, substance abuse, or plastic surgery — and gives the character of

Rayna the dignity of a real person, taking on a real professional challenge. Rayna has to work even harder to stay relevant; there is no such thing as resting on laurels, especially for a female celebrity over the age of thirty. And, as always, Rayna rises to the challenge, writing more songs, evolving her sound, taking more risks, going on tour. When faced with a challenge, Rayna does not break down; she steels herself and takes it on, and she succeeds — not by chance or wiles, but by hard work and force of will.

For Juliette — young, hot, and unattached — the challenges are different. More than anything, Juliette wants to be taken seriously: by her record label, by her employees, by her colleagues, by reviewers, by her fans. Her youth is a major part of her problem: her male-dominated world (her boss at the label, her manager, her roadies, her band, the predominately male reviewers) do not want to take her seriously. But, even more problematic for a young woman like Juliette is her attitude. She knows what she wants, and she does what she wants without thinking of the consequences.

Juliette's behavior is not always perfect, but her slips in judgment are exacerbated by her gender and her age, and these mistakes drive the show's examination of social and professional double standards. Were Juliette a man, she would be described as "driven" and "demanding" when she fires her manager or changes her set list at the last minute; instead, since she is a woman, she is seen as irrational. Were she a man, she would be called a "bad boy" for her brushes with the law and her late nights clubbing; since she is a woman, this behavior threatens to ruin her career and her image. When Juliette's ex-boyfriend blackmails her over a sex tape he secretly filmed, the show takes on one of the most gendered celebrity scandals: a sex tape for a male celebrity means almost nothing, but becomes part of a woman's permanent record.

Even when exploring the rivalry between Rayna and Juliette — one of *Nash-* 20 *ville*'s central plotlines — the show treats the women with sophistication and dignity, making it clear from the start that it's a professional rivalry. It would be ideal if all women — or, for that matter, all people — could support each other even in competition, but in the world in which Rayna and Juliette operate, that isn't an option. This kind of competition is particularly endemic to women and particularly brutal, but professional competition transcends gender. Record labels only have so much promotional money to put behind artists; magazines only have so many pages to dedicate to female country music stars. In the plotline that will wrap up this season, Rayna and Juliette are both nominated for Female Country Music Artist of the Year. This turn of events is a brilliant move by the show in that it brings their competition to the forefront.

The show's recognition of this contest — and also the way the rivalry unfolds — again defies the typical portrayal of female envy. The very fact that competition is the major plot point of the show recognizes that women can compete in the first place — that women don't always "play nice," that a woman can want to be number one. Beyond that initial recognition, the rivalry itself is handled with sophistication and dignity. Other than a few snippy comments in the first few episodes when the show was finding its footing, both women are refreshingly direct (the gendered thing to say here would be that they aren't catty) about their relationship. Other than a few offhand statements, neither of them really talks about the other behind her back; when one of them is frustrated or angry at the other, she says so to her rival's face.

Most refreshingly, the competition stays entirely in the professional sphere. When Juliette is confronted with a giant billboard of Rayna's face as a celebrity endorsement, she does not react by commenting on Rayna's appearance or her age; she is pissed, but she is pissed because she wants an endorsement deal and a billboard of her own. When Rayna is forced to fly on Juliette's plane, she is also unhappy, but mostly about the fact that she doesn't have her own jet. Even when Juliette beds Rayna's long-ago love, the story focuses more on both women wanting him as a bandleader and song-writer—in a professional capacity—than a sexual or romantic rivalry.

In fact, in a brilliantly self-aware move, this season's closing plotline about Rayna and Juliette's award rivalry perfectly appropriates real-world media commentary about the show itself. When the show debuted in the fall, *Nashville*'s creator Khouri and stars Connie Britton and Hayden Panettiere both had to spend a lot of time (an inordinate amount of time) telling interviewers that the show was not about a "catfight" between the two women. In a recent episode, as Britton's Rayna and Panettiere's Juliette walked a red carpet together, reporters ask them how it feels to compete and Rayna, echoing Britton's real-life remarks, tells them, "If you're expecting a catfight, you're not going to get it."

Not only does this statement provide a new meta-commentary on female-driven narratives, but also continues the themes established in "Wrong Song" of defying traditional expectations for women, both for the way women act and the way women are represented—and represent themselves. In other words, if viewers come to *Nashville* looking for the same old soapy female tropes—catfights, bitchiness, seduction, backstabbing—then they've got the wrong show.

READING THE TEXT

1. According to Stanford, how do the fictional *Nashville* characters Rayna James and Juliette Barnes compare with real-life country music stars Tammy Wynette and Dolly Parton?

2. Why does Stanford claim that the word "'feminism' is now so loaded with meaning, confusion, and incorrect associations that it has become all too common, especially among young women, to disavow the term entirely" (para. 1)?

3. Summarize in your own words the conventional motifs of mainstream country music. In what ways does *Nashville* depart from the genre's conventions?

4. What does Stanford mean by saying that "Wrong Song" adds "a meta-layer of commentary on country music (and music in general)" (para. 9)?

READING THE SIGNS

1. In class, list on the board the connotations class members attach to the word "feminism." What do you think the sources of these connotations may be? Do you detect any differences between male and female students; if so, how do you account for them?

2. In an essay, argue for your own response to Stanford's question about *Nashville*: "Can a show that is so ostensibly interested in the 'feminine' . . . also be feminist?" (para. 4). As an alternative, focus your argument on a different program that features women characters, such as *Orange Is the New Black*.

3. Using Stanford's critique of femininity and feminism as a critical framework, analyze some songs popularized by current real-life country music artists such as Carrie Underwood or Taylor Swift. As an alternative, conduct a survey of country music lyrics by both male and female performers, and write an essay analyzing the gender politics implicit in these lyrics.

4. Write a semiotic analysis of a music superstar such as Lady Gaga who is overtly political in her public persona and actions. In what ways might your object of analysis reflect "the themes established in 'Wrong Song' of defying traditional expectations for women, both for the way women act and the way women are represented — and represent themselves" (para. 24)?

5. **CONNECTING TEXTS**   Adopting Stanford's perspective, analyze the gender dynamics you see in a different show that focuses on Southern female characters, *Here Comes Honey Boo Boo*. To what extent does this show replicate or defy "the same old soapy female tropes" (para. 24)? To develop your ideas, read Michelle Dean's "Here Comes the Hillbilly, Again" (below).

SOUTHERN WOMAN

MICHELLE DEAN

Here Comes the Hillbilly, Again

From *The Beverly Hillbillies* to *Hee Haw* to *Duck Dynasty*, Americans have liked television hillbillies. But when *Here Comes Honey Boo Boo* became a surprise TV hit in 2012, things got sticky, causing enough of a "fuss" that Michelle Dean figured she'd better have a look at the show. And in this review for *Slate*, Dean reveals that, to her surprise, she found herself relating to Honey and her family, while at the same time seeing that, like *Jersey Shore* and *Teen Mom*, *Here Comes Honey*

macmillanhighered.com/signsoflife
How does a vintage TV show mine the hillbilly stereotype for comedy?
e-readings > *The Beverly Hillbillies,* "Getting Settled" [TV episode]

Boo Boo is very much a TV show for our times. This is an era when the increasing gap between the haves and the have-nots has the haves laughing at the have-nots, and the have-nots clinging precariously to the notion that the American dream isn't over for them yet, even when the reality is otherwise. Michelle Dean is an editor-at-large for *Flavorwire* and a writer whose work appears in *Slate*, the *New Yorker*, the *Nation*, and *Hazlitt*.

Somehow America always goes a little off the rails in the allegedly slow month of August, and this year's party is as wild as any. Republicans can't figure out how babies are made; cutting-and-pasting an article from the *New Yorker* into your *Time* column is no longer a fireable offense; and all the way down in McIntyre, Ga., there is a mother who feeds her child a Mountain Dew-and-Red Bull concoction before the 6-year-old gets onstage at beauty pageants. June Shannon, who stars with her daughter Alana "Honey Boo Boo Child" Thompson in TLC's controversial hit *Here Comes Honey Boo Boo*, would have provoked a firestorm even if what she calls "go-go juice" were the only sin she was broadcasting all over Christendom. All that caffeine, pop-culture commentators everywhere clucked, and all that sugar.

Lost in the outrage is just how squarely "go-go juice" fits into America's long tradition of "white trash" entertainment, which for decades has elevated characters like Honey Boo Boo into the nation's objects of fun. The Pepsi Co. borrowed the Mountain Dew brand-name from slang for moonshine; in the 1960s, it was explicitly advertised as a "hillbilly" drink. The campaign's entertaining TV ads, which you can watch on YouTube, were scored by twangy banjos and errant buckshot and plotted around a "stone-hearted gal" who will open her heart to you if you only take a swig. Watching these old videos after an episode or two of *Honey Boo Boo* makes at least one thing clear: The hillbilly has regained the spotlight in American culture.

As Anthony Harkins observes in *Hillbilly: A Cultural History of an American Icon*, one of the hillbilly's signature moves is to peak, popularity-wise, just when Americans sense that things in general are headed south. Its first true zenith came in the depressed 1930s, a handmaiden to the birth of commercial country music. Another arrived in the turbulent 1960s, when *The Beverly Hillbillies* and *Green Acres* and *Hee Haw* were in their prime. (Those are hardly the only examples, of course: It also popped up in the Ma and Pa Kettle films of the 1940s and 1950s and Paul Webb's 1930s *Esquire* cartoons about "The Mountain Boys," among other places.)

Though the term first referred to mountaineers in the Appalachians and the Ozarks, the hillbilly trope spread to cover pretty much all non-urban territory in America, joined by its cousins in cultural iconography, the "redneck" and "white trash." Today, people even apply that last term to residents of certain New Jersey beachfronts, for instance. Yet, as Harkins points out, no matter where an alleged country bumpkin comes from, he will be derided for his crass behavior. And such ridicule has always been politically coded:

The hillbilly figure allows middle-class white people to offload the venality and sin of the nation onto some other constituency, people who live somewhere — anywhere — else. The hillbilly's backwardness highlights the progress more upstanding Americans in the cities or the suburbs have made. These fools haven't crawled out of the muck, the story goes, because they don't want to.

This idea that the hillbilly's poverty is a choice allows more upscale Americans to feel comfortable while laughing at the antics before them. It also pushes some people to embrace the stereotype as a badge of honor. "Guitars, Cadillacs, hillbilly music / It's the only thing that keeps me hangin' on," Dwight Yoakam once sang. For more contemporary examples of reappropriation, you can attend any number of Tea Party rallies. The classist term "redneck," originally coined to indicate those who worked so hard and so long in the sun that they sported sunburns in the designated anatomical location, likewise has been adopted in the name of all that's good and holy. What's more American than a hard day's work?

June Shannon is a reappropriator *par excellence*. One of her signature phrases on *Here Comes Honey Boo Boo* is a call to, as she puts it, "Redneck-ognize." And yet all the cultural chatter that's attended Honey Boo Boo has been less than affectionate. The word of the day across the media is "apocalypse" — that is, the show is a sign of it. It's not just the caffeine highs, either. It's a family of six chopping up a roadkill deer for dinner, bellyflopping in the mud, and — those with delicate constitutions may want to avert their eyes for this next part — farting *in public*. Even critics who enjoy the show do so from a crouched, defensive posture. People seem to think this has all gone a little too far. Even the *Today Show* is starting to wonder if reality television just might be "exploitative."

I'm not a *Toddlers & Tiaras* fan, so I missed out on Alana's big splash on that show earlier this year. Beauty pageants in general are foreign and noxious to me: I can barely muster the energy to put on lip gloss and mascara. But I watched *Honey Boo Boo* out of curiosity about the fuss, and found myself, somewhat surprisingly, relating to Alana and her milieu. I have fond memories of that Dwight Yoakam song playing softly on my parents' radio as we drove home through the dark from a visit to my grandparents' house in rural Quebec. My family isn't from the South — we're not even from the United States — but I know enough of the land Honey Boo Boo lives in to be dubious of simple accusations of bad parenting and worse morals.

The practices are different, of course, and no, I'm not wild about the caffeine and sugar thing, either. Alana's little-girl grandiosity must become exhausting when experienced in more than 30-minute increments. But the people raising her are clearly aware of your disdain. Shannon can be delightfully funny when she self-consciously plays with her hillbilly image, warning the audience that she's about to "scratch her bugs," or speaking of her beauty routine: "Granted, I ain't the most beautimous out the box, but a little paint on this barn, shine it back to its original condition. 'Cause it shines up like it's brand new."

5

That's not to say the humor is always comfortable or even funny. Alana's trademark phrases and mannerisms — "a dollar makes me holler," a particular head swivel she does — are informed by racist stereotypes of black women. This ambiguous borrowing from black culture has always been part of the hillbilly trope as well. Early commercial country music borrowed liberally from black folk music. (Hank Williams learned to play guitar, he said, from a black street performer.) And this borrowing often turned into racist mimicry: The Grand Ole Opry included minstrelsy shows in the 1920s and 1930s. Interestingly, the term "white trash" may have been coined by black slaves in the early 19th century to describe poor white people in the South; American attitudes toward poor white people have long been tangled up with "the race problem."

And hillbilly stereotypes have always made it easier for middle-class whites 10 to presume that racism is the exclusive province of "that kind" of person. As Ta-Nehisi Coates has written, "It is comforting to think of racism as a species of misanthropy, or akin to child molestation, thus exonerating all those who bear no real hatred in their heart. It's much more troubling to think of it as it's always been — a means of political organization and power distribution."

As that distribution of power becomes more and more unequal, it's no surprise to see the hillbilly here again — on *Here Comes Honey Boo Boo*, on *Jersey Shore*, on MTV's *16 & Pregnant* and *Teen Mom* franchises. These shows reassure us that our struggle is worth it, all economic evidence to the contrary — if only because *we would never* belly-flop into the mud on cable television. *Here Comes Honey Boo Boo* casts this socio-economic divide in especially sharp relief, since the show is rooted partly in beauty pageant culture, which, in its own idiosyncratic way, indulges the American belief that you can work and spend your way to greatness. If you can afford the entry fees, the glitter, the makeup, the coach, and the stylists, you will be the Ultimate Supreme, as they say in the business. You'll have the sash to prove it.

But tiny, 6-year-old Alana is too crass and happy to get it. She is a terrible pageant queen. Her wigs are always askew, her daisy-dukes ill-fitting, and sometimes she grinds her fake teeth. Those rhinestone-studded bootstraps simply can't pull her up the way she needs them to.

READING THE TEXT

1. What are the typical characteristics of "hillbilly" culture, as you glean them from Dean's description?

2. Dean uses the terms "hillbilly," "white trash," and "redneck," offering some explanations of how they differ. In a chart, tease out the different connotations of these terms, especially as they may be interpreted by people of differing ethnic or socioeconomic groups.

3. According to Dean, how has hillbilly culture appropriated black culture?

4. What does Dean mean by saying that media representations of hillbilly culture are "politically coded" (para. 4)?

5. How do TV programs like *Honey Boo Boo* exploit the impoverished and offer them unrealistic hope for the future, in Dean's view?

READING THE SIGNS

1. Watch an episode of *Honey Boo Boo*, and write an essay in which you agree, disagree, or modify Dean's claim that the program exploits hillbilly, redneck, or white trash stereotypes. As an alternative, do the same analysis on an older TV show that Dean mentions, such as *The Beverly Hillbillies* or *Hee Haw*.

2. **CONNECTING TEXTS**   Compare Dean's analysis of the social significance of a show like *Honey Boo Boo* with Nick Serpe's reading of shows like *Repo Games* (p. 268). To what extent do the shows use similar class stereotypes? To develop your analysis, consult Michael Parenti's "Class and Virtue" (p. 361).

3. Dean suggests similarities between *Honey Boo Boo*, a show located in the deep American South, and *Jersey Shore*, a program situated in a mid-Atlantic state. Write an essay in which you evaluate her connection between these programs. Do both use signs of "white-trashiness"? If so, how do they do that? If you see divergences, explain them.

4. Dean suggests that viewing a 1960s Mountain Dew commercial can be enlightening. Watch such an older commercial and then a current ad for Mountain Dew. Analyze them, and in an essay explain how the ads have used, modified, or changed the image of the "hillbilly."

CARL MATHESON
The Simpsons, *Hyper-Irony, and the Meaning of Life*

Don't have a cow or anything, but most comedy, as Carl Matheson points out in this analysis of *The Simpsons*, which first appeared in *The Simpsons and Philosophy* (2001), is based in cruelty. And while Matheson doesn't "mean to argue that the makers of *The Simpsons* intended the show primarily as a theater of cruelty," he does "imagine that they did." At any rate, Matheson suggests, the pervasive irony that makes the program funny should serve as a warning to anyone who believes that this ever-popular cartoon sitcom is a warm endorser of family values. Carl Matheson is a professor in, and chair of, the department of philosophy at the University of Manitoba. He has published essays in the *British Journal of Aesthetics*, the *Journal of Aesthetics and Art Criticism*, and *Philosophy and Literature*.

DISAFFECTED YOUTH #1: Here comes that cannonball guy. He's cool.
DISAFFECTED YOUTH #2: Are you being sarcastic, dude?
DISAFFECTED YOUTH #1: I don't even know anymore.

— "Homerpalooza," Season 7

What separates the comedies that were shown on television fifty, forty, or even twenty-five years ago from those of today? First, we may notice technological differences, the difference between black-and-white and color, the difference between film stock (or even kinescope) and video. Then there are the numerous social differences. For instance, the myth of the universal traditional two-parent family is not as secure as it was in the 1950s and 1960s, and the comedies of the different eras reflect changes in its status — although even early comedies of the widow/widower happy fifties, sixties, and seventies were full of nontraditional families, such as are found in *The Partridge Family*, *The Ghost and Mrs. Muir*, *Julia*, *The Jerry van Dyke Show*, *Family Affair*, *The Courtship of Eddie's Father*, *The Andy Griffith Show*, *The Brady Bunch*, *Bachelor Father*, and *My Little Margie*. Also, one may note the ways in which issues such as race have received different treatments over the decades.

But I would like to concentrate on a deeper transformation: today's comedies, at least most of them, are funny in different ways from those of decades past. In both texture and substance the comedy of *The Simpsons* and *Seinfeld* is worlds apart from the comedy of *Leave It to Beaver* and *The Jack Benny Show*, and is even vastly different from much more recent comedies, such as *MASH* and *Maude*. First, today's comedies tend to be highly *quotational*: many of today's comedies essentially depend on the device of referring to or quoting other works of popular culture. Second, they are *hyper-ironic*: the flavor of humor offered by today's comedies is colder, based less on a shared sense of humanity than on a sense of world-weary cleverer-than-thouness. In this essay I would like to explore the way in which *The Simpsons* uses both quotationalism and hyper-ironism and relate these devices to currents in the contemporary history of ideas.

Quotationalism

Television comedy has never completely foregone the pleasure of using pop culture as a straight man. However, early instances of quotation tended to be opportunistic; they did not comprise the substance of the genre. Hence, in sketch comedy, one would find occasional references to popular culture in *Wayne and Shuster* and *Johnny Carson*, but these references were really treated as just one more source of material. The roots of quotationalism as a main source of material can be found in the early seventies with the two visionary comedies, *Mary Hartman Mary Hartman*, which lampooned soap operas by being an ongoing soap opera, and *Fernwood 2Night*, which, as a small-budget talk show, took on small-budget talk shows. Quotationalism then came much more to the attention of the general public between the mid-seventies and early eighties through *Saturday Night Live*, *Late Night with David Letterman*, and *SCTV*. Given the mimical abilities of its cast and its need for weekly material, the chief comedic device of *SNL* was parody — of genres (the nightly news, television debates), of particular television shows (*I Love Lucy*, *Star Trek*) and of movies (*Star Wars*). The type of quotationalism employed by Letterman was more abstract and less based on particular shows. Influenced by the much earlier absurdism of such hosts as Dave Garroway, Letterman immediately took the formulas of television and cinema beyond their logical conclusions (*The Equalizer Guy*, chimp cam, and spokesperson Larry "Bud" Melman).

However, it was *SCTV* that gathered together the various strains of quotationalism and synthesized them into a deeper, more complex, and more mysterious whole. Like *Mary Hartman*, and unlike *SNL*, it was an ongoing series with recurring characters such as Johnny Larue, Lola Heatherton, and Bobby Bittman. However, unlike *Mary Hartman*, the ongoing series was about the workings of a television station. *SCTV* was a television show about the process of television. Through the years, the models upon which characters like Heatherton and Bittman were based vanished somewhat into the background, as Heatherton and Bittman started to breathe on their own, and therefore, came to occupy a shadowy space between real (fictional) characters and simulacra. Furthermore, *SCTV*'s world came to intersect the real world as some of the archetypes portrayed (such as Jerry Lewis) were people in real life. Thus, *SCTV* eventually produced and depended upon patterns of inter-textuality and cross-referencing that were much more thoroughgoing and subtle than those of any program that preceded it.

The Simpsons was born, therefore, just as the use of quotationalism was 5 maturing. However, *The Simpsons* was not the same sort of show as *SNL* and *SCTV*. One major difference, of course, was that *The Simpsons* was animated while the others were (largely) not, but this difference does not greatly affect the relevant potential for quotationalism — although it may be easier to draw the bridge of the U.S.S. *Enterprise* than to rebuild it and re-enlist the entire original cast of *Star Trek*. The main difference is that as an ostensibly ongoing family comedy, *The Simpsons* was both plot and character driven, where the other shows, even those that contained ongoing characters, were largely sketch driven. Furthermore, unlike *Mary Hartman Mary Hartman*, which existed to parody soap operas, *The Simpsons* did not have the raison d'être of parodying the family-based comedies of which it was an instance. The problem then was this: How does one transform an essentially non-quotational format into an essentially quotational show?

The answer to the above question lies in the form of quotationalism employed by *The Simpsons*. By way of contrast, let me outline what it was definitively not. Take, for instance, a *Wayne and Shuster* parody of Wilde's *The Picture of Dorian Gray*. In the parody, instead of Gray's sins being reflected in an artwork, while he remains pure and young in appearance, the effects of Gray's overeating are reflected in the artwork, while he remains thin. The situation's permissions and combinations are squeezed and coaxed to produce the relevant gags and ensuing yuks. End of story. Here the quotationalism is very direct; it is the source both of the story line and of the supposedly humorous contrast between the skit and the original novel. Now, compare this linear and one-dimensional use of quotation for the purposes of parody with the pattern of quotation used in a very short passage from an episode from *The Simpsons* entitled "A Streetcar Named Marge." In the episode, Marge is playing Blanche Dubois opposite Ned Flanders's Stanley in *Streetcar!*, her community theatre's musical version of the Tennessee Williams play. In need of day care for little Maggie, she sends Maggie to the Ayn Rand School for Tots, which is run by the director's sister. Headmistress Sinclair, a strict disciplinarian and believer in infant self-reliance, confiscates all of the tots' pacifiers, which causes an enraged Maggie to lead her classmates in a highly organized reclamation mission, during which the theme from *The Great Escape* plays in the background. Having re-acquired the pacifiers, the group sits, arrayed in rows, making little sucking sounds, so that when Homer arrives to pick up Maggie, he is confronted with a scene from Hitchcock's *The Birds*.

The first thing that one can say about these quotations is that they are very funny. . . . To see that these quotations are funny just watch the show again. Second, we note that these quotations are not used for the purpose of parody.[1] Rather, they are allusions, designed to provide unspoken metaphorical elaboration and commentary about what is going on in the scene. The allusion to Ayn Rand underscores the ideology and personal rigidity of Headmistress Sinclair. The theme music from *The Great Escape* stresses the determination of Maggie and her cohort. The allusion to *The Birds* communicates the threat of the hive-mind posed by many small beings working as one. By going outside of the text via these nearly instantaneous references, *The Simpsons* manages to convey a great deal of extra information extremely economically. Third, the most impressive feature of this pattern of allusion is its pace and density, where this feature has grown more common as the series has matured. Early episodes, for instance the one in which Bart saws the head off the town's statue of Jebediah Springfield, are surprisingly free of quotation. Later episodes derive much of their manic comic energy from their rapid-fire sequence of allusions. This density of allusion is perhaps what sets *The Simpsons* most apart from any show that has preceded it.

However, the extent to which *The Simpsons* depends on other elements of pop culture is not without cost. Just as those readers who are unfamiliar with Frazer's *Golden Bough* will be hindered in their attempt to understand Eliot's "The Waste Land," and just as many modern-day readers will be baffled by many of the Biblical and classical allusions that play important roles in the history of literature, many of today's viewers won't fully understand much of what goes on in *The Simpsons* due to an unfamiliarity with the popular culture that forms the basis for the show's references. Having missed the references, these people may interpret *The Simpsons* as nothing more than a slightly off-base family comedy populated with characters who are neither very bright

---

[1] I don't mean to say that *The Simpsons* does not make use of parody. The episode currently under discussion contains a brilliant parody of Broadway adaptations, from its title to the show-stopping tune "A Stranger Is Just a Friend You Haven't Met!"

nor very interesting. From these propositions they will probably derive the theorem that the show is neither substantial nor funny, and also the lemma that the people who like the show are deficient in taste, intelligence, or standards of personal mental hygiene. However, not only do the detractors of the show miss a great deal of its humor, they also fail to realize that its pattern of quotations is an absolutely essential vehicle for developing character and for setting a tone. And, since these people are usually not huge fans of popular culture to begin with, they will be reluctant to admit that they are missing something significant. Oh well. It is difficult to explain color to a blind man, especially if he won't listen. On the other hand, those who enjoy connecting the quotational dots will enjoy their task all the more for its exclusivity. There is no joke like an in-joke: The fact that many people don't get *The Simpsons* might very well make the show both funnier and better to those who do.

Hyper-Ironism and the Moral Agenda

Without the smart-ass, comedy itself would be impossible. Whether one subscribes, as I do, to the thesis that all comedy is fundamentally cruel, or merely to the relatively spineless position that only the vast majority of comedy is fundamentally cruel, one has to admit that comedy has always relied upon the joys to be derived from making fun of others. However, usually the cruelty has been employed for a positive social purpose. In the sanctimonious *MASH*, Hawkeye and the gang were simply joking to "dull the pain of a world gone mad," and the butts of their jokes, such as Major Frank Burns, symbolized threats to the liberal values that the show perpetually attempted to reinforce in the souls of its late-twentieth-century viewers. In *Leave It to Beaver*, the link between humor and the instillation of family values is didactically obvious. A very few shows, most notably *Seinfeld*, totally eschewed a moral agenda.[2] *Seinfeld*'s ability to maintain a devoted audience in spite of a cast of shallow and petty characters engaged in equally petty and shallow acts is miraculous. So, as I approach *The Simpsons*, I would like to resolve the following questions. Does *The Simpsons* use its humor to promote a moral agenda? Does it use its humor to promote the claim that there is no justifiable moral agenda? Or, does it stay out of the moral agenda game altogether?

These are tricky questions, because data can be found to affirm each 10 of them. To support the claim that *The Simpsons* promotes a moral agenda, one usually need look no further than Lisa and Marge. Just consider Lisa's speeches in favor of integrity, freedom from censorship, or any variety of touchy-feely social causes, and you will come away with the opinion that *The Simpsons* is just another liberal show underneath a somewhat thin but

[2]For a different view, see Robert A. Epperson, "Seinfeld and the Moral Life," in William Irwin, ed., *Seinfeld and Philosophy: A Book about Everything and Nothing* (Chicago: Open Court, 2000), pp. 163–74.

tasty crust of nastiness. One can even expect Bart to show humanity when it counts, as when, at military school, he defies sexist peer pressure to cheer Lisa on in her attempt to complete an obstacle course. The show also seems to engage in self-righteous condemnation of various institutional soft targets. The political system of Springfield is corrupt, its police chief lazy and self-serving, and its Reverend Lovejoy ineffectual at best. Property developers stage a fake religious miracle in order to promote the opening of a mall. Mr. Burns tries to increase business at the power plant by blocking out the sun. Taken together, these examples seem to advocate a moral position of caring at the level of the individual, one which favors the family over any institution.

However, one can find examples from the show that seem to be denied accommodation within any plausible moral stance. In one episode, Frank Grimes (who hates being called "Grimey") is a constantly unappreciated model worker, while Homer is a much beloved careless slacker. Eventually, Grimes breaks down and decides to act just like Homer Simpson. While "acting like Homer" Grimes touches a transformer and is killed instantly. During the funeral oration by Reverend Lovejoy (for "Gri-yuh-mee, as he liked to be called") a snoozing Homer shouts out "Change the channel, Marge!" The rest of the service breaks into spontaneous and appreciative laughter, with Lenny saying "That's our Homer!" End of episode. In another episode, Homer is unintentionally responsible for the death of Maude Flanders, Ned's wife. In the crowd at a football game, Homer is eager to catch a T-shirt being shot from little launchers on the field. Just as one is shot his way, he bends over to pick up a peanut. The T-shirt sails over him and hits the devout Maude, knocking her out of the stands to her death. These episodes are difficult to locate on a moral map; they certainly do not conform to the standard trajectory of virtue rewarded.

Given that we have various data, some of which lead us toward and others away from the claim that *The Simpsons* is committed to caring, liberal family values, what should we conclude? Before attempting to reach a conclusion, I would like to go beyond details from various episodes of the show to introduce another form of possibly relevant evidence. Perhaps, we can better resolve the issue of *The Simpsons*' moral commitments by examining the way it relates to current intellectual trends. The reader should be warned that, although I think that my comments on the current state of the history of ideas are more or less accurate, they are greatly oversimplified. In particular, the positions that I will outline are by no means unanimously accepted.

Let's start with painting. The influential critic Clement Greenberg held that the goal of all painting was to work with flatness as the nature of its medium, and he reconstructed the history of painting so that it was seen to culminate in the dissolution of pictorial three-dimensional space and the acceptance of total flatness by the painters of the mid-twentieth century. Painters were taken to be like scientific researchers whose work furthered the progress of their medium, where the idea of artistic progress was to be taken as literally as that of scientific progress. Because they were fundamentally unjustifiable and because they put painters into a straitjacket, Greenberg's positions gradually lost their hold, and no other well-supported candidates for the essence of painting could be found to take their place. As a result painting (and the other arts) entered a phase that the philosopher of art Arthur Danto has called "the end of art." By this Danto did not mean that art could no longer be produced, but rather that art could no longer be subsumed under a history of progress toward some given end.[3] By the end of the 1970s, many painters had turned to earlier, more representational styles, and their paintings were as much commentaries on movements from the past, like expressionism, and about the current vacuum in the history of art, as they were about their subject matter. Instead of being about the essence of painting, much of painting came to be about the history of painting. Similar events unfolded in the other artistic media as architects, filmmakers, and writers returned to the history of their disciplines.

However, painting was not the only area in which long-held convictions concerning the nature and inevitability of progress were aggressively challenged. Science, the very icon of progressiveness, was under attack from a number of quarters. Kuhn held (depending on which interpreter of him you agree with) either that there was no such thing as scientific progress, or that if there was, there were no rules for determining what progress and scientific rationality were. Feyerabend argued that people who held substantially different theories couldn't even understand what each other was saying, and hence that there was no hope of a rational consensus; instead he extolled the anarchistic virtues of "anything goes." Early sociological workers in the field of science studies tried to show that, instead of being an inspirational narrative of the disinterested pursuit of truth, the history of science was essentially a story of office-politics writ large, because every transition in the history of science could be explained by appeal to the personal interests and allegiances of the participants.[4] And, of course, the idea of philosophical progress has continued to be challenged. Writing on Derrida, the American philosopher Richard Rorty argues that anything like *the* philosophical truth is either unattainable, non-existent, or uninteresting, that philosophy itself is a literary genre, and that philosophers should reconstrue themselves as writers who elaborate and re-interpret the writings of other philosophers. In other words, Rorty's version of Derrida recommends that philosophers view themselves as historically aware participants in a conversation, as opposed to quasi-scientific researchers.[5] Derrida himself favored a method known as deconstruction, which was popular several years ago, and which consisted of a

---

[3]See Arthur Danto, *After the End of Art* (Princeton: Princeton University Press, 1996).

[4]Thomas Kuhn, *The Structure of Scientific Revolutions*, second edition (Chicago: University of Chicago Press, 1970). Paul Feyerabend, *Against Method* (London: NLB, 1975). For a lively debate on the limits of the sociology of knowledge, see James Robert Brown (ed.), *Scientific Rationality: The Sociological Turn* (Dordrecht: Reidel, 1984).

[5]Richard Rorty, "Philosophy as a Kind of Writing," pp. 90–109 in *Consequences of Pragmatism* (Minneapolis: University of Minnesota Press, 1982).

highly technical method for undercutting texts by revealing hidden contradictions and unconscious ulterior motives. Rorty questions whether, given Derrida's take on the possibility of philosophical progress, deconstruction could be used only for negative purposes, that is, whether it could be used for anything more than making philosophical fun of other writings.

Let me repeat that these claims about the nature of art, science, and philosophy are highly controversial. However, all that I need for my purposes is the relatively uncontroversial claim that views such as these are now in circulation to an unprecedented extent. We are surrounded by a pervasive crisis of authority, be it artistic, scientific or philosophical, religious or moral, in a way that previous generations weren't. Now, as we slowly come back to earth and *The Simpsons*, we should ask this: If the crisis I described were as pervasive as I believe it to be, how might it be reflected generally in popular culture, and specifically in comedy?

We have already discussed one phenomenon that may be viewed as a consequence of the crisis of authority. When faced with the death of the idea of progress in their field, thinkers and artists have often turned to a reconsideration of the history of their discipline. Hence artists turn to art history, architects to the history of design, and so on. The motivation for this turn is natural; once one has given up on the idea that the past is merely the inferior pathway to a better today and a still better tomorrow, one may try to approach the past on its own terms as an equal partner. Additionally, if the topic of progress is off the list of things to talk about, an awareness of history may be one of the few things left to fill the disciplinary conversational void. Hence, one may think that quotationalism is a natural offshoot of the crisis of authority, and that the prevalence of quotationalism in *The Simpsons* results from that crisis.

The idea that quotationalism in *The Simpsons* is the result of "something in the air" is confirmed by the stunning everpresence of historical appropriation throughout popular culture. Cars like the new Volkswagen Beetle and the PT Cruiser quote bygone days, and factories simply can't make enough of them. In architecture, New Urbanist housing developments try to re-create the feel of small towns of decades ago, and they have proven so popular that only the very wealthy can buy homes in them. The musical world is a hodgepodge of quotations of styles, where often the original music being quoted is simply sampled and re-processed.

To be fair, not every instance of historical quotationalism should be seen as the result of some widespread crisis of authority. For instance, the New Urbanist movement in architecture was a direct response to a perceived erosion of community caused by the deadening combination of economically segregated suburbs and faceless shopping malls; the movement used history in order to make the world a better place for people to live with other people. Hence, the degree of quotationalism in *The Simpsons* could point toward a crisis in authority, but it could also stem from a strategy for making the world better, like the New Urbanism, or it could merely be a fashion accessory, like retro-khaki at the Gap.

No, if we want to plumb the depths of *The Simpsons'* connection with the crisis in authority we will have to look to something else, and it is at this point that I return to the original question of this section: Does *The Simpsons* use its humor to promote a moral agenda? My answer is this: *The Simpsons* does not promote anything, because its humor works by putting forward positions only in order to undercut them. Furthermore, this process of undercutting runs so deeply that we cannot regard the show as merely cynical; it manages to undercut its cynicism too. This constant process of undercutting is what I mean by "hyper-ironism."

To see what I mean, consider "Scenes from the Class Struggle in Spring- 20 field," an episode from the show's seventh season. In this episode Marge buys a Coco Chanel suit for $90 at the Outlet Mall. While wearing the suit, she runs into an old high-school classmate. Seeing the designer suit and taking Marge to be one of her kind, the classmate invites Marge to the posh Springfield Glen Country Club. Awed by the gentility at the Club, and in spite of sniping from club members that she always wears the same suit, Marge becomes bent on social climbing. Initially alienated, Homer and Lisa fall in love with the club for its golf course and stables. However, just as they are about to be inducted into the club, Marge realizes that her newfound obsession with social standing has taken precedence over her family. Thinking that the club also probably doesn't want them anyway, she and the family walk away. However, unbeknownst to the Simpsons, the club has prepared a lavish welcome party for them, and is terribly put out that they haven't arrived — Mr. Burns even "pickled the figs for the cake" himself.

At first glance, this episode may seem like another case of the show's reaffirmation of family values: after all, Marge chooses family over status. Furthermore, what could be more hollow than status among a bunch of shallow inhuman snobs? However, the people in the club turn out to be inclusive and fairly affectionate, from golfer Tom Kite who gives Homer advice on his swing despite the fact that Homer has stolen his golf clubs — and shoes — to Mr. Burns, who thanks Homer for exposing his dishonesty at golf. The jaded cynicism that seems to pervade the club is gradually shown to be a mere conversational trope; the club is prepared to welcome the working-class Simpsons with open arms — or has it realized yet that they are working class? Further complicating matters are Marge's reasons for walking away. First, there is the false dilemma between caring for her family and being welcomed by the club. Why should one choice exclude the other? Second is her belief that the Simpsons just don't belong to such a club. This belief seems to be based on a classism that the club itself doesn't have. This episode leaves no stable ground upon which the viewer can rest. It feints at the sanctity of family values and swerves closely to class determinism, but it doesn't stay anywhere. Furthermore, upon reflection, none of the "solutions" that it momentarily holds is satisfactory. In its own way, this episode is as cruel and cold-blooded as the Grimey episode. However, where the Grimey episode wears its heartlessness upon its sleeve, this episode conjures up illusions of satisfactory heart-warming resolution only to undercut them immediately. In my view, it stands as a paradigm of the real *Simpsons*.

I think that, given a crisis of authority, hyper-ironism is the most suitable form of comedy. Recall that many painters and architects turned to a consideration of the history of painting and architecture once they gave up on the idea of a fundamental trans-historical goal for their media. Recall also that once Rorty's version of Derrida became convinced of the non-existence of transcendent philosophical truth, he reconstructed philosophy as an historically aware conversation which largely consisted of the deconstruction of past works. One way of looking at all of these transitions is that, with the abandonment of *knowledge* came the cult of *knowingness*. That is, even if there is no ultimate truth (or method for arriving at it) I can still show that I understand the intellectual rules by which you operate better than you do. I can show my superiority over you by demonstrating my awareness of what makes you tick. In the end, none of our positions is ultimately superior, but I can at least show myself to be in a superior position for now on the shifting sands of the game we are currently playing. Hyper-irony is the comedic instantiation of the cult of knowingness. Given the crisis of authority, there are no higher purposes to which comedy can be put, such as moral instruction, theological revelation, or showing how the world is. However, comedy can be used to attack anybody at all who thinks that he or she has any sort of handle on the answer to any major question, not to replace the object of the attack with a better way of looking at things, but merely for the pleasure of the attack, or perhaps for the sense of momentary superiority mentioned earlier. *The Simpsons* revels in the attack. It treats nearly everything as a target, every stereotypical character, every foible, and every institution. It plays games of one-upmanship with its audience members by challenging them to identify the avalanche of allusions it throws down to them. And, as "Scenes from the Class Struggle in Springfield" illustrates, it refrains from taking a position of its own.

However, to be fair to those who believe *The Simpsons* takes a stable moral stance, there are episodes that seem not to undercut themselves at all. Consider, for instance, the previously mentioned episode in which Bart helps Lisa at military school. In that episode, many things are ridiculed, but the fundamental goodness of the relationship between Bart and Lisa is left unquestioned. In another episode, when Lisa discovers that Jebediah Springfield, the legendary town founder, was a sham, she refrains from announcing her finding to the town when she notices the social value of the myth of Jebediah Springfield. And, of course, we must mention the episode in which jazzman Bleeding Gums Murphy dies, which truly deserves the Simpsonian epithet "worst episode ever." This episode combines an uncritical sentimentality with a naïve adoration of art-making, and tops everything off with some unintentionally horrible pseudo-jazz which would serve better as the theme music for a cable-access talk show. Lisa's song "Jazzman" simultaneously embodies all three of these faults, and must count as the worst moment of the worst episode ever. Given these episodes and others like them, which occur too frequently to be dismissed as blips, we are still left with the conflicting data with which we started. . . . Is *The Simpsons* hyper-ironic or not? One could argue that the hyper-ironism is a trendy fashion accessory, irony from the Gap, which does not reflect the ethos of the show. Another critically well-received program, *Buffy the Vampire Slayer* is as strongly committed to a black and white distinction between right and wrong as only teenagers can be. Its dependence on wisecracks and subversive irony is only skin deep. Underneath the surface, one will find angst-ridden teens fighting a solemn battle against evil demons who want to destroy the world. Perhaps, one could argue, beneath the surface irony of *The Simpsons* one will find a strong commitment to family values.

I would like to argue that Simpsonian hyper-ironism is not a mask for an underlying moral commitment. Here are three reasons, the first two of which are plausible but probably insufficient. First, *The Simpsons* does not consist of a single episode, but of over two hundred episodes spread out over more than ten seasons. There is good reason to think that apparent resolutions in one episode are usually undercut by others.[6] In other words, we are cued to respond ironically to one episode, given the cues provided by many other episodes. However, one could argue that this inter-episodic undercutting is itself undercut by the show's frequent use of happy family endings.

Second, as a self-consciously hip show, *The Simpsons* can be taken to be aware of and to embrace what is current. Family values are hardly trendy, so there is little reason to believe that *The Simpsons* would adopt them wholeheartedly. However, this is weak confirmation at best. As a trendy show, *The Simpsons* could merely flirt with hyper-irony without fully adopting it. After all, it is hardly hyper-ironic to pledge allegiance to any flag, including the flag of hyper-ironism. Also, in addition to being a self-consciously hip show, it is also a show that must live within the constraints of prime-time American network television. One could argue that these constraints would force *The Simpsons* toward a commitment to some sort of palatable moral stance. Therefore, we cannot infer that the show is hyper-ironic from the lone premise that it is self-consciously hip.

The third and strongest reason for a pervasive hyper-ironism and against the claim that *The Simpsons* takes a stand in favor of family values is based on the perception that the comedic energy of the show dips significantly whenever moral closure or didacticism rise above the surface (as in the Bleeding Gums Murphy episodes). Unlike *Buffy the Vampire Slayer*, *The Simpsons* is fundamentally a comedy. *Buffy* can get away with dropping its ironic stance, because it is an adventure focused on the timeless battle between good and evil. *The Simpsons* has nowhere else to go when it stops being funny. Thus, it's very funny when it celebrates physical cruelty in any given *Itchy and Scratchy Show*. It's very funny when it ridicules Krusty and the marketing geniuses who

---

[6]Thanks to my colleague and co-contributor, Jason Holt, for first suggesting this to me.

broadcast *Itchy and Scratchy*. It's banal, flat, and not funny when it tries to deal seriously with the issue of censorship arising from *Itchy and Scratchy*. The lifeblood of *The Simpsons*, and its astonishing achievement, is the pace of cruelty and ridicule that it has managed to sustain for over a decade. The prevalence of quotationalism helps to sustain this pace, because the show can look beyond itself for a constant stream of targets. When the target-shooting slows down for a wholesome message or a heart-warming family moment, the program slows to an embarrassing crawl with nary a quiver from the laugh-meter.

I don't mean to argue that the makers of *The Simpsons* intended the show primarily as a theater of cruelty, although I imagine that they did. Rather, I want to argue that, as a comedy, its goal is to be funny, and we should read it in a way that maximizes its capability to be funny. When we interpret it as a wacky but earnest endorsement of family values, we read it in a way that hamstrings its comedic potential. When we read it as a show built upon the twin pillars of misanthropic humor and oh-so-clever intellectual one-upmanship, we maximize its comedic potential by paying attention to the features of the show that make us laugh. We also provide a vital function for the degree of quotationalism in the show, and as a bonus, we tie the show into a dominant trend of thought in the twentieth century.

But, if the heart-warming family moments don't contribute to the show's comedic potential, why are they there at all? One possible explanation is that they are simply mistakes; they were meant to be funny but they aren't. This hypothesis is implausible. Another is that the show is not exclusively a comedy, but rather a family comedy — something wholesome and not very funny that the whole family can pretend to enjoy. This is equally implausible. Alternatively, we can try to look for a function for the heart-warming moments. I think there is such a function. For the sake of argument, suppose that the engine driving *The Simpsons* is fueled by cruelty and one-upmanship. Its viewers, although appreciative of its humor, might not want to come back week after week to such a bleak message, especially if the message is centered on a family with children. *Seinfeld* never really offered any hope; its heart was as cold as ice. However, *Seinfeld* was about disaffected adults. A similarly bleak show containing children would resemble the parody of a sitcom in Oliver Stone's *Natural Born Killers*, in which Rodney Dangerfield plays an alcoholic child-abuser. Over the years, such a series would lose a grip on its viewers, to say the least. I think that the thirty seconds or so of apparent redemption in each episode of *The Simpsons* is there mainly to allow us to soldier on for twenty-one and a half minutes of maniacal cruelty at the beginning of the next episode. In other words, the heart-warming family moments help *The Simpsons* to live on as a series. The comedy does not exist for the sake of a message; the occasional illusion of a positive message exists to enable us to tolerate more comedy. Philosophers and critics have often talked of the paradox of horror and the paradox of tragedy. Why do we eagerly seek out art forms that arouse unpleasant emotions in us like pity, sadness, and fear? I think that, for at least certain forms of comedy, there is an equally important paradox of comedy. Why do we seek out art that makes us laugh at the plight of unfortunate people in a world without redemption? The laughter here seems to come at a high price. *The Simpsons'* use of heart-warming family endings should be seen as its attempt to paper over the paradox of comedy that it exemplifies so well.

I hope to have shown that quotationalism and hyper-ironism are prevalent, inter-dependent, and jointly responsible for the way in which the humor in *The Simpsons* works. The picture I have painted of *The Simpsons* is a bleak one, because I have characterized its humor as negative, a humor of cruelty and condescension — but really funny cruelty and condescension. I have left out a very important part of the picture, however. *The Simpsons*, consisting of a not-as-bright version of the Freudian id for a father, a sociopathic son, a prissy daughter, and a fairly dull but innocuous mother, is a family whose members love each other. And, we love them. Despite the fact that the show strips away any semblance of value, despite the fact that week after week it offers us little comfort, it still manages to convey the raw power of the irrational (or nonrational) love of human beings for other human beings, and it makes us play along by loving these flickering bits of paint on celluloid who live in a flickering hollow world. Now *that's* comedy entertainment.

READING THE TEXT

1. Write an outline of Matheson's essay, being sure to note how Matheson establishes differences and similarities in relation to other pop culture phenomena. Compare your outline with those produced by the rest of the class.

2. Explain in your own words what Matheson means by "quotationalism" and "hyper-ironism" (para. 2). How do those words relate to the current term "sampling"?

3. What does Matheson mean by "historical appropriation" (para. 17)?

4. Matheson outlines recent intellectual trends in the study of art, science, and philosophy. What are those trends, and what relationship does Matheson find between them and a TV program such as *The Simpsons*?

5. What connection does Matheson see between the "crisis of authority" (para. 15) and hyper-irony?

READING THE SIGNS

1. Write an argumentative essay that supports, challenges, or complicates Matheson's position that "heart-warming family moments" appear in *The Simpsons* "mainly to allow us to soldier on for twenty-one and a half minutes of maniacal cruelty" (para. 28).

2. In class, brainstorm other TV shows and films that are hyper-ironic, and use the list as the basis for your own essay in which you argue whether their popularity is a barometer of the current cultural mood in America or whether it is an aberration.

3. Watch an episode of *The Simpsons*, and analyze the extent to which it supports Matheson's belief that, rather than promoting a moral stance, the show "does not promote anything" (para. 19).

4. Visit a Web site devoted to *The Simpsons*, such as www.thesimpsons.com, and study the comments fans make about the program. To what extent do your observations support Matheson's belief that "those who enjoy connecting the quotational dots will enjoy their task all the more for its exclusivity" (para. 8)?

5. Compare and contrast the humor in *The Simpsons* with that of another TV show such as *Family Guy*. Do the shows appeal to different audiences, and if so, why?

NATASHA SIMONS
Mad Men *and the Paradox of the Past*

> *Mad Men*, a dramatic re-creation of early 1960s America, when the country was poised upon the brink of a cultural revolution but had not quite tipped over yet, is a deeply ambiguous television series. Does it represent an exposé of the bad old days of rampant sexual harassment in the workplace and casual racism, when everyone smoked too much and men called all the shots? Or does the show's appeal lie in nostalgia for a bygone era on the other side of a vast cultural divide? As Natasha Simons observes in this article that originally appeared in the *National Review*, it depends upon who is viewing it. Thus, as Simons notes, "Conservatives and liberals just can't help but see *Mad Men* differently: the former with apprehension, the latter with anticipation." Even the show's creator, Matthew Weiner, seems divided, Simons claims. Basically a liberal, Weiner likes his main character, Don Draper, too much to make it clear just which side he's on. Such is the stuff of which pop culture paradoxes are made. Natasha Simons is an assistant editor at Simon and Schuster.

Mad Men is a show about an unbending generation on the cusp of dissolution; Matthew Weiner, the show's head writer, has often said that the majority of America in the early '60s was still, by and large, living in the domestic '50s. Weiner, a baby boomer, has a conflicted relationship with this time period. Because it is the generation of his parents, he wants to explore it and pore over it; because it's the generation that, through Weiner's specific political prism, reflects a hypocritical façade, he'd like it to form a gangway for the liberation to come. This ambivalence creates a divide in the audience's responses to the show, which tend to fall along political lines.

Conservatives and liberals just can't help but see *Mad Men* differently: the former with apprehension, the latter with anticipation. The show inspires a certain self-satisfaction in the type of viewers who would observe each instance of sexism, racism, and general prejudice as just more foundation for an interpretation many critics have arrived at: "The show explains why the '60s had to happen." Rod Dreher says, "For unreflective liberals, *Mad Men* is only temporarily tragic. It has a happy ending. Deliverance from all this sexism and repression and cigarette smoke draws nigh."

The show, and in particular, the third season, is shot through with references to that impending deliverance. Don Draper says, "New York City is decaying." Paul Kinsey says, "This city has no memory." The World's Fair in New York, given passing lip service on the show, turned out to be a bust, the old-money business class's last hurrah at corralling an innocent kind of fun already beset by the counterculture. Its slogan? "Man in a Shrinking Globe in an Expanding Universe." That's not only a pointed assessment of modern fear, but a wonderful précis of the theme of *Mad Men*. And it's difficult to ignore the ambitious allusions to the prototypical decayed society of ancient Rome, which made a few cameos in the past season. Don's daughter, Sally, reads to her grandfather the beginning of a passage from *The History of the Decline and Fall of the Roman Empire*: "The Praetorian bands, whose licentious fury was the first symptom and cause of the decline of the Roman empire . . ."

The Praetorian guards, of course, were a specially chosen group of soldiers who abused their imperial power over Rome. *Mad Men* depicts a group of men who have great influence over what they consider their particular citizenry—consumers—and their particular emperor—consumerism. By cataloging this group's "licentious" excesses (imbibing during the workday, hiring prostitutes on the company dime, etc.), general indifference to the burgeoning youth counterculture (think: Bertram Cooper's horror at Kennedy's lack of hat), and miring themselves in the past (Roger Sterling's unfortunate minstrel show in "My Old Kentucky Home"), Weiner, consciously or unconsciously, is demonstrating the ways in which America's Old Guard is leading the '50s generation to its end by stubbornly refusing to go forward. Weiner has remarked of that generation of people, "[They were saying,] 'We don't want to be that way. We'd rather fail.'"

Clearly, Don Draper is the starring figure of this collapse. He is the Man in the Grey Flannel Suit, an Ayn Rand–ian allegory of a stoic firmly in the past. He is the prototype '50s representative male, confident in his role without, and in turmoil within. Don is a member of a dying breed who wants to play by the old business rules, and he can barely conceive of the ways in which advertising is inexorably moving (unlike, say, fellow ad man Pete Campbell). He is a relic waiting to be phased out.

But Weiner's flaw is that he loves Don Draper too much to make him that relic, as intended—he is clearly not going to leave Don in the past, if season-four promotional posters are any indication. So the show attempts to imbue him with the sympathy of the audience, despite his stodgy '50s limits —which leads to all sorts of annoying contradictions. Don looks down on Roger for the blackface, yet behaves dismissively toward his own black servant; Don assaults his mistress in a bathroom and demands women not speak to him "like that," despite facilitating his former secretary Peggy's surge upward through the ranks; Don lectures his wife about being a good parent even as he picks up strangers in his car and recklessly partakes of some unidentified drugs. These frustrating contradictions can't simply be chalked up to mere nuance of human character, either; it seems clear that Weiner started out by using Don as an emblem of the '50s, defining him in opposition to the '60s to come.

Which brings us again to the main political schism for viewers of this show: Conservatives and liberals cannot see the inevitability of the '60s the same way. The hedonism, the "licentious fury" set up in these soldiers of such terrible, soul-destroying consumerism, is about to give way to the tortured emoting of Frank O'Hara and reggae-inspired coffee commercials, both of which have been featured in the past few seasons. But conservatives understand that the hedonism is only just beginning. The Me Generation is about to swing into full effect, after which we lose both the unrepentant ambition and

A promotional still from *Mad Men*.

Photofest

charming earnestness of the American Dream — a phrase never to be uttered without a small smirk again.

True, the keeping-up-with-the-Joneses mentality was unsustainable, simply because of the practical problem of the single income that families were expected to fulfill the traditional iteration of the American Dream on. And, often, the unwavering values of the '50s resulted in an outwardly homogenous appearance that left many marginalized parties gasping for air. But the '60s, with their relentless concentration on the self and self-expression, shaped individualistic tendencies in consumers that brought them out of the follow-the-leader consumption of the '50s into a gluttonous consumption merely for selfish purposes. So which is better? And is that really the redemption the show hopes to establish, and what liberal viewers gaze backward and clutch the edges of their seats in anticipation of?

Weiner's chosen narrative posits that our present is much better than the '50s zeitgeist he portrays, but the essential paradox is that he portrays it with so much love and tenderness that it is sometimes impossible to pull out the theme of generational decay. The audience is caught between a mislaid nostalgia for the often sexist and bigoted environment and an equally mislaid moral desire to see it all disappear. As Benjamin Schwarz pointed out in the *Atlantic*, the show invites us to "indulge in a most unlovely — because wholly unearned — smugness."

Mad Men has lost its way a bit; Weiner, wrapped up in adoring his main   10
character and the intricacies of a period he wants to evaporate, has fallen into a quicksand trap, not wanting to move on, despite his obvious political loyalties to the '60s generation. Critics remarked that the pace of *Mad Men* has recently slowed to a ponderous crawl, perhaps to allow Weiner time to languish a while. But he is definitely plunging forward now, having commented in an interview that "It's got to be something different. . . . Life is change." Here's hoping that the fourth season marks that change with the same ambivalence we've seen prior, which would prove Weiner is interested in portraying history with a fair hand. Falling into a rote '60s nostalgia would be wholly unwelcome for a show that has come to be known for its nuance.

READING THE TEXT

1. What significance for *Mad Men* does Simons see in scriptwriter Matthew Weiner's status as a baby boomer?

2. Summarize in your own words the ways in which conservatives and liberals interpret *Mad Men*, according to Simons.

3. What does Simons mean when she says that *Mad Men* character Don Draper "is the Man in the Grey Flannel Suit" (para. 5)?

4. In class, discuss whether Simons is presenting an objective analysis of *Mad Men*, as you would want to do in an academic essay, or whether she betrays a bias favoring or opposing the program. Use this discussion of objectivity as a guide when you write your own essay on the program.

READING THE SIGNS

1. Simons claims that conservatives and liberals interpret *Mad Men* in diametrically opposed ways. Interview at least ten viewers of the program, preferably half who identify as conservative and half who identify as liberal, asking them about their reading of and reaction to it. Use your results to assess the validity of Simons's claim.

2. Write an essay in which you support, refute, or modify Simons's claim that *Mad Men*'s "audience is caught between a mislaid nostalgia for the often sexist and bigoted environment and an equally mislaid moral desire to see it all disappear" (para. 9).

3. Read Sloan Wilson's novel *The Man in the Gray Flannel Suit* (1955). To what extent does *Mad Men* reflect the discontented business culture depicted in that novel, as Simons asserts? Alternatively, read Vance Packard's *The Hidden Persuaders* (1957). Do you find that book to reflect the advertising industry's practices as they are depicted in *Mad Men*?

4. Write a semiotic analysis of a current episode of *Mad Men* that features a diverse cast, focusing on the depiction of nonwhite characters. To what extent do you find those depictions to be realistic or stereotypical? To develop your analysis, consult Michael Omi's "In Living Color: Race and American Culture" (p. 538).

5. Many critics of *Mad Men* focus on the show's depiction of female characters. Drawing on Aaron Devor's "Gender Role Behaviors and Attitudes" (p. 504), write an essay in which you analyze the prevailing mythology of gender roles as the program presents them.

JANE HU

Reality Hunger: On Lena Dunham's Girls

In its own way, *Girls* is a lot like *Friends*, but without the fun, for both programs feature white middle-class young adults coming of age in an era of reduced economic expectations. Still, in Jane Hu's review of *Girls* for the *Los Angeles Review of Books*, it is hard to sort out just how much the series speaks for an entire generation of millennials and how much it speaks for its creator, Lena Dunham, and her more particular milieu. Leaving the matter open for further analysis, Hu points out that for all the talk about sex on *Girls*, there's also an awful lot on food and eating, making for a very different, and ambiguous, kind of hunger games. Jane Hu is a freelance writer who writes for *Slate* and other online publications.

Most reviews of Lena Dunham's new HBO show *Girls* so far have focused on its "realism," which immediately begs questions. If Dunham's show is meant to be realistic, then we're obliged to judge whether it's either refreshingly on target or entirely missing the mark. Do we, the viewers, feel represented and reflected by the conversations and scenarios that *Girls* presents? Or do we feel alienated from them? Do we identify? Or do we feel something in between?

In the promotional trailer for the series, Dunham's character Hannah Horvath sits before her parents and proclaims: "I think I may be the voice of my generation," only to retreat instantly behind the modification: "or at least *a* voice . . . of *a* generation." This line, tagged as the catchphrase of *Girls* in the lead up to its pilot, was received almost as a dare. Someone, finally, was going to take on the challenge of speaking the real and raw truth for recession-era youth! For all its overwhelming narcissism, though, the line also anticipates the mix of recklessness and reluctance that the show cultivates. *Girls* wants to have it both ways: it wants to be both brash and unsure of itself, universal and specific, speaking (when it wants to) for a generation but reserving the right not to specify which one.

Based on the internet chatter, there seems to be a voracious desire to find oneself in *Girls*, implying an urgency to locate a voice for this generation, a generation that understands itself to be diverse. As *The Hairpin*'s Jenna Wortham says about these *Girls*: "They are us but they are not us. They are me but they are not me." The show's representations of race, class, and gender have generated an expansive range of reactions, not least because of the show's monolithic middle-class whiteness. It seems like the one thing anyone can agree on is that, unlike Hannah Horvath, *they* don't eat cupcakes in the bathtub.

But if we're looking for what's truly universal in Dunham's depiction of young, white, upper-middle-class life in New York City, then maybe the cupcake isn't such a bad place to start. Eating is, after all, about as universal as it gets. The overwhelming excitement about and immediate backlash to Dunham's show both seem to suggest a profound hunger on the part of its audience for something nourishing, sustaining, and nutritious, prepared especially for them. This is fitting, because hunger, in all its manifestations, drives *Girls*. As with all lost generations, there seems to be a profound sense of lack among Hannah's friends. Hannah showcases her appetite for attention, sex, and food, none of which prove exclusive to one another.

The first shot of the pilot shows Hannah in an upscale restaurant seated   5
in front of multiple plates of food, inhaling alternating mouthfuls from each plate. Her mother tells her to slow down: "You're eating like they're going to take it away from you." To which Hannah responds (childishly, mid-bite): "I'm a growing girl." For her, eating and talking are inseparable from the process of growing up. Hannah is, in turn, interrupted mid-bite, for her parents have chosen dinner as the opportunity to announce that they will no longer be supporting her unpaid internship in New York, or as her mother describes it, "bankrolling your groovy lifestyle." Shocked and outraged in all of her un-self-aware entitlement, Hannah announces to her parents that she cannot

see them tomorrow evening since she has a "dinner thing" and then will be "too busy becoming who I am." This scene of furious public ingestion looks forward to a future of relaxed, private digestion: Hannah needs to eat, and then she needs to figure her shit out. Throughout the *Girls* pilot, there is a sense that the world as we know it will slip away if we do not get to — and through — it fast enough. What these *Girls* are running toward, and who they are busy becoming, they have yet to discover. But resources are scarce, and no one is getting younger.

Consuming and facing the reality that there might not be enough left to consume are seemingly incompatible in Hannah's world. When she's let go from her internship after her request for a paying position is denied, Hannah's boss (played by Chris Eigeman, familiar as a privileged slacker from Whit Stillman and Noah Baumbach movies) assures her: "When you get hungry enough, you'll figure it out." To which she responds: "Do you mean like physically hungry or like hungry for the job?" The line is played for comic effect, but it also expresses Hannah's confusion about exactly what she might get hungry for. An appetite, and an appetitive drive, is what Hannah and her fellow *Girls* need in order to "become who they are." If you lack hunger, then you just might be lost. But, then again, you might still be anyway.

No matter: talking and eating will keep us distracted from the object of our hunger. Later on, Hannah tells her roommates in a typically melodramatic moment: "I can last in New York for three and a half more days — maybe seven if I don't eat lunch." The running joke behind these statements is that Hannah's livelihood is not actually at stake (even her roommates roll their eyes during this moment of self-pity) since, when push comes to shove, Hannah's parents could just take back what they said about buying a lake-house and bail her out instead. Yet Hannah's fixation on ingestion is no less real or urgent. Food, as both a metaphoric notion and a real, onscreen substance, is essential to *Girls*. The tentative title of Hannah's memoir-in-progress is, after all, *Midnight Snack*. A title is supposed to be suggestive and representative of a body of work, but really all Hannah's (unfinished) *Midnight Snack* indicates is that she still has not learned how or when to eat like an adult. As for talking, she has only just begun.

The paradox in writing about — or filming — scenes of eating is that any meal is, narratively speaking, a snack, in that it's not an end in itself but a brief interruption of some more crucial ongoing action. Exceptions, such as Louis Malle's *My Dinner with Andre* and Francis Veber's *Le dîner de cons*, only emphasize the latent narrative potential surrounding cultures of eating. Jim Jarmusch's *Coffee and Cigarettes* — a film that strings together vignettes of café scenes — finds the narratability in visualizing a break or snack. Snacks are by definition inessential, unstructured, and irregular: you never know when the next one might come. The snack does not offer satisfaction or closure; in fact, it demands a more responsible future that might justify the present indulgence.

Food is meant to help us fuel up so we can get on with life, but food in *Girls* becomes the very excuse to avoid the mundane reality of growing up.

Scenes of eating, which abound in the pilot, are pauses in the real work that constitutes a bread-earning life. Rather than showcase the necessary regularity of eating, however, *Girls* uses food scenes as a way of driving plot and exploring character development. A meal is an opportunity for Hannah's parents to tell her "No. More. Money." (and, by extension, no more food). When the waiter asks if they would like more of anything, Hannah's mother drives the message home and speaks on her behalf: "No, she's fine." Food is also the gateway to Hannah's method of coping with her new economic status. After twenty-four hours of being financially cut off, Hannah comes home (notably late for her "dinner thing") and drinks a cup of cooked opium leaves upon mishearing that it "tastes like Twix." (It, surprisingly, does not.) Where a proper, scheduled restaurant dinner facilitates Hannah's "final push" into adulthood, she responds by consuming a drug (masked in the form of a drink, or a chocolate bar, or even better, a midnight snack). Characters' motivations and affective responses are, here and elsewhere, displaced onto food.

In terms of development — narrative, character, and otherwise — food is a   10 means to an end. It will bring the girls of *Girls* together, but it also differentiates them. Hannah eats her bathtub cupcake while complaining about her situation (and her body) to roommate Marnie. At the dinner party for their returning friend Jessa, a last-minute invitee occupies a seat at the table that was never meant for her, though this finally matters little as her presence feels inconsequential since she will not eat: "I didn't mean to be rude. I'm just not really into eating this week." Unsurprisingly, further development of this character stops at this sentence.

As pauses, eating is both what keeps us from attaining our ideals, as well as the literal driving force for life, and thus living the good life, itself. For all that is clichéd and flat about the show's glancing portrayal of Joy Lin, the Asian intern who got hired because of her Photoshopping skills, the show establishes common ground between Joy and the rest of the girls through her privileged relationship to food. Her one line in the pilot — "Will you get me a Luna bar, and a SmartWater, and Vitamin Water?" — indexes her socioeconomic status more precisely than it does her racial one. A health bar and two types of bottled water? If Joy can care about what she consumes, it's because, as a skilled and paid employee, she can afford to. As a point of fixation, food becomes an excuse and distraction to keep Hannah from facing up to her imminent shift in financial conditions. Again, the joke is that there is always enough food around to provide a distraction from worries about not having enough food.

The intermingling of appetites for food and for sex in fiction, film, and even television long predates *Girls*. A few examples: François Rabelais's *Gargantua and Pantagruel*, Thomas Mann's *The Magic Mountain*, Marco Ferreri's *La grande bouffe*, *I Love Lucy*, and, like, all of Evelyn Waugh. What makes narrative so directly contingent on physical drives? ("You're tired of eating him out," Hannah tells Marnie about her submissive boyfriend, "because he has a vagina.")

If our culture has mostly neglected food in its discussion of *Girls* thus far, it's got sex pretty well covered. Coinciding with the broadcast of the pilot,

Katie Roiphe wrote an article on submissive sexual appetites for *Newsweek* and, following the premiere, another on the performance of sadomasochistic sex in *Girls* for *Slate*. While many have responded to Roiphe's ideas on female fantasies of sexual domination with appropriate rage, more have received it as mostly dull and uncritical. In comparison to Roiphe's earlier pieces, which seem controversial and infuriating because they struck something about her generation's ideas of modern womanhood, her latest take on heteronormative desire seems to be getting tired. In Troy Patterson's take on *Girls* (also for *Slate*), he both quotes and comments on Roiphe's loss of steam:

> "The movement against date rape is a symptom of a more general anxiety about sex. . . . The crisis is not a rape crisis, but a crisis in sexual identity." I think that Roiphe had a strong point back then. It is unclear to me what she is saying, now, in lamenting the awkward sex of *Girls*. She is lamenting human nature? She is disappointed that non-marital sex still had yet to achieve zipless perfection?

Roiphe's retrograde reading of female desire does not take into account the possibilities of displacement and suppression that could lead to conclusions other than, simply, that women wish to be dominated. *Girls* might really represent a generational shift that diverges from, or at least complicates, Roiphe's concepts of female submission and, more importantly, sexual identity in general that get us talking again. Who is eating whom out anymore in *Girls*?

What is seen as realism in *Girls* is exactly what we would not expect to be able to see in our everyday interactions with others: uncomfortable scenes involving food and sex. Sex is explicitly bad and unsatisfying in *Girls*, but in an unfazed way. Dunham's camera takes us into the bathtub and the bedroom as though she were just narrating another chapter in our shared diary. In the sex scenes between Hannah and her "boyfriend" Adam, *Girls* plays on the expectations of erotic submission but fails to go all the way. Through mimicking, rather badly, the narratives of submissive sex, the show exposes the potential for disengagement and humor in sadomasochism through its over-performance. Indeed, sex for Hannah seems to feed her appetite to analyze her environment. (At one point, mid-thrust, Adam tells Hannah: "Let's play the quiet game.") In turn for the bad pornographic script that Adam feeds her, Hannah responds with her own. She wants to focus on the talk that occurs not just around — but also during — the act of sleeping with another person. When Adam offers Hannah a Gatorade after a particularly unappetizing round of sex for the latter, Hannah pauses then responds: "No thanks I'm good." An exercise in pleasure for Adam means he'll need a snack to replenish; but Hannah not only does not need a drink, her rejection of nutrients also signals an implicit rejection of the sex to which it would be a response. For Hannah, talking is a way of coming to terms with, and owning, her appetites.

These scenes, lurid in their will to show what is unsexy about sex, are [15] outside our ordinary purview, except, as *Girls* seems to suggest, when girls are with their closest female friends. Even when Hannah is having sex with

Adam, there is still a sense that her best friend, Marnie, is there with them as a judgmental third. Sitting back in her apartment, Marnie tells her own boyfriend: "I know exactly where she is. She's off having gross sex with that animal." For all that writers have spoken about *Girls'* appetite for sex — bad or good — these scenes often seem like just another appetite that drives the show's deeper dynamic of female friendship. Men are often only the catalyst through which women connect. Marnie's boyfriend Charlie is, literally, the outsider, who keeps trying to insert himself where he does not belong. He interrupts Marnie conversing with another girl in the bathroom not once, but twice; first sharing the bathtub with Hannah, and again just after Jessa, on the toilet, confesses to being pregnant (he is shooed out with a disgruntled wave of Marnie's hand). "Dude, it's never 'just your girlfriend' in here," Hannah tells Charlie, and really, it seems like he would know this by now. Unlike the men that interrupt Hannah and her girlfriends, however, Dunham's camera is allowed to stay inside with her female protagonists, inviting viewers to become a part of the talk that happens behind closed bathroom doors.

The camera's ability to insert viewers in intensely, even uncomfortably, intimate scenes of female bonding is at the heart of Dunham's art. Unloading your shit is a process that takes place in more than one form, with more than one body, in the bathrooms of *Girls*. Dunham's visualization of these moments of too-closeness is, however, how she prompts moments of visceral identification from her audience. In his article, Patterson compares Dunham's interaction with the camera as

> kind of like an *SNL* player doing body art [. . .] Has any of the commentary around Dunham's use of her nude or naked body in her work bothered to compare her to Tracey Emin, Pipilotti Rist, Vanessa Beecroft, Marina Abramović, or for that matter Matthew Barney?

The cast of *Girls*.

Photofest

As a type of performance art, Dunham's manipulation of her body engages viewers because she treats her body wholly irreverently. Like Hannah, Dunham has a desire to "take control of her shape," and she does this through bold portrayals of her naked body, in bizarre contortions, on screen. As the person who gets to script, direct, block, and portray her own body, all the arguments about Dunham's resolve to degrade herself fall apart on screen. Viewers might not have a hard time deciding what they think about Hannah's use of her body, but they will have a harder time locating Hannah's, or Dunham's, own take on sex since these acts are never fixed in the sexual identity of one body. Like body art, Dunham's directing of Hannah's body, alongside the psychological characterization she attributes to it, undoes any clear notion of what it is that body is doing and why.

Patterson's placement of Dunham among the pantheon of feminist body artists might, however, be slightly off key, as Dunham, ultimately, communicates her body via a television character. The immediacy of body art is precipitated by the real, physical fact of viewers' confrontation with the live body of the performer before them. What makes *Girls* a piece of art (and entertainment) of its time is precisely its ability to maintain a distance and anonymity from its viewers by virtue of the televisual medium.

The second episode of *Girls* concludes with Dunham lying flat on a gynecologist's table, while she makes a characteristically insensitive, and provocative, remark about her body. Though a large part of *Girls* runs on forcing the audience to contend with Dunham's body, Hannah, in this moment of vulnerability, wants nothing more than to escape her corporeality: "Maybe I'm actually not scared of AIDS. Maybe I thought I was scared of AIDS, but really what I am is . . . wanting AIDS." This is not Ron Athey or Tim Miller, however, whose performance art demanded one's response to the very real, very immediate consequences of AIDS. Like Dunham's treatment of food and sex, AIDS now stands as just another vehicle for her fantasy of escaping the current moment. Dunham goes on to tell her gynecologist that her fear of AIDS is like a *"Forrest Gump"* — that is, a cinematic — type of fear, one that only occurs when you are detached from the real, distanced from the object that prompts this fear. The scene is stunning in its portrayal of Hannah's narcissism, but it also shows Dunham's complete unawareness that her privilege lies in her ability to dramatize disease, starvation, and sexual degradation as forms of liberation.

Though its first season might be scripted, shot and ready to air, *Girls* — like its characters — is still feeling out a precarious situation, trying to find a space of identification for viewers that is neither too insular and restrained nor so expansive and universal that it stops signifying anything meaningful at all. So far the show seems stuck somewhere between its characters' sense of the emergency of the present moment and the magical ability to postpone emergency, seemingly indefinitely, because they have the economic and cultural resources to do so. Talk about *Girls*, too, is coming at us hard and fast in a way that forestalls, rather than forecloses, our developing sense of what it's about. If *Girls* truly resembles performance art, as Patterson suggests, it is in its ability to precipitate lively talk about itself almost instantaneously. Our responses are vital and urgent, but provisional, and we should remember that Dunham's show is still becoming what it is. Writing about *Girls* instantaneously on the internet, however, we might be chewing on a lot — and for a long time — before we get a chance to look down and really examine what it is that we've been digesting. Maybe we're afraid they'll take it away from us.

Reading the Text

1. How, according to Hu, does food function as a narrative and thematic leit-motif in *Girls*?

2. What does Hu mean by saying that "*Girls* wants to have it both ways: it wants to be both brash and unsure of itself, universal and specific, speaking (when it wants to) for a generation but reserving the right not to specify which one" (para. 2)?

3. Hu claims that in *Girls* "talking and eating will keep us distracted from the object of our hunger" (para. 7). What, in your own words, does Hu mean by "hunger"?

4. In her final paragraph, Hu says "Our responses [to *Girls*] are vital and urgent, but provisional" (para. 20). How might that comment reflect her own analysis of this TV show?

Reading the Signs

1. Both *Girls* and the earlier TV program *Friends* focus on the lives of young people who face economic difficulties living in an urban environment. In an essay, conduct a semiotic analysis of these two shows; you might focus on gender relations, economic forces, or both. What do these shows say about the times in which they appeared? How are they similar and different, and what do any differences signify?

2. Hu quotes *Girls*' protagonist, Hannah, who claims to be "at least *a* voice . . . of *a* generation" (para. 2) in the show's pilot episode. That generation is millennials. For an essay, first interview four or five acquaintances about their view on whether *Girls* indeed reflects the lifestyles and problems of millennials. Use your interviews as the foundation of an essay that argues for, disputes, or modifies the proposition that the show indeed accurately reflects the millennial experience.

3. Research the two articles by Katie Roiphe about *Girls* that Hu mentions. Write an essay in which you support, oppose, or modify Hu's assertion that Roiphe proposes a "retrograde reading of female desire [that] does not take into account the possibilities of displacement and suppression that could lead to conclusions other than, simply, that women wish to be dominated" (para. 13).

4. Hu mentions that commentary about *Girls* often focuses on the show's "realism" and adds, "What is seen as realism in *Girls* is exactly what we would not

expect to be able to see in our everyday interactions with others: uncomfortable scenes involving food and sex" (para. 14). After watching a few episodes of *Girls*, write an argumentative essay in which you take a position on the extent to which the program can be labeled "realistic." Be sure to define how you use the word "realism" in your essay.

5. After quoting commentator Troy Patterson's discussion of *Girls*' cinematography, Hu dubs the program an example of "performance art" (para. 17). Write an essay in which you assess the validity of this claim, being sure to research performance art if you are unfamiliar with the genre.

6. **CONNECTING TEXTS**   Hu claims that *Girls* has been criticized for its "monolithic middle-class whiteness" (para. 3). Adopting the perspective of Michael Parenti (see "Class and Virtue," p. 361), analyze the racial and class dynamics that you see in *Girls*.

WILLA PASKIN
Devious Maids *Skewers the One Percent*

Even when American television sets out to be subversive, it usually ends up celebrating the status quo. Take Lifetime's *Devious Maids*, a semi-soap in the tradition of *Desperate Housewives*, which manages to suggest, in Willa Paskin's words, that "[e]ven if the rich are bitches, . . . we should still aspire to be them." Indeed, the Latina maids who star in the series never seem to leave Beverly Hills, and their plans are to get just as wealthy as the unpleasant women who employ them. It all looks like *workers of the world, move up*, which is hardly the stuff of revolution. Willa Paskin is a staff writer specializing in television for *Salon*, where this selection first appeared.

I was recently having a conversation about working class people and television, and how it has become nearly impossible to find the former on the latter. Sitcoms used to have a blue-collar tradition, from *All in the Family* to *Roseanne*, but in recent years that's been all but abandoned. People on television are usually rich, nearly so, or becoming so. They are typically untroubled by financial practicalities or only marginally bothered by them. Into this desert of class diversity comes Lifetime's cheeky new melodrama *Devious Maids*, premiering Sunday, which features five working class Latina women but still just flickers in and out of class consciousness.

Devious Maids comes from Marc Cherry, the creator of *Desperate Housewives* and a man who clearly believes in sticking to certain naming conventions. Tonally, the shows are very similar: comedic super-soaps about a group of women with a central murder mystery, crazy plot turns, and a knowing, winking tone. The stars of *Devious Maids* are not housewives but Latina domestic servants, all working for crazy rich people in Beverly Hills. In the first minutes of the pilot, a maid, Flora, is murdered by a person unknown. When her employer, a camp character on the order of Cruella De Vil, breaks down, it's not because of the death, but the mess: "My maid was murdered! Who is going to clean all this up?" she screeches.

Soon thereafter, Marisol (*Ugly Betty*'s Ana Ortiz) appears on the scene, eager to find out more about Flora's murder and ingratiate herself with the other women who work nearby. These include the bratty Carmen (*Without a Trace*'s Roselyn Sanchez), an ultra-ambitious singer who has gained employment in a superstar's house, hoping she'll be able to get him to hear her music; Rosie (Dania Ramirez), a kind, widowed nanny working to bring her small son to America from Mexico while she cares for the son of a soap actor (*Melrose Place*'s Grant Show) and his bitchy, selfish wife; and Zoila (*Scrubs*' Judy Reyes) and her daughter Valentina (Edy Ganem), who work in the home of a histrionic woman (soap legend Susan Lucci) and her rich son, who Valentina loves even though her mother insists it will never work out.

Devious Maids has already been accused of perpetuating stereotypes for having all five Latina characters be domestic servants (though I suspect that Marisol, who in a flashback appears to have a maid of her own, is secretly rich), and been defended from these charges by executive producer Eva Longoria. But there's a second-order stereotyping going on of the well-meaning and yet still totally ghettoizing variety, as June Thomas points out in her review for *Slate*. The show is a parade of "Latina maids who are both devious and pure of heart, and of their Caucasian employers, who are all selfish, utterly detestable, entitled snobs." In other words, while the nasty white people get all the ridiculous, over-the-top lines and complicated, knotty emotions, the "good" Hispanic characters are largely straitjacketed into having no fun, imprisoned by their ethical superiority.

Having watched *Desperate Housewives*, I suspect that the goody-two- 5
shoes nature of the Latina characters will be short-lived: Marc Cherry churns through too much plot to leave anyone pristine. Carmen, already, is a straight manipulator on the make not at all interested in being a maid—"you guys know how to be poor," she tells her friend, "I do not."—and willing to use a nice guy to get her way. But for now, the bias toward boring is definitely at work. Cherry should look at *Scandal*, a show in which everyone of every color gets to be troubled and naughty and still expect our sympathy, to see how to improve.

Until then, there is something really fascinating about at least one half of *Devious Maids*' stereotyping: the part that turns it into the "indulge your vitriol for white ladies with too much money" hour. In one scene, Rosie's boss won't let Rosie go see a lawyer about her son's immigration because the boss has a facial appointment she refuses to cancel. Another woman doesn't want to hire Marisol because she has no accent and sounds like "she went to college" and thus appears to have "attitude." Wherever we are, culturally speaking, it appears to be a place where a TV show aspiring to be frothy, escapist and fun can get its dramatic climaxes and moments of triumph from a bunch of rich bitches — whose husbands are, by and large, much, much nicer than them — getting theirs. Gleefully skewering the one percent of obnoxious white ladies — and obnoxious, in the pilot anyway, is the only way they come — must have market-tested just fine.

This is not to suggest that *Devious Maids* has something larger to say about the inequity of American society. This is a TV show about class that does not for one minute want to leave the safe haven of real estate porn. Even if the rich are bitches, the show implies, we should still aspire to be them. *Devious Maids* may star people who have to work for a living, but since three of the five women are live-in maids, we never have to leave Beverly Hills. None of the domestics seem concerned about money. Rosie's efforts to bring her son to America get back-burnered by the second episode. And Carmen and Valentina are pursuing affluence as hard as they can. *Devious Maids* finds a way to have all its stars sitting in lounge chairs by a pool — it may not make sense, but at least it looks like *Sex and the City*. The message of *Devious Maids* is not quite that the rich are no better than anyone else, but that anyone else — in this case, five maids — would make for better rich people than the already rich, which also happens to be one of the guiding fantasies of American life. I think this show, however flawed, just might be a big hit.

READING THE TEXT

1. Summarize in your own words the stereotypes that Paskin sees in the characters featured in *Devious Maids*.

2. In your own words, explain how *Devious Maids* actually endorses the values it seems to satirize, according to Paskin.

3. What parallels does Paskin draw between *Devious Maids* and *Desperate Housewives*?

4. What does Paskin mean by saying that *Devious Maids* engages in both typical stereotypes of Latinas and a "second-order stereotyping" (para. 4)?

READING THE SIGNS

1. **CONNECTING TEXTS** Watch an episode or two of *Devious Maids*, and then write your own analysis of its depiction of class differences. To what extent does your viewing support, undercut, or modify Paskin's claim that the show's message is "not quite that the rich are no better than anyone else, but that anyone else — in this case, five maids — would make for better rich people than the already rich, which also happens to be one of the guiding fantasies of American life" (para. 7). To develop your ideas, consult Michael Parenti's "Class and Virtue" (p. 361).

2. View an episode of *Ugly Betty*, and then write an analytic essay that considers whether that program and *Devious Maids* perpetuate class and racial stereotypes.

3. **CONNECTING TEXTS**   Using Michael Omi's "In Living Color: Race and American Culture" (p. 538) as a critical framework, analyze the racial dimensions that you view in *Devious Maids*. To what extent does the show exemplify his categories of racial stereotyping, such as overt and inferential racism? Given that the show's debut occurred nearly twenty-five years after Omi first published his essay, do you think that the show has moved beyond the stereotypes Omi describes?

4. In class, discuss the merits of Paskin's claim that "gleefully skewering the one percent of obnoxious white ladies . . . must have market-tested just fine" (para. 6). In other words, to what extent do you think that the popularity of a show such as *Devious Maids* might relate to an increasing class division in America? Use your discussion as a jumping-off point for your own essay that addresses Paskin's claim.

5. In the first paragraph, Paskin refers to earlier TV programs that featured working-class characters. Watch an episode of *All in the Family*, *Roseanne*, or *Laverne and Shirley*, and write an essay that compares the depiction of these characters with the maids as Paskin describes them. What ethnic and class differences do you see? How do you explain any such observations?

NEAL GABLER
The Social Networks

Remember *Friends*, that sprightly comedy in which no one ever seemed to be alone? Or *Sex and the City*, wherein busy Manhattan professional women always seemed to have time to share a glass of water and some lettuce? Indeed, even today, wherever you look on television, Neal Gabler notes in this essay that originally appeared in the *Los Angeles Times*, you are certain to see "lots of folks spending the better part of their day surrounded by their friends and family in happy conviviality." Yet oddly enough, this sort of programming is appearing "at a time when it is increasingly difficult to find this kind of deep social interaction anyplace but on TV." Clearly, Gabler suggests, television is providing some sort of compensation for the social atomization that it itself has contributed to, and thus, all the simulated conviviality, while being a pleasant "dream," is "pure wish fulfillment," indeed, rather "phony," and, perhaps, sad. The author of *An Empire of Their Own: How the Jews Invented Hollywood* (1989), *Winchell: Gossip,*

Power and the Culture of Celebrity (1994), *Life the Movie: How Entertainment Conquered Reality* (1998), and *Walt Disney: The Triumph of the American Imagination* (2006), Neal Gabler is a well-known analyst and historian of American cinema and popular culture.

With the new television season upon us, here are a few things you are virtually certain to see again and again and again: lots of folks spending the better part of their day surrounded by their friends and family in happy conviviality; folks wandering into the unlocked apartments and homes of friends, family, and neighbors at any time of the day or night as if this were the most natural thing in the world; friends and family sitting down and having lots of tearful heart-to-hearts; Little League games, school assemblies, and dance recitals, all attended by, you guessed it, scads of friends and family.

You're going to be seeing these scenes repeatedly because the basic unit of television is not the lone individual or the partnership or even the nuclear family. The basic unit of television is the flock — be it the extended family of brothers and sisters, grandfathers and grandmothers, nieces, nephews, and cousins, or the extended circle of friends, and, rest assured, it is always a circle. On television friends never come in pairs; they invariably congregate in groups of three or more.

That television has become quite possibly the primary purveyor in American life of friendship and of the extended family is no recent blip. Over the last twenty years, beginning with *Seinfeld* and moving on through *Friends, Sex and the City,* and more recently to *Desperate Housewives, Glee, The Big Bang Theory, How I Met Your Mother, Cougartown,* and at least a half-dozen other shows, including this season's newbies *Raising Hope* and *Better with You,* television has become a kind of friendship machine dispensing groups of people in constant and intimate contact with one another, sitting around in living rooms, restaurants, and coffee shops, sharing everything all the time. You might even say that friendship has become the basic theme of television, certainly of broadcast television, though cable has its own friendship orgies like *Men of a Certain Age, My Boys,* and *It's Always Sunny in Philadelphia.* Friendship is what television is about.

What makes this so remarkable is that it has been happening at a time when it is increasingly difficult to find this kind of deep social interaction anyplace but on TV. Nearly a decade ago, Harvard professor Robert Putnam observed in his classic *Bowling Alone* that Americans had become more and more disconnected from one another and from their society. As Putnam put it, "For the first two-thirds of the twentieth century a powerful tide bore Americans into ever deeper engagement in the life of their communities, but a few decades ago — silently, without warning — that tide reversed and we were overtaken by a treacherous current." It was a current that pulled Americans apart.

Moreover, the current that Putnam observed has, according to more recent studies, only intensified in the last decade. One study found that 5

Americans had one-third fewer nonfamily confidants than they had twenty years earlier, and 25 percent had no one in whom to confide whatsoever. Another study of 3,000 Americans found that on average they had only four close social contacts, but these included family members like one's own spouse. This decline in real friendships may account in part for the dramatic rise of virtual friendships like those on social-networking sites where being "friended" is less a sign of personal engagement than a quantitative measure of how many people your life has brushed and how many names you can collect, but this is friendship lite. Facebook, in fact, only underscores how much traditional friendship — friendship in which you meet, talk, and share — has become an anachronism and how much being "friended" is an ironic term.

Among the reasons Putnam cited for the increasing atomization in American life were economic pressures and anxieties; women entering the workplace in full-time employment by necessity and thus disengaging from their friends and neighbors; metropolitan sprawl, which meant more time spent commuting, greater social segregation, and the disruption of community boundaries; and last but by no means least, the rise of television itself, especially its splintering influence on later generations who have grown up addicted to the tube. It is no secret that watching television is not exactly a communal activity. Rather, we often use it to fill a communal void. But instead of bringing comfort, it seems only to remind us of our alienation. In Putnam's view, based on several studies, "TV is apparently especially attractive for people who feel unhappy, particularly when there is nothing else to do."

It's not that we prefer television to human contact. The laugh track attests that most people don't really want to be alone in front of their TV sets. They want to be part of a larger community. Yet another study indicates that TV provides a sort of simulacrum of community because the relationship between the TV viewer and the people he or she watches on the screen competes with and even substitutes for physical encounters with real people. It is Facebook with hundreds of "friends" but without any actual contact with any of them, only the virtual contact of watching.

But what none of these theories of television has noticed is that TV has learned how to compensate for the increasing alienation it seems to induce. And it compensates not by letting us kill time with "friends" on-screen but by providing us with those nonstop fantasies of friendship, which clearly give us a vicarious pleasure. Watch *Seinfeld* or *Friends* or *Sex and the City* or *Community* or *Men of a Certain Age* — the list is endless — and you'll see people who not only are never ever alone but people whose relationships are basically smooth, painless, uninhibited and deeply, deeply intimate — the kind of friendships we may have had in college but that most of us can only dream about now. How many adults do you know who manage to hang out with their friends every single day for hour after hour?

Or watch the incomparable *Modern Family* or *Brothers and Sisters* or *Parenthood* and you'll see big, happy family gatherings with lots of bonhomie and jokes and an outpouring of love. On the last there seems to be a huge extended family dinner every other night where most families would be lucky to have one such get-together each year at Thanksgiving. And don't forget those school assemblies, already mentioned, which everyone in the family takes off work to attend en masse or the weekend birthday parties where attendance is also compulsory.

One feels a little churlish pointing out how phony most of this intimacy is. 10 After all, these shows, even one as observant as *Modern Family*, aren't about realism. They aren't about the genuine emotional underpinnings of friendship or family, and they certainly aren't about the rough course that almost every relationship, be it with a friend or family member, takes — the inevitable squabbles, the sometimes long and even permanent ruptures, the obtuseness, the selfishness, the reprioritization, the expectations of reciprocity, the drifting apart, the agonizing sense of loneliness even within the flock. These shows are pure wish fulfillment. They offer us friends and family at one's beck and call but without any of the hassles. It is friendship as we want it to be.

For the fact is that we miss the friendships we no longer have, and we know that Facebook or e-mails cannot possibly compensate for the loss. So we sit in front of our television sets and enjoy the dream of friendship instead: a dream where we need never be alone, where there are a group of people who would do anything for us, and where everyone seems to understand us to our very core, just like Jerry and George, Chandler and Joey, Carrie and her girls, or the members of the McKinley High glee club. It is a powerful dream, and it is one that may now be the primary pleasure of television.

READING THE TEXT

1. Summarize in your own words what Gabler means by saying, "The basic unit of television is the flock" (para. 2).

2. How does Robert Putnam's research on friendship in America inform Gabler's argument?

3. Why does Gabler say that "being 'friended' is an ironic term" (para. 5)?

4. How does Gabler use concession to strengthen his argument?

5. In your own words, explain what Gabler means by "simulacrum of community" (para. 7)?

READING THE SIGNS

1. Write an argumentative essay in which you assess the validity of Gabler's claim that "instead of bringing comfort, [television] seems only to remind us of our alienation" (para. 6). To support your argument, you might interview friends or acquaintances about their reasons for watching television.

2. In an essay, analyze an episode of one of the friend-heavy TV programs that Gabler mentions, such as *Desperate Housewives*, *Glee*, or *Modern Family*. To

what extent does it confirm Gabler's assertion that "these shows are pure wish fulfillment" (para. 10)?

3. Write an essay in which you support, oppose, or complicate Gabler's belief that Facebook offers "friendship lite" (para. 5). To develop your ideas, read "Students Addicted to Social Media" (p. 403).

4. **CONNECTING TEXTS** Adopting Gabler's perspective, analyze the friendships and interpersonal relations depicted in Lena Dunham's *Girls*. To what extent do they replicate or deviate from the ones represented in the shows "The Social Networks" discusses? How do you think Gabler would explain any differences you see among these TV shows? To develop your ideas, read Jane Hu's "Reality Hunger: On Lena Dunham's *Girls*" (p. 304).

THE HOLLYWOOD SIGN
The Culture of American Film

One Enchanted Evening

By the first half of 2013, *Iron Man 3*, *Man of Steel*, *Oz*, *Star Trek: Into Darkness*, *The Croods*, *Monsters University*, and *World War Z* were, respectively, America's first, second, third, fifth, sixth, seventh, and tenth top-grossing movies. In 2012, the top ten included *The Avengers* (1), *The Dark Knight Rises* (2), *The Hobbit* (5), *Breaking Dawn–Part 2* (6), and *The Amazing Spider-Man* (7). Similarly, in 2011, 2010, 2009, 2008, and so on back to the year 2000, most of the top-grossing movies were, in some way, fantasy or science fiction films, featuring superheroes, vampires, wizards, and whatnot. By contrast, in 1975, the only top-ten movie with a fantasy theme was *Monty Python and the Holy Grail*, which, as a send-up of sword-and-sorcery storytelling, hardly counts. In the previous five years, not a single top-five film could be counted as a fantasy film, unless you include Disney's *The Aristocats* (number 5 in 1970). In the 1960s, the fantasy genre was virtually nonexistent in the box office bonanza sweepstakes (our source for this information is leesmovieinfo.net /WBOYearly).

The turning point seemed to occur in 1977, when George Lucas combined the spirit of J. R. R. Tolkien's *Lord of the Rings* trilogy with the short-lived *Star Trek* television series to create *Star Wars: Episode IV–A New Hope* — a movie that took advantage of new developments in film technology to help transform the old, rather cheesy, B-movie tradition of science fiction into A-list entertainment. From then on, we find an ever-increasing share of Hollywood movie production devoted to fantasy, and, as is so often the case in **semiotic** analysis, such a shift, or **difference**, points to cultural significance.

Here is the key to a semiotic analysis: finding a pattern or detail that stands out and practically begs to be analyzed. The question now is simply: Why have American audiences turned so decisively to fantasy in recent decades? What does this shift tell us?

A full analysis of such a question would take us beyond the scope of this Introduction, but a few **abductive** explanations might be offered. First, in the rise of what traditionally was regarded as a children's genre, we can find a reflection of the evolution of America's youth culture, a culture that places great value upon childhood and adolescence as a period of innocence apart from adult experience (the late J. D. Salinger played a major role in this evolution). Essentially a form of escapism, fantasy plays upon a sense of childhood wonder and enchantment, and in the popularity of fantasy among adult audiences we can accordingly find the desire of adults to escape from the realities of their ordinary lives into an enchanted realm wherein the imagination, rather than reality, reigns.

This desire for enchantment can thus also be seen as a **sign** of a certain cultural disenchantment that has emerged in an era of economic contraction, political dysfunction, social divisiveness, and global terrorism. In such times, it should not be surprising that Americans are seeking not only distractions from the grim realities of their lives but also simple solutions to complex problems that resist real-life resolution. And that is the ultimate fantasy. (See Christine Folch's article on p. 378 for a divergent reading.)

Donald Sutherland as President Snow in *The Hunger Games: Catching Fire.*

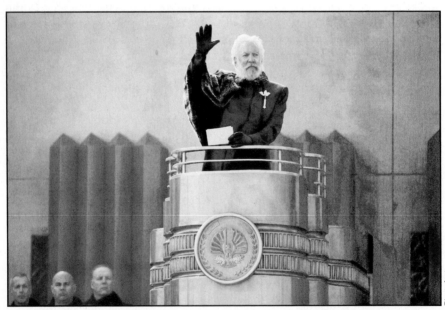

Photofest

The Culture Industry

Filmmakers have been providing Americans with entertainments that have both reflected and shaped their desires for over a century. Long before the advent of TV, movies offered viewers the glamour, romance, and sheer excitement that modern life seems to deny. So effective have movies been in molding audience desire that such early culture critics as Theodor Adorno and Max Horkheimer[1] accused them of being part of a vast, Hollywood-centered "culture industry" whose products successfully distracted their audiences from the inequities of modern life and thus effectively maintained the social status quo under capitalism by drawing everyone's attention away from it.

More recent analysts, however, are far less pessimistic. Indeed, for many cultural studies "populists," films, along with the rest of popular culture, can represent a kind of mass resistance to the political dominance — or what is often called the *hegemony* — of the social and economic powers-that-be. For such critics, films can provide utopian visions of a better world, stimulating their viewers to imagine how their society might be improved, and so, perhaps, inspiring them to go out and do something about it.

Whether you believe that films distract us from the real world or inspire us to imagine a better one, their central place in contemporary American culture demands interpretation, for their impact goes well beyond the movie theater or Netflix rental. Far from being mere entertainments, movies constitute a profound part of our everyday lives, with every film festival and award becoming major news, and each major release becoming the talk of the country. Just think of the pressure you might feel to discuss the latest film sensation among your friends. Consider how, if you decide to save a few bucks, not watch the latest hit, and wait for the DVD release or watch it online, you can lose face and be seriously on the social outs. No, nothing is frivolous about the movies. You've been watching them all your life: Now's the time to start thinking about them semiotically.

Interpreting the Signs of American Film

Interpreting a movie or a group of movies is not unlike interpreting a television program or group of programs. Again, you should suspend your personal feelings and aesthetic judgments about your subject. As with any semiotic analysis, your goal is to interpret the cultural significance of your topic, not to give it a thumbs-up or a thumbs-down. Thus, you may find it more rewarding to interpret films that promise to be culturally meaningful than to simply examine your favorite flick. Determining whether a movie is culturally

---

[1]**Theodor Adorno** (1903–1969) and **Max Horkheimer** (1895–1973) authored *Dialectic of Enlightenment* (1947), a book whose analyses included a scathing indictment of the culture industry. — EDS.

Discussing the Signs of Film

In any given year, one film may dominate the Hollywood box office, becoming a blockbuster that captures that public's cinematic imagination. In class, discuss which film would be your choice as this year's top hit. Then analyze the film semiotically. Why has *this* film so successfully appealed to so many moviegoers?

---

meaningful in the prewriting stage, of course, may be a hit-or-miss affair; you may find that your first choice does not present any particularly interesting grounds for interpretation. That's why it can be helpful to consider reasons a particular movie is special, such as enormous popularity or widespread critical attention. Of course, cult favorites, while often lacking in critical or popular attention, can also be signs pointing toward their self-selected audiences and thus are strong candidates for analysis. Academy Award nominees are also reliable as cultural signs.

Your interpretation of a movie or group of movies should begin with a construction of the *system* in which it belongs — that is, those movies, past and present, with which it can be *associated*. While tracing those associations, be on the lookout for striking *differences* from films that are otherwise like what you are analyzing, because those differences are what often reveal the significance of your subject.

Archetypes are useful features for film analysis as well. An archetype is anything that has been repeated in storytelling from ancient times to the present. There are character archetypes, such as the wise old man, which include such figures as Yoda and Gandalf, and plot archetypes, such as the heroic quest, which is the archetypal backbone of films like *The Lord of the Rings* trilogy. All those male buddy films — from *Butch Cassidy and the Sundance Kid* to *Lethal Weapon* to *Men in Black* — hark back to archetypal male bonding stories as old as *The Epic of Gilgamesh* (from the third millennium B.C.E.) and the *Iliad*, while Cruella de Vil from *101 Dalmatians* is sister to the Wicked Witch of the West, Snow White's evil stepmother, and every other witch or crone dreamed up by the patriarchal imagination. All those sea monsters, from Jonah's "whale" to Moby Dick to the great white shark in *Jaws*, are part of the same archetypal phylum, and every time a movie hero struggles to return home after a long journey — Dorothy to Kansas, Lassie to Timmy — a story as old as Exodus and the *Odyssey* is retold.

Hollywood is well aware of the enduring appeal of archetypes (see Linda Seger's selection in this chapter for a how-to description of archetypal scriptwriting), and director George Lucas's reliance on the work of anthropologist Joseph Campbell in his creation of the *Star Wars* saga is widely known. But it is not always the case that either creators or consumers are consciously aware of the archetypes before them. Part of a culture's collective unconscious, archetypal stories can send messages that their audiences only subliminally understand. A heavy dosage of male-bonding films in a given Hollywood season, for instance, can send the unspoken cultural message that a man can't really make friends with a woman and that women are simply the sexual reward for manly men. Similarly, too many witches in a given Hollywood season can send the antifeminist message that there are too many bitches. Conversely, the modification of an archetype, as in the *female*-bonding film *Thelma and Louise*, can signify a feminist emergence.

Repetition with a Difference

Just as movies frequently repeat ancient archetypal character and plot types, they also may refer to other movies and modern cultural artifacts in what is referred to as a **postmodern** manner. Postmodernism is, in effect, both a historical period and an attitude. As a historical period, postmodernism refers to the culture that emerged in the wake of the advent of mass media, one obsessed with electronic imagery and the products of mass culture. As an attitude, postmodernism rejects the values of the past, not to support new values but instead to ironize value systems as such. Thus, in the postmodern worldview, our traditional hierarchical distinctions valuing high culture over low culture, say, or creativity over imitation, tend to get flattened out. What was once viewed in terms of an oppositional hierarchy (origination is opposed to emulation and is superior to it) is reconceived and deconstructed. Postmodern artists, accordingly, tend to reproduce, with an ironic or parodic twist, already-existing cultural images in their work, especially if they can be drawn from mass culture and mass society. Roy Lichtenstein's cartoon canvases, for instance, parody popular cartoon books, and Andy Warhol's tomato soup paintings repeat the familiar labels of the Campbell Soup Company — thus mixing high culture and mass culture in a new, nonoppositional, relation.

To put this another way, the postmodern worldview holds that it is no longer possible or desirable to create new images; rather, one surveys the vast range of available images that mass culture has to offer, and repeats them, but with a difference. Postmodern filmmakers accordingly allude to existing films in their work, as in the final scene of Tim Burton's *Batman*, which directly alludes to Alfred Hitchcock's *Vertigo*, or Oliver Stone and Quentin Tarantino's *Natural Born Killers*, which recalls *Bonnie and Clyde*. Such allusions to, and repetitions of, existing cultural images in postmodern cinema are called *double-coding*, because of the way that the postmodern artifact simultaneously refers to existing cultural **codes** and recasts them in new contexts. The conclusion of *Batman*, for example, while echoing *Vertigo*'s climactic scene, differs dramatically in its significance, turning from Hitchcock's tragedy to Burton's quasi-farce.

Exploring the Signs of Film

In your journal, list your favorite movies. Then consider your list: What does it say about you? What **cultural mythologies** do the movies tend to reflect, and why do you think those myths appeal to you? What signs particularly appeal to your emotions? What sort of stories about human life do you most respond to?

Movies as Metaphors

Sometimes movies can also be seen as metaphors for larger cultural concerns. Consider the grade-B horror flicks of the 1950s, such as the original *Godzilla*. If we were to study only its plot, we would see little more than a cheesy horror story featuring a reptilian monster that is an archetypal kin of the dragons in medieval literature. But Godzilla was no mere dragon transported to the modern world. The dragons that populated the world of medieval storytelling were themselves often metaphors for the satanic serpent in the Garden of Eden, but Godzilla was a wholly different sort of metaphor. Created by Japanese filmmakers, Godzilla was originally a metaphor for the nuclear era. A female mutant creation of nuclear poisoning, Godzilla rose over her Japanese audiences like a mushroom cloud, symbolizing the potential for future mushroom clouds both in Japan and around the world in the Cold War era.

For their part, 1950s American filmmakers had their own metaphors for the nuclear era. Whenever some "blob" threatened to consume New York or

Reading Film Online

Most major films now released in the United States have their own Web sites. You can find them listed online under the film's title or in print ads for the film. Select a current film, find the Web address, log on, and analyze the film's site semiotically. What images are used to attract your interest in the film? What interactive strategies, if any, are used to increase your commitment to the film? If you've seen the movie, how does the site's presentation of it compare with your experience of viewing it either in a theater or on video? Alternatively, analyze the posters designed to attract attention to a particular film; a useful resource is the Movie Poster Page (www.musicman.com/mp/mp.html).

some especially toxic slime escaped from a laboratory, the suggestion that science — especially nuclear science — was threatening to destroy the world filled the theater along with the popcorn fumes. And if it wasn't science that was the threat, Cold War filmmakers could scare us with Communists, as films like *Invasion of the Body Snatchers* metaphorically suggested through its depiction of a town in which everyone looked the same but had really been taken over by aliens. "Beware of your neighbors," the movie seemed to warn. "They could be Communists."

In such ways, an entire film can be a kind of metaphor, but you can find many smaller metaphors at work in the details of a movie as well. Early film-makers, for example, used to put a tablecloth on the table in dining scenes to signify that the characters at the table were good, decent people (you can find such a metaphor in Charlie Chaplin's *The Kid*, where an impoverished tramp who can't afford socks or a bathrobe still has a nice tablecloth on the break-fast table). Sometimes a director's metaphors have a broad political signifi-cance, as at the end of the Rock Hudson / James Dean / Elizabeth Taylor classic *Giant*, where the parting shot presents a tableau of a white baby goat standing next to a black baby goat, which is juxtaposed with the image of a white baby standing in a crib side by side with a brown baby. Since the human babies are both the grandchildren of the film's protagonist (one of whose sons has married a Mexican woman, the other an Anglo), the goats are added to under-score metaphorically (if rather heavy-handedly) the message of racial recon-ciliation that the director wanted to send.

Reading a film, then, is much like reading a novel. Both are texts filled with intentional and unintentional signs, metaphors, and archetypes, and both are cultural signifiers. The major difference is in their medium of expression. Literary texts are cast entirely in written words; films combine verbal language, visual imagery, and sound effects. Thus, we perceive literary and cinematic texts differently, for the written sign is perceived in a linear fashion that relies on one's cognitive and imaginative powers, while a film primarily targets the senses: One sees and hears (and sometimes even smells!). That film is such a sensory experience often conceals its textuality. One is tempted to sit back and go with the flow, to say that it's only entertainment and doesn't have to "mean" anything at all. But even the most cartoonish cinematic entertainment can harbor a rather profound cultural significance. To see how, let's look at that recurring subject for Hollywood moviemaking concerning a banker who dresses up in a bat costume — yes, a bat suit — in order to fight crime.

Batman: The Dark Knight

There are a lot of *Batman* movies to choose from, of course, including the Tim Burton version we have already referred to. And as we write these words, a new version is in the works that will bring a new actor to the role (Ben Affleck), while the latest version to have hit the theaters so far is still *The*

Dark Knight Rises (2012). We are choosing to present an analysis of a Batman movie from 2008 because that film addresses an especially powerful social dilemma for Americans, a dilemma that will still affect us all into the foreseeable future, making that movie as culturally cogent in the years to come as it was when it first appeared.

We can begin with a movie poster. One of the posters used to advertise *Batman: The Dark Knight* featured the familiar figure of Batman, in full regalia, standing in front of a high-rise office tower whose upper floors are on fire. This image would be immediately recognizable to audiences as alluding to the September 11, 2001, attacks on the World Trade Center and is a key signifier of what was different about this entry into the long history of Batman movies and television shows. As always, this difference is crucial to understanding the cultural significance of the film.

Heath Ledger's Joker provides an especially good figure with which to start. In the early days of the Batman saga, when Batman was still simply a children's comic book hero, the Joker was one of a group of villains who were little more than cartoon clowns. Like Burgess Meredith's Penguin in the 1960s *Batman* television series, the Joker was not really very frightening and mostly out for a fast buck. Ledger's Joker belongs to this system and thus can be associated with all the other Jokers and villains within it. But we can see a striking difference. This Joker is no clown; he is an out-of-control homicidal maniac, and although he robs banks, he most certainly is not motivated by a desire for money. Something else is going on.

Ledger's Joker, of course, was not pulled out of a hat. Before Ledger there was Jack Nicholson, and before Nicholson there was *Arkham Asylum*. That graphic novel introduced a far more disturbing Joker into the system, a psychopath rather than a mere criminal. Jack Nicholson's Joker in Tim Burton's *Batman* surely displayed some of the maniacal energy of the *Arkham* Joker, and he was far more violent and sadistic than any Joker in the past. Still, Nicholson's Joker was motivated by desires that his audience could understand: He wanted money, he wanted power, and he wanted revenge. We see him ruthlessly taking over the organized crime syndicate in Gotham City because he wants to be at its head. His war with Batman is fueled by an earlier duel with the Caped Crusader that left him disfigured for life. We may not be on his side, but we can understand him.

And we can also laugh with him. His epic attack on an art gallery is just plain funny, and his ability to run rings around everyone in Gotham City, especially the news media, makes Nicholson's Joker something like a stand-up comedian — a murderous comedian, but a comedian all the same.

Heath Ledger's Joker is no comedian. He is never funny. Much more importantly, he does not seem to have any motives for his actions. He doesn't want power, as is evident from the fact that while he makes war on the mob, he does not attempt to build his own organization. Rather, he continually murders his own subordinates, along with the mob leaders whose organization he is taking over. And he doesn't want money, which is dramatically symbolized

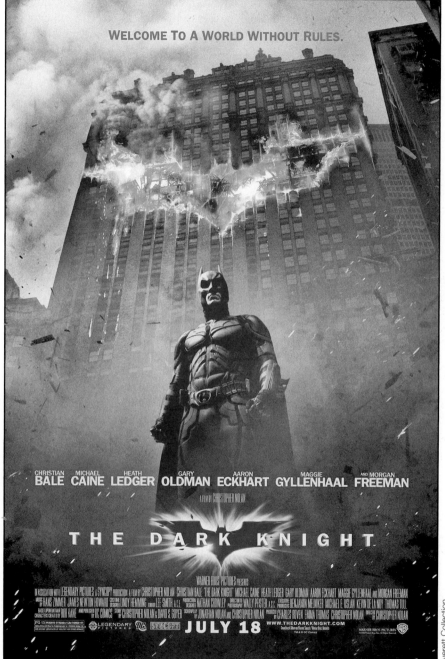

by his setting fire to a huge pile of cash atop which sits the mob's accountant. He doesn't really seem to want revenge (even his indications that he was cruelly raised — thereby suggesting a possible revenge motive emerging from his childhood — are undercut by later speeches that make it clear that he will say just about anything, no matter how untrue). And he doesn't want sex (Nicholson's Joker had a girlfriend, though she was horribly abused; Ledger's Joker is completely unattached). Basically, all he wants to do is create mayhem and make people suffer as much as possible.

So it is quite a journey from the comic book criminal-clowns of the past to Ledger's Joker. The semiotic question is: What does this journey mean?

The key change here is one of ever-increasing violence. When we look at popular culture more generally, we can find innumerable instances of ever-more-violent entertainment with which the Batman saga can be associated. Consider the difference between the horror films of the 1950s and today's splatter films, or even between Hitchcock's *Psycho* and Van Sant's. And then there's Dexter, who manages to out-Hannibal Hannibal Lecter. The difference lies not only in the enhanced ability to simulate violence in modern moviemaking due to advances in film technology but also in the fact that today's audiences don't want much to be left to the imagination. The more graphically gruesome, the better. What is more, audiences today are attracted to representations of emotional along with physical torture — as seen in such movies as *Hostel*, parts 1 and 2, and the *Saw* franchise, as well as in the way that Ledger's Joker emotionally tortures his victims, such as the civilians on a ferryboat who are forced to choose between the destruction of their boat or that of one carrying a group of criminals being evacuated from a prison.

Does this mean that people are more violent today than in the past or more evil? No, not really. Violence has always been a staple of low cultural entertainment (indeed, for the ancient Romans, violent entertainment was literally violent and not merely a simulation). But Americans have traditionally chosen to restrict the level of violence that they allow in their entertainments. The Hays Code of the 1930s, for example, represented a self-imposed censorship by the film industry, restricting not only the sexual content of movies but their violent content as well. But with the passing of the years those restrictions have been considerably loosened. Why?

As always, the answer is **overdetermined**. Part of it lies in an increasing sophistication in American audiences, who will no longer accept as realistic a highly toned-down representation of violence. In 1950s TV Westerns, for example, when a man was shot at close range by a .45 caliber bullet, audiences were satisfied with a small spot of blood where the bullet entered. Now they want to see what a .45 caliber bullet really does at close range.

But there is another explanation as well. Remember, history shows that the appeal of violent entertainment is universal, which implies that at any time there will be an audience for it. Until relatively recently, American values held that such a desire should not be satisfied, that extremely violent entertainment should not be allowed in a civilized society. So what changed?

Jack Nicholson (left) and Heath Ledger (right) had vastly different takes on *Batman* arch-villain the Joker.

Here we might consider a primary contradiction in American culture: the contradiction between America's "spiritual" and "materialistic" values. One side sees that it is better for the spirit to repress our violent proclivities. But the other side sees that a lot of money can be made precisely by catering to those ancient desires. The fact that we can find the materialistic calculation overriding the spiritual principle throughout contemporary popular culture is a striking sign of the power of modern capitalism.

And yet, there is still more. Let's return to the movie poster for *Batman: The Dark Knight*. That poster, as we have seen, was immediately evocative of one of the most violent days in American history; with such violence (and more) to be found in the real world, it should not be surprising to find a demand for its realistic representation in our entertainment. Here the difference between Nicholson's and Ledger's Jokers comes back into play, for Ledger's Joker is very much a reflection of the terroristic violence of our times. Simply stated, Ledger's Joker is a terrorist, and as such he raises an important question that is explicitly presented in the movie—namely, how can a society fight terrorism without becoming terroristic itself?

Batman: The Dark Knight both reflects and addresses this larger cultural dilemma by dramatizing the choices that civilized societies must make when battling enemies who do not seem to respect any limits. Thus, while Batman is willing to break some rules to fight the Joker, he is not willing to kill him when he has him at his mercy (the Joker even anticipates this as he dares Batman to kill him and so become like the Joker himself). Reflecting the dilemma that Americans face when confronted by shadowy organizations like al-Qaeda, *Batman: The Dark Knight* is ultimately a profoundly *political* film that raises questions about the conduct of America's war on terror.

The fact that *Batman: The Dark Knight* contains both "official" and "outlaw" heroes, however, strongly indicates that it does not intend to subvert that war. As Robert B. Ray argues in "The Thematic Paradigm" (included in Chapter 6 of this book), an official hero is someone who serves and protects society from within its institutions. As the district attorney of Gotham City, Harvey Dent is just such a hero. His courageous war on the mob differentiates him from the bumbling and/or corrupt officials in Tim Burton's *Batman*, a difference that reflects the general rehabilitation of official heroes after the 9/11 terror attacks (such television series as the *CSI* franchise, *Criminal Minds*, and any show featuring sympathetic cops, FBI agents, or any other branch of law enforcement are all signifiers of this return to the official hero in popular culture). That Harvey Dent is eventually corrupted to become Two Face does not really contradict this because the audience can see that he has a very strong motive for going "bad," and he is only after those who have hurt him (which much ameliorates his change). What is more, we see plenty of other officials in the movie who are innocent victims of the Joker (for example, the chief of police and a judge), and, in the end, it is Batman who decides that the people of Gotham City *need* an official hero, and so conspires to conceal the truth about Harvey Dent / Two Face and take the blame for Two Face's deeds so that the people will not become overwhelmed with despair and disillusionment.

Batman himself is what Ray calls an "outlaw hero," someone who may serve and protect society, but only on his or her own terms, even if this means breaking the law. Batman is a pure outlaw hero, in that he has no official connection with law enforcement, while figures like Dirty Harry and Jack Bauer (of *24*) are outlaw heroes who work for official law enforcement institutions. Outlaw heroes have been steadily gaining favor over official heroes in American popular culture ever since the cultural revolution of the 1960s, which dethroned most if not all of America's traditional official heroes and replaced them with a variety of outlaw heroes. It was this shift that vaulted Batman over Superman in the 1980s as America's favorite cartoon superhero.

Interestingly, in *Batman: The Dark Knight* the official hero and the outlaw hero are symbolically *combined* when Dent declares during a press conference that *he* is Batman. This union of official and outlaw hero offers a satisfying mediation of the conflict between the two heroic types in the post–9/11 era, when Americans have turned once more to official heroes like police, firefighters, Homeland Security personnel, and soldiers, while not abandoning the outlaw heroes made popular by the cultural revolution.

Thus, the evidence is that *Batman: The Dark Knight* does not represent a metaphoric challenge to the war on terror. Rather, it reassures its audience in troubling times that they have not been abandoned. Heroic men and women are on the case, fighting for the rest of us. It's all rather sentimental and unrealistic — in short, a fantasy — but as a popular expression of American angst and desire in an era of unprecedented conflict, this *Batman* is no mere entertainment. It is a sign of a society desperately in need of cathartic reassurance in times that often seem apocalyptic.

The Readings

Linda Seger's how-to guide for the creation of the kind of archetypal characters that made *Star Wars* one of the most popular movies of all time opens this chapter's readings. A paired set of readings follow, in which Jessica Hagedorn surveys a tradition of American filmmaking that stereotypes Asian women as either tragic or trivial, and Helena Andrews compares the critical reactions to *The Butler* and *The Help*, revealing how complicated attitudes toward race and gender have affected the two films' receptions. Matt Zoller Seitz is next with a critical exposé of cinema's "'Magical Negro': a saintly African-American character who acts as a mentor to a questing white hero." Michael Parenti then takes a social-class-based approach to the codes of American cinema, noting the caste biases inherent in such popular hits as *Pretty Woman*, while David Denby explains in "High-School Confidential" why generations of teenagers flock to all those jocks-and-cheerleaders-versus-the-nerds movies. Michael Agresta surveys the rise and fall of the once-mighty Western, a genre that even *The Lone Ranger* (not to mention Johnny Depp) has been unable to save as America comes to terms with its own history. And Christine Folch concludes the chapter with an analysis of the cultural differences that make sci-fi and fantasy movies all the rage in America but nothing special in India.

LINDA SEGER

Creating the Myth

To be a successful screenwriter, Linda Seger suggests in this selection from *Making a Good Script Great* (1987), you've got to know your archetypes. Seger reveals the secret behind the success of such Hollywood creations as *Star Wars'* Luke Skywalker and tells you how you can create such heroes yourself. In this how-to approach to the cinema, Seger echoes the more academic judgments of such semioticians of film as Umberto Eco — the road to popular success in mass culture is paved with cultural myths and clichés. A script consultant and author who has given professional seminars on filmmaking around the world, Seger has also published *Creating Unforgettable Characters* (1990), *When Women Call the Shots: The Developing Power and Influence of Women in Television and Film* (1996), and *Writing Subtext: What Lies Beneath* (2011).

All of us have similar experiences. We share in the life journey of growth, development, and transformation. We live the same stories, whether they involve the search for a perfect mate, coming home, the search for fulfillment, going after an ideal, achieving the dream, or hunting for a precious treasure. Whatever our culture, there are universal stories that form the basis for all our particular stories. The trappings might be different, the twists and turns that create suspense might change from culture to culture, the particular characters may take different forms, but underneath it all, it's the same story, drawn from the same experiences.

Many of the most successful films are based on these universal stories. They deal with the basic journey we take in life. We identify with the heroes because we were once heroic (descriptive) or because we wish we could do what the hero does (prescriptive). When Joan Wilder finds the jewel and saves her sister, or James Bond saves the world, or Shane saves the family from the evil ranchers, we identify with the character, and subconsciously recognize the story as having some connection with our own lives. It's the same story as the fairy tales about getting the three golden hairs from the devil, or finding the treasure and winning the princess. And it's not all that different a story from the caveman killing the woolly beast or the Roman slave gaining his freedom through skill and courage. These are our stories — personally and collectively — and the most successful films contain these universal experiences.

e macmillanhighered.com/signsoflife
How do B-movies critique society?
e-readings > **Louis J. Gasnier and Arthur Hoerl,** *Reefer Madness* [film clip]
George A. Romero and John A. Russo, *Night of the Living Dead* [film clip]

Some of these stories are "search" stories. They address our desire to find some kind of rare and wonderful treasure. This might include the search for outer values such as job, relationship, or success; or for inner values such as respect, security, self-expression, love, or home. But it's all a similar search.

Some of these stories are "hero" stories. They come from our own experiences of overcoming adversity, as well as our desire to do great and special acts. We root for the hero and celebrate when he or she achieves the goal because we know that the hero's journey is in many ways similar to our own.

We call these stories *myths*. Myths are the common stories at the root of 5 our universal existence. They're found in all cultures and in all literature, ranging from the Greek myths to fairy tales, legends, and stories drawn from all of the world's religions.

A myth is a story that is "more than true." Many stories are true because one person, somewhere, at some time, lived it. It is based on fact. But a myth is more than true because it is lived by all of us, at some level. It's a story that connects and speaks to us all.

Some myths are true stories that attain mythic significance because the people involved seem larger than life, and seem to live their lives more intensely than common folk. Martin Luther King, Jr., Gandhi, Sir Edmund Hillary, and Lord Mountbatten personify the types of journeys we identify with, because we've taken similar journeys — even if only in a very small way.

Other myths revolve around make-believe characters who might capsulize for us the sum total of many of our journeys. Some of these make-believe characters might seem similar to the characters we meet in our dreams. Or they might be a composite of types of characters we've met.

In both cases, the myth is the "story beneath the story." It's the universal pattern that shows us that Gandhi's journey toward independence and Sir Edmund Hillary's journey to the top of Mount Everest contain many of the same dramatic beats. And these beats are the same beats that Rambo takes to set free the MIAs, that Indiana Jones takes to find the Lost Ark, and that Luke Skywalker takes to defeat the Evil Empire.

In *Hero with a Thousand Faces*, Joseph Campbell traces the elements that 10 form the hero myth. In their own work with myth, writer Chris Vogler and seminar leader Thomas Schlesinger have applied this criteria to *Star Wars*. The myth within the story helps explain why millions went to see this film again and again.

The hero myth has specific story beats that occur in all hero stories. They show who the hero is, what the hero needs, and how the story and character interact in order to create a transformation. The journey toward heroism is a process. This universal process forms the spine of all the particular stories, such as the *Star Wars* trilogy.

The Hero Myth

1. In most hero stories, the hero is introduced in ordinary surroundings, in a mundane world, doing mundane things. Generally, the hero begins as a

Star Wars, 1977.

nonhero; innocent, young, simple, or humble. In *Star Wars*, the first time we see Luke Skywalker, he's unhappy about having to do his chores, which consist of picking out some new droids for work. He wants to go out and have fun. He wants to leave his planet and go to the Academy, but he's stuck. This is the setup of most myths. This is how we meet the hero before the call to adventure.

2. Then something new enters the hero's life. It's a catalyst that sets the story into motion. It might be a telephone call, as in *Romancing the Stone*, or the German attack in *The African Queen*, or the holograph of Princess Leia in *Star Wars*. Whatever form it takes, it's a new ingredient that pushes the hero into an extraordinary adventure. With this call, the stakes are established, and a problem is introduced that demands a solution.

3. Many times, however, the hero doesn't want to leave. He or she is a reluctant hero, afraid of the unknown, uncertain, perhaps, if he or she is up to the challenge. In *Star Wars*, Luke receives a double call to adventure. First, from Princess Leia in the holograph, and then through Obi-Wan Kenobi, who says he needs Luke's help. But Luke is not ready to go. He returns home, only to find that the Imperial Stormtroopers have burned his farmhouse and slaughtered his family. Now he is personally motivated, ready to enter into the adventure.

4. In any journey, the hero usually receives help, and the help often 15 comes from unusual sources. In many fairy tales, an old woman, a dwarf, a witch, or a wizard helps the hero. The hero achieves the goal because of this help, and because the hero is receptive to what this person has to give.

There are a number of fairy tales where the first and second sons are sent to complete a task, but they ignore the helpers, often scorning them. Many times they are severely punished for their lack of humility and unwillingness to accept help. Then the third son, the hero, comes along. He receives the help, accomplishes the task, and often wins the princess.

In *Star Wars*, Obi-Wan Kenobi is a perfect example of the "helper" character. He is a kind of mentor to Luke, one who teaches him the Way of the Force and whose teachings continue even after his death. This mentor character appears in most hero stories. He is the person who has special knowledge, special information, and special skills. This might be the prospector in *The Treasure of the Sierra Madre*, or the psychiatrist in *Ordinary People*, or Quint in *Jaws*, who knows all about sharks, or the Good Witch of the North who gives Dorothy the ruby slippers in *The Wizard of Oz*. In *Star Wars*, Obi-Wan gives Luke the light saber that was the special weapon of the Jedi Knight. With this, Luke is ready to move forward and do his training and meet adventure.

5. The hero is now ready to move into the special world where he or she will change from the ordinary into the extraordinary. This starts the hero's transformation, and sets up the obstacles that must be surmounted to reach the goal. Usually, this happens at the first Turning Point of the story, and leads into Act Two development. In *Star Wars*, Obi-Wan and Luke search for a pilot to take them to the planet of Alderaan, so that Obi-Wan can deliver the plans to Princess Leia's father. These plans are essential to the survival of the Rebel Forces. With this action, the adventure is ready to begin.

6. Now begin all the tests and obstacles necessary to overcome the enemy and accomplish the hero's goals. In fairy tales, this often means getting past witches, outwitting the devil, avoiding robbers, or confronting evil. In Homer's *Odyssey*, it means blinding the Cyclops, escaping from the island of the Lotus-Eaters, resisting the temptation of the singing Sirens, and surviving a shipwreck. In *Star Wars*, innumerable adventures confront Luke. He and his cohorts must run to the *Millennium Falcon*, narrowly escaping the Stormtroopers before jumping into hyperspace. They must make it through the meteor shower after Alderaan has been destroyed. They must evade capture on the Death Star, rescue the Princess, and even survive a garbage crusher.

7. At some point in the story, the hero often hits rock bottom. He often [20] has a "death experience," leading to a type of rebirth. In *Star Wars*, Luke seems to have died when the serpent in the garbage-masher pulls him under, but he's saved just in time to ask R2D2 to stop the masher before they're crushed. This is often the "black moment" at the second turning point, the point when the worst is confronted, and the action now moves toward the exciting conclusion.

8. Now, the hero seizes the sword and takes possession of the treasure. He is now in charge, but he still has not completed the journey. Here Luke has the Princess and the plans, but the final confrontation is yet to begin. This starts the third-act escape scene, leading to the final climax.

9. The road back is often the chase scene. In many fairy tales, this is the point where the devil chases the hero and the hero has last obstacles to overcome before really being free and safe. His challenge is to take what he has learned and integrate it into his daily life. He *must* return to renew the

mundane world. In *Star Wars*, Darth Vader is in hot pursuit, planning to blow up the Rebel Planet.

10. Since every hero story is essentially a transformation story, we need to see the hero changed at the end, resurrected into a new type of life. He must face the final ordeal before being "reborn" as the hero, proving his courage and becoming transformed. This is the point, in many fairy tales, where the Miller's Son becomes the Prince or the King and marries the Princess. In *Star Wars*, Luke has survived, becoming quite a different person from the innocent young man he was in Act One.

At this point, the hero returns and is reintegrated into his society. In *Star Wars*, Luke has destroyed the Death Star, and he receives his great reward.

This is the classic "Hero Story." We might call this example a *mission* or *task* 25 *myth*, where the person has to complete a task, but the task itself is not the real treasure. The real reward for Luke is the love of the Princess and the safe, new world he had helped create.

A myth can have many variations. We see variations on this myth in James Bond films (although they lack much of the depth because the hero is not transformed), and in *The African Queen*, where Rose and Allnutt must blow up the *Louisa*, or in *Places in the Heart*, where Edna overcomes obstacles to achieve family stability.

The *treasure myth* is another variation on this theme, as seen in *Romancing the Stone*. In this story, Joan receives a map and a phone call which forces her into the adventure. She is helped by an American birdcatcher and a Mexican pickup-truck driver. She overcomes the obstacles of snakes, the jungle, waterfalls, shootouts, and finally receives the treasure, along with the "prince."

Whether the hero's journey is for a treasure or to complete a task, the elements remain the same. The humble, reluctant hero is called to an adventure. The hero is helped by a variety of unique characters. S/he must overcome a series of obstacles that transform him or her in the process, and then face the final challenge that draws on inner and outer resources.

The Healing Myth

Although the hero myth is the most popular story, many myths involve healing. In these stories, some character is "broken" and must leave home to become whole again.

The universal experience behind these healing stories is our psychological 30 need for rejuvenation, for balance. The journey of the hero into exile is not all that different from the weekend in Palm Springs, or the trip to Hawaii to get away from it all, or lying still in a hospital bed for some weeks to heal. In all cases, something is out of balance and the mythic journey moves toward wholeness.

Being broken can take several forms. It can be physical, emotional, or psychological. Usually, it's all three. In the process of being exiled or hiding out in the forest, the desert, or even the Amish farm in *Witness*, the person becomes whole, balanced, and receptive to love. Love in these stories is both a healing force and a reward.

Think of John Book in *Witness*. In Act One, we see a frenetic, insensitive man, afraid of commitment, critical and unreceptive to the feminine influences in his life. John is suffering from an "inner wound" which he doesn't know about. When he receives an "outer wound" from a gunshot, it forces him into exile, which begins his process of transformation.

At the beginning of Act Two, we see John delirious and close to death. This is a movement into the unconscious, a movement from the rational, active police life of Act One into a mysterious, feminine, more intuitive world. Since John's "inner problem" is the lack of balance with his feminine side, this delirium begins the process of transformation.

Later in Act Two, we see John beginning to change. He moves from his highly independent lifestyle toward the collective, communal life of his Amish hosts. John now gets up early to milk the cows and to assist with the chores. He uses his carpentry skills to help with the barn building and to complete the birdhouse. Gradually, he begins to develop relationships with Rachel and her son, Samuel. John's life slows down and he becomes more receptive, learning important lessons about love. In Act Three, John finally sees that the feminine is worth saving, and throws down his gun to save Rachel's life. A few beats later, when he has the opportunity to kill Paul, he chooses a nonviolent response instead. Although John doesn't "win" the Princess, he has nevertheless "won" love and wholeness. By the end of the film, we can see that the John Book of Act Three is a different kind of person from the John Book of Act One. He has a different kind of comradeship with his fellow police officers, he's more relaxed, and we can sense that somehow, this experience has formed a more integrated John Book.

Combination Myths

Many stories are combinations of several different myths. Think of *Ghost-* 35 *busters*, a simple and rather outrageous comedy about three men saving the city of New York from ghosts. Now think of the story of "Pandora's Box." It's about the woman who let loose all manner of evil upon the earth by opening a box she was told not to touch. In *Ghostbusters*, the EPA man is a Pandora figure. By shutting off the power to the containment center, he inadvertently unleashes all the ghosts upon New York City. Combine the story of "Pandora's Box" with a hero story, and notice that we have our three heroes battling the Marshmallow Man. One of them also "gets the Princess" when Dr. Peter Venkman finally receives the affections of Dana Barrett. By looking at these combinations, it is apparent that even *Ghostbusters* is more than "just a comedy."

Tootsie is a type of reworking of many Shakespearean stories where a woman has to dress as a man in order to accomplish a certain task. These Shakespearean stories are reminiscent of many fairy tales where the hero becomes invisible or takes on another persona, or wears a specific disguise to hide his or her real qualities. In the stories of "The Twelve Dancing Princesses" or "The Man in the Bearskin," disguise is necessary to achieve a goal. Combine these elements with the transformation themes of the hero myth where a hero (such as Michael) must overcome many obstacles to his success as an actor and a human being. It's not difficult to understand why the *Tootsie* story hooks us.

Archetypes

A myth includes certain characters that we see in many stories. These characters are called *archetypes*. They can be thought of as the original "pattern" or "character type" that will be found on the hero's journey. Archetypes take many forms, but they tend to fall within specific categories.

Earlier, we discussed some of the helpers who give advice to help the hero—such as the *wise old man* who possesses special knowledge and often serves as a mentor to the hero.

The female counterpart of the wise old man is the *good mother*. Whereas the wise old man has superior knowledge, the good mother is known for her nurturing qualities, and for her intuition. This figure often gives the hero particular objects to help on the journey. It might be a protective amulet, or the ruby slippers that Dorothy receives in *The Wizard of Oz* from the Good Witch of the North. Sometimes in fairy tales it's a cloak to make the person invisible, or ordinary objects that become extraordinary, as in "The Girl of Courage," an Afghan fairy tale about a maiden who receives a comb, a whetstone, and a mirror to help defeat the devil.

Many myths contain a *shadow figure*. This is a character who is the opposite of the hero. Sometimes this figure helps the hero on the journey; other times this figure opposes the hero. The shadow figure can be the negative side of the hero which could be the dark and hostile brother in "Cain and Abel," the stepsisters in "Cinderella," or the Robber Girl in "The Snow Queen." The shadow figure can also help the hero, as the whore with the heart of gold who saves the hero's life, or provides balance to his idealization of woman. 40

Many myths contain *animal archetypes* that can be positive or negative figures. In "St. George and the Dragon," the dragon is the negative force which is a violent and ravaging animal, not unlike the shark in *Jaws*. But in many stories, animals help the hero. Sometimes there are talking donkeys, or a dolphin which saves the hero, or magical horses or dogs.

The *trickster* is a mischievous archetypical figure who is always causing chaos, disturbing the peace, and generally being an anarchist. The trickster uses wit and cunning to achieve his or her ends. Sometimes the trickster is a harmless prankster or a "bad boy" who is funny and enjoyable. More often, the trickster is a con man, as in *The Sting*, or the devil, as in *The Exorcist*, who demanded all the skills of the priest to outwit him. The "Till Eulenspiegel" stories revolve around the trickster, as do the Spanish picaresque novels. Even the tales of Tom Sawyer have a trickster motif. In all countries, there are stories that revolve around this figure, whose job it is to outwit.

"Mythic" Problems and Solutions

We all grew up with myths. Most of us heard or read fairy tales when we were young. Some of us may have read Bible stories, or stories from other religions or other cultures. These stories are part of us. And the best way to work with them is to let them come out naturally as you write the script.

Of course, some filmmakers are better at this than others. George Lucas and Steven Spielberg have a strong sense of myth and incorporate it into their films. They both have spoken about their love of the stories from childhood, and of their desire to bring these types of stories to audiences. Their stories create some of the same sense of wonder and excitement as myths. Many of the necessary psychological beats are part of their stories, deepening the story beyond the ordinary action-adventure.

Myths bring depth to a hero story. If a filmmaker is thinking only about 45 the action and excitement of a story, audiences might fail to connect with the hero's journey. But if the basic beats of the hero's journey are evident, a film will often inexplicably draw audiences, in spite of critics' responses to the film.

Take *Rambo*, for instance. Why was this violent, simple story so popular with audiences? I don't think it was because everyone agreed with its politics. I do think Sylvester Stallone is a master at incorporating the American myth into his filmmaking. That doesn't mean it's done consciously. Somehow he is naturally in sync with the myth, and the myth becomes integrated into his stories.

Clint Eastwood also does hero stories, and gives us the adventure of the myth and the transformation of the myth. . . . Eastwood's films have given more attention to the transformation of the hero, and have been receiving more serious critical attention as a result.

All of these filmmakers — Lucas, Spielberg, Stallone, and Eastwood — dramatize the hero myth in their own particular ways. And all of them prove that myths are marketable.

Application

It is an important part of the writer's or producer's work to continually find opportunities for deepening the themes within a script. Finding the myth beneath the modern story is part of that process.

To find these myths, it's not a bad idea to reread some of Grimm's fairy 50 tales or fairy tales from around the world to begin to get acquainted with various myths. You'll start to see patterns and elements that connect with our own human experience.

Also, read Joseph Campbell and Greek mythology. If you're interested in Jungian psychology, you'll find many rich resources within a number of books on the subject. Since Jungian psychology deals with archetypes, you'll find many new characters to draw on for your own work.

With all of these resources to incorporate, it's important to remember that the myth is not a story to force upon a script. It's more a pattern which you can bring out in your own stories when they seem to be heading in the direction of a myth.

As you work, ask yourself:

Do I have a myth working in my script? If so, what beats am I using of the hero's journey? Which ones seem to be missing?

Am I missing characters? Do I need a mentor type? A wise old man? A wizard? Would one of these characters help dimensionalize the hero's journey?

Could I create new emotional dimensions to the myth by starting my character as reluctant, naïve, simple, or decidedly "unheroic"?

Does my character get transformed in the process of the journey?

Have I used a strong three-act structure to support the myth, using the first turning point to move into the adventure and the second turning point to create a dark moment, or a reversal, or even a "near-death" experience?

Don't be afraid to create variations on the myth, but don't start with the myth itself. Let the myth grow naturally from your story. Developing myths is part of the rewriting process. If you begin with the myth, you'll find your writing becomes rigid, uncreative, and predictable. Working with the myth in the rewriting process will deepen your script, giving it new life as you find the story within the story.

READING THE TEXT

1. How does Seger define the "hero myth" (para. 11)?
2. In your own words, explain what Seger means by "the healing myth" (para. 29).
3. What is an "archetype" in film (para. 37)?

READING THE SIGNS

1. Seger is writing to aspiring screenwriters. How does her status as an industry insider affect her description of heroic archetypes?
2. **CONNECTING TEXTS** Focusing on gender issues, compare Seger's formulation of heroes with Robert B. Ray's in "The Thematic Paradigm" (p. 450). To what extent do Seger and Ray adequately explain the role of women — and men — in movies?

3. **CONNECTING TEXTS**   Review Michael Parenti's "Class and Virtue" (p. 361), and write an essay identifying the myths behind the modern story *Pretty Woman* (1990) or *Juno* (2007).

4. Watch *Titanic* or a segment of the *Lord of the Rings* trilogy, and write an essay in which you explain the myths and archetypal characters the film includes. How might archetypal and mythic patterns explain the film's success?

5. Seger recommends that aspiring screenwriters read Grimm's fairy tales for inspiration. You can find them online. Read some of Grimm's tales, and then write an argument assessing the suitability of such tales as inspiration for films today.

6. Watch one of the *Hunger Games* films, focusing particularly on character types. In an essay, analyze the film's use of archetypes. To what extent does it replicate, reinvent, or otherwise complicate archetypal characters?

GENDER AND RACE IN FILM

JESSICA HAGEDORN

Asian Women in Film: No Joy, No Luck

Why do movies always seem to portray Asian women as tragic victims of history and fate? Jessica Hagedorn asks in this essay, which originally appeared in *Ms.* Even such movies as *The Joy Luck Club*, based on Amy Tan's breakthrough novel that elevated Asian American fiction to best-seller status, reinforce old stereotypes of the powerlessness of Asian and Asian American women. A screenwriter and novelist, Hagedorn calls for a different kind of storytelling that would show Asian women as powerful controllers of their own destinies. Jessica Hagedorn's publications include the novels *Dogeaters* (1990), *The Gangster of Love* (1996), *Dream Jungle* (2003), and *Toxicology* (2011); *Danger and Beauty* (1993), a collection of poems; *Fresh Kill* (1994), a screenplay; and *Charlie Chan Is Dead 2: At Home in the World* (2004) and *Manila Noir* (2013) (as editor).

Pearl of the Orient. Whore. Geisha. Concubine. Whore. Hostess. Bar Girl. Mamasan. Whore. China Doll. Tokyo Rose. Whore. Butterfly. Whore. Miss Saigon. Whore. Dragon Lady. Lotus Blossom. Gook. Whore. Yellow Peril. Whore. Bangkok Bombshell. Whore. Hospitality Girl. Whore. Comfort Woman. Whore. Savage. Whore. Sultry. Whore. Faceless. Whore. Porcelain. Whore. Demure. Whore. Virgin. Whore. Mute. Whore. Model Minority. Whore. Victim. Whore. Woman Warrior. Whore. Mail-Order Bride. Whore. Mother. Wife. Lover. Daughter. Sister.

As I was growing up in the Philippines in the 1950s, my fertile imagination was colonized by thoroughly American fantasies. Yellowface variations on the exotic erotic loomed larger than life on the silver screen. I was mystified and enthralled by Hollywood's skewed representations of Asian women: sleek, evil goddesses with slanted eyes and cunning ways, or smiling, sarong-clad South Seas "maidens" with undulating hips, kinky black hair, and white skin darkened by makeup. Hardly any of the "Asian" characters were played by Asians. White actors like Sidney Toler and Warner Oland played "inscrutable Oriental detective" Charlie Chan with taped eyelids and a singsong, chop suey accent. Jennifer Jones was a Eurasian doctor swept up in a doomed "interracial romance" in *Love Is a Many Splendored Thing*. In my mother's youth, white actor Luise Rainer played the central role of the Patient Chinese Wife in the 1937 film adaptation of Pearl Buck's novel *The Good Earth*. Back then, not many thought to ask why; they were all too busy being grateful to see anyone in the movies remotely like themselves.

Cut to 1960: *The World of Suzie Wong*, another tragic East/West affair. I am now old enough to be impressed. Sexy, sassy Suzie (played by Nancy Kwan) works out of a bar patronized by white sailors, but doesn't seem bothered by any of it. For a hardworking girl turning nightly tricks to support her baby, she manages to parade an astonishing wardrobe in damn near every scene, down to matching handbags and shoes. The sailors are also strictly Hollywood, sanitized and not too menacing. Suzie and all the other prostitutes in this movie are cute, giggling, dancing sex machines with hearts of gold. William Holden plays an earnest, rather prim, Nice Guy painter seeking inspiration in The Other. Of course, Suzie falls madly in love with him. Typically, she tells him, "I not important," and "I'll be with you until you say—Suzie, go away." She also thinks being beaten by a man is a sign of true passion and is terribly disappointed when Mr. Nice Guy refuses to show his true feelings.

Next in Kwan's short-lived but memorable career was the kitschy 1961 musical *Flower Drum Song*, which, like *Suzie Wong*, is a thoroughly American commercial product. The female roles are typical of Hollywood musicals of the times: women are basically airheads, subservient to men. Kwan's counterpart is the Good Chinese Girl, played by Miyoshi Umeki, who was better playing the Loyal Japanese Girl in that other classic Hollywood tale of forbidden love, *Sayonara*. Remember? Umeki was so loyal, she committed double suicide with actor Red Buttons. I instinctively hated *Sayonara* when I first saw it as a child; now I understand why. Contrived tragic resolutions were the only way Hollywood got past the censors in those days. With one or two exceptions, somebody in these movies always had to die to pay for breaking racial and sexual taboos.

Until the recent onslaught of films by both Asian and Asian American filmmakers, Asian Pacific women have generally been perceived by Hollywood with a mixture of fascination, fear, and contempt. Most Hollywood movies either trivialize or exoticize us as people of color and as women. Our intelligence is underestimated, our humanity overlooked, and our diverse cultures treated as interchangeable. If we are "good," we are childlike, submissive, silent, and eager for sex (see France Nuyen's glowing performance as

Liat in the film version of *South Pacific*) or else we are tragic victim types (see *Casualties of War*, Brian De Palma's graphic 1989 drama set in Vietnam). And if we are not silent, suffering doormats, we are demonized dragon ladies—cunning, deceitful, sexual provocateurs. Give me the demonic any day—Anna May Wong as a villain slithering around in a slinky gown is at least gratifying to watch, neither servile nor passive. And she steals the show from Marlene Dietrich in Josef von Sternberg's *Shanghai Express*. From the 1920s through the 1930s, Wong was our only female "star." But even she was trapped in limited roles, in what filmmaker Renee Tajima has called the dragon lady/lotus blossom dichotomy.

Cut to 1985: There is a scene toward the end of the terribly dishonest but weirdly compelling Michael Cimino movie *Year of the Dragon* (cowritten by Oliver Stone) that is one of my favorite twisted movie moments of all time. If you ask a lot of my friends who've seen that movie (especially if they're Asian), it's one of their favorites too. The setting is a crowded Chinatown nightclub. There are two very young and very tough Jade Cobra gang girls in a shoot-out with Mickey Rourke, in the role of a demented Polish American cop who, in spite of being Mr. Ugly in the flesh—an arrogant, misogynistic bully devoid of any charm—wins the "good" Asian American anchorwoman in the film's absurd and implausible ending. This is a movie with an actual disclaimer as its lead-in, covering its ass in advance in response to anticipated complaints about "stereotypes."

My pleasure in the hard-edged power of the Chinatown gang girls in *Year of the Dragon* is my small revenge, the answer to all those Suzie Wong "I want to be your slave" female characters. The Jade Cobra girls are mere background to the white male foreground/focus of Cimino's movie. But long after the movie has faded into video-rental heaven, the Jade Cobra girls remain defiant, fabulous images in my memory, flaunting tight metallic dresses and spiky cock's-comb hairdos streaked electric red and blue.

Mickey Rourke looks down with world-weary pity at the unnamed Jade Cobra
    girl (Doreen Chan) he's just shot who lies sprawled and bleeding on the
    street: "You look like you're gonna die, beautiful."
JADE COBRA GIRL: "Oh yeah? [blood gushing from her mouth] I'm proud of it."
ROURKE: "You are? You got anything you wanna tell me before you go, sweet-
    heart?"
JADE COBRA GIRL: "Yeah. [pause] Fuck you."

Cut to 1993: I've been told that like many New Yorkers, I watch movies with the right side of my brain on perpetual overdrive. I admit to being grouchy and overcritical, suspicious of sentiment, and cynical. When a critic like Richard Corliss of *Time* magazine gushes about *The Joy Luck Club* being "a fourfold *Terms of Endearment*," my gut instinct is to run the other way. I resent being told how to feel. I went to see the 1993 eight-handkerchief movie version of Amy Tan's bestseller with a group that included my ten-year-old

Anna May Wong.

daughter. I was caught between the sincere desire to be swept up by the turbulent mother-daughter sagas and my own stubborn resistance to being so obviously manipulated by the filmmakers. With every flashback came tragedy. The music soared; the voice-overs were solemn or wistful; tears, tears, and more tears flowed on-screen. Daughters were reverent; mothers carried dark secrets.

I was elated by the grandness and strength of the four mothers and the luminous actors who portrayed them, but I was uneasy with the passivity of the Asian American daughters. They seemed to exist solely as receptors for

Michelle Yeoh, *Tomorrow Never Dies*, 1997.

their mothers' amazing life stories. It's almost as if by assimilating so easily into American society, they had lost all sense of self.

In spite of my resistance, my eyes watered as the desperate mother played by Kieu Chinh was forced to abandon her twin baby girls on a country road in war-torn China. (Kieu Chinh resembles my own mother and her twin sister, who suffered through the brutal Japanese occupation of the Philippines.) So far in this movie, an infant son had been deliberately drowned, a mother played by the gravely beautiful France Nuyen had gone catatonic with grief, a concubine had cut her flesh open to save her dying mother, an insecure daughter had been oppressed by her boorish Asian American husband, another insecure daughter had been left by her white husband, and so on. . . . The overall effect was numbing as far as I'm concerned, but a man sitting two rows in front of us broke down sobbing. A Chinese Filipino writer even more grouchy than me later complained, "Must ethnicity only be equated with suffering?"

Because change has been slow, *The Joy Luck Club* carries a lot of cultural baggage. It is a big-budget story about Chinese American women, directed by a Chinese American man, cowritten and coproduced by Chinese American women. That's a lot to be thankful for. And its box office success proves that an immigrant narrative told from female perspectives can have mass appeal. But my cynical side tells me that its success might mean only one thing in Hollywood: more weepy epics about Asian American mother-daughter relationships will be planned.

That the film finally got made was significant. By Hollywood standards (think white male; think money, money, money), a movie about Asian Americans even when adapted from a bestseller was a risky proposition. When I asked a producer I know about the film's rumored delays, he simply said, "It's still an *Asian* movie," surprised I had even asked. Equally interesting was director Wayne Wang's initial reluctance to be involved in the project; he told the *New York Times*, "I didn't want to do another Chinese movie."

Maybe he shouldn't have worried so much. After all, according to the media, the nineties are the decade of "Pacific Overtures" and East Asian chic. Madonna, the pop queen of shameless appropriation, cultivated Japanese high-tech style with her music video "Rain," while Janet Jackson faked kitschy orientalia in hers, titled "If." Critical attention was paid to movies from China, Japan, and Vietnam. But that didn't mean an honest appraisal of women's lives. Even on the art house circuit, filmmakers who should know better took the easy way out. Takehiro Nakajima's 1992 film *Okoge* presents one of the more original film roles for women in recent years. In Japanese, "okoge" means the crust of rice that sticks to the bottom of the rice pot; in pejorative slang, it means fag hag. The way "okoge" is used in the film seems a reappropriation of the term; the portrait Nakajima creates of Sayoko, the so-called fag hag, is clearly an affectionate one. Sayoko is a quirky, self-assured woman in contemporary Tokyo who does voice-overs for cartoons, has a thing for Frida Kahlo paintings, and is drawn to a gentle young gay man named Goh. But the other women's roles are disappointing, stereotypical "hysterical females" and the movie itself turns conventional halfway through. Sayoko sacrifices herself to a macho brute Goh desires, who rapes her as images of Frida Kahlo paintings and her beloved Goh rising from the ocean flash before her. She gives birth to a baby boy and endures a terrible life of poverty with the abusive rapist. This sudden change from spunky survivor to helpless, victimized woman is baffling. Whatever happened to her job? Or that arty little apartment of hers? Didn't her Frida Kahlo obsession teach her anything?

Then there was Tiana Thi Thanh Nga's *From Hollywood to Hanoi*, a self-serving but fascinating documentary. Born in Vietnam to a privileged family that included an uncle who was defense minister in the Thieu government and an idolized father who served as press minister, Nga (a.k.a. Tiana) spent her adolescence in California. A former actor in martial arts movies and fitness teacher ("Karaticize with Tiana"), the vivacious Tiana decided to make a record of her journey back to Vietnam.

From Hollywood to Hanoi is at times unintentionally very funny. Tiana 15 includes a quick scene of herself dancing with a white man at the Metropole hotel in Hanoi, and breathlessly announces: "That's me doing the tango with Oliver Stone!" Then she listens sympathetically to a horrifying account of the My Lai massacre by one of its few female survivors. In another scene, Tiana cheerfully addresses a food vendor on the streets of Hanoi: "Your hairdo is so pretty." The unimpressed, poker-faced woman gives a brusque, deadpan reply: "You want to eat, or what?" Sometimes it is hard to tell the difference between Tiana Thi Thanh Nga and her Hollywood persona: The real Tiana still seems to be playing one of her B-movie roles, which are mainly fun because they're fantasy. The time was certainly right to explore postwar Vietnam from a Vietnamese woman's perspective; it's too bad this film was done by a Valley Girl.

Nineteen ninety-three also brought Tran Anh Hung's *The Scent of Green Papaya*, a different kind of Vietnamese memento — this is a look back at the peaceful, lush country of the director's childhood memories. The film opens in Saigon, in 1951. A willowy ten-year-old girl named Mui comes to work for a troubled family headed by a melancholy musician and his kind, stoic wife. The men of this bourgeois household are idle, pampered types who take naps while the women do all the work. Mui is male fantasy: She is a devoted servant, enduring acts of cruel mischief with patience and dignity; as an adult, she barely speaks. She scrubs floors, shines shoes, and cooks with loving care and never a complaint. When she is sent off to work for another wealthy musician, she ends up being impregnated by him. The movie ends as the camera closes in on Mui's contented face. Languid and precious, *The Scent of Green Papaya* is visually haunting, but it suffers from the director's colonial fantasy of women as docile, domestic creatures. Steeped in highbrow nostalgia, it's the arty Vietnamese version of *My Fair Lady* with the wealthy musician as Professor Higgins, teaching Mui to read and write.

And then there is Ang Lee's tepid 1993 hit, *The Wedding Banquet* — a clever culture-clash farce in which traditional Chinese values collide with contemporary American sexual mores. The somewhat formulaic plot goes like this: Wai-Tung, a yuppie landlord, lives with his white lover, Simon, in a chic Manhattan brownstone. Wai-Tung is an only child and his aging parents in Taiwan long for a grandchild to continue the family legacy. Enter Wei-Wei, an artist who lives in a grungy loft owned by Wai-Tung. She slugs tequila straight from the bottle as she paints and flirts boldly with her young, uptight landlord, who brushes her off. "It's my fate. I am always attracted to handsome gay men," she mutters. After this setup, the movie goes downhill, all edges blurred in a cozy nest of happy endings. In a refrain of Sayoko's plight in *Okoge*, a pregnant, suddenly complacent Wei-Wei gives in to family pressures — and never gets her life back.

"It takes a man to know what it is to be a real woman."
— SONG LILING in *M. Butterfly*

Ironically, two gender-bending films in which men play men playing women reveal more about the mythology of the prized Asian woman and the superficial trappings of gender than most movies that star real women. The slow-moving *M. Butterfly* presents the ultimate object of Western male desire as the spy/opera diva Song Liling, a Suzie Wong/Lotus Blossom played by actor John Lone with a five o'clock shadow and bobbing Adam's apple. The best and most profound of these forays into cross-dressing is the spectacular melodrama *Farewell My Concubine*, directed by Chen Kaige. Banned in China, *Farewell My Concubine* shared the prize for Best Film at the 1993 Cannes Film Festival with Jane Campion's *The Piano*. Sweeping through fifty years of tumultuous history in China, the story revolves around the lives of two male Beijing Opera stars and the woman who marries one of them. The three characters make an unforgettable triangle, struggling over love, art, friendship, and politics against the bloody backdrop of cultural upheaval. They are as capable of casually betraying each other as they are of selfless, heroic acts. The androgynous Dieyi, doomed to play the same female role of concubine over and over again, is portrayed with great vulnerability, wit, and grace by male Hong Kong pop star Leslie Cheung. Dieyi competes with the prostitute Juxian (Gong Li) for the love of his childhood protector and fellow opera star, Duan Xiaolou (Zhang Fengyi).

Cheung's highly stylized performance as the classic concubine-ready-to-die-for-love in the opera within the movie is all about female artifice. His sidelong glances, restrained passion, languid stance, small steps, and delicate, refined gestures say everything about what is considered desirable in Asian women — and are the antithesis of the feisty, outspoken woman played by Gong Li. The characters of Dieyi and Juxian both see suffering as part and parcel of love and life. Juxian matter-of-factly says to Duan Xiaolou before he agrees to marry her: "I'm used to hardship. If you take me in, I'll wait on you hand and foot. If you tire of me, I'll . . . kill myself. No big deal." It's an echo of Suzie Wong's servility, but the context is new. Even with her back to the wall, Juxian is not helpless or whiny. She attempts to manipulate a man while admitting to the harsh reality that is her life.

Dieyi and Juxian are the two sides of the truth of women's lives in most 20 Asian countries. Juxian in particular — wife and ex-prostitute — could be seen as a thankless and stereotypical role. But like the characters Gong Li has played in Chinese director Zhang Yimou's films, *Red Sorghum*, *Raise the Red Lantern*, and especially *The Story of Qiu Ju*, Juxian is tough, obstinate, sensual, clever, oafish, beautiful, infuriating, cowardly, heroic, and banal. Above all, she is resilient. Gong Li is one of the few Asian Pacific actors whose roles have been drawn with intelligence, honesty, and depth. Nevertheless, the characters she plays are limited by the possibilities that exist for real women in China.

"Let's face it. Women still don't mean shit in China," my friend Meeling reminds me. What she says so bluntly about her culture rings painfully true, but in less obvious fashion for me. In the Philippines, infant girls aren't drowned, nor were their feet bound to make them more desirable. But sons were and are cherished. To this day, men of the bourgeois class are coddled and prized, much like the spoiled men of the elite household in *The Scent of Green Papaya*. We do not have a geisha tradition like Japan, but physical beauty is overtreasured. Our daughters are protected virgins or primed as potential beauty queens. And many of us have bought into the image of the white man as our handsome savior: G.I. Joe.

Buzz magazine recently featured an article entitled "Asian Women/L.A. Men," a report on a popular hangout that caters to white men's fantasies of nubile Thai women. The lines between movies and real life are blurred. Male screenwriters and cinematographers flock to this bar-restaurant, where the waitresses are eager to "audition" for roles. Many of these men have been to Bangkok while working on film crews for Vietnam War movies. They've come back to L.A., but for them, the movie never ends. In this particular fantasy the boys play G.I. Joe on a rescue mission in the urban jungle, saving the whore from herself. "A scene has developed here, a kind of R-rated *Cheers*," author Alan Rifkin writes. "The waitresses audition for sitcoms. The customers date the waitresses or just keep score."

Colonization of the imagination is a two-way street. And being enshrined on a pedestal as someone's Pearl of the Orient fantasy doesn't seem so demeaning, at first; who wouldn't want to be worshipped? Perhaps that's why Asian women are the ultimate wet dream in most Hollywood movies; it's no secret how well we've been taught to play the role, to take care of our men. In Hollywood vehicles, we are objects of desire or derision; we exist to provide sex, color, and texture in what is essentially a white man's world. It is akin to what Toni Morrison calls "the Africanist presence" in literature. She writes: "Just as entertainers, through or by association with blackface, could render permissible topics that otherwise would have been taboo, so American writers were able to employ an imagined Africanist persona to articulate and imaginatively act out the forbidden in American culture." The same analogy could be made for the often titillating presence of Asian women in movies made by white men.

Movies are still the most seductive and powerful of artistic mediums, manipulating us with ease by a powerful combination of sound and image. In many ways, as females and Asians, as audiences or performers, we have learned to settle for less — to accept the fact that we are either decorative, invisible, or one-dimensional. When there are characters who look like us represented in a movie, we have also learned to view between the lines, or to add what is missing. For many of us, this way of watching has always been a necessity. We fill in the gaps. If a female character is presented as a mute, willowy beauty, we convince ourselves she is an ancestral ghost — so smart she doesn't have to speak at all. If she is a whore with a heart of gold, we claim her as a tough feminist icon. If she is a sexless, sanitized, boring nerd, we embrace her as a role model for our daughters, rather than the tragic whore. And if she is presented as an utterly devoted saint suffering nobly in silence, we lie and say she is just like our mothers. Larger than life. Magical and insidious. A movie is never just a movie, after all.

READING THE TEXT

1. Summarize in your own words Hagedorn's view of the traditional images of Asian women as presented in American film.

2. What is the chronology of Asian women in film that Hagedorn presents, and why do you think she gives us a historical overview?

3. Why does Hagedorn say that the film *The Joy Luck Club* "carries a lot of cultural baggage" (para. 11)?

4. What sort of images of Asian women does Hagedorn imply that she would prefer to see?

READING THE SIGNS

1. Watch *The Joy Luck Club*, and write an essay in which you support, refute, or modify Hagedorn's interpretation of the film. Alternatively, view another film featuring Asian characters, such as *Better Luck Tomorrow* or *Gran Torino*, or a TV show with an Asian character, such as *The Big Bang Theory*, and use Hagedorn's article as a critical framework to evaluate your choice's representation of Asian characters.

2. **CONNECTING TEXTS** In class, form teams and debate the proposition that Hollywood writers and directors have a social responsibility to avoid stereotyping ethnic characters. To develop your team's arguments, brainstorm films that depict various ethnicities, and then discuss whether the portrayals are damaging or benign. You might also consult Michael Omi's "In Living Color: Race and American Culture" (p. 538).

3. Study a magazine that targets Asian American readers, such as *Tea*, *Hyphen*, or *Yolk*. Then write an essay in which you analyze whether Asian women in the magazine fit the stereotypes that Hagedorn describes, keeping in mind the magazine's intended readership (businessmen, twentysomethings of both sexes, and so forth).

4. **CONNECTING TEXTS**   Watch one of the gender-bending films Hagedorn mentions (such as *M. Butterfly*), and write your own analysis of the gender roles portrayed in the film. To develop your ideas, consult Aaron Devor's "Gender Role Behaviors and Attitudes" (p. 504).

5. Few American films have featured Asian characters as protagonists. Watch an exception to this trend, *Harold & Kumar Go to White Castle* (2004), and write a semiotic analysis of the racial depictions in this film. To what extent does this film replicate or avoid the stereotypes Hagedorn discusses?

GENDER AND RACE IN FILM

HELENA ANDREWS

The Butler versus *The Help*: Gender Matters

> Though both movies shared much, including commercial success, *The Butler*, in Helena Andrews's words, was critically "toasted," while "*The Help* was trashed." Finding the critical dichotomy grounded in gender biases that undervalue "women's work" — the lead character in *The Help* is a maid — Andrews situates *The Butler* in a system of recent films featuring black men that give the benefit of the doubt to their lead characters, even as black actresses are still criticized for playing "mammy"-like roles. Helena Andrews is a contributing editor at *The Root*, where this article first appeared, and the author of *Bitch Is the New Black* (2011).

Like many of the films in the "it's complicated" historical-fiction genre, *Lee Daniels' The Butler* uses broad strokes to paint a decidedly unpretty picture — the cinematic equivalent of an Instagram filter.

But despite the artistic liberties and Forrest Gump–like rendering of the life of White House butler Cecil Gaines — based upon the true story of Eugene Allen — in its first week out *The Butler* has seemed to bob and weave past the reflexive reproof such movies usually attract.

Almost immediately, I noticed the stark difference in tone between critical discussion of *The Butler* and another similarly entitled film, *The Help*. Whereas this most recent film, jam-packed with big first names like Oprah, Cuba and Forest, has been toasted, *The Help* was trashed.

Early criticism of *The Help* — starring Viola Davis, who was nominated for an Academy Award for her leading role as Aibileen, a maid — was swift and unrelenting. As part of her publicity blitz in the lead up to the film's release and the ensuing awards season, Davis spent as much time defending her choice to play Aibileen as she did promoting the film.

In an interview with newsman Tavis Smiley—who pointedly told Davis 5
and her co-star, Octavia Spencer, "I want you to win, but I'm ambivalent
about what you are winning for"—Davis had to explain herself.

"The black artist cannot live in a place, in a revisionist place. The black
artist can only tell the truth about humanity, and humanity is messy, people
are messy," said Davis. At this point the actress had had a lot of practice being
on the defense.

"I've been under assault that the maid, the mammy, is a tired image,
to which I respond and have responded that I created a character, a human
being, and this is an important story to tell. It's an important dialogue to
have," said Davis in an interview with the *Wall Street Journal* right before the
2011 awards season.

None of Davis' defensive tactics have been necessary for Forest Whitaker
during the full-court publicity press for *The Butler*.

While on ABC's *The View*, Whitaker said early positive responses to the
film had been "universal." In an interview with the *New York Times*, the actor
was asked about his methods, how he was able to convey his character's
"pride and struggle," and not why he'd decided to take on such a role. *Rolling Stone* film critic Peter Travers asked Whitaker in an interview about the
research involved in playing Cecil Gaines.

So far the most popular sentiment from the film—repeated in several 10
interviews—is the notion that black domestics serving white families were, in
fact, subversive.

"Just by their presence, by their dignity, by their dedication to their work,
they were able to move things forward," explained Whitaker on *Good Morning
America*.

This is a radical shift in thought when applied to the debate about the
lack of nonstereotypical roles in mainstream Hollywood. From Hattie McDaniel onward, the debate about whether or not black actors and actresses (along
with screenwriters, directors and producers) should ever play the roles of the
maid or the butler has been ongoing. Davis couldn't escape the backlash for
her role in *The Help* in 2011, but just two years later Whitaker has.

The most obvious difference between Davis' Aibileen and Whitaker's
Cecil is the characters' gender. Then comes the issue of class and access. Aibileen is a maid in a middle-class enclave in Jackson, Miss., serving up chicken
salad and changing diapers. Cecil is a tuxedoed butler at the most famous
address in the United States, serving tea in fine china to the leaders of the free
world. They both wear the uniform. They both wear two faces.

But Aibileen's world is dominated by women. She does "women's
work"—cleaning, cooking, care-giving. Cecil, though just as invisible, occupies space crowded by men. He's "in service" and "serving his country," as
President Ronald Reagan (played by Alan Rickman) puts it.

I don't think it's too far of a stretch to think that for most—despite the 15
effusive testaments to the legacy of maids delivered by Oprah and the film's
director, Lee Daniels—the role of the maid, no matter how dignified, is still

considered less significant. It's a story that audiences, especially black ones, believe has been told before.

To be fair, *The Help* and *The Butler* are two distinct narratives. The white characters, though presidents and first ladies they may be, are ancillary to Cecil's story. *The Butler* is woven around Cecil's life. By contrast, in *The Help*, Aibileen's story is tightly tied to those of the white women around her, a narrative device that didn't sit well with some because it reinforces the notion that black women's stories cannot stand on their own.

Still, the onslaught of accolades for the recent batch of films starring black men in historically complicated roles, from Jamie Foxx's Django to Whitaker's Cecil and Chiwetel Ejiofor's Solomon Northup in the upcoming *12 Years a Slave*, says something about how films featuring black actresses in similarly uncomfortable roles are perceived. And in a creative landscape where Harriet Tubman gets a "sex tape" instead of a starring role, I'm not sure if it says something good.

READING THE TEXT

1. Summarize in your own words how the critical response to *The Butler* and *The Help* differed, in Andrews's estimation.

2. What does Viola Davis mean by saying, "The black artist cannot live . . . in a revisionist place" (para. 6)?

3. What evidence does Andrews provide to support her contention that attitudes toward gender and class have influenced the different responses to these two films?

4. Define in your own words the "mammy" (para. 6) role in films.

READING THE SIGNS

1. Analyze reviews of *The Butler* and *The Help* (using a site like Rotten Tomatoes), and write an essay in which you support, refute, or complicate Andrews's claims about the critical reception of these films. Alternatively, read reviews of another film focused on African American characters, such as *12 Years a Slave* (2013), and analyze their response to the portrayal of blacks in the film.

2. **CONNECTING TEXTS**   Andrews refers to an ongoing "debate about whether or not black actors and actresses (along with screenwriters, directors and producers) should ever play the roles of the maid or the butler" (para. 12). In an argumentative essay, present your own position in this debate, being sure to ground your claims in an analysis of specific characters. To develop your ideas, read Michael Omi's "In Living Color: Race and American Culture" (p. 538) and Matt Zoller Seitz's "The Offensive Movie Cliché That Won't Die" (p. 356).

3. **CONNECTING TEXTS**   Andrews suggests that attitudes toward class also influenced viewers' responses to *The Help* and *The Butler*. Adopting the perspective of Michael Parenti in "Class and Virtue" (p. 361), conduct your own analysis of how the two films use class-based signs to shape their characters' identities.

Lee Daniels' The Butler

READING THE SIGNS

1. Based on this poster for *Lee Daniels' The Butler*, how would you characterize the subject matter of this film? Does the poster make you want to see the film? Why or why not?

2. If you have read Helena Andrews's "*The Butler* versus *The Help*: Gender Matters" (p. 352), then you already know a little bit about the plot of this film, the story of an African American White House butler. In your opinion, how is the central figure in the poster (the butler of the film's title) portrayed in the poster? What are we supposed to think about this character from the poster alone?

3. Judging from this poster for *The Butler*, who in your opinion is the intended audience for this film? Why? What elements in this poster appeal to that intended audience?

4. Consider the caption on this poster: "One quiet voice can ignite a revolution." In your opinion, is this caption effective as a teaser? Why or why not? How is the language in this caption designed to stoke interest in the film?

MATT ZOLLER SEITZ

The Offensive Movie Cliché That Won't Die

You've seen a satirical portrayal of him on *The Simpsons*, in the guise of Bleeding Gums Murphy, and he has appeared quite seriously in such movies as *The Legend of Bagger Vance*, *The Green Mile*, and *Legendary*. He's the "Magical Negro": "a saintly African American character who acts as a mentor to a questing white hero" in many recent movies. First identified as such by Spike Lee, as Matt Zoller Seitz observes in this critique of the character, the "Magical Negro" has his roots in such figures as Uncle Remus and Bill "Bojangles" Robinson, and his persistence in American popular culture can be read as a signifier of a larger cultural negotiation in which, Seitz argues, white America, finding itself no longer in complete control of the cultural and political agenda, is trying to strike a "deal." Matt Zoller Seitz is a freelance critic and film editor and the founder of the online publication *The House Next Door*.

"You always know the right things to say," says Cal Chetley (Devon Graye), the high school wrestler hero of *Legendary*, in conversation with Harry "Red" Newman (Danny Glover), a local fisherman.

The hero seems bewildered and delighted as he says this. He's about to compete in an important match, reeling from melodramatic blows. When

Harry shows up out of nowhere to give Cal a pep talk, the stage is set for a *Rocky*-style, go-the-distance ending. But if Cal had thought about Harry in terms of pop culture stereotypes, he could have answered his own implied question: *How come you're always there when I need you, even though I barely know you?* Harry seems to stand apart from the rest of the community, even though he's a familiar and beloved part of it. The only character who speaks to Harry directly is Cal, and their conversations are always about Cal and his well-being. He's such the benevolent guardian angel figure that the cynical viewer half-expects him to be revealed as a figment of Cal's imagination.

He's not imaginary. He's a "Magical Negro": a saintly African American character who acts as a mentor to a questing white hero, who seems to be disconnected from the community that he adores so much, and who often seems to have an uncanny ability to say and do exactly what needs to be said or done in order to keep the story chugging along in the hero's favor.

We have Spike Lee to thank for popularizing this politically incorrect but very useful term. Lee used it in a 2001 appearance at college campuses. He was blasting a then-recent wave of such characters, played by the likes of Cuba Gooding Jr., in *What Dreams May Come* (a spirit guide helping Robin Williams rescue his wife from Hell), Will Smith in *The Legend of Bagger Vance* (a sherpa-on-the-green, mentoring Matt Damon's golfer), Laurence Fishburne in *The Matrix* (Obi-Wan to Keanu Reeves' Luke Skywalker), and Michael Clarke Duncan in *The Green Mile* (a gentle giant on death row whose touch heals white folks' illnesses).

The word choice is deliberately anachronistic — "negro" started to fall out 5 of fashion about forty years ago. But that's why it's so devastating. The word "negro" was a transitional word that fell between the white-comforting "colored" and the more militantly self-determined and oppositional "black." It asked for dignity and autonomy without going that extra step asserting that it existed anyway, with or without white America's approval. "Negro" fits the sorts of characters that incensed Lee. Even though the movies take pains to insist that the African American character is as much a flesh-and-blood person as the white hero, the relationship is that of a master and servant. And not a *real* servant, either: one that really, truly lives to serve, has no life to speak of beyond his service to Da Man, and never seems to trouble himself with doubts about the cause to which he's devoting his time and energy. "How is it that black people have these powers but they use them for the benefit of white people?" Lee asked sarcastically.

The Magical Negro character (or as Lee called him, the "super-duper magical negro") wasn't invented in the 1990s. He's been around for at least a hundred years, accumulating enough examples (from Uncle Remus in *Song of the South* through the clock-keeper played by Bill Cobbs in *The Hudsucker Proxy*) to merit snarky lists, an entry in the urban dictionary, and a detailed Wikipedia page (turns out Stephen King's fiction has been a Magical Negro factory). The term gained an even wider audience when a candidate to chair the Republican National Committee mailed out a song titled "Barack the Magic Negro," with lyrics to the tune of the Peter, Paul and Mary hit. Outraged liberals

A scene from *The Green Mile*.

focused on the surface racism encoded in the song title, ignoring the possibility that the song, however lead-footed in its humor, was rooted in something real.

What got lost in the flap over the song was the phrase's relevance to Obama's candidacy: There was (among Democrats, at least) a widespread sense that replacing George W. Bush with the Illinois senator would send a definitive signal that everything was different now, that it was time to rebuild, repair, rejuvenate, and move forward, not just toward a post-Bush society, but a post-racial one. It was an absurd hope, one that Obama himself seemed to resist endorsing at first, only to relent and begin publicly playing up his pioneer status as the first not-entirely-Caucasian man to pursue and then win the Democratic presidential nomination. Frequent *Salon* commenter

David Ehrenstein tackled this subject in a memorable 2007 *Los Angeles Times* piece that called Obama a "magic negro" almost a year before that RNC ditty appeared. Likening Obama to a spiritual descendant of the noble, kind-hearted, often sexless black men portrayed by pioneering leading man Sidney Poitier, he wrote, "Like a comic-book superhero, Obama is there to help, out of the sheer goodness of a heart we need not know or understand. For as with all Magic Negroes, the less real he seems, the more desirable he becomes."

Suffice to say Obama's election triggered a paroxysm of paranoia, insecurity, and rage in roughly half the population (maybe more, if polls on immigration and the Park51 project are to be believed). These flare-ups of privilege (wherein an almost entirely white sector of the populace descended from once-despised immigrants embraces the idea that "we" have to protect or reclaim "our" country from "them") cast retrospective light on the Magical Negro resurgence, which flowered in earnest during the last Democratic administration and has been going full-steam ever since.

Between demographers' projections of a twenty-first-century majority-minority swap, Clinton's unprecedented (un-presidented?) comfort with African American culture (which he made official during the 1992 campaign, in an effective bit of pandering stagecraft, by playing sax on *The Arsenio Hall Show*), and hip-hop's supplanting rock as the country's unofficial national soundtrack, there was a sense, even in the pre-Internet era, that the white man either wasn't in control anymore or soon wouldn't be. Whitey was just going to have to deal.

Things haven't played out quite so simply, of course. In every aspect of   10
quality of life that can be measured, nonwhite folks have always tended to be worse off than whites. That hasn't changed in the aughts, and the recession/depression has hit black men especially hard.

Looking back over the last twenty years' worth of cultural and demographic unrest, the M. N. phenomenon seems a form of psychological jujitsu—one that takes a subject that some white folks find unpleasant or even troubling to ponder (justifiably resentful black people's status in a country that, fifty years after the start of the modern civil rights struggle, is still run by, and mostly for, whites) and turns it into a source of gentle reassurance. Do "they" hate us? Oh, no! In fact, deep down they want "us" to succeed, and are happy to help "us" succeed, as long as we listen well and are polite. That's why Whoopi Goldberg put her life on hold to help Demi Moore get in touch with her dead boyfriend in *Ghost*, and Jennifer Hudson lived to serve Sarah Jessica Parker in the first *Sex and the City* movie. And it's why Danny Glover's character—one of but a few black men in an otherwise white town—takes such a keen interest in the life of a bantamweight high school wrestler who has apparently lived in the same town with Harry his entire life and recognizes him as a local eccentric, yet never bothered to get to know him before now.

People that enjoyed *Legendary* may say I'm being unfair to Harry, that there's more to him than Magical Negro-hood. And yes, it's true, at the end—spoiler alert!—we're told that he's not just a gravel-voiced sweetheart who likes to hang out by the local creek, catching fish and dispensing words of wisdom. He's actually quite influential — not *literally* magical, but nevertheless demi-godlike in his influence over the town and its history. But the specifics of Harry's character don't refute the label; quite the contrary. The revelation of Harry's influence is a nifty trick, one that's common in nearly all movies featuring nonwhite mentor / sidekick / deus ex machina characters. It seems appealing enough in the abstract. But it's weak soup when you look at such a character's role in the totality of the story.

Danny Glover, arguably one of cinema's most versatile and likable character actors, gets to play something close to God (he even narrates the story and turns out to have had a hand in three generations of local lives). But he doesn't get a good scene with anybody but the hero, doesn't get even the intimation of a private life, and barely speaks to anyone in the town that supposedly adores and respects him. Like the clock-tender in *The Hudsucker Proxy*, the HIV-stricken painter/saint from *In America*, and Ben Vereen's characters in *Pippin* and *All That Jazz*, Harry's aura of omnipotence is compensation for being shut out of the movie. It's a screenwriter's distraction that obscures the character's detachment from the heart of the narrative — and the character's essentially decorative nature. Like the hot-tempered black police captain who demands the maverick white detective's badge and the stern black woman judge who dresses down the kooky but irresponsible white heroine and warns her to get her life together, the Magical Negro is a glorified walk-on role, a narrative device with a pulse. The M. N. doesn't really drive the story, but is a glorified hood ornament attached to the end of a car that's being driven by white society, vigorously turning a little steering wheel that's not attached to anything.

Which might be a harsh but accurate metaphor for our current president, come to think of it.

READING THE TEXT

1. In your own words, define the term "Magical Negro" (para. 3). Why is it considered "anachronistic" (para. 5)?

2. What evidence does Seitz offer to suggest that the Danny Glover character in *Legendary* is a Magical Negro?

3. Why did some commentators dub Barack Obama, who was not a cinematic character, a Magical Negro during the 2008 presidential race?

4. Characterize Seitz's tone in this selection. In what ways does it affect your response to his argument?

READING THE SIGNS

1. Write your own interpretation of the representation of African American characters in *Legendary*, *Ghost*, *Sex in the City*, *All That Jazz*, or another film that Seitz refers to. To develop your ideas, consult Michael Omi's "In Living Color: Race and American Culture" (p. 538). To what extent do the characters in the

film you've selected display traits of "overt" or "inferential" racism, as Omi describes those concepts?

2. Both the Magical Negro and the black domestic servant are exaggerated versions of racial stereotypes. In class, compare and contrast these stereotypes. What underlying myths regarding racial difference do they display? Use your discussion to jump-start your own essay about the extent to which these stereotypes perpetuate racial myths. To develop your ideas, read Helena Andrews's "*The Butler* versus *The Help*: Gender Matters" (p. 352).

3. Seitz attributes the recurrence of the Magical Negro stereotype, in part, to concern about changing demographics whereby Caucasians would no longer be the dominant ethnic group in America. Considering today's political landscape, what signs do you see that support or complicate this explanation? Be sure to consider both national voting patterns and movements like the Tea Party.

4. Seitz comments parenthetically that "Stephen King's fiction has been a Magical Negro factory" (para. 6). Read at least one King novel that includes African American characters. Write an essay in which you support, refute, or modify this assertion.

5. Seitz is critical of the Magical Negro stereotype, but it has been argued that this particular representation of African Americans is a positive response to accusations that this demographic group too often is portrayed with overtly negative, violent stereotypes. Write an essay in which you evaluate this argument, taking care to base your claims on an analysis of specific films and characters.

MICHAEL PARENTI
Class and Virtue

In 1993, a movie called *Indecent Proposal* presented a story in which a billionaire offers a newly poor middle-class woman a million dollars if she'll sleep with him for one night. In Michael Parenti's terms, what was really indecent about the movie was the way it showed the woman falling in love with the billionaire, thus making a romance out of a class outrage. But the movie could get away with it, partly because Hollywood has always conditioned audiences to root for the ruling classes and to ignore the inequities of class privilege. In this selection from *Make-Believe Media: The Politics of Entertainment* (1992), Parenti argues that Hollywood has long been in the business of representing the interests of the ruling classes. Whether it is forgiving the classist behavior in *Pretty Woman* or glamorizing the lives of the wealthy, Hollywood makes sure its audiences leave the theater thinking you can't be too rich. Michael Parenti is a writer who lectures widely at university campuses around the country. His publications include *Power and the Powerless* (1978), *Inventing Reality: The Politics of the News Media* (1986), *Against Empire* (1995), *Dirty Truths* (1996), *America Besieged* (1998), *The Culture Struggle* (2006), *Democracy for the Few* (2007), *God and His Demons* (2010), *The Face of Imperialism* (2011), and *Waiting for Yesterday: Pages from a Street Kid's Life* (2013).

Class and Virtue ← look this word to help out with paper

The entertainment media present working people not only as unlettered and uncouth but also as less desirable and less moral than other people. Conversely, virtue is more likely to be ascribed to those characters whose speech and appearance are soundly middle- or upper-middle class.

Even a simple adventure story like *Treasure Island* (1934, 1950, 1972) manifests this implicit class perspective. There are two groups of acquisitive persons searching for a lost treasure. One, headed by a squire, has money enough to hire a ship and crew. The other, led by the rascal Long John Silver, has no money—so they sign up as part of the crew. The narrative implicitly assumes from the beginning that the squire has a moral claim to the treasure, while Long John Silver's gang does not. After all, it is the squire who puts up the venture capital for the ship. Having no investment in the undertaking other than their labor, Long John and his men, by definition, will be "stealing" the treasure, while the squire will be "discovering" it.

To be sure, there are other differences. Long John's men are cutthroats. The squire is not. Yet, one wonders if the difference between a bad pirate and a good squire is itself not preeminently a matter of having the right amount of disposable income. The squire is no less acquisitive than the conspirators. He just does with money what they must achieve with cutlasses. The squire and his associates dress in fine clothes, speak an educated diction, and drink brandy. Long John and his men dress slovenly, speak in guttural accents, and drink rum. From these indications alone, the viewer knows who are the good guys and who are the bad. Virtue is visually measured by one's approximation to proper class appearances.

Sometimes class contrasts are juxtaposed within one person, as in *The Three Faces of Eve* (1957), a movie about a woman who suffers from multiple personalities. When we first meet Eve (Joanne Woodward), she is a disturbed, strongly repressed, puritanically religious person, who speaks with a rural, poor-Southern accent. Her second personality is that of a wild, flirtatious woman who also speaks with a rural, poor-Southern accent. After much treatment by her psychiatrist, she is cured of these schizoid personalities and emerges with a healthy third one, the real Eve, a poised, self-possessed, pleasant woman. What is intriguing is that she now speaks with a cultivated, affluent, Smith College accent, free of any low-income regionalism or ruralism, much like Joanne Woodward herself. This transformation in class style and speech is used to indicate mental health without any awareness of the class bias thusly expressed.

Mental health is also the question in *A Woman under the Influence* (1974), the story of a disturbed woman who is married to a hard-hat husband. He cannot handle — and inadvertently contributes to — her emotional deterioration. She is victimized by a spouse who is nothing more than an insensitive, working-class bull in a china shop. One comes away convinced that every unstable woman needs a kinder, gentler, and above all, more *middle-class* hubby if she wishes to avoid a mental crack-up.

Class prototypes abound in the 1980s television series *The A-Team*. In each episode, a Vietnam-era commando unit helps an underdog, be it a Latino immigrant or a disabled veteran, by vanquishing some menacing force such as organized crime, a business competitor, or corrupt government officials. As always with the make-believe media, the A-Team does good work on an individualized rather than collectively organized basis, helping particular victims by thwarting particular villains. The A-Team's leaders are two white males of privileged background. The lowest ranking members of the team, who do none of the thinking nor the leading, are working-class palookas. They show they are good with their hands, both by punching out the bad guys and by doing the maintenance work on the team's flying vehicles and cars. One of them, "B.A." (bad ass), played by the African American Mr. T., is visceral, tough, and purposely bad-mannered toward those he doesn't like. He projects an image of crudeness and ignorance and is associated with the physical side of things. In sum, the team has a brain (the intelligent white leaders) and a body with its simpler physical functions (the working-class characters), a hierarchy that corresponds to the social structure itself.[1]

Sometimes class bigotry is interwoven with gender bigotry, as in *Pretty Woman* (1990). A dreamboat millionaire corporate raider finds himself all alone for an extended stay in Hollywood (his girlfriend is unwilling to join him), so he quickly recruits a beautiful prostitute as his playmate of the month. She is paid three thousand dollars a week to wait around his super-posh hotel penthouse ready to perform the usual services and accompany him to business dinners at top restaurants. As prostitution goes, it is a dream gig. But there is one cloud on the horizon. She is low-class. She doesn't know which fork to use at those CEO power feasts, and she's bothersomely fidgety, wears tacky clothes, chews gum, and, y'know, doesn't talk so good. But with some tips from the hotel manager, she proves to be a veritable Eliza Doolittle in her class metamorphosis. She dresses in proper attire, sticks the gum away forever, and starts picking the right utensils at dinner. She also figures out how to speak a little more like Joanne Woodward without the benefit of a multiple personality syndrome, and she develops the capacity to sit in a poised, wordless, empty-headed fashion, every inch the expensive female ornament.

[1]Gina Marchetti, "Class, Ideology and Commercial Television: An Analysis of *The A-Team*," *Journal of Film and Video* 39, Spring 1987, pp. 19–28.

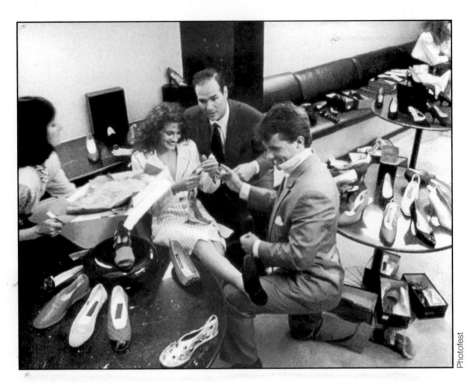

Photofest

A scene from *Pretty Woman* (1990).

She is still a prostitute but a classy one. It is enough of a distinction for the handsome young corporate raider. Having liked her because she was charmingly cheap, he now loves her all the more because she has real polish and is a more suitable companion. So suitable that he decides to do the right thing by her: set her up in an apartment so he can make regular visits at regular prices. But now she wants the better things in life, like marriage, a nice house, and, above all, a different occupation, one that would allow her to use less of herself. She is furious at him for treating her like, well, a prostitute. She decides to give up her profession and get a high school diploma so that she might make a better life for herself — perhaps as a filing clerk or receptionist or some other of the entry-level jobs awaiting young women with high school diplomas.[2]

After the usual girl-breaks-off-with-boy scenes, the millionaire prince returns. It seems he can't concentrate on making money without her. He even abandons his cutthroat schemes and enters into a less lucrative but supposedly more productive, caring business venture with a struggling old-time entrepreneur. The bad capitalist is transformed into a good capitalist. He then carries off his ex-prostitute for a lifetime of bliss. The moral is a familiar one, updated for post-Reagan yuppiedom: A woman can escape from economic

[2]See the excellent review by Lydia Sargent, *Z Magazine*, April 1990, pp. 43–45.

and gender exploitation by winning the love and career advantages offered by a rich male. Sexual allure goes only so far unless it develops a material base and becomes a class act.[3]

READING THE TEXT

1. According to Parenti, what characteristics are typically attributed to working-class and upper-class film characters?
2. How does Parenti see the relationship between "class bigotry" and "gender bigotry" (para. 7) in *Pretty Woman*?
3. What relationship does Parenti see between mental health and class values in films?

READING THE SIGNS

1. Watch *Wall Street*, *Unstoppable*, or *The Fighter*, and analyze the class issues that the movie raises. Alternatively, watch an episode of *The Apprentice*, and perform the same sort of analysis.
2. Do you agree with Parenti's interpretation of *Pretty Woman*? Write an argumentative essay in which you defend, challenge, or complicate his reading of the film.
3. **CONNECTING TEXTS**   Read Aaron Devor's "Gender Role Behaviors and Attitudes" (p. 504). How would Devor explain the gender bigotry that Parenti finds in *Pretty Woman*?
4. Watch the 1954 film *On the Waterfront* with your class. How are labor unions and working-class characters portrayed in that film? Does the film display the class bigotry that Parenti describes?
5. **CONNECTING TEXTS**   Read Michael Omi's "In Living Color: Race and American Culture" (p. 538). Then write an essay in which you create a category of cinematic racial bigotry that corresponds to Parenti's two categories of class and gender bigotry. What films have you seen that illustrate your new category?

[3]Ibid.

DAVID DENBY

High-School Confidential: Notes on Teen Movies

Face it: High school for most of us is one extended nightmare, a long-playing drama starring cheerleaders and football players who sneer at the mere mortals who must endure their haughty reign. So it's little wonder that, as David Denby argues in this *New Yorker* essay from 1999, teen movies so often feature loathsome cheerleaders and football stars who, one way or another, get theirs in this ever-popular movie genre. Indeed, Denby asks, "Who can doubt where Hollywood's twitchy, nearsighted writers and directors ranked—or feared they ranked—on the high-school totem pole?" Nerds at the bottom, where else, like the millions of suffering kids who flock to their films. A staff writer and film critic for the *New Yorker*, David Denby is the author of *The Great Books: My Adventures with Homer, Rousseau, Woolf, and Other Indestructible Writers of the Western World* (1996), *American Sucker* (2003), and *Snark: It's Mean, It's Personal, and It's Ruining Our Conversation* (2009).

The most hated young woman in America is a blonde—well, sometimes a redhead or a brunette, but usually a blonde. She has big hair flipped into a swirl of gold at one side of her face or arrayed in a sultry mane, like the magnificent pile of a forties movie star. She's tall and slender, with a waist as supple as a willow, but she's dressed in awful, spangled taste: her outfits could have been put together by warring catalogues. And she has a mouth on her, a low, slatternly tongue that devastates other kids with such insults as "You're vapor, you're Spam!" and "Do I look like Mother Teresa? If I did, I probably wouldn't mind talking to the geek squad." She has two or three friends exactly like her, and together they dominate their realm—the American high school as it appears in recent teen movies. They are like wicked princesses, who enjoy the misery of their subjects. Her coronation, of course, is the senior prom, when she expects to be voted "most popular" by her class. But, though she may be popular, she is certainly not liked, so her power is something of a mystery. She is beautiful and rich, yet in the end she is preëminent because . . . she is preëminent, a position she works to maintain with Joan Crawford–like tenacity. Everyone is afraid of her; that's why she's popular.

She has a male counterpart. He's usually a football player, muscular but dumb, with a face like a beer mug and only two ways of speaking—in a conspiratorial whisper, to a friend; or in a drill sergeant's sudden bellow. If her weapon is the snub, his is the lame but infuriating prank—the can of Sprite emptied into a knapsack, or something sticky, creamy, or adhesive deposited in a locker. Sprawling and dull in class, he comes alive in the halls and in the cafeteria. He hurls people against lockers; he spits, pours, and sprays; he has a projectile relationship with food. As the crown prince, he claims the best-looking girl for himself, though in a perverse display of power he may invite an outsider or an awkward girl—a "dog"—to the prom, setting her up for some special humiliation. When we first see him, he is riding high, and virtually the entire school colludes in his tyranny. No authority figure—no teacher or administrator—dares correct him.

Thus the villains of the recent high-school movies. Not every American teen movie has these two characters, and not every social queen or jock shares all the attributes I've mentioned. (Occasionally, a handsome, dark-haired athlete can be converted to sweetness and light.) But as genre figures these two types are hugely familiar; that is, they are a common memory, a collective trauma, or at least a social and erotic fantasy. Such movies of the past year [1999] as *Disturbing Behavior*, *She's All That*, *Ten Things I Hate about You*, and *Never Been Kissed* depend on them as stock figures. And they may have been figures in the minds of the Littleton shooters, Eric Harris and Dylan Klebold, who imagined they were living in a school like the one in so many of these movies—a poisonous system of status, snobbery, and exclusion.

Do genre films reflect reality? Or are they merely a set of conventions that refer to other films? Obviously, they wouldn't survive if they didn't provide emotional satisfaction to the people who make them and to the audiences who watch them. A half century ago, we didn't need to see ten Westerns a year in order to learn that the West got settled. We needed to see it settled ten times a year in order to provide ourselves with the emotional gratifications of righteous violence. By drawing his gun only when he was provoked, and in the service of the good, the classic Western hero transformed the gross tangibles of the expansionist drive (land, cattle, gold) into a principle of moral order. The gangster, by contrast, is a figure of chaos, a modern, urban person, and in the critic Robert Warshow's formulation he functions as a discordant element in an American society devoted to a compulsively "positive" outlook. When the gangster dies, he cleanses viewers of their own negative feelings.

High-school movies are also full of unease and odd, mixed-up emotions. They may be flimsy in conception; they may be shot in lollipop colors, garlanded with mediocre pop scores, and cast with goofy young actors trying to make an impression. Yet this most commercial and frivolous of genres harbors a grievance against the world. It's a very specific grievance, quite different from the restless anger of such fifties adolescent-rebellion movies as *The Wild One*, in which someone asks Marlon Brando's biker "What are you rebelling against?" and the biker replies "What have you got?" The fifties teen outlaw was against anything that adults considered sacred. But no movie teenager now revolts against adult authority, for the simple reason that adults have no authority. Teachers are rarely more than a minimal, exasperated presence, administrators get turned into a joke, and parents are either absent or distantly benevolent. It's a teen world, bounded by school, mall, and car, with occasional moments set in the fast-food outlets where the kids work, or in the kids' upstairs bedrooms, with their pinups and rack stereo systems. The enemy is not authority; the enemy is other teens and the social system that they impose on one another.

The bad feeling in these movies may strike grownups as peculiar. After all, from a distance American kids appear to be having it easy these days. The teen audience is facing a healthy job market; at home, their parents are stuffing the den with computers and the garage with a bulky SUV. But most teens aren't thinking about the future job market. Lost in the eternal swoon of late adolescence, they're thinking about their identity, their friends, and their clothes. Adolescence is the present-tense moment in American life. Identity and status are fluid: abrupt, devastating reversals are always possible. (In a teen movie, a guy who swallows a bucket of cafeteria coleslaw can make himself a hero in an instant.) In these movies, accordingly, the senior prom is the equivalent of the shoot-out at the O.K. Corral; it's the moment when one's worth as a human being is settled at last. In the rather pedestrian new comedy *Never Been Kissed*, Drew Barrymore, as a twenty-five-year-old newspaper reporter, goes back to high school pretending to be a student, and immediately falls into her old, humiliating pattern of trying to impress the good-looking rich kids. Helplessly, she pushes for approval, and even gets herself chosen prom queen before finally coming to her senses. She finds it nearly impossible to let go.

Genre films dramatize not what happens but how things feel — the emotional coloring of memory. They fix subjectivity into fable. At actual schools, there is no unitary system of status; there are many groups to be a part of, many places to excel (or fail to excel), many avenues of escape and self-definition. And often the movies, too, revel in the arcana of high-school cliques. In last summer's *Disturbing Behavior*, a veteran student lays out the cafeteria ethnography for a newcomer: Motorheads, Blue Ribbons, Skaters, Micro-geeks ("drug of choice: Stephen Hawking's *A Brief History of Time* and a cup of jasmine tea on Saturday night"). Subjectively, though, the social system in *Disturbing Behavior* (a high-school version of *The Stepford Wives*) and in the other movies still feels coercive and claustrophobic: humiliation is the most vivid emotion of youth, so in memory it becomes the norm.

The movies try to turn the tables. The kids who cannot be the beautiful ones, or make out with them, or avoid being insulted by them — these are the heroes of the teen movies, the third in the trio of character types. The female outsider is usually an intellectual or an artist. (She scribbles in a diary, she draws or paints.) Physically awkward, she walks like a seal crossing a beach, and is prone to drop her books and dither in terror when she stands before a handsome boy. Her clothes, which ignore mall fashion, scandalize the social queens. Like them, she has a tongue, but she's tart and grammatical, tending toward feminist pungency and precise diction. She may mask her sense of vulnerability with sarcasm or with Plathian rue (she's stuck in the bell jar), but even when she lashes out she can't hide her craving for acceptance.

The male outsider, her friend, is usually a mass of stuttering or giggling sexual gloom: he wears shapeless clothes; he has an undeveloped body, either stringy or shrimpy; he's sometimes a Jew (in these movies, still the generic outsider). He's also brilliant, but in a morose, preoccupied way that suggests masturbatory absorption in some arcane system of knowledge. In a few special cases, the outsider is not a loser but a disengaged hipster, either saintly or satanic. (Christian Slater has played this role a couple of times.) This outsider wears black and keeps his hair long, and he knows how to please women. He sees through everything, so he's ironic by temperament and genuinely indifferent to the opinion of others — a natural aristocrat, who transcends the school's contemptible status system. There are whimsical variations on the outsider figure, too. In the recent *Rushmore*, an obnoxious teen hero, Max Fischer (Jason Schwartzman), runs the entire school: he can't pass his courses but he's a dynamo at extracurricular activities, with a knack for staging extraordinary events. He's a con man, a fund-raiser, an entrepreneur — in other words, a contemporary artist.

In fact, the entire genre, which combines self-pity and ultimate vindication, might be called "Portrait of the Filmmaker as a Young Nerd." Who can doubt where Hollywood's twitchy, nearsighted writers and directors ranked — or feared they ranked — on the high-school totem pole? They are still angry, though occasionally the target of their resentment goes beyond the jocks and cheerleaders of their youth. Consider this anomaly: the young actors and models on the covers of half the magazines published in this country, the shirtless men with chests like burnished shields, the girls smiling, glowing, tweezed, full-lipped, full-breasted (but not too full), and with skin so honeyed that it seems lacquered — these are the physical ideals embodied by the villains of the teen movies. The social queens and jocks, using their looks to dominate others, represent an American barbarism of beauty. Isn't it possible that the detestation of them in teen movies is a veiled strike at the entire abs-hair advertising culture, with its unobtainable glories of perfection? A critic of consumerism might even see a spark of revolt in these movies. But only a spark.

My guess is that these films arise from remembered hurts which then get recast in symbolic form. For instance, a surprising number of the outsider heroes have no mother. Mom has died or run off with another man; her child, only half loved, is ill equipped for the emotional pressures of school. The motherless child, of course, is a shrewd commercial ploy that makes a direct appeal to the members of the audience, many of whom may feel like outsiders, too, and unloved, or not loved enough, or victims of some prejudice or exclusion. But the motherless child also has powers, and will someday be a success, an artist, a screenwriter. It's the wound and the bow all over again, in cargo pants.

As the female nerd attracts the attention of the handsomest boy in the senior class, the teen movie turns into a myth of social reversal — a Cinderella fantasy. Initially, his interest in her may be part of a stunt or a trick: he is leading her on, perhaps at the urging of his queenly girlfriend. But his gaze lights her up, and we see how attractive she really is. Will she fulfill the eternal American fantasy that you can vault up the class system by removing your specs? She wants her prince, and by degrees she wins him over, not just with her looks but with her superior nature, her essential goodness. In the male version of the Cinderella trip, a few years go by, and a pale little nerd (we see him at a reunion) has become rich. All that poking around with chemicals paid off. Max Fischer, of *Rushmore*, can't miss being richer than Warhol.

So the teen movie is wildly ambivalent. It may attack the consumerist ethos that produces winners and losers, but in the end it confirms what it is attacking. The girls need the seal of approval conferred by the converted jocks; the nerds need money and a girl. Perhaps it's no surprise that the outsiders can be validated only by the people who ostracized them. But let's not be too schematic: the outsider who joins the system also modifies it, opens it up to the creative power of social mobility, makes it bend and laugh, and perhaps this turn of events is not so different from the way things work in the real world, where merit and achievement stand a good chance of trumping appearance. The irony of the Littleton shootings is that Klebold and Harris, who were both proficient computer heads, seemed to have forgotten how the plot turns out. If they had held on for a few years they might have been working at a hip software company, or have started their own business, while the jocks who oppressed them would probably have wound up selling insurance or used cars. That's the one unquestionable social truth the teen movies reflect: geeks rule.

There is, of course, a menacing subgenre, in which the desire for revenge turns bloody. Thirty-one years ago, Lindsay Anderson's semi-surrealistic *If . . .* was set in an oppressive, class-ridden English boarding school, where a group of rebellious students drive the school population out into a courtyard and open fire on them with machine guns. In Brian De Palma's 1976 masterpiece *Carrie*, the pale, repressed heroine, played by Sissy Spacek, is courted at last by a handsome boy but gets violated — doused with pig's blood — just as she is named prom queen. Stunned but far from powerless, Carrie uses her telekinetic powers to set the room afire and burn down the school. *Carrie* is the primal school movie, so wildly lurid and funny that it exploded the clichés of the genre before the genre was quite set: The heroine may be a wrathful avenger, but the movie, based on a Stephen King book, was clearly a grinning-gargoyle fantasy. So, at first, was *Heathers*, in which Christian Slater's satanic outsider turns out to be a true devil. He and his girlfriend (played by a very young Winona Ryder) begin gleefully knocking off the rich, nasty girls and the jocks, in ways so patently absurd that their revenge seems a mere wicked dream. I think it's unlikely that these movies had a direct effect on the actions of the Littleton shooters, but the two boys would surely have recognized the emotional world of *Heathers* and *Disturbing Behavior* as their own. It's a place where feelings of victimization join fantasy, and you experience the social élites as so powerful that you must either become them or kill them.

But enough. It's possible to make teen movies that go beyond these fixed polarities — insider and outsider, blond-bitch queen and hunch-shouldered nerd. In Amy Heckerling's 1995 comedy *Clueless*, the big blonde played by Alicia Silverstone is a Rodeo Drive clotheshorse who is nonetheless possessed of extraordinary virtue. Freely dispensing advice and help, she's almost ironically good — a designing goddess with a cell phone. The movie offers a sunshiny satire of Beverly Hills affluence, which it sees as both absurdly swollen and generous in spirit. The most original of the teen comedies, *Clueless* casts away self-pity. So does *Romy and Michele's High School Reunion* (1997), in which two gabby, lovable friends, played by Mira Sorvino and Lisa Kudrow, review the banalities of their high-school experience so knowingly that they might be criticizing the teen-movie genre itself. And easily the best American film of the year so far is Alexander Payne's *Election*, a high-school movie that inhabits a different aesthetic and moral world altogether from the rest of these pictures. *Election* shreds everyone's fantasies and illusions in a vision of high school that is bleak but supremely just. The movie's villain, an overachieving girl (Reese Witherspoon) who runs for class president, turns out to be its covert heroine, or, at least, its most poignant character. A cross between Pat and Dick Nixon, she's a lower-middle-class striver who works like crazy and never wins anyone's love. Even when she's on top, she feels excluded. Her loneliness is produced not by malicious cliques but by her own implacable will, a condition of the spirit that may be as comical and tragic as it is mysterious. *Election* escapes all the clichés; it graduates into art.

READING THE TEXT

1. Describe in your own words the stereotypical male and female villains common in teen movies.
2. What does Denby mean by the comment, "Adolescence is the present-tense moment in American life" (para. 6)?
3. What sort of characters are typically the heroes in teen films, in Denby's view?
4. In what ways does a Cinderella fantasy influence teen films?
5. What is the "menacing subgenre" (para. 14) of teen movies?

READING THE SIGNS

1. Using Denby's description of stock character types in teen movies as your critical framework, analyze the characters in a teen TV program, such as *The Carrie Diaries*, *Awkward*, or *90210*. Do you see the same conventions at work? How do you account for any differences you might see?
2. In class, brainstorm a list of current teen films. Then, using the list as evidence, write an essay in which you assess the validity of Denby's claim: "The

enemy [in teen films] is not authority; the enemy is other teens and the social system that they impose on one another" (para. 5).

3. Watch *The Perks of Being a Wallflower* (2012), and write an essay in which you argue whether it can be categorized as a teen film, at least as Denby defines the genre.

4. Denby asks, "Do genre films reflect reality? Or are they merely a set of conventions that refer to other films?" (para. 4). Write an essay in which you propose your own response to these questions, using as evidence your high school experience and specific teen films. In addition, you can consider as evidence teen-based TV programs such as *Glee*.

MICHAEL AGRESTA

How the Western Was Lost — and Why It Matters

The Western, once one of Hollywood's favorite and most reliable film genres, is in trouble. With such highly promoted box-office disappointments as *The Lone Ranger* (2013) and *Cowboys & Aliens* (2011), among others, the Western just isn't what it was. In this analysis of both the genre and the particular example of *The Lone Ranger*, Michael Agresta sets out to determine what happened. The trouble, primarily, is history, because while the Western is all about history, that history, in Agresta's words, has become "embarrassing to us." The conquest of the West was a messy, and racist, process, so toxic a subject that any film that takes it on has to use extraordinary measures (as, for example, transporting it to another planet, like *Avatar*'s Pandora) to save it. Hi-ho, Silver, away! A freelance writer on popular culture and the arts, Michael Agresta has written for such publications as *Slate*, the *Wall Street Journal*, and the *Atlantic*, where this selection originally appeared.

The Lone Ranger's failure at the box office earlier this month not only dealt a blow to mega-budget Hollywood blockbusters, Johnny Depp's career, and Disney. The Jerry Bruckheimer–Gore Verbinski flop — which cost a reported $250 million to make and brought in just $50 million opening on a holiday weekend — also may mark a decisive chapter in the sad story of how the Western was lost.

Since the dawn of film, the Western has been one of the great, durable movie genres, but its audience seems to be finally drying up. *The Lone Ranger* is the third Western to flop in four summers, and the most expensive, capping a trend set by *Cowboys & Aliens* and *Jonah Hex*. (Remember them? Exactly.) Western fans are getting older and whiter with respect to the overall population, and as any Republican political consultant will tell you, that doesn't bode well for the future. Other, newer genres like superhero movies and fighting-robot flicks have cowboy movies outgunned with younger generations and international audiences.

Now the genre finds itself in the ironic position of needing a hero to save it, and quick. If *The Lone Ranger* goes down in history as the last of the big-budget oaters, it'll be a sad milestone for moviemaking — and for America. For a century plus, we have relied on Westerns to teach us our history and reflect our current politics and our place in the world. We can ill afford to lose that mirror now, especially just because we don't like what we see staring back at us.

Westerns provide many timeless pleasures — tough guy heroes, action set pieces on horseback, adventures in magnificent landscapes, good triumphing over evil. It's all there already in arguably the first narrative film ever made, *The Great Train Robbery*.

But to discuss Westerns as if they just boiled down to heroic stories of 5 saving the homestead from savages, tracking the bad guy through the wilderness, or finding the treasure in the mountains would be to miss the real meaning of the genre. Westerns have earned their place at the heart of the national culture and American iconography abroad because they've provided a reliable vehicle for filmmakers to explore thorny issues of American history and character. In the enduring examples of the genre, the real threat to the homestead, we learn, is an economic system that is being rigged for the wealthy, or the search for the bad guy becomes a search for meaning in a culture of violent retribution, or the treasure of the Sierra Madre is a diabolical mirage of the American dream.

Through the past century of Western movies, we can trace America's self-image as it evolved from a rough-and-tumble but morally confident outsider in world affairs to an all-powerful sheriff with a guilty conscience. After World War I and leading into World War II, Hollywood specialized in tales of heroes taking the good fight to savage enemies and saving defenseless settlements in the process. In the Great Depression especially, as capitalism and American exceptionalism came under question, the cowboy hero was often mistaken for a criminal and forced to prove his own worthiness — which he inevitably did. Over the '50s, '60s, and '70s however, as America enforced its dominion over half the planet with a long series of coups, assassinations, and increasingly dubious wars, the figure of the cowboy grew darker and more complicated. If you love Westerns, most of your favorites are probably from this era — *Shane*, *The Searchers*, *Butch Cassidy and the Sundance Kid*, *McCabe & Mrs. Miller*, the spaghetti westerns, etc. By the height of the Vietnam protest era, cowboys were antiheroes as often as they were heroes.

The dawn of the 1980s brought the inauguration of Ronald Reagan and the box-office debacle of the artsy, overblown *Heaven's Gate*. There's a sense of disappointment to the decade that followed, as if the era of revisionist Westerns had failed and a less nuanced patriotism would have to carry the day. Few memorable Westerns were made in the '80s, and Reagan himself proudly associated himself with an old-fashioned, pre-Vietnam cowboy image. But victory in the Cold War coincided with a revival of the genre, including the revisionist strain, exemplified in Clint Eastwood's career-topping *Unforgiven*. A new, gentler star emerged in Kevin Costner, who scored a postcolonial megahit with *Dances with Wolves*. Later, in the 2000s, George W. Bush reclaimed the image of the cowboy for a foreign policy far less successful than Reagan's, and the genre retreated to the art house again.

Under the presidency of Barack Obama, there has been a short-lived Western revival that would seem to match America's tentative new moral authority. If the genre in this era can be said to have a unifying aim, it's to divest itself and its audiences of a strictly white, male, heterosexual perspective on history, and by extension on present day conflicts. *Cowboys & Aliens* is a cynical attempt at a post-racial Western—just take the Indians out of the equation so we can be good guys again!—but with more sincerity. *True Grit, Django Unchained*, and now *The Lone Ranger* have all put non-male, non-white perspectives front and center. (Two other notable movies from the past 15 years, the wonderful *Brokeback Mountain* and the awful *Wild Wild West*, also fit this model.) It's worth pointing out, however, that all of these examples (except *Brokeback Mountain*) were directed by white men, and *The Lone Ranger* has Tonto played by an actor with only the slightest claim to American Indian ancestry.

Although end-of-year prestige movies like *True Grit* and *Django Unchained* have broken through to achieve critical acclaim, Oscars, and substantial return on investment, the Obama era has not been kind to newfangled Westerns that aimed for large audiences. Exacerbating the problem is the rejection of cowboy movies by international audiences, particularly the Chinese. So even as filmmakers have become more interested in incorporating a diversity of viewpoints, they have hit against what appears a global demographic ceiling. It's another reason why *The Lone Ranger* will probably be the last attempt to build a true summer tent-pole in the genre.

Nobody likes a weak ending, and this is especially true for cowboy movies. 10 A sad outcome we can accept, even the death of a genre, but at least let our hero meet his challenge, fulfill his destiny, stand his (or her) ground. Watching *The Lone Ranger* slink off into the sunset, it's hard to feel any sense of resolution for the Western.

It's always difficult to diagnose the reason for a movie's success or failure. Did the audience dislike what *The Lone Ranger* tried to do, or the fact that it executed its aims poorly? Since it bombed definitively on opening weekend (long before China got a look at it, too) it seems safest to base conclusions in part on the movie's advertising and the media storylines surrounding its release.

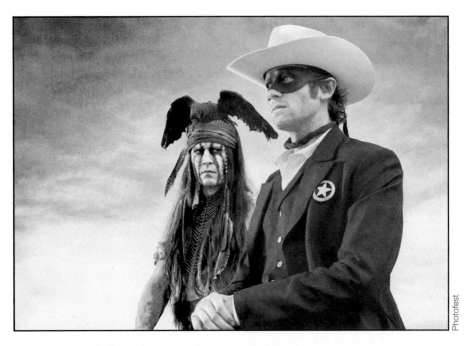

Armie Hammer and Johnny Depp in *The Lone Ranger* (2013).

Three contributing factors stand out. First, there was some coverage of an outcry about racism in Depp's portrayal of Tonto, which conceivably made audiences less comfortable laughing along with the pidgin English. Second, advertising leaned heavily on the association with the *Pirates of the Caribbean* franchise, touting the movie as a family-friendly adventure yarn, but word quickly spread that *The Lone Ranger* was not safe for kids. Finally, the 149-minute runtime can't have helped.

The irony is that the very factors that helped make *The Lone Ranger* a bomb also helped make it much more interesting than typical summer fare. (Mild spoilers follow.) The runtime ballooned because the filmmakers wouldn't dispense with a time-consuming framing story that shows Depp's Tonto, in old-man makeup and a historically inappropriate headdress, wilting away inside a Museum of Natural History–style display called "The Noble Savage in His Native Habitat." The scenes deemed unsafe for children included two graphic depictions of American Indian genocide. The character of Tonto came to the filmmakers with heavy racist baggage, and, rather than tossing him out altogether, they took on the challenge of trying to carry that baggage while walking the tightrope of commenting on a stereotype through the performance of that same stereotype.

This is not to say that any of these bold moves are executed adeptly. The framing story never goes anywhere; the Indian genocide scenes are distastefully incidental to the plot, especially one scene of mass slaughter that provides the heroes cover to get out of a pickle; Depp's winking performance is still fundamentally problematic, as if he or any other white actor had done a modern Mr. Bojangles, blackface and all, and tried to get actual laughs out of it.

Still, in simple terms, *The Lone Ranger* went there. And there. And over there. *The Lone Ranger* did not fail for being timid. In this cautious, sequel-dominated era of summer movies, that's a recommendation in itself. Even if they weren't particularly clever about it, Verbinski and his collaborators deserve credit for engaging critically with the history involved, both the 19th-century Indian massacres and the legacy of racism from the early 20th-century source material.

This is also a tribute to the genre. The ground rules of the Western more or less forced Verbinski and company into that treacherous territory. They could make, say, a movie about Caribbean pirates without addressing the slave trade, even though such pirates often held slaves as cargo. That's fine, because pirate movies are about gold, not slaves. Everyone knows that. Westerns, on the contrary, are traditionally about cowboys and Indians, or at least homesteaders and land and railroad barons, the kinds of men who built the cities we live in today.

It's the task of Westerns to address that history, even as decade by decade that history becomes more and more embarrassing to us. In theory, it's a beautiful thing, though in practice it means cowboy movies are easy to bungle, because by now they all take place on contested ground. Every Western must find its own way to reconcile itself to the founding contradictions of America. A certain kind of escapism becomes impossible.

Unless, of course, we stop making and watching Westerns. The genres that currently rule the box office do other things well — sci-fi movies can address the ecological crisis and challenges of new technology, for instance, and superhero movies can provide never-ending glosses on the core myth of American exceptionalism — but none are particularly engaged with history, especially pre–World War II. And none can boast the richness of symbolic language developed by Westerns over the course of a century at the heart of film culture.

It would be a terrible thing to give up on that language, especially now, in the wake of *The Lone Ranger*'s failure. Isn't there anyone, perhaps a female or non-white director, capable of making a great mass-audience Western for the Obama era? Or, if it's too late for that, then for whatever era comes next? If neither, here's hoping that filmmakers will keep trying at the art-house level and on cable television.

The other great theme of the Western, after that of the conquering of native peoples and the establishment of civilization in the desert, is that of loss and of nostalgia for a certain way of life — the early freedoms of the West, the idea of riding across an unfenced landscape, the infinite possibilities of the frontier. That "West," of course, is already gone, fallen, conquered. It has been for decades, even though holding onto some sense of it seems crucial to our identity as Americans. Movie Westerns have been tracking that loss for a century.

Now, as *The Lone Ranger* leaves theaters this month, that sense of loss begins to expand to cowboy movies themselves. The train is leaving the station, and the thing we rely on to help make sense of ourselves in the world is tied to the tracks. Is there a hero on the horizon?

READING THE TEXT

1. Why does Agresta say that the Western has been "a reliable vehicle for film-makers to explore thorny issues of American history and character" (para. 5)?

2. In your own words, trace the history of the American Western, as Agresta describes it.

3. What does the term "American exceptionalism" (para. 18) mean?

4. In what ways have modern Westerns changed the motifs and patterns of classic Westerns?

5. According to Agresta, why was 2013's *The Lone Ranger* a box-office failure?

READING THE SIGNS

1. Watch *The Lone Ranger*, and write an essay in which you take on Agresta's contention that "the very factors that helped make *The Lone Ranger* a bomb also helped make it much more interesting than typical summer fare" (para. 13).

2. **CONNECTING TEXTS**   Watch one of the recent films that Agresta mentions, such as *Django Unchained* (2012) or *Brokeback Mountain* (2005), and write a semiotic analysis of the film's depiction of race relations. To develop your ideas, read Michael Omi's "In Living Color: Race and American Culture" (p. 538).

3. Write a semiotic analysis of *Avatar* (2009). In what ways does it resemble a conventional Western? How does it differ? Alternatively, write an essay that asks the same questions of the TV show *The Walking Dead*.

4. Both Agresta and Christine Folch ("Why the West Loves Sci-Fi and Fantasy: A Cultural Explanation," p. 378) offer cultural explanations for what Americans find most compelling in films. Write an essay in which you synthesize their views, developing your own cultural explanations as well.

CHRISTINE FOLCH

Why the West Loves Sci-Fi and Fantasy: A Cultural Explanation

> Hollywood loves sci-fi and fantasy; Bollywood doesn't. Just why the
> Indian movie industry (which is the world's largest) is so uninterested
> in fantasy is an anthropological question that Christine Folch sets
> out to answer in this *Atlantic* analysis. The key, Folch believes, lies in
> history, a history that in the West has included a post-Enlightenment
> reign of scientific rationalism that has led to a general disenchant-
> ment with things-as-they-are, which fantasy strives to reverse by
> "re-enchant[ing] the world." Experiencing a different kind of history
> without this disenchantment, Indians, Folch suggests, feel no need
> for cinematic fantasy, so Bollywood doesn't bother much with it.
> Christine Folch is an assistant professor of anthropology at Wheaton
> College.

Hollywood's had a long love affair with sci-fi and fantasy, but the romance has
never been stronger than it is today. A quick glance into bookstores, television lineups, and upcoming films shows that the futuristic and fantastical is
everywhere in American pop culture. In fact, of Hollywood's top earners since
1980, a mere eight have *not* featured wizardry, space or time travel, or apocalyptic destruction caused by aliens/zombies/Robert Downey Jr.'s acerbic wit.
Now, with *Man of Steel*, it appears we will at last have an effective reboot of
the most important superhero story of them all.

These tales of mystical worlds and improbable technological power appeal universally, right? Maybe not. Bollywood, not Hollywood, is the largest
movie industry in the world. But only a handful of its top hits of the last four
decades have dealt with science fiction themes, and even fewer are fantasy or
horror. American films in those genres make much of their profits abroad, but
they tend to underperform in front of Indian audiences.

This isn't to say that there aren't folk tales with magic and mythology in
India. There are. That makes their absence in Bollywood and their overabun-
dance in Hollywood all the more remarkable. Whereas Bollywood takes quotidian family dramas and imbues them with spectacular tales of love and wealth
found-lost-regained amidst the pageantry of choreographed dance pieces,
Hollywood goes to the supernatural and futurism. It's a sign that longing for
mystery is universal, but the taste for science fiction and fantasy is cultural.

Cultural differences are fascinating because even as we learn about others, we learn about ourselves. As an anthropologist, I want to flip this conversation: Why are *we* so into science fiction and fantasy? Nineteenth-century

German sociologist Max Weber had a useful theory about this: The answer may be that we in the West are "disenchanted." The world in which we live feels explainable, predictable, and boring. Weber posited that because of modern science, a rise in secularism, an impersonal market economy, and government administered through bureaucracies rather than bonds of loyalty, Western societies perceived the world as knowably rational and systematic, leading to a widespread loss of a sense of wonder and magic. Because reality is composed of processes that can be identified with a powerful-enough microscope or calculated with a fast-enough computer, so Weber's notion of disenchantment goes, there is no place for mystery. But this state of disenchantment is a difficult one because people seem to *like* wonder.

And so we turn to science fiction and fantasy in an attempt to re-enchant the world. Children and childhood retain mystery, and so one tactic has been to take fairytales and rewrite them for adults and here we get the swords and sorcery of modern fantasy. Another strategy was to reinsert the speculative unknown into the very heart of scientific processes. But just because *we* have mined myth for magic — and, remember, even what we define as *myth* would have been called *religion* two millennia earlier (and the very fact that we think those two terms equivalent is also cultural) — does not mean that this fills the same need for wonder elsewhere. 5

India has developed many of the same features as America: a capitalist economy, an enormous bureaucratic government, and cutting-edge scientific expertise. But its intellectual history is different. Weber's argument is much more nuanced and substantive than the cursory description I have given here, but, in sum, disenchantment is rooted in the intellectual tradition of the 18th-century European Enlightenment with its struggles over the place of religion versus rationality. The aftermath of that contest in the West was to relegate the supernatural mysterious to a lower position than material-based reason. The key point is that this is a particular moment in cultural history, not some necessary and universal stage of human societal "development." Similarly, for that reason, I'd guess Japan's vibrant tradition of the supernatural in its anime, and China's recent taste for American FX spectacles, results from those countries' specific cultural contexts rather than from disenchantment. (And some of the ways the West looks to the non-West for re-enchantment are another, Orientalist can of worms best left for a different day.)

Anyone looking to debunk cultural explanations for the American/Indian sci-fi gap might point out that Hollywood has had the big-budget, dragons-and-droids market flooded for years. Perhaps Bollywood, for commercial reasons, doesn't want to jump in. Average production costs for American superhero blockbusters hover around $200 million these days, and audiences have come to expect the computer-generated spectacle that kind of money buys. But . . . *Star Wars* was made for $11 million in 1977 (less than $40 million now) and 25 percent of *Iron Man 3*'s $200 million budget was Robert Downey Jr.'s salary. Surely there's enough technical expertise and financial muscle in India to digitize a realistic Mars landing when the country's space program is on track to launch a real spacecraft (unmanned) to the red planet this upcoming November.

What about the fact that American blockbusters make tons of money worldwide? For films like *Avatar* and *The Hobbit*, foreign sales equal or exceed domestic U.S. sales. But India, the world's ninth-largest economy and second-most populous country, does not even rank in the top 12 foreign markets for the genre. The list of those markets reads like the attendees of a G-8 summit (plus some key trading partners): the United Kingdom, Japan, France, Germany, Italy, Mexico, Brazil, Spain, South Korea, Russia, Australia, and China. *Avatar* (2009) set the high-water mark for India, where South Asian audiences purchased $24 million worth of tickets — about 10 percent of foreign ticket sales worldwide. But for most science fiction, countries with smaller GDPs than India (Australia, Mexico, South Korea) are higher consumers. Of *Avengers'* (2012) $888 million worldwide, $12 million came from India; *Iron Man 3* is on track with similar numbers; and, to their credit, Indian audiences contributed a paltry $2.8 million to *Transformers 3*'s $434 million. Fantasy fares much worse. *The Hobbit* (2012) made $714 million worldwide; it took home $1.8 million in India. That is barely more than Croatia's $1.4 million.

The simplest conclusion to draw from this is that Bollywood doesn't produce science fiction and fantasy because Indian audiences aren't as keen on it. Local cultural production doesn't just result from economic wherewithal; desires and needs also matter. And desires and needs are cultural. This sometimes feels hard to accept because desires and needs feel so *natural*. Often we think that the way we live is normal and not cultural; this is what anthropologists call "tacit ethnocentrism," when we are not *trying* to be prejudiced, but we have unquestioned assumptions that somehow we are the normal human baseline and others somehow deviate from that.

Hollywood continues to make science fiction and fantasy movies because 10 disenchantment creates a demand for these stories, but disenchantment predates Hollywood. We were journeying ten thousand leagues under the sea or scarcely surviving a war of the worlds before the film industry began. If the uptick of *Hunger Games*–inspired archery lessons and the CDC's humorous-but-practical Zombie Preparedness Guide are any indication, this is not going away any time soon. Re-enchantment delivers something more important than escapism or entertainment. Through its promise of a world of mystery and wonder, it offers the hope that we haven't seen all that there is.

READING THE TEXT

1. Explain in your own words Max Weber's notion of "disenchantment" (para. 4).
2. What is Folch's explanation for why Western film audiences find the supernatural and futurism appealing?
3. According to Folch, what are the cultural reasons Indian film audiences are not "keen on" science fiction and fantasy?

4. What was the Enlightenment, and how did it affect Western consciousness?

5. What does Folch mean by the anthropological term "tacit ethnocentrism" (para. 9)?

READING THE SIGNS

1. Research the last ten years of American movies, and determine how many of the most successful films were fantasies. Use your findings to write your own argument about why fantasy films appeal to American audiences, basing your claims on an analysis of particular movies.

2. Write an essay in which you support, refute, or modify the claim that the rise of fantasy films in America reflects market forces pandering to immature cinematic tastes.

3. Watch a Bollywood film such as *Dhoom 3* (2013), the all-time most popular Indian film, or *Chennai Express* (2013). In an essay, analyze the nature of its appeal to Indian audiences, using Folch's selection as a critical framework. What cultural needs and desires does the film seem to satisfy?

4. Folch claims that "Bollywood takes quotidian family dramas and imbues them with spectacular tales of love and wealth found-lost-regained amidst the pageantry of choreographed dance pieces" (para. 3). In an essay, compare an Indian film like *Devdas* (2002) with an American movie such as *My Big Fat Greek Wedding* (2002). How do the films you select depict family and interpersonal relations? What cultural explanations can you offer for your observations?

PAY ATTENTION WHILE WALKING

YOUR FACEBOOK STATUS UPDATE CAN WAIT.

 Metropolitan Etiquette Authority

THE CLOUD

Semiotics and the New Media

The New Panopticon

In the spring of 2013, an obscure government subcontractor named Edward Snowden blew the cover on the National Security Agency. A hero to some and a traitor to others, Snowden not only created some very odd political bed-fellows through his revelation that the NSA had been collecting and storing data for years on every phone call and digital transaction made in America (congressional Democrats joined Libertarians in seeking new NSA restrictions after the leak, while Republicans joined the White House in resisting those efforts), but also indirectly revealed just how deeply digital technology has invaded our lives. Because here was a revelation that put a new edge on the already-widespread knowledge that such digital titans as Google, Facebook, and Apple were mining user data and selling that information to anyone willing to pay for it. It raised to a whole new level the sense that there is a price to pay for all the pleasures and conveniences of the digital age. That price is our privacy, whether it is sold for the benefit of businesses that want to know what we are doing so they can more efficiently market goods and services to us, or given to the government on behalf of national security. And with the arrival of Google Glass, ordinary citizens will be all the more able to invade the privacy of anyone around them, surreptitiously recording and posting to YouTube everything in their path. Thus, one way or another, the new media are transforming America into what the late Michel Foucault called a "Panopticon": a society that is under constant surveillance, like a prison.

And yet, that isn't the way that many, if not most, people see it. Rather—especially for those who have spent their lives within the digital era — their smartphones, tablets, e-readers, laptops, and even desktops are not merely sources of pleasure or convenience; they are necessities, required not only for work, school, and play, but for existence itself. Who cares if someone's watching as long as the connection is still up, and they can remain enveloped in the vast, round-the-clock social network in which no one ever has to be alone? It isn't a Panopticon; it's a global village that's revolutionizing human life all over the world.

So which is it: prison or village? An abuse of power or a triumph of social evolution? Like all technological interventions — such as the automobile or television — that have made an indelible impact on society, digital technology is not easy to assess, but there may be no subject as important to think about semiotically in an era when the new media are expanding into every corner of our lives with a velocity that some think will soon become infinite. Indeed, your analyses of the new media could well begin with questions just like these.

The Global Hive

Grasping the impact of the new media isn't made any easier by the conflicting signals that have been sent by media history itself. In 1962, when Marshall McLuhan launched the modern era of media studies with his groundbreaking book *The Gutenberg Galaxy*, the situation looked pretty straightforward. At the time, television, cinema, radio, and stereos were the dominant electronic media, so it was only natural that McLuhan would focus on the shift he saw taking place from a text, or print-based, culture to an aural and image-based culture. Such a culture would mark a radical change in consciousness, he predicted, a departure from the logical form of thinking fostered by the linear structure of alphabetic writing and a return of sorts to a more ancient oral/visual consciousness in what he was the first to call the "global village."

With the rise of the Internet and related digital technologies, however, McLuhan's predictions have become considerably complicated. While digital technology, too, is an electronic medium saturated with visual images and aural content, it has also brought the (digitally) printed word back into popular culture and consciousness. Indeed, before the full blossoming of the Internet as we know it today, word processing and, subsequently, print-based e-mail, constituted the leading edge of the digital revolution. And with the rise of the blogosphere in the late 1990s, not to mention the online posting of such traditional print media as newspapers, magazines (does anyone remember "zines"?), and fiction (does anyone remember "hypertexts"?) and the rise of texting (often at the expense of telephonic talking), the digital proliferation of print appeared to refute one of McLuhan's most fundamental observations about media history. Indeed, things seemed to be going *back* to Gutenberg.

With the obliteration of MySpace — which in its heyday tended to be plastered with visual imagery and aural content — at the hands of Facebook, which made printed text the dominant feature on the screen "page," this return of the font appeared to be closer to accomplishment. Sure, there was still YouTube, but Facebook was really getting much of the attention.

But while it is far too early to predict the eventual demise of Facebook, a new trend is appearing, a differential shift in the high-speed history of digital culture. This **difference** involves the emergence of such sites as Twitter (still print based but reduced to a kind of digital shorthand) and Tumblr, which, in its presentation of "microblogs," is heavy on uploaded images and light on printed text. Facebook, for its part, has largely supplanted the much more text-based world of the original blogging site, and individual Facebook pages can be filled with photos and videos in a kind of semi-return to the MySpace era. Add the continued popularity of YouTube and the emergence of many other sites, like Instagram, Snapchat, and Flickr, devoted to the uploading of an endless image stream contributed by a ubiquitous arsenal of iPhones, Droids, Galaxys, and other devices, and you have a veritable tsunami of pixels, not fonts.

The ability to upload your own images instantly with the same device that took the pictures has further enhanced the "village-like" nature of the cloud in a socially profound manner as well. We call it "sharing," but it is more than that, because the tendency to post images of your personal experiences even as you experience them is an expression and intensification of what sociologists call the "heterodirectedness" of our culture. A heterodirected society is one in which members live their lives predominantly in relation to others, constantly seeking their approval and recognition. In contrast with the autonomous individualist, who isn't concerned with what others think, the heterodirected person lives his or her life within a social web where everyone is in contact with everyone else, not only sharing with others but ultimately judging them. It is not unlike the premodern experience of small-town or village life, where everyone knew everyone else, but now, thanks to new technologies, the scale is global, with people all over the world living their lives in relation to the often-anonymous others who share their experiences via those tiny digital boxes that they can never seem to put down.

So maybe it is premature to rule McLuhan out entirely. Perhaps the global village has arrived in the form of a global hive, a buzzing crowd of digitally connected Netizens who appear to be unable to let go for a few minutes to concentrate on an actual here-and-now as they hook up with a virtual elsewhere.

Of course, you hardly need to be told about how digital technology has revolutionized the ways in which people communicate with each other and consume entertainment. You really don't need to be told about the latest, and hottest, social networking sites. Indeed, even if we try to identify what those sites are, by the time this book is published that information would be dated, as we discovered when composing the Introduction to our initial chapter on digital technology for the sixth edition of *Signs of Life in the U.S.A.* At that time, MySpace was the eight-hundred-pound gorilla of social networking, with hundreds of millions of mostly youthful members. Facebook was an out-lier, something for some college students in the Northeast and a few adults. But by the time the sixth edition appeared, Facebook had become a world-wide behemoth, and MySpace was on the way out. Even as we prepare the eighth edition of this text, however, Facebook is showing some signs of losing its hegemony, with such sites as Twitter, Instagram, Pinterest, Tumblr, Snap-chat, and Reddit looming large, but we expect that at least some will be old hat by the time this book comes out, and that new names will dominate the Internet, which will, in turn, rise to dizzying heights of popularity and then subside.

So, when considering the semiotics of digital technology and social media, the point is not to identify what's hot and what's not; instead, you should explore the cultural significance of digitality. Consider for a moment the basic setup, the experiential situation of online communication through social media sites. They weren't always called "social media," by the way. In the early days of the Internet, they were called "chat rooms."

Whose Space?

The first chat rooms were rather primitive places. Austere, you might say, with no images, music, or decoration of any kind, just plain text boxes where words materialized as if from out of nowhere. Visiting such places was a bit of an adventure, a pioneering voyage into cyberspace and the uncharted expanses of the electronic frontier.

Until the advent of the now-ubiquitous smartphone and tablet, these excursions were carried out indoors, in homes and offices via stationary desk-top computers. Today, of course, thanks to mobile devices operating within a cloud computing environment, the journey can be taken anywhere — in the street, in the classroom, in a club, in a park, in a restaurant, in an airport — literally everywhere. Yet, either way, via desktop or smartphone, navigating the cloud through an ever-expanding number of social networking sites dis-rupts some very ancient codes governing the use of social space, deconstruct-ing not only the old demarcations between public and private space but the meaning of social experience itself.

Consider for a moment an ordinary public road: It isn't just a ribbon of asphalt; it's a complex structure of codes for pedestrians. These codes tell you that you may walk down the street, but must stick to the side (or sidewalk if there is one), and that it's best to stay to the right to avoid oncoming foot traffic. If there are private houses on the street, you may approach the front door, but you're not supposed to cut through the yard, and you're certainly not allowed to enter without permission. You may enter the public space of a store, shopping center, or post office, but you probably need to pay to enter a museum, and you must pass through a security checkpoint if you are entering a courthouse or an airline terminal.

Now consider your own physical personal space: There, you set the rules. You determine who enters it and what can be done there. You might actually write out the rules that govern your space (as in posting a NO SMOKING sign), but those rules are more likely to be obeyed if you are personally present. Indeed, the most basic personal space rule is that no unauthorized person should be in it when you are absent.

The spaces of everyday life, both public and private, are, in short, packed with codes that we violate or ignore at our peril. These codes all originate in the way that human beings define their territories. A *territory* is a space that has been given meaning through having been claimed by an individual or group of individuals. Unclaimed, unmarked space is socially meaningless, but put up a building or a fence and the uncircumscribed landscape becomes a bounded territory, a human habitat with its own rules for permitted and unpermitted behavior. Anyone unaware of those rules can't survive for long in human society.

But what sort of territory is a social networking site, and what rules govern it? In a sense, it is a place where its users are all hosts and guests simultaneously, with the rules accordingly being quite confusing. A host is hospitable; a guest is polite and follows the host's guidance. But with no one in the cloud being entirely host or entirely guest, things can easily go wrong. You don't insult people in their own homes, but online flaming occurs all too often. Indeed, many sites and forums where people socialize and communicate are described as being like the Wild West — a wide-open space known for its lack of clear rules of conduct and the way in which it challenges traditional conceptions of social space. The result has been a blurring of the traditional lines between the uses of public and private space and, with that, much confusion about how to behave in the essentially public arena of digital communication. Just read responses people make in the feedback or comments sections of popular Web sites like YouTube. Certainly, the old rules about public courtesy no longer apply.

This is one reason so many people flocked to Facebook in the latter half of the first decade of the new millennium. Since everyone is the administrator of his or her Facebook page, it feels like you are in control there, that your Facebook page is like your own home: a private space whose rules you control. But it really isn't. Not only does Facebook periodically change how its privacy protections work, but the company can, and does, overstep those protections all the time in order to sell your information to virtually anyone who wants it, and the company will give it to the government as well. So even though your Facebook page may feel private and controllable, it is actually quite public — as all too many Facebook users have learned to their distress.

Or consider the very common phenomenon of someone (perhaps yourself) in an ostensibly public setting — say, sitting with a group of friends — while engaging in an essentially private activity on a mobile device. Whether texting, tweeting, posting to Instagram, updating your Facebook page, or doing any one of an almost-unlimited number of online activities, you

---

Exploring the Signs of the Cloud

If you have a Facebook page, describe it in your journal and discuss why you designed it as you did. What signs did you choose to communicate your identity, and why? Did you deliberately avoid including some signs? If so, why? If you chose not to join Facebook or another such site, why did you make that choice?

---

have, once again, turned a public social space into a private one, moving back and forth between what were once separate spheres (after all, you can share what you are doing on your Galaxy, or even put it aside for a moment and talk to the people around you) as if there were no difference between them.

Thus, one way or another, the private/public divide is being undone, and the old rules governing the use of social space are becoming obsolete. This is all happening so quickly that not only is it easy to take for granted, but there hasn't been sufficient time to constitute new rules to take the place of the old ones. Given that society cannot function without such codes, this change is of profound social significance, a problem that cannot be addressed without first realizing that it exists.

Tweeting with the Stars

Then there is the disruptive nature of the way that we socialize in the cloud. While the invention of the telephone began the disruption in the nineteenth century, today's social networking greatly magnifies the possibilities of socializing in the absence of anyone being physically present. You can tweet to the whole world, but no one is necessarily listening. You can have thousands of Facebook "friends," without actually meeting any of them. You can even "tweet with the stars," though the chances that any celebrity tweeter will know who you are, or care, are tiny. Often, then, that sense of intimacy with others in the cloud is, in reality, an illusion, especially given the way that people can stage-manage their online profile. How, in such conditions, can you know for certain whether those profiles of "friends" whom you have never met are accurate or true?

Thus, the lack of actual spatial proximity in digital communication produces what could be called a "proxemic disruption" within human history. **Proxemics**, a field loosely related to semiotics, is the study of how we communicate with others in face-to-face situations, including such means as body language, facial expression, and tone of voice. Because these social cues are absent in the cloud, social communication itself is being revolutionized in ways that are not yet entirely clear. Certainly, there has been a loss of civility due to the proxemic disruption, thanks to the lack of the controlling influence of the threat of direct retaliation for rude or insulting behavior that exists in face-to-face communication, while the possibility for misunderstanding has also increased. Indeed, a phenomenon known as "Poe's Law"—which refers to the difficulty of determining whether someone is being ironic or not in the cloud—is a particularly striking example of how the lack of physical contact can lead to less, not more, effective communication, in spite of the apparently limitless opportunities for social interaction that the cloud provides.

What is more, much of the communication that does take place in the cloud is either a form of shorthand (as on Twitter or on microblogging sites like Tumblr) or simply an exchange of pictures. Then there is the fact that those whom you allow to "speak" on your Facebook page more often than not do not speak at all: They just give you a thumbs-up. And if people say anything you don't like, you can silence them. This is profoundly different from traditional communication among peers, which cannot be individually controlled and requires much more complete verbalization. In some ways, then, communication in the cloud has become a highly segregated activity where only those who already agree with each other are allowed to "speak," and they don't have to say much because everyone already agrees.

And yet, the cloud doesn't *feel* exclusive to the innumerable people who "live" there. In fact, it feels all-inclusive, like a vast buzzing hive of closely related "friends." Clearly, part of the appeal of the new media is that they make people feel connected, with family, with friends, and with online communities that may be based on little more than shared interests—instantly postable to sites like Pinterest that encourage the passing around of information like a vast chain letter—but that can be very real communities all the same. Human beings are social animals, after all, but nothing in our genes says that those with whom we socialize have to be physically present. The addictive nature of digital technology, the way that its users suffer something like drug withdrawal when they are deprived of it, is a powerful testimony to the deep appeal of socializing in the cloud. Whether this compelling draw of digital socializing will eventually lead to a whole new definition of "society," a whole new way of relating to other people, is anyone's guess at this point, but there is no doubt that it has become a very effective way of making money for those who control the networks. Which leads us to yet another semiotic question.

Top-Down After All?

Traditionally, the mass media have been structured in a top-down manner, with corporate elites providing passive consumers with the news, entertainments, and products that they consume, along with the advertisements that promote them. But now the top-down news has turned into a bottom-up conversation in which anyone can become a pundit, while newspapers and online news sites invite input from their readers. Broadband Internet access has turned video creativity over to the masses in such a way that you no longer have to be a famous director or producer to present your own television shows or films to a wide audience, and you don't have to be an authorized critic to respond, with YouTube, Rotten Tomatoes, and related sites offering unlimited opportunities to critique what you find there. In short, what was once a passive and vicarious media experience for the mass of consumers is now active and participatory.

Another way of putting this is that until recently our relationship with the mass media has been more or less a one-way street. Those with the power to control the media (TV networks, radio stations, movie studios, newspaper owners, corporate sponsors with advertising dollars to spend) have broadcast their signals to us (TV and radio programs, films, newspapers, and ads), and we have passively received them, without being able to answer back. The late semiologist and sociologist Jean Baudrillard (1929–2007) regarded this situation as one of the essential conditions of postmodern times and used it as a basis for his analyses of contemporary society. But with so much of the mass media now actively eliciting responses from their audiences, and with consumers of the mass media able to create and disseminate their own media content — indeed, now an ordinary news story can be remixed into memes that go viral and become news stories of their own, like the "Bed Intruder Song" in 2010, which turned an interview with the brother of a victim of sexual assault into an international sensation — it certainly appears that something post-postmodern is emerging beyond Baudrillard's perceptions.

But while the new media are definitely opening up channels for democratic communication and expression that previously did not exist, they have also created new elites whose wealth and power depend upon their ability to exploit the mass of people who use the technologies they offer. We have already referred here to the price we all have to pay for personal privacy thanks to the panoptic capabilities of digital technology, but there is also the way that technology tycoons seek to monopolize daily life and shut down older, predigital forms of commerce and professional activity. We're referring here to the assaults on "brick-and-mortar" retailing via online shopping sites, print journalism via online news outlets, and face-to-face education via massive open online courses (MOOCs) as just three prominent examples.

Partly, what has made the creation of the new media elites possible has been the consumer expectation (and demand) that "information should be free." While consumers do not balk at paying for the tangible commodities they purchase online, they do feel that such intangible commodities as education, music, and written texts should be accessible without cost (which is why so many people regarded Aaron Swartz, who hacked into MIT's servers to release copyrighted articles, as a martyr to the open access movement when he committed suicide in 2013). Already trained by commercial TV and radio to expect free content, American consumers were immediately receptive to the similar business models of the new media, taking for granted the free use of online services, not realizing that those services have a cost and that they are not really free at all. Thus, traditional media (like newspapers) that paid for and profited by charging directly for their operation are going out of business, while the new media titans that have found ways to monetize their operations without any direct out-of-pocket costs to consumers are replacing them.

At the same time, once-populist, user-generated sites have tended to become dominated by social and corporate elites very quickly. Twitter is an example. Though it is still a site where anyone can tweet (if he or she is a registered user, that is) and still serves as a premier source of breaking news stories from the people who experience them first, the major news organizations now present news stories in the form of tweets from their reporters in the field; similarly, celebrity tweeters and politicians like Sarah Palin have pretty well hogged vast spaces of Twitterland in recent years.

And so we have a paradox: Top-down has met bottom-up in a cloud that is at once democratic and hierarchical, your space and corporate space. The democratic, user-generated spaces in the cloud are simultaneously revolutionary and business as usual. Users pass around their own content (often not self-created), but they do so on sites that are owned by huge corporations that require registration so that their services can be monetized. Somehow, the future doesn't seem to be what it used to be.

In the famous 1984 Super Bowl commercial that introduced the Macintosh, Apple Computer promised that the future was going to belong to the people, not to rigid, profit-seeking corporate powers. Web 1.0 and Web 2.0 were both built, in large part, by people who believed in this vision of a sort of anticorporate utopia. But that isn't what happened at all. The Macintosh ad, after all, featured a big screen with an image of Big Brother hectoring a room full of hypnotized viewers. Is that so very different from the billions of people who compulsively stare into their digital devices, knowing that those devices are looking back at the behest of corporate elites who want to use their information to profit from, and control, their behavior?

We are all living in the midst of a gigantic social experiment whose significance can be determined only by careful critical thinking. Often uncritically celebrated as a "disruption," the brave new world of digital technology is easy to take for granted, but the profound differences that it has introduced into our lives call for semiotic attention. In its own way, the cloud is the most

Discussing the Signs of the Cloud

Critics of online social networking sites have expressed concern that excessive online networking will diminish participants' ability to socialize normally in face-to-face environments. In class, discuss the legitimacy of this concern, drawing upon your personal experiences with social networking.

Reading the Cloud

YouTube allows users to create their own "television" content, yet the site is filled with content taken from other sources, such as television clips, concert footage, and the like. Conduct a survey of YouTube content to estimate the ratio of user-created content to postings of professional performers. Analyze and interpret your results semiotically. What are the implications of your findings for the bottom-up versus top-down debate over Web 2.0 "democracy"?

important popular cultural topic you can semiotically analyze. This chapter is designed to prompt you to do that.

The Readings

S. Craig Watkins opens the chapter with a look at today's always turned-on and tuned-in world of digital entertainment, wondering if it isn't all leading to an epidemic of Continuous Partial Attention. The International Center for Media and the Public Agenda and Simon Dumenco follow with a paired set of readings, with the former reporting on experimental data that suggest digital usage may be literally addictive, and the latter looking at the way Facebook "guilts" its inactive users into logging back in as it seeks to maintain its social media supremacy. Next, danah boyd reveals the surprising racial coding that separates rival social networking sites Facebook and MySpace, and that has led to the near demise of the latter. Salvador Rodriguez follows with a personal essay on lost romances that refuse to disappear when it comes to the almost-ineradicable traces they leave on the Internet, while Richard Rushfield blogs on what he sees as social networking overkill — that is, the tendency of the Internet to talk just about any subject to death. Daniel D'Addario's rumination on the way that the word "trolling" has become overused and abused in Internet discourse is next, and Henry Jenkins concludes this chapter with an analysis of the phenomenon that he calls "convergence culture," a world where old and new media come together.

S. CRAIG WATKINS

Fast Entertainment and Multitasking in an Always-On World

Thanks to digital technology, a veritable universe of entertainment is now available to us whenever and wherever we want it. S. Craig Watkins, in this excerpt from his book *The Young and the Digital* (2009), calls this cornucopia of always-on diversion "fast entertainment," focusing here on the multitasking ways of its youthful consumers. But, Watkins warns, "like fast food, fast entertainment is easy to get, all around us, and typically cheap, but not always good for you." Something to keep in mind while studying for finals. S. Craig Watkins is a professor at the University of Texas at Austin, where he teaches in the departments of Radio-Television-Film, Sociology, and the Center for African and African American Studies. His previous books include *Hip Hop Matters* (2005) and *Representing: Hip Hop Culture and the Production of Black Cinema* (1998).

For the younger generation of multitaskers, the great electronic din is an expected part of everyday life. And given what neuroscience and anecdotal evidence have shown us, this state of constant intentional self-distraction could well be of profound detriment to individual and cultural well-being.

—CHRISTINE ROSEN, Senior Editor of *The New Atlantis*[1]

Laptop computers, mobile phones, and iPods deliver a vast assortment of digital media content in unprecedented speed — now! Today, we can view video clips, listen to our favorite music downloads, squeeze in a game, access user-generated content, or just about anything else in smaller and quicker doses, thus making these digital delights all-pervading and irresistible. A 2007 *Wired* magazine cover story titled "Snack Culture" celebrates the rise of what it calls bite-size entertainment and the emergent world of one-minute media. "We now devour our pop culture," writes Nancy Miller, "the same way we enjoy candy and chips — in conveniently packaged bite-size nuggets made to be munched easily with increased frequency and maximum speed."[2] *Wired* calls it snack culture. I call it fast entertainment — this ever-widening menu of media content that we can consume easily and on the go.

No matter where we are, fast entertainment is generally just a click away. I liken the efficient delivery of digital media content to another staple in the

---

[1] Christine Rosen, "The Myth of Multitasking," *New Atlantis* no. 20 (Spring 2008): 105–10.
[2] Nancy Miller, "Minifesto for a New Age," *Wired*, March 2007.

daily American diet: fast food. Like fast food, fast entertainment is easy to get, all around us, and typically cheap, but not always good for you.

It is hard to know which came first—our appetite for speedy entertainment or the widespread manufacturing and aggressive marketing of it. Mobile technologies are ideal platforms for delivering bite-size media easily and effectively. For much of its early life, fast entertainment was the primary domain of technology companies, Silicon Valley start-ups, and Web entrepreneurs. Known for its user-generated content, a major part of YouTube's success can also be attributed to the creation of a space that supplies an endless stream of short video clips that complement our desire to consume a lot very quickly. Yahoo! is also a favorite online destination to grab a quick video clip, music playlist, or game. Social-network sites allow users to share a wide range of content with their fellow users casually and throughout the day. Come across a funny video and send it to your Facebook friends. Discover a cool new underground hip-hop band and spread the word through MySpace. Nowhere is the hegemony of fast entertainment more evident than in the rise of Apple's iTunes Store, one of the most prolific platforms for delivering digital media content.

In his book *The Perfect Thing: How the iPod Shuffles Commerce, Culture, and Coolness*, *Newsweek* chief technology correspondent Steven Levy explains how the music industry insiders dismissed the idea of selling digital downloads. Apple's CEO, Steve Jobs, told Levy, "When we first approached the labels, the online music business was a disaster. Nobody had ever sold a song for ninety-nine cents. Nobody ever really sold a *song*."[3] When Apple launched the iTunes Store in 2003, the service developed a reputation for delivering digital music downloads quickly, reliably, legally, and cheaply. From day one the iTunes Store was a huge success, reportedly selling 275,000 downloads in its first eighteen hours of operation. By day five, the number of downloads reached one million. In six short years, iTunes went from being nonexistent to surpassing the retail behemoth, Walmart, to become the number one music retailer in the United States.

In 2005 the iTunes Store began offering downloads of music videos and 5 popular television programs for the iPod. Soon after that the store expanded to include movies, podcasts, audiobooks, and games, among other things. Apple's iPhone has been an even bigger hit and distributor of fast entertainment. In just nine months iPhone users downloaded more than one billion applications, many from categories like games, music, and entertainment. Apple's iPod and iPhone made it convenient and cool to carry our entire inventory of media and entertainment in our pocket. No matter if you are at home or on the road, access to your media entertainment library is just a touch of a button away. Technology companies such as YouTube, Yahoo!, and Apple were among the first to superserve our desire to quickly and constantly consume media. After

---

[3]Steven Levy, *The Perfect Thing: How the iPod Shuffles Commerce, Culture, and Coolness* (New York: Simon & Schuster, 2006), 135.

realizing our desire to consume content on the go and in smaller bites, the old media guard is responding.

From the big music labels to the network television industry, the major media companies are investing, strategically and financially, in fast entertainment by offering up their own versions of bite-size media. In 2007 Sony Corporation and its production studio, Sony Pictures Television, tossed its hat in the fast entertainment ring. The studio announced that it would begin sifting through its massive inventory to produce three-to-five-minute versions of programs that once filled the thirty-minute and hour-length programming slots in the primetime schedule. Sony executives call these tiny TV episodes minisodes. According to the studio, minisodes are not clips but rather full episodes containing a discernible narrative structure consisting of a beginning, middle, and end. The initial roster of miniature programs included old television series like *Charlie's Angels*, *T.J. Hooker*, and *Starsky & Hutch*.

Sony executives characterize the minisodes as campy and fun, but the decision to produce them is a serious response to how young people enjoy their media. In many ways, the creation of three-to-five-minute episodes are influenced by a video-clip culture that is a staple in the online experiences of many young people. From Lime Wire to BitTorrent, the adoption of file-sharing platforms not only alters how the young and the digital consume media content; it also reflects a greater interest on their part to manage, share, and engage content.

One of the more intriguing paradoxes of today's digital media environment is that we consume more and less at the same time. How is this possible? The rise of YouTube, founded in February 2005 by Chad Hurley and Steve Chen, is a great illustration. They launched the video file-sharing site to empower users of social media to do with videos what they were doing with photos—create, manage, and share them with peers. You name it—music videos, sports highlights, news segments, political speeches, user-generated content, clips from television and film—and YouTube users share it. According to comScore, "Americans viewed more than 11.4 billion videos for a total duration of 558 million hours during the month of July 2008."[4] Five billion, or 44 percent, of the videos were watched on YouTube. More precisely, 91 million viewers watched a YouTube video, which averages out to about fifty-five videos per person. The average length of a video watched in July 2008: 2.9 minutes. In short, Americans watched a ton of online videos, the vast majority of them short clips. In the digital media age, more equals less.

In addition to consuming less of more, we are constantly consuming. We have evolved from a culture of instant gratification to one of constant gratification. Fast entertainment encourages an insatiable desire to be entertained no matter where we are (at work) or what we are doing (driving a car). While the scientific merits of Internet addiction are still being measured, analyzed, and

[4]*YouTube Draws 5 Billion U.S. Online Video Views in July 2008* (Reston, VA: comScore Media Metrix, September 10, 2008), www.comscore.com/press/release.asp?press=2444.

assessed, one thing is undeniable: the desire for fast entertainment is widespread and voracious. We not only want our media content now, we expect it now. Not that long ago, consuming media on the go was a luxury. Today, it is a standard feature of daily life.

In many ways, the social- and mobile-media lifestyle represents a new 10 cultural ethos and a profound shift in how we consume media—in smaller and steadier portions and on smaller and more mobile screens. Along with changing how we consume media, fast entertainment changes where we consume media. Two developments defined the post-war boom Americans experienced starting around the 1950s: a rapid increase in home ownership and a bustling consumer economy. By the 1950s Americans were furnishing their new homes with all kinds of appliances that helped to establish a more modern and socially mobile lifestyle. Beginning with the radio, the phonograph, and then the television, Americans also filled their homes with media. Over the next half century, Americans participated in a flourishing home-centered media consumer culture that redefined leisure and household life.

Not that long ago we typically left our homes to purchase a wide array of media—music, books, magazines, videocassettes, games, DVDs—and then returned home to enjoy it. Today, however, the reverse is increasingly more common. We collect content from the comfort and convenience of our home, via digital downloads and peer-to-peer networks, to take with us when we leave our home. Throughout the last two decades of the twentieth century, Americans turned their homes into what media technology professor Jorge Schement calls the wired castle. Our homes became the ultimate leisure space. But in an always-on world, any place can be a good place to grab a quick bite of entertainment.

Despite all the euphoria over iTunes, iPods, iPhones, Webisodes, minisodes, minigames, and one-minute media, is the ability to be entertained constantly and no matter where you are really a good thing?

Young people are media rich. They own music players, computers, mobile phones, TVs, and game consoles. Young people's media environment is like a kid who wakes up one day and finds himself in a candy store. Surrounded by so many tasty options, what does he do? Naturally, he devours as much of it as he can, any way that he can. And that is essentially what we are seeing young people do with media. Immersed in a world of media, they use as much of it as they can, any way that they can. Innovative as ever, the one sure way for young people to use all of the media and technology they own is to use it simultaneously. One study, for example, found that American youth report spending about six hours a day with media. If you include the simultaneous use of media, that figure grows to about eight hours a day. Communication scholars refer to this as media multitasking.

We all media multitask. As I work on this chapter, my e-mail box, music player, photo application, and several tabs on my two favorite browsers are all open on my computer screen. But the young and the digital are widely viewed as masterful multitaskers, capable of managing several technologies, screens, and conversations fluidly and simultaneously. They multitask habitually and according to many observers, they also do it instinctively.

Donald F. Roberts, a Stanford University communications professor, has [15] studied the media behaviors of children and adolescents for more than thirty years. Roberts believes that adolescents' multitasking ways began to really take shape as the media in their homes migrated into their bedrooms. With the use of ethnographic techniques, time diaries, and surveys, researchers began building more nuanced portraits of the media environment in American homes in the 1970s. A 1972 study of southern California sixth graders found that 6 percent of the sample had a television in their bedrooms.[5] Since then, the flow of media into children's bedrooms has continued at a steady clip. In his study of media use by youth, Roberts and his colleagues found that no matter if they were especially young, ages two to seven, or older, ages eleven to fourteen, kids in America access a lot of media from their bedrooms.[6]

At least a third of young children, for example, can watch television or listen to music from their own bedroom. Similarly, three-quarters of older children are able to watch TV or play a videogame from the comforts of their bedroom.[7] By the year 2000, about 20 percent of older youth, ages twelve to eighteen, were accessing computers from their bedrooms. Assessing the state of young people's media environment by the start of the new millennium, Roberts writes, "Compared with even a few years ago, the sheer numbers of children and adolescents possessing personal media is remarkable."[8] The movement of media into children's bedrooms creates the context for more frequent, intense, unsupervised, and in the view of some researchers, unhealthy media behaviors.

Until recently the data on media multitasking was extremely limited. How much do young people media multitask? According to a 2006 study by the Kaiser Family Foundation, a lot.

The San Mateo, California–based research unit surveyed a national cross-section of 2,032 school-age kids ages eight to eighteen. In addition, Kaiser analyzed data from a self-selected subsample of 694 respondents who completed a seven-day diary of their media use. Here are some of the study's findings. Children and teenagers spend at least a quarter of their time with multiple media.[9] On a typical day, Kaiser reports, eight in ten school-age children media multitask. Predictably, young people do a lot of their multitasking when they are using a computer. Older children, ages fourteen to eighteen,

[5]J. Lyle and H. R. Hoffman, "Children's Use of Television and Other Media," in E. A. Rubinstein, G. A. Comstock, and J. P. Murray, eds., *Television and Social Behavior*, vol. 4, *Television in Day-to-Day Life: Patterns and Use* (Washington, DC: U.S. Government Printing Office, 1972): 129–256.

[6]Roberts and Foehr, *Kids and Media in America*, 42–48.

[7]Ibid., 42–43.

[8]Ibid., 42.

[9]For a detailed assessment of media multitasking among young people, see Foehr, *Media Multitasking Among American Youth.*

multitask more, but by the age of ten, their desire to multitask is strong. Young multitaskers tend to use other media — such as television or music — while on the computer. Even when using the computer is the only activity, it is common for young people to shuffle back and forth between instant messaging, their favorite Web sites, online videos, and games, all while managing a wealth of digital content such as photos and music files.

Tweens and teens are not the only ones multitasking their media. Our surveys and in-depth conversations show that college students are avid users of multiple media too. They multitask with just about every media they use — the Internet, music, television, and books and magazines. A decisive majority, 95 percent, listen to music either most or some of the time when using the computer. Seventy-two percent of our survey respondents said they watch television most or some of the time when using a computer is their primary activity. And when television is the primary activity, 81 percent of our respondents said they use a computer either most or some of the time. That is what Justin, a twenty-one-year-old psychology major, does.

"I multitask the most with the computer and television," Justin explained.   20 When there are commercials he usually goes online. "In that gap of time, I am normally on instant messenger talking to friends."

Twenty-one-year-old Andrea, an advertising major, uses television and the Internet at the same time too. "For me, the television works as background noise and the Internet allows me to be connected at all times," she said. When she gets bored with television, her computer is never too far away. Different media require different cognitive loads. For example, the load needed to listen to music is considered less than the cognitive resources needed to read a book. One thing is consistently clear in our research: among college students, using one media almost always means interacting with other media too.

Multitasking media habits are formed relatively early and right around the time young teens begin to develop their own peer networks, media interests, and greater independence from their parents. Among the young people we met, media multitasking is widely accepted as a fact of everyday life. Johnson, a nineteen-year-old, summed up multitasking this way: "I don't really think about it. It's just something that I've always done." Twenty-two-year-old Justine's multitasking skills are at once typical and amazing. "At one time I can be banking, paying bills, checking my e-mail, Facebooking, e-mailing my parents, talking online to my friends, checking the *TV Guide* on the Internet, and researching possible graduate schools," she said. As one young woman put it when referring to her generation, "Multitasking is easy and natural for us."

She's right. Multitasking for the young and the digital is easy and it certainly appears natural. But a growing body of evidence provokes the question, is media multitasking effective? More important, is it healthy?

When we asked young people why they multitask, the response was consistent: to accomplish more things efficiently. Twenty-two-year-old Brandon said, "I would never get anything done if I did not multitask." Most of us, in fact, multitask as a way to more effectively manage our time. And yet, even as humans continue managing multiple screens, media, and tasks simultaneously, cutting-edge brain research is beginning to confirm what some say is obvious: doing several things at once actually reduces task efficiency and proficiency. There is growing evidence that multitasking may not only slow down the completion of tasks but may also impair our performance. Addressing our incessant desire to multitask in a piece that appears in the *Atlantic*, Walter Kirn writes, "The great irony of multitasking — that its overall goal, getting more done in less time, turns out to be chimerical."[10]

In 2007 a team of psychology professors working from the Human Infor- 25 mation Processing Laboratory at Vanderbilt University conducted a series of test trials to assess the brain's capacity to perform multiple tasks. For years brain specialists have suspected that the brain contains a bottleneck function that keeps us from concentrating on two different things at once. Dr. René Marois, one of the principal investigators from the Vanderbilt lab, focuses on the neural basis of attention and information processing in the human brain. More precisely, Marois and his colleagues seek to more fully understand why humans appear unable to execute more than one mental task at a time. Using functional magnetic resonance imaging (fMRI) of the brain, Marois and his colleagues identified what doctors believe is the mechanism that prohibits humans from processing two or more things at the same time, the central bottleneck of information processing.

To determine what happens when we ask our brain to execute two tasks at the same time, the Vanderbilt researchers conducted dual-task trials.[11] In the first task participants were instructed to touch the appropriate button in response to a sound stimulus. In the second task participants were asked to select the appropriate vocal response to a visual stimulus. Compared to the complex information processing that takes place daily, each task in the trials is easy to perform. Hear a sound, push a particular button. See an image, utter a specific word. Easy, right? But the Vanderbilt team made things more interesting and challenging by varying the time interval in between these two simple tasks. In some instances participants were given 300 milliseconds in between tasks, while others were allotted more time, on average about 1560 milliseconds.

Among the test subjects with very little time in between the first and second tasks, there was a statistically significant delay in executing the second task. The experiments along with the brain scanning data from the fMRI provide neural evidence of what researchers call dual-task interference. That is, when we try to process two pieces of information simultaneously, a traffic

[10]Walter Kirn, "The Autumn of the Multitaskers," *Atlantic*, November 2007, www .theatlantic.com/doc/200711/multitasking.

[11]Paul E. Dux et al., "Isolation of a Central Bottleneck of Information Processing with Time-Resolved fMRI," *Neuron* 52 (December 21, 2006): 1109–20.

jam ensues in the brain. Conversely, among the subjects allotted more time in between each task, there was no significant delay in their execution of the second task. In addition to executing the trial experiments more efficiently, the subjects with a longer interval between tasks were more likely to push the correct button or execute the right vocal response. In short, subjects with more time in between tasks were much more efficient and proficient. Our brains, it turns out, are not wired to process dual information simultaneously. Results of the study were published in the December 2007 issue of the medical journal *Neuron*.

In the summary section of the peer-reviewed article, the Vanderbilt researchers write, "When humans attempt to perform two tasks at once, execution of the first task usually leads to postponement of the second one." The results of the trial experiments, the doctors maintain, "suggest that a neural network of frontal lobe areas acts as a central bottleneck of information processing that severely limits our ability to multitask."[12]

The significance of these findings extends well beyond medical labs and scientific journals. Multitasking has real-life implications both for our brains and our world. Think about how frequently we multitask throughout the day. In some situations multitasking—say, responding to e-mails while eating lunch—may be quite useful in managing a busy day. In other situations multitasking may be inappropriate and even fatal. That was certainly the case on September 20, 2008, when twenty-five people were killed after Metrolink III crashed head-on with an oncoming Union Pacific freight train in Chatsworth, California. It was the worst California train disaster in fifty years. An investigation revealed that, seconds before the crash, the Metrolink engineer at the helm of the train was sending and receiving text messages. Concentrating on his phone messages meant that he could not focus on his path and a series of warning signals that would have almost certainly prevented the accident.

At this point and time there are as many questions as there are answers 30 when it comes to understanding the neurological implications of multitasking. For instance, some brain specialists believe that constant multitasking may be stretching our neural capabilities beyond their outer limits and subtly changing the machinations of our brain. Studies show that certain regions of the human brain are wired to process information, whereas other regions facilitate our ability to recall information. There is growing speculation in the medical community that young multitaskers may be conditioning their brains to quickly access, manage, and process information while underdeveloping the neural ability to recall and understand the information that they find.

Popular notions of media multitasking are misleading. The person using a computer while watching television and responding to text messages on their phone actually uses one screen at a time. Multitasking involves switching one's attention back and forth from one platform to another. In reality,

[12]Ibid., 1109.

the issue media multitasking raises is not simultaneous media use per se, but rather the ability of humans to pay attention in an always-on, always-connected digital-media environment. Underscoring this very issue, Christine Rosen, senior editor of the *New Atlantis*, writes, "When we talk about multitasking, we are really talking about attention: the art of paying attention, the ability to shift our attention, and, more broadly, to exercise judgment about what objects are worthy of our attention."[13]

Now that anytime, anywhere technology and fast entertainment are pervasive parts of our cultural environment, deciding what to pay attention to is more challenging than ever. Linda Stone, a communication technology thought leader and consultant, believes that the constant efforts by humans to manage our time—a main reason we multitask—should be accompanied by an equally zealous effort to better manage our attention. In an age of multiplying screens, constant connections, and content overload, Stone, a former Apple researcher, believes that humans suffer severe lapses in attention. She even has a name for this particular state of being: continuous partial attention, or CPA. Whether or not humans are genuinely addicted to the Web is still a major source of debate, but one thing is undeniable—managing our attention in a world of anytime, anywhere technology is one of the great challenges of modern life.

Stone makes a distinction between multitasking and CPA. With multitasking, she maintains, "we are motivated by a desire to be more productive and more efficient."[14] We multitask to save time. Conversely, Stone writes, "we pay continuous partial attention in an effort NOT TO MISS ANYTHING." She adds that CPA "is an always-on, anywhere, anytime, anyplace behavior that involves an artificial sense of constant crisis. We are always in high alert when we pay continuous partial attention."[15] CPA describes a familiar yet relatively recent state of being—the constantly tethered to technology lifestyle. No matter if it's sending a text message, responding to e-mails, tagging the latest batch of pictures posted by a friend online, or downloading the latest application for your cool new phone, the digital world is a busy world. The nonstop access to content and comrades via smaller and more mobile screens keeps us on constant alert. Meanwhile, our attention stays on the move, constantly shifting from one task to the next, one conversation to the next, one screen to the next.

Whereas CPA is an increasingly normal state of being, it is not a very healthy state of being. As a result of CPA, Stone argues that "in a 24/7, always-on world, continuous partial attention used as our dominant attention mode contributes to a feeling of [being overwhelmed], over-stimulation and to a sense of being unfulfilled."[16]

Along with understanding the neurological implications of multitasking, 35 we need to understand the sociological implications too. Millions of people talking on their phones while driving make the roads less safe. Multitasking

[13]Rosen, "Myth of Multitasking."
[14]http://continuouspartialattention.jot.com/WikiHome.
[15]Ibid.
[16]Ibid.

while doing homework, a common behavior these days, can contribute to poor academic performance. For robust multitaskers like the young and the digital the stakes are even higher, the outcomes potentially more profound. As Rosen notes, "For the younger generation of multitaskers, the great electronic din" is a common aspect of life. Rosen notes, however, that "when people do their work only in the 'interstices of their mind-wandering,' with crumbs of attention rationed out among many competing tasks, their culture may gain in information, but it will surely weaken in wisdom."[17]

READING THE TEXT

1. In your own words, what do the terms "fast entertainment" and "snack culture" (para. 1) mean?
2. What does Watkins mean by saying, "In the digital media age, more equals less" (para. 8)?
3. Summarize the results of the scientific studies of the brain's ability to handle multiple tasks simultaneously.
4. What does the term "continuous partial attention" mean, according to the article, and why is it "not a very healthy state of being" (paras. 32–34)?

READING THE SIGNS

1. In an essay, write your own response to Watkins's question: "Is the ability to be entertained constantly and no matter where you are really a good thing?" (para. 12).
2. In your journal, explore your own ability to multitask. For you, is multitasking "a fact of everyday life" (para. 22) that makes completing daily activities more efficient? Or do you tend to avoid multitasking and prefer concentrating on one activity at a time? How do you explain your behavioral choices?
3. Write an argumentative essay that supports, refutes, or complicates Watkins's concluding quote from editor Christine Rosen: "When people do their work only . . . with crumbs of attention rationed out among many competing tasks, their culture may gain in information, but it will surely weaken in wisdom" (para. 35).
4. **CONNECTING TEXTS**   In an essay, discuss the extent to which University of Maryland students (see "Students Addicted to Social Media," p. 403) who participated in a research study on social media are "addicted" to their electronic toys.
5. **CONNECTING TEXTS**   Watkins claims that "we have evolved from a culture of instant gratification to one of constant gratification" (para. 9). Drawing upon Laurence Shames's "The More Factor" (p. 80), write an essay analyzing whether "consuming media on the go" is a twenty-first century extension of "the hunger for more."

---

[17]Rosen, "Myth of Multitasking."

INTERNATIONAL CENTER FOR MEDIA AND THE PUBLIC AGENDA

Students Addicted to Social Media

It's official: The use of digital technology is addictive, or so concludes a 2010 study by the International Center for Media and the Public Agenda at the University of Maryland. After two hundred University of Maryland students willingly gave up their digital devices for twenty-four hours, journalism professor Susan D. Moeller found them virtually traumatized by the experience. Indeed, as one student wrote, "Texting and IM-ing my friends gives me a constant feeling of comfort. . . . When I did not have those two luxuries, I felt quite alone and secluded from my life. Although I go to a school with thousands of students, the fact that I was not able to communicate with anyone via technology was almost unbearable." Maybe iPhones should come with a warning from the Surgeon General?

American college students today are addicted to media, describing their feelings when they have to abstain from using media in literally the same terms associated with drug and alcohol addictions: *In withdrawal, Frantically craving, Very anxious, Extremely antsy, Miserable, Jittery, Crazy.*

A new study out today from the International Center for Media and the Public Agenda (ICMPA) at the University of Maryland concludes that most college students are not just unwilling, but functionally unable to be without their media links to the world. "I clearly am addicted and the dependency is sickening," said one student in the study. "I feel like most people these days are in a similar situation, for between having a BlackBerry, a laptop, a television, and an iPod, people have become unable to shed their media skin."

The new ICMPA study, "24 Hours: Unplugged," asked 200 students at the College Park campus to give up all media for 24 hours. After their 24 hours of abstinence, the students were then asked to blog on private class Web sites about their experiences: to report their successes and admit to any failures. The 200 students wrote more than 110,000 words: in aggregate, about the same number of words as a 400-page novel.

Without Digital Ties, Students Feel Unconnected Even to Those Who Are Close By

"We were surprised by how many students admitted that they were 'incredibly addicted' to media," noted the project director Susan D. Moeller, a

403

journalism professor at the University of Maryland and the director of the International Center for Media and the Public Agenda which conducted the study. "But we noticed that what they wrote at length about was how they hated losing their personal connections. Going without media meant, in their world, going without their friends and family."

"The students did complain about how boring it was to go anywhere and   5 do anything without being plugged into music on their MP3 players," said Moeller. "And many commented that it was almost impossible to avoid the TVs on in the background at all times in their friends' rooms. But what they spoke about in the strongest terms was how their lack of access to text messaging, phone calling, instant messaging, e-mail, and Facebook, meant that they couldn't connect with friends who lived close by, much less those far away."

"Texting and IM-ing my friends gives me a constant feeling of comfort," wrote one student. "When I did not have those two luxuries, I felt quite alone and secluded from my life. Although I go to a school with thousands of students, the fact that I was not able to communicate with anyone via technology was almost unbearable."

The student responses to the assignment showed not just that 18–21-year-old college students are constantly texting and on Facebook — with calling and e-mail distant seconds as ways of staying in touch, especially with friends — but that students' lives are wired together in such ways that opting out of that communication pattern would be tantamount to renouncing a social life.

News: Accessed via Connections with Friends & Family

Very few students in the study reported that they regularly watched news on television or read a local or national newspaper (although a few said they regularly read *The Diamondback*, the University of Maryland student newspaper). They also didn't mention checking mainstream media news sites or listening to radio news while commuting in their cars. Yet student after student demonstrated knowledge of specific news stories. How did they get the information? In a disaggregated way, and not typically from the news outlet that broke or committed resources to a story. "To be entirely honest I am glad I failed the assignment," wrote one student, "because if I hadn't opened my computer when I did I would not have known about the violent earthquake in Chile from an informal blog post on Tumblr."

"Students expressed tremendous anxiety about being cut off from information," observed Ph.D. student Raymond McCaffrey, a former writer and editor at *The Washington Post*, and a current researcher on the study. "One student said he realized that he suddenly 'had less information than everyone else, whether it be news, class information, scores, or what happened on *Family Guy*.'"

"They care about what is going on among their friends and families and   10 even in the world at large," said McCaffrey. "But most of all they care about being cut off from that instantaneous flow of information that comes from all sides and does not seem tied to any single device or application or news outlet."

That's the real takeaway of this study for journalists: Students showed no significant loyalty to a news program, news personality or even news platform. Students have only a casual relationship to the originators of news, and in fact rarely distinguished between news and more general information.

While many in the journalism profession are committing significant resources to deliver content across media platforms — print, broadcast, online, mobile — the young adults in this study appeared to be generally oblivious to branded news and information. For most of the students reporting in the study, information of all kinds comes in an undifferentiated wave to them via social media. If a bit of information rises to a level of interest, the student will pursue it — but often by following the story via "unconventional" outlets, such as through text messages, their e-mail accounts, Facebook, and Twitter.

Students said that only the most specific or significant news events — for example, a medal event at the Olympics — merited their tuning in to a mainstream outlet. Even news events that students cared about were often accessed via their personal interactions. To learn about the Maryland vs. Virginia Tech basketball game, for example, one student told of "listening to someone narrate the game from a conversation they were having on their own phone" (although he would have preferred watching it on TV) and another student told of calling her father to learn more about the earthquake in Chile.

Study Background

The University of Maryland is a large state university campus, and the class, *JOUR 175: Media Literacy*, that undertook this 24-hour media-free assignment, is a "core course" for the entire student body — which means it enrolls undergraduate students across majors. It is, in short, a class of 200 students, characterized by a diversity of age, race, ethnicity, religion, and nationality. According to the assignment, students had to go media-free for a full day (or had to try to go media-free), but they were allowed to pick which 24 hours in a nine-day period, from February 24–March 4. By coincidence that period saw several major news events, including the earthquake in Chile on February 27, and the close of the Vancouver Olympics on February 28.

According to separately obtained demographic data on the student class, 15 75.6 percent of the students in JOUR 175 self-identify as Caucasian/White, 9.4 percent as Black, 6.3 percent as Asian, 1.6 percent as Latino, 3.1 percent as Mixed Race, and 3.9 percent as Other. Students who self-reported themselves as non-American said they were from China, South Korea, Sri Lanka, and Ethiopia. Women outnumbered men, 55.9 percent to 44.1 percent.

44.1 percent of the class reported that their parents or guardians earned over $100,000 or more; 28.3 percent reported that their parents or guardians earned between $75–$100,000; 22 percent reported coming from a household with an income between $50–75,000; and 5.5 percent reported that their families' income was between $25–50,000.

40.9 percent of the students who responded to the demographic survey reported that they were first-year students, 40.9 percent reported that they were sophomores, 11 percent reported that they were juniors, and 7.1 percent reported that they were seniors or beyond. Most students reported their ages as between 18–21; the average class age was 19.5.

When asked about what types of media devices they own, 43.3 percent of the students reported that they had a "smart phone" (e.g., a BlackBerry or an iPhone), and 56.7 percent said they did not.

Prof. Susan Moeller led the study research team, and the six teaching assistants for the course acted as researchers/authors, conducting a qualitative content analysis of the student responses. Those six TAs, all Ph.D. students in the Philip Merrill College of Journalism, were: Ms. EunRyung Chong, Mr. Sergei Golitsinski, Ms. Jing Guo, Mr. Raymond McCaffrey, Mr. Andrew Nynka, and Ms. Jessica Roberts.[1]

READING THE TEXT

1. What are the symptoms of addiction to social media, according to the International Center for Media and the Public Agenda study conducted at the University of Maryland?

2. What can journalists learn from this study?

3. What is the primary reason for the use of digital media for the students in this study?

4. In your own words, how can people's reliance on social media be considered an "addiction"?

READING THE SIGNS

1. Write a journal entry in which you reflect upon your own use of text messaging, social media, and other forms of electronic media. Why do you use such media? Would you consider yourself "addicted"? If you do not use them, or do so rarely, why is that your preference?

2. Conduct a similar experiment in your class, having everyone give up their use of all digital media for twenty-four hours. Then use your course Web site to blog about your experiences (or discuss them in class). To what extent does your experiment replicate the results of the University of Maryland study? If your results differ, how do you account for that difference?

[1] The study is available online at http://www.withoutmedia.wordpress.com.

3. Write an essay that assesses students' reliance on text messaging and social media as their primary source for news of the world rather than mainstream news sources. You might base your essay on interviews with acquaintances about which news sources they typically rely on.

4. **CONNECTING TEXTS** In "Fast Entertainment and Multitasking in an Always-On World" (p. 393), S. Craig Watkins asks whether media multitasking is "healthy." In an essay, write your own response to his query, using the University of Maryland study as your evidence.

5. Do some research on the clinical definition of "addiction," and then write an essay in which you argue whether reliance on electronic media can accurately be classified as addictive.

SIMON DUMENCO

If We're All So Sick of You, Facebook, Why Can't We Quit You?

The death of Facebook has been highly exaggerated, as Simon Dumenco notes in this essay for *Advertising Age*, and the question is, what accounts for Facebook's continuing success even as its PR tanks? The company's success is no accident, Dumenco proposes, because Facebook actively pursues its dormant users, bombarding them with e-mails designed to get them to log back in, while social media and marketing consultants continue to intone the mantra "You *have* to be on Facebook." And so, the social media behemoth that growing numbers of people love to hate, can moan — all the way to the bank. Simon Dumenco is a media columnist for *Advertising Age*.

Facebook is one of the digital world's great shape-shifters — it's endlessly changed its user interface, its business strategy and (notoriously) its privacy policies over the years — but one thing has remained constant: We all love to complain about it.

In fact, hinting at, or outright predicting, the eventual demise of Facebook has become something of an obsession for a lot of the media. *Business Insider*, for instance, recently ran a post titled. "You Have to Believe This Chart Makes Mark Zuckerberg Slightly Anxious." The graphic came from Kleiner Perkins' Mary Meeker and it plots the results of a survey of 2,000 social-media users, age 12 to 64, who were asked in 2011 and then again in 2012 which social-media products they use. YouTube, Twitter, Google +, LinkedIn,

Pinterest, Instagram, Tumblr, Foursquare and even MySpace all gained. But Facebook actually shrunk a bit.

Though surveys about self-reported media usage obviously should be taken with a grain of salt, the chart still would seem to jibe with data Nielsen released last month, which said that Facebook shed more than 10 million U.S. users from March 2012 to March 2013 — going from 153 million monthly uniques to 142 million.

But wait! For every Facebook-is-in-trouble story, there is, of course, a counter-narrative. As the *Wall Street Journal*'s Tom Gara wrote in response to the Nielsen figures, "While some web traffic numbers might be down, it's a mistake to read this as a peak in usage. The company is undergoing an amazing boom in mobile usage."

And the revenue is following. As my colleague Cotton Delo reported last month, 30 percent of Facebook's first-quarter ad revenue came from mobile ads, up from 23 percent last quarter. The company pulled in $1.46 billion in revenue last quarter, vs. $1.06 billion in the same quarter a year ago.

So, basically: Facebook usage in the U.S. might be down, or maybe it's just flat, but mobile is growing, and revenue is up. Which means, what, exactly? What's missing from our big-picture understanding of Facebook? Some thoughts:

We don't have access to the right data, really.

Speaking of self-reporting, Facebook itself claims "1.11 billion monthly active users as of March 2013." That, of course, includes users who visit Facebook as infrequently as once every four weeks or so — the kind of users who think of Facebook as less of an immersive hangout and more as a sort of monolithic directory that's occasionally useful for tracking people down (because "everyone's on Facebook"). A utility, of sorts.

Facebook's other most recent self-reported start — "655 million daily active users on average in March 2013" — offers a little more insight, but not much. Mainly because Facebook doesn't break that number down country-by-country (though it does concede that "79 percent of our daily active users are outside the U.S. and Canada"). And also because "daily active" . . . well, that covers everyone from the status-updating, picture-posting addict to the time-strapped user who, say, quickly checks her Facebook inbox every morning as a matter of habit.

Facebook stalks people into being "active."

You know the Morrissey song "The More You Ignore Me, the Closer I Get"? That's Facebook's modus operandi. If you don't log in for a while, Facebook guilts you into visiting with its vaguely desperate "You have notifications pending" emails, which name-check friends and colleagues who have "posted statuses, photos and more on Facebook." In one recent two-week period, for example, during which I stayed away from Facebook, I got four such emails (on May 19, 23, 28 and 29). In essence, Facebook is using the oldest trick in the digital-marketing book — email — to keep those users who are sick of Facebook from abandoning it entirely.

Facebook's big mobile push lets it be a "must-spend" in a whole new way. But for how long?

"You have to be on Facebook." Self-appointed social-media and marketing "experts" still say that sort of thing, even though it's increasingly clear that Facebook is helpful for certain kinds of products and pretty useless for others.

There's still a lot of experimental marketing spend flooding into social media, but by becoming, almost overnight, a company with significant mobile revenue, Facebook can now also partake of the ongoing mobile-marketing frenzy/paranoia.

Remember, before mobile, before Facebook, there were marketing "experts" who were saying, "You have to be on MySpace." And to rewind to the dawn of digital-marketing time, in the '90s their forebears were saying, "You have to be on AOL." 15

AOL posted some amazing numbers during its go-go years because a lot of marketers really believed the hype about advertising on AOL being almost mandatory. Until, you know, they didn't.

These days, if you're a CMO who has been questioning the "You have to be on Facebook" dogma, well, there's a new faith — "You have to be on mobile" — and continuing to spend on the newly mobile-first Facebook satisfies that imperative.

For the time being, at least.

READING THE TEXT

1. What evidence does Dumenco advance to demonstrate — and complicate — the "Facebook-is-in-trouble" story?

2. In your own words, how does Facebook "stalk" users into remaining constant fans?

3. Characterize Dumenco's tone here. How does it affect your response to his article?

4. What are the implications for Facebook that Dumenco sees in the history of MySpace and AOL?

READING THE SIGNS

1. In class, discuss the validity of Dumenco's opening claim that "we all love to complain about [Facebook]"? Do you think that Facebook receives as much criticism as Dumenco implies? If so, how might Facebook's business practices contribute to that response? If not, why not?

2. Individuals are not the only ones with Facebook pages; big institutions like universities, businesses, and governmental entities have them as well. In an essay, explore the extent to which the ubiquity of such pages pressures people to join Facebook.

3. Facebook has largely replaced the open-to-all world of blogging, which means that much of what once appeared to any viewer in blogs now is visible only to Facebook members. In a contemplative essay, explore the extent to which this restriction limits the exchange of opinion and information.

danah boyd

Implications of User Choice: The Cultural Logic of "MySpace or Facebook?"

Once upon a time, everyone was on MySpace. Or almost everyone. Oh, there was Friendster and Facebook, but Facebook was for networking adults and a few Ivy League college students. Then, suddenly, everyone was on Facebook. Well, not everyone, of course, and in this 2009 study of the shift from MySpace to Facebook, danah boyd explains what happened. Interviewing numerous Facebook users, boyd concludes that a good deal of racial and class snobbery was involved, with Facebook users referring, somewhat shamefacedly, to MySpace as a "ghetto." So maybe the world of social networking isn't really drawing people together after all; it may only be reproducing ancient conflicts and divisions. A researcher at Microsoft Research, a research assistant professor in media, culture, and communication at New York University, and a fellow at Harvard University's Berkman Center, danah boyd specializes in the sociology of the Internet.

Many of us have had our lives transformed by technology. And many of us are also enamored of the transformative potential of technology, which has led us to develop technology and become advocates of technological practices. As we become more enveloped in and by technology, it's easy to feel excited about what's going on. Yet we must also be cautious.

The rhetoric around technology often makes it out to be the great equalizer of society, suggesting that technology can in and of itself make the world a better place. Let's ignore the technological determinist overtones for a moment and note that this rhetoric fails to capture the complex ways in which the actual adoption of technology tends to mirror and magnify a whole suite of societal issues.

It is crucial that we begin accounting for how technology actually reveals social stratification and reproduces social divisions. For decades we've assumed that inequality in relation to technology has everything to do with access and that if we fix the access problem, all will be fine. This is the grand narrative of politicized concepts like the digital divide. Yet, increasingly, we're seeing people with similar levels of access engage with technology in very different ways. And we're experiencing a social media landscape in which participation "choice" leads to a digital reproduction of social divisions, which already pervade society.

Rather than staying in the land of the abstract, let's go concrete with a specific case study: the differential adoption of MySpace and Facebook among American teens. I have been doing ethnographic fieldwork on various aspects

410

of social network sites since 2003. Starting in 2005, I began specifically focusing on the social media practices of American high school–age teenagers. During the 2006–2007 school year, I started noticing a trend. In each school, in each part of the country, there were teens who opted for MySpace and teens who opted for Facebook. There were also plenty of teens who used both. At the beginning of the school year, teens were asking "Are you on MySpace? Yes or No?" At the end of the school year, the question had changed to "MySpace or Facebook?"

In analyzing my data, one can reasonably see this as a matter of individual choice in a competitive market. There are plenty of teenagers who will tell you that they are on one or the other as a matter of personal preference having to do with features, functionality, design, and usability. For example, Justin (15, Austin) prefers Facebook because of the unlimited pictures while Anindita (17, Los Angeles) likes that MySpace is "more complex" while "Facebook is just plain white and that's it."

Teens will also talk about their perceptions of different sites, about what they think certain affordances mean, or how they perceive the sites in relation to values they hold, such as safety. For example, Cachi (18, Iowa) likes that "Facebook is less competitive than MySpace" while Tara (16, Michigan) thinks that Facebook seems safer.

For all of the technology-specific commentary teens offer, the dominant explanation teens will give to justify their choice has to do with their friends. Simply put, they go where their friends are:

KEVIN (15, Seattle): I'm not big on Facebook; I'm a MySpace guy. I have a Facebook and I have some friends on it, but most of my friends don't check it that often so I don't check it that often.

RED (17, Iowa): I am on Facebook and MySpace. I don't talk to people on MySpace anymore. . . . The only reason I still have my MySpace is because my brother's on there.

In choosing to go where their friends are, teens reproduce preexisting social networks. Yet their choice is not neutral. Teens do not randomly select their friends; they connect with people who are like them. This is the basis of the sociological concept of "homophily," which highlights that "birds of a feather stick together." By the time most teens join MySpace or Facebook, they already know someone who is on the site. They are attracted to the site because of the people there. Thus, the early adopters of the sites and the network effects of adoption fundamentally shaped each site's tenor.

MySpace came out first and quickly attracted urban twenty-somethings. It spread to teenagers through older siblings and cousins as well as those who were attracted to indie rock and hip-hop culture. Facebook started at Harvard and spread to the Ivies before spreading more broadly, first to other colleges, then to companies, then elite high schools, and then the unwashed masses. The first teenagers to hear about Facebook were those connected to the early adopters of Facebook (i.e., the Ivy League–bound). Thus, the desirability of the site spread from people who were heading to college. As the two sites grew, they initially attracted different audiences. But by early 2007, teens were choosing between the sites. And while that choice was driven by friendship, it also reinforced distinctions.

Teens recognize that MySpace and Facebook attracted different populations: 10

KAT (14, Massachusetts): I was the first one of my friends to get a Facebook, and then a lot of people got one afterwards. . . . The people who use MySpace—again, not in a racist way—but are usually more like ghetto and hip-hop rap lovers group. And pretty much everyone else might have a Facebook. But there's some people that aren't that. All the rockers, too, will have a MySpace.

In trying to describe what distinguishes the two groups, Kat chooses words that signal that those on MySpace are from a lower socio-economic background and, most probably, black. This is reinforced both by her apology for the racial connotation of her distinction and also by her reference to a different group of youth defined by music, who are presumably not lumped into the group she marks as "ghetto."

The structure of social relations in the United States is shaped by race, socio-economic status, education, and lifestyle. Given the network-driven adoption of MySpace and Facebook, it is not surprising that the adoption patterns also play out along these lines. What is interesting is what happened when some teens chose to move from MySpace to Facebook.

Social media is faddish. MySpace came first and many teens chose to embrace it. When Facebook came along, plenty of teens adopted it as the "new thing." In doing so, some chose to leave MySpace, while others simply maintained two profiles. Yet Facebook did not simply usurp MySpace. In May 2009—two and a half years after teens began splitting—comScore reported that MySpace and Facebook had roughly equal numbers of unique visitors. In other words, while a shift did occur, not all MySpace users left for Facebook, and not all who joined after both were available opted for the newer site.

Those teens who left were not abstractly driven by fads; they were driven by their social networks. Thus, the shift that took place was also shaped by race, socio-economic status, education, and lifestyle. Here is where the division solidified, marked by social categories and distinctions:

ANASTASIA (17, New York): My school is divided into the "honors kids" (I think that is self-explanatory), the "good not-so-honors kids," "wangstas" (they pretend to be tough and black but when you live in a suburb in Westchester you can't claim much hood), the "latinos/hispanics" (they tend to band together even though they could fit into any other groups), and the "emo kids" (whose lives are alllllways filled with woe). We were all in MySpace with our own little social networks, but when Facebook opened its doors to high schoolers, guess who moved and guess who stayed behind. . . . The first two groups were the first to go and then the "wangstas" split with half of them on Facebook and the rest on MySpace. . . . I shifted with the rest of my school to Facebook and it became the place where the "honors kids" got together and discussed how they were procrastinating over their next AP English essay.

In choosing between the two sites, teens marked one as for "people like 15 me," which suggested that the other was for the "other" people. Teens — and adults — use social categories and labels to identify people with values, tastes, and social positions. As teens chose between MySpace and Facebook, these sites began reflecting the cultural frames of those social categories. Nowhere is this more visible than in the language of those who explicitly chose Facebook over MySpace.

CRAIG (17, California): The higher castes of high school moved to Facebook. It was more cultured, and less cheesy. The lower class usually were content to stick to MySpace. Any high school student who has a Facebook will tell you that MySpace users are more likely to be barely educated and obnoxious. Like Peet's is more cultured than Starbucks, and jazz is more cultured than bubblegum pop, and like Macs are more cultured than PCs, Facebook is of a cooler caliber than MySpace.

Craig's description focuses on a comparison of MySpace and Facebook to a series of lifestyle brands. Taste identification is a way in which people self-segregate. Yet, as with social networks, taste is highly correlated with race, socio-economic status, and education. Social networks also drive taste; people like what their friends like. Thus, in choosing Facebook, teens were both connecting with their friends and identifying with a particular lifestyle brand.

The mere fact that network effects, shaped by homophily, resulted in a self-segregation of teens across two social network sites should not be particularly surprising. Yet it ruptures a well-loved fantasy that the Internet would be a great equalizer in which race and class would no longer matter. Furthermore, it presents new challenges for those seeking to address the costs of social stratification in American society.

Social network sites are not like e-mail, where it doesn't matter if you're on Hotmail or Yahoo (although there are connotations implied, with AOL conveying a different signal than Gmail). These are walled gardens. Those who use MySpace can't communicate with those on Facebook, and vice versa. So choosing to participate in one but not the other introduces a hurdle for communication across social divisions. This is further magnified when educators and politicians and universities and organizations choose to use social network sites to connect with their students/constituents/customers. Choosing one becomes political, because choosing only one means excluding those who opted for the other. Consider, for example, the universities that are doing all of their high school recruiting through Facebook. Or the public officials who use just one platform to reach all constituents, thinking that everyone is or will be present. It's one thing to make this choice to reach a specific demographic; it's another to do so blindly and think that everyone is at the table simply because people like you are.

We cannot expect to suddenly eradicate inequality from society, and it is not surprising that technology reflects persistent social stratification. In raising these issues, I'm not arguing that technology can or should be the great equalizer. Instead, I want us to all recognize that it is not. The technologies that we build are never neutral—they are infused with the values and ideas of the creators and the actions and goals of the users. Network effects of adoption patterns further shape technology. As people begin to identify with specific technologies, they take on specific frames in society and begin to reflect them in everyday life. Understanding that divisions are taking place does not necessarily mean trying to "fix" them; there are perfectly rational explanations for self-segregating. Rather, recognizing social divisions means being conscious of the underlying factors and vigilant in thinking of the implications.

We can ignore the fact that social divisions are taking place, but in doing 20 so we fail to realize that we shape what's unfolding. We are building systems in which social stratification will be reproduced and reenacted even if we do not design it that way. We often launch our systems first to those who are like us; the early adopters who set the norms are baking specific cultural values into our systems. These values can alienate people who are not like us, and the choices we make can thus reinforce social divisions. We are shaping the public dialogue about these technologies and our attitudes reflect our personal structural positions, often at the expense of people who are not like us. Knowing how the technologies we create mirror and shape society is crucial to being an ethical technologist. Even if we don't know how to tackle large societal issues, the least we can do is be conscious of their presence in the environments we create and respect the choices and attitudes of those who aren't like us.

READING THE TEXT

1. How, according to boyd's research, do digital choices reflect existing social divisions?

2. What is the image of MySpace for such young Facebook users as Kat and Anastasia? How do they view the users of Facebook?

3. What does boyd mean by the word "homophily" (para. 8)?

4. In your own words, how are MySpace and Facebook "walled gardens" (para. 18)?

5. What is the social effect of universities' use of Facebook but not MySpace for recruiting purposes, according to boyd?

READING THE SIGNS

1. In your journal, discuss why you prefer to use MySpace, Facebook, or another social networking site. What is your view of sites that you do not use? If you do not use social networking sites, discuss why you are not attracted to them.

2. Write an essay in which you support, refute, or complicate boyd's claim that Facebook and MySpace reproduce racial divisions in America.

3. Watch the movie *The Social Network*, and write a paper arguing for or against the proposition that the prestige of Facebook's Harvard origins has been a significant cause of its rise in popularity and the decline of MySpace.

4. Conduct a class debate in which you address the proposition that technology "reveals social stratification and reproduces social divisions" (para. 3). To develop your ideas, consult the introduction to this chapter. Use the debate as a jumping-off point for your own essay that responds to this proposition

5. Write a comparative essay that analyzes today's Facebook and MySpace. Do the appearances of the sites continue to reflect teenager Craig's opinion that Facebook "was more cultured, and less cheesy" than MySpace (para. 15)?

SALVADOR RODRIGUEZ

In the Digital Age, Breaking Up Is Hard to Do

If only love were as enduring as the digital archive, but alas, as Salvador Rodriguez reports in this personal attestation to the recalcitrance of the social network for couples who have cut the knot, it isn't so. From shared lists to search engines, Dropbox to Google +, the cloud has got your, and your former significant other's, numbers, and it won't let go. Yes, you can try to delete all traces of your love's labor lost, but it's a painful business, Rodriguez laments, and it's likely that you won't get it all anyway. The best way forward, sometimes, is just to log off for a while. Salvador Rodriguez is a technology writer for the *Los Angeles Times*, where this article first appeared.

It's Valentine's Day, and I'm not celebrating. A few weeks ago my fiancée and I broke up.

It was a difficult breakup, so I immediately stopped following her on Facebook, Twitter and Instagram, and deleted her name from my iPhone address book.

I thought that would be enough to disconnect her from my digital life. But I'm finding out — as many others have in the age of smartphones and social networks — that connecting is easy, but severing ties online is nearly impossible. Take even the basic task of doing an Internet search. When I type in the letter "T" into my Web browser, Google suggests Twitter and just below that it

🄴 macmillanhighered.com/signsoflife
How does online courtship resemble dating IRL?
e-readings > Nancy Schwartzman and Isaac Mathes, *xoxosms* [documentary film trailer]

lists my former fiancée's Twitter handle. Other social media platforms serve up similar uncomfortable reminders. It feels like no matter what I do, I run into her online.

Ka-Yuet Liu, a sociologist who studies social networks at UCLA, said I'm not alone. Social networks have taken away some of the controls that we have over our social lives. As soon as we post information, it is forever on the Internet somewhere, she said. That means you can't undo or wipe away a memory by merely pressing the delete button.

Adrian Miller, who runs a Studio City Web branding firm, recently ended   5 a relationship with his longtime girlfriend, leading him to swear off social media so that he can focus his attention on other things. "I just have not looked at Facebook, Twitter, Instagram or any of that, and I'm not going to for another, at least, month," the Los Feliz resident said. "Do something else. Go to a movie, get in the community. At the end of the day, you cannot let social media dictate you or your life."

Miller, 43, said that disconnecting is tough because many people rely on the Internet to manage a great deal of their social lives, so they share too much personal information. He has kept busy working on HeartBreakSecrets .com, a new website he created that gives users who are dealing with break-ups a place to go to write about their experiences anonymously. "Just bleed your heart, tell your story," he said. "Because you don't want to do that on your Facebook page."

But it's not just romantic breakups that can be distressing when it comes to disconnecting. A few years back, Miller left a job under less than friendly terms. In the years before social networking, he would have naturally stopped seeing his former colleagues and hearing about them unless he sought them out. But because he was friends with them on Facebook, Miller said he had to manually delete all of them, one by one. "I just didn't want to deal with any of those people anymore," he said. "I don't want to see their respective timelines and feeds."

Or in my case, efforts by social networks to make it easier for me to connect has made it impossible for me to disconnect from my former fiancée.

After my breakup, when I typed "V" (the initial of my former fiancée's first name) into the Twitter search feature, her profile was the first suggestion that popped up.

When I use Facebook's Messenger app, her name is the first suggestion when   10 I want to start a new chat, even though we're no longer connected on Facebook.

On Spotify, a music streaming service, I was able to delete the playlists I shared with her and unfollow her so I won't see what she's listening to. But I have not been able to block her from seeing what I'm enjoying.

On Dropbox, the cloud storage service, are hundreds of photos of us together shot with my phone that it backed up for me automatically, along with countless other photos. I've stopped trying to go through them and delete them one by one. Google + does the same, and it also stores some GIFs, or short slide shows, of my proposal to her. It will be a while before I browse through my photos on either of these services.

We've been apart for a few weeks now, but the most recent instance of randomly coming across her on the Web was one that was particularly devastating. It came courtesy of LinkedIn, the social network for professionals.

I logged into LinkedIn because I hadn't used the service in a while and I had a ton of notifications that needed attention. I went through dozens of connection requests and was feeling very proud of myself for clearing them out. I finished the last request, and that's when I felt like *Fight Club*'s Tyler Durden had punched me right in the stomach.

"Join V . . . , Dustin and 313 others who have found people they already 15 know," the service said, hoping to keep me on its website a little longer.

When I saw her avatar right below that suggestion, LinkedIn nearly brought me to tears.

READING THE TEXT

1. Why did Rodriguez assume that it would be easy to disconnect his former fiancée from his digital life?

2. How do social media platforms manage to hold on to one's personal information, according to Rodriguez?

3. In your own words, explain what sociologist Ka-Yuet Liu means by saying that "social networks have taken away some of the controls that we have over our social lives" (para. 4).

4. In what ways does Rodriguez's personal tale of a broken relationship shape your response to his selection?

READING THE SIGNS

1. Rodriguez laments that postings on social media sites remain "forever" and that a user has little control over his or her own online content. In class, brainstorm a set of guidelines that people should consider when posting personal or romantic material online. To what extent do class members already follow these guidelines? Why? If the class had difficulty drafting such guidelines, what problems emerged?

2. Snapchat is an app that supposedly avoids the "online forever" problem that Rodriguez describes because it almost instantaneously deletes posts. Study Snapchat, and then write an essay analyzing whether it can indeed protect you from the problems Rodriguez cites and why that protection may be appealing.

3. Interview friends who are active on social media sites about their motivation for posting personal information. Based on your results, to what extent do they acknowledge sociologist Ka-Yuet Liu's claim that "[s]ocial networks have taken away some of the controls that we have over our social lives" (para. 4)?

4. **CONNECTING TEXTS** Read Rachel Lowry's "Straddling Online and Offline Profiles, Millennials Search for Identity" (p. 500). Assuming the perspective of Lowry's interviewee Mariah Hanaike, write a letter to Rodriguez in which you offer him advice on how to handle the difficulty of stopping a romantic relationship in the digital age.

RICHARD RUSHFIELD

Toward a Unified Theory of How the Internet Makes Everything Terrible

> Watching television isn't bird-watching, but you'd be forgiven for
> thinking it was, with all the tweeting that goes on every time a
> popular show like *Game of Thrones* airs. And this, Richard Rushfield
> believes, is too much — too much media frenzy "articulating the
> frenzy of the mob." It's *Sharknado* out there on the Internet, Rush-
> field believes, and the only way to stop it is by simply "shutting the
> hell up." Richard Rushfield is the author of the blog *Rushfield Babylon:
> Where It All Went Wrong*, in which this plea for a sense of proportion
> first appeared.

I have nothing bad to say about *Breaking Bad*. I was completely gripped by
Sunday night's episode. I've watched it twice and enjoyed it more the second
time. I think when the show concludes it is certain to go down as one of the
great dramas in TV history. What quibbles I have with the show I recognize as
just that — quibbles.

So why on Monday did the Internet make me ashamed to have watched
the show, much less to have liked it? Part of the revulsion is no doubt due to
some vestigial adolescent need to feel myself ahead of the crowd and just getting cranky when I find my tastes are actually not particularly unique or special.

But beyond that, I think there is something terrifying about the way the
Internet turns out for these events and cranks up the GIF, meme, Tweet and
think piece machines like some sort of disembodied 4th of July parade. These
moments carry a desperation with them; the logical conclusion of the *Bowling Alone* thing, where now living our lives glued to our individual screens cut
off from actual human interaction, we are desperate to find ways to march
together. I've noticed that these events — awards shows, series premieres,
etc. — are becoming bigger and bigger group phenomena. Super Bowl ratings
have never been higher. The Grammies for chrissake inch upwards. We want
to watch together. In our own homes, in front of our own multiple screens.
All to some extent harmless enough. If the world (or the upscale, urban sub-
sub-subset of the world) can find some comfort in cheering on an episode of
gritty drama together, then good for it for finding some in this cold machine-
driven world. But here are the downsides as I see them.

In our desperation to make a community out of watching an episode of
a TV show, we pour more of our hopes and desires into that show than any
hour of entertainment can bear. We meme the life out of whatever is original and striking about a work within minutes, overexposing it so much it

becomes noxious. In olden times, it took years for enough VHS copies of *Scarface* to trickle back to frat houses so that every brother could do a passably awful Tony Montana imitation and make you wince when you heard the real thing. And in the meantime people could talk about the film, consider it, pass judgment and change their mind before the re-use of the film became this world-devouring thing apart from the show itself. Today, "I'm the one who knocks" and "say my name" are reproduced in every form upside down and backwards literally before the show is even over and any hope of a quiet place to take it in is in vain.

The fancy media, instead of calming the crowd, now only stokes the flames. Once they could have put things in perspective, but now they see their job as articulating the frenzy of the mob. What is the good of having a blog or a Twitter account if you're going to be the only corner of this corner of the Internet not enjoying the hooplah? And if you're a professional reviewer and get screeners in advance you can actually get ahead of the mob by declaring an episode the best thing since Euripides before anyone else has even watched it, and hope that your words are printed on banners in the parade.

Frenzied mobs, history has shown us, are not always just about fun, games and watching TV together. Now and then, they can have a dark side. Once we say this is all about us just piling on together for some kind of group ecstatic transformation, that can lead to all kinds of places, and as I have noted in the past, Twitter's less attractive tendency to transform into a lynch mob at the drop of a hat. Its hunger for fresh blood has not in the least abated.

Of late, its hunger has actually become an industry. *Sharknado* represents the Internet now creating material for itself to mock. In olden times again, the camp fun of watching old disaster films was mocking the dead serious overacting and unintentionally hamfisted actions. Now at Twitter's demand, networks are producing intentionally hamfisted and overacted pieces so the Internet can tear them apart. They are even letting us—in a contest—pick the name that we find most mockable. So we pick the thing we most want to rip to shreds, like a school bully making a nerd dress up in the most ridiculous costume, so we can make fun of him for wearing it.

What is the solution? Well, as America's leading anti–First Amendment crusader I have advocated the power and dignity of shutting the hell up many times before. Short of that catching fire, we can pray the Internet continues to be merely annoying and only sporadically dangerous. And short of that, networks that want their shows to be appreciated by the people and not just the subject of a mass spectacle should stop sending screeners to critics. That part of the conversation at least we can put a lid on.

READING THE TEXT

1. What does Rushfield's title signify to you, and why do you think he used this title for this essay?

2. In your own words, why do you think Rushfield objects to the Internet response to an episode of *Breaking Bad*? In what general media trend does he locate this particular incident?

3. Characterize Rushfield's tone in this selection. To what extent does it affect your response as a reader? How do you suppose Rushfield meant his readers to take his essay?

4. Rushfield states, "The fancy media, instead of calming the crowd, now only stokes the flames" (para. 5). Why does he say this?

READING THE SIGNS

1. **CONNECTING TEXTS**   Adopt the perspective of S. Craig Watkins ("Fast Entertainment and Multitasking in an Always-On World," p. 393), and analyze the effect of instant media-generated responses to media products. How would Watkins interpret the plethora of awards shows, premieres, tweet fests, and the like?

2. Rushfield identifies "Twitter's less attractive tendency to transform into a lynch mob at the drop of a hat" and observes that "its hunger for fresh blood has not in the least abated" (para. 6). In an essay, support, refute, or modify Rushfield's criticism.

3. Rushfield claims that today "[w]e want to watch together. In our own homes, in front of our own multiple screens" (para. 3). In an argumentative essay, discuss whether or how this behavior exemplifies a form of digital addiction. To develop your ideas, consult the International Center for Media and the Public Agenda's "Students Addicted to Social Media" (p. 403).

DANIEL D'ADDARIO
Everything Is "Trolling" Now

What is "trolling?" Well, it's rather hard to say, Daniel D'Addario believes, now that we use the word *trolling* so frequently "its meaning seems to evaporate into air." Providing a concise history of the popular Internet term — from how it began to where it went wrong — D'Addario illustrates how a once-useful word can become useless once it gets overused. We can only hope that this article doesn't bring the trolls out. Daniel D'Addario is a staff reporter for *Salon*, in which this article originally appeared.

If everyone is a troll, maybe no one is.

In the past few years, accusations of "trolling" have flown across the Internet fast and furious; recently, the targets have included a *New York Times* feature about the popularity of chopped salads, just about everything *Vice* does, and a cover of *Rolling Stone* featuring Dzhokhar Tsarnaev.

But for a word that's tossed around so frequently, its meaning seems to evaporate into air when grasped at. Trolling is bad. Trolling provokes a reaction, usually negative. Trolling is apparently quite easy to do. But, if only to better gird one's own defenses against it—what *is* trolling?

"I think that it started with a pretty clear definition—which is somebody who goes into a place that shares a particular ideology and says something they don't believe just to get a reaction," said Sady Doyle, a feminist blogger and staff writer for *In These Times*.

"Originally, it was, like, racist Reddit kids going into r/blackgirls—that was old-school trolling, a very specific online behavior," said Matt Buchanan, a tech blogger for the *New Yorker*, referring to the popular message board and clearinghouse for human pathologies in which racist, sexist or homophobic vitriol flowed freely. On Reddit, clearly defined groups sort themselves according to demographics, identity and ideology—a troll would attempt to disrupt these groups, and order as normal. Trolls, as classically defined, could insert themselves into any number of milieus; the classic *New York Times Magazine* piece documenting the state of the troll in 2008 recorded instances like self-defined trolls hacking the Epilepsy Foundation's website in order to fill it with flashing lights, triggers for epileptics. As an action designed to harm and upset a specific group of people, it wasn't exactly a newspaper piece about salad.

"It's one of those semi-useful but also dumb Internet words that just kind of means whatever you want it to mean," said Shani Hilton, an editor at *BuzzFeed*. "It's a good shorthand for a kind of thing that's been going on for a long time at more contrarian publications." Consider the case of *Newsweek*, the publication that got attention for splashy covers (like the one featuring a resurrected Princess Diana, aged 50, or the one calling Barack Obama "The First Gay President"). Those were frustrating—so too was *Newsweek*'s online arm the *Daily Beast* publishing a gallery of "magazine controversies" today after spending years trying to provoke. But whose existence or fixed ideas were they upending?

"People have come to use the word 'troll' to mean, 'It made me angry on the Internet,'" said Doyle. "And that's pretty broad. It's a big and noisy Internet."

During the rise of the troll, the Internet was less in the thrall of legacy media than it is today; legacy media outlets, by their very nature, broadcast to a wide audience rather than a narrow and self-selecting community. If the visually striking, provocative and attention-getting *Rolling Stone* cover is trolling, what, then, are the visually striking, provocative and attention-getting covers George Lois designed for *Esquire* in the mid-20th century? (Lois recently told *New York* magazine the cover should "maybe have a devil's tongue or horns. I'm not saying I would do that, but you better do something"—such a visual frippery would, if the media outrage cycle behaved as normal, likely only further elicit calls of trolling.)

"When people accuse publications of trolling," said Doyle, "it's a weird rhetorical move that erases the content and says, 'You made me angry, you must have meant to, I don't need to engage with the content of the article.'"

"It's a cheap shot," said Maria Bustillos, whose recent sympathetic inter- 10
view of a pickup artist on *The Awl* came in for that very criticism. "You have
to come out and say, 'I want to have a productive conversation on this topic.'
And to have to say that is silly. We're all adults. It takes the whole conversation down a notch.

"There's certain writers accused of it, publications accused of it—for
instance, the *Daily Caller*—there's worthy stuff in there in it. It's hard to
believe the whole publication's not worth reading, that it's all trolling. They do
have polemicists, but there's stuff worth reading."

The distinction is important; perhaps a polemicist, a politically minded
columnist whose very purpose is not merely to engage in the world of ideas
but stir the blood of a self-selected few and poke at the other side, can be
a troll. But is it really possible to "troll" when broadcasting to the universe?
If so, perhaps the Internet has evolved too quickly; though we're in a vast
and free-form space, we all still believe we're in walled gardens. When anything upsetting invades that garden, we don't discuss the emotions or ideas
aroused by the image of an alleged terrorist as tousled-haired boy, or reflect
on what it means to live in an age when the variegations of salad-choppings
and -toppings are endlessly debatable among a certain class. We tend to reach
for something a bit more ad hominem.

But perhaps sometimes trolling can be good. Said Bustillos, "Some people
use it as a slur. It's not always meant that way. A lot of people on Twitter use it
to mean 'You're a provocateur.' I'm perfectly happy being called that. It's not
uniformly pejorative."

The distinction Bustillos draws—between a conversation, one that's ultimately productive through the painful process of challenging assumptions, and
the sort of personal, targeted hate that trolling historically had been—is a difficult one for Internet users. It's your Internet. *Everything* seems personal. But,
said Doyle, it's more difficult than accusers think to get people's hackles up.

"I can't ever think of a published piece as trolling," she said. "Someone 15
must have wanted to write this piece enough to commit to a deadline and commit to an editing process. It's a heck of a lot of work to get a couple people
angry. It's not in the best interest of a publication or a writer's career to do that.
But maybe I'm naive."

As for the future, "trolling" may literally be redefined in exactly the way "literally" has (though as Buchanan notes, many Internet-savvy folks are already
using it as a joke, saying anything that even mildly offends them is "trolling").
The term may move from conflating malevolent actions and pageview-
baiting to simply describing the second. "It's the best way to describe it," said
Buchanan, "a certain, compact way of describing! It's why we use German
words. It's such a good descriptor!"

READING THE TEXT

1. According to D'Addario, how has the meaning of the word *troll*, in the context
   of the Internet, evolved?

2. What does D'Addario mean by the term "legacy media" (para. 8)?

3. How does Maria Bustillos distinguish between Internet trolling and criticism delivered in a published piece? How convincing do you find that distinction?

4. What does D'Addario mean when he says, "As for the future, 'trolling' may literally be redefined in exactly the way 'literally' has" (para. 16)?

READING THE SIGNS

1. In small groups in class, compose your own definition of online trolling, being sure to provide specific examples for illustration. Compare the groups' results. Which definitions would you consider accurate and current? Why?

2. Write an essay in which you support, refute, or complicate Maria Bustillos's contention that trolling can have benefits.

3. Visit a political Web site or forum, and study the level of decorum you observe. To what extent do you find that trolling has become the new normal for Internet communication?

4. The comments sections of everything from online news pages and newspapers to YouTube are filled with violent and hostile posts that could be described as "trolling." Write an essay in which you present your own argument for, against, or complicating the proposition that such comments should be moderated.

HENRY JENKINS
Convergence Culture

You're watching *American Idol* and a text message comes in informing you that AmericanIdolWatch.com reports that the guy who sings like Alvin the Chipmunk is outpolling your favorite contestant, so you log in to check the report and then phone in your vote to *American Idol* before "Alvin" can move on to the next level. Though it may seem pretty routine to you, your movement from television screen, to text messaging, to the Internet, to cell phone constitutes a newly emerging mixture of old and new media that Henry Jenkins calls "convergence culture." In this selection from his book of the same title, Jenkins describes the new multi–mixed media and their possible effects on society and human consciousness. A self-avowed fan of the new media, Henry Jenkins is the founder of MIT's Comparative Media Studies Program, and he is currently the provost's professor of communication, journalism, and cinematic arts at the University of Southern California. He is the author of numerous books, including *Textual Poachers: Television Fans and Participatory Culture* (1998), *Convergence Culture: Where Old and New Media Collide* (2006), *The Wow Climax: Tracing the Emotional Impact of Popular Culture* (2007), and *Spreadable Media: Creating Value and Meaning in a Networked Culture* (2013, coauthored with Sam Ford and Joshua Green).

Worship at the Altar of Convergence
— Slogan, the New Orleans Media Experience (2003)

The story circulated in the fall of 2001: Dino Ignacio, a Filipino-American high school student created a Photoshop collage of *Sesame Street*'s (1970) Bert interacting with terrorist leader Osama Bin Laden as part of a series of "Bert Is Evil" images he posted on his homepage. Others depicted Bert as a Klansman, cavorting with Adolph Hitler, dressed as the Unabomber, or having sex with Pamela Anderson. It was all in good fun.

In the wake of September 11, a Bangladesh-based publisher scanned the Web for Bin Laden images to print on anti-American signs, posters, and T-shirts. *Sesame Street* is available in Pakistan in a localized format; the Arab world, thus, had no exposure to Bert and Ernie. The publisher may not have recognized Bert, but he must have thought the image was a good likeness of the al-Qaeda leader. The image ended up in a collage of similar images that was printed on thousands of posters and distributed across the Middle East.

CNN reporters recorded the unlikely sight of a mob of angry protestors marching through the streets chanting anti-American slogans and waving signs depicting Bert and Bin Laden (Fig. 1). Representatives from the Children's Television Workshop, creators of the *Sesame Street* series, spotted the CNN footage and threatened to take legal action: "We're outraged that our characters would be used in this unfortunate and distasteful manner. The people responsible for this should be ashamed of themselves. We are exploring all legal options to stop this abuse and any similar abuses in the future." It was not altogether clear whom they planned to sic their intellectual property attorneys on — the young man who had initially appropriated their images, or the terrorist supporters who deployed them. Coming full circle, amused fans produced a number of new sites, linking various *Sesame Street* characters with terrorists.

From his bedroom, Ignacio sparked an international controversy. His images crisscrossed the world, sometimes on the backs of commercial media, sometimes via grassroots media. And, in the end, he inspired his own cult following. As the publicity grew, Ignacio became more concerned and ultimately decided to dismantle his site: "I feel this has gotten too close to reality. . . . 'Bert Is Evil' and its following has always been contained and

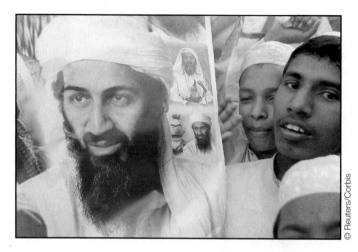

FIGURE 1 Ignacio's collage surprisingly appeared in CNN coverage of anti-American protests following September 11.

distanced from big media. This issue throws it out in the open."[1] Welcome to convergence culture, where old and new media collide, where grassroots and corporate media intersect, where the power of the media producer and the power of the media consumer interact in unpredictable ways. . . .

By convergence, I mean the flow of content across multiple media platforms, the cooperation between multiple media industries, and the migratory behavior of media audiences who will go almost anywhere in search of the kinds of entertainment experiences they want. Convergence is a word that manages to describe technological, industrial, cultural, and social changes depending on who's speaking and what they think they are talking about. . . . 5

In the world of media convergence, every important story gets told, every brand gets sold, and every consumer gets courted across multiple media platforms. Think about the circuits that the Bert Is Evil images traveled — from *Sesame Street* through Photoshop to the World Wide Web, from Ignacio's bedroom to a print shop in Bangladesh, from the posters held up by anti-American protestors that are captured by CNN and into the living rooms of people around the world. Some of its circulation depended on corporate strategies, such as the localization of *Sesame Street* or the global coverage of CNN. Some of its circulation depended on tactics of grassroots appropriation, whether in North America or in the Middle East.

[1]Josh Grossberg, "The Bert–Bin Laden Connection?" E Online, October 10, 2001, http://www.eonline.com/News/Items/0,1,8950,00.html. For a different perspective on Bert and Bin Laden, see Roy Rosenzweig, "Scarcity or Abundance? Preserving the Past in a Digital Era," *American Historical Review* 108 (June 2003).

This circulation of media content — across different media systems, competing media economies, and national borders — depends heavily on consumers' active participation. I . . . argue here against the idea that convergence should be understood primarily as a technological process bringing together multiple media functions within the same devices. Instead, convergence represents a cultural shift as consumers are encouraged to seek out new information and make connections among dispersed media content. . . .

The term *participatory culture*, contrasts with older notions of passive media spectatorship. Rather than talking about media producers and consumers as occupying separate roles, we might now see them as participants who interact with each other according to a new set of rules that none of us fully understands. Not all participants are created equal. Corporations — and even individuals within corporate media — still exert greater power than any individual consumer or even the aggregate of consumers. And some consumers have greater abilities to participate in this emerging culture than others.

Convergence does not occur through media appliances, however sophisticated they may become. Convergence occurs within the brains of individual consumers and through their social interactions with others. Each of us constructs our own personal mythology from bits and fragments of information extracted from the media flow and transformed into resources through which we make sense of our everyday lives. Because there is more information on any given topic than anyone can store in their head, there is an added incentive for us to talk among ourselves about the media we consume. This conversation creates buzz that is increasingly valued by the media industry. Consumption has become a collective process — and that's what [I mean] by *collective intelligence*, a term coined by French cybertheorist Pierre Lévy. None of us can know everything; each of us knows something; and we can put the pieces together if we pool our resources and combine our skills. Collective intelligence can be seen as an alternative source of media power. We are learning how to use that power through our day-to-day interactions within convergence culture. Right now, we are mostly using this collective power through our recreational life, but soon we will be deploying those skills for more "serious" purposes. . . .

Convergence Talk

Another snapshot of convergence culture at work: In December 2004, a hotly [10] anticipated Bollywood film, *Rok Sako To Rok Lo* (2004), was screened in its entirety to movie buffs in Delhi, Bangalore, Hyderabad, Mumbai, and other parts of India through EDGE-enabled mobile phones with live video streaming facility. This is believed to be the first time that a feature film had been fully accessible via mobile phones.[2]

[2]"RSTRL to Premier on Cell Phone," IndiaFM News Bureau, December 6, 2004, http://www.indiafm.com/scoop/04/dec/0612rstrlcell/index.shtml.

Over the past several years, many of us have watched as cell phones have become increasingly central to the release strategies of commercial motion pictures around the world, as amateur and professional cell phone movies have competed for prizes in international film festivals, as mobile users have been able to listen in to major concerts, as Japanese novelists serialize their work via instant messenger, and as game players have used mobile devices to compete in augmented and alternative reality games. Some functions will take root; others will fail.

Call me old-fashioned. The other week I wanted to buy a cell phone — you know, to make phone calls. I didn't want a video camera, a still camera, a Web access device, an MP3 player, or a game system. I also wasn't interested in something that could show me movie previews, would have customizable ring tones, or would allow me to read novels. I didn't want the electronic equivalent of a Swiss army knife. When the phone rings, I don't want to have to figure out which button to push. I just wanted a phone. The sales clerks sneered at me; they laughed at me behind my back. I was told by company after mobile company that they don't make single-function phones anymore. Nobody wants them. This was a powerful demonstration of how central mobiles have become to the process of media convergence.

You've probably been hearing a lot about convergence lately. You are going to be hearing even more.

The media industries are undergoing another paradigm shift. It happens from time to time. In the 1990s, rhetoric about a coming digital revolution contained an implicit and often explicit assumption that new media were going to push aside old media, that the Internet was going to displace broadcasting, and that all of this would enable consumers to more easily access media content that was personally meaningful to them. A best-seller in 1995, Nicholas Negroponte's *Being Digital* drew a sharp contrast between "passive old media" and "interactive new media," predicting the collapse of broadcast networks in favor of an era of narrowcasting and niche media on demand: "What will happen to broadcast television over the next five years is so phenomenal that it's difficult to comprehend."[3] At one point, he suggests that no government regulation will be necessary to shatter the media conglomerates: "The monolithic empires of mass media are dissolving into an array of cottage industries. . . . Media barons of today will be grasping to hold onto their centralized empires tomorrow. . . . The combined forces of technology and human nature will ultimately take a stronger hand in plurality than any laws Congress can invent."[4] Sometimes, the new media companies spoke about convergence, but by this term, they seemed to mean that old media would be absorbed fully and completely into the orbit of the emerging technologies. George Gilder, another digital revolutionary, dismissed such claims: "The computer industry is converging with the television industry in the same sense that

[3]Nicholas Negroponte, *Being Digital* (New York: Alfred A. Knopf, 1995), p. 54.
[4]Ibid., pp. 57–58.

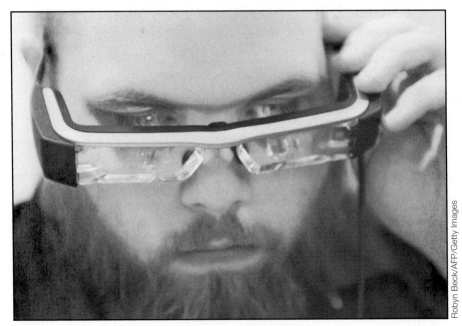

Robyn Beck/AFP/Getty Images

An attendee of the 2014 Consumer Electronics Show tries the Epson Moverio BT-200 smart glasses. Each lens has its own display right in the user's field of vision.

the automobile converged with the horse, the TV converged with the nickelodeon, the word-processing program converged with the typewriter, the CAD program converged with the drafting board, and digital desktop publishing converged with the linotype machine and the letterpress."[5] For Gilder, the computer had come not to transform mass culture but to destroy it.

The popping of the dot-com bubble threw cold water on this talk of a digital revolution. Now, convergence has reemerged as an important reference point as old and new media companies try to imagine the future of the entertainment industry. If the digital revolution paradigm presumed that new media would displace old media, the emerging convergence paradigm assumes that old and new media will interact in even more complex ways. The digital revolution paradigm claimed that new media were going to change everything. After the dot-com crash, the tendency was to imagine that new media had changed nothing. As with so many things about the current media environment, the truth lay somewhere in between. More and more, industry

[5]George Gilder, "Afterword: The Computer Juggernaut: Life after *Life after Television*," added to the 1994 edition of *Life after Television: The Coming Transformation of Media and American Life* (New York: W. W. Norton), p. 189. The book was originally published in 1990.

leaders are returning to convergence as a way of making sense of a moment of disorienting change. Convergence is, in that sense, an old concept taking on new meanings. . . .

The Prophet of Convergence

If *Wired* magazine declared Marshall McLuhan the patron saint of the digital revolution, we might well describe the late MIT political scientist Ithiel de Sola Pool as the prophet of media convergence. Pool's *Technologies of Freedom* (1983) was probably the first book to lay out the concept of convergence as a force of change within the media industries:

> A process called the "convergence of modes" is blurring the lines between media, even between point-to-point communications, such as the post, telephone, and telegraph, and mass communications, such as the press, radio, and television. A single physical means — be it wires, cables or air-waves — may carry services that in the past were provided in separate ways. Conversely, a service that was provided in the past by any one medium — be it broadcasting, the press, or telephony — can now be pro-vided in several different physical ways. So the one-to-one relationship that used to exist between a medium and its use is eroding.[6]

Some people today talk about divergence rather than convergence, but Pool understood that they were two sides of the same phenomenon.

"Once upon a time," Pool explained, "companies that published news-papers, magazines, and books did very little else; their involvement with other media was slight."[7] Each medium had its own distinctive functions and mar-kets, and each was regulated under different regimes, depending on whether its character was centralized or decentralized, marked by scarcity or plenti-tude, dominated by news or entertainment, and owned by governmental or private interests. Pool felt that these differences were largely the product of political choices and preserved through habit rather than any essential char-acteristic of the various technologies. But he did see some communications technologies as supporting more diversity and a greater degree of participa-tion than others: "Freedom is fostered when the means of communication are dispersed, decentralized, and easily available, as are printing presses or microcomputers. Central control is more likely when the means of commu-nication are concentrated, monopolized, and scarce, as are great networks."[8]

Several forces, however, have begun breaking down the walls separating these different media. New media technologies enabled the same content to

[6]Ithiel de Sola Pool, *Technologies of Freedom: On Free Speech in an Electronic Age* (Cam-bridge, Mass.: Harvard University Press, 1983), p. 23.
[7]Ibid.
[8]Ibid., p. 5.

flow through many different channels and assume many different forms at the point of reception. Pool was describing what Nicholas Negroponte calls the transformation of "atoms into bytes" or digitization.[9] At the same time, new patterns of cross-media ownership that began in the mid-1980s, during what we can now see as the first phase of a longer process of media concentration, were making it more desirable for companies to distribute content across the various channels rather than within a single media platform. Digitization set the conditions for convergence; corporate conglomerates created its imperative.

Much writing about the so-called digital revolution presumed that the outcome of technological change was more or less inevitable. Pool, on the other hand, predicted a period of prolonged transition, during which the various media systems competed and collaborated, searching for the stability that would always elude them: "Convergence does not mean ultimate stability or unity. It operates as a constant force for unification but always in dynamic tension with change. . . . There is no immutable law of growing convergence; the process of change is more complicated than that."[10]

As Pool predicted, we are in an age of media transition, one marked by tactical decisions and unintended consequences, mixed signals and competing interests, and most of all, unclear directions and unpredictable outcomes.[11] Two decades later, I find myself reexamining some of the core questions Pool raised — about how we maintain the potential of participatory culture in the wake of growing media concentration, about whether the changes brought about by convergence open new opportunities for expression or expand the power of big media. Pool was interested in the impact of convergence on political culture; I am more interested in its impact on popular culture, but the lines between the two have now blurred.

It is beyond my abilities to describe or fully document all of the changes that are occurring. My aim is more modest. I want to describe some of the ways that convergence thinking is reshaping American popular culture and, in particular, the ways it is impacting the relationship between media audiences, producers, and content. My goal is to help ordinary people grasp how convergence is impacting the media they consume and, at the same time, to help industry leaders and policymakers understand consumer perspectives on these changes. This has been challenging because everything seems to be changing at once and there is no vantage point that takes me above the fray. Rather than trying to write from an objective vantage point, I describe what this process looks like from various localized perspectives — advertising executives struggling to reach a changing market, creative artists discovering new ways

20

---

[9]Negroponte, *Being Digital.*

[10]Pool, *Technologies of Freedom*, pp. 53–54.

[11]For a fuller discussion of the concept of media in transition, see David Thorburn and Henry Jenkins, "Towards an Aesthetics of Transition," in David Thorburn and Henry Jenkins (eds.), *Rethinking Media Change: The Aesthetics of Transition* (Cambridge, Mass.: MIT Press, 2003).

to tell stories, educators tapping informal learning communities, activists deploying new resources to shape the political future, religious groups contesting the quality of their cultural environs, and, of course, various fan communities who are early adopters and creative users of emerging media.

I can't claim to be a neutral observer in any of this. For one thing, I am not simply a consumer of many of these media products; I am also an active fan. The world of media fandom has been a central theme of my work for almost two decades — an interest that emerges from my own participation within various fan communities as much as it does from my intellectual interests as a media scholar. During that time, I have watched fans move from the invisible margins of popular culture and into the center of current thinking about media production and consumption. For another, through my role as director of the MIT Comparative Media Studies Program, I have been an active participant in discussions among industry insiders and policymakers; I have consulted with some of the companies discussed; my earlier writings on fan communities and participatory culture have been embraced by business schools and are starting to have some modest impact on the way media companies are relating to their consumers; many of the creative artists and media executives I interviewed are people I would consider friends. At a time when the roles between producers and consumers are shifting, my job allows me to move among different vantage points. Yet, readers should also keep in mind that my engagement with fans and producers alike necessarily colors what I say. My goal here is to document conflicting perspectives on media change rather than to critique them. I don't think we can meaningfully critique convergence until it is more fully understood; yet if the public doesn't get some insights into the discussions that are taking place, they will have little to no input into decisions that will dramatically change their relationship to media.

The Black Box Fallacy

Almost a decade ago, science fiction writer Bruce Sterling established what he calls the Dead Media Project. As his Web site (http://www.deadmedia.org) explains, "The centralized, dinosaurian one-to-many media that roared and trampled through the twentieth century are poorly adapted to the postmodern technological environment."[12] Anticipating that some of these "dinosaurs" were heading to the tar pits, he constructed a shrine to "the media that have died on the barbed wire of technological change." His collection is astounding, including relics like "the phenakistoscope, the telharmonium, the Edison wax cylinder, the stereopticon, . . . various species of magic lantern."[13]

[12]Bruce Sterling, "The Dead Media Project: A Modest Proposal and a Public Appeal," http://www.deadmedia.org/modest-proposal.html.
    [13]Ibid.

Yet, history teaches us that old media never die—and they don't even necessarily fade away. What dies are simply the tools we use to access media content—the 8-track, the Beta tape. These are what media scholars call *delivery technologies*. Most of what Sterling's project lists falls under this category. Delivery technologies become obsolete and get replaced; media, on the other hand, evolve. Recorded sound is the medium. CDs, MP3 files, and 8-track cassettes are delivery technologies.

To define media, let's turn to historian Lisa Gitelman, who offers a model   25 of media that works on two levels: on the first, a medium is a technology that enables communication; on the second, a medium is a set of associated "protocols" or social and cultural practices that have grown up around that technology.[14] Delivery systems are simply and only technologies; media are also cultural systems. Delivery technologies come and go all the time, but media persist as layers within an ever more complicated information and entertainment stratum.

A medium's content may shift (as occurred when television displaced radio as a storytelling medium, freeing radio to become the primary showcase for rock and roll), its audience may change (as occurs when comics move from a mainstream medium in the 1950s to a niche medium today), and its social status may rise or fall (as occurs when theater moves from a popular form to an elite one), but once a medium establishes itself as satisfying some core human demand, it continues to function within the larger system of communication options. Once recorded sound becomes a possibility, we have continued to develop new and improved means of recording and playing back sounds. Printed words did not kill spoken words. Cinema did not kill theater. Television did not kill radio.[15] Each old medium was forced to coexist with the emerging media. That's why convergence seems more plausible as a way of understanding the past several decades of media change than the old digital revolution paradigm had. Old media are not being displaced. Rather, their functions and status are shifted by the introduction of new technologies.

The implications of this distinction between media and delivery systems become clearer as Gitelman elaborates on what she means by "protocols." She writes: "Protocols express a huge variety of social, economic, and material relationships. So telephony includes the salutation 'Hello?' (for English speakers, at least) and includes the monthly billing cycle and includes the wires and cables that materially connect our phones. Cinema includes everything from the sprocket holes that run along the sides of film to the widely shared sense of being able to wait and see 'films' at home on video. And

[14]Lisa Gitelman, "Introduction: Media as Historical Subjects," in *Always Already New: Media, History and the Data of Culture* (Cambridge, Mass.: MIT Press, 2006).
[15]For a useful discussion of the recurring idea that new media kill off old media, see Priscilla Coit Murphy, "Books Are Dead, Long Live Books," in David Thorburn and Henry Jenkins (eds.), *Rethinking Media Change: The Aesthetics of Transition* (Cambridge, Mass.: MIT Press, 2003).

protocols are far from static."[16] I have less to say about the technological dimensions of media change than about the shifts in the protocols by which we are producing and consuming media.

Much contemporary discourse about convergence starts and ends with what I call the Black Box Fallacy. Sooner or later, the argument goes, all media content is going to flow through a single black box into our living rooms (or, in the mobile scenario, through black boxes we carry around with us everywhere we go). If folks could just figure out which black box will reign supreme, then everyone can make reasonable investments for the future. Part of what makes the black box concept a fallacy is that it reduces media change to technological change and strips aside the cultural levels we are considering here.

I don't know about you, but in my living room, I am seeing more and more black boxes. There are my VCR, my digital cable box, my DVD player, my digital recorder, my sound system, and my two game systems, not to mention a huge mound of videotapes, DVDs and CDs, game cartridges and controllers, sitting atop, laying alongside, toppling over the edge of my television system. (I would definitely qualify as an early adopter, but most American homes now have, or soon will have, their own pile of black boxes.) The perpetual tangle of cords that stands between me and my "home entertainment" center reflects the degree of incompatibility and dysfunction that exists between the various media technologies. And many of my MIT students are lugging around multiple black boxes — their laptops, their cells, their iPods, their Game Boys, their BlackBerrys, you name it.

As Cheskin Research explained in a 2002 report, "The old idea of convergence was that all devices would converge into one central device that did everything for you (à la the universal remote). What we are now seeing is the hardware diverging while the content converges. Your e-mail needs and expectations are different whether you're at home, work, school, commuting, the airport, etc., and these different devices are designed to suit your needs for accessing content depending on where you are — your situated context."[17] This pull toward more specialized media appliances coexists with a push toward more generic devices. We can see the proliferation of black boxes as symptomatic of a moment of convergence: because no one is sure what kinds of functions should be combined, we are forced to buy a range of specialized and incompatible appliances. On the other end of the spectrum, we may also be forced to deal with an escalation of functions within the same media appliance, functions that decrease the ability of that appliance to serve its original function, and so I can't get a cell phone that is just a phone.

Media convergence is more than simply a technological shift. Convergence alters the relationship between existing technologies, industries, markets, genres, and audiences. Convergence alters the logic by which media industries

[16]Gitelman, "Introduction."
[17]Cheskin Research, "Designing Digital Experiences for Youth," *Market Insights Series,* Fall 2002, pp. 8–9.

operate and by which media consumers process news and entertainment. Keep this in mind: convergence refers to a process, not an endpoint. There will be no single black box that controls the flow of media into our homes. Thanks to the proliferation of channels and the portability of new computing and telecommunications technologies, we are entering an era where media will be everywhere. Convergence isn't something that is going to happen one day when we have enough bandwidth or figure out the correct configuration of appliances. Ready or not, we are already living within a convergence culture.

Our cell phones are not simply telecommunications devices; they also allow us to play games, download information from the Internet, and take and send photographs or text messages. Increasingly they allow us to watch previews of new films, download installments of serialized novels, or attend concerts from remote locations. All of this is already happening in northern Europe and Asia. Any of these functions can also be performed using other media appliances. You can listen to the Dixie Chicks through your DVD player, your car radio, your Walkman, your iPod, a Web radio station, or a music cable channel.

Fueling this technological convergence is a shift in patterns of media ownership. Whereas old Hollywood focused on cinema, the new media conglomerates have controlling interests across the entire entertainment industry. Warner Bros. produces film, television, popular music, computer games, Web sites, toys, amusement park rides, books, newspapers, magazines, and comics.

In turn, media convergence impacts the way we consume media. A teenager doing homework may juggle four or five windows, scan the Web, listen to and download MP3 files, chat with friends, word-process a paper, and respond to e-mail, shifting rapidly among tasks. And fans of a popular television series may sample dialogue, summarize episodes, debate subtexts, create original fan fiction, record their own soundtracks, make their own movies—and distribute all of this worldwide via the Internet.

Convergence is taking place within the same appliances, within the same   35 franchise, within the same company, within the brain of the consumer, and within the same fandom. Convergence involves both a change in the way media are produced and a change in the way media are consumed.

The Cultural Logic of Media Convergence

Another snapshot of the future: Anthropologist Mizuko Ito has documented the growing pace of mobile communications among Japanese youth, describing young couples who remain in constant contact with each other throughout the day, thanks to their access to various mobile technologies.[18] They

---

[18]Mizuko Ito, "Mobile Phones, Japanese Youth and the Re-Placement of the Social Contract," in Rich Ling and Per Petersen (eds.), *Mobile Communications: Re-Negotiation of the Social Sphere* (forthcoming). http://www.itofisher.com/mito/archives/mobileyouth.pdf.

wake up together, work together, eat together, and go to bed together even though they live miles apart and may have face-to-face contact only a few times a month. We might call it telecocooning.

Convergence doesn't just involve commercially produced materials and services traveling along well-regulated and predictable circuits. It doesn't just involve the mobile companies getting together with the film companies to decide when and where we watch a newly released film. It also occurs when people take media in their own hands. Entertainment content isn't the only thing that flows across multiple media platforms. Our lives, relationships, memories, fantasies, desires also flow across media channels. Being a lover or a mommy or a teacher occurs on multiple platforms.[19] Sometimes we tuck our kids into bed at night and other times we Instant Message them from the other side of the globe.

And yet another snapshot: Intoxicated students at a local high school use their cell phones spontaneously to produce their own soft-core porn movie involving topless cheerleaders making out in the locker room. Within hours, the movie is circulating across the school, being downloaded by students and teachers alike, and watched between classes on personal media devices.

When people take media into their own hands, the results can be wonderfully creative; they can also be bad news for all involved.

For the foreseeable future, convergence will be a kind of kludge — a jerry-rigged relationship among different media technologies — rather than a fully integrated system. Right now, the cultural shifts, the legal battles, and the economic consolidations that are fueling media convergence are preceding shifts in the technological infrastructure. How those various transitions unfold will determine the balance of power in the next media era.

The American media environment is now being shaped by two seemingly contradictory trends: on the one hand, new media technologies have lowered production and distribution costs, expanded the range of available delivery channels, and enabled consumers to archive, annotate, appropriate, and recirculate media content in powerful new ways. At the same time, there has been alarming concentration of the ownership of mainstream commercial media, with a small handful of multinational media conglomerates dominating all sectors of the entertainment industry. No one seems capable of describing both sets of changes at the same time, let alone show how they impact each other. Some fear that media are out of control, others that it is too controlled. Some see a world without gatekeepers, others a world where gatekeepers have unprecedented power. Again, the truth lies somewhere in between.

---

[19]For a useful illustration of this point, see Henry Jenkins, "Love Online," in Henry Jenkins (ed.), *Fans, Gamers, and Bloggers* (New York: New York University Press, 2005).

Another snapshot: People around the world are affixing stickers show-ing yellow arrows (http://global.yellowarrow.net) alongside public monuments and factories, beneath highway overpasses, onto lamp posts. The arrows pro-vide numbers others can call to access recorded voice messages — personal annotations on our shared urban landscape. They use it to share a beautiful vista or criticize an irresponsible company. And increasingly, companies are co-opting the system to leave their own advertising pitches.

Convergence, as we can see, is both a top-down corporate-driven process and a bottom-up consumer-driven process. Corporate convergence coexists with grassroots convergence. Media companies are learning how to accelerate the flow of media content across delivery channels to expand revenue oppor-tunities, broaden markets, and reinforce viewer commitments. Consumers are learning how to use these different media technologies to bring the flow of media more fully under their control and to interact with other consumers. The promises of this new media environment raise expectations of a freer flow of ideas and content. Inspired by those ideals, consumers are fighting for the right to participate more fully in their culture. Sometimes, corporate and grassroots convergence reinforce each other, creating closer, more rewarding relations between media producers and consumers. Sometimes, these two forces are at war and those struggles will redefine the face of American popu-lar culture.

Convergence requires media companies to rethink old assumptions about what it means to consume media, assumptions that shape both program-ming and marketing decisions. If old consumers were assumed to be passive, the new consumers are active. If old consumers were predictable and stayed where you told them to stay, then new consumers are migratory, showing a declining loyalty to networks or media. If old consumers were isolated indi-viduals, the new consumers are more socially connected. If the work of media consumers was once silent and invisible, the new consumers are now noisy and public.

Media producers are responding to these newly empowered consumers 45 in contradictory ways, sometimes encouraging change, sometimes resisting what they see as renegade behavior. And consumers, in turn, are perplexed by what they see as mixed signals about how much and what kinds of partici-pation they can enjoy.

As they undergo this transition, the media companies are not behaving in a monolithic fashion; often, different divisions of the same company are pursuing radically different strategies, reflecting their uncertainty about how to proceed. On the one hand, convergence represents an expanded opportu-nity for media conglomerates, since content that succeeds in one sector can spread across other platforms. On the other, convergence represents a risk since most of the media fear a fragmentation or erosion of their markets. Each time they move a viewer from television to the Internet, say, there is a risk that the consumer may not return.

Industry insiders use the term "extension" to refer to their efforts to expand the potential markets by moving content across different delivery systems, "synergy" to refer to the economic opportunities represented by their ability to own and control all of those manifestations, and "franchise" to refer to their coordinated effort to brand and market fictional content under these new conditions. Extension, synergy, and franchising are pushing media industries to embrace convergence.

You are now entering convergence culture. It is not a surprise that we are not yet ready to cope with its complexities and contradictions. We need to find ways to negotiate the changes taking place. No one group can set the terms. No one group can control access and participation.

Don't expect the uncertainties surrounding convergence to be resolved anytime soon. We are entering an era of prolonged transition and transformation in the way media operate. Convergence describes the process by which we will sort through these options. There will be no magical black box that puts everything in order again. Media producers will only find their way through their current problems by renegotiating their relationship with their consumers. Audiences, empowered by these new technologies, occupying a space at the intersection between old and new media, are demanding the right to participate within the culture. Producers who fail to make their peace with this new participatory culture will face declining goodwill and diminished revenues. The resulting struggles and compromises will define the public culture of the future.

READING THE TEXT

1. Define in your own words what Jenkins means by "convergence culture," and create a list of current media examples that would constitute that culture.

2. What contradictions does Jenkins find in convergence culture?

3. Explain how convergence culture is both top-down and bottom-up.

4. Describe Jenkins's tone, considering the extent to which it may be neutral or biased. How does it affect your response to the concept of convergence culture?

5. In your own words, define what industry insiders mean by "extension," "synergy," and "franchise" (para. 47), and explain how they apply to the new media.

READING THE SIGNS

1. In your journal, reflect on your own experience with new media. What participatory media do you engage in, and why? If you avoid such media, what are the reasons behind your behavior?

2. Jenkins's claim that "when people take media into their own hands, the results can be wonderfully creative; they can also be bad news for all involved" (para. 39) presents the two outcomes as equally possible. Write an essay in which you support Jenkins's assumption or weigh the outcomes and

decide that one is more likely. If you argue the latter position, what tips the balance in favor of the side you chose?

3. **CONNECTING TEXTS** Write an essay arguing for or against the proposition that "concentration of the ownership of mainstream commercial media" (para. 41) is turning the Cloud into just another way for the corporate world to make money. To develop your ideas, consult the introduction to this chapter.

4. A significant proportion of the videos on YouTube and similar sites consist of copyrighted material. Write an essay in which you support, oppose, or modify the position that ordinary copyright law should apply to the use of such material on YouTube.

5. Since Jenkins wrote the book from which this selection is taken, Facebook and Twitter have joined cell phones and other media as tools of political revolution — for example, in the revolutions against the governments of Egypt, Tunisia, and Libya in 2011. Picking one such revolution, research how social and other media were used, and write an essay that evaluates the effectiveness of electronic media as a political force.

Navigating On- and Offline Lives

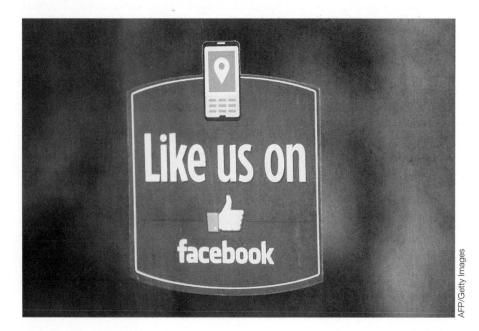

AFP/Getty Images

READING THE SIGNS

1. How often on a daily basis do you encounter stickers, signs, or posters like this one, which asks you to link up some sort of real-world experience with

your social media account? What types of things are you most likely to "like," and why?

2. Think about all the companies, services, and entertainments that you've "liked." What inferences might a stranger make about you based on these "likes"? How do they contribute to a fuller picture of "you" on social media?

3. **CONNECTING TEXTS** Write an essay in which you argue whether or not signs like this one are a part of what Henry Jenkins calls "convergence culture" (p. 423).

6

HEROES AND VILLAINS

Encoding Our Conflicts

Saving the World

The first full-fledged hero of written storytelling was Gilgamesh, the legendary king of the Mesopotamian kingdom of Uruk, whose exploits are recounted in the various cuneiform texts that make up *The Epic of Gilgamesh*. Like many superheroes today, Gilgamesh was described as having superhuman strength (indeed, he is more than half divine in his origins), and he was a monster slayer. Many modern readers might question whether Gilgamesh is really the good guy in the story (after all, he is an oppressor of his own people, and his slaying of Humbaba, the guardian of the Cedars of Lebanon, leads to his destruction of the entire forest). Nonetheless, he does defend his city from the Bull of Heaven who has been sent to destroy it, thus becoming the first of many heroes whose job is to "save the world."

Saving the world (or, at least, a city or society) appears to have been a primary duty of ancient heroes, whether the threat came from nature (as symbolized by such figures as Humbaba), from demons (like the mysterious Grendel and his mother), from dragons (a symbol for evil itself in Western society), or simply from enemy warriors (like Goliath). That's still the job description, especially in popular culture, of many modern heroes, who fight monstrous forces of nature (*Jaws*), demons (*World War Z*), dragons (*The Hobbit*), and enemy warriors/nations (*G.I. Joe: The Rise of Cobra*). Whether they operate alone — as what Robert B. Ray, in "The Thematic Paradigm," calls "outlaw heroes" — or from within established social institutions — Ray's "official heroes" — heroes represent the best in us — courage, skill, altruism — defending and protecting their societies against whatever threatens them.

Exploring the Signs of Heroes and Villains

In your journal, jot down four or five fictional heroes whom you admire, then list a similar number of real-life heroes whom you also regard as outstanding. Study your two lists: What traits do they share? What values do these heroes embody, and what do those values reveal about your own worldview? In addition (or as an alternate), do the same with fictional and real-life villains. If you have difficulty creating such lists, explore in your journal why you think that is the case.

Ugly Is as Ugly Does

But saving the world requires someone (or something) to save the world *from*, and in the modern era that is more often a human threat, not a natural or a nonhuman one. This threat is the *villain*, the hero's necessary antagonist, and the history of storytelling is as filled with vivid villains as it is with heroes. They are usually easy to spot, because if the hero is conventionally coded by his or her physical attractiveness (by whatever standard of beauty a society holds), the villain is often simply ugly (equally often a matter of social construction). Consider Sauron and the Orcs in *The Lord of the Rings* versus the cute Hobbits, beautiful elves, and handsome warriors like Aragorn and the Riders of Rohan. Even the two wizards, Gandalf and Saruman, who are superficially similar, can be distinguished: Gandalf is grandfatherly when still gray, distinguished when white; Saruman, on the other hand, has the wrong nose (too long, too hooked) and the wrong fingernails (too long, too pointed). Or take Batman (buff, tall, dark, and handsome) versus Bane (who looks like something out of a WWE promoter's worst nightmare). Or Iron Man versus Mandarin. Luke Skywalker versus Darth Vader (in spite of the family relationship). Glinda, the Good Witch of the North, versus the Wicked Witch of the West. The list is endless.

It's a crude code, of course, and an obvious one, but it is extremely common in popular cultural representation, so common that currently a not uncommon gambit is to deliberately turn it upside down in order to make a point. Take Shrek.

The whole point of the Shrek stories is to reverse the codes of good versus evil and thus expose the social constructions of beauty and ugliness that can lie behind them. Here the hero is literally an ogre, an ugly troll with funny ears, while the villain can be a blond and handsome Prince Charming. Something similar goes on in the *Despicable Me* franchise with the Minions, who, in their apparent amalgamation of Alvin and the Chipmunks with Pac-Man and the Budweiser Ferret, are very cute parodies of the "evil-must-be-ugly" tradition. But the jokes work (and the reversals in *Shrek* and *Despicable Me* are jokes) precisely because they are reversals, transpositions of the usual signs of good and evil in popular storytelling.

The coding of evilness through ugliness and of goodness through beauty is such a universal convention of storytelling that it is often easy to forget that in reality things don't really work out that way. For one, real-life villains are simply human beings, and beautiful people can be evil while unattractive ones can be very good indeed. What is more, in conflicts among human beings, one man's villain is likely to be another's hero, and vice versa. This is usually not a problem in traditional storytelling, which is generally unconcerned with the niceties of moral relativity, but it most certainly is in contemporary narratives, which frequently serve as metaphors for real-world conflicts. Often reflecting an uneasy apprehension that perhaps good and evil aren't so easily distinguished after all, such stories feature a new kind of hero — one who isn't precisely a hero at all.

Enter the Antihero

Such protagonists as *Mad Men*'s Don Draper, *Dexter*'s Dexter, *Breaking Bad*'s Walter White, *The Sopranos*' Tony Soprano, and *The Sons of Anarchy*'s Jax Teller are prominent examples of recent protagonists who embody a *mixture* of good and evil. They commit patently evil acts and are hardly heroes in the ordinary sense of the term, yet they aren't simply villains either. Indeed, even when they are behaving badly, usually there is someone worse in the room, as it were, to make it clear who the *real* villain is. Often referred to as "antiheroes," these characters offer an interesting counterpoint to the hordes of cartoonish superheroes who have cast so large a shadow on contemporary popular culture.

The dichotomy between superheroes and antiheroes can be explained, in part, by the different media in which they typically appear. Cinema tends to be the superhero's prime domain; the antiheroes mentioned above, on the other hand, all come from television — to be more precise, from cable networks, not the traditional commercial TV stations. The distinction is significant, because unlike commercially sponsored television, cable has its own guaranteed revenue stream provided by viewer subscriptions. Unbeholden to commercial sponsors, who are themselves vulnerable to pressure groups and the threat of consumer boycotts, the producers of cable TV series are much freer to experiment with more controversial, complex, and, quite simply, mature story concepts. Thus, they are able to show human beings in all their complexity, mixing good and bad, strength and frailty, vision and blindness, kindness and cruelty.

The movies, on the other hand, lack this freedom, not because they are held hostage to corporate sponsors but because they cost so much to produce in an era when audiences demand all sorts of expensive special effects

---

Discussing the Signs of Antiheroes

Antiheroes, who are most commonly the protagonists of television series and movies, are effectively heroes in that the audience is expected to sympathize with them. In class, discuss the consequences for social behavior when Americans sympathize and identify with deeply flawed (including illegal and psychopathic) behavior on the part of a fictional protagonist (who, by definition, is the focal character who shapes the viewers' emotional responses).

(including, of course, 3-D technology) and high-priced stars. By contrast, cable TV, with its cheaper production costs and — at least initially — relatively cheap actor salaries, is far less expensive and can thus take greater risks than movies can. With so much at stake financially, American moviemakers have increasingly turned to simplistic formulas that are calculated to attract multiple demographics to the theaters. To appeal to adults and children, simple confrontations between handsome heroes and ugly villains are the safest bet, combined with stories taken from already-proven cartoon series and children's books that are also popular with adults (Batman, Spider-Man, Iron Man, the Avengers, the X-Men, Superman, Harry Potter, and so on).

Thus, the rise of the antihero suggests a more nuanced level of understanding in its audience, along with a certain cultural resignation and weariness, fostered by a growing apprehension that no one is perfect and that there is some evil in all of us. At a time when so many ordinary Americans are under stress and finding themselves facing their own temptations to test the boundaries of civil society, popular culture's exploration of the antihero's flawed behavior can be especially enticing. It's as if there were a bit of Walter White in all of us.

At the same time, the popularity of the antihero may also reflect a certain rising cynicism as well, a diminishing interest in old-fashioned morality and a growing fascination with no-holds-barred freedom, because the antihero, who violates the law and does what he wants when he wants and as he wants, is, in effect, an ultra-individualist: exactly the sort of protagonist one might expect to find in an era of widespread libertarian tendencies. Either way, the antihero stands as a signifier of a society that is losing its traditional certitudes and becoming resigned instead to that gray area of moral uncertainty in which pure heroes cannot thrive.

The Capitalist Villain to the Rescue

But the rise of the antihero doesn't mean that the villain has disappeared; indeed, without the villain there is often no story to tell at all. The problem, however, lies in who gets cast *as* the villain, which can be a very sensitive matter indeed. With their long history of racist stereotyping, for example, Hollywood filmmakers are far less likely today to cast nonwhite actors as villains. During the Cold War, the Soviet Union provided a source of villains for many James Bond and other spy films, but that pretty much came to an end with the fall of the Soviet Union. Evil white Southern sheriffs were popular villains in the 1960s to 1970s, while Colombian drug dealers were the villains of choice in many an action flick in the 1980s. And the Mafia has provided a steady stream of Hollywood villains, much to the dismay of many Italian Americans, who see themselves being negatively stereotyped.

In recent years, another kind of villain has stepped up to the plate, one that can be called the "capitalist villain." Unlike a conventional criminal such as a bank robber or murderer, the capitalist villain is not a social outsider: He is an *insider*, a businessman whose crimes are the crimes of corporate capitalism itself. Movies like *Avatar*, *The Lone Ranger*, *Iron Man 3*, and *White House Down* and TV shows like *Arrested Development* and *Sons of Anarchy* feature this new variety of villain. This is not at all surprising in the wake of the Great Recession, an economic catastrophe that continues to brutalize most Americans and is decimating the middle class. While some corporate leaders have expressed irritation that now *they* are being unfairly stereotyped, they have provided what appears to be a convenient source of new villains for entertainment purposes, villains who, as members of the dominant culture, cannot effectively complain that they are being persecuted.

And they are needed, for one way or another, American entertainment today is packed with stories of heroes and villains locked in violent conflict. Such stories point to a society in crisis, a divided people who feel threatened but are unable to agree on the source of the threat. Such a society will be drawn to simplistic stories where the difference between good and evil is obvious (call out the Avengers!) or to more cynical narratives (like *The Walking Dead*) where evil is everywhere and it's "every man for himself." All of which leads to

Lord Business, the capitalist villain of *The Lego Movie* (2014).

Photofest

yet another semiotic question: What has so divided the American people, leading to so many narratives—both fictional and real—involving irreconcilable conflict?

This Is the End of the Innocence

Though often neglected today, America's experience in the Vietnam War was a watershed in American history. Prior to that, Americans had no difficulty identifying who were the heroes in their wars and who were the villains. (Even during the Civil War, Northerners and Southerners alike had no difficulty making this distinction: They simply lined up on different sides.) But Vietnam was different. Unlike World War II, which really did represent a war between the forces of evil and its opponents, Vietnam turned into a moral quagmire. Popular cultural representations of war changed accordingly with movies (and TV series) like *M*A*S*H* serving as metaphors for a conflict that divided America and shook our trust in the American government as well.

In the same era, America also split apart over the effects of a cultural revolution that included the civil rights movement, the women's movement, and sexual liberation. The backlash against this profound disruption in cultural history produced a "silent majority" that had evolved into the Moral Majority by the late 1970s. Ever since, America has been so fractured that a tendency to divide the country into sets of heroes and villains—rather than citizens who happen to disagree—has taken hold.

Just look at some popular news media. On one side, for instance, we have Fox News, and on the other MSNBC. For the fans of Fox News, such current and former MSNBC personalities as Keith Olbermann, Chris Matthews, and Al Sharpton—not to mention politicians like Barack Obama, Hillary Clinton, and Nancy Pelosi—are absolute villains, while such figures as Glenn Beck, Rush Limbaugh, Bill O'Reilly, and Sarah Palin are heroes. Of course, this is exactly reversed for MSNBC fans. The Fox News versus MSNBC conflict is but a microcosm of a larger one whereby Americans apparently can't simply agree to disagree but are inclined to treat all politics as some sort of WWE smackdown or out-and-out war.

What's Red and Blue and Mad All Over?

This split between hostile political ideologies has been directly reflected in national elections that have produced the red-state and blue-state divide, a cultural division that was first officially noted after the 2000 presidential election. At the time, maps color-coded the states that voted Republican in red and the states that voted Democratic in blue. Since then it has become common to refer to "red state" and "blue state" regions of America, with the former generally considered conservative, and the latter liberal or progressive.

Exploring Heroes Online

Visit a Web site that proposes historical heroes, such as "History's Heroes" (http://historysheroes.e2bn.org/), "Heroes of History" (www .heroesofhistory.com), or "100 Greatest Heroes" (www.adherents.com /people/100_heroes.html). Evaluate the choices you find. What criteria does the site seem to use to define a "hero"? Do you agree with the site's judgments? Why or why not? Alternatively, compare two of the sites: What differences in their choices do you find, if any?

Although these terms run the risk of stereotyping, red and blue states do tend to take different sides in relation to America's cultural and ideological conflicts, reflecting their opposing positions on some very fundamental American values. These values include a number of highly contradictory cultural **mythologies** that exist in hostile relation to each other and, consequently, underpin a great deal of the political conflict in America today. Knowing what those contradictions are can be an important step in your analysis of many current tales of heroes and villains.

Three Basic Contradictions

Perhaps the values that especially divide Americans today can be boiled down to three fundamental conflicts over attitudes toward the **body**, toward the **mind**, and toward **community**. Let's take them in order.

MYTHOLOGIES OF THE BODY

Prior to the sexual revolution of the 1960s to 1970s, the prevailing mythology of the body in America could be characterized as one of modesty and repression. Valuing bodily health and hygiene ("cleanliness is next to godliness"), this mythology celebrates sports and recreation but frowns on erotic display and expression. Clearly reflected in Hollywood's Hays Code, which restricted the sexual content of movies from the 1930s onwards, this puritanical streak in the American character led many people to disapprove of the sexual energy of rock and roll in the 1950s and, notoriously, caused broadcasters to film Elvis Presley from the waist up when he first performed on *The Ed Sullivan Show* (they objected to the King's vigorous pelvic gyrations). Within the terms of the mythology, the body's fundamental sexual instincts must be controlled through prohibitions on premarital sex and channeled into state-approved monogamous and procreative marital relationships.

But in the wake of the "Summer of Love" in 1967, a sexual revolution swept America, a revolution that divides sexually repressive red-state and sexually liberated blue-state attitudes to this day. In the view of the new mythology, the body need not be covered up and its instinctive desires need not be constrained — in fact, both body and desire can be commodified and exploited. This transformation is especially apparent in our popular culture, where sexually explicit entertainments and clothing fashions paradoxically reflect not only the triumph of the progressive spirit of the sexual revolution but also the prevalence of the conservative capitalistic profit motive over traditional morality, which once put values above profits. Lady Gaga, who has so successfully commodified her own body, is an apt emblem of this complex contradiction, exemplifying both a capitalistic exploitation of erotic desire and a socially progressive position on sexual freedom. Accordingly, she has become a heroine to some and an object of revulsion to others, like members of the Florida Family Association, who protested her Born This Way tour in 2013.

MYTHOLOGIES OF THE MIND

Closely related to our conflicting mythologies of the body, American attitudes toward the mind, or spirit, divide along a faith versus reason axis. Upholders of a sexually modest and repressive ideology of the body tend to embrace orthodox religious beliefs that put piety of mind above rationality and science. A conflict ingrained within an American history that includes both the theocratic Puritans of the Massachusetts Bay Colony and such Enlightenment nation builders as Benjamin Franklin and Thomas Jefferson, who created America upon the basis of a separation of church and state, this division is expressed in the battle over the teaching of evolution in public schools and in the red-state-tending rejection of scientific research on global warming and climate change. In such an environment, evangelical leaders like Pat Robertson can be heroes to many and villains to others, while scientists like Albert Einstein and Richard Feynman and technology pioneers like Steve Jobs and Elon Musk can be culture heroes.

MYTHOLOGIES OF COMMUNITY

Although you would hardly know it from listening to much of the social conversation these days, America has a history of social altruism — the communitarian ethos that led to the establishment of such entitlements as Social Security, Medicare, and federal and state welfare programs — along with the individualistically grounded libertarianism that underlies the emergence of such political movements as the Tea Party Patriots. The conflict between these two ideologies came to a dramatic head in the battle over the Affordable Care Act ("Obamacare"), which made President Barack Obama a heroic figure to those blue-state Americans who believe in socially guaranteed health care, and an arch-villain to its libertarian opponents, with such red-state politicians as Senator Ted Cruz vying for the hero role among those who shared his opposition to a governmentally organized health system.

Faced with such ideological conflicts, Americans today do not simply argue — they demonize each other, turning opponents into "villains" and supporters into "heroes." They become dragon slayers, as it were, putting all ideological opponents to the sword. Such real-life conflict inevitably makes its way into our popular culture, but there it is often mediated into a less controversial form, as in the movie *Gettysburg*, which treats both Union and Confederate soldiers alike as heroes in order to avoid alienating a large portion of the potential audience, conveniently soft-pedaling the fact that one side was fighting for slavery and the other against it. Or, much more commonly still, popular cultural narratives avoid reality altogether by presenting cartoonish Hitlerian villains who are so obviously evil that the battle against them can be entertainingly uncomplicated and uncontroversial. Thus, while vaguely aware that something is wrong, American audiences can be beguiled into a feeling that problems can be resolved quite simply, and they can be distracted from the uncomfortable fact that in America today, as *Pogo* cartoonist Walt Kelly put it so well many years ago, "we have met the enemy, and he is us."

The Readings

Robert B. Ray's analysis of the "official hero" and "outlaw hero" begins this chapter, providing a solid foundation for the analysis of the complexities of heroism in popular culture. Stevie St. John comes next with her analysis of Wonder Woman, a superhero who in spite of decades of popularity still hasn't had her own feature film. A paired set of readings on a third kind of popular hero — the antihero — follows, with Heather Havrilesky providing an in-depth reading of *Breaking Bad*'s Walter White, and Laura Bennett arguing that the term "antihero" has become an almost-meaningless buzzword. George Packer's "Celebrating Inequality" takes a trenchant look at today's celebrities — an exclusive "superclass" of entertainers, corporate executives, politicians, and a handful of intellectuals, whom Packer finds to be anything but heroic. Then, looking at the villains from three high-profile movies of 2013 — *Iron Man 3*, *White House Down*, and *The Lone Ranger* — Noah Gittell notes the emergence of a new kind of Hollywood villain: the greedy and corrupt businessman. Tim Layden's "A Patriot's Tale" follows, telling the story of a family of New York City firefighters, real-life heroes who risked their lives during the September 11 terror attack on the World Trade Center. And Lorraine Devon Wilke concludes the readings with a critique of what she sees as the overly simplistic, black-and-white assessments of the actions of Edward Snowden, whose embrace as an out-and-out hero by some and denunciation as a villain by others gloss over the broadly gray moral dimensions of his exposure of the NSA.

ROBERT B. RAY
The Thematic Paradigm

Usually we consider movies to be merely entertainment, but as Robert B. Ray demonstrates in this selection from his book *A Certain Tendency of the Hollywood Cinema* (1985), American films have long reflected fundamental patterns and contradictions in our society's myths and values. Whether in real life or on the silver screen, Ray explains, Americans have always been ambivalent about the value of civilization, celebrating it through official heroes like George Washington and Jimmy Stewart, while at the same time questioning it through outlaw heroes like Davy Crockett and Huck Finn. Especially when presented together in the same film, these two hero types help mediate America's ambivalence, providing a mythic solution. Ray's analyses show how the movies are rich sources for cultural interpretation. Robert B. Ray is a professor of English at the University of Florida at Gainesville. His publications include *The Avant Garde Finds Andy Hardy* (1995), *How a Film Theory Got Lost and Other Mysteries in Cultural Studies* (2001), and, most recently, *Walden × 40: Essays on Thoreau* (2011).

The dominant tradition of American cinema consistently found ways to overcome dichotomies. Often, the movies' reconciliatory pattern concentrated on a single character magically embodying diametrically opposite traits. A sensitive violinist was also a tough boxer (*Golden Boy*); a boxer was a gentle man who cared for pigeons (*On the Waterfront*). A gangster became a coward because he was brave (*Angels with Dirty Faces*); a soldier became brave because he was a coward (*Lives of a Bengal Lancer*). A war hero was a former pacifist (*Sergeant York*); a pacifist was a former war hero (*Billy Jack*). The ideal was a kind of inclusiveness that would permit all decisions to be undertaken with the knowledge that the alternative was equally available. The attractiveness of Destry's refusal to use guns (*Destry Rides Again*) depended on the tacit understanding that he could shoot with the best of them, Katharine Hepburn's and Claudette Colbert's revolts against conventionality (*Holiday*, *It Happened One Night*) on their status as aristocrats.

Such two-sided characters seemed particularly designed to appeal to a collective American imagination steeped in myths of inclusiveness. Indeed, in creating such characters, classic Hollywood had connected with what Erik Erikson has described as the fundamental American psychological pattern:

> The functioning American, as the heir of a history of extreme contrasts and abrupt changes, bases his final ego identity on some tentative combination of dynamic polarities such as migratory and sedentary, individualistic and standardized, competitive and co-operative, pious and free-thinking, responsible and cynical, etc. . . .

> To leave his choices open, the American, on the whole, lives with two sets of "truths."[1]

The movies traded on one opposition in particular, American culture's traditional dichotomy of individual and community that had generated the most significant pair of competing myths: the outlaw hero and the official hero.[2] Embodied in the adventurer, explorer, gunfighter, wanderer, and loner, the outlaw hero stood for that part of the American imagination valuing self-determination and freedom from entanglements. By contrast, the official hero, normally portrayed as a teacher, lawyer, politician, farmer, or family man, represented the American belief in collective action, and the objective legal process that superseded private notions of right and wrong. While the outlaw hero found incarnations in the mythic figures of Davy Crockett, Jesse James, Huck Finn, and all of Leslie Fiedler's "Good Bad Boys" and Daniel Boorstin's "ring-tailed roarers," the official hero developed around legends associated with Washington, Jefferson, Lincoln, Lee, and other "Good Good Boys."

An extraordinary amount of the traditional American mythology adopted by Classic Hollywood derived from the variations worked by American ideology around this opposition of natural man versus civilized man. To the extent that these variations constituted the main tendency of American literature and legends, Hollywood, in relying on this mythology, committed itself to becoming what Robert Bresson has called "the Cinema."[3] A brief description of the competing values associated with this outlaw hero–official hero opposition will begin to suggest its pervasiveness in traditional American culture.

1. *Aging*: The attractiveness of the outlaw hero's childishness and propensity to whims, tantrums, and emotional decisions derived from America's cult of childhood. Fiedler observed that American literature celebrated "the notion that a mere falling short of adulthood is a guarantee of insight and even innocence." From Huck to Holden Caulfield, children in American literature were privileged, existing beyond society's confining rules. Often, they set the plot in motion (e.g., *Intruder in the Dust*, *To Kill a Mockingbird*), acting for the adults encumbered by daily affairs. As Fiedler also pointed out, this image of childhood "has impinged upon adult life itself, has become a 'career' like everything else in America,"[4] generating stories like *On the Road*

---

[1]Erik H. Erikson, *Childhood and Society* (New York: Norton, 1963), p. 286.

[2]Leading discussions of the individual–community polarity in American culture can be found in *The Contrapuntal Civilization: Essays Toward a New Understanding of the American Experience*, ed. Michael Kammen (New York: Crowell, 1971). The most prominent analyses of American literature's use of this opposition remain Leslie A. Fiedler's *Love and Death in the American Novel* (New York: Stein and Day, 1966) and A. N. Kaul's *The American Vision* (New Haven: Yale University Press, 1963).

[3]Robert Bresson, *Notes on Cinematography*, trans. Jonathan Griffin (New York: Urizen Books, 1977), p. 12.

[4]Leslie A. Fiedler, *No! In Thunder* (New York: Stein and Day, 1972), pp. 253, 275.

The "outlaw hero," Davy Crockett, portrayed by Fess Parker.

or *Easy Rider* in which adults try desperately to postpone responsibilities by clinging to adolescent lifestyles.

While the outlaw heroes represented a flight from maturity, the official heroes embodied the best attributes of adulthood: sound reasoning and judgment, wisdom and sympathy based on experience. Franklin's *Autobiography* and *Poor Richard's Almanack* constituted this opposing tradition's basic texts, persuasive enough to appeal even to outsiders (*The Great Gatsby*). Despite the legends surrounding Franklin and the other Founding Fathers, however, the scarcity of mature heroes in American literature and mythology indicated American ideology's fundamental preference for youth, a quality that came to be associated with the country itself. Indeed, American stories often distorted the stock figure of the Wise Old Man, portraying him as mad (Ahab), useless (Rip Van Winkle), or evil (the Godfather).

2. *Society and Women*: The outlaw hero's distrust of civilization, typically represented by women and marriage, constituted a stock motif in American mythology. In his *Studies in Classic American Literature*, D. H. Lawrence detected the recurring pattern of flight, observing that the Founding Fathers had come to America "largely to get *away*. . . . Away from what? In the long

run, away from themselves. Away from everything."[5] Sometimes, these heroes undertook this flight alone (Thoreau, *Catcher in the Rye*); more often, they joined ranks with other men: Huck with Jim, Ishmael with Queequeg, Jake Barnes with Bill Gorton. Women were avoided as representing the very entanglements this tradition sought to escape: society, the "settled life," confining responsibilities. The outlaw hero sought only uncompromising relationships, involving either a "bad" woman (whose morals deprived her of all rights to entangling domesticity) or other males (who themselves remained independent). Even the "bad" woman posed a threat, since marriage often uncovered the clinging "good" girl underneath. Typically, therefore, American stories avoided this problem by killing off the "bad" woman before the marriage could transpire (*Destry Rides Again*, *The Big Heat*, *The Far Country*). Subsequently, within the all-male group, women became taboo, except as the objects of lust.

The exceptional extent of American outlaw legends suggests an ideological anxiety about civilized life. Often, that anxiety took shape as a romanticizing of the dispossessed, as in the Beat Generation's cult of the bum, or the characters of Huck and "Thoreau," who worked to remain idle, unemployed, and unattached. A passage from Jerzy Kosinski's *Steps* demonstrated the extreme modern version of this romanticizing:

> I envied those [the poor and the criminals] who lived here and seemed so free, having nothing to regret and nothing to look forward to. In the world of birth certificates, medical examinations, punch cards, and computers, in the world of telephone books, passports, bank accounts, insurance plans, wills, credit cards, pensions, mortgages and loans, they lived unattached.[6]

In contrast to the outlaw heroes, the official heroes were preeminently worldly, comfortable in society, and willing to undertake even those public duties demanding personal sacrifice. Political figures, particularly Washington and Lincoln, provided the principal examples of this tradition, but images of family also persisted in popular literature from *Little Women* to *Life with Father* and *Cheaper by the Dozen*. The most crucial figure in this tradition, however, was Horatio Alger, whose heroes' ambition provided the complement to Huck's disinterest. Alger's characters subscribed fully to the codes of civilization, devoting themselves to proper dress, manners, and behavior, and the attainment of the very things despised by the opposing tradition: the settled life and respectability.[7]

---

[5]D. H. Lawrence, *Studies in Classic American Literature* (New York: Viking/Compass, 1961), p. 3. See also Fiedler's *Love and Death in the American Novel* and Sam Bluefarb's *The Escape Motif in the American Novel: Mark Twain to Richard Wright* (Columbus: Ohio State University Press, 1972).

[6]Jerzy Kosinski, *Steps* (New York: Random House, 1968), p. 133.

[7]See John G. Cawelti, *Apostles of the Self-Made Man: Changing Concepts of Success in America* (Chicago: University of Chicago Press, 1965), pp. 101–23.

3. *Politics and the Law*: Writing about "The Philosophical Approach of the 10 Americans," Tocqueville noted "a general distaste for accepting any man's word as proof of anything." That distaste took shape as a traditional distrust of politics as collective activity, and of ideology as that activity's rationale. Such a disavowal of ideology was, of course, itself ideological, a tactic for discouraging systematic political intervention in a nineteenth-century America whose political and economic power remained in the hands of a privileged few. Tocqueville himself noted the results of this mythology of individualism which "disposes each citizen to isolate himself from the mass of his fellows and withdraw into the circle of family and friends; with this little society formed to his taste, he gladly leaves the greater society to look after itself."[8]

This hostility toward political solutions manifested itself further in an ambivalence about the law. The outlaw mythology portrayed the law, the sum of society's standards, as a collective, impersonal ideology imposed on the individual from without. Thus, the law represented the very thing this mythology sought to avoid. In its place, this tradition offered a natural law discovered intuitively by each man. As Tocqueville observed, Americans wanted "to escape from imposed systems . . . to seek by themselves and in themselves for the only reason for things . . . in most mental operations each American relies on individual effort and judgment" (p. 429). This sense of the law's inadequacy to needs detectable only by the heart generated a rich tradition of legends celebrating legal defiance in the name of some "natural" standard: Thoreau went to jail rather than pay taxes, Huck helped Jim (legally a slave) to escape, Billy the Kid murdered the sheriff's posse that had ambushed his boss, Hester Prynne resisted the community's sexual mores. This mythology transformed all outlaws into Robin Hoods, who "correct" socially unjust laws (Jesse James, Bonnie and Clyde, John Wesley Harding). Furthermore, by customarily portraying the law as the tool of villains (who used it to revoke mining claims, foreclose on mortgages, and disallow election results — all on legal technicalities), this mythology betrayed a profound pessimism about the individual's access to the legal system.

If the outlaw hero's motto was "I don't know what the law says, but I do know what's right and wrong," the official hero's was "We are a nation of laws, not of men," or "No man can place himself above the law." To the outlaw hero's insistence on private standards of right and wrong, the official hero offered the admonition, "You cannot take the law into your own hands." Often, these official heroes were lawyers or politicians, at times (as with Washington and Lincoln), even the executors of the legal system itself. The values accompanying such heroes modified the assurance of Crockett's advice, "Be sure you're right, then go ahead."

[8]Alexis de Tocqueville, *Democracy in America*, ed. J. P. Mayer, trans. George Lawrence (Garden City, N.Y.: Anchor/Doubleday, 1969), pp. 430, 506. Irving Howe has confirmed Tocqueville's point, observing that Americans "make the suspicion of ideology into something approaching a national creed." *Politics and the Novel* (New York: Avon, 1970), p. 337.

In sum, the values associated with these two different sets of heroes contrasted markedly. Clearly, too, each tradition had its good and bad points. If the extreme individualism of the outlaw hero always verged on selfishness, the respectability of the official hero always threatened to involve either blandness or repression. If the outlaw tradition promised adventure and freedom, it also offered danger and loneliness. If the official tradition promised safety and comfort, it also offered entanglements and boredom.

The evident contradiction between these heroes provoked Daniel Boorstin's observation that "never did a more incongruous pair than Davy Crockett and George Washington live together in a national Valhalla." And yet, as Boorstin admits, "both Crockett and Washington were popular heroes, and both emerged into legendary fame during the first half of the nineteenth century."[9]

The parallel existence of these two contradictory traditions evinced the general pattern of American mythology: the denial of the necessity for choice. In fact, this mythology often portrayed situations requiring decision as temporary aberrations from American life's normal course. By discouraging commitment to any single set of values, this mythology fostered an ideology of improvisation, individualism, and ad hoc solutions for problems depicted as crises. American writers have repeatedly attempted to justify this mythology in terms of material sources. Hence, Irving Howe's "explanation":

> It is when men no longer feel that they have adequate choices in their styles of life, when they conclude that there are no longer possibilities of honorable maneuver and compromise, when they decide that the time has come for "ultimate" social loyalties and political decisions — it is then that ideology begins to flourish. Ideology reflects a hardening of commitment, the freezing of opinion into system. . . . The uniqueness of our history, the freshness of our land, the plenitude of our resources — all these have made possible, and rendered plausible, a style of political improvisation and intellectual free-wheeling.[10]

Despite such an account's pretext of objectivity, its language betrays an acceptance of the mythology it purports to describe: "honorable maneuver and compromise," "hardening," "freezing," "uniqueness," "freshness," and "plenitude" are all assumptive words from an ideology that denies its own status. Furthermore, even granting the legitimacy of the historians' authenticating causes, we are left with a persisting mythology increasingly discredited by historical developments. (In fact, such invalidation began in the early nineteenth century, and perhaps even before.)

The American mythology's refusal to choose between its two heroes went beyond the normal reconciliatory function attributed to myth by Lévi-Strauss. For the American tradition not only overcame binary oppositions; it systematically mythologized the certainty of being able to do so. Part of this process

---

[9]Daniel J. Boorstin, *The Americans: The National Experience* (New York: Random House, 1965), p. 337.

[10]*Politics and the Novel*, p. 164.

involved blurring the lines between the two sets of heroes. First, legends often brought the solemn official heroes back down to earth, providing the sober Washington with the cherry tree, the prudent Franklin with illegitimate children, and even the upright Jefferson with a slave mistress. On the other side, stories modified the outlaw hero's most potentially damaging quality, his tendency to selfish isolationism, by demonstrating that, however reluctantly, he would act for causes beyond himself. Thus, Huck grudgingly helped Jim escape, and Davy Crockett left the woods for three terms in Congress before dying in the Alamo for Texas independence. In this blurring process, Lincoln, a composite of opposing traits, emerged as the great American figure. His status as president made him an ex officio official hero. But his Western origins, melancholy solitude, and unaided decision-making all qualified him as a member of the other side. Finally, his ambivalent attitude toward the law played the most crucial role in his complex legend. As the chief executive, he inevitably stood for the principle that "we are a nation of laws and not men"; as the Great Emancipator, on the other hand, he provided the prime example of taking the law into one's own hands in the name of some higher standard.

Classic Hollywood's gallery of composite heroes (boxing musicians, rebellious aristocrats, pacifist soldiers) clearly derived from this mythology's rejection of final choices, a tendency whose traces Erikson detected in American psychology:

> The process of American identity formation seems to support an individual's ego identity as long as he can preserve a certain element of deliberate tentativeness of autonomous choice. The individual must be able to convince himself that the next step is up to him and that no matter where he is staying or going he always has the choice of leaving or turning in the opposite direction if he chooses to do so. In this country the migrant does not want to be told to move on, nor the sedentary man to stay where he is; for the life style (and the family history) of each contains the opposite element as a potential alternative which he wishes to consider his most private and individual decision.[11]

The reconciliatory pattern found its most typical incarnation, however, in one particular narrative: the story of the private man attempting to keep from being drawn into action on any but his own terms. In this story, the reluctant hero's ultimate willingness to help the community satisfied the official values. But by portraying this aid as demanding only a temporary involvement, the story preserved the values of individualism as well.

Like the contrasting heroes' epitomization of basic American dichotomies, the reluctant hero story provided a locus for displacement. Its most famous version, for example, *Adventures of Huckleberry Finn*, offered a typically individualistic solution to the nation's unresolved racial and sectional anxieties, thereby helping to forestall more systematic governmental measures. In adopting this story, Classic Hollywood retained its censoring power, using it, for example,

---

[11] *Childhood and Society*, p. 286.

in *Casablanca* to conceal the realistic threats to American self-determination posed by World War II.

Because the reluctant hero story was clearly the basis of the Western, American literature's repeated use of it prompted Leslie Fiedler to call the classic American novels "disguised westerns."[12] In the movies, too, this story appeared in every genre: in Westerns, of course (with *Shane* its most schematic articulation), but also in gangster movies (*Angels with Dirty Faces*, *Key Largo*), musicals (*Swing Time*), detective stories (*The Thin Man*), war films (*Air Force*), screwball comedy (*The Philadelphia Story*), "problem pictures" (*On the Waterfront*), and even science fiction (the Han Solo character in *Star Wars*). *Gone with the Wind*, in fact, had two selfish heroes who came around at the last moment, Scarlett (taking care of Melanie) and Rhett (running the Union blockade), incompatible only because they were so much alike. The natural culmination of this pattern, perfected by Hollywood in the 1930s and early 1940s, was *Casablanca*. Its version of the outlaw hero–official hero struggle (Rick versus Laszlo) proved stunningly effective, its resolution (their collaboration on the war effort) the prototypical Hollywood ending.

The reluctant hero story's tendency to minimize the official hero's role (by making him dependent on the outsider's intervention) suggested an imbalance basic to the American mythology: Despite the existence of both heroes, the national ideology clearly preferred the outlaw. This ideology strove to make that figure's origins seem spontaneous, concealing the calculated, commercial efforts behind the mythologizing of typical examples like Billy the Kid and Davy Crockett. Its willingness, on the other hand, to allow the official hero's traces to show enables Daniel Boorstin to observe of one such myth, "There were elements of spontaneity, of course, in the Washington legend, too, but it was, for the most part, a self-conscious product."[13] 20

The apparent spontaneity of the outlaw heroes assured their popularity. By contrast, the official values had to rely on a rational allegiance that often wavered. These heroes' different statuses accounted for a structure fundamental to American literature, and assumed by Classic Hollywood: a split between the moral center and the interest center of a story. Thus, while the typical Western contained warnings against violence as a solution, taking the law into one's own hands, and moral isolationism, it simultaneously glamorized the outlaw hero's intense self-possession and willingness to use force to settle what the law could not. In other circumstances, Ishmael's evenhanded philosophy paled beside Ahab's moral vehemence, consciously recognizable as destructive.

D. H. Lawrence called this split the profound "duplicity" at the heart of nineteenth-century American fiction, charging that the classic novels evinced "a tight mental allegiance to a morality which all [the author's] passion goes to destroy." Certainly, too, this "duplicity" involved the mythology's pattern of obscuring the necessity for choosing between contrasting values. Richard

[12] *Love and Death in the American Novel*, p. 355.
[13] *The Americans: The National Experience*, p. 337.

Chase has put the matter less pejoratively in an account that applies equally to the American cinema:

> The American novel tends to rest in contradictions and among extreme ranges of experience. When it attempts to resolve contradictions, it does so in oblique, morally equivocal ways. As a general rule it does so either in melodramatic actions or in pastoral idylls, although intermixed with both one may find the stirring instabilities of "American humor."[14]

Or, in other words, when faced with a difficult choice, American stories resolved it either simplistically (by refusing to acknowledge that a choice is necessary), sentimentally (by blurring the differences between the two sides), or by laughing the whole thing off.

READING THE TEXT

1. In your own words, describe the two basic hero types in American cinema that Ray describes.
2. How do these two hero types relate to America's "psychological pattern" (para. 2)?
3. Explain why, according to Ray, the outlaw hero typically mistrusts women.
4. Define what Ray means by the "reluctant hero" (para. 17).

READING THE SIGNS

1. What sort of hero is Katniss in *The Hunger Games*? Write an essay in which you apply Ray's categories of hero to her character, supporting your argument with specific references to both films in the series.
2. In class, brainstorm on the board official and outlaw heroes you've seen in movies. Then categorize these heroes according to characteristics they share (such as race, gender, profession, or social class). What patterns emerge in your categories, and what is the significance of those patterns?
3. Ray focuses on film, but his categories of hero can be used as a critical framework to analyze other media, including television. What kinds of heroes are the heroes in the program *Sons of Anarchy*? Alternatively, consider a character such as Dexter Morgan in *Dexter*. How might he fit Ray's definitions of a hero?
4. Cartoon television series like *The Simpsons* and *South Park* feature characters that don't readily fit Ray's two main categories of hero. Invent a third type of hero to accommodate such characters.
5. In class, brainstorm a list of female heroes from film and television. Then try to categorize them according to Ray's article. Do the characters easily fit the categories Ray mentions, or do they seem to be mismatches? Do you feel a need to create an additional category? If so, what would it be?

[14]Richard Chase, *The American Novel and Its Tradition* (Garden City, N.Y.: Anchor/Double-day, 1957), p. 1.

STEVIE ST. JOHN

Out of Character: Wonder Woman's Strength Is Her Compassion — What Happened?

At a time when filmmakers are mining the comic book archives for just about any as-yet-unexploited superhero on which to hang a movie, it is odd that Wonder Woman, who has had her own TV series and has been a prominent popular cultural character for decades, is only scheduled to appear in her first feature film in 2016, and even then may not really have the starring role. In this essay exploring the history and significance of Wonder Woman, Stevie St. John invites us to wonder whether a preference for testosterone-charged violence in our superheroes has had something to do with this filmic marginalization of Wonder Woman, who has traditionally been distinctive for her compassionate reluctance to get tough. But now that even Wonder Woman is getting "harder" in the DC comics in which she appears, it remains to be seen which one — violent warrior or compassionate woman — will be featured on the big screen. Stevie St. John is a freelance writer who writes for such publications as *Bitch*, in which this essay first appeared in 2014.

It seems like a given that the best-known and longest-running female superhero would have made it to the big screen by now, especially considering the box-office supremacy of American superhero films in the past decade. Yet while comics fans watched the Dark Knight rise, Captain America soldier forth, and Spider-Man get his own trilogy — twice — Wonder Woman is only now hitting the big screen, and she's not even in the spotlight. The as-yet unnamed 2016 Batman/Superman project will feature Gal Gadot, best known for her work in the *Fast & Furious* series, in the iconic role.

Many hope Gadot will star in her own Wonder Woman film soon, especially because she signed a three-picture deal. But for now it's not clear whether the new film is the prelude to a Wonder Woman project or if she'll just be making a cameo alongside Henry Cavill's Superman and Ben Affleck's Batman.

But it's not just the big picture that has fans apprehensive. Director Zack Snyder isn't exactly known for complex female characters (see: past projects *300* and his *Watchmen* adaptation). "I don't see the director or writers having the desire to grasp the nuances of [Wonder Woman]," says DC Women Kicking Ass blogger Sue, who declined to give her last name due to past issues with online harassment. "And it isn't her story, so I fear she'll be written more as a plot device than a fleshed-out character."

Susie Rantz, PR manager of Geek Girl Con, has similar concerns. "Certainly Wonder Woman has physical strength—but what I always associate more with Wonder Woman is her strength of character. Unlike other superheroes, Wonder Woman always fights for peace. Sometimes that means bringing down the villain, but oftentimes it means unlocking the potential inside every person she encounters." When it comes to the silver screen, Rantz wonders if Wonder Woman will be "physically strong and focused on peace, justice, and equality."

And that's what has folks most worried. Like any superhero who's been around for seven decades, Wonder Woman and her alter ego, Diana Prince, have gone through many transformations, carrying with them the expectations of comic-book fans, new readers, and feminists alike. What's always stuck out isn't her physical prowess but her strength as a leader who inspires others and never betrays her beliefs.

"Wonder Woman represents the best of humanity," says Rantz. "She is strong but also compassionate. She elevates the voices of those who are underrepresented. She comes at every situation with an optimism about our human potential, not a preconceived and pessimistic view of an individual. And she is focused on promoting the idea that women should support other women."

It's this essence of her character that fans are afraid will be missing from her long-awaited film debut. And if her recent turn in comics is any indication, their fears are not unfounded.

Certainly Wonder Woman's story in the pages of DC Comics has left many disappointed. In recent story lines, Wonder Woman appears more angry than amused and has a much quicker trigger for when to use physical force. Her original creator, William Marston, didn't arm the Amazon with ropes and chains just for a kinky subtext: He favored them because they were less violent than other weapons, like guns. In the original Wonder Woman stories, villains were usually sent to Reform Island for rehabilitation—inflicting physical harm was generally a last resort.

But in DC's New 52 series, which launched in 2011, Wonder Woman's first appearance comes when a scantily clad woman in peril wakes the slumbering superhero. Although she eventually aids the distressed woman, her first reaction is to swiftly grab and lift the woman by the neck. Later, Wonder Woman smashes a broken wineglass into a villain's hand and draws blood. Notably, it's done in anger, not to deflect an imminent physical threat.

Self-proclaimed "Wonder Woman evangelist" Boston Blake, who gives a Wonder Woman presentation called "The Kink in the Golden Lasso" at fan conventions and academic settings, describes the new series as "all about being stronger, being tougher—not necessarily being wiser." He describes the revamped Wonder Woman as a "butt-kicking piece of ass"—and Snyder's interpretation will likely reflect that as well.

Phil Jimenez, who first became enamored with Wonder Woman through Lynda Carter's 1970s television show, has worked on several superhero titles for both DC Comics and Marvel (credits include *X-Men* and *Spider-Man*). "The

Lynda Carter Wonder Woman was incredibly likable," Jimenez says. "Her great strength [was that] when she walked into a room, you just wanted to be around her. And when she left, you wanted to be a different person. You wanted to be a *better* person."

Jimenez was elated to work on *Wonder Woman* comics between 2000 and 2003, and he coauthored *The Essential Wonder Woman Encyclopedia* (2010). But his take didn't always mesh with what DC Comics envisioned.

Jimenez noticed a shift in the industry shortly after 9/11. As with many depictions of New York in pop culture at the time, several adjustments were made to the art for DC's *Superman*, issue no. 175, published in December 2001. Buildings and falling debris were taken out, as were any deaths shown as the result of the Joker flying a plane into Times Square. Significantly, though, Jimenez's editor asked him to change a scene where Wonder Woman embraces her friend Superman, who is shedding tears for lost lives. Jimenez thought it was "a very Superman/Wonder Woman moment" that "seemed like a genuine expression of these two characters" — but his editor thought it made the Man of Steel look weak. Jimenez fought for the original image and ultimately prevailed, but the art still needed to be adjusted: "He couldn't look fetal; he couldn't cry. He had to look like he was ready for battle, angry — clenched fists, screaming anger, etc."

The impact of 9/11 on comics went further than a single issue: Villains were more likely to be killed than reformed, and superheroes — including Wonder Woman — became "harder."

Terrorism and wars aren't the only factors making modern comics more violent or Wonder Woman's strength more defined by physicality. Jimenez says it's just easier to sell comics with shocking violence than with the complex qualities that originally drew him to Wonder Woman.

Whatever the reason, the New 52 Wonder Woman storyline certainly has a different sensibility — grittier, more violent — than past iterations. Even the titles of the graphic novel compilations of the new series reflect the darker tone: *Blood*, *Guts*, *Iron*, and *War*. More troubling, though, are the changes to Wonder Woman's origin story — a story that's intrinsic to earlier visions of the character and what she stands for. Marston's Paradise Island, the land of Amazons, was a peaceful matriarchy where the Amazons had eternal life, advanced technology, rich natural resources, and no conflict or war. To Marston, these were the results of an all-female society. He assumed the male-wrought ills of society could be ameliorated by women, who possessed innate qualities of love and compassion.

Of course, as KL Pereira writes in "Female Bonding: The Strange History of Wonder Woman" (*Bitch*, no. 33), Marston's version of feminism was "less about advocating gender equality and fighting sexism than it was a variant of the 19th-century temperance movement, which held that women were morally superior to men and, as such, responsible for controlling their appetites."

Still, Marston's Amazon mythology has been important to Wonder Woman's feminist fans for ages. And while there were supernatural aspects to

15

Marston's Diana, her physical strength, speed, and agility were gained through sheer training. Jimenez says this was "a huge part of the original mythology," and a way to connect to the audience. It told readers that if you worked hard, "you, too, could be a 'wonder woman.'"

But this isn't the case with the comics reboot, says DC Women Kicking Ass blogger Sue. "The writer chose to present [the Amazons] as sirenlike creatures that lured soldiers into sex to get pregnant, murdered them after intercourse, and then traded their boy babies for guns. Not only did [this] radically revamp the Amazons from what Wonder Woman's creator had meant them to be, it revamped them into a set of antifeminist tropes."

Susan Polo, managing editor of TheMarySue.com, a "Girl Guide to Geek Culture," admits that the utopia concept is also problematic—any society built on the idea of exclusion is bound to encounter some trouble—but systematically murdering men and bartering with babies takes it to quite an extreme. "[I'm] really not into the idea of Amazons as [embodying the] greatest fears of the men's rights movement." She has taken the comic off of her pull list. [20]

And instead of a fatherless birth—the original Diana Prince was sculpted out of clay from the Amazons' queen—in the reboot, Diana Prince is another spawn of Zeus, the clay birth a clever ruse to protect her from the jealous rage of Zeus's wife, Hera. She's essentially born out of female rivalry, rather than solidarity. Also, instead of being trained alongside her Amazon sisters, she is trained by Ares, god of war.

Some readers see this as a return to the Greek myth that inspired Marston. However, as Les Daniels explains in *Wonder Woman: The Complete History* (2000), Marston's origin story was itself a subversion of a sexist myth, as "the Amazons in ancient legend and literature . . . were said to be a band of self-mutilating child murderers who launched violent, ultimately suicidal attacks on the social order." The lesson of these older myths was that women should know their place. Daniels concluded that "modern feminists who view Amazons as an ideal may well owe more to comic books than to ancient myths."

Ironically, Marston's subversion of sexist mythology has itself been upended. And the results are hard to reconcile with the ideals that spawned the character and then made her a feminist powerhouse.

As Pereira wrote, male superheroes are "revered for their incredible strength and X-ray vision, their mild-mannered alter egos serve as foils to their super selves . . . making it clear to the reader that no amount of pumping iron or fancy cars could ever transform him into his male hero." Diana Prince, however, "encouraged the women she met to realize that while their talents and hard work were important, a positive attitude and confidence in oneself was what really got the job done."

Of course, Diana Prince has evolved through many eras and identities. After Marston's death in 1947, Wonder Woman was taken up by other writers who didn't quite know what to do with the wasp-waisted Amazon. In [25] the 1950s, the comics focused largely on Diana Prince's love life with the inept Steve Trevor. And in the late 1960s, she gave up her powers and iconic swimsuit costume for mod dresses. ("Talk about bondage!" quipped comics historian Trina Robbins about this dark era in Diana's history.) Switching to jumpsuit apparel in the '70s, Emma Peel–style, she continued defeating criminals while also running a clothing store.

It was around then that Gloria Steinem picked up the Wonder Woman mantle. "We discovered that she had fallen on very hard times," says Steinem dryly in Kristy Guevara-Flanagan's 2012 documentary *Wonder Women! The Untold Story of American Superheroines.* "We [had to] practically march in the street to get her magical powers back." When Wonder Woman graced the cover of *Ms.* magazine's inaugural 1972 issue, it was also the beginning of a feminist interpretation of her origin story.

A few years later came the debut of the lovably campy TV series anchored by Lynda Carter. Like the Wonder Woman from the original comic pages, Carter's character confidently stood up for what she believed in without taking anything too seriously. In the pilot, she thwarts bank robbers then comments on how silly it is that the police expect her — and not the robbers — to fill out paperwork: "What a country this is!"

Boston Blake, like so many others, fell in love with Carter's portrayal, but laments that her carefree crime-fighting days seem over. "This is a sad time to be a Wonder Woman fan," he says. "We're really divided."

Tim Hanley, whose new book *Wonder Woman Unbound: The Curious History of the World's Most Famous Heroine* traces the development of Wonder Woman's character over the decades, is looking on the bright side. "A comic book read by 30,000 people isn't going to affect the millions of people who know Wonder Woman as an icon of feminism and female empowerment. Her comic-book iterations come and go, but the icon is bigger than any of them."

And while Hanley can see how the New 52 Wonder Woman "would easily ₃₀ fit into the dark, violent, joyless world Zack Snyder created in *Man of Steel*," he doesn't necessarily think the movies will reflect the comics. That being said, "Wonder Woman could be the Pollyanna of superhero comics and Snyder would still make her sexy and violent above all else."

As for a film starring the Amazon princess, The Mary Sue's Susan Polo is hedging her bets. "It's so far in the future and there are so many maybes. . . . I'm not getting excited about it yet."

With a string of false-start Wonder Woman projects dotting pop culture history, it's no surprise that some Wonder Woman enthusiasts have an I'll-believe-it-when-I-see-it attitude. Two TV pilots have been axed: a CW pilot called *Amazon* and an NBC Wonder Woman pilot from David E. Kelley. The highest-profile disappointment was a Wonder Woman film attached to *Buffy the Vampire Slayer* creator Joss Whedon, who told *Rookie* magazine that his version of Wonder Woman would have emphasized her humanity and vulnerability. A goddess on earth, Diana Prince would "look at us and the way we kill each other and the way we let people starve and the way the world is run and she'd just be like, 'None of this makes sense to me.'" Whedon said that through Diana's relationship with Steve Trevor, the film would have focused on "what it's like when you are weak, when you do have all these forces controlling you and there's nothing you can do about it. That was the sort of central concept: [Trevor] teaching her humanity and [Wonder Woman] saying, okay, great, but we can still do better."

Jimenez understands why valuing a female superhero for embodying stereotypically feminine traits might rankle some people. But the fact that Wonder Woman was loving and compassionate was what he always loved about the heroine. "That's not seen as valid anymore," he says. "I think more people should be like that."

READING THE TEXT

1. In your own words, summarize the reasons Hollywood producers have had difficulty in deciding how to present a female hero, as St. John describes them.

2. What does the PR manager Susie Rantz mean in saying, "Wonder Woman represents the best of humanity" (para. 6)? How do you respond to this claim?

3. What impact did the 9/11 terrorist attacks on America have on the comic industry, according to cartoonist Phil Jimenez?

4. Summarize in your own words the history of Wonder Woman, according to St. John.

5. What is the significance of the Amazons, as St. John explains it?

READING THE SIGNS

1. Compare Wonder Woman with another female superhero, such as Catwoman, Elektra, or Emma Frost. To what extent does your choice exhibit either compassion, on the one hand, or a gritty penchant for violence, as many male superheroes do?

2. **CONNECTING TEXTS** Read or reread Robert B. Ray's "The Thematic Paradigm" (p. 450), and write an essay in which you argue whether Wonder Woman should be categorized as an official or outlaw hero. Do those categories even apply to this character?

3. Cartoonist Phil Jimenez claims that the 9/11 terrorist attacks changed the depiction of violence in cartoons specifically and popular culture more generally. In an essay, explore the extent to which popular culture serves as an accurate sign of political attitudes. Be sure to ground your argument in an analysis of particular media examples.

4. **CONNECTING TEXTS** To what extent does Wonder Woman reproduce, change, or complicate traditional gender codes? To develop your argument, read or reread Aaron Devor's "Gender Role Behavior and Attitudes" (p. 504).

5. **CONNECTING TEXTS** Read or reread Mariah Burton Nelson's "I Won. I'm Sorry" (p. 524). Adopting Nelson's perspective, write a response to cartoonist Phil Jimenez's endorsement of female superheroes that embody stereotypical feminine traits.

HEATHER HAVRILESKY
No Sympathy for the Devil

Ever since HBO's *The Sopranos* managed to make millions of viewers identify with a violent criminal who would have been the villain of any conventional crime drama, television producers have been churning out flawed protagonists — like *Mad Men*'s Don Draper and *Breaking Bad*'s Walter White — who, though often called antiheroes in the tradition of Tony Soprano, may simply be doomed and degraded men unworthy of our sympathy. That, at least, is the conclusion that Heather Havrilesky draws in this 2013 assessment of TV's recent crop of flawed protagonists, and if Don Draper and Walter White have been unable to elicit the kind of viewer identification that Tony Soprano did, so be it, Havrilesky believes. As she suggests, that is what real life is all about. Indeed, those who are brave enough to explore the depths have shown that modern television has the potential to reach literary status — to be art as well as entertainment — and that can be a very good thing. Heather Havrilesky is the author of *Disaster Preparedness: A Memoir* (2011) and a journalist who writes for such publications as *Salon* and *Bookforum*.

A moderately bad man knows he is not very good: a thoroughly bad man thinks he is all right.

— C. S. LEWIS

For the past decade, TV has been awash with deeply flawed antiheroes: philandering ad men and pill-popping nurses, meth-cooking chemistry teachers and mob boss suburban dads. But when you launch a show that's centered on an unethical protagonist, how do you keep viewers engaged and invested in that character indefinitely — or at least through six seasons?

Because for every show like *The Sopranos* and *The Shield* that made us cheer for a rotten scoundrel, there were five or six others that failed to engage us. Dark dramedies like *Californication, Shameless, Weeds, American Horror Story, Nurse Jackie*, and *Nip/Tuck* have plenty of redeeming qualities — a wicked sense of humor, an irresistible visual style, a delicious knack for realistic marital spats. But the second we determine that our antihero is nothing but an irredeemable loser and/or we conclude that his or her choices will never make a shred of sense, we're lost. Every plot twist feels arbitrary and impossible to care about, like watching Bart Simpson burn his finger over and over again without learning a thing about cause and effect.

Despite Edie Falco's great performance on *Nurse Jackie*, which made Jackie far more likable and believable than she would've been otherwise, it was tough to understand why this very practical woman was popping pills and sleeping around on her perfectly good husband. Eventually it became hard to watch. Likewise, Hank Moody's high jinx on *Californication* were only amusing until his total lack of a soul and somewhat repetitive insistence on deadpan debauchery reduced him to a caricature. The two antiheroes of *Nip/Tuck* navigated their shiny, shallow world with irresistible swagger, but the arrogance and slickness that drew us in were exactly what drove us away in the end. The drama *Dexter*'s perverse sense of humor (its perverse sense of everything, really) kept us in a serial killer's thrall far longer than seemed plausible, but that show's appeal started to crumble once our antihero's antics landed his wife, a reliable source of comic relief, in mortal danger.

But what did we expect from a show about a serial killer? Hugging and learning? Isn't it a little unfair to lose interest in *Dexter* the second it stops looking like a darkly comical revenge fantasy and starts to look more like a gory horror movie featuring a baby in a pool of blood?

Unfair or not, maintaining an audience's interest can require self-restraint 5 in storytelling. Carmela of *The Sopranos* never ended up with her throat slit, and if she did, our feelings about her husband would've been irretrievably altered.

In truth, the likability of any given protagonist represents one of the most subjective assessments you can make about a TV show. Debating how hateful Vic Mackey, Walter White, Nancy Botwin, or Don Draper is can feel like squabbling over whether a tasteless joke is funny or not. Gut checks depend on what's at stake for viewers, how many ethical lapses are tolerable to them, how interesting they find it to watch a person's principles bend and then break, and which personality strengths (and weaknesses) they judge as redemptive, where others are judged as unforgivable.

And as easy as it is to pinpoint when *Weeds* or *Nip/Tuck* stopped commanding our interest, it's a little more thorny when two of the best shows on television, *Breaking Bad* and *Mad Men*, repeatedly grapple with the same problem of character likability.

Breaking Bad presents a particularly fascinating example because its protagonist, Walter White (Bryan Cranston), was never supposed to charm us, enthrall us, or appear remotely heroic. The hard sell of *Breaking Bad* is that it offers up a painfully regular, geeky school teacher who sees himself as a big failure (and he's dying of cancer to boot). Our antihero is *anti-hero* in the literal sense: He is clumsy, stutters, and rarely saves the day. And who better to occupy the role of sidekick than a self-interested, shallow kid like Jesse Pinkman (Aaron Paul)? Jesse is the epitome of a thug: uneducated, naïve, and brutish.

Even though *Breaking Bad*'s pilot was much more comedic than the subsequent series proved to be, an acute sense of the absurd seems to drive the show. Throw in its gorgeous cinematography, its poetic appreciation of little

Photofest

Bryan Cranston as Walter White in *Breaking Bad*.

details (a stuffed animal's eyeball in a swimming pool, a pizza fermenting on a garage rooftop), its unerring grasp of dramatic tension, of nuanced dialogue, of escalating stakes, and you've got one of the strangest, most riveting shows on TV. *Breaking Bad* is so good, in part, because of creator Vince Gilligan's insistence on ignoring every TV convention in the book. What we see on our screen are two essentially unlikable, not very attractive human beings, placed in ethically indefensible situations over and over again, each of which unfolds at an extremely patient pace.

But even as Walt stretches our patience to the breaking point, he never 10 gets to enjoy the spoils of his crimes. Unlike Tony Soprano, who eats and cheats and drinks and indulges his own vanity and self-delusion over and over, Walt is usually focused on digging his way out of one mess or another, trying to win his family back, trying to hide his crimes from them so they never know just how far he's fallen. This fact alone can be exhausting. But if Walt were vain or wasteful, or if any of his choices felt ego-driven at the outset, we'd never stay on his side. He's not appealing enough to pull that off. He's more of a blank slate than a character, someone we can project our own longing or frustration onto.

Slowly over the course of the show, Walter goes from desperate man in a tight spot to a true criminal — killing somewhat blameless people out of convenience. Jesse, on the other hand, proclaims at the start of season three, "I'm the bad guy," but by the end of that season, he's the one trying to convince

Walt not to commit murder. Over the course of the show, Jesse develops from typical scumbag to something else, a lonely guy who's smart enough to know better but who keeps falling short of his best intentions. For all of his flaws, Jesse is usually more sympathetic than Walt, because he's actively trying to connect with other people, even if he does so by falling in love with a manipulative junkie or throwing hundred dollar bills in the air. Walt is troubling because the guilt and moral compass he has at the start of the series melts off him until his choices feel purely pragmatic. But he no longer has a choice. He boards this crazy train and then he can't get off without destroying his entire family.

Because *Breaking Bad* doesn't take pains to show us Walt's vulnerabilities and the root causes of his damage the way *The Sopranos* did with Tony, we rarely feel that much sympathy for the man. We do want him to find a way out of each mess (unlike Dexter, who we sometimes wish would get caught). But we don't look into his eyes and feel heartbroken the way we felt with Tony Soprano. James Gandolfini was a master of showing us Tony's mixed emotions and regrets and guilt, and David Chase served up at least one vivid, guilt-inducing moment per episode (Tony says the wrong thing to Meadow and immediately cringes at his own gall; Tony orders a hit and then can't sleep at night, etc.).

But Walt isn't a giant puppy dog in mob boss clothing. He's not supposed to be lovable. While *Breaking Bad* veers into unrelenting darkness so often that it can be tough to stomach, that's kind of the point. The daring of *Breaking Bad* lies in its insistence on making its protagonists scrape and claw and make awful compromises without any retreat into giant plates of pasta or reassuringly mundane family bickering or self-doubting therapy sessions.

Tony's very relatable vices — laziness, gluttony, adultery — offered the recurring impression of an indulged child who refused to grow up. We were meant to see our own lapses reflected in Tony, and to empathize with him despite his obvious repugnant choices. Our feeling of connection to him was necessary, thanks to how extreme his flaws were. He was vengeful, ego-driven, short-sighted, and sometimes even casually reprehensible, striking people down out of mere convenience. The trick that David Chase pulled off with *The Sopranos* was that he made us feel protective, affectionate love for a bad, bad guy, a guy who wanted to grow but couldn't, a guy who, at the end of the day, just wanted to daydream about the good old days and stuff his face with onion rings. When Tony had a panic attack or missed the ducks in his pool or got beat up or embarrassed, it made us feel terribly sorry for him in spite of ourselves. That's not how we feel about Walter White. But that's not how we're supposed to feel about him.

Just as Walt wasn't designed to occupy the same place in our hearts as Tony Soprano, neither was Don Draper of *Mad Men*. But because Matthew Weiner and the show's other writers take pains to show us why Don does what he does, it's more of a problem when we come away from these character sketches feeling unmoved. In the show's sixth season, Don didn't necessarily make bigger mistakes than he ever had, but his hungry ego and his weaknesses were on full display like never before. Aside from being called a monster by Peggy and assuming the fetal position toward the end of the season, Don didn't register guilt or awareness of his own terrible behavior that often. Even though it may be Weiner's intention to demonstrate the limitations of Don's consciousness, even though *Mad Men* is arguably guided by ideas more than emotions, and Don's shortcomings are meant to embody the shortcomings of not just an entire generation but also late capitalist American society itself, the exercise can grow tiresome when Don is less likable than the writers seem to believe.

That's arguably a minor quibble, considering that *Mad Men* is an ensemble show, and Peggy and Joan and Roger and even Pete continue to draw us in thoroughly despite (and even because of) their flaws. Still, Don's story lines would be more satisfying if the show's awkward attempts to have us understand him — via flashbacks to a not-all-that-sympathetic kid in a whore house — didn't fail about half the time. Weiner and company seemed to assume that we'd tolerate Don's repeated hypocritical behavior in the absence of any hint of how alone he felt in the world. As Don cheated on his second wife, betrayed his new friend, demeaned his new lover, disappointed his co-workers and horrified his daughter, we needed some offsetting moments of feeling sad for him. We needed to see him wishing for something that he couldn't quite have (something other than another man's wife). We needed to see him relying on someone for help (other than the man whose wife he was sleeping with). Instead, we got the same repeating close-up of his perplexed face. In the show's sixth season, the writers set out to make Don the victim, but they accidentally made him the enemy instead.

Maybe it's time to admit that we've been spoiled by Chase, who made Tony sympathetic from the very first episode of *The Sopranos*. Chase tricked showrunners into thinking they could make audiences feel sympathy for a truly awful person. It wasn't as easy as Chase and Gandolfini made it look.

And to be fair, Walter White and Don Draper aren't designed to elicit the same kind of affection that Tony Soprano is. At the end of *The Sopranos,* the show's audience was on the edge of their seats, wondering whether Tony would be killed or not because, by then, for better or for worse, Tony felt like part of the family. When *Breaking Bad* ends with Walt doing something so reprehensible it makes our teeth hurt, or *Mad Men* ends with Don leaping from his office window to his death or leaving his fourth wife for his eleventh secretary, we're unlikely to feel quite as wound up about it. Most likely, Walt will simply continue suffering, and Don will continue to believe his own hero complex despite all evidence to the contrary. These characters were made to disappoint us, even if the shows they occupy rarely do.

We might wish for a prettier picture, or hope for some closure, but redemption is not at the heart of either of these shows, and that's exactly what makes them so mesmerizingly different from more typical, saccharine fare. Neither show is perfect; both Don Draper and Walter White could be humanized more. But as *Breaking Bad* and *Mad Men* enter their home stretches, it might make sense to step back and accept that these are both dark portrayals of doomed men. We're not going to be treated to a heart-warming indie pop ballad as Skyler White drives off into the sunset in a Prius like Claire Fisher on the *Six Feet Under* finale. Instead, we should expect an unnerving ending, and feel grateful that such unapologetically bleak, literary stories now occupy the small screen. Because this picture was never pretty to begin with.

READING THE TEXT

1. How does Havrilesky explain why some TV shows that feature antiheroes succeed and others fail?
2. Havrilesky only implicitly offers her own definition of hero or antihero. Read through her essay, and summarize in your own words the definition of hero/antihero that seems to govern her selection.
3. Explain in your own words what Havrilesky means by "redemptive" (para. 6).
4. According to Havrilesky, how do TV antiheroes contribute to a more realistic and more artistic entertainment than simple heroes and villains?
5. Explain in your own words the reasons that shows like *Mad Men* and *Breaking Bad* have enjoyed a loyal fan base, while audiences eventually tired of programs like *Nurse Jackie*.

READING THE SIGNS

1. Havrilesky claims that "the likability of any given protagonist represents one of the most subjective assessments you can make about a TV show" (para. 6). In an essay, evaluate the plausibility of this claim, based on a careful analysis of a TV show protagonist of your choice. To what extent does "likability" influence an audience's response to a program?
2. Watch a few of the final episodes of *The Sopranos*, and write your own analysis of what kind of hero Tony Soprano is. Does your interpretation support, oppose, or modify Havrilesky's analysis of this character? Alternatively, write an analysis of *Breaking Bad* or *Mad Men*, again comparing your reading with Havrilesky's.
3. **CONNECTING TEXTS** In class, brainstorm a list of current TV shows that feature antihero protagonists. Use the list as the basis of your own essay in which you argue for your explanation for why antiheroes have become so dominant on TV, focusing on your interpretation of two or three programs. How is their dominance a sign of the times? To develop your ideas, consult Laura Bennett's "Against Antiheroes" (p. 471).

LAURA BENNETT

Against Antiheroes

Antiheroes are hot, and Laura Bennett thinks that it's high time we stepped back and chilled out a bit about it all. When book agents and TV network publicists promote practically everything they've got going as antiheroic, and journalists lasso the likes of Edward Snowden and Bradley Manning into the antihero corral, this once-useful label has become little more than a buzzword, Bennett believes. Maybe it's time to retire the term and coin a fresher and more specific word. Laura Bennett is an author and designer whose books include *Didn't I Feed You Yesterday? A Mother's Guide to Sanity in Stilettos* (2010) and *Handmade Chic: Fashionable Projects That Look High-End, Not Home-spun* (2012).

I recently received an email from the publicist for Junot Diaz's *This Is How You Lose Her* declaring that "the protagonist, Yunior, is also a bit of an anti-hero, which makes these topics all the more interesting and relatable." There it was again: antihero, that vague and fashionable word, with its connotation of middle-aged family men and their shadowy consciences. To be clear, Diaz's Yunior is not an antihero. He is a vulnerable, likeable protagonist with human flaws, as most every protagonist in the history of literature has been. But it was hardly surprising that a publicist, in search of an easy toehold on the zeitgeist, would deploy the word. Somehow "antihero" has come to represent an impossibly broad characterological range: from psychopathic drug lords to well-meaning serial killers to wayward Dominican kids who sometimes mistreat women because of culturally ingrained misogyny.

More than a decade after Tony Soprano cried about ducks and several weeks before Walter White completes his infernal transformation, this is perhaps the most overused term in all of pop culture. I should clarify that I also say this in response to myself, as I recently wrote an essay about "Breaking Bad" that featured "antihero" in the headline. And granted, the TV obsession with troubled bad boys borders on self-parody. AMC teased its new drama, "Low Winter Sun," in ways that felt like a comically transparent attempt to get in on the antihero hype: "Good man. Cop. Killer," the ads proclaimed. But the sheer volume of antihero references over the past few months seems like evidence of a current tendency in cultural criticism to rely too heavily on pre-established archetypes. At this point, "antihero" barely means anything at all.

The recent books *Difficult Men* by Brett Martin and *The Revolution Was Televised* by Alan Sepinwall, which both chart the golden age of TV drama, have launched countless essays about our era of antiheroes; TV showrunners themselves have even been characterized as the antiheroes of showbiz.

471

An article in *The American Spectator* was titled "In Defense of the Antihero," though today's antiheroes scarcely need defending. The *Global Post* weighed in on "Snowden, Manning, and the Rise of the American Antihero." Amazon lists some three hundred titles containing the word over the past few years alone.

What, exactly, does "antihero" mean? *Merriam-Webster* traces its first appearance back to 1714 and murkily defines it as "a protagonist or notable figure who is considerably lacking in heroic qualities." Some books on the subject claim that the term has its roots in the idea of the Byronic hero, though this is a far more concrete and specific type: Byron's leading men are melancholic loners with a distaste for authority, struggling to overcome their own dark pasts. In Hollywood, the concept has been around at least since films of the '40s and '50s began exploring the new post-war cynicism, and an action film actually titled "Anti-hero" appeared in 1999. *Britannica* cites as some early antiheroes Satan in *Paradise Lost*, Heathcliff in *Wuthering Heights*, and Don Quixote, none of whom are particularly useful analogues for the wretched, morally bankrupt leading men of cable drama. And the men of HBO and AMC are not as similar in their sinfulness as they have been made out to be. Walter White is by now less an antihero than a straightforward villain, a macho foil for Hank. "Antihero" implies that a character encourages a conflicted sympathy; Walt forfeited our sympathy long ago.

Even Emily Nussbaum — who it should be said, is singularly skilled at 5 inventing her own critical archetypes, à la the "Hummingbird theory" — wrote a piece on "Sex and the City" that identified Carrie as the "first female antihero," the one frustrating bit of an otherwise lovely essay. Carrie could be irksome as a character, but "Sex and the City" was defensive of its protagonist in a way that "Breaking Bad" and "The Sopranos" never were, permitting Carrie to be abrasive and vain only to rein her in at the last minute with a pat, chastened ending; the other shows pushed us to see just what it would take to sever our emotional attachment to their protagonists, while Carrie's reprehensibility was always a learning experience. It is hard to deny that seeing "antihero" applied to Carrie provides a quick, simple thrill of analytical recognition. But in the end, it confuses more than it reveals.

Over-reliance on buzzwords is not specific to pop culture — academia is an echo chamber of scholars responding to and recasting each others' jargon — but the world of online cultural coverage is so breakneck and ephemeral that the pressure to find quick reference points is particularly intense. So instead of describing a phenomenon on its own terms, the impulse is to locate it in relation to some other, louder phenomenon, to riff on an old paradigm instead of devising a new one. Another similarly abused term is "manic pixie dream girl," coined by Nathan Rabin in a 2007 *A.V. Club* essay, which has had an absurdly long half-life, applied to every female, free-spirited weirdo to cavort across our screens.

This one even engendered spin-off archetypes: A lengthy essay in *Grantland* identified the new trend of the "manic pixie dream guy." (To name a few: the boys of One Direction, Ben Wyatt of "Parks and Recreation," Joseph Gordon-Levitt, and Ryan Gosling.) An article in *Flavorwire* announced the arrival of the "nerdy doormat dream girl." It's hard to blame critics for fever-ishly trying to come up with formulations that stick, an impulse rooted in the sorry Internet-age assumption that every concept must be crammed into some neat, buzzy category in order to be understood amid a sea of fruit-fly attention spans. But the result is a narrowness of interpretation, a critical cul-ture of shortcuts. If Yunior is an antihero and Ryan Gosling is a manic pixie dream guy, it's probably time to retire these phrases for good.

READING THE TEXT

1. Trace the evolution of the term "antihero," as Bennett describes it.

2. What reasons does Bennett provide for her proposal to abandon the word "antihero"?

3. In your own words, explain what Bennett means when she claims that critics have "an impulse rooted in the sorry Internet-age assumption that every con-cept must be crammed into some neat, buzzy category in order to be under-stood amid a sea of fruit-fly attention spans" (para. 7).

4. Characterize Bennett's tone in this selection. How does it affect your response to her ideas?

READING THE SIGNS

1. Write an essay that supports, rejects, or modifies Bennett's claim that the term "antihero" is being overused. You might use as evidence some reviews of films or TV programs that purportedly include antihero protagonists. If you agree with her, explain why; if not, propose your own explanation for why antiheroes are part of today's cultural zeitgeist.

2. Read one of the texts focused on antiheroes that Bennett mentions in paragraph 3. Analyze its use of the term, and in an essay discuss whether Bennett's indictment of the term is valid, overblown, or something else.

3. **CONNECTING TEXTS**   Bennett briefly notes the history of antiheroes in film and literature. Adopting the perspective of Linda Seger in "Creating the Myth" (p. 334), write an essay that evaluates the proposition that antiheroes are an enduring character archetype that deserves its nomenclature.

GEORGE PACKER
Celebrating Inequality

Are celebrities heroes? No, not at all, George Packer suggests, but in tough times like today's, when the gap between the rich and the poor yawns ever wider, celebrities loom larger on the social horizon than they do in more equitable times, overshadowing the rest of us. And we're not just talking about entertainers. Indeed, as Packer quips in this 2013 essay for the *New York Times*, "Our age is lousy with celebrities"; they include bankers, computer engineers, real estate developers, media executives, journalists, politicians, scientists, and even chefs. And as the new celebrity deities gobble up whatever opportunities are left in America, Packer believes, America itself is turning backward to the days of the Jazz Age and Jay Gatsby. So, meet the new celebrity gods; same as the old celebrity gods — or "something far more perverse." George Packer is a staff writer for the *New Yorker* and the author of numerous books, including *The Assassins' Gate: America in Iraq* (2006) and the National Book Award–winning *The Unwinding: An Inner History of the New America* (2013).

The Roaring '20s was the decade when modern celebrity was invented in America. F. Scott Fitzgerald's *The Great Gatsby* is full of magazine spreads of tennis players and socialites, popular song lyrics, movie stars, paparazzi, gangsters and sports scandals — machine-made by technology, advertising and public relations. Gatsby, a mysterious bootlegger who makes a meteoric ascent from Midwestern obscurity to the palatial splendor of West Egg, exemplifies one part of the celebrity code: it's inherently illicit. Fitzgerald intuited that, with the old restraining deities of the 19th century dead and his generation's faith in man shaken by World War I, celebrities were the new household gods.

What are celebrities, after all? They dominate the landscape, like giant monuments to aspiration, fulfillment and overreach. They are as intimate as they are grand, and they offer themselves for worship by ordinary people searching for a suitable object of devotion. But in times of widespread opportunity, the distance between gods and mortals closes, the monuments shrink closer to human size and the centrality of celebrities in the culture recedes. They loom larger in times like now, when inequality is soaring and trust in institutions — governments, corporations, schools, the press — is falling.

The Depression that ended Fitzgerald's Jazz Age yielded to a new order that might be called the Roosevelt Republic. In the quarter-century after World War II, the country established collective structures, not individual monuments, that channeled the aspirations of ordinary people: state universities, progressive taxation, interstate highways, collective bargaining, health insurance for the elderly, credible news organizations.

One virtue of those hated things called bureaucracies is that they oblige everyone to follow a common set of rules, regardless of station or background; they are inherently equalizing. Books like William H. Whyte's *The Organization Man* and C. Wright Mills's *White Collar* warned of the loss of individual identity, but those middle-class anxieties were possible only because of the great leveling. The "stars" continued to fascinate, especially with the arrival of TV, but they were not essential. Henry Fonda, Barbara Stanwyck, Bette Davis, Jimmy Stewart, Perry Como, Joe DiMaggio, Jack Paar, Doris Day and Dick Clark rose with Americans — not from them — and their successes and screw-ups were a sideshow, not the main event.

Our age is lousy with celebrities. They can be found in every sector of 5 society, including ones that seem less than glamorous. We have celebrity bankers (Jamie Dimon), computer engineers (Sergey Brin), real estate developers/conspiracy theorists (Donald J. Trump), media executives (Arianna Huffington), journalists (Anderson Cooper), mayors (Cory A. Booker), economists (Jeffrey D. Sachs), biologists (J. Craig Venter) and chefs (Mario Batali).

There is a quality of self-invention to their rise: Mark Zuckerberg went from awkward geek to the subject of a Hollywood hit; Shawn Carter turned into Jay-Z; Martha Kostyra became Martha Stewart, and then *Martha Stewart Living*. The person evolves into a persona, then a brand, then an empire, with the business imperative of grow or die — a process of expansion and commodification that transgresses boundaries by substituting celebrity for institutions. Instead of robust public education, we have Mr. Zuckerberg's "rescue" of Newark's schools. Instead of a vibrant literary culture, we have Oprah's book club. Instead of investments in public health, we have the Gates Foundation. Celebrities either buy institutions, or "disrupt" them.

After all, if you *are* the institution, you don't need to play by its rules. Mr. Zuckerberg's foundation myth begins with a disciplinary proceeding at Harvard, which leads him to drop out and found a company whose motto is "Move fast and break things." Jay-Z's history as a crack dealer isn't just a hard-luck story — it's celebrated by fans (and not least himself) as an early sign of hustle and smarts. Martha Stewart's jail time for perjury merely proved that her will to win was indomitable. These new celebrities are all more or less start-up entrepreneurs, and they live by the hacker's code: ask forgiveness, not permission.

The obsession with celebrities goes far beyond supermarket tabloids, gossip Web sites and reality TV. It obliterates old distinctions between high and low culture, serious and trivial endeavors, profit making and philanthropy, leading to the phenomenon of being famous for being famous. An activist singer (Bono) is given a lucrative role in Facebook's initial public offering. A patrician politician (Al Gore) becomes a plutocratic media executive and tech investor. One of America's richest men (Michael R. Bloomberg) rules its largest city.

This jet-setting, Davos-attending crowd constitutes its own superclass, who hang out at the same TED talks, big-idea conferences and fund-raising galas, appear on the same talk shows, invest in one another's projects, wear one another's brand apparel, champion one another's causes, marry and cheat on one another. *The New Digital Age*, the new guide to the future by Eric Schmidt and Jared Cohen of Google, carries blurbs from such technology experts as Henry A. Kissinger and Tony Blair. The inevitable next step is for Kim Kardashian to sit on the board of a tech start-up, host a global-poverty-awareness event and write a book on behavioral neuroscience.

This new kind of celebrity is the ultimate costume ball, far more exclu- 10 sive and decadent than even the most potent magnates of Hollywood's studio era could have dreamed up. Their superficial diversity dangles before us the myth that in America, anything is possible—even as the American dream quietly dies, a victim of the calcification of a class system that is nearly hereditary.

As mindless diversions from a sluggish economy and chronic malaise, the new aristocrats play a useful role. But their advent suggests that, after decades of widening income gaps, unequal distributions of opportunity and reward, and corroding public institutions, we have gone back to Gatsby's time—or something far more perverse. The celebrity monuments of our age have grown so huge that they dwarf the aspirations of ordinary people, who are asked to yield their dreams to the gods: to flash their favorite singer's corporate logo at concerts, to pour open their lives (and data) on Facebook, to adopt Apple as a lifestyle. We know our stars aren't inviting us to think we can be just like them. Their success is based on leaving the rest of us behind.

READING THE TEXT

1. In your own words, trace the evolution of the celebrity from the 1920s to the post–World War II era to today, as Packer describes it.

2. What does Packer mean when he asserts that today a celebrity "evolves into a persona, then a brand, then an empire, with the business imperative of grow or die" (para. 6)?

3. Why does Packer consider today's celebrities their "own superclass" (para. 9)?

4. What relation does Packer find between the plethora of celebrities today and economic conditions?

5. Why does Packer say that America today is returning to the ethos of the Jazz Age (or, perhaps, becoming even worse)?

READING THE SIGNS

1. In class, discuss the meanings of the terms "celebrities" and "heroes." Using that conversation as a starting point, write an essay that argues for your own definition of the two terms, taking care to delineate distinctions between them. Be sure to ground your discussion in real-life examples of both categories, as Packer does in his essay.

2. As Packer mentions, one kind of current celebrity is the person who is "famous for being famous" (para. 8). In class, brainstorm a list of current such celebrities and discuss what they have in common. Use this discussion to jump-start your own essay on what this sort of fame signifies about the values and world-view of modern America.

3. Write an essay in which you support, refute, or complicate Packer's claim that "this new kind of celebrity is the ultimate costume ball. . . . Their superficial diversity dangles before us the myth that in America, anything is possible" (para. 10). To develop your ideas, consult the introduction to this chapter.

4. Select one of the recent celebrities whom Packer mentions, such as Martha Stewart or Bono, and research the public relations surrounding the individual. Use your findings to endorse, refute, or modify Packer's contention that "these new celebrities are all more or less start-up entrepreneurs, and they live by the hacker's code: ask forgiveness, not permission" (para. 7).

5. In your journal, ruminate about which celebrities you admire and why. Then, in an essay, subject one or two of your choices to Packer's critique of today's celebrities. Do they survive his accusation that they "have grown so huge that they dwarf the aspirations of ordinary people, who are asked to yield their dreams to the gods" (para. 11)? Alternatively, if you do not admire any celebrities, write an essay in which you explain why, basing your comments on examples of particular "celebrity monuments of our age" (para. 11).

NOAH GITTELL

The Lone Ranger *Seals It: America's New Favorite Villain Is a Rich Guy*

Even as life gets better and better for the CEO class, its image gets worse and worse. Indeed, as Noah Gittell observes in this 2013 movie review for the *Atlantic*, it appears that corrupt business executives are taking over as the villain of choice in Hollywood blockbusters. This shouldn't be too surprising, given the role of big business in the making of the Great Recession, and so, in a fairly typical irony of entertainment logic, a good way of making money for large corporate studios like Disney and Sony is to make movies about greedy corporations. Go figure. Noah Gittell is the editor of the blog *Reel Change*.

Writer Ian Fleming is known to have once said, "Once is happenstance. Twice is coincidence. Three times is enemy action." If that's the case, three recently released Hollywood films — *Iron Man 3*, *White House Down*, and now *The Lone Ranger* — show that American moviegoers and moviemakers have identified a new enemy of the moment, and it doesn't come from overseas. These would-be summer blockbusters convey a leftward turn in thinking about the militarization and the War on Terror. The real enemy, Hollywood seems to be telling us, is within.

In discussing the progressive politics of *The Lone Ranger*, most critics have focused on the depiction of Native Americans, and with good reason. Over the history of the American Western, Native Americans have often been depicted as faceless savages whose efforts to defend themselves were merely obstacles to America's Manifest Destiny. Some cinematic efforts have been made to subvert this convention (*The Searchers* and *Dances with Wolves* are probably the most famous examples), but *The Lone Ranger* takes things a step further, making Tonto and John Reid (who will become the eponymous hero) dual protagonists. There is room for debate on this; some critics still feel that Depp's performance, with its use of "red face" and halted speaking style, is dehumanizing, but the increased role for Tonto is at least a step in the right direction.

This depiction of Native Americans in *The Lone Ranger* actually serves an even deeper revision of the genre, as it posits war as the underlying oppressor in American society. Here's how it's done: In making Tonto and Reid equals, the filmmakers are able to give them a mutual enemy. This is Cole (Tom Wilkinson), a railroad magnate trying to lay tracks from Texas to California. A treaty between the U.S. and the Indian tribes has prevented him from building on tribal lands, so he makes it look like the Comanches — Tonto's tribe — have broken the agreement, thus opening up their land for train travel. The turn of events will lead to war — and Indian genocide at the hands of the U.S. Cavalry. But who could make a fuss over the survival of an indigenous people when there are American dollars to be made?

It comes across like a Western as told by Howard Zinn, a shocking change for a genre that has leaned conservative in all things. Unlike previous Westerns, in which Indians were seen as an obstacle to American economic expansion, the historical perspective inherent in *The Lone Ranger* shows the same story from the other side and suggests that American business interests were the driving force behind the Indian massacres. There may be a lot of professors at liberal arts colleges who agree, but you'll be unable to find that point of view in more than a couple of movies through the Western's long history.

This may be a new perspective for its genre, but a variant of it has been 5 amazingly common in other summer blockbusters, particularly those released *this year*. And its implications hit far closer to home than the events of the 19th century. You can learn a lot about a film's values from examining the motivations of its villains, and you can learn a lot about a society — or at least what Hollywood thinks society wants to hear — when it produces three mainstream movies in a few months that give its villains the exact same motivation. *Iron Man 3*, *White House Down*, and *The Lone Ranger* span cinematic categories — respectively, we have a comic-book film, a political action thriller, and a Western — but each of their stories portrays war, and implicitly the War on Terror, as caused by corporations and greed.

In *Iron Man 3*, we are introduced to an Osama Bin Laden–like terrorist named the Mandarin (played by Ben Kingsley), who is carrying out attacks on American military bases. But halfway through the film, we learn — spoiler alert — that the Mandarin is just a decoy character dreamed up by a scientist to provide cover for his experimentation on war veterans. The film's writer/director Shane Black explained this major plot twist as "a message that's more interesting for the modern world, because I think there's a lot of fear that's generated toward very available and obvious targets, which could perhaps be directed more intelligently at what's behind them." The *Iron Man* franchise laid the groundwork for this subtext from its first film, which featured Jeff Bridges as a greedy arms dealer who was arming a Taliban-like terrorist group to drive sales.

White House Down shows just how deeply this notion of villainy has taken root, particularly in contrast to past entries in its genre. The film initially offers a smorgasbord of motivations for its team of villains who hold the White House hostage — one is a white supremacist, and another is a disgruntled ex-soldier — but it ultimately shines a light on the collusion between corrupt government officials and defense contractors who are trying to launch a war in the Middle East to keep their coffers filled with money from government contracts. Again, the War on Terror is shown to be nothing more than a scheme by profiteers, not an ideological struggle and certainly not a necessary war. In explaining the issue to his buddy, President Sawyer (Jamie Foxx) even calls those profiteers out by name. "You ever hear of the military-industrial complex?" We have now, Mr. President.

It is quite a contrast to *Die Hard*, the 1988 action classic to which *White House Down* is most often compared. That film employed German thieves as the source of its terrorism, which fit nicely amid the Reagan era's popular support for increased defense spending to fend off a Communist threat. Similar films like *Air Force One* ("*Die Hard* in the president's plane") or *Toy Soldiers* ("*Die Hard* in a prep school") also address the fight against terrorism, but in their pre-9/11 mind-set, the villains are foreigners with clear-cut political goals.

Though people often forget it, Westerns are also war movies, as they take place during the American-Indian Wars of the 18th and 19th centuries. So it should be no surprise that *The Lone Ranger* uses the same moral template as *Iron Man 3* and *White House Down*. With the stated goal of becoming the wealthiest man in America, Cole launches a battle that seems a stand-in for all of the violence between American settlers and Indian populations. The message we leave with is that both U.S. soldiers and foreign enemies are pawns in the rich man's eternal quest to get even more for himself.

READING THE TEXT

1. Why does Gittell claim that *The Lone Ranger* presents "American business interests" (para. 2) as the real villain of the film?

2. What characteristics do the villains share in the three films Gittell discusses?

3. What historical conditions have led to the rise of the "rich guy" as a new kind of villain?

4. Gittell claims, "You can learn a lot about a film's values from examining the motivations of its villains, and you can learn a lot about a society — or at least what Hollywood thinks society wants to hear — when it produces three mainstream movies in a few months that give its villains the exact same motivation" (para. 5). In what way is he voicing a fundamental semiotic principle in this statement?

READING THE SIGNS

1. Gittell and Michael Agresta ("How the Western Was Lost — and Why It Matters," p. 372) discuss the genre of movie Westerns as a sign of American attitudes and mythologies. In an essay, compare and contrast their treatment of the Western. How do you account for any differences you might observe?

2. Gittell acknowledges that the three films he analyzes belong to rather different cinematic genres: "a comic-book film, a political action thriller, and a Western" (para. 5). In an essay, explore the extent to which this generic diversity strengthens, weakens, or complicates his argument about "a new enemy of the moment" (para. 1). Does this generic diversity make his argument seem more universal or less plausible? To support your argument, refer to current films that present moneyed American corporate interests as the villain.

3. **CONNECTING TEXTS** Watch *The Wolf of Wall Street* (2013), focusing your analysis on the protagonist Jordan Belfort. In an essay, write a semiotic analysis of his character. Is he the sort of "rich guy" villain Gittell describes? Or might he be better described as a hero or an antihero? To develop your ideas, read or reread Robert B. Ray's "The Thematic Paradigm" (p. 450).

TIM LAYDEN

A Patriot's Tale

With so many superheroes, antiheroes, outlaw heroes, and ultra-villains running around in American entertainment, one might well wonder whether there are any real, *ordinary* heroes left. So, if you're looking for some real-life heroes, you could start with the Andruzzi brothers—Marc, Billy, and Jimmy—New York City firefighters who were right in the thick of it when the World Trade Center towers were attacked and destroyed on September 11, 2001. Though their brother Joe, a former NFL player, is a lot better known, Tim Layden profiles the firefighting brothers—"official heroes," in Robert B. Ray's terms—here. (As the founder of the Joe Andruzzi Foundation, which provides funding for cancer research and cancer patients, Joe has been no slouch as a real-life hero either.) Tim Layden is a writer for *Sports Illustrated.*

The Andruzzis grew up the best kind of brothers, four boys wedged into two small bedrooms in their Staten Island home, loving and fighting, best friends and worst enemies. They spent long Saturday afternoons at the Little League field and Sundays at home, eating their mother's ritual macaroni and meatballs. They handed down paper routes and school clothes through four mini-generations. They were the sons of a New York City cop who sometimes worked three jobs at once to keep them all in parochial school, and their neighborhood was filled with the children of policemen and firefighters. Fathers were sometimes hurt or lost in the line of duty; that was part of life. Many sons would follow the same path.

Three of the Andruzzi boys became New York City firemen, Jimmy, 30, was first, graduating from the academy in October 1995. Billy, the oldest, at 32, first worked as a case manager for the New York City welfare department, but when he saw how much Jimmy loved his job, he joined the firefighting ranks in the summer of '99. The baby, Marc, 24, finished eight weeks of academy training in early September and is a "probie," beginning the probationary period that precedes graduation. "Their father was a cop, and now three sons are in the fire department," says their mother, Mary Ann, with a look of pride in her eyes. "My boys love to help people."

Joe, 26, would be the odd one. He kept growing long after his 200-pound brothers stopped, played football as an offensive lineman at Southern Connecticut State and clawed his way into the NFL as an undrafted free agent in 1997, making the roster of the Super Bowl champion Green Bay Packers. Despite three knee surgeries, he is the starting right guard for the New England Patriots, a 6'3", 315-pound contradiction of weekday calm and Sunday mayhem. "If I didn't play football, I would be teaching special education," says Joe. "I'm the black sheep, I guess. I wouldn't be a firefighter."

Still, he admires his brothers as much as they do him. "What's important is that my brothers are happy in what they do, and I know they are," says Joe. "A lot of people hate their jobs. I know my brothers are excited when they go to work. I'm excited when I get up on Sunday morning and know I've got a game to play. And I know they're excited when they go into a building to put out a fire." Nonetheless, he fights guilt over the opulence made possible by his profession. "I see them driving old cars, scrounging for second jobs," says Joe of his siblings. "The wage difference, it doesn't feel right for what they do."

Joe was in a dentist's chair on the morning of Tuesday, Sept. 11, when he 5
heard a radio report of a fire at the World Trade Center. He rushed back to his
house in North Attleboro, Mass., with his wife, Jen, and their children, Hunter, 3,
and Breanna, 17 months, and they watched coverage of the attacks. Both towers were still standing but soon would fall. Joe knew that Jimmy was stationed
in lower Manhattan (Engine 5, on East 14th Street). "I was thinking Jimmy
could be in the middle of all that," says Joe. "I knew he had to be close. My
heart was in my throat." Five hours passed before Joe learned that his brothers
were all safe and that Jimmy had, indeed, been terrifyingly close to death.

On the day after the disaster, Joe sleepwalked through meetings and practice in preparation for a game at Carolina that he hoped would not take place.
"I was there, but not really there," he says. When the NFL announced the next
day that its games were canceled, Joe drove to Staten Island. Late last Friday
afternoon he was sitting in the living room of his parents' modest split-level
house when Jimmy walked through the door and stopped at the entrance to
the room. He raised his right hand and held his thumb and index finger less
than an inch apart, wordlessly demonstrating the margin of his survival as his
lip trembled and his eyes watered. Both men began to cry, and they embraced
in the center of the room, sobbing for longer than either could ever remember.

On the morning of the attack, Jimmy was scheduled to work a nine-to-six
shift, but firefighters all know that means showing up at eight. Just after 8:30
Jimmy and his squad were called to a smoky apartment on East 19th Street.
Food left on a stove. They put out the fire and, as they climbed back onto the
truck, heard a jet screaming overheard. Awfully low, they said to one another.
Seconds later, the engine radio sounded. *Engine 10, Ladder 10, a plane has
hit Tower 1 of the World Trade Center.* Engine 10 is in the shadow of the twin
towers; firefighters from that company saw the first plane hit. Engine 5, fresh
from the kitchen fire, was not far away. Within minutes the two companies
were at the base of Tower 1, the first building that was struck.

Five days later Jimmy Andruzzi sat on a couch in his parents' living room,
unshaven, wearing denim shorts and a white T-shirt. His brothers, Joe and
Billy, sat nearby. Their father, Bill, 13 years retired from the police force, was
on his way home from his sales job. Their mother was in the kitchen, making the Sunday macaroni and meatballs, seeking blessed routine even as
a newspaper lay open on a table showing pictures of dozens of the missing,
many of them friends of the Andruzzis.

In a soft voice Jimmy described the events of Sept. 11.

"We're on the rig, and we look up and see the first tower burning, and my 10
buddy, Derek Brogan, says to me, 'We're going to the biggest disaster in the
history of New York City.' Once we're there, we're thinking about the proto-
col for a high-rise: command post in the lobby, another command post three
floors below the fire. They told us the bottom of the fire was on the 79th floor.

We're in the lobby when we hear another huge explosion. I figured out later that was the second plane hitting. I'm thinking, When we practice terrorist scenarios, they always tell us, 'First responders will be casualties.' The building is shaking, and nobody wants to go up now. They tell us, 'Engine 5, go with Engine 10 to 79. Put that fire out.' So we go up the stairs, me and Derek and Manny Delvalle and Gerard Gorman and Eddie Mecner and Lieutenant Bob Bohak. That's what we do. We put out fires.

"People are coming down the stairs. They're saying, 'You guys are so brave, thank you, thank you.' The stairwell is narrow — one line going up, another line going down. At the ninth floor Derek's getting chest pains. The lieutenant tells him to stop, but he keeps going. We're carrying 160 pounds of equipment, and it's hot. We get to the 23rd floor, and Derek is worse. The lieutenant radios for oxygen and tells the cops who bring up the oxygen to bring Derek back down. We start up again, maybe four more floors before we hear the biggest, loudest, most intense sound I've ever heard in my life. I didn't know at the time, but that was Tower 2 coming down. We thought it was our building coming down or a huge bomb. I figured I was dead right there. That's it.

"Lieutenant Bohak says, 'Drop your hoses and get out! Right now! Out!' We start running down the stairs, and it's all black smoke. [Here Jimmy begins to sob loudly.] We're leaving all those firemen behind, and they're still going up. All those guys, those guys, going up, but we had to leave. Those poor guys. . . . [He pauses to compose himself.] We get to the fourth floor, and the door out of the stairwell to the lobby is locked. I feel this rumble, like thunder, and the walls start cracking and the beams are bending. Some guy, not a firefighter — God bless him, he was an angel — points out another door, and we got through that into the lobby. I ran out into the street and kept going, and the whole building came down, maybe 45 seconds behind me. All those firemen got killed, and I'm alive because Derek got chest pains and because my lieutenant told us to get out and that guy was on the fourth floor. [Long pause as he begins crying again.] It's not supposed to happen. Terrorists aren't supposed to fly jet planes into a building full of innocent people, and the World Trade Center isn't supposed to fall down. It's just not supposed to happen."

Firefighters have two families: one at home, one at the station house. "My brothers, they're blood," says Jimmy. "But the guys in the station house, they're my brothers too. Everybody knows everything about everybody else. You know who's got a new girlfriend, you know whose kids are sick. The guys with seniority, they get all the respect. The probies, they get their balls broken a lot. Thin skin doesn't play in the station house."

When Jimmy exited onto the street that Tuesday morning, he found that among his group from the stairwell, only Delvalle was missing. Five days later he was still missing, along with Engine 5 lieutenant Paul Mitchell, who was off duty at the time of the crash but rushed to the site to help. They were two of the more than 300 New York City firefighters lost in the disaster, equal to more than a third of all previous casualties in the department's history. "Probably 100 of them were friends of mine," says Jimmy, who has worked at four station houses in his six-plus years with the department. "That's true of a lot of guys."

At the core of this immeasurable disaster, the missing firefighters were 15 at once heroes and victims, symbols of bravery and tragedy. It will be years before their ranks fully recover the experience and skill that was lost. Two days after the towers fell, Jimmy joined the thousands of firemen and other volunteers searching through the rubble for survivors and bodies. Standing atop a pile of twisted steel and compacted concrete, he felt another rumble, similar to what he had felt 48 hours earlier. He ran from the pile in terror and promised not to return soon.

His brothers Billy and Marc have done multiple shifts on what rescue and recovery workers have come to call "the mountain," their name for the pile of rubble that had been the tallest buildings in the city. "I hate to say that it's hard to appreciate what it's like down there," said Billy on Sunday, "but television does not do justice to how terrible it is."

The previous evening he had held a fellow firefighter's ankles as the man reached deep into the wreckage and scooped intestines out of a detached torso for DNA identification. In another place he picked up a single tooth. "By the end of my shift down there, I smelled like death," he said, and then he too began to cry.

On a cool, crystal-clear Sunday morning, Joe went with Jimmy to the Engine 5 station house, a three-story building that is one of the oldest firehouses in the city. He found tough men, scarred but battling for their sanity. "There were guys there who said they'd been crying for three days and it was time to stop," Joe said later. They were also worried about Jimmy, who had taken things harder than most. "They said he's not back yet," said Joe. "They said he needs more time. I hope it helps him to talk about it."

Joe sat on the steps of his mom and dad's home. A soft breeze ruffled the American flag on the front of the house. Inside, the table was set for dinner. Soon Joe would return to Massachusetts to begin preparing for this Sunday's game against the New York Jets in Foxboro. Football business. "Regular game week," said Joe.

Normalcy beckons, but reaching it will take longest for those survivors 20 who were closest to the flame.

READING THE TEXT

1. How does Joe Andruzzi characterize himself in comparison to his brothers?

2. Describe the organization and narration of events of this article. To what extent do they work to create an emotional impact on the reader?

3. Layden begins the article not by describing his main subject, the firefighter heroes, but by focusing on their football-player brother. What effect does this opening have on you as a reader?

4. In your own words, explain why Layden sees the firefighters missing in the wreckage as having symbolic status.

READING THE SIGNS

1. **CONNECTING TEXTS**   Well over a decade has passed since the September 11, 2001, terrorist attacks, and press coverage devoted to police, firefighters, and other rescue workers is now limited to the 9/11 anniversary. In class, discuss whether these workers still have the heroic status they were granted in the immediate aftermath of the attacks. Reflect on your class discussion, and write an essay in which you explore whether America's devotion to its heroes is deep-rooted and genuine or, alternatively, subject to trends. To develop your ideas, consult Lorraine Devon Wilke's "Snowden's a Hero, Obama's a Villain" (below).

2. In class, brainstorm a list of students' personal heroes, and then analyze the results. What areas of life do they hail from (politics, sports, entertainment, medicine, military, and so forth)? To what extent do students mention "ordinary" people, like the 9/11 rescuers, who found themselves in extraordinary circumstances? Use the results as the basis for an essay in which you argue for your own explanation of the criteria Americans use to identify heroes.

3. In an essay, present your own argument in response to this question: How do the identities of real-life heroes compare with those of fictional heroes? To develop your ideas, consult the introduction to this chapter and any of the readings in this chapter; be sure to base your argument on specific examples, both human and fictional.

LORRAINE DEVON WILKE

Snowden's a Hero, Obama's a Villain

Heroes and villains tend to be locked in simple black-and-white binary pairs, the one being defined by the other. But that is precisely the problem, Lorraine Devon Wilke argues, when considering such real-life antagonists as Edward Snowden and the Obama administration. Because if you think that Snowden is a hero for spilling the beans on the NSA, then you are likely to think that Obama must be a villain, but the whole matter is rather more complicated than that, with a whole lot of gray to go around. It's time to grow up, Wilke suggests, and stop demanding clear-cut distinctions between not-so-clear-cut opponents. Lorraine Devon Wilke is an actor, a singer-songwriter, and a columnist for the *Huffington Post*, where this selection first appeared.

As the long and winding road of Edward Snowden's journey continues to play out, trending opinions seem to be keeping pace with his ever-so-fluid travel itinerary. Back in the early days, fist-pumpers on both sides of the political divide — or, rather, *all* sides (we mustn't forget libertarians in this chorus) — were uncharacteristically joined in the certainty that he was a hero, a brave whistleblower who blew the lid off nefarious back-room dealings done to the detriment of Americans and countries the world over. Never mind that the dealings he was denouncing were largely protected by existing law, his hero status was cemented in a cultural climate that frames most things within the palette of black and white, good guys and bad guys. Gray area, nuance, intent between the lines, even fact or truth, are pushed aside for the extreme of belief.

To believe Edward Snowden, to define him as a hero, one must conversely believe that Obama and his administration are villains, as, it seems, Snowden supporters, by and large, do. Of course, swiping Obama et al. with the brush of tyranny has become a convenient meme; we've had "scandals" and conspiracy theories of every ilk occupying our attention, with calls for impeachment and various other forms of mass hysteria, none of which have resulted in much more than wide-ranging and colorful news cycles and a lot of noise that ultimately became deflective and distracting.

But that's where we are as a country: black-and-white thinking, a mode of perspective that comes with grand presumptions that we all know *all* the truth about everything, even things we couldn't possibly know all the truth about. But we make that presumption because we're Americans; we're arrogant and entitled.

When I hear opinionated movie stars and college professors encouraging people not to vote based on their purportedly deep knowledge and arcane understanding of the details and minutia of policies and decisions made behind closed doors of the White House and other government institutions, I can't help but wonder how they got the inside track on an inside track they could not possibly have an inside track to. And yet . . . they speak as if they do. They're little Zeligs, magically present when presidents make globally impacting decisions or ponder the right moves regarding national security. They *know*. Because they're Americans and they just . . . well . . . *know*! And with that mysterious know-it-all knowledge, they put a black hat on the president and others and we're told not to vote for the lot of 'em.

We've got citizens who "just know" the World Trade Center was brought 5 down by Bush and Cheney, that Michael Hastings was blown up by the FBI,

macmillanhighered.com/signsoflife
What happens when you try to map the superhero genre onto real-life dangers?
e-readings > United States Immigration and Customs Enforcement, *iGuardians* [video]

that Obama is secretly out to confiscate ALL guns, and that the illuminati is running the whole damn show anyway. You can't argue with this thinking because it's stated in unequivocal black and white; it allows for no persuasion, no debate, no logic. Because it's not based on fact; it's based on conjecture, presumption, guessing, and . . . just knowing.

We are quite knowledgeable, we arrogant, entitled Americans.

As for Snowden, while large numbers "just knew" the truth about him — that he was a hero, that he saved the world by exposing the over-reaching surveillance of the NSA; that he should be honored, protected and deified along with other truth-seeking whistleblowers — other Americans, the less black-and-white thinkers, took a more circumspect view. They said, "Let's wait and see how this all plays out before we jump on any bandwagons," and as they took their reflective, patient pose, they were sometimes maligned by those who'd already made up their minds. Liberals went after liberals, Republicans (who wanted so desperately to side with any side sided against Obama) started in-fighting over exactly *what* Snowden was, and even libertarians got squeamish at the revelations that Snowden was dumping info at the doorsteps of less-than-friendly governments.

Now as his fans carry on about an angry South America inviting him in and Glenn Greenwald of *The Guardian* continues to front for his boy, the black and whiteness of it all is getting a bit muddied.

A recent *Huffington Post* / YouGov poll reveals for the first time a slip in the "hero" numbers:

According to the new poll, 38 percent of Americans think that Snowden, 10 a former contractor for the National Security Agency, did the wrong thing, while 33 percent said he did the right thing. Still, 29 percent of Americans remain unsure about Snowden's actions.

Much of the drop in support for Snowden's actions since the earlier poll appears to have taken place among Republicans, who were divided, 37 percent to 37 percent, on whether Snowden did the right thing in the previous poll, but in the latest poll said by a 44 percent to 29 percent margin that he did the wrong thing.

Ah . . . red staters stirring a little gray into the mix. Fascinating.

In a compelling piece at *Addicting Info* titled "Have We All Been Fooled by Edward Snowden?," the writer references some illuminating information that frames his motivations as less noble than some would have us believe. In public chat rooms, long before he hit the front pages, he made clear his deep disdain for Obama, his support of Ron Paul, his Second Amendment fanaticism, his (truly vile) revulsion about seniors sucking off Social Security; his antipathy for the *New York Times* for "reporting classified shit" (ironic, isn't it?!), followed by put-downs of Wikileaks (his current BFFs) and his support of Bush's warrantless wiretapping. Yes. Really. I know . . . getting grayer all the time. I urge you to read the whole article; the chats alone are worth the click.

Edward Snowden, the hero, the whistleblower, the do-gooder doing good for the good of America seems to have been a very different fellow not all that long ago. What are we to make of that? My first impulse is to say, "Like everything that happens in life, we are to watch, listen, pay attention, open our minds, get past our partisan impulses, and wait for enough information to arrive at an intelligent, fact-based opinion." Turns out that's my second impulse too.

Because there's very little that comes in true black and white. That we 15 Americans persist in believing that, demanding that others believe in that, indicates a sort of cultural arrested development . . . like children who only see in broad strokes of good or bad (no child believes Daddy can be dastardly). Most people — those we hate, those we love and all those in between — have at least some shades of gray. We've just got to be willing to see past the black and white to notice.

READING THE TEXT

1. How does the scandal surrounding Edward Snowden's revelation of NSA practices complicate the definitions of "hero" and "villain" in this case, according to Wilke?

2. Why does Wilke say, "That's where we are as a country: black and white thinking, a mode of perspective that comes with grand presumptions that we all know *all* the truth about everything, even things we couldn't possible know all the truth about" (para. 3)?

3. How does Wilke connect reactions to the Edward Snowden case to modern conspiracy theories?

4. Wilke states that, in reaction to Edward Snowden, "liberals went after liberals, Republicans . . . started in-fighting over exactly *what* Snowden was" (para. 7). According to Wilke, why did people react this way?

READING THE SIGNS

1. In class, discuss writing strategies you can use both to avoid black-and-white thinking and to present a more nuanced argument that recognizes shades of gray. Use your findings to evaluate an op-ed piece in a general-interest newspaper (such as the *Washington Post* or the *New York Times*) or, alternatively, an opinion piece on a pointed political site such as Fox News.

2. When this selection first appeared in the *Huffington Post*, some bloggers responded that Wilke herself could be accused of black-and-white thinking, while others praised her nuanced view. In an essay of your own, evaluate the evenhandedness of her essay.

3. In an essay, argue for your own evaluation of the Edward Snowden affair, taking heed of Wilke's admonition that we consider "at least some shades of gray" (para. 15). Alternatively, do the same for a different polarizing debate, such as same-sex marriage.

4. Write an essay supporting, refuting, or complicating the proposition that making the hero-villain dichotomy "grayer" can risk a lack of commitment and moral indecisiveness.

5. In class, brainstorm non-gray distinctions of political heroes and villains. Then use your results to analyze a current topic that tends to invite dichotomous responses (consider, for instance, the split between Fox News and MSNBC supporters), using fan comments as evidence.

MY SELFIE, MY SELF

Ma(s)king Identity in the New Millennium

Who Are You?

You are not your self-portrait, but if you are at all like tens of millions of other people who own smartphones, it is quite likely that you have presented yourself to the world by way of a digital image taken, quite literally, at arm's length: your selfie. And since that image has the power to define who you are to an incalculable number of people the world over, you probably took a good deal of care in constructing it before posting it to Instagram or Snapchat or Facebook or wherever. "Here I am," says your selfie. "This is me, my unique self." But, in truth, a selfie cannot tell anyone much about who you are, and, paradoxically enough, one selfie really looks quite like another, often featuring the same poses and facial expressions framed within the strict limits imposed by a tiny camera held less than two feet from your face. So you have to go beyond your selfie to let other people know who you are, but that's a lot more difficult, isn't it? Who are you, anyway?

We like to think, especially in America where individualism is such a prized **mythology**, that our identity is completely within our control, autonomous and self-constructed. But it isn't that simple, because a large part of who you are is shaped socially and externally from your many experiences in life. Your social class, for example, influences what life experiences you may (or may not) have had, and these experiences play a strong role in shaping your consciousness and sense of self. Your race, too, has a powerful effect; because humans have not yet created a post-racial society, the way people treat you is affected by your ethnicity and influences how you identify yourself. And your gender and sexual orientation, too, can profoundly affect your experience and identity.

It is easy to forget the ways our identities began to be constructed in childhood, and all human cultures have their ways of influencing that process. Such institutions as family, religion, and education, for example, all tell you who you are and what you should expect of life. But in an entertainment culture like that of contemporary America, popular culture has emerged as an equally potent shaper of individual identity and desire.

Just think of all those children's television programs you may have watched even before you could walk or talk. When America's (and, increasingly, the world's) children spend hours in front of a TV set (which has been called "the great pacifier"), watching programs whose plots and characters subtly communicate to them how to behave — from appropriate gender roles to appropriate professional careers — the role of popular culture in shaping personal identity can be enormous. And at the same time that children are exposed to all that television, they are also absorbing a great deal of advertising. These ads are carefully constructed not only to shape children as consumers when they grow up but also to "brand" them as consumers of the products they see advertised, in the expectation of a lifetime of brand loyalty. Much the same can happen with kiddie flicks, which so often inculcate traditional social norms even as they dazzle young viewers' eyes with today's technological wizardry.

The products you consume in your youth can also have a powerful effect on your sense of identity. Your favorite clothing fashions, for example, are not only personal forms of expression but **signs** of your identification with the various youth cohorts who share your tastes. In a sense, using consumption as a badge of your identity can be considered a form of self-stereotyping (have you ever summed someone up as a "skater" or a "geek"?), but if we are the ones adopting the signs, it doesn't feel like stereotyping. The difference is the belief that we have a choice in the matter, and the desire for the freedom to choose our own identities is especially prevalent in America today. Consider, for example, some recent challenges to the gender codes that have traditionally defined our identities as gendered subjects.

Gender Codes

A **gender code** is a culturally constructed system that prescribes the appropriate roles and behaviors for men and women in society. Assuming both a continuity between your biological sex and your gender awareness or identity, as well as a normative heterosexual orientation, such codes tell you how to conduct yourself as a male or a female: *Boys don't cry; girls wear makeup. Boys are aggressive; girls are passive. Boys play sports; girls are cheerleaders. Men go out to work; women stay at home and raise children.* The list is long, and it has shaped your gender identity since your birth.

But challenges by transgender people to the assumption that biological sexual identity determines psychological gender identity have disrupted the authority of the traditional codes, leading to a multiplicity of possible identities that can be chosen rather than received. The popularity of such reality TV programs as *RuPaul's Drag Race* is a striking sign of this disruption of the old gender codes, for here we find a transgender performer whose flamboyant defiance of traditional gender behavior — which would have once subjected him to social marginalization — has made him both popular and successful.

Similarly, disruptions of the heteronormative assumptions that have traditionally governed sexual identity are also changing the cultural landscape. The success of television programs like *Modern Family*, the increasing number of athletes and politicians coming out to their fans and constituents, and the growing number of Americans who endorse same-sex marriage all signify an emerging acceptance of the freedom to differ from mainstream notions of sexual identity and desire.

But this is not to say that traditional gender codes have disappeared from popular culture. They are still very much at work and are particularly evident in advertising campaigns. Consider, for example, a current campaign for Axe grooming products. Denotatively, Axe is simply a perfume, but since the traditional gender codes specify that perfume is a woman's product, the marketing of Axe fragrances tries to connote a hypermasculine identity for its male consumers. Thus, like Brute before it, Axe products are given a name traditionally associated with such masculine-coded traits as violence and aggression. One famous Axe ad featured a swarm of passionate women running frantically toward a beach where a single man stands dousing himself in Axe fragrance, reinforcing the gender-coded belief that an unmarried man should "score" as often as possible (a woman who behaves in the same way can be called all kinds of unpleasant names).

Similarly, products (especially cosmetics) aimed at women play up the traditional gender-coded prescription that a woman's primary concern, and role, in life is to attract the gaze of a man — that is, to look beautiful. This is so glaringly obvious in women's magazines that it has stimulated its own

---

Exploring the Signs of Gender

In your journal, explore the expectations about gender roles that you grew up with. What gender norms were you taught by your family or the media, either overtly or implicitly? Have you ever had any conflicts with your parents over "natural" gender roles? If so, how did you resolve them? Do you think your gender-related expectations today are the same as those you had when you were a child?

backlash in the well-known Dove "Campaign for Real Beauty." But, while the campaign does feature more ordinary models than do other beauty product ads, it does not abandon the focus on physical attractiveness that the traditional code demands — and, it might also be pointed out, the same company that constructed the Dove campaign is also behind the Axe line of products.

Maybe things haven't changed so much after all.

Postfeminist or Third Wave?

The continuing tendency of American popular culture to tell girls and women that their primary identities lie in their ability to be sexually attractive to men through endless images of eroticized female bodies presents a particular challenge to cultural theory. For, given the attempts of the feminist movement in the 1970s to challenge such messages — which are reflections of what journalist Ariel Levy has called a "raunch culture" — the current era might seem to be more postfeminist than feminist when it comes to female identity in America. That is, some of the current signs (for instance, the notorious performance of Miley Cyrus at the 2013 VMA ceremony) suggest that America may have abandoned feminist goals and reverted to the most conservative of gender-coded prescriptions.

But it may not be that simple, because it is also the case that traditional gender codes insist that female sexuality must be tightly controlled by male masters, whereas for many women who embrace what is often called third wave feminism, the confident display of their sexuality is actually empowering rather than degrading, a taking charge rather than a knuckling under — an attitude that was behind the immense popularity, among women, of the TV hit *Sex and the City* and many similar books, movies, and TV series, like *Girls*. Thus, third wave feminists regard themselves as representing an evolution within the women's movement itself, not a movement away from it, arguing that being proud of her body and using it to get what she wants is part of a woman's empowerment and a valid identity choice. More traditional feminists are not persuaded by this argument, however, and point out that, by focusing their attention on their bodies rather than their minds, women may subject themselves to the tyranny of a youth-worshipping culture that will reject them once they are past the peak of their sexually appealing years. It is no accident that the vast majority of the images of women we see in popular culture are of very young women. There are a lot more Betty Boops than Betty Whites.

The Space for Race

Despite claims that race is no longer a significant factor in American life, with some commentators insisting that America has reached a "post-racial" condition in which race no longer matters, plenty of evidence shows that racial identity is still a profound, and often painful, part of American identity formation and politics. One only needs to look at the national obsession with the 2013 trial for Trayvon Martin's killing (itself a kind of inverse reproduction of the fascination with the O. J. Simpson trials of the 1990s) to see this. And while some see the election of Barack Obama as evidence that America has finally gotten beyond race, the sometimes-hysterical reaction against the first black American president has been widely interpreted as being racially motivated.

Even within the context of a popular culture that includes such race-transcending stars as Denzel Washington, Halle Berry, and Beyoncé, racial identity — especially when it appears in the form of racial stereotyping — continues to be a major issue in American entertainment. Having endured long histories of negative stereotyping in Hollywood, African Americans, Asian Americans, Native Americans, and Latin Americans can still find themselves being stereotyped by directors and scriptwriters who by now presumably should be aware of the problem. Complaints about the character Jar Jar Binks in the *Star Wars* saga, for example, were based upon a perception that it perpetrated a derisive stereotype of Afro-Caribbean culture, while even *Avatar*, with its sympathetic depiction of a nonwhite society under siege by white invaders, has been compared to *Dances with Wolves* as yet another example of a stereotypical story in which a group of nonwhites needs a white hero to lead them. In 2013, Disney's box-office failure with *The Lone Ranger* was also attributed, at least in part, to its revival of the always racially problematic character of Tonto.

But while the representation of race in popular culture is still a politically potent topic, certain changes in racial identity itself are altering the landscape. With increasing numbers of Americans identifying themselves as being of mixed race (while President Barack Obama identified himself as "Black, African Am or Negro" on his 2010 census form, he could have chosen "mixed race" as well), the traditional racial categories, like those of gender, are in a state of flux. Indeed, even the term "minority" is becoming obsolete in a country that will have no racial majority by midcentury. Such a demographic shift will have a profound effect on racial consciousness in America, an effect whose traces will be increasingly visible in popular culture in the years to come, shaping and reshaping Americans' sense of who they are.

Discussing the Signs of Race

Demographers predict that, by the middle of the twenty-first century, America will no longer have any racial or ethnic majority population. In class, discuss what effects this may have on Americans' sense of this country's history, culture, and identity.

The Great Divide

More subtly, but arguably just as profoundly, your social class also shapes your identity. But unlike such identifying categories as race and gender, class has historically been underplayed, even denied, as a component in American life. Obscured by the mythology of the American dream, which promises an opportunity for upward social mobility, class has been the great blind spot in American history ever since Michel-Guillaume-Jean de Crèvecoeur (an eighteenth-century French aristocrat who wrote glowingly of his experiences in America) declared that America was a land of economic equality that had transcended Europe's great gulf between rich and poor.

The inability of Americans to recognize the role that social class plays (and has always played) in their lives was dramatically altered in the wake of the Great Recession that broke over America like a tidal wave after the near-meltdown of our economy in 2008. Movements like Occupy Wall Street, which has famously divided America into "the 99 percent" and "the 1 percent," have finally brought class to the forefront. But the class divide that such twenty-first-century movements have brought to popular attention has been growing for a far longer time than merely the past few years. Indeed, we can trace it back to at least the 1970s, when the historic post–World War II expansion of the American middle class hit the skids thanks to the stagflation economy that beset the country after the Vietnam War. Since that period, the real wages of most Americans have scarcely grown at all.

But in the 1980s, thanks to a combination of the Reagan-era tax cuts for the wealthy and the restructuring of the American economy from an industrial to a postindustrial one, the wealth of America's top earners skyrocketed. This is when the 1 percent versus the 99 percent divide that the Occupy movement refers to originated, and this divide represents a profound disruption of what Americans have always thought themselves to be. For America has always considered itself a land of equality: That principle has been a key part of our national identification. But in the past forty years or so, that belief has been seriously challenged by the reality of a class divide that is changing the identity of America itself.

But so pertinacious are cultural mythologies that the America of vast class differences is still not very visible in popular culture. The movie *Batman: The Dark Knight Rises* certainly alluded to the class divide in 2012, but, as a number of critics noted at the time, it characterized the class revolution of Bane and company as brutally terroristic, thus potentially undermining those with a serious desire to promote class equality. Generally, one can argue that while American popular culture is eager to present itself as progressive about race and gender, it is not so eager to reveal the effects of class inequality — which is not so very surprising when so many members of the entertainment industry belong to that 1 percent.

Be Whatever You Want to Be

Race, class, and gender form a triad of identifiers that are especially prominent in cultural studies. But plenty of evidence in popular culture suggests that
American youth are not terribly preoccupied with them. For one, these forms
of identification are based in demographic categorization, while the signs are
indicating that millennials are more concerned with their own highly individual identities as expressed through the self-constructions that appear on social
networking sites from LinkedIn to Facebook, Instagram to Snapchat, Twitter
to Tumblr, and everything in between and beyond. In short, in the world of
the selfie, the emphasis is on self-advertising, not demographic classification.
And this opens up a whole new territory in identity formation.

On the Internet, you can be pretty much what you want to be. From
online gaming sites (like World of Warcraft) where you can adopt a host of
identities, to the Facebook profiles where you can present to the world an
idealized version of your life, the Internet has revolutionized the traditional
restrictions on identity formation. With no one able to see you in person, you
can adopt whatever personae you like, exchanging identities as if you were
changing your clothes. Such freedom to present yourself in whatever way you
like has been a fundamental appeal of the Internet from its beginnings.

But just as the Internet creates the opportunity for self-making, it also
offers users the possibility of disguise — a masked *non-identity* that seems

Science fiction fans wear elaborate costumes at the annual Comic-Con convention.

AP Photo/Denis Poroy

to unleash some of our most antisocial tendencies. Just read the comments that follow online news stories, YouTube videos, or just about anything on the Internet. You will find the same aggression, vile language, flame wars, and hate and hostility, no matter what the topic. This "keyboard courage" is made possible by the anonymity that the Internet confers upon its users, who feel emboldened to say things that they would not say face-to-face because non-virtual society has ways of policing itself that the Internet does not (a lot of rude comments on the Internet would get their posters punched out if delivered in person; others would get them fired).

Paradoxically, then, the Internet offers to its users a kind of non-identity in its offer of anonymity. And since identification is also a form of social control (think of your driver's license — it is your ID, and without it you cannot legally drive your car or board a commercial airplane), the outbursts that fill the Internet are signifiers not only of all the conflict out there but also of a resentment against the restrictions that come with social identity. Such resentment bears a close relation to that fundamental American mythology of individualism, which can be found at work so often in American culture, for it is our individualism that guides our cherishing of our liberty. The possibility of escaping identity, of having a non-identity, offers an immense freedom — even if that freedom is expressed only as a license to rant in public.

The Supermarket of IDs

But let's look again at your ability to construct your own online identity. You pay a price for the self-making you can do on the Internet. As you advertise yourself, the social networking site on which you do so is mining your data to sell to others who want to advertise to you. Rather than setting up your own Web page — which is what people did in the Internet's early days — you build your social networking identity upon mass-produced platforms that offer ease and convenience in exchange for your life details. Ironically, your identity is a commodity for sale, and you sold it without even knowing it.

In short, identity itself has become a commodity in America. The mining of our private information can be very disturbing to members of a society

---

Reading Identity Online

Many Internet sites are devoted to the culture of a particular ethnicity, gender, or cultural subgroup. Visit several such sites and survey the breadth of information available within them. Is there any information that you wish would appear online but could not find? Do you find any material problematic?

in which individualism and independence are so highly valued, but it is routinely shrugged off by consumers who are pleased to have advertising tailored to their online profiles. This isn't very surprising in a consumer culture wherein people have been trained from the cradle to *identify* themselves as consumers.

And so we come full circle to what it really means to live in a consumer society and why the study and understanding of popular culture, so much of which is involved with consumption, is important. Although one American tradition, a mythology that goes back to the roots of this nation, clings desperately to a sense of individualism within a mass culture, another more recent development — the advent of consumerism — is taking that all away. And if that worries you, just look online: At fearandclothing.com, you can buy a T-shirt that reads "I'm Not a Number." The shirt refers to a popular television program from the 1960s: *The Prisoner*.

The Readings

Rachel Lowry opens the readings with a news feature on millennials who "may be suffering from an identity crisis" due to the difference between their online profiles and their more authentic, and private, selves. In a paired set of readings, Aaron Devor analyzes gender roles and the ways men and women manipulate the signs by which we traditionally communicate our gender identity, while Deborah Blum suggests that biology *does* play a role in gender identity and that we can best understand the gender gap by looking at both the cultural and the physiological determinants of human behavior. Kevin Jennings follows with a personal memoir that chronicles his struggles with growing up gay in conflict with his family's traditionalist construction of male heterosexual identity. Next, Mariah Burton Nelson's essay on the predicament of women athletes points out the cultural contradictions that women must negotiate when they enter the world of competitive sport, while Alfred Lubrano offers a reflection on the personal disruptions in moving out of the working class into a new middle-class identity. Michael Omi's historical survey of racial stereotyping in American entertainment provides an essential foundation for the analysis of race in popular culture, and Dani McClain's journalistic exploration of "the intersection of blackness, gender expression and sexual orientation" unveils the risks incurred by LGBTQ African Americans. Then, Theresa Celebran Jones calls for more mixed-race representation on television, celebrating Nickelodeon's *Sanjay and Craig*, an animated series about a mixed-race boy and his "best friend / talking pet snake." And Aymar Jean Christian concludes the chapter with an argument that the era of "post-identity" television — that is, shows that play down demographic differences and specificities — is coming to an end, as new programs like *Girls*, *The Misadventures of Awkward Black Girl*, *Buppies*, and *Afro City* make race, gender, and sexual orientation explicit topics for TV and online entertainment.

RACHEL LOWRY

Straddling Online and Offline Profiles, Millennials Search for Identity

It's hard to know who you really are when everyone counsels you to market yourself on such social networking sites as LinkedIn and Facebook, which is pretty much the fate of most of the people who belong to the generation of millennials. And so, as Rachel Lowry reports in this feature for *Deseret News*, a lot of millennials, who have spent their entire lives with digital technology and self-hyped social networking profiles, have begun to wonder just who their authentic selves really are. Sometimes it's best just to find some time to be alone, but that's not easy to do when you're online all the time. So maybe it's time to turn that smartphone off, once in a while, so you can look for yourself. Rachel Lowry is a magazine editor for *Graphis*.

Twenty-year-old Mariah Hanaike waits in the disconcerting silence of a temporary employment agency lobby in Redwood City, Calif. Though the interview has not yet begun, Hanaike said she knows she is being scrutinized before she shakes the hand of a potential employer. "You know the person you're going to meet is somewhere close in the building preparing for you, maybe by looking you up on Facebook or Googling your name, possibly reading an embarrassing entry about you on your mom's blog or being surprised to not find you on LinkedIn," said Hanaike. "I can't just be myself where and when I want because anything I do has the potential to end up on some site somewhere where anyone can look at it and judge. I feel like I need to water down who I am."

Millennials, the term given for those born between 1980 and 2000, may be suffering from an identity crisis as they search for their authentic self. According to a recent online study, one out of four millennials say they can only be their true self when alone. As today's twenty-somethings create online identities to market themselves professionally, as well as socially, some fear that the disparity between the two can prevent a young person from finding authentic self-definition.

Living Life Publicly

As today's younger generation navigates the transition to adulthood, reconciling between online and offline identities can be difficult.

Nearly 25 percent of all millennials say they can only be their true self when alone, Belgium researcher Joeri Van den Bergh found. In his book,

500

Millennials: How Cool Brands Stay Hot, Branding to Generation Y, Van den Bergh argues that authenticity is key for brands to connect with millennials. "The key concept behind authenticity is to stay true to yourself, so we wanted to know when Millennials stay true to themselves," he said.

Van den Bergh asked 4,056 people, ages 15 to 25, when they felt they   5
were or weren't being authentic online or offline, with friends, parents, partners or employers. Identity, he found, was strongly influenced by the back-and-forth of these two spheres. "Millennials are pre-wired to achieve and create success stories in their lives," Van den Bergh said. "They would rather blow up some stories or pretend they are having fun on Instagram and Facebook than admit they had a boring night out to the friends and immediate social circle." This can alter authenticity in identity, Van den Bergh found. Only half of the millennials surveyed believe themselves to be authentic and real. "[It's] a response to the social society in which private moments are rare and everything is transparent and in the open on social media," Van den Bergh said.

For Victor Ruiz, 25, a student at Utah State University, social media perpetuates the problem. "We live in a capitalist society," Ruiz said. "People don't want to be singled out, especially in a negative way, so they will try to make themselves look better and good to impress. They would try to make their online pages look as though they are living the American dream and not expose weakness." It's a "fluffy portrayal of reality," said 27-year-old Angie Rideout, a hairstylist in Salt Lake City. "It shows what we value, how we spend our time and who we spend our time with."

If you don't participate online, you risk being uninvolved and out of touch, said Hanaike, who is also attending LDS Business College in Salt Lake City. "Nobody will show you to others for you, so you will be voiceless and unseen." Hanaike said online media can be detrimental to her offline identity. "I am perfectly capable of representing myself without a domain name or URL," she said. "But I do not have that option. My freedom is definitely being infringed upon. I can't just be myself where and when I want because literally anything I do has the potential to end up on some site somewhere where anyone can look at it and judge."

Twenty-three-year-old Braden Bissegger, a student at LDS Business College, agrees. "You're required to define yourself to be involved: Build a Facebook page and Twitter account and post your thoughts and show the world who you are," Bissegger said. "But what if that's inaccurate? What if we are all purporting to be something we're not? Yes, we are certainly in an identity crisis."

Linking In

Hanaike is one of 80 million millennials, ages 18 to 24, in the U.S., many of whom are competing for the job market, according to a 2010 U.S. Census Bureau report. How to get a leg up? Many say self-promotion through online media can be huge. "It's standard procedure for hiring managers to check out your Facebook, Twitter and LinkedIn profiles," wrote Jenna Goudreau in a recent *Forbes* article. "Simply sifting through job postings and sending out applications en masse was never a good route to success, and is even less so now," wrote Phyllis Korkki, an employment editor for the *New York Times*. "One of the most important questions that many job seekers can ask these days is this: How searchable am I?"

Professional self-branding and social networking is necessary no matter 10 what the economy looks like, according to David Lake, a 25-year-old marketer in Lindon. "When tools like these are available you can either keep up with the times and use them for your benefit, or you can let others take advantage of the opportunity," Lake said. "The days of a paper resume and a blind interview are over. With social media platforms and personal websites, interviewers can know a lot about who you are before the interview even starts."

For many millennials, however, self-branding can bleed into narcissism or the creation of a false persona. "It is upsetting to think that an employer can base their decision to hire me on who I appear to be on online media. That is not the person that they are hiring," said Hanaike. "I don't want to appear narcissistic when I talk to a potential employer," said Duncan Purser, 25, a student of managerial financial accounting. "But with the way applying for jobs goes in today's technological work, you have to promote yourself and continually go for presence."

Thoren Williams, a 22-year-old studying accounting at LDS Business College, agrees. "If you don't update your LinkedIn when applying for jobs, your personality doesn't come through on social media platforms and it can seem as if you don't have one," Williams said. "Potential employers may assume they know what type of an employee you would be because they've checked out your resume on LinkedIn."

It's almost necessary to be a little bit narcissistic, Hanaike said. "If you want to get noticed, or if you want someone to see your qualifications, you have to show them, lest you get swept away with the tide." For Hanaike, this can lead to a disparity between online and offline identity.

Reconciling Identities

So how do you reconcile the two identities and maintain a true center?

For Mutual Leonard, a 29-year-old actuarial analyst living in Salt Lake City, 15 culture can be a strong source of identity. "Mormons with pioneer heritage, for example, say 'My grandmother walked across the plains. I'm not giving up my religion for anything. This is my identity.'" Leonard said culture prepares youth for adulthood, preparing boys to be men through priesthood duties in a church, or hunting for your first kill as initiation into a tribe. "Psychologically, you need that kind of a thing," he said, noting that identity requires an outward focus. "You will establish identity as soon as you focus on something beyond yourself."

Katie Greer, a nation-wide Internet and technology safety trainer, recommends tolerance. "I could follow someone's entire day online, seeing when they wake up, eat, what they wear and the traffic they hit," said Greer. "Perhaps we should lift our eyes from our screens more often and live the lives we are purporting." Reconciliation, Greer said, requires creating an identity worth owning up to online. "I'm 30 years old and it's really bizarre to think of all the things in my life that have formed my identity: Soccer, politics, clubs, sports, friends," Greer said. "I worked really hard to prove who I was, for myself, my friends, my family, the colleges I've applied to. Can I just put all that effort into saying I am something I'm not online? It's kind of like cheating." The things today's twenty-somethings do can later define you, Greer warned. Being cautious about what one posts online can avoid false labels and assumptions.

Millennials, themselves, are learning how to create a consistent identity across the many platforms before them. "I meet people who seem to be in a sort of fog because they are so focused on Facebook and getting likes," Bissegger said. "But then I've also seen many people who are not trying to boast or brag about themselves, but trying to show how they are contributing to something or giving of themselves and social media is one of their most effective platforms." In fact, those who are able to see social media as a means of getting beyond yourself are the ones who are confident in their identity, Hanaike said. "We've been given a lot of crap, as millennials, but if we want our future to be something significant and if we want our lives to be great, we have to have self-confidence," she said. "It takes a certain level of self-awareness to think I am going to provide something for the community and the world that no one else is, so that I can do the best job of doing this. That is the antithesis of an identity crisis."

For David Lake, the two platforms can actually enhance one's identity both online and offline. "Facebook and other social networks give a voice and confidence to many people that didn't previously have either of those things," Lake said. "They might be shy or naturally lacking in confidence. Now that they have a stage to project their voice, we really get to see who those people are."

READING THE TEXT

1. Summarize in your own words Lowry's explanation for why millennials feel that they are losing touch with their essential selves.
2. What does researcher Joeri Van den Bergh mean by saying, "Millennials are pre-wired to achieve and create success stories in their lives" (para. 5)?
3. Why does interviewee Mutual Leonard claim that culture can ground one's sense of identity?
4. In your own words, explain how concerns about future job prospects can affect millennials' profiles on social network sites such as Facebook and LinkedIn.

READING THE SIGNS

1. In a journal entry, describe how you might have profiled yourself on a social network site. Did you try to "improve" your self-image, or did you just describe yourself as accurately as you could? Then consider why you chose that profile. If you have not constructed a social network profile, discuss why you preferred to avoid that venue.

2. In an essay, explore how the job-related stress that Lowry discusses supports or deviates from the proposition that social media controls our lives more than users control social media. As evidence, you might interview some upper-division students who are contemplating entering the job market and ask them about their social media profiles.

3. Lowry suggests that millennials feel pressured by job counselors, teachers, and parents to use social media to market themselves. But young people are also influenced by their peers. In an essay, evaluate the influence adults and peers have on engagement with social media. In your essay, you should base your analysis on interviews with social media users, perhaps analyzing how they behaved in high school and in college.

4. **CONNECTING TEXTS** Both Lowry and Salvador Rodriguez ("In the Digital Age, Breaking Up Is Hard to Do," p. 415) write journalistic accounts, based on individuals' experiences, to elucidate ways that online communication can be problematic. As brainstorming, first synthesize the ways that Facebook and other sites have affected millennials' sense of and projection of identity. Then use your thoughts to support an essay in which you argue your own position on how social media affect millennials' sense of identity. For further ideas, consult "Students Addicted to Social Media" by the International Center for Media and the Public Agenda (p. 403).

PERFORMING GENDER

AARON DEVOR

Gender Role Behaviors and Attitudes

"Boys will be boys, and girls will be girls": Few of our cultural mythologies seem as natural as this one. But in this exploration of the gender signals that traditionally tell what a "boy" or "girl" is supposed to look and act like, Aaron Devor shows how these signals are not "natural" at all but instead are cultural constructs. While the classic cues of masculinity — aggressive posture, self-confidence, a tough appearance — and the traditional signs of femininity — gentleness, passivity, strong nurturing instincts — are often considered "normal," Devor explains that they are by no means biological or psychological necessities. Indeed, he suggests, they can be richly mixed and varied, or to paraphrase the old Kinks song "Lola," "Boys can be girls and girls can be boys." Devor is professor of sociology, former dean of graduate studies, and the founder and academic director of the Transgender Archives at the University of Victoria and author of *Gender Blending: Confronting the Limits of Duality* (1989), from which this selection is excerpted, and *FTM: Female-to-Male Transsexuals in Society* (1997).

Gender Role Behaviors and Attitudes

The clusters of social definitions used to identify persons by gender are collectively known as "femininity" and "masculinity." Masculine characteristics are used to identify persons as males, while feminine ones are used as signifiers for femaleness. People use femininity or masculinity to claim and communicate their membership in their assigned, or chosen, sex or gender. Others recognize our sex or gender more on the basis of these characteristics than on the basis of sex characteristics, which are usually largely covered by clothing in daily life.

These two clusters of attributes are most commonly seen as mirror images of one another with masculinity usually characterized by dominance and aggression, and femininity by passivity and submission. A more evenhanded description of the social qualities subsumed by femininity and masculinity might be to label masculinity as generally concerned with egoistic dominance and femininity as striving for cooperation or communion.[1] Characterizing femininity and masculinity in such a way does not portray the two clusters of characteristics as being in a hierarchical relationship to one another but rather as being two different approaches to the same question, that question being centrally concerned with the goals, means, and use of power. Such an alternative conception of gender roles captures the hierarchical and competitive masculine thirst for power, which can, but need not, lead to aggression, and the feminine quest for harmony and communal well-being, which can, but need not, result in passivity and dependence.

Many activities and modes of expression are recognized by most members of society as feminine. Any of these can be, and often are, displayed by

---

[1]Eleanor Maccoby, *Social Development: Psychological Growth and the Parent-Child Relationship* (New York: Harcourt, 1980), p. 217. Egoistic dominance is a striving for superior rewards for oneself or a competitive striving to reduce the rewards for one's competitors even if such action will not increase one's own rewards. Persons who are motivated by desires for egoistic dominance not only wish the best for themselves but also wish to diminish the advantages of others whom they may perceive as competing with them.

---

e macmillanhighered.com/signsoflife
Is gender a learned performance?
e-readings > Sut Jhally, *The Codes of Gender* [documentary film clip]

persons of either gender. In some cases, cross-gender behaviors are ignored by observers, and therefore do not compromise the integrity of a person's gender display. In other cases, they are labeled as inappropriate gender role behaviors. Although these behaviors are closely linked to sexual status in the minds and experiences of most people, research shows that dominant persons of either gender tend to use influence tactics and verbal styles usually associated with men and masculinity, while subordinate persons, of either gender, tend to use those considered to be the province of women.[2] Thus it seems likely that many aspects of masculinity and femininity are the result, rather than the cause, of status inequalities.

Popular conceptions of femininity and masculinity instead revolve around hierarchical appraisals of the "natural" roles of males and females. Members of both genders are believed to share many of the same human characteristics, although in different relative proportions; both males and females are popularly thought to be able to do many of the same things, but most activities are divided into suitable and unsuitable categories for each gender class. Persons who perform the activities considered appropriate for another gender will be expected to perform them poorly; if they succeed adequately, or even well, at their endeavors, they may be rewarded with ridicule or scorn for blurring the gender dividing line.

The patriarchal gender schema currently in use in mainstream North   5
American society reserves highly valued attributes for males and actively supports the high evaluation of any characteristics which might inadvertently become associated with maleness. The ideology underlying the schema postulates that the cultural superiority of males is a natural outgrowth of the innate predisposition of males toward aggression and dominance, which is assumed to flow inevitably from evolutionary and biological sources. Female attributes are likewise postulated to find their source in innate predispositions acquired in the evolution of the species. Feminine characteristics are thought to be intrinsic to the female facility for childbirth and breastfeeding. Hence, it is popularly believed that the social position of females is biologically mandated to be intertwined with the care of children and a "natural" dependency on men for the maintenance of mother-child units. Thus the goals of femininity and, by implication, of all biological females are presumed to revolve around heterosexuality and maternity.[3]

Femininity, according to this traditional formulation, "would result in warm and continued relationships with men, a sense of maternity, interest in caring for children, and the capacity to work productively and continuously

[2]Judith Howard, Philip Blumstein, and Pepper Schwartz, "Sex, Power, and Influence Tactics in Intimate Relationships," *Journal of Personality and Social Psychology* 51 (1986), pp. 102–9; Peter Kollock, Philip Blumstein, and Pepper Schwartz, "Sex and Power in Interaction: Conversational Privileges and Duties," *American Sociological Review* 50 (1985), pp. 34–46.

[3]Nancy Chodorow, *The Reproduction of Mothering: Psychoanalysis and the Sociology of Gender* (Berkeley: U of California P, 1978), p. 134.

in female occupations."[4] This recipe translates into a vast number of pro-scriptions and prescriptions. Warm and continued relations with men and an interest in maternity require that females be heterosexually oriented. A het-erosexual orientation requires women to dress, move, speak, and act in ways that men will find attractive. As patriarchy has reserved active expressions of power as a masculine attribute, femininity must be expressed through modes of dress, movement, speech, and action which communicate weakness, dependency, ineffectualness, availability for sexual or emotional service, and sensitivity to the needs of others.

Some, but not all, of these modes of interrelation also serve the demands of maternity and many female job ghettos. In many cases, though, feminin-ity is not particularly useful in maternity or employment. Both mothers and workers often need to be strong, independent, and effectual in order to do their jobs well. Thus femininity, as a role, is best suited to satisfying a mascu-line vision of heterosexual attractiveness.

Body postures and demeanors which communicate subordinate status and vulnerability to trespass through a message of "no threat" make people appear to be feminine. They demonstrate subordination through a minimiz-ing of spatial use: People appear feminine when they keep their arms closer to their bodies, their legs closer together, and their torsos and heads less verti-cal than do masculine-looking individuals. People also look feminine when they point their toes inward and use their hands in small or childlike gestures. Other people also tend to stand closer to people they see as feminine, often invading their personal space, while people who make frequent appeasement gestures, such as smiling, also give the appearance of femininity. Perhaps as an outgrowth of a subordinate status and the need to avoid conflict with more socially powerful people, women tend to excel over men at the ability to cor-rectly interpret, and effectively display, nonverbal communication cues.[5]

Speech characterized by inflections, intonations, and phrases that con-vey nonaggression and subordinate status also make a speaker appear more feminine. Subordinate speakers who use more polite expressions and ask more questions in conversation seem more feminine. Speech characterized by sounds of higher frequencies are often interpreted by listeners as femi-nine, childlike, and ineffectual.[6] Feminine styles of dress likewise display

[4]Jon K. Meyer and John E. Hoopes, "The Gender Dysphoria Syndromes: A Position Statement on So-Called 'Transsexualism,'" *Plastic and Reconstructive Surgery* 54 (Oct. 1974), pp. 444–51.

[5]Erving Goffman, *Gender Advertisements* (New York: Harper, 1976); Judith A. Hall, *Non-Verbal Sex Differences: Communication Accuracy and Expressive Style* (Baltimore: Johns Hop-kins UP, 1984); Nancy M. Henley, *Body Politics: Power, Sex and Non-Verbal Communication* (Englewood Cliffs, N.J.: Prentice, 1979); Marianne Wex, *"Let's Take Back Our Space": "Female" and "Male" Body Language as a Result of Patriarchal Structures* (Berlin: Frauenliteraturverlag Hermine Fees, 1979).

[6]Karen L. Adams, "Sexism and the English Language: The Linguistic Implications of Being a Woman," in *Women: A Feminist Perspective*, 3rd ed., ed. Jo Freeman (Palo Alto, Calif.: Mayfield, 1984), pp. 478–91; Hall, pp. 37, 130–37.

Rearing children is work typically done by women, but not always.

subordinate status through greater restriction of the free movement of the body, greater exposure of the bare skin, and an emphasis on sexual character-istics. The more gender distinct the dress, the more this is the case.

Masculinity, like femininity, can be demonstrated through a wide variety [10] of cues. Pleck has argued that it is commonly expressed in North American society through the attainment of some level of proficiency at some, or all, of the following four main attitudes of masculinity. Persons who display success and high status in their social group, who exhibit "a manly air of toughness, confidence, and self-reliance" and "the aura of aggression, violence, and dar-ing," and who conscientiously avoid anything associated with femininity are seen as exuding masculinity.[7] These requirements reflect the patriarchal ide-ology that masculinity results from an excess of testosterone, the assumption being that androgens supply a natural impetus toward aggression, which in turn impels males toward achievement and success. This vision of masculin-ity also reflects the ideological stance that ideal maleness (masculinity) must remain untainted by female (feminine) pollutants.

Masculinity, then, requires of its actors that they organize themselves and their society in a hierarchical manner so as to be able to explicitly quantify the achievement of success. The achievement of high status in one's social group requires competitive and aggressive behavior from those who wish to obtain it. Competition which is motivated by a goal of individual achievement, or egoistic dominance, also requires of its participants a degree of emotional insensitivity to feelings of hurt and loss in defeated others, and a measure of emotional insularity to protect oneself from becoming vulnerable to manip-ulation by others. Such values lead those who subscribe to them to view

[7]Joseph H. Pleck, *The Myth of Masculinity* (Cambridge, Mass.: MIT P, 1981), p. 139.

feminine persons as "born losers" and to strive to eliminate any similarities to feminine people from their own personalities. In patriarchally organized societies, masculine values become the ideological structure of the society as a whole. Masculinity thus becomes "innately" valuable and femininity serves a contrapuntal function to delineate and magnify the hierarchical dominance of masculinity.

Body postures, speech patterns, and styles of dress which demonstrate and support the assumption of dominance and authority convey an impression of masculinity. Typical masculine body postures tend to be expansive and aggressive. People who hold their arms and hands in positions away from their bodies, and who stand, sit, or lie with their legs apart—thus maximizing the amount of space that they physically occupy—appear most physically masculine. Persons who communicate an air of authority or a readiness for aggression by standing erect and moving forcefully also tend to appear more masculine. Movements that are abrupt and stiff, communicating force and threat rather than flexibility and cooperation, make an actor look masculine. Masculinity can also be conveyed by stern or serious facial expressions that suggest minimal receptivity to the influence of others, a characteristic which is an important element in the attainment and maintenance of egoistic dominance.[8]

Speech and dress which likewise demonstrate or claim superior status are also seen as characteristically masculine behavior patterns. Masculine speech patterns display a tendency toward expansiveness similar to that found in masculine body postures. People who attempt to control the direction of conversations seem more masculine. Those who tend to speak more loudly, use less polite and more assertive forms, and tend to interrupt the conversations of others more often also communicate masculinity to others. Styles of dress which emphasize the size of upper body musculature, allow freedom of movement, and encourage an illusion of physical power and a look of easy physicality all suggest masculinity. Such appearances of strength and readiness to action serve to create or enhance an aura of aggressiveness and intimidation central to an appearance of masculinity. Expansive postures and gestures combine with these qualities to insinuate that a position of secure dominance is a masculine one.

Gender role characteristics reflect the ideological contentions underlying the dominant gender schema in North American society. That schema leads us to believe that female and male behaviors are the result of socially directed hormonal instructions which specify that females will want to have children and will therefore find themselves relatively helpless and dependent on males for support and protection. The schema claims that males are innately aggressive and competitive and therefore will dominate over females. The social hegemony of this ideology ensures that we are all raised to practice gender roles which will confirm this vision of the nature of the sexes. Fortunately, our training to gender roles is neither complete nor uniform. As a result, it

[8]Goffman; Hall; Henley; Wex.

is possible to point to multitudinous exceptions to, and variations on, these themes. Biological evidence is equivocal about the source of gender roles; psychological androgyny is a widely accepted concept. It seems most likely that gender roles are the result of systematic power imbalances based on gender discrimination.[9]

READING THE TEXT

1. List the characteristics that Devor describes as being traditional conceptions of "masculinity" and "femininity" (para. 1).
2. What relationship does Devor see between characteristics that are considered masculine and feminine?
3. How does Devor explain the cultural belief in the "superiority" (para. 5) of males?
4. How, in Devor's view, do speech and dress communicate gender roles?

READING THE SIGNS

1. In small same-sex groups, brainstorm lists of traits that you consider to be masculine and feminine, and then have each group write its list on the board. Compare the lists produced by male and female groups. What patterns of differences or similarities do you see? To what extent do the traits presume a heterosexual orientation? How do you account for your results?
2. Study the speech patterns, styles of dress, and other nonverbal cues communicated by your friends during a social occasion, such as a party, trying not to reveal that you are observing them for an assignment. Then write an essay in which you analyze these cues used by your friends. To what extent do your friends enact the traditional gender codes Devor describes?
3. **CONNECTING TEXTS**   Study a popular magazine such as *Vanity Fair*, *Rolling Stone*, or *Maxim* for advertisements depicting men and women interacting with each other. Then write an essay in which you interpret the body postures of the models, using Devor's selection as your framework for analysis. How do males and females typically stand? To what extent do the models enact stereotypically masculine or feminine stances? To develop your essay, consult Steve Craig's "Men's Men and Women's Women" (p. 182).
4. **CONNECTING TEXTS**   Devor argues that female fashion traditionally has restricted body movement while male styles of dress usually allow freedom of movement. In class, discuss whether this claim is still true today, being sure to consider a range of clothing types (such as athletic wear, corporate dress, party fashion, and so forth). To develop your ideas, consult Mariah Burton Nelson's "I Won. I'm Sorry" (p. 524).

[9]Howard, Blumstein, and Schwartz; Kollock, Blumstein, and Schwartz.

DEBORAH BLUM

The Gender Blur: Where Does Biology End and Society Take Over?

There's an old argument over whether nature or nurture is more important in determining human behavior. Nowhere is this argument more intense than in gender studies, where proponents of the social construction of gender identities are currently exploring the many ways in which our upbringing shapes our behavior. But after watching her two-year-old son emphatically choose to play only with carnivorous dinosaur toys and disdainfully reject the "wimpy" vegetarian variety, Deborah Blum decided that nurture couldn't be all that there was to it. Exploring the role of biology in the determination of human behavior, Blum argues that both nature and nurture have to be taken into account if we are to understand gender differences. A Pulitzer Prize–winning professor of journalism at the University of Wisconsin at Madison, Blum is the author of several books, including *Sex on the Brain: The Biological Differences between Men and Women* (1997), *Ghost Hunters: William James and the Search for Scientific Proof of Life after Death* (2006), and *The Poisoner's Handbook: Murder and the Birth of Forensic Medicine in Jazz Age New York* (2010).

I was raised in one of those university-based, liberal elite families that politicians like to ridicule. In my childhood, every human being—regardless of gender—was exactly alike under the skin, and I mean exactly, barring his or her different opportunities. My parents wasted no opportunity to bring this point home. One Christmas, I received a Barbie doll and a softball glove. Another brought a green enamel stove, which baked tiny cakes by the heat of a lightbulb, and also a set of steel-tipped darts and competition-quality dartboard. Did I mention the year of the chemistry set and the ballerina doll?

It wasn't until I became a parent—I should say, a parent of two boys—that I realized I had been fed a line and swallowed it like a sucker (barring the part about opportunities, which I still believe). This dawned on me during my older son's dinosaur phase, which began when he was about two-and-a-half. Oh, he loved dinosaurs, all right, but only the blood-swilling carnivores. Plant-eaters were wimps and losers, and he refused to wear a T-shirt marred by a picture of a stegosaur. I looked down at him one day, as he was snarling around my feet and doing his toddler best to gnaw off my right leg, and I thought: This goes a lot deeper than culture.

Raising children tends to bring on this kind of politically incorrect reaction. Another friend came to the same conclusion watching a son determinedly bite his breakfast toast into the shape of a pistol he hoped would blow away — or at least terrify — his younger brother. Once you get past the guilt part — Did I do this? Should I have bought him that plastic allosaur with the oversized teeth? — such revelations can lead you to consider the far more interesting field of gender biology, where the questions take a different shape: Does love of carnage begin in culture or genetics, and which drives which? Do the gender roles of our culture reflect an underlying biology, and, in turn, does the way we behave influence that biology?

The point I'm leading up to — through the example of my son's innocent love of predatory dinosaurs — is actually one of the most straightforward in this debate. One of the reasons we're so fascinated by childhood behaviors is that, as the old saying goes, the child becomes the man (or woman, of course). Most girls don't spend their preschool years snarling around the house and pretending to chew off their companion's legs. And they — mostly — don't grow up to be as aggressive as men. Do the ways that we amplify those early differences in childhood shape the adults we become? Absolutely. But it's worth exploring the starting place — the faint signal that somehow gets amplified.

"There's plenty of room in society to influence sex differences," says 5 Marc Breedlove, a behavioral endocrinologist at the University of California at Berkeley and a pioneer in defining how hormones can help build sexually different nervous systems. "Yes, we're born with predispositions, but it's society that amplifies them, exaggerates them. I believe that — except for the sex differences in aggression. Those [differences] are too massive to be explained simply by society."

Aggression does allow a straightforward look at the issue. Consider the following statistics: Crime reports in both the United States and Europe record between ten and fifteen robberies committed by men for every one by a woman. At one point, people argued that this was explained by size difference. Women weren't big enough to intimidate, but that would change, they predicted, with the availability of compact weapons. But just as little girls don't routinely make weapons out of toast, women — even criminal ones — don't seem drawn to weaponry in the same way that men are. Almost twice as many male thieves and robbers use guns as their female counterparts do.

Or you can look at more personal crimes: domestic partner murders. Three-fourths of men use guns in those killings; 50 percent of women do. Here's more from the domestic front: In conflicts in which a woman killed a man, he tended to be the one who had started the fight — in 51.8 percent of the cases, to be exact. When the man was the killer, he again was the likely first aggressor, and by an even more dramatic margin. In fights in which women died, they had started the argument only 12.5 percent of the time.

Enough. You can parade endless similar statistics but the point is this: Males are more aggressive, not just among humans but among almost all species on earth. Male chimpanzees, for instance, declare war on neighboring troops, and one of their strategies is a warning strike: They kill females and infants to terrorize and intimidate. In terms of simple, reproductive genetics, it's an advantage of males to be aggressive: You can muscle your way into dominance, winning more sexual encounters, more offspring, more genetic future. For the female — especially in a species like ours, with time for just one successful pregnancy a year — what's the genetic advantage in brawling?

Thus the issue becomes not whether there is a biologically influenced sex difference in aggression — the answer being a solid, technical "You betcha" — but rather how rigid that difference is. The best science, in my opinion, tends to align with basic common sense. We all know that there are extraordinarily gentle men and murderous women. Sex differences are always generalizations: they refer to a behavior, with some evolutionary rationale behind it. They never define, entirely, an individual. And that fact alone should tell us that there's always — even in the most biologically dominated traits — some flexibility, an instinctive ability to respond, for better and worse, to the world around us.

This is true even with physical characteristics that we've often assumed are nailed down by genetics. Scientists now believe height, for instance, is only about 90 percent heritable. A person's genes might code for a six-foot-tall body, but malnutrition could literally cut that short. And there's also some evidence, in girls anyway, that children with stressful childhoods tend to become shorter adults. So while some factors are predetermined, there's evidence that the prototypical male/female body design can be readily altered. 10

It's a given that humans, like most other species — bananas, spiders, sharks, ducks, any rabbit you pull out of a hat — rely on two sexes for reproduction. So basic is that requirement that we have chromosomes whose primary purpose is to deliver the genes that order up a male or a female. All other chromosomes are numbered, but we label the sex chromosomes with the letters X and Y. We get one each from our mother and our father, and the basic combinations are these: XX makes female, XY makes male.

There are two important — and little known — points about these chromosomal matches. One is that even with this apparently precise system, there's nothing precise — or guaranteed — about the physical construction of male and female. The other point makes that possible. It appears that sex doesn't matter in the early stages of embryonic development. We are unisex at the point of conception.

If you examine an embryo at about six weeks, you see that it has the ability to develop in either direction. The fledgling embryo has two sets of ducts — Wolffian for male, Muellerian for female — an either/or structure, held in readiness for further development. If testosterone and other androgens are released by hormone-producing cells, then the Wolffian ducts develop into the channel that connects penis to testes, and the female ducts wither away.

Without testosterone, the embryo takes on a female form; the male ducts vanish and the Muellerian ducts expand into oviducts, uterus, and vagina. In other words, in humans, anyway (the opposite is true in birds), the female is the default sex. Back in the 1950s, the famed biologist Alfred Jost showed that if you castrate a male rabbit fetus, choking off testosterone, you produce a completely feminized rabbit.

We don't do these experiments in humans — for obvious reasons — but 15 there are naturally occurring instances that prove the same point. For instance: In the fetal testes are a group of cells, called Leydig cells, that make testosterone. In rare càses, the fetus doesn't make enough of these cells (a defect known as Leydig cell hypoplasia). In this circumstance we see the limited power of the XY chromosome. These boys have the right chromosomes and the right genes to be boys; they just don't grow a penis. Obstetricians and parents often think they see a baby girl, and these children are routinely raised as daughters. Usually, the "mistake" is caught about the time of puberty, when menstruation doesn't start. A doctor's examination shows the child to be internally male; there are usually small testes, often tucked within the abdomen. As the researchers put it, if the condition had been known from the beginning, "the sisters would have been born as brothers."

Just to emphasize how tricky all this body-building can get, there's a peculiar genetic defect that seems to be clustered by heredity in a small group of villages in the Dominican Republic. The result of the defect is a failure to produce an enzyme that concentrates testosterone, specifically for building the genitals. One obscure little enzyme only, but here's what happens without it: You get a boy with undescended testes and a penis so short and stubby that it resembles an oversized clitoris.

In the mountain villages of this Caribbean nation, people are used to it. The children are usually raised as "conditional" girls. At puberty, the secondary tide of androgens rises and is apparently enough to finish the construction project. The scrotum suddenly descends, the phallus grows, and the child develops a distinctly male body — narrow hips, muscular build, and even slight beard growth. At that point, the family shifts the child over from daughter to son. The dresses are thrown out. He begins to wear male clothes and starts dating girls. People in the Dominican Republic are so familiar with this condition that there's a colloquial name for it: *guevedoces*, meaning "eggs (or testes) at twelve."

It's the comfort level with this slip-slide of sexual identity that's so remarkable and, I imagine, so comforting to the children involved. I'm positive that the sexual transition of these children is less traumatic than the abrupt awareness of the "sisters who would have been brothers." There's a message of tolerance there, well worth repeating, and there are some other key lessons, too.

These defects are rare and don't alter the basic male-female division of our species. They do emphasize how fragile those divisions can be. Biology allows flexibility, room to change, to vary and grow. With that comes room for error as well. That it's possible to live with these genetic defects, that they don't merely kill us off, is a reminder that we, male and female alike, exist on a continuum of biological possibilities that can overlap and sustain either sex.

Marc Breedlove points out that the most difficult task may be separat- 20
ing how the brain responds to hormones from how the brain responds to the
results of hormones. Which brings us back, briefly, below the belt: In this context, the penis is just a result, the product of androgens at work before birth.
"And after birth," says Breedlove, "virtually everyone who interacts with that
individual will note that he has a penis, and will, in many instances, behave
differently than if the individual was a female."

Do the ways that we amplify physical and behavioral differences in childhood shape who we become as adults? Absolutely. But to understand that,
you have to understand the differences themselves—their beginning and the
very real biochemistry that may lie behind them.

Here is a good place to focus on testosterone—a hormone that is both
well-studied and generally underrated. First, however, I want to acknowledge
that there are many other hormones and neurotransmitters that appear to
influence behavior. Preliminary work shows that fetal boys are a little more
active than fetal girls. It's pretty difficult to argue socialization at that point.
There's a strong suspicion that testosterone may create the difference.

And there are a couple of relevant animal models to emphasize the point.
Back in the 1960s, Robert Goy, a psychologist at the University of Wisconsin at
Madison, first documented that young male monkeys play much more roughly
than young females. Goy went on to show that if you manipulate testosterone level—raising it in females, damping it down in males—you can reverse
those effects, creating sweet little male monkeys and rowdy young females.

Is testosterone the only factor at work here? I don't think so. But clearly
we can argue a strong influence, and, interestingly, studies have found that
girls with congenital adrenal hypoplasia—who run high in testosterone—

Shoppers gather at the opening of an American Girl doll store in Colorado.

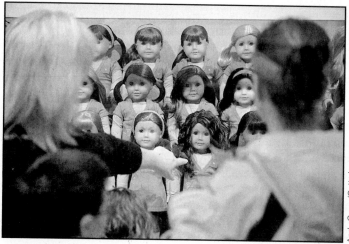

Andy Cross/Getty Images

tend to be far more fascinated by trucks and toy weaponry than most little girls are. They lean toward rough-and-tumble play, too. As it turns out, the strongest influence on this "abnormal" behavior is not parental disapproval, but the company of other little girls, who tone them down and direct them toward more routine girl games.

And that reinforces an early point: If there is indeed a biology to sex differ- 25 ences, we amplify it. At some point — when it is still up for debate — we gain a sense of our gender, and with it a sense of "gender-appropriate" behavior.

Some scientists argue for some evidence of gender awareness in infancy, perhaps by the age of twelve months. The consensus seems to be that full-blown "I'm a girl" or "I'm a boy" instincts arrive between the ages of two and three. Research shows that if a family operates in a very traditional, Beaver Cleaver kind of environment, filled with awareness of and association with "proper" gender behaviors, the "boys do trucks, girls do dolls" attitude seems to come very early. If a child grows up in a less traditional family, with an emphasis on partnership and sharing — "We all do the dishes, Joshua" — children maintain a more flexible sense of gender roles until about age six.

In this period, too, relationships between boys and girls tend to fall into remarkably strict lines. Interviews with children find that three-year-olds say that about half their friendships are with the opposite sex. By the age of five, that drops to 20 percent. By seven, almost no boys or girls have, or will admit to having, best friends of the opposite sex. They still hang out on the same playground, play on the same soccer teams. They may be friendly, but the real friendships tend to be boy-to-boy or girl-to-girl.

There's some interesting science that suggests that the space between boys and girls is a normal part of development; there are periods during which children may thrive and learn from hanging out with peers of the same sex. Do we, as parents, as a culture at large, reinforce such separations? Is the pope Catholic? One of my favorite studies looked at little boys who asked for toys. If they asked for a heavily armed action figure, they got the soldier about 70 percent of the time. If they asked for a "girl" toy, like a baby doll or a Barbie, their parents purchased it maybe 40 percent of the time. Name a child who won't figure out how to work *that* system.

How does all this fit together — toys and testosterone, biology and behavior, the development of the child into the adult, the way that men and women relate to one another?

Let me make a cautious statement about testosterone: It not only has 30 some body-building functions, it influences some behaviors as well. Let's make that a little less cautious: These behaviors include rowdy play, sex drive, competitiveness, and an in-your-face attitude. Males tend to have a higher baseline of testosterone than females — in our species, about seven to ten times as much — and therefore you would predict (correctly, I think) that all of those behaviors would be more generally found in men than in women.

But testosterone is also one of my favorite examples of how responsive biology is, how attuned it is to the way we live our lives. Testosterone, it turns out, rises in response to competition and threat. In the days of our ancestors, this might have been hand-to-hand combat or high-risk hunting endeavors. Today, scientists have measured testosterone rise in athletes preparing for a game, in chess players awaiting a match, in spectators following a soccer competition.

If a person — or even just a person's favored team — wins, testosterone continues to rise. It falls with a loss. (This also makes sense in an evolutionary perspective. If one was being clobbered with a club, it would be extremely unhelpful to have a hormone urging one to battle on.) Testosterone also rises in the competitive world of dating, settles down with a stable and supportive relationship, climbs again if the relationship starts to falter.

It's been known for years that men in high-stress professions — say, police work or corporate law — have higher testosterone levels than men in the ministry. It turns out that women in the same kind of strong-attitude professions have higher testosterone than women who choose to stay home. What I like about this is the chicken-or-egg aspect. If you argue that testosterone influenced the behavior of those women, which came first? Did they have high testosterone and choose the law? Or did they choose the law, and the competitive environment ratcheted them up on the androgen scale? Or could both be at work?

And, returning to children for a moment, there's an ongoing study by Pennsylvania researchers, tracking that question in adolescent girls, who are being encouraged by their parents to engage in competitive activities that were once for boys only. As they do so, the researchers are monitoring, regularly, two hormones: testosterone and cortisol, a stress hormone. Will these hormones rise in response to this new, more traditionally male environment? What if more girls choose the competitive path; more boys choose the other? Will female testosterone levels rise, male levels fall? Will that wonderful, unpredictable, flexible biology that we've been given allow a shift, so that one day, we will literally be far more alike?

We may not have answers to all those questions, but we can ask them, 35 and we can expect that the answers will come someday, because science clearly shows us that such possibilities exist. In this most important sense, sex differences offer us a paradox. It is only through exploring and understanding what makes us different that we can begin to understand what binds us together.

READING THE TEXT

1. What effect do Blum's opening personal anecdotes have on the persuasiveness of her argument?

2. What evidence does Blum offer to support her contention that males are naturally more aggressive than females?

3. How does testosterone affect human behavior, according to Blum?

4. In Blum's view, how do the cultural choices that humans make, such as engaging in sports or other competitive activities, affect hormone balances?

READING THE SIGNS

1. In your journal, reflect on the way your upbringing shaped your sense of appropriate gender behavior.

2. **CONNECTING TEXTS** Blum's selection challenges the common cultural studies position that gender behavior is socially constructed. Write an essay in which you defend, qualify, or reject Blum's point of view. To develop your ideas, consult Aaron Devor's "Gender Role Behaviors and Attitudes" (p. 504) and Kevin Jennings's "American Dreams" (p. 519).

3. Write an essay describing how you would raise a boy to counteract his stereotypical tendencies to aggressive behavior. Alternatively, describe how you would raise a girl to avoid the common stereotypes associated with females.

4. Visit the library, and investigate recent research on the possible genetic basis for homosexuality. Then write an essay in which you extend Blum's argument for the biological basis of gendered behavior to sexual orientation.

5. **CONNECTING TEXTS** Read or reread Lorraine Devon Wilke's "Snowden's a Hero, Obama's a Villain" (p. 485), focusing on her plea that we avoid black-and-white thinking. In an essay, analyze Blum's approach to argumentation: To what extent does her selection satisfy Wilke's notion of a balanced argument?

Gender Identity Online

Dan Habib/Concord Monitor/Corbis

READING THE SIGNS

1. In February 2014, Facebook made headlines when it expanded its number of gender categories to more than fifty, including "pangender," "gender fluid," and "transgender." This photo shows Facebook software engineer Brielle Harrison demonstrating the new options for gender identity, and the original caption for this photo indicated that she planned to switch her identifier to "Trans Woman." How does such a move by Facebook challenge traditional ideas of gender identity?

2. Visit your Facebook page and explore these gender identity labels yourself. Pick a few and research them. How do they differ from one another? Why do you think Facebook chose to add so many fine variations in gender identity for users to choose from?

KEVIN JENNINGS
American Dreams

When Ellen DeGeneres became the first television star to come out of the closet on prime-time TV, gay men and lesbians around the country celebrated what appeared to be a major step forward for one of America's most marginalized communities. But the firestorm of protest that also attended Ellen's coming-out equally demonstrated just how far homosexuals have to go before winning full acceptance into American society. In this personal narrative (first published in 1994) of what it means to grow up gay in America, Kevin Jennings reveals the torment endured by a child forced to conceal his difference from everyone around him, especially his own parents. With years of self-denial and one suicide attempt behind him, Jennings shows how he eventually came to accept himself as he is and in so doing achieved his own version of the American dream. Kevin Jennings is founder of the Gay, Lesbian, and Straight Education Network (GLSEN) and author (with Pat Shapiro) of *Always My Child: A Parent's Guide to Understanding Your Gay, Lesbian, Bisexual, Transgendered, or Questioning Son or Daughter* (2003). His most recent book is *Mama's Boy, Preacher's Son: A Memoir* (2007). He is the assistant deputy secretary for the Office of Safe and Drug-Free Schools at the U.S. Department of Education.

When I was little, I honestly thought I would grow up to be the president. After all, I lived in a land of opportunity where anyone, with enough determination and hard work, could aspire to the highest office in the land. I planned to live out the American Dream.

I realized, however, that something was amiss from an early age. I grew up in the rural community of Lewisville, North Carolina, just outside the city of Winston-Salem. As you might guess from the city's name, Winston-Salem, Winston-Salem makes its living from the tobacco industry: It was cigarettes that propelled local conglomerate RJR-Nabisco to its status as one of the world's largest multinational corporations. Somehow this rising tide of prosperity never lapped at our doors, and the Jennings family was a bitter family indeed. Poor whites descended from Confederate veterans, we eagerly sought out scapegoats for our inexplicable failure to "make it" in the land of opportunity. My uncles and cousins joined the Ku Klux Klan, while my father, a fundamentalist minister, used religion to excuse his prejudices — against blacks, against Jews, against Catholics, against Yankees, against Communists and liberals (basically the same thing, as far as he was concerned), and, of course, against gays. Somehow the golden rule of "Do unto others as you would have them do unto you" never made it into his gospel. Instead, I remember church services filled with outbursts of paranoia, as we were warned about the evils of those whom we (incorrectly) held responsible for our very real oppression. I grew up believing that there was a Communist plot undermining our nation, a Jewish conspiracy controlling the banks and the media, and that black men — whom I unself-consciously referred to as "niggers" — spent their days plotting to rape white women. In case this seems like a history lesson on the Stone Age, please consider that I was born in 1963 and graduated from high school in 1981. Hardly the ancient past!

My father's profession as a traveling minister never left much money for luxuries like college tuition. Nevertheless, my mother was determined that I, her last chance, was going to make good on the Dream that had been denied to her and to my four older siblings — that one of her children would be the first member of our extended family ever to go to college. Not that it was going to be easy: my father died when I was eight, and my mother went to work at McDonald's (the only job she could get with her limited credentials). Every penny was watched carefully; dinner was often leftover quarter-pounders that she didn't have to pay for. I'm the only person I know who sees the Golden Arches, takes a bite, and thinks, "Mmm, just like Mom used to make!"

Throughout high school, I was determined to make it, determined to show my mother — and myself — that the American Dream really could come true. I worked hard and got ahead, earning a scholarship to Harvard after I had remade myself into the image of what I was told a successful person was like. Little did I realize at that point the price I was paying to fit in.

The first thing to go was any sign of my Southern heritage. As I came into 5 contact with mainstream America, through high school "gifted and talented" programs and, later, at college in Massachusetts, I began to realize that we Southerners were different. Our home-cooked meals — grits, turnip greens, red-eye gravy — never seemed to show up in frozen dinners, and if a character

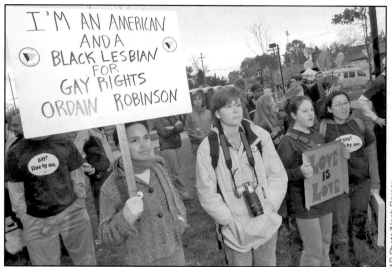

AP Photo/Noah Berger

LGBTQ protestors march in favor of ordaining and consecrating the Rev. Gene Robinson, the first openly gay Bishop in the Anglican church.

on television spoke with a Southern accent, that immediately identified him or her as stupid or as comic relief. As the lesbian writer Blanche Boyd put it:

> When television programs appeared, a dreadful truth came clear to me: Southerners were not normal people. We did not sound like normal people . . . [and] what we chose to talk about seemed peculiarly different also. I began to realize we were hicks. Television took away my faith in my surroundings. I didn't want to be a hick. I decided to go North, where people talked fast, walked fast, and acted cool. I practiced talking like the people on television. . . . I became desperate to leave the South.

Like Blanche Boyd, I deliberately erased my accent and aped the false monotone of television newscasters. I never invited college friends home to North Carolina for fear they might meet my family and realize they were worthless, ignorant hicks — which is how I'd come to view those whom I loved. I applied to colleges on the sole criterion that they not be in the South. I ran as far from Lewisville, North Carolina, as I could.

But there were some things about myself I could not escape from or change, no matter how hard I tried — among them the fact that I am gay.

I had always known I was gay, even before I had heard the word or knew what it meant. I remember that at age six or seven, the "adult" magazines that so fascinated my older brothers simply didn't interest me at all, and I somehow knew that I'd better hide this feeling from them. As I grew older and began to understand what my feelings meant, I recoiled in horror from myself. After all, my religious upbringing as a Southern Baptist had taught me that gay people were twisted perverts destined for a lifetime of eternal damnation.

Being as set as I was on achieving the American Dream, I was not about to accept the fact that I was gay. Here is where I paid the heaviest price for my Dream. I pursued what I thought was "normal" with a vengeance in high school, determined that, if the spirit was weak, the flesh would be more willing at the prospect of heterosexuality. I dated every girl I could literally get my hands on, earning a well-deserved reputation as a jerk who tried to see how far he could get on the first date. I attacked anyone who suggested that gay people might be entitled to some rights, too, and was the biggest teller of fag jokes at Radford High. But what I really hated was myself, and this I couldn't escape from, no matter how drunk or stoned I got, which I was doing on an almost daily basis by senior year.

That was also the year I fell in love for the first time, with another boy in my class. It turned out he was gay, too, and we made love one night in late May. I woke up the next morning and realized that it was true — I really was a fag after all. I spent that day trying to figure out how I was going to live the American Dream, which seemed impossible if I was homosexual. By nightfall I decided it *was* impossible, and without my Dream I couldn't see a reason why I'd want to be alive at all. I went to my family's medicine cabinet, took the new bottle of aspirin out, and proceeded to wash down 140 pills with a glass of gin. I remember the exact number — 140 — because I figured I could only get down about ten at one swallow, so I carefully counted out fourteen little stacks before I began. Thanks to a friend who got to me in time, I didn't die that night. My story has a happy ending — but a lot of them don't. Those moments of desperation helped me understand why one out of every three gay teens tries to commit suicide.

At Harvard, the most important lessons I learned had little to do with Latin American or European history, which were my majors. Instead, I learned the importance of taking control of my own destiny. I met a great professor who taught me that as long as I stayed in the closet, I was accepting the idea that there was something wrong with me, something that I needed to hide. After all, as my favorite bisexual, Eleanor Roosevelt, once said, "No one can make you feel inferior without your consent." By staying closeted, I was consenting to my own inferiority. I realized that for years, I had let a Dream — a beautiful, seductive, but ultimately false Dream — rule my life. I had agreed to pay its price, which was the rejection of my family, my culture, and eventually myself. I came to understand that the costs of the Dream far outweighed its rewards. I learned that true freedom would be mine only when I was able to make my own decisions about what I wanted out of life instead of accepting those thrust upon me by the Dream. Since I made that realization, I have followed my own path instead of the one I had been taught was "right" all my life.

Once I started down this new path, I began to make some discoveries about the society in which I was raised, and about its notions of right and wrong. I began to ask many questions, and the answers to these questions were not always pleasant. Why, for example, did my mother always earn less than men who did the same exact work? Why did I learn as a child that to cheat someone was to "Jew" them? Why was my brother ostracized when he

10

fell in love with and later married a black woman? Why did everyone in my family work so hard and yet have so little? I realized that these inequalities were part of the game, the rules of which were such that gays, blacks, poor people, women, and many others would always lose to the wealthy white heterosexual Christian men who have won the Presidency forty-two out of forty-two times. Those odds — 100 percent — are pretty good ones to bet on. No, I discovered that true freedom could not be achieved by a Dream that calls on us to give up who we are in order to fit in and become "worthy" of power. Holding power means little if women have to become masculine "iron ladies" to get it, if Jews have to "Americanize" their names, if blacks have to learn to speak so-called Standard English (though we never acknowledge *whose* standard it is), or if gays and lesbians have to hide what everyone else gets to celebrate — the loves of their lives.

Real freedom will be ours when the people around us — and when we ourselves — accept that we, too, are "real" Americans, and that we shouldn't have to change to meet anyone else's standards. In 1924, at age twenty-two, the gay African American poet Langston Hughes said it best, in his poem "I, Too":

> Tomorrow,
> I'll be at the table
> When company comes.
> Nobody'll dare
> Say to me,
> "Eat in the kitchen,"
> Then.
> Besides,
> They'll see how beautiful I am
> And be ashamed —
> I, too, am America.

By coming out as a gay man and demanding my freedom, I realize that I have done the most American thing of all. And while I have come a long way since the days when I dreamed of living in the White House, I have discovered that what I'm fighting for now is the very thing I thought I'd be fighting for if I ever became President — "liberty and justice for all."

READING THE TEXT

1. According to Jennings, how did his Southern upbringing influence his goals for the future?

2. Why did Jennings feel he had to eschew his Southern heritage?

3. In what ways did Jennings deny to himself his sexual orientation, and why did he do so?

4. In your own words, trace the evolution of Jennings's understanding of the American dream as he grew up.

5. What is the relationship between the excerpt from Langston Hughes's "I, Too" and Jennings's story?

READING THE SIGNS

1. In your journal, write your own account of how you responded to normative gender codes as a high school student. To what extent did you feel pressure to conform to or to renounce traditional expectations — or to do both?

2. Jennings describes his early attempts to deny his sexual orientation. In class, discuss how other minority or underprivileged groups — ethnic minorities, women, the disabled — sometimes try to erase their identities. What social and cultural forces motivate such self-denial? Use the discussion as a springboard for an essay in which you explore why one might be motivated to do so.

3. In class, brainstorm two lists: films or TV shows that reinforce heterosexuality as normative and those that present homosexuality positively. Then compare your lists. What conclusions do you draw about popular culture's influence on American gender codes?

4. In his conclusion, Jennings states his desideratum: "Real freedom will be ours when the people around us — and when we ourselves — accept that we, too, are 'real' Americans, and that we shouldn't have to change to meet anyone else's standards" (para. 12). Research the current status of efforts to legalize same-sex marriage, and write an essay in which you make an argument about the extent to which Jennings's goal has been realized.

MARIAH BURTON NELSON
I Won. I'm Sorry.

Athletic competition, when you come right down to it, is about winning, which is no problem for men, whose gender codes tell them that aggression and domination are admirable male traits. But "how can you win, if you're female?" Mariah Burton Nelson asks, when the same gender codes insist that women must be feminine, "not aggressive, not victorious." And so women athletes, even when they do win, go out of their way to signal their femininity by dolling themselves up and smiling a lot. Beauty and vulnerability seem to be as important to today's female athlete as brawn and gold medals, Nelson complains, paradoxically contradicting the apparent feminist gains that women athletes have made in recent years. A former Stanford University and professional basketball player, Mariah Burton Nelson is the author of six books, including *We Are All Athletes* (2002) and *Making Money on the Sidelines* (2008). She is vice president for innovation and planning at ASAE: the Center for Association Leadership. This piece originally appeared in *Self* magazine.

When Sylvia Plath's husband, Ted Hughes, published his first book of poems, Sylvia wrote to her mother: "I am so happy that HIS book is accepted FIRST. It will make it so much easier for me when mine is accepted. . . ."

After Sylvia killed herself, her mother published a collection of Sylvia's letters. In her explanatory notes, Aurelia Plath commented that from the time she was very young, Sylvia "catered to the male of any age so as to bolster his sense of superiority." In seventh grade, Aurelia Plath noted, Sylvia was pleased to finish second in a spelling contest. "It was nicer, she felt, to have a boy first."

How many women still collude in the myth of male superiority, believing it's "nicer" when boys and men finish first? How many of us achieve but only in a lesser, smaller, feminine way, a manner consciously or unconsciously designed to be as nonthreatening as possible?

Since I'm tall, women often talk to me about height. Short women tell me, "I've always wanted to be tall — but not as tall as you!" I find this amusing, but also curious. Why not? Why not be six-two?

Tall women tell me that they won't wear heels because they don't want   5 to appear taller than their husbands or boyfriends, even by an inch. What are these women telling me — and their male companions? Why do women regulate their height in relation to men's height? Why is it still rare to see a woman who is taller than her husband?

Women want to be tall enough to feel elegant and attractive, like models. They want to feel respected and looked up to. But they don't want to be so tall that their height threatens men. They want to win — to achieve, to reach new heights — but without exceeding male heights.

How can you win, if you're female? Can you just do it? No. You have to play the femininity game. Femininity by definition is not large, not imposing, not competitive. Feminine women are not ruthless, not aggressive, not victorious. It's not feminine to have a killer instinct, to want with all your heart and soul to win — neither tennis matches nor elected office nor feminist victories such as abortion rights. It's not feminine to know exactly what you want, then go for it.

Femininity is about appearing beautiful and vulnerable and small. It's about winning male approval.

One downhill skier who asked not to be identified told me the following story: "I love male approval. Most women skiers do. We talk about it often. There's only one thing more satisfying than one of the top male skiers saying, 'Wow, you are a great skier. You rip. You're awesome.'

"But it's so fun leaving 99 percent of the world's guys in the dust — oops,"   10 she laughs. "I try not to gloat. I've learned something: If I kick guys' butts and lord it over them, they don't like me. If, however, I kick guys' butts then act 'like a girl,' there is no problem. And I do mean girl, not woman. Nonthreatening."

Femininity is also about accommodating men, allowing them to feel bigger than and stronger than and superior to women, not emasculated by them.

Femininity is unhealthy, obviously. It would be unhealthy for men to act passive, dainty, obsessed with their physical appearance, and dedicated to bolstering the sense of superiority in the other gender, so it's unhealthy for women too. These days, some women are redefining femininity as strong, as athletic, as however a female happens to be, so that "feminine" becomes synonymous with "female." Other women reject both feminine and masculine terms and stereotypes, selecting from the entire range of human behaviors instead of limiting themselves to the "gender-appropriate" ones. These women smile only when they're happy, act angry when they're angry, dress how they want to. They cling to their self-respect and dignity like a life raft.

But most female winners play the femininity game to some extent, using femininity as a defense, a shield against accusations such as bitch, man-hater, lesbian. Feminine behavior and attire mitigate against the affront of female victory, soften the hard edges of winning. Women who want to win without losing male approval temper their victories with beauty, with softness, with smallness, with smiles.

Serena Williams at Wimbledon.

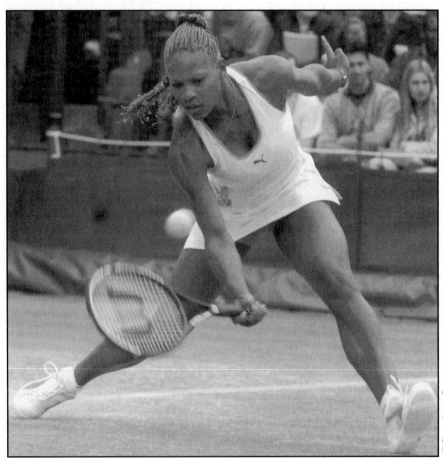

AP Photo/Noah Berger

In the fifties, at each of the Amateur Athletic Union's women's basketball championships, one of the players was crowned a beauty queen. (This still happens at Russian women's ice hockey tournaments.) Athletes in the All-American Girls Baseball League of the forties and fifties slid into base wearing skirts. In 1979, professional basketball players with the California Dreams were sent to John Robert Powers' charm school. Ed Temple, the legendary coach of the Tennessee State Tigerbelles, the team that produced Wilma Rudolph, Wyomia Tyus, Willye White, Madeline Manning, and countless other champions, enforced a dress code and stressed that his athletes should be "young ladies first, track girls second."

Makeup, jewelry, dress, and demeanor were often dictated by the male   15
coaches and owners in these leagues, but to some extent the players played along, understanding the trade-off: in order to be "allowed" to compete, they had to demonstrate that they were, despite their "masculine" strivings, real ("feminine") women.

Today, both men and women wear earrings, notes Felshin, "but the media is still selling heterosexism and 'feminine' beauty. And if you listen carefully, in almost every interview" female athletes still express apologetic behavior through feminine dress, behavior, and values.

Florence Griffith-Joyner, Gail Devers, and other track stars of this modern era dedicate considerable attention to portraying a feminine appearance. Basketball star Lisa Leslie has received more attention for being a model than for leading the Americans to Olympic victory. Steffi Graf posed in bikinis for the 1997 *Sports Illustrated* swimsuit issue. In a Sears commercial, Olympic basketball players apply lipstick, paint their toenails, rock babies, lounge in bed, and pose and dance in their underwear. Lisa Leslie says, "Everybody's allowed to be themselves. Me, for example, I'm very feminine."

In an Avon commercial, Jackie Joyner Kersee is shown running on a beach while the camera lingers on her buttocks and breasts. She tells us that she can bench-press 150 pounds and brags that she can jump farther than "all but 128 men." Then she says: "And I have red toenails." Words flash on the screen: "Just another Avon lady." Graf, Mary Pierce, Monica Seles, and Mary Jo Fernandez have all played in dresses. They are "so much more comfortable" than skirts, Fernandez explained. "You don't have to worry about the shirt coming up or the skirt being too tight. It's cooler, and it's so feminine."

"When I put on a dress I feel different — more feminine, more elegant, more ladylike — and that's nice," added Australia's Nicole Bradtke: "We're in a sport where we're throwing ourselves around, so it's a real asset to the game to be able to look pretty at the same time."

Athletes have become gorgeous, flirtatious, elegant, angelic, darling — and   20
the skating commentators' favorite term: "vulnerable." Some think this is good news: proof that femininity and sports are compatible. "There doesn't have to be such a complete division between 'You're beautiful and sexy' and 'you're athletic and strong,'" says Linda Hanley, a pro beach volleyball player who also appeared in a bikini in the 1997 *Sports Illustrated* swimsuit issue.

Athletes and advertisers reassure viewers that women who compete are still willing to play the femininity game, to be cheerleaders. Don't worry about us, the commercials imply. We're winners but we'll still look pretty for you. We're acting in ways that only men used to act but we'll still act how you want women to act. We're not threatening. We're not lesbians. We're not ugly, not bad marriage material. We're strong but feminine. Linguists note that the word "but" negates the part of the sentence that precedes it.

There are some recent examples of the media emphasizing female power in an unambiguous way. "Women Muscle In," the *New York Times Magazine* proclaimed in a headline. The *Washington Post* wrote, "At Olympics, Women Show Their Strength." And a new genre of commercials protests that female athletes are NOT cheerleaders, and don't have to be. Olympic and pro basketball star Dawn Staley says in a Nike commercial that she plays basketball "for the competitiveness" of it. "I need some place to release it. It just builds up, and sports is a great outlet for it. I started out playing with the guys. I wasn't always accepted. You get criticized, like: 'You need to be in the kitchen. Go put on a skirt.' I just got mad and angry and went out to show them that I belong here as much as they do."

Other commercials tell us that women can compete like conquerors. A Nike ad called "Wolves" shows girls leaping and spiking volleyballs while a voice says, "They are not sisters. They are not classmates. They are not friends. They are not even the girls' team. They are a pack of wolves. Tend to your sheep." Though the athletes look serious, the message sounds absurd. When I show this commercial to audiences, they laugh. Still, the images do depict the power of the volleyball players: their intensity, their ability to pound the ball almost through the floor. The script gives the players (and viewers) permission not to be ladylike, not to worry about whether their toenails are red.

But in an American Basketball League commercial, the Philadelphia Rage's female basketball players are playing rough; their bodies collide. Maurice Chevalier sings, "Thank heaven for little girls." The tag line: "Thank heaven, they're on our side."

Doesn't all this talk about girls and ladies simply focus our attention on 25 femaleness, femininity, and ladylike behavior? The lady issue is always there in the equation: something to redefine, to rebel against. It's always present, like sneakers, so every time you hear the word *athlete* you also hear the word *lady* — or feminine, or unfeminine. It reminds me of a beer magazine ad from the eighties that featured a photo of Olympic track star Valerie Brisco-Hooks. "Funny, she doesn't look like the weaker sex," said the print. You could see her impressive muscles. Clearly the intent of the ad was to contrast an old stereotype with the reality of female strength and ability. But Brisco-Hooks was seated, her legs twisted pretzel style, arms covering her chest. But in that position, Brisco-Hooks didn't look very strong or able. In the line, "Funny, she doesn't look like the weaker sex," the most eye-catching words are funny, look, weaker, and sex. Looking at the pretzel that is Valerie, you begin to think that she looks funny. You think about weakness. And you think about sex.

When she was young, Nancy Kerrigan wanted to play ice hockey with her older brothers. Her mother told her, "You're a girl. Do girl things."

Figure skating is a girl thing. Athletes in sequins and "sheer illusion sleeves" glide and dance, their tiny skirts flapping in the breeze. They achieve, but without touching or pushing anyone else. They win, but without visible signs of sweat. They compete, but not directly. Their success is measured not by confrontation with an opponent, nor even by a clock or a scoreboard. Rather, they are judged as beauty contestants are judged: by a panel of people who interpret the success of the routines. Prettiness is mandatory. Petite and groomed and gracious, figure skaters — like cheerleaders, gymnasts, and aerobic dancers — camouflage their competitiveness with niceness and prettiness until it no longer seems male or aggressive or unseemly.

The most popular sport for high school and college women is basketball. More than a million fans shelled out an average of $15 per ticket in 1997, the inaugural summer of the Women's National Basketball Association. But the most televised women's sport is figure skating. In 1995 revenue from skating shows and competitions topped six hundred million dollars. In the seven months between October 1996 and March 1997, ABC, CBS, NBC, Fox, ESPN, TBS, and USA dedicated 162.5 hours of programming to figure skating, half of it in prime time. Kerrigan earns up to three hundred thousand dollars for a single performance.

Nearly 75 percent of the viewers of televised skating are women. The average age is between twenty-five and forty-five years old, with a household income of more than fifty thousand dollars. What are these women watching? What are they seeing? What's the appeal?

Like golf, tennis, and gymnastics, figure skating is an individual sport favored by white people from the upper classes. The skaters wear cosmetics, frozen smiles, and revealing dresses. Behind the scenes they lift weights and sweat like any serious athlete, but figure skating seems more dance than sport, more grace than guts, more art than athleticism. Figure skating allows women to compete like champions while dressed like cheerleaders.

In women's figure skating, smiling is part of "artistic expression." In the final round, if the competitors are of equal merit, artistry weighs more heavily than technique. Midori Ito, the best jumper in the history of women's skating, explained a weak showing at the 1995 world championships this way: "I wasn't 100 percent satisfied. . . . I probably wasn't smiling enough."

The media portray female figure skaters as "little girl dancers" or "fairy tale princesses" (NBC commentator John Tesh); as "elegant" (Dick Button); as "little angels" (Peggy Fleming); as "ice beauties" and "ladies who lutz" (*People* magazine). Commentators frame skaters as small, young, and decorative creatures, not superwomen but fairy-tale figments of someone's imagination.

After Kerrigan was assaulted by a member of Tonya Harding's entourage, she was featured on a *Sports Illustrated* cover crying "Why me?" When she recovered to win a silver medal at the Olympics that year, she became "America's sweetheart" and rich to boot. But the princess turned pumpkin shortly after midnight, as soon as the ball was over and she stopped smiling and started speaking. Growing impatient during the Olympic medal ceremony while everyone waited for Baiul, Kerrigan grumbled, "Oh, give me a break, she's just going to cry out there again. What's the difference?"

What were Kerrigan's crimes? She felt too old to cavort with cartoon characters. Isn't she? She expressed anger and disappointment — even bitterness and bad sportsmanship — about losing the gold. But wasn't she supposed to want to win? What happens to baseball players who, disappointed about a loss, hit each other or spit on umpires? What happens to basketball players and football players and hockey players who fight? Men can't tumble from a princess palace because we don't expect them to be princesses in the first place, only athletes.

Americans fell out of love with Kerrigan not because they couldn't adore 35 an athlete who lacked grace in defeat, but because they couldn't adore a female athlete who lacked grace in defeat.

Female politicians, lawyers, and businesswomen of all ethnic groups also play the femininity game. Like tennis players in short dresses, working women seem to believe it's an asset to look pretty (but not too pretty) while throwing themselves around. The female apologetic is alive and well in corporate boardrooms, where women say "I'm sorry, maybe someone else already stated this idea, but . . ." and smile while they say it.

When Newt Gingrich's mother revealed on television that Newt had referred to Hillary Clinton as a bitch, how did Hillary respond? She donned a pink suit and met with female reporters to ask how she could "soften her image." She seemed to think that her competitiveness was the problem and femininity the solution.

So if you want to be a winner and you're female, you'll feel pressured to play by special, female rules. Like men, you'll have to be smart and industrious, but in addition you'll have to be "like women": kind, nurturing, accommodating, nonthreatening, placating, pretty, and small. You'll have to smile. And not act angry. And wear skirts. Nail polish and makeup help, too.

READING THE TEXT

1. Summarize in your own words the contradictory messages about appropriate gender behavior that women athletes must contend with, according to Nelson.

2. Nelson begins her article with an anecdote about poet Sylvia Plath. How does this opening frame her argument about women in sports?

3. What is the "femininity game" (para. 7), in Nelson's view, and how do the media perpetuate it?

4. What sports are coded as "feminine," according to Nelson, and why?

READING THE SIGNS

1. Watch a women's sports event on television, such as an LPGA match, analyzing the behavior and appearance of the athletes. Use your observations as

evidence in an essay in which you assess the validity of Nelson's claims about the contradictory gender role behaviors of female athletes.

2. If you are a female athlete, write a journal entry exploring whether you feel pressure to act feminine and your responses to that pressure. If you are not a female athlete, reflect on the behavior and appearance of women athletes on your campus. Do you see signs that they are affected by the femininity game?

3. Obtain a copy of a magazine that focuses on women's sports, such as *Sports Illustrated Women*, or visit an online magazine such as sportsister.com or womensportreport.com. Analyze the articles and the ads in the magazine, noting models' and athletes' clothing, physical appearance, and speech patterns. Using Nelson's argument as a critical framework, write an essay in which you analyze whether the magazine perpetuates traditional gender roles or presents sports as an avenue for female empowerment.

4. Interview women athletes on your campus, and ask them whether they feel pressured by the femininity game. Have they been accused of being lesbians or bitches simply because they are athletes? Do they feel pressure to be physically attractive or charming? Do you see any correlation between an athlete's sport and her responses? Use your observations as the basis of an argument about the influence of traditional gender roles on women athletes at your school.

ALFRED LUBRANO

The Shock of Education: How College Corrupts

One of America's most fundamental contradictions lies at the heart of the American dream itself. That is, America's promise of social mobility compels those who begin at the bottom to leave behind their origins in order to succeed, which entails giving up a part of oneself and leaving one's home behind. It can be a wrenching transition, and in this reflection on what it means to achieve the dream, Alfred Lubrano describes the strain of moving between two worlds, relating both his own experiences moving from working-class Brooklyn to an Ivy League school and those of other working-class "straddlers" who moved into the middle class. The son of a bricklayer, Lubrano is a journalist and National Public Radio commentator. He is the author of *Limbo: Blue-Collar Roots, White-Collar Dreams* (2004), from which this selection is taken.

College is where the Great Change begins. People start to question the blue-collar take on the world. Status dissonance, the sociologists call it. Questions arise: Are the guys accurate in saying people from such-and-such a race are really so bad?

Was Mom right when she said nice girls don't put out? Suddenly, college opens up a world of ideas—a life of the mind—abstract and intangible. The core blue-collar values and goals—loyalty to family and friends, making money, marrying, and procreating—are supplanted by stuff you never talked about at home: personal fulfillment, societal obligation, the pursuit of knowledge for knowledge's sake, and on and on. One world opens and widens; another shrinks.

There's an excitement and a sadness to that. The child, say Sennett and Cobb, is deserting his past, betraying the parents he is rising above, an unavoidable result when you're trying to accomplish more with your life than merely earning a paycheck.[1] So much will change between parent and child, and between peers, in the college years. "Every bit of learning takes you further from your parents," says Southwest Texas State University history professor Gregg Andrews, himself a Straddler. "I say this to all my freshmen to start preparing them." The best predictor of whether you're going to have problems with your family is the distance between your education and your parents', Jake Ryan says. You may soon find yourself with nothing to talk to your folks or friends about.

This is the dark part of the American story, the kind of thing we work to hide. Mobility means discomfort, because so much has to change; one can't allow for the satisfactions of stasis: You prick yourself and move, digging spurs into your own hide to get going, forcing yourself to forget the comforts of the barn. In this country, we speak grandly of this metamorphosis, never stopping to consider that for many class travelers with passports stamped for new territory, the trip is nothing less than a bridge burning.

Fighting Self-Doubt

When Columbia plucked me out of working-class Brooklyn, I was sure they had made a mistake, and I remained convinced of that throughout most of my time there. My high school was a gigantic (4,500 students) factory; we literally had gridlock in the halls between classes, kids belly to back between history and English class. A teacher once told me that if every one of the reliable corps of truant students actually decided to show up to class one day, the school could not hold us all. (We were unofficially nicknamed "the Italian Army." When our football guys played nearby New Utrecht, which boasted an equivalent ethnic demographic, kids dubbed the game the "Lasagna Bowl.") Lafayette High School roiled with restless boys and girls on their way to jobs in their parents' unions or to secretaries' desks. How could you move from that to an elite college?

At night, at home, the difference in the Columbia experiences my father and I were having was becoming more evident. The family still came together

[1] Richard Sennett and Jonathan Cobb, *The Hidden Injuries of Class* (New York: Alfred A. Knopf, 1972), 131.

for dinner, despite our disparate days. We talked about general stuff, and I learned to self-censor. I'd seen how ideas could be upsetting, especially when wielded by a smarmy freshman who barely knew what he was talking about. No one wanted to hear how the world worked from some kid who was first learning to use his brain; it was as unsettling as riding in a car with a new driver. When he taught a course on Marx, Sackrey said he used to tell his students just before Thanksgiving break not to talk about "this stuff at the dinner table" or they'd mess up the holiday. Me mimicking my professors' thoughts on race, on people's struggle for equality, or on politics didn't add to the conviviality of the one nice hour in our day. So I learned to shut up.

After dinner, my father would flip on the TV in the living room. My mom would grab a book and join him. And I'd go looking for a quiet spot to study. In his autobiography, *Hunger of Memory: The Education of Richard Rodriguez*, the brilliant Mexican-American Straddler, writer, and PBS commentator invokes British social scientist Richard Hoggart's "scholarship boys," finding pieces of himself in them. Working-class kids trying to advance in life, the scholarship boys learned to withdraw from the warm noise of the gathered family to isolate themselves with their books.[2] (Read primarily as a memoir of ethnicity and — most famously — an anti–affirmative action tract, the book is more genuinely a dissertation on class. At a sidewalk café in San Francisco, Rodriguez himself tells me how often his book is miscatalogued.) Up from the immigrant working class, Rodriguez says in our interview, the scholarship boy finds himself moving between two antithetical places: home and school. With the family, there is intimacy and emotion. At school, one learns to live with "lonely reason." Home life is in the now, Rodriguez says; school life exists on an altogether different plane, calm and reflective, with an eye toward the future.

The scholarship boy must learn to distance himself from the family circle in order to succeed academically, Rodriguez tells me. By doing this, he slowly loses his family. There's a brutality to education, he says, a rough and terrible disconnect. Rodriguez says he despised his parents' "shabbiness," their inability to speak English. "I hated that they didn't know what I was learning," he says. He thought of D. H. Lawrence's *Sons and Lovers*, and of Paul Morel, the coal miner's son. Lawrence is a model for Rodriguez, in a way. Rodriguez remembers the scene in which the son watches his father pick up his schoolbooks, his rough hands fingering the volumes that are the instruments separating the two men. Books were establishing a disharmony between the classroom and Rodriguez's house. Preoccupation with language and reading is an effeminacy not easily understood by workers. "It sears your soul to finally decide to talk like your teacher and not your father," Rodriguez says. "I'm not talking about anything less than the grammar of the heart."

[2]Richard Rodriguez, *Hunger of Memory: The Education of Richard Rodriguez* (New York: Bantam Books, 1983), 46. Rodriguez himself quotes from Richard Hoggart, *The Uses of Literacy* (London: Chatto and Windus, 1957), chap. 10.

Myself, I studied in the kitchen near the dishwasher because its white noise drowned out the television. As long as the wash cycle ran, I could not hear Mr. T and the A-Team win the day. I did not begrudge my father his one indulgence; there wasn't much else that could relax him. He was not a drinker. TV drained away the tumult and hazard of his Columbia day [he was a bricklayer]. My own room was too close to the living room. My brother's small room was too crowded for both of us to study in. You never went in your parents' bedroom without them in it, inviting you. When the dishes were clean and the kitchen again too quiet to beat back the living room noise, I'd go downstairs to my grandparents' apartment. If they were both watching the same TV show on the first floor, then the basement was free. Here was profound and almost disquieting silence. I could hear the house's systems rumble and shake: water whooshing through pipes, the oil burner powering on and off, and the refrigerator humming with a loud efficiency. Down in the immaculate redwood-paneled kitchen/living room, which sometimes still smelled of the sausages and peppers my grandfather may have made that night (my grandparents cooked and ate in their basement, something that never seemed unusual to us), I was ninety minutes from my school and two floors below my family in a new place, underscoring my distance from anything known, heightening my sense of isolation — my limbo status. I read Homer, Shakespeare, and Molière down there. I wrote a paper on landscape imagery in Dante's *Inferno*. In my self-pitying, melodramatic teenager's mind, I thought I had been banished to a new, lonely rung of hell that Dante hadn't contemplated.

By 11 p.m., I'd go back upstairs. My mother would be in bed, my father asleep on his chair. I'd turn off the TV, which awakened my dad. He'd walk off to bed, and I'd study for a couple more hours. His alarm would go off before 5 a.m., and he'd already be at Columbia by the time I woke up at 6:30. That's how our Ivy League days ended and began. When my father was done with Columbia, he moved on to another job site. When I was done with Columbia, I was someone else. I'd say I got the better deal. But then, my father would tell you, that was always the plan. . . .

Macbeth and Other Foolishness

Middle-class kids are groomed for another life. They understand, says Patrick Finn, why reading *Macbeth* in high school could be important years down the road. Working-class kids see no such connection, understand no future life for which digesting Shakespeare might be of value. Very much in the now, working-class people are concerned with immediate needs. And bookish kids are seen as weak.

Various education studies have shown that schools help reinforce class. 10 Teachers treat the working class and the well-to-do differently, this work demonstrates, with the blue-collar kids getting less attention and respect. It's no secret, education experts insist, that schools in poorer areas tend to employ teachers who are less well-trained. In these schools, the curriculum is test-based and uncreative. Children are taught, essentially, to obey and fill in blanks. By fourth grade, many of the children are bored and alienated; nothing in school connects to their culture. Beyond that, many working-class children are resistant to schooling and uncooperative with teachers, experts say. They feel pressure from other working-class friends to not participate and are told that being educated is effeminate and irrelevant. Educators have long understood that minority children have these problems, says Finn. But they rarely understand or see that working-class white kids have similar difficulties. "So we're missing a whole bunch of people getting screwed by the education systems," he says.

In our conversations, Finn explains that language is a key to class. In a working-class home where conformity is the norm, all opinions are dictated by group consensus, by what the class says is so. There's one way to do everything, there's one way to look at the world. Since all opinions are shared, there's never a need to explain thought and behavior. You talk less. Language in such a home, Finn says, is implicit.

Things are different in a middle-class home. There, parents are more willing to take the time to explain to little Janey why it's not such a good idea to pour chocolate sauce on the dog. If Janey challenges a rule of the house, she's spoken to like an adult, or at least not like a plebe at some military school. (Working-class homes are, in fact, very much like the military, with parents barking orders, Straddlers tell me. It's that conformity thing again.) There is a variety of opinions in middle-class homes, which are more collaborative than conformist, Finn says. Middle-class people have a multiviewed take on the world. In such a home, where one needs to express numerous ideas and opinions, language is by necessity explicit.

When it's time to go to school, the trouble starts. The language of school—of the teachers and the books—is explicit. A child from a working-class home is at a huge disadvantage, Finn says, because he's used to a narrower world of expression and a smaller vocabulary of thought. It's little wonder that kids from working-class homes have lower reading scores and do less well on SATs than middle-class kids, Finn says.

In high school, my parents got me a tutor for the math part of the SATs, to bolster a lackluster PSAT score. That sort of thing happens all the time in middle-class neighborhoods. But we were setting precedent among our kind. Most kids I knew from the community were not taking the SATs, let alone worrying about their scores. If you're from the middle class, you do not feel out of place preparing for college. Parents and peers help groom you, encourage you, and delight in your progress. Of course, when you get to freshman year, the adjustments can be hard on anyone, middle-class and working-class kids alike. But imagine going through freshman orientation if your parents are ambivalent—or hostile—about your being there, and your friends aren't clear about what you're doing.

It was like that for my friend Rita Giordano, forty-five, also a journal- 15
ist, also from Brooklyn. Her world, like mine, was populated by people who
thought going from 60th to 65th Streets was a long journey. So when Rita
took sojourns into Greenwich Village by herself on Saturday mornings as a
teenager, she made sure not to tell any of her friends. It was too oddball to
have to explain. And she'd always come back in time to go shopping with
everyone. She couldn't figure out why she responded to the artsy vibe of the
Village; she was just aware that there were things going on beyond the neighborhood. When it came time for college, she picked Syracuse University
because it was far away, a new world to explore. That bothered her friends,
and she'd have to explain herself to them on trips back home. "What do you
do up there?" they asked her. "Don't you get homesick?" Suddenly, things
felt awkward among childhood friends who had always been able to talk. "It
was confusing to come home and see people thinking that you're not doing
what they're doing, which meant you're rejecting them," said Rita, a diminu-
tive, sensitive woman with large, brown eyes. "'Don't they see it's still me?' I
wondered. I started feeling like, how do I coexist in these two worlds, college
and home? I mean, I could talk to my girlfriends about what color gowns their
bridesmaids would wear at their fantasy weddings. But things like ambition
and existential questions about where you fit in the world and how you make
your mark—we just didn't go there."

And to make matters more complicated, there was a guy. Rita's decision
to go to Syracuse didn't sit well with the boyfriend who was probably always
going to remain working class. "In true Brooklyn fashion, he and his friends
decided one night they were going to drive four hundred miles to Syracuse to
bring me back, or whatever. But on the way up, they totaled the car and my
boyfriend broke his leg. He never got up there, and after that, the idea of him
bringing me to my senses dissipated."

Another Straddler, Loretta Stec, had a similar problem with a blue-collar
lover left behind. Loretta, a slender thirty-nine-year-old English professor at
San Francisco State University with delicate features and brown hair, needed
to leave the commotion of drugs and friends' abortions and the repressed religious world of Perth Amboy, New Jersey, for the calm life of the mind offered
by Boston College. The only problem was Barry. When Loretta was seventeen, she and Barry, an older construction worker, would ride motorcycles
in toxic waste dumps. He was wild and fine—what every working-class girl
would want. But Loretta knew life had to get better than Perth Amboy, so she
went off to Boston. Barry and she still got together, though. They even worked
on the same taping crew at a construction site during the summer between
Loretta's freshman and sophomore years. But the differences between them
were growing. All the guys on the job—Barry included—thought it was weird
that Loretta would read the *New York Times* during lunch breaks. "What's with
that chick?" people asked.

By the time Loretta returned to Boston for her second year, she knew
she was in a far different place than Barry. The working class was not for her.

Hanging around with this guy and doing construction forever — it sounded awful. "I was upwardly mobile, and I was not going to work on a construction crew anymore," Loretta says. She tried to break it off, but Barry roared up I-95 in a borrowed car to change her mind. Loretta lived in an old Victorian with middle-class roommates who had never met anyone like Barry. When he showed up with a barking Doberman in tow, she recalled he was screaming like Stanley Kowalski in *A Streetcar Named Desire* that he wanted Loretta back. The women became terrified. Loretta was able to calm first Barry, then her roommates. Afterward, the couple went to listen to some music. In a little place on campus, a guitar trio started performing a Rolling Stones song. Suddenly, Barry turned to Loretta and began scream-singing about wild horses not being able to drag him from her, really loud, trying to get her to see his resolve. "People were wondering who was this guy, what's his deal?" Loretta says. "It pointed out the clash between my new world and the old. You don't do stuff like that. It was embarrassing, upsetting, and confusing. I didn't want to hurt him. But I knew it wasn't going to work for me." They walked around campus, fighting about things coming to an end. At some point, she recalls, Barry noticed that a college student with a nicer car than his — Loretta can't remember exactly what it was — had parked behind his car, blocking him. Already ramped up, Barry had a fit and smashed a headlight of the fancy machine with a rock. There Loretta was, a hundred feet from her campus Victorian, newly ensconced in a clean world of erudition and scholarship, far from the violence and swamps of central Jersey. Her bad-boy beau, once so appealing, was raving and breathing hard, trying to pull her away from the books, back down the turnpike to the working class.

"That was really the end of it," Loretta says. "I couldn't have a guy around who was going to act like that. He was wild and crazy and I was trying to make my way." Barry relented, and left Loretta alone. They lost touch, and Loretta later learned that Barry had died, the cause of death unknown to her. It was such a shock.

READING THE TEXT

1. What is your response to Lubrano's title, and why do you think he chose it for his essay?

2. Summarize in your own words the difference between Lubrano's high school and college experiences.

3. What does Richard Rodriguez mean by saying, "There's a brutality to education" (para. 6)?

4. Why did Lubrano avoid discussing his Columbia University experiences with his family?

5. How does child rearing differ in blue-collar and in middle-class families, in Lubrano's view? What evidence does he advance to support his claims?

READING THE SIGNS

1. In your journal, reflect on the effects—positive or negative—that attending college may have had on your relationship with your family and high school friends. How do you account for any changes that may have occurred?

2. In an argumentative essay, support, challenge, or complicate Gregg Andrews's statement that "every bit of learning takes you further from your parents" (para. 1).

3. Write a synthesis of the personal tales of Lubrano, Loretta Stec, and Rita Giordano. Then use your synthesis as the basis of an essay in which you explain how their collective experiences combine to demonstrate Lubrano's position that "for many class travelers with passports stamped for new territory, the trip is nothing less than a bridge burning" (para. 2).

4. Interview students from both blue-collar and middle- or upper-class backgrounds about the effect that attending college has had on their relationship with their family and high school friends. Use your findings to support your assessment of Lubrano's position that college can create divisions between blue-collar students and their families but that it tends not to have that effect on other classes.

5. Analyze Lubrano's use of evidence and quotations. Who is quoted directly? Who is quoted indirectly? What sources and experts are consulted? Use your observations for support in an argumentative essay in which you analyze what Lubrano's article implies about expertise and authority.

MICHAEL OMI

In Living Color: Race and American Culture

Though many like to think that racism in America is a thing of the past, Michael Omi argues that racism is a pervasive feature in our lives, one that is both overt and inferential. Using race as a sign by which we judge a person's character, inferential racism invokes deep-rooted stereotypes, and as Omi shows in his survey of American film, television, and music, our popular culture is hardly immune from such stereotyping. Indeed, when ostensibly "progressive" programs like *Saturday Night Live* can win the National Ethnic Coalition of Organizations' "Platinum Pit Award" for racist stereotyping in television, and shock jocks such as Howard Stern command big audiences and salaries, one can see popular culture has a way to go before it becomes color-blind. The author of *Racial Formation in the United States: From the 1960s to the 1990s* (with Howard Winant, 1986, 1994), Michael Omi is a professor of comparative ethnic studies at the University of California, Berkeley.

In February 1987, Assistant Attorney General William Bradford Reynolds, the nation's chief civil rights enforcer, declared that the recent death of a black man in Howard Beach, New York, and the Ku Klux Klan attack on civil rights marchers in Forsyth County, Georgia, were "isolated" racial incidences. He emphasized that the places where racial conflict could potentially flare up were "far fewer now than ever before in our history," and concluded that such a diminishment of racism stood as "a powerful testament to how far we have come in the civil rights struggle."[1]

Events in the months following his remarks raise the question as to whether we have come quite so far. They suggest that dramatic instances of racial tension and violence merely constitute the surface manifestations of a deeper racial organization of American society — a system of inequality which has shaped, and in turn been shaped by, our popular culture.

In March, the NAACP released a report on blacks in the record industry entitled "The Discordant Sound of Music." It found that despite the revenues generated by black performers, blacks remain "grossly underrepresented" in the business, marketing, and A&R (Artists and Repertoire) departments of major record labels. In addition, few blacks are employed as managers, agents, concert promoters, distributors, and retailers. The report concluded that:

> The record industry is overwhelmingly segregated and discrimination is rampant. No other industry in America so openly classifies its operations on a racial basis. At every level of the industry, beginning with the separation of black artists into a special category, barriers exist that severely limit opportunities for blacks.[2]

Decades after the passage of civil rights legislation and the affirmation of the principle of "equal opportunity," patterns of racial segregation and exclusion, it seems, continue to characterize the production of popular music.

The enduring logic of Jim Crow is also present in professional sports. In April, Al Campanis, vice president of player personnel for the Los Angeles Dodgers, explained to Ted Koppel on ABC's *Nightline* about the paucity of blacks in baseball front offices and as managers. "I truly believe," Campanis said, "that [blacks] may not have some of the necessities to be, let's say, a field manager or perhaps a general manager." When pressed for a reason, Campanis offered an explanation which had little to do with the structure of opportunity or institutional discrimination within professional sports:

> [W]hy are black men or black people not good swimmers? Because they don't have the buoyancy. . . . They are gifted with great musculature and various other things. They're fleet of foot. And this is why there are a lot

---

[1] Reynolds's remarks were made at a conference on equal opportunity held by the Bar association in Orlando, Florida. *The San Francisco Chronicle* (February 7, 1987). Print.

[2] Economic Development Department of the NAACP, "The Discordant Sound of Music (A Report on the Record Industry)," (Baltimore, Maryland: The NAACP, 1987), pp. 16–17. Print.

of black major league ballplayers. Now as far as having the background to become club presidents, or presidents of a bank, I don't know.[3]

Black exclusion from the front office, therefore, was justified on the basis of biological "difference."

The issue of race, of course, is not confined to the institutional arrangements [5] of popular culture production. Since popular culture deals with the symbolic realm of social life, the images which it creates, represents, and disseminates contribute to the overall racial climate. They become the subject of analysis and political scrutiny. In August, the National Ethnic Coalition of Organizations bestowed the "Golden Pit Awards" on television programs, commercials, and movies that were deemed offensive to racial and ethnic groups. *Saturday Night Live*, regarded by many media critics as a politically "progressive" show, was singled out for the "Platinum Pit Award" for its comedy skit "Ching Chang," which depicted a Chinese storeowner and his family in a derogatory manner.[4]

These examples highlight the *overt* manifestations of racism in popular culture — institutional forms of discrimination which keep racial minorities out of the production and organization of popular culture, and the crude racial caricatures by which these groups are portrayed. Yet racism in popular culture is often conveyed in a variety of implicit, and at times invisible, ways. Political theorist Stuart Hall makes an important distinction between *overt* racism, the elaboration of an explicitly racist argument, policy, or view, and *inferential* racism, which refers to "those apparently naturalized representations of events and situations relating to race, whether 'factual' or 'fictional,' which have racist premises and propositions inscribed in them as a set of *unquestioned assumptions*." He argues that inferential racism is more widespread, common, and indeed insidious since "it is largely *invisible* even to those who formulate the world in its terms."[5]

Race itself is a slippery social concept which is paradoxically both "obvious" and "invisible." In our society, one of the first things we notice about people when we encounter them (along with their sex/gender) is their *race*. We utilize race to provide clues about *who* a person is and *how* we should relate to her/him. Our perception of race determines our "presentation of *self*," distinctions in status, and appropriate modes of conduct in daily and institutional life. This process is often unconscious; we tend to operate off of an unexamined set of *racial beliefs*.

---

[3]Campanis's remarks on *Nightline* were reprinted in *The San Francisco Chronicle* (April 9, 1987). Print.

[4]Ellen Wulfhorst, "TV Stereotyping: It's the 'Pits,'" *The San Francisco Chronicle* (August 24, 1987). Print.

[5]Stuart Hall, "The Whites of Their Eyes: Racist Ideologies and the Media," in George Bridges and Rosalind Brunt, eds., *Silver Linings* (London: Lawrence and Wishart, 1981), pp. 36–37. Print.

Racial beliefs account for and explain variations in "human nature." Differences in skin color and other obvious physical characteristics supposedly provide visible clues to more substantive differences lurking underneath. Among other qualities, temperament, sexuality, intelligence, and artistic and athletic ability are presumed to be fixed and discernible from the palpable mark of race. Such diverse questions as our confidence and trust in others (as salespeople, neighbors, media figures); our sexual preferences and romantic images; our tastes in music, film, dance, or sports; indeed our very ways of walking and talking are ineluctably shaped by notions of race.

Ideas about race, therefore, have become "common sense"—a way of comprehending, explaining, and acting in the world. This is made painfully obvious when someone disrupts our common sense understandings. An encounter with someone who is, for example, racially "mixed" or of a racial/ethnic group we are unfamiliar with becomes a source of discomfort for us, and momentarily creates a crisis of racial meaning. We also become disoriented when people do not act "black," "Latino," or indeed "white." The content of such stereotypes reveals a series of unsubstantiated beliefs about who these groups are, what they are like, and how they behave.

The existence of such racial consciousness should hardly be surprising. 10 Even prior to the inception of the republic, the United States was a society shaped by racial conflict. The establishment of the Southern plantation economy, Western expansion, and the emergence of the labor movement, among other significant historical developments, have all involved conflicts over the definition and nature of the *color line*. The historical results have been distinct and different groups have encountered unique forms of racial oppression—Native Americans faced genocide, blacks were subjected to slavery, Mexicans were invaded and colonized, and Asians faced exclusion. What is common to the experiences of these groups is that their particular "fate" was linked to historically specific ideas about the significance and meaning of race.[6] Whites defined them as separate "species," ones inferior to Northern European cultural stocks, and thereby rationalized the conditions of their subordination in the economy, in political life, and in the realm of culture.

A crucial dimension of racial oppression in the United States is the elaboration of an ideology of difference or "otherness." This involves defining "us" (i.e., white Americans) in opposition to "them," an important task when distinct racial groups are first encountered, or in historically specific periods where preexisting racial boundaries are threatened or crumbling.

Political struggles over the very definition of who an "American" is illustrate this process. The Naturalization Law of 1790 declared that only free *white* immigrants could qualify, reflecting the initial desire among Congress to create and maintain a racially homogeneous society. The extension of

[6]For an excellent survey of racial beliefs see Thomas F. Gossett, *Race: The History of an Idea in America* (New York: Shocken, 1965). Print.

eligibility to all racial groups has been a long and protracted process. Japanese, for example, were finally eligible to become naturalized citizens after the passage of the Walter-McCarran Act of 1952. The ideological residue of these restrictions in naturalization and citizenship laws is the equation within popular parlance of the term "American" with "white," while other "Americans" are described as black, Mexican, "Oriental," etc.

Popular culture has been an important realm within which racial ideologies have been created, reproduced, and sustained. Such ideologies provide a framework of symbols, concepts, and images through which we understand, interpret, and represent aspects of our "racial" existence.

Race has often formed the central themes of American popular culture. Historian W. L. Rose notes that it is a "curious coincidence" that four of the "most popular reading-viewing events in all American history" have in some manner dealt with race, specifically black/white relations in the south.[7] Harriet Beecher Stowe's *Uncle Tom's Cabin*, Thomas Ryan Dixon's *The Clansman* (the inspiration for D. W. Griffith's *The Birth of a Nation*), Margaret Mitchell's *Gone with the Wind* (as a book and film), and Alex Haley's *Roots* (as a book and television miniseries) each appeared at a critical juncture in American race relations and helped to shape new understandings of race.

Emerging social definitions of race and the "real American" were reflected in American popular culture of the nineteenth century. Racial and ethnic stereotypes were shaped and reinforced in the newspapers, magazines, and pulp fiction of the period. But the evolution and ever-increasing sophistication of visual mass communications throughout the twentieth century provided, and continue to provide, the most dramatic means by which racial images are generated and reproduced.   15

Film and television have been notorious in disseminating images of racial minorities which establish for audiences what these groups look like, how they behave, and, in essence, "who they are." The power of the media lies not only in their ability to reflect the dominant racial ideology, but in their capacity to shape that ideology in the first place. D. W. Griffith's aforementioned epic *Birth of a Nation*, a sympathetic treatment of the rise of the Ku Klux Klan during Reconstruction, helped to generate, consolidate, and "nationalize" images of blacks which had been more disparate (more regionally specific, for example) prior to the film's appearance.[8]

In television and film, the necessity to define characters in the briefest and most condensed manner has led to the perpetuation of racial caricatures, as racial stereotypes serve as shorthand for scriptwriters, directors, and actors. Television's tendency to address the "lowest common denominator" in order

---

[7]W. L. Rose, *Race and Religion in American Historical Fiction: Four Episodes in Popular Culture* (Oxford: Clarendon, 1979). Print.

[8]Melanie Martindale-Sikes, "Nationalizing 'Nigger' Imagery through *Birth of a Nation*," paper prepared for the 73rd Annual Meeting of the American Sociological Association (September 4–8, 1978) in San Francisco.

to render programs "familiar" to an enormous and diverse audience leads it regularly to assign and reassign racial characteristics to particular groups, both minority and majority.

Many of the earliest American films deal with racial and ethnic "difference." The large influx of "new immigrants" at the turn of the century led to a proliferation of negative images of Jews, Italians, and Irish which were assimilated and adapted by such films as Thomas Edison's *Cohen's Advertising Scheme* (1904). Based on an old vaudeville routine, the film featured a scheming Jewish merchant, aggressively hawking his wares. Though stereotypes of these groups persist to this day,[9] by the 1940s many of the earlier ethnic stereotypes had disappeared from Hollywood. But, as historian Michael Winston observes, the "outsiders" of the 1890s remained: "the ever-popular Indian of the Westerns; the inscrutable or sinister Oriental; the sly, but colorful Mexican; and the clowning or submissive Negro."[10]

In many respects the "Western" as a genre has been paradigmatic in establishing images of racial minorities in film and television. The classic scenario involves the encircled wagon train or surrounded fort from which whites bravely fight off fierce bands of Native American Indians. The point of reference and viewer identification lies with those huddled within the circle—the representatives of "civilization" who valiantly attempt to ward off the forces of barbarism. In the classic Western, as writer Tom Engelhardt observes, "the viewer is forced behind the barrel of a repeating rifle and it is from that position, through its gun sights, that he receives a picture history of Western colonialism and imperialism."[11]

Westerns have indeed become the prototype for European and American excursions throughout the Third World. The cast of characters may change, but the story remains the same. The "humanity" of whites is contrasted with the brutality and treachery of nonwhites; brave (i.e., white) souls are pitted against the merciless hordes in conflicts ranging from Indians against the British Lancers to Zulus against the Boers. What Stuart Hall refers to as the imperializing "white eye" provides the framework for these films, lurking outside the frame and yet seeing and positioning everything within; it is "the unmarked position from which . . . 'observations' are made and from which, alone, they make sense."[12]

Our "common sense" assumptions about race and racial minorities in the United States are both generated and reflected in the stereotypes presented

[9]For a discussion of Italian, Irish, Jewish, Slavic, and German stereotypes in film, see Randall M. Miller, ed., *The Kaleidoscopic Lens: How Hollywood Views Ethnic Groups* (Englewood, N.J.: Jerome S. Ozer, 1980). Print.

[10]Michael R. Winston, "Racial Consciousness and the Evolution of Mass Communications in the United States," *Daedalus*, vol. III, No. 4 (Fall 1982). Print.

[11]Tom Engelhardt, "Ambush at Kamikaze Pass," in Emma Gee, ed., *Counterpoint: Perspectives on Asian America* (Los Angeles: Asian American Studies Center, UCLA, 1976), p. 270. Print.

[12]Hall, "Whites of Their Eyes," p. 38. Print.

by the visual media. In the crudest sense, it could be said that such stereotypes underscore white "superiority" by reinforcing the traits, habits, and predispositions of nonwhites which demonstrate their "inferiority." Yet a more careful assessment of racial stereotypes reveals intriguing trends and seemingly contradictory themes.

While all racial minorities have been portrayed as "less than human," there are significant differences in the images of different groups. Specific racial minority groups, in spite of their often interchangeable presence in films steeped in the "Western" paradigm, have distinct and often unique qualities assigned to them. Latinos are portrayed as being prone toward violent outbursts of anger; blacks as physically strong, but dim-witted; while Asians are seen as sneaky and cunningly evil. Such differences are crucial to observe and analyze. Race in the United States is not reducible to black/white relations. These differences are significant for a broader understanding of the patterns of race in America, and the unique experience of specific racial minority groups.

It is somewhat ironic that *real* differences which exist within a racially defined minority group are minimized, distorted, or obliterated by the media. "All Asians look alike," the saying goes, and indeed there has been little or no attention given to the vast differences which exist between, say, the Chinese and Japanese with respect to food, dress, language, and culture. This blurring within popular culture has given us supposedly Chinese characters who wear kimonos; it is also the reason why the fast-food restaurant McDonald's can offer "Shanghai McNuggets" with teriyaki sauce. Other groups suffer a similar fate. Professor Gretchen Bataille and Charles Silet find the cinematic Native American of the Northeast wearing the clothing of the Plains Indians, while living in the dwellings of Southwestern tribes:

> The movie men did what thousands of years of social evolution could not do, even what the threat of the encroaching white man could not do; Hollywood produced the homogenized Native American, devoid of tribal characteristics or regional differences.[13]

The need to paint in broad racial strokes has thus rendered "internal" differences invisible. This has been exacerbated by the tendency for screenwriters to "invent" mythical Asian, Latin American, and African countries. Ostensibly done to avoid offending particular nations and peoples, such a subterfuge reinforces the notion that all the countries and cultures of a specific region are the same. European countries retain their distinctiveness, while the Third World is presented as one homogeneous mass riddled with poverty and governed by ruthless and corrupt regimes.

While rendering specific groups in a monolithic fashion, the popular cultural imagination simultaneously reveals a compelling need to distinguish

---

[13]Gretchen Bataille and Charles Silet, "The Entertaining Anachronism: Indians in American Film," in Randall M. Miller, ed., *Kaleidoscopic Lens*, p. 40. Print.

and articulate "bad" and "good" variants of particular racial groups and individuals. Thus each stereotypic image is filled with contradictions: The bloodthirsty Indian is tempered with the image of the noble savage; the *bandido* exists along with the loyal sidekick; and Fu Manchu is offset by Charlie Chan. The existence of such contradictions, however, does not negate the one-dimensionality of these images, nor does it challenge the explicit subservient role of racial minorities. Even the "good" person of color usually exists as a foil in novels and films to underscore the intelligence, courage, and virility of the white male hero.

Another important, perhaps central, dimension of racial minority stereo- 25
types is sex/gender differentiation. The connection between race and sex has traditionally been an explosive and controversial one. For most of American history, sexual and marital relations between whites and nonwhites were forbidden by social custom and by legal restrictions. It was not until 1967, for example, that the U.S. Supreme Court ruled that antimiscegenation laws were unconstitutional. Beginning in the 1920s, the notorious Hays Office, Hollywood's attempt at self-censorship, prohibited scenes and subjects which dealt with miscegenation. The prohibition, however, was not evenly applied in practice. White men could seduce racial minority women, but white women were not to be romantically or sexually linked to racial minority men.

Women of color were sometimes treated as exotic sex objects. The sultry Latin temptress — such as Dolores Del Rio and Lupe Velez — invariably had boyfriends who were white North Americans; their Latino suitors were portrayed as being unable to keep up with the Anglo-American competition. From Mary Pickford as Cho-Cho San in *Madame Butterfly* (1915) to Nancy Kwan in *The World of Suzie Wong* (1961), Asian women have often been seen as the gracious "geisha girl" or the prostitute with a "heart of gold," willing to do anything to please her man.

By contrast, Asian men, whether cast in the role of villain, servant, sidekick, or kung fu master, are seen as asexual or, at least, romantically undesirable. As Asian American studies professor Elaine Kim notes, even a hero such as Bruce Lee played characters whose "single-minded focus on perfecting his fighting skills precludes all other interests, including an interest in women, friendship, or a social life."[14]

The shifting trajectory of black images over time reveals an interesting dynamic with respect to sex and gender. The black male characters in *The Birth of a Nation* were clearly presented as sexual threats to "white womanhood." For decades afterward, however, Hollywood consciously avoided portraying black men as assertive or sexually aggressive in order to minimize controversy. Black men were instead cast as comic, harmless, and nonthreatening figures exemplified by such stars as Bill "Bojangles" Robinson, Stepin Fetchit, and Eddie "Rochester" Anderson. Black women, by contrast, were

---

[14]Elaine Kim, "Asian Americans and American Popular Culture," in Hyung-Chan Kim, ed., *Dictionary of Asian American History* (New York: Greenwood, 1986), p. 107. Print.

divided into two broad character types based on color categories. Dark black women such as Hattie McDaniel and Louise Beavers were cast as "dowdy, frumpy, dumpy, overweight mammy figures"; while those "close to the white ideal," such as Lena Horne and Dorothy Dandridge, became "Hollywood's treasured mulattoes" in roles emphasizing the tragedy of being of mixed blood.[15]

It was not until the early 1970s that tough, aggressive, sexually assertive black characters, both male and female, appeared. The "blaxploitation" films of the period provided new heroes (e.g., *Shaft*, *Superfly*, *Coffy*, and *Cleopatra Jones*) in sharp contrast to the submissive and subservient images of the past. Unfortunately, most of these films were shoddy productions which did little to create more enduring "positive" images of blacks, either male or female.

In contemporary television and film, there is a tendency to present and 30 equate racial minority groups and individuals with specific social problems. Blacks are associated with drugs and urban crime, Latinos with "illegal" immigration, while Native Americans cope with alcoholism and tribal conflicts. Rarely do we see racial minorities "out of character," in situations removed from the stereotypic arenas in which scriptwriters have traditionally embedded them. Nearly the only time we see young Asians and Latinos of either sex, for example, is when they are members of youth gangs, as *Boulevard Nights* (1979), *Year of the Dragon* (1985), and countless TV cop shows can attest to.

Racial minority actors have continually bemoaned the fact that the roles assigned them on stage and screen are often one-dimensional and imbued with stereotypic assumptions. In theater, the movement toward "blind casting" (i.e., casting actors for roles without regard to race) is a progressive step, but it remains to be seen whether large numbers of audiences can suspend their "beliefs" and deal with a Latino King Lear or an Asian Stanley Kowalski. By contrast, white actors are allowed to play anybody. Though the use of white actors to play blacks in "black face" is clearly unacceptable in the contemporary period, white actors continue to portray Asian, Latino, and Native American characters on stage and screen.

Scores of Charlie Chan films, for example, have been made with white leads (the last one was the 1981 *Charlie Chan and the Curse of the Dragon Queen*). Roland Winters, who played Chan in six features, was once asked to explain the logic of casting a white man in the role of Charlie Chan: "The only thing I can think of is, if you want to cast a homosexual in a show, and you get a homosexual, it'll be awful. It won't be funny . . . and maybe there's something there."[16]

Such a comment reveals an interesting aspect about myth and reality in popular culture. Michael Winston argues that stereotypic images in the visual media were not originally conceived as representations of reality, nor were they initially understood to be "real" by audiences. They were, he suggests,

[15]Donald Bogle, "A Familiar Plot (A Look at the History of Blacks in American Movies)," *The Crisis*, Vol. 90, No. 1 (January 1983), p. 15. Print.
[16]Frank Chin, "Confessions of the Chinatown Cowboy," *Bulletin of Concerned Asian Scholars*, Vol. 4, No. 3 (Fall 1972). Print.

ways of "coding and rationalizing" the racial hierarchy and interracial behavior. Over time, however, "a complex interactive relationship between myth and reality developed, so that images originally understood to be unreal, through constant repetition began to *seem* real."[17]

Such a process consolidated, among other things, our "common sense" understandings of what we think various groups should look like. Such presumptions have led to tragicomical results. Latinos auditioning for a role in a television soap opera, for example, did not fit the Hollywood image of "real Mexicans" and had their faces bronzed with powder before filming because they looked too white. Model Aurora Garza said, "I'm a real Mexican and very dark anyway. I'm even darker right now because I have a tan. But they kept wanting to make my face darker and darker."[18]

Historically in Hollywood, the fact of having "dark skin" made an actor or 35 actress potentially adaptable for numerous "racial" roles. Actress Lupe Velez once commented that she had portrayed "Chinese, Eskimos, Japs, squaws, Hindus, Swedes, Malays, and Japanese."[19] Dorothy Dandridge, who was the first black woman teamed romantically with white actors, presented a quandary for studio executives who weren't sure what race and nationality to make her. They debated whether she should be a "foreigner," an island girl, or a West Indian.[20] Ironically, what they refused to entertain as a possibility was to present her as what she really was, a black American woman.

The importance of race in popular culture is not restricted to the visual media. In popular music, race and race consciousness have defined, and continue to define, formats, musical communities, and tastes. In the mid-1950s, the secretary of the North Alabama White Citizens Council declared that "Rock and roll is a means of pulling the white man down to the level of the Negro."[21] While rock may no longer be popularly regarded as a racially subversive musical form, the very genres of contemporary popular music remain, in essence, thinly veiled racial categories. "R & B" (Rhythm and Blues) and "soul" music are clearly references to *black* music, while Country & Western or heavy metal music are viewed, in the popular imagination, as *white* music. Black performers who want to break out of this artistic ghettoization must "cross over," a contemporary form of "passing" in which their music is seen as acceptable to white audiences.

The airwaves themselves are segregated. The designation "urban contemporary" is merely radio lingo for a "black" musical format. Such categorization affects playlists, advertising accounts, and shares of the listening market. On cable television, black music videos rarely receive airplay on MTV, but are

---

[17]Winston, "Racial Consciousness," p. 176. Print.

[18]*The San Francisco Chronicle* (September 21, 1984). Print.

[19]Quoted in Allen L. Woll, "Bandits and Lovers: Hispanic Images in American Film," in Miller, ed., *Kaleidoscopic Lens*, p. 60. Print.

[20]Bogle, "Familiar Plot," p. 17.

[21]Dave Marsh and Kevin Stein, *The Book of Rock Lists* (New York: Dell, 1981), p. 8. Print.

confined instead to the more marginal BET (Black Entertainment Television) network.

In spite of such segregation, many performing artists have been able to garner a racially diverse group of fans. And yet, racially integrated concert audiences are extremely rare. Curiously, this "perverse phenomenon" of racially homogeneous crowds takes place despite the color of the performer. Lionel Richie's concert audiences, for example, are virtually all-white, while Teena Marie's are all-black.[22]

Racial symbols and images are omnipresent in popular culture. Commonplace household objects such as cookie jars, salt and pepper shakers, and ashtrays have frequently been designed and fashioned in the form of racial caricatures. Sociologist Steve Dublin in an analysis of these objects found that former tasks of domestic service were symbolically transferred onto these commodities.[23] An Aunt Jemima–type character, for example, is used to hold a roll of paper towels, her outstretched hands supporting the item to be dispensed. "Sprinkle Plenty," a sprinkle bottle in the shape of an Asian man, was used to wet clothes in preparation for ironing. Simple commodities, the household implements which help us perform everyday tasks, may reveal, therefore, a deep structure of racial meaning.

A crucial dimension for discerning the meaning of particular stereotypes and images is the *situation context* for the creation and consumption of popular culture. For example, the setting in which "racist" jokes are told determines the function of humor. Jokes about blacks where the teller and audience are black constitute a form of self-awareness; they allow blacks to cope and "take the edge off" of oppressive aspects of the social order which they commonly confront. The meaning of these same jokes, however, is dramatically transformed when told across the "color line." If a white, or even black, person tells these jokes to a white audience, it will, despite its "purely" humorous intent, serve to reinforce stereotypes and rationalize the existing relations of racial inequality.

Concepts of race and racial images are both overt and implicit within popular culture — the organization of cultural production, the products themselves, and the manner in which they are consumed are deeply structured by race. Particular racial meanings, stereotypes, and myths can change, but the presence of a *system* of racial meanings and stereotypes, of racial ideology, seems to be an enduring aspect of American popular culture.

The era of Reaganism and the overall rightward drift of American politics and culture has added a new twist to the question of racial images and meanings. Increasingly, the problem for racial minorities is not that of misportrayal, but of "invisibility." Instead of celebrating racial and cultural diversity, we

[22]*Rock & Roll Confidential*, No. 44 (February 1987), p. 2. Print.
[23]Steven C. Dublin, "Symbolic Slavery: Black Representations in Popular Culture," *Social Problems*, Vol. 34, No. 2 (April 1987). Print.

are witnessing an attempt by the right to define, once again, who the "real" American is, and what "correct" American values, mores, and political beliefs are. In such a context, racial minorities are no longer the focus of sustained media attention; when they do appear, they are cast as colored versions of essentially "white" characters.

The possibilities for change—for transforming racial stereotypes and challenging institutional inequities—nonetheless exist. Historically, strategies have involved the mobilization of political pressure against an offending institution(s). In the late 1950s, for instance, "Nigger Hair" tobacco changed its name to "Bigger Hare" due to concerted NAACP pressure on the manufacturer. In the early 1970s, Asian American community groups successfully fought NBC's attempt to resurrect Charlie Chan as a television series with white actor Ross Martin. Amidst the furor generated by Al Campanis's remarks cited at the beginning of this essay, Jesse Jackson suggested that a boycott of major league games be initiated in order to push for a restructuring of hiring and promotion practices.

Partially in response to such action, Baseball Commissioner Peter Ueberroth announced plans in June 1987 to help put more racial minorities in management roles. "The challenge we have," Ueberroth said, "is to manage change without losing tradition."[24] The problem with respect to the issue of race and popular culture, however, is that the *tradition* itself may need to be thoroughly examined, its "common sense" assumptions unearthed and challenged, and its racial images contested and transformed.

READING THE TEXT

1. Describe in your own words the difference between "overt racism" and "inferential racism" (para. 6).
2. Why, according to Omi, is popular culture so powerful in shaping America's attitudes toward race?
3. What relationship does Omi see between gender and racial stereotypes?
4. How did race relations change in America during the 1980s, in Omi's view?

READING THE SIGNS

1. In class, brainstorm stereotypes, both positive and negative, attributed to specific racial groups. Then discuss the possible sources of these stereotypes. In what ways have they been perpetuated in popular culture, including film, TV, advertising, music, and consumer products? What does your discussion reveal about popular culture's influence on our most basic ways of seeing the world?
2. **CONNECTING TEXTS** Using Omi's essay as your critical framework, write an essay in which you explore how the film *12 Years a Slave* (2013) may reflect or

[24]*The San Francisco Chronicle* (June 13, 1987). Print.

redefine American attitudes toward racial identity and race relations. Alternatively, watch *Malcolm X*, *Mi Familia*, or another film that addresses race relations.

3. Study an issue of a magazine targeted to a specific ethnic readership, such as *Essence*, *Ebony*, *Latina*, or *Jade*, analyzing both its articles and advertising. Then write an essay in which you explore the extent to which the magazine accurately reflects that ethnicity or, in Omi's words, appeals to readers as "colored versions of essentially 'white' characters" (para. 42).

4. Omi claims that "in contemporary television and film, there is a tendency to present and equate racial minority groups and individuals with specific social problems" (para. 30). In class, brainstorm films and TV shows that have characters that are ethnic minorities; pick one example and watch it. Does Omi's claim apply to that example, or does it demonstrate different patterns of racial representation?

5. Watch the film *Avatar*, and then, using Omi's categories of "overt" and "inferential" racism, write your own analysis of the race relations in this movie.

DANI McCLAIN

Being "Masculine of Center" While Black

The U.S. Census form asks questions about your race and gender, but it presumes that such questions (especially with respect to sex) invite straightforward either/or answers. But what if you are a black female whose gender expression is "masculine of center": that is, male in manner and dress? This is the identity situation that Dani McClain investigates in this report, interviewing women whose masculine-of-center identities lead to hostility and even threats toward them in a world where "black or white" and "male or female" are the norm, with little space for the queer space between. Dani McClain is a fellow with the Nation Institute and a writer for such publications as the *Miami Herald*, *The Root*, *AlterNet*, and *On the Issues*.

The weekend after the George Zimmerman verdict came down, Erica Woodland of Oakland stayed close to home. She could identify with the righteous anger expressed at the protests. But rather than join in, she canceled plans with family, postponed a trip to the laundromat and limited outings to work and the grocery store. "I decided for my own safety, I need to stay in the house," Woodland recalls. "I knew I could be putting myself at risk for anything."

The possibility of being targeted by police or by a fearful, overzealous civilian on account of her race was one consideration for Woodland, who is black. But so was gender. She describes herself as masculine of center, which means that her way of expressing herself — clothes, mannerisms — falls toward that side of the spectrum. It also means that like many of the black men and boys at the center of the recent conversation advanced by everyone from President Obama to Questlove, she's been profiled as criminal or suspicious. "We walk through the world and some of us pass as male," Woodland, 33, says. "We get left out of this conversation."

Somewhere at the intersection of blackness, gender expression and sexual orientation is a heightened risk for harassment and bias-driven violence. According to National Coalition of Anti-Violence Program's 2012 report on hate violence, LGBTQ people of color are nearly twice as likely as their white counterparts to experience physical violence. Last year, nearly three-fourths of anti-LGBTQ homicide victims were people of color and just over half were black.

People who are perceived as feminine — including femme lesbians and trans women — are certainly at risk, as the case of CeCe McDonald brought to national attention last year. But trans men and masculine of center women experience discrimination and harassment in ways that often map more clearly to mainstream narratives about black men. Chai Jindasurat, co-director of organizing and advocacy at the New York City Anti-Violence Project, says this shows up most clearly in the context of police interactions. "They're stopped, searched and arrested, and sometimes they experience police violence as a result of that," says Jindasurat, whose organization is part of a New York City coalition working to address this problem. "It's a combination of both identities that contribute to that disproportionate impact of violence."

Police can be a threat, but more often aggression comes from strangers 5 in public places. In situations where an offender is unknown, nearly three-fourths of assailants are strangers, followed by police at 24 percent, according to the Anti-Violence Project report. Morgan Willis says she's been confronted by random aggressors at bars, in subway cars and on sidewalks. But there's one demographic she tries her best to steer clear of in public spaces: white, intoxicated men in groups. "It's a group of the most powerful people in the world who are not in their right mind and who feel empowered to do whatever they want," says Willis, 29. "Not only do I have to be extremely cautious with my safety; I end up feeling like if for some reason whatever happens escalates to violence, I'm going to get in trouble."

Willis lives in Detroit and works with a collective of masculine of center people called Bklyn Boihood. She said experience has led her to believe that any official first responder or bystander would side with her attackers or otherwise fail to support her safety or version of events. "They're going to be the ones that walk away and I'm going to have to start a campaign online to get people to acknowledge that something actually happened."

Something along those lines unfolded in Oakland five days after the Zimmerman verdict was announced. Veteran community organizer Malkia Cyril says she was verbally and physically attacked outside a downtown bar after she accidentally backed her car into a parked motorcycle. That bar had had its windows smashed by protestors responding to the verdict earlier in the week, and tensions in the neighborhood were high. None of which excuses what unfolded after Cyril got out of her car to assess the damage.

One of the bar's employees, a white man named Issa Eismont, admits he called her a "bitch" and stood in front of her car door, blocking her from being able to reenter. After hearing the crash, he approached the scene and thought she was trying to flee the scene, he said. Cyril says she was also called a "dyke" and "stupid" by bystanders in the crowd that gathered, many of whom were white and male, according to Cyril and another witness. Cyril says a black male employee of the bar pushed and restrained her. Of her version of events, that employee — who was off-duty at the time and would only give his first name as Marcus — told me a week later, "I'm not going to dispute anything. I kind of forgot about what happened."

But Cyril hasn't, and she has ideas about why a simple auto accident escalated so quickly to insults and physical aggression. "They were reading me as a butch. They were reading me as a black woman. They were reading me as a masculine woman," Cyril, 39, says. "The combination of those things is why they felt they could be so physical toward me."

She eventually exchanged insurance information with the bike's owner 10 and continued on to her original destination — a panel on media portrayals of black masculinity. And later that night, she shared her account of what happened with her more than 3,000 Facebook friends and named the bar in question. By the next day, the bar's owner issued a public apology on its own Facebook page and Eismont had reached out to Cyril to apologize.

This kind of online organizing around individual incidents matters, and so do more systemic efforts to shift perceptions and institutions. Jindasurat of the Anti-Violence Project mentions a public awareness campaign run out of the Washington, DC, Office of Human Rights and a legislative campaign advanced by New York City's Communities United for Police Reform as bright spots.

But two groups doing some of the most innovative work in the country with trans men and masculine of center women of color are actually focused inward rather than on advocacy. Willis, of Bklyn Boihood, says that collective is more interested in building community than in confronting head-on the harassment and violence that many in her community consistently face. "If this happens 100 times, I don't have the energy to articulate and to make this call to arms and action 100 times," Willis says. "A lot of times it doesn't feel valuable to take to task something that's happening all the time everywhere." Woodland, who is field building director at an Oakland-based national organization called Brown Boi Project, expresses a similar belief that her energy is better spent shifting the culture of privilege within masculine of center communities of color than on challenging the broader culture. Still, she acknowledges that someone needs to organize in response to the violence, the threats and the humiliations.

"Because we are always responding to events, we don't have any healing going on," Woodland says. "How do we reframe the conversation, first for ourselves?"

READING THE TEXT

1. Summarize in your own words what the term "masculine of center" means.
2. What does McClain mean by "mainstream narratives about black men" (para. 4)?
3. What experiences do black women who appear male have in the black community, as McClain describes them?
4. Why do some members of the masculine of center community devote their energies to in-group politics rather than engaging with mainstream America?

READING THE SIGNS

1. In an essay, evaluate the term "masculine of center." To what extent does it adequately describe the women profiled in McClain's selection? If you think the term is inadequate, can you suggest and defend your own term?

2. **CONNECTING TEXTS** As of this writing, Facebook has more than fifty categories for a user's gender identification. Study that list, and use it as a basis for an essay in which you explore the traditional binary distinction of male/female. Do you think the traditional distinction or Facebook's categories are more valid? How does Facebook's list complicate the traditional definitions of gender identity? To develop your ideas, consult Aaron's Devor's "Gender Role Behaviors and Attitudes" (p. 504) and Deborah Blum's "The Gender Blur: Where Does Biology End and Society Take Over?" (p. 511).

3. **CONNECTING TEXTS** While discussing two rather different groups, both McClain and Mariah Burton Nelson (p. 524) describe the experiences of women who violate conventional norms surrounding gender identity. Drawing upon both selections, write an essay in which you analyze the experiences of both groups of women. If you find differences, how do you account for them? What reasons can you advance for the response to such women?

4. McClain says that "LGBTQ people of color are nearly twice as likely as their white counterparts to experience physical violence" (para. 3). Research the National Coalition of Anti-Violence Program's studies on the causes of such violence. Use your results as the basis of an essay that proposes your own argument about how gender and ethnic identities affect people's attitudes toward others.

5. Central to McClain's essay is the notion of "intersectionality," or the idea that race, gender, and sexuality considered together provide a clearer picture of particular needs and issues facing minority groups. Research this term, and write an essay in which you discuss why advocates might favor this model over others. Use examples from the essays in this chapter.

THERESA CELEBRAN JONES

Sanjay and Craig: *Nickelodeon's Hilarious New Mixed-Race Heroes*

With more and more Americans identifying as "mixed race," one might expect that television would be filled with mixed-race characters. But while that hasn't happened yet, Theresa Celebran Jones has been happy to find such Nickelodeon offerings as *Sanjay and Craig*, a children's program featuring an Anglo-Indian boy and his pet snake. In fact, Jones observes, if you are looking for progressive racial programming, preschool shows like *Sesame Street* and *Yo Gabba Gabba* are the best places to look, but avoid tween sitcoms. Theresa Celebran Jones is a columnist for *Hyphen: Asian America Unabridged*.

We need more mixed-race families and kids on television. Nickelodeon is leading the way.

Surely by now you've all heard about the Cheerios commercial featuring a biracial family that received a depressing amount of racist backlash. To refresh your memory, the ad was a pretty benign spot that merely featured a white mother, a black father, and a crazy adorable mixed girl talking about cereal. It was beloved by many, but ended up being a pretty decent barometer for the current state of race relations in America — and it was surprising only to the people who don't have to deal with race on a daily basis (namely white people).

Like it or not, mixed-race families are an ever-growing reality in America. Asian Americans have struggled for a long time (and we continue to struggle) to show there is a demand to see people like us on television, and the controversy over the Cheerios ad shows the fight for mixed-race families is just beginning. The controversy of the Cheerios ad (as well as its Streisand effect) demonstrated the potential for success when you simply show a good-looking mixed-race family on television. The backlash from the ad was disheartening to be sure, but then I discovered Nickelodeon's new show, *Sanjay and Craig*.

Let me first acknowledge that kids' television is generally a mixed bag when it comes to race. Shows for the preschool set (*Sesame Street*; *Yo Gabba Gabba*; *Ni Hao, Kai-Lan*; *Dora the Explorer*) are usually great at being inclusive and reflecting diversity, while, for some reason, tween sitcoms (*iCarly*, *Victorious*, *Jessie*) tend to be the worst offenders when it comes to perpetuating racist stereotypes. Cartoon shows for older kids lie somewhere in the middle, but seem to have the most creative leeway and therefore the most potential for debunking stereotypes.

554

Enter *Sanjay and Craig*. The show follows the hijinks of a boy (Sanjay) and ₅ his best friend / talking pet snake (Craig). In the first episode, Sanjay and Craig sneak into a hospital disguised as doctors to watch a butt transplant being performed, and end up performing the butt transplant themselves. Not much is made of Sanjay's background in the first episode, so I had to watch it twice to make sure, but I'd picked up that Sanjay's father is Indian, his mother is white, and she's a surgeon.

Naturally, my five-year-old thought the episode was hilarious, and the show earned her stamp of approval. The hugeness of the mixed-race family was entirely lost on her, which may speak to how well the show is written.

That being said, the show is really only groundbreaking in its featuring a mixed-race family without making it A Big Deal, and is otherwise pretty standard kid fare, fairly indistinguishable from *Adventure Time* or *Regular Show*. Watching the show gave me a similar feeling to watching *Better Luck Tomorrow* for the first time — it was simply refreshing to see POCs tell a normal story without having to comment on race. I loved what I saw and I hope the show continues on for multiple seasons, but I can't say it's the most original show I've ever seen.

And I think it's important to note that the show's creators are white, and while it would be nice to have more Asian American representation in all parts of the production process, it does go to show that it's really not that difficult for white writers to create a normal damn television show that features people of color that are three-dimensional characters and not just racist caricatures, or simply as vehicles for teaching white people lessons about race.

READING THE TEXT

1. Why do you think Jones says that white people "don't have to deal with race on a daily basis" (para. 2)?

2. What does Jones mean by the "Streisand effect" (para. 3)?

3. Jones comments that *Sanjay and Craig* features mixed-race characters "without making it A Big Deal" (para. 7). Why is this important, according to Jones?

4. Why does Jones find it significant that *Sanjay and Craig*'s creators are white?

READING THE SIGNS

1. Watch an episode or two of *Sanjay and Craig*. Relying on your observation of specific details of those episodes, write an essay in which you defend, oppose, or modify Jones's assumption that the program eschews typical ethnic stereotypes and "features people of color that are three-dimensional characters and not just racist caricatures" (para. 8).

2. **CONNECTING TEXTS** Read or reread Jessica Hagedorn's "Asian Women in Film: No Joy, No Luck" (p. 343). Adopting Hagedorn's perspective on the depiction of Asian characters in media, assess Jones's selection and its approval of the way *Sanjay and Craig* represents Asian characters.

3. Write an essay that demonstrates, refutes, or complicates the proposition that *Sanjay and Craig* represents a positive, subtler representation of racial identity in mass media. To develop a historical context for your argument, read or reread Michael Omi's "In Living Color: Race and American Culture" (p. 538).

AYMAR JEAN CHRISTIAN
The End of Post-Identity Television

For a while, if you went by television casting strategies, racial and gender identity appeared to be disappearing as anything of significance in popular TV shows like *Grey's Anatomy*. But in more recent years, with shows like *Girls* and *The Misadventures of Awkward Black Girl*, TV and Web TV may be leaving the "post-identity era," Aymar Jean Christian believes, and that's a good thing, especially in a time of LGBTQ emergence. Identity still matters, Christian argues, and that's a positive, he concludes. Aymar Jean Christian is an assistant professor in Northwestern University's School of Communication. His writings have appeared in such publications as *Continuum*, *Transformative Works and Cultures*, *Newsweek*, the *Washington Post*, the *Wall Street Journal*, and *Bloomberg BusinessWeek*.

Nothing ever "ends" in culture — and nothing is ever new. Conditions change. Culture changes, sometimes.

Still, it does feel like a certain era is ending. That era might be called the post-identity era, which, in television, had its prime in the 2000s. "Post-identity" here refers to the casting of characters without focusing on cultural difference — the much-discussed trifecta academics like to call "race, gender, sexuality" (almost always in that order, for some reason).

What's Happening

Years ago when *Grey's Anatomy* premiered, much was made about creator Shonda Rhimes' open casting strategy: characters written black were cast Asian, vice versa, and every which way. The idea was the characters were written broadly, and their races were essentially interchangeable, at least for the beginning of the show. For shows about women and GLBT-identified individuals, this meant writing characters who were either feminist (working women) or post-feminist (freed from the burden of labor, think *SATC*) archetypes). For gays, it meant presenting them as "normal" or "just like you" — married, with kids, or wanting kids. (For more on this, see Suzanna Walters' *All the Rage* and Douglas' *Enlightened Sexism*.)

All of this, was, really, fine. Television reflected our ideals, the belief that our differences had melted away, that we'd learned how we're all, fundamentally, the same. (I've tried to find something redeeming in this idea.) This was particularly true of broadcast networks, who tried to grab mass audiences as cable networks heavily invested in scripted programming.

But in reality, people do feel, recognize and debate cultural differences. If ⁵ *Survivor* didn't bust that myth, recent television shows — online and on-air — have certainly put it into question.

The Economics of Identity Television

With more and more cable channels creating television, the need to hit a niche has steadily increased. Smaller niches mean smaller audiences and production budgets, but also more creative freedom for producers and auteurs. It's been happening for well over a decade, but we're hitting a crucial turning point — maybe.

So we get *Girls*. We've had plenty of great shows and women and gender politics — *Mary Tyler Moore*, *Roseanne*, *Murphy Brown*, and, yes, *Sex and the City*, many referenced in the *Girls* pilot — but *Girls* arrives at a moment when the need to be "frank" about gender and class is not only necessary, but possible. *Girls* is the television show as thesis statement: it's a critical work about a very, very specific type of woman. Its super-niche focus on upper-middle-class young women allows it to hone in on the minutiae of growing up as an educated girl in the warped US economy. It's uncomfortable. It allows — arguably, encourages — viewers to despise its privileged leads, something only a few critics have decided to do.

When Chuck Lorre obnoxiously lamented the surfeit of lady comedies on TV, what he was really talking about was the explicitness with which these shows address "gender problems": *2 Broke Girls*, *Girls*, *Whitney*, *Parks and Recreation*, *30 Rock*, *Enlightened*, *New Girl*, *Awkward.*, *Web Therapy*, *Don't Trust the B — in Apartment 23* and *Up All Night* are all saturated with story lines about the complications of being a professional woman today. Some of them even manage to approach some realism (*Girls* wins there, hands down). Because unlike in TV's leading procedurals — *The Closer*, *Rizzoli & Isles*, *The Good Wife*, etc. — most women aren't able to conquer the workplace with such elegance and ease.

Down the Long Tail, to the Web

The market for explicitly lady comedy is strong on TV right now, and many of the shows are doing well. One only need look at FX's interest in web comedy hit *Broad City* — one of many borough-centric web shows — to see the trend is in full swing.

But you'd be missing half the story if you stopped there. Look to the 10 incredible success of *The Misadventures of Awkward Black Girl*, and you'll notice basically every non-white-straight-dude is hankering for shows that speak intimately to their lives. With hundreds of thousands of fans, *Awkward Black Girl* is an incredibly well-written show. Like *Girls*, it gets at the ambivalences and complications of gender and race today, and does so in ways perhaps too explicit for TV. It uses the words "bitch" and "nigga" liberally, and explicitly calls out racism and prejudice with humor.

"But, as was demonstrated by some of the Shorty Award tweets, some people can't get past the 'black' in the title. The bewilderment that our show not only exists, but that it could actually be good is indicative of how mainstream media thinks. I'm pretty sure none of the people tweeting that I'd only get three-fifths of my award had even seen an episode of our show, but they were 100 percent positive that it couldn't be as good as whatever it is someone who didn't look like me produced," creator Issa Rae wrote in *xojane*.

If "black" in *ABG* has been a problem — too explicit for a postracial age — it might not be for longer. Before it announced its 2012 programming slate, which includes its first scripted programs, BET got interested in *Single Black Female*, a Gabrielle Union–vehicle now called *Being Mary Jane*.

Web producers have no such restrictions, and of the scores of black, gay, and Latina series, a number call out race outright, like BET's first web show, *Buppies*, *Afro City* (which built a fan base before its first episode even aired) and the new *Unwritten Rules*, about a black woman navigating a white workplace. Jane Espenson's *Husbands* might be inspired by *The Honeymooners* or *I Love Lucy*, but there's no question it's gay, gay, gay. Gayer, it seems, than most of gay television, whose characters are nestled in straight shows like *Modern Family* and *Glee*. (Indeed, NBC has in development a Sean Hayes–starrer that's basically the same thing.) Indie shows like *Gay's Anatomy*, *The Real Girl's Guide to Everything Else*, *Drama Queenz*, and *Two Jasperjohns* are much more nuanced and grounded examinations of being gay-identified than most of what's on TV.

Of course, things change slowly. Logo for its part is moving away from gays to the broader category of women. And aside from *Girls*, few of these shows are particularly challenging or bracing, in the way that series like *Roseanne* and *All in the Family* shook up audiences decades ago. For that matter, class remains a bit of a third rail, particularly in shows without white guy leads.

Why?

In politics, we're debating contraception, stay-at-home moms and a wom- 15 an's right-to-choose. In crime, we're grappling with two chilling alleged hate crimes. And that's just the tip of the iceberg.

Quite simply, we, or the media, have been forced to realize that identity matters — still. It may not be the 1960s, but if you're watching *Mad Men*, it's starting to look a little familiar.

It helps that we have a glut of media outlets today, including tons of blogs for pretty much every interest. Niche, implicitly social media have been integral to pushing awareness to the fore.

We're starting a new decade! And the one thing we know about culture is: anything can change.

READING THE TEXT

1. In your own words, what does Christian mean by "post-identity" television?

2. How has the increasing number of TV channels and the rise in niche marketing, especially on cable, changed the character of programs aired, in Christian's view?

3. Explain what Christian means by saying "*Girls* is the television show as thesis statement" (para. 7).

4. According to Christian, how have TV shows evolved in their depiction of black, gay, and Latina characters?

READING THE SIGNS

1. **CONNECTING TEXTS** Write an essay that supports, refutes, or complicates Christian's assumption that mass media have entered a "post-identity" phase in which they are less inclined to rely on conventional categories of gender, ethnicity, sexual orientation, and other demographics. To develop your ideas, consult the introduction to this chapter, in addition to the other readings in this chapter.

2. Christian says that "*Girls* is the television show as thesis statement" (para. 7). In an essay, argue for, against, or complicate his view of *Girls*. To develop your ideas, consult Jane Hu's "Reality Hunger: On Lena Dunham's *Girls*" (p. 304).

3. **CONNECTING TEXTS** Write an essay in which you propose your own explanation for why "post-identity" TV shows that feature black characters tend to receive short shrift from both viewers and critics. To develop your argument, consult Michael Omi's "In Living Color: Race and American Culture" (p. 538).

4. Use Christian's essay as a critical lens to analyze one or two high school teen movies, as David Denby does in "High-School Confidential: Notes On Teen Movies" (p. 366). To what extent have such films embraced the "post-identity" phase that Christian proposes? How do you explain your findings?

5. As a capstone essay, review the selections in this chapter, along with the introduction to this chapter. Synthesize your response to these readings, and write an essay in which you make an argument about the extent to which America has indeed become a post-identity culture.

GLOSSARY

abduction (n.)   A form of logical inference, first proposed by Charles Sanders Peirce, by which one seeks the most likely explanatory hypothesis or cause for a phenomenon. For example, the most likely explanation for the fact that in teen horror movies the first victims of the murderous monster are the cheerleader and the football player is that the majority of the teen audience enjoys the imaginative revenge of seeing snooty high school types done in.

archetype (n.)   A recurring character type or plot pattern found in literature, mythology, and popular culture. Sea monsters like Jonah's whale and Moby Dick are archetypes, as are stories that involve long sea journeys or descents into the underworld.

canon (n.)   Books or works that are considered essential to a literary tradition, as the plays of Shakespeare are part of the canon of English literature.

class (n.)   A group of related objects or people. Those who share the same economic status in a society are said to be of the same social class: for example, working class, middle class, upper class. Members of a social class tend to share the same interests and political viewpoints.

code (n.)   A system of **signs** or values that assigns meanings to the elements that belong to it. Thus, a traffic code defines a red light as a "stop" signal and a green light as a "go," while a fashion code determines whether an article of clothing is stylish. To *decode* a system is to figure out its meanings, as in interpreting the tattooing and body-piercing fads.

commodification (n.)   The transforming of an abstraction or behavior into a product for sale. For example, selling mass-produced hamburgers as an expression of rule-breaking defiance and individualism. See also **hypercapitalism**.

connotation (n.)   The meaning suggested by a word, as opposed to its objective reference, or **denotation**. Thus, the word *flag* might connote (or suggest) feelings of patriotism, while it literally denotes (or refers to) a pennant-like object.

consumption (n.)   The use of products and services, as opposed to their production. A *consumer culture* is one that consumes more than it produces. As a consumer culture, for example, America uses more goods such as computers and stereos than it manufactures, which results in a trade deficit with those *producer cultures* (such as China) with which America trades.

context (n.)   The environment in which a **sign** can be interpreted. In the context of a college classroom, for example, T-shirts, jeans, and sneakers are interpreted as ordinary casual dress. Wearing the same outfit in the context of a job interview at an investment bank would be interpreted as meaning that you're not serious about wanting the job.

cultural studies (n.)   The academic study of ordinary, everyday culture rather than **high culture**. See also **culture**; **culture industry**; **mass culture**; **popular culture**.

culture (n.)   The overall system of values and traditions shared by a group of people. Not exactly synonymous with *society*, which can include numerous cultures within its boundaries, a culture encompasses the worldviews of those who belong to it. Thus, the United States, which is a multicultural society, includes the differing worldviews of people of African, Asian, Native American, and European descent. See also **cultural studies**; **culture industry**; **high culture**; **mass culture**; **popular culture**.

culture industry (n.)   The commercial forces behind the production of **mass culture** or entertainment. See also **cultural studies**; **culture**; **high culture**; **mass culture**; **popular culture**.

denotation (n.)   The particular object or class of objects to which a word refers. Contrast with **connotation**.

discourse (n.)   The words, concepts, and presuppositions that constitute the knowledge and understanding of a particular community, often academic or professional.

dominant culture (n.)   The group within a **multicultural** society whose traditions, values, and beliefs are held to be normative, as the European tradition is the dominant culture in the United States.

Eurocentric (adj.)   Related to a worldview founded on the traditions and history of European culture, usually at the expense of non-European cultures.

function (n.)   The utility of an object, as opposed to its cultural meaning. Spandex or Lycra shorts, for example, have a functional value for cyclists because they're lightweight and aerodynamic. On the other hand, such shorts are a general fashion item for both men and women because of their cultural meaning, not their function. Many noncyclists wear spandex to project an image of hard-bodied fitness, sexiness, or just plain trendiness, for instance.

gender (n.)   One's sexual identity and the roles that follow from it, as determined by the norms of one's culture rather than by biology or genetics. The assumption that women should be foremost in the nurturing of children is a gender norm; the fact that only women can give birth is a biological phenomenon.

high culture (n.)   The products of the elite arts, including classical music, literature, drama, opera, painting, and sculpture. See also **cultural studies; culture; culture industry; mass culture; popular culture**.

hypercapitalism (n.)   Introduced by Jeremy Rifkin, hypercapitalism refers to a society in which the values of capitalism, especially the profit motive and the commodification of experience, have come to override all other values.

icon (n.), **iconic** (adj.)   In **semiotics**, a **sign** that visibly resembles its referent, as a photograph looks like the thing it represents. More broadly, an icon is someone (often a celebrity) who enjoys a commanding or representative place in popular culture. Michael Jackson and Madonna are music video icons. Contrast with **symbol**.

ideology (n.)   The beliefs, interests, and values that determine one's interpretations or judgments and that are often associated with one's social class. For example, in the ideology of modern business, a business is designed to produce profits, not social benefits.

image (n.)   Literally, a pictorial representation; more generally, the identity that one projects to others through such things as clothing, grooming, speech, and behavior.

mass culture (n.)   A subset of **popular culture** that includes the popular entertainments that are commercially produced for widespread consumption. See also **cultural studies; culture; culture industry; high culture**.

mass media (n. pl.)   The means of communication, often controlled by the **culture industry**, that include newspapers, popular magazines, radio, television, film, and the Internet.

multiculturalism (n.), **multicultural** (adj.)   In American education, the movement to incorporate the traditions, history, and beliefs of the United States' non-European cultures into a traditionally *monocultural* (or single-culture) curriculum dominated by European thought and history.

mythology (n.)   The overall framework of values and beliefs incorporated in a given cultural system or worldview. Any given belief within such a structure — like the belief that "a woman's place is in the home" — is called a *myth*.

overdetermination (n.)   Originally a term from Freudian psychoanalytic theory to describe the multiple causes of a psychological affect, overdetermination more generally describes the multiplicity of possible causes for any social phenomenon. Combined with abductive reasoning, overdetermination is a key element in **semiotic** interpretation. See also **abduction**.

politics (n.)   Essentially, the practice of promoting one's interests in a competitive social environment. Not restricted to electioneering; there may be office politics, classroom politics, academic politics, and sexual politics.

popular culture (n.)   That segment of a **culture** that incorporates the activities of everyday life, including the consumption of consumer goods and the production and enjoyment of mass-produced entertainments. See also **cultural studies; culture industry; high culture; mass culture**.

postmodernism (n.), **postmodern** (adj.)   The worldview behind contemporary literature, art, music, architecture, and philosophy that rejects traditional attempts to make meaning out of human history and experience. For the *postmodern* artist, art does not attempt to create new explanatory myths or **symbols** but rather recycles or repeats existing images, as does the art of Andy Warhol.

proxemics (n.)   The study of human uses of space in interactions with other humans, including body language, facial expression, distance between subjects, gestures, and so on.

semiotics (n.)   In short, the study of **signs**. Synonymous with *semiology*, semiotics is concerned with both the theory and the practice of interpreting linguistic, cultural, and behavioral sign systems. One who practices *semiotic analysis* is called a *semiotician* or *semiologist*.

sign (n.)   Anything that bears a meaning. Words, objects, images, and forms of behavior are all signs whose meanings are determined by the particular **codes**, or **systems**, in which they appear.

symbol (n.), **symbolic** (adj.)   A **sign**, according to semiotician Charles Sanders Peirce, whose significance is arbitrary. The meaning of the word *bear*, for example, is arbitrarily determined by those who use it. Contrast with **icon**.

system (n.)   The **code**, or network, within which a **sign** functions and so achieves its meaning through its associational and differential relations with other signs. The English language is a sign system, as is a fashion code.

text (n.)   A complex of **signs**, which may be linguistic, imagistic, behavioral, and/or musical, that can be read or interpreted.

Acknowledgments

Michael Agresta, "How the Western Was Lost—And Why It Matters" from the *Atlantic*. Copyright © 2013 The Atlantic Media Co., as first published in The Atlantic Magazine. All rights reserved. Distributed by Tribune Content Agency, LLC. Reprinted with permission.

Helena Andrews, "*The Butler* vs. *The Help*: Gender Matters" from *The Root*. Copyright © 2013 by Helena Andrews. Used by permission. All rights reserved.

Laura Bennett, "Against Antiheroes" from *The New Republic*, Aug. 17, 2013. Copyright © 2013 by The New Republic. Reprinted with permission.

Deborah Blum, "The Gender Blur: Where Does Biology End and Society Take Over?" from *Utne Reader*, Sept./Oct. 1998. Copyright © 1998 by Deborah Blum. Used by permission. All rights reserved.

danah boyd, "Implications of User Choice: The Cultural Logic of 'MySpace or Facebook?'" from http://interactions.acm.org, Vol. 16, Issue 6, Nov./Dec. 2009. Reprinted by permission of the author. http://interactions.acm.org/content/?p = 1302.

Patti S. Caravello, "Judging Quality on the Web" by Patti Schifter Caravello, UCLA Research Library. Reprinted with permission.

Aymar Jean Christian, "The End of Post-Identity Television" from tvisual.org. Copyright © 2012 by Aymar Jean Christian. Reused with permission of the author.

Stephanie Clifford and Quentin Hardy, "Attention, Shoppers: Store Is Tracking Your Cell" from the *New York Times* online, July 14, 2013. Copyright © 2013 by The New York Times. All rights reserved. Used by permission and protected by the Copyright Laws of the United States. The printing, copying, redistribution, or retransmission of this Content without express written permission is prohibited. http://nytimes.com.

Julia B. Corbett, "A Faint Green Sell: Advertising in the Natural World" from *Enviropop: Studies in Environmental Rhetoric and Popular Culture*, eds. Mark Meister & Phyllis K. Japp, pp. 81–94. Copyright © 2002 by Mark Meister & Phyllis K. Japp. Reproduced with permission of ABC-CLIO, LLC.

Steve Craig, "Men's Men and Women's Women: How TV Commercials Portray Gender to Different Audiences" from *Issues and Effects of Mass Communication: Other Voices* by Steve Craig. Reprinted by permission of the author.

Daniel D'Addario, "Everything Is 'Trolling' Now" from *Salon*. This article first appeared in Salon.com, at http://Salon.com. An online version remains in the Salon archives. Reprinted with permission.

Michelle Dean, "Here Comes the Hillbilly, Again" from *Slate*. Copyright © 2012 The Slate Group. All rights reserved. Used by permission and protected by the Copyright Laws of the United States. The printing, copying, redistribution, or retransmission of this Content without express written permission is prohibited.

David Denby, "High-School Confidential: Notes on Teen Movies" published by the *New Yorker*, May 31, 1999. Copyright © 1999 by David Denby. Reprinted by permission of the author.

Aaron Devor, "Gender Role Behaviors and Attitudes" from *Gender Blending: Confronting the Limits of Duality* by Aaron Devor. Copyright © 1989 by Indiana University Press. Reprinted with permission of Indiana University Press.

Simon Dumenco, "If We're All So Sick of You, Facebook, Why Can't We Quit You?" from *Advertising Age*, June 10, 2013. Copyright © 2013 by Simon Dumenco. Reprinted with permission.

Christine Folch, "Why the West Loves Sci-Fi and Fantasy: A Cultural Explanation" from the *Atlantic*. Copyright © 2013 The Atlantic Media Co., as first published in The Atlantic Magazine. All rights reserved. Distributed by Tribune Content Agency, LLC. Reprinted with permission.

Thomas Frank and Matt Weiland, "Commodify Your Dissent" published as "Why Johnny Can't Dissent" in the *Baffler*, 1997. Copyright © 1997 The Baffler Literary Magazine, Inc. Reprinted with permission.

Neal Gabler, "The Social Networks" from the *Los Angeles Times*, Oct. 17, 2010. Copyright © 2010 by the Los Angeles Times. Reprinted with permission.

Mariah Burton Nelson, "I Won. I'm Sorry." Was originally published in *Self* Magazine, 1998. Reprinted by permission of the author.

Anne Norton, excerpts from *Republic of Signs*. Copyright © 1993 by the University of Chicago. Reprinted by permission of the University of Chicago Press.

Michael Omi, "In Living Color: Race and American Culture" from *Cultural Politics in Contemporary America*, ed. Ian Angus and Sut Jhally. Copyright © 1989 by Michael Omi. Reprinted by permission of the author.

Michael Parenti, "Class and Virtue" from *Make-Believe Media: The Politics of Entertainment*, 1st ed., by Michael Parenti. Copyright © 1992 by Wadsworth. Reprinted by permission of Wadsworth, a part of Cengage Learning, Inc. Reproduced by permission. www.cengage.com /permissions.

Willa Paskin, "*Devious Maids* Skewers the One Percent." This article first appeared in Salon. com, at http://Salon.com. An online version remains in the Salon archives. Reprinted with permission.

Jennifer L. Pozner, "Dove's 'Real Beauty' Backlash" from *Bitch: Feminist Response to Pop Culture*, Issue 30, Fall 2005. Copyright © 2005. Reprinted by permission of the author.

Robert B. Ray, excerpts from "Formal and Thematic Paradigms" from *A Certain Tendency of the Hollywood Cinema 1930–1980*. Copyright © 1985 Princeton University Press. Reprinted by permission of Princeton University Press.

James A. Roberts, "The Treadmill of Consumption," pages 95–101 from *Shiny Objects* by James A. Roberts. Copyright © 2011 by James A. Roberts. Reprinted by permission of HarperCollins Publishers.

Salvador Rodriguez, "In the Digital Age, Breaking Up Is Hard to Do" from the *Los Angeles Times*, published Feb. 13, 2014. Copyright © The Los Angeles Times. Reprinted with permission.

Richard Rushfield, "Toward a Unified Theory of How the Internet Makes Everything Terrible" from http://rushfieldbabylon.com. Copyright © 2013 by Richard Rushfield. Reprinted by permission of the author.

Juliet B. Schor, "Tony the Tiger to Slime Time Live: The Content of Commercial Messages in Children's Advertising" from *Born to Buy: The Commercialized Child and the New Consumer Culture* by Juliet Schor. Copyright © 2004 by Juliet Schor. All rights reserved. Reprinted with permission of Scribner Publishing Group.

Matt Zoller Seitz, "The Offensive Movie Cliché That Won't Die" first appeared in Salon.com, at http://Salon.com. An online version remains in the Salon archives. Reprinted with permission.

Linda Seger, "Creating the Myth" from *Making a Good Script Great*. Copyright © 1987 by Linda Seger. Reprinted by permission of the author.

Nick Serpe, "Reality Pawns: The New Money TV" from *Dissent Magazine*, Summer 2013. Copyright © 2013 by Nick Serpe. Reprinted with permission of the University of Pennsylvania Press.

Laurence Shames, "The More Factor" from *The Hunger for More: Searching for Values in an Age of Greed*. Copyright © 1989 by Laurence Shames. Reprinted by permission of the Stuart Krichevsky Agency, Inc.

Natasha Simons, "*Mad Men* and the Paradox of the Past" from *National Review* online, July 19, 2010. Reprinted by permission of the publisher.

Jack Fisher Solomon, "Masters of Desire: The Culture of American Advertising" from *The Signs of Our Time* by Jack Fisher Solomon. Copyright © 1988 by Jack Solomon. Used by permission of Jeremy P. Tarcher, an imprint of Penguin Group (USA) Inc.

Gloria Steinem, "Sex, Lies, and Advertising" from *Ms.* Magazine, July/August 1990. Copyright © 1990 by Gloria Steinem. Reprinted by permission of the author.

Stevie St. John, "Out of Character" from *Bitch Magazine*, Summer 2014, Issue 63. Copyright © 2014 by Bitch Media. Reprinted with permission.

"Students Addicted to Social Media—New UM Study," Apr. 21, 2010, http://www.newsdesk .umd.edu/sociss/release.cfm?ArticleID=2144. Reprinted with permission, Susan D. Moeller, "24 Hours: Unplugged" study.

Joseph Turow, "Introduction" from *The Daily You: How the New Advertising Industry Is Defining Your Identity and Your Worth* by Joseph Turow. Copyright © 2012 by Joseph Turow. Reprinted by permission of Yale University Press.

James B. Twitchell, "What We Are to Advertisers" from *Lead Us into Temptation: The Triumph of American Materialism* by James B. Twitchell. Copyright © 1999 by James B. Twitchell. Reprinted by permission of the author.

S. Craig Watkins, "Now! Fast Entertainment and Multitasking in an Always-On World" from *The Young and the Digital* by S. Craig Watkins. Copyright © 2009 by S. Craig Watkins. Reprinted by permission of Beacon Press, Boston.

INDEX OF AUTHORS AND TITLES

Missing something? Instructors may assign the online materials that accompany this text. For access to them, visit **macmillanhighered.com /signsoflife8e**.

Inside LaunchPad Solo for *Signs of Life* in the *USA*

Tutorials

Critical Reading

Active Reading Skills

Reading Visuals: Purpose

Reading Visuals: Audience

Documentation and Working with Sources

Do I Need to Cite That?

How to Cite an Article in MLA Style

How to Cite a Book in MLA Style

How to Cite a Database in MLA Style

How to Cite a Database in APA Style

How to Cite a Web Site in MLA Style

How to Cite a Web Site in APA Style

Digital Writing

Photo Editing Basics with GIMP

Audio Editing with Audacity

Presentations

Word Processing

Online Research Tools

Job Search/Personal Branding

LearningCurve

Critical Reading

Topic Sentences and Supporting Details

Topics and Main Ideas

Working with Sources (MLA)

Working with Sources (APA)

Commas

Fragments

Run-Ons and Comma Splices

Active and Passive Voice

Appropriate Language

Subject-Verb Agreement

E-readings

Gene Brockhoff, *Shop 'Til You Drop* [DOCUMENTARY FILM CLIP]

Ford Motor Company, *Two-Ford Freedom* [VINTAGE ADVERTISEMENT]

The Beverly Hillbillies, Getting Settled [TV EPISODE]

Louis J. Gasnier and Arthur Hoerl, *Reefer Madness* [FILM CLIP]

George A. Romero and John A. Russo, *Night of the Living Dead* [FILM CLIP]

Nancy Schwartzman and Isaac Mathes, *xoxosms* [DOCUMENTARY FILM TRAILER]

U.S. Immigration and Customs Enforcement, *iGuardians* [VIDEO]

Sut Jhally, *The Codes of Gender* [DOCUMENTARY FILM CLIP]